W9-ACG-603

Annual Review of

INFORMATION
SCIENCE AND
TECHNOLOGY

Annual Review of
INFORMATION SCIENCE AND TECHNOLOGY

Volume 37 • 2003
Blaise Cronin, Editor

Published on behalf of the
American Society for Information Science and Technology
by Information Today, Inc.

Information Today, Inc.
Medford, New Jersey

Copyright © 2002
by the American Society for Information Science and Technology

ISBN: 1-57387-154-0
ISSN: 0066-4200
CODEN: ARISBC
LC No. 66-25096

Published and distributed by
Information Today, Inc.
143 Old Marlton Pike
Medford, NJ 08055-8750

On behalf of

The American Society for Information Science and Technology
1320 Fenwick Lane, Suite 510
Silver Spring, MD 20910-3602, U.S.A.

Table of Contents

SECTION I:
Language and Representation

SECTION II:
Dynamics of Scholarly Communication

SECTION III:
Information Systems

SECTION IV:
Theorizing Information and Information Use

Introduction

Blaise Cronin

The 11 chapters that make up this volume of the *Annual Review of Information Science and Technology* cover topics old and new, and do so in ways—and from perspectives—that are sometimes new.

The relationship between language and representation is central to both the theoretical and applied bases of information science, and, of course, it is a subject that has been treated in these pages previously. The three chapters in Section I: Language and Representation—all written by well-known information scientists—help to remind us of the long-standing links between linguistics, epistemology, and information science. David Blair's contribution, "Information Retrieval and the Philosophy of Language," is distinctive by virtue of its detailed examination of the work of Ludwig Wittgenstein and the implications for research in information retrieval (IR). Had the author had his way, I would surely have written "*the life and work* of Ludwig Wittgenstein" in the preceding sentence, but space constraints prevented us from including some of the fascinating biographical information about the 20th century's most celebrated philosopher that the original draft of Blair's chapter contained. In fairness, then, let me recommend a short and charming book that weaves the lives of Wittgenstein and Karl Popper around the celebrated poker incident, which occurred at the October 1946 meeting of the Moral Science Club at the University of Cambridge

(Edmonds & Eidinow, 2001). Now, you may be asking yourself, is that poker as in "card game" or poker as in ...?

Words, how we use them, what we mean by them, and what others make of them, are the stuff of information retrieval. If words were, well, just words, we wouldn't have the problem of false drops, and translating Seamus Heaney's poetry into Urdu wouldn't be such a difficult task. In a perfect world—one free of false drops—Representative Dick Armey's Web page wouldn't be mistaken for a pornographic site and a voluptuous Rubens nude wouldn't be blocked by image recognition software designed to protect children from explicit sexual representations. These are not simply abstruse technicalities, but issues that can have an impact on public policy, as evidenced by the debate swirling around the Children's Internet Protection Act (CIPA). Unfortunately, if understandably, most retrieval and filtering software packages are differentially constrained when it comes to semantic analysis, and that poses enormous challenges for, among others, researchers working in the area of cross-language information retrieval, machine translation, and artificial intelligence, as Gobinda Chowdhury describes in his chapter, "Natural Language Processing."

Indexing was difficult enough when information scientists were dealing with bounded collections, but with the advent of the Internet and World Wide Web, the universe of indexable materials has mushroomed unmanageably. Even the best Web search engines pick up only a fraction of available content—content, moreover, that is dynamically changing. The Web is rather different from, say, the INSPEC database or the contents of your local public library; we typically comprehend the dimensions of the latter two, but not of the former, which creates difficulty when it comes to evaluating retrieval performance. This, as Edie Rasmussen suggests in her chapter, "Indexing and Retrieval for the Web," means that we may need to look beyond classical measures of recall and precision when dealing with Web-based information resources.

The two chapters in Section II: Dynamics of Scholarly Communication, feature a quintet of authors new to *ARIST*. Although the subject matter may not be altogether new, the approach in each case is rather different from yore. My colleagues Rob Kling and Ewa Callahan provide a much-needed and highly nuanced dissection of the concept of "the electronic journal" in their chapter, "Electronic Journals, the Internet, and

Scholarly Communication." Their sociotechnical analysis of the scholarly publishing ecosystem should provide a road map for other researchers, and, at the very least, lead to greater clarity of thought and expression in the discourse of electronic communication. Communication is an inherently social phenomenon. The ways in which scholars interact is not merely a function of available toolsets, but reflects the material practices and prevailing norms of their disciplines. In short, no single electronic publishing system is likely to work for, and be adopted in equal measure by, all disciplinary tribes.

Information visualization is a topic that should be familiar to *ARIST* readers, but the chapter by Katy Börner, Chaomei Chen, and Kevin Boyack, "Visualizing Knowledge Domains," comes with a novel twist or two. Their contribution is a combination of (a) the traditional literature review, (b) a tutorial—the reader is introduced to the strengths and limitations of a range of information visualization tools by having them applied to the subject matter of the chapter, domain visualization—and (c) original research: the authors have created a task-specific database with which to illustrate their key points. Because *ARIST* (for now, at any rate) cannot accommodate color artwork and space is limited, the authors have graciously provided a Web-based repository of data and color images to support the printed text (http://www.asis.org/Publications/ARIST/Vol37/BornerFigures.html). If a picture is worth a thousand words, this hybrid chapter must surely amount to the longest in *ARIST* history.

Last year's *ARIST* included a chapter on health informatics, and this year, in Section III: Information Systems, we turn the spotlight on two very different but equally intriguing domains, rich in informatics-related developments: museums and music. The chapter by Paul Marty, Boyd Rayward, and Michael Twidale picks up the socio-technical, or, if you prefer, social informatics, theme developed by Kling and Callahan. Museums are rewarding sites in which to observe how social practices and information technology are, to use the terminology of the moment, mutually constitutive. The authors raise a number of important issues relating to the nature and mission of the museum in the digital age as they examine the organizational, behavioral, and pedagogic implications of interactive media for the world of museums. They also explore the kinds of relationships that exist—and will exist—between museums, both physical and virtual, and their diverse user populations.

Music information retrieval is a fast-growing, multidisciplinary research field, one that exhibits early signs of institutionalization, as Stephen Downie documents in his crisply written chapter on the subject. Retrieving music (whether a Wagnerian leitmotif, the words of a Beatles song, or the opening bars of a lullaby) poses a host of technical challenges, challenges that seem set to occupy information scientists, musicologists, and computer scientists—not to mention, in a post-Napster era, intellectual property rights management experts—for years to come.

There are many professors, departments, and associations of information science, but little agreement as to what information is, or what the foundational elements of the putative science of information are. Thus, a chapter, or section, devoted to information theory has become a common feature of *ARIST* volumes. Definitions of information abound; some are enumerative and pragmatic in character—think of Harold Borko's (1968, p. 5): "the generation, collection, organization, interpretation, storage, retrieval, dissemination, transformation, and use of information." Others are memorably pithy—think of Gregory Bateseon's (1972, p. 459) definition of information as "a difference which makes a difference." Consensus, however, is absent. Both of these oft-quoted definitions, and many others, are critically appraised by Rafael Capurro and Birger Hjørland in their chapter, "The Concept of Information," which opens with an etymological exploration of the focal term, from classical times, through the Middle Ages, to the present. With some reluctance we pruned the opening sections of this chapter, removing not a few Latin and Greek references, but what remains nonetheless constitutes a worthwhile historical overview in and of itself, not to mention a very effective entrée to the ontological and epistemological discussion that follows.

Section IV: Theorizing Information and Information Use contains three further chapters, the first of which, "Task-Based Information Searching," by Pertti Vakkari, makes a strong case for foregrounding the tasks—both work-related and personal/avocational—that give rise to information seeking behaviors and mold users' search tactics. Vakkari has crafted a well-structured critique of the sprawling information seeking literature, its dominant paradigms—from ASK (anomalous states of knowledge), through behavioral models, to the cognitive approach—and the related methodological issues.

Trust—how it is constituted and sustained—has recently emerged as a key research topic in areas such as electronic commerce, online education, and, more generally, computer-mediated communication. Whom and what can we believe on the Web? Can we trust those we interact with online, where social presence is weak and identities can be easily masked? Trust is a salient issue in information systems effectiveness, but it has not been treated heretofore in the pages of *ARIST*. The chapter by Stephen Marsh and Mark Dibben, "The Role of Trust in Information Science and Technology," combines a theoretical analysis of trust—drawing, in particular, on literature from philosophy, psychology, sociology, and management—with a critical assessment of the place of trust in information systems design and development. More concretely, the authors attempt to show why and how trust, a multifaceted construct, can be embedded in a variety of information systems. Undoubtedly, this is a topic that we shall revisit in the not too distant future, as—to take but one example—research in embodied conversational agents moves rapidly ahead.

The concluding chapter in Volume 37, "Information and Equity," by Leah Lievrouw and Sharon Farb, is a timely effort to conceptualize notions of information equality and information equity. The authors resist the easy ideological posturing, which metaphors such as the digital divide can sometimes invite, to examine what we mean by equity. They draw upon the writings of, among others, Amartya Sen and John Rawls to move beyond the polarizing rhetoric of "information rich" and "information poor," arguing convincingly that equity—informational or otherwise—is not synonymous with quantitatively equal distribution of resources for the very good reason that no two individuals may need, or choose to use, a particular parcel of information resources in the same way.

In the concluding sentence of last year's introduction, I said that the 2003 volume would include several new topics and a number of first-time contributors to *ARIST*. We have managed to deliver on that promise, and I am confident that we shall be able to do so again with respect to Volume 38.

Blaise Cronin
Editor

References

Bateson, G. (1972). *Steps to an ecology of mind*. New York: Ballantine Books.

Borko, H. (1968). Information science: What is it? *American Documentation, 3*, 5.

Edmonds, D. & Eidinow, J. (2001). *Wittgenstein's poker: The story of a ten-minute argument between two great philosophers*. London: Faber & Faber.

Acknowledgments

Many individuals are involved in the production of *ARIST*. In particular, I should like to acknowledge the sterling contributions of both our Advisory Board members and our many outside reviewers. Their names are listed in the pages that follow. Maryam Fakouri and Shaun McMahon helped us greatly with copyediting and bibliographic checking, and Amy Novick has created a fine index. As before, Debora Shaw, my associate editor, has proved herself to be indispensable.

ARIST Advisory Board

Helen Barsky Atkins
HighWire Press, Stanford University, USA

Micheline Beaulieu
University of Sheffield, UK

Pierrette Bergeron
Université de Sherbrooke, Québec, Canada

Elisabeth Davenport
Napier University, Edinburgh, UK

Susan Dumais
Microsoft Research, Redmond, Washington, USA

Glynn Harmon
University of Texas at Austin, USA

Peter Ingwersen
Royal School of Library and Information Science, Copenhagen, Denmark

Paul B. Kantor
Rutgers University, New Brunswick, New Jersey, USA

Jane Klobas
Curtin University of Technology, Perth, Australia

Ray R. Larson
University of California at Berkeley, USA

Leah A. Lievrouw
University of California at Los Angeles, USA

Robert M. Losee
University of North Carolina at Chapel Hill, USA

Peter Lyman
University of California at Berkeley, USA

Victor Rosenberg
University of Michigan, Ann Arbor, USA

Chapter Reviewers

Judit Bar-Ilan

David Bearman

Micheline Beaulieu

Christine Borgman

Donald Byrd

Tony Cawkell

Elfreda Chatman

G. Sayeed Choudhury

Ian Cornelius

Timothy Craven

Elisabeth Davenport

Ron Day

Susan Dumais

Don Fallis

Jonathan Furner

Denham Grey

Stephanie Haas

Glynn Harmon

Carol Hert

Peter Ingwersen

Jane Klobas

Elin Jacob

Ray Larson

Kjell Lemström

Peter Lyman

John Paolillo

Robin Peek

Alice Robbin

Howard Rosenbaum

Fytton Rowland

Harmeet Sawhney

Henry Small

Paul Solomon

Jean Umiker-Sebeok

Lynn Ann Underwood

Keith van Rijsbergen

Julian Warner

Barbara Wildemuth

Patrick Wilson

Contributors

David C. Blair is Professor of Computer and Information Systems in the Graduate School of Business of the University of Michigan, Ann Arbor. He holds the Jack Sparks Research Professorship and is a Faculty Fellow of the Graduate Interdisciplinary Institute. While at the University of Michigan, he has held appointments in the Industrial Technology Institute, the School of Information, and UTEP (the Urban, Technology and Environmental Planning Program). Professor Blair's doctoral degree is from the University of California, Berkeley, School of Information Systems and Management. In 1999, he received the American Society for Information Science and Technology's Research Award.

Katy Börner is Assistant Professor of Information Science at Indiana University. She holds a Ph.D. in computer science from the University of Kaiserslautern. Her principal research area is information visualization with special focus on knowledge domain visualizations and visual interfaces to digital libraries. She utilizes three-dimensional (3-D) virtual environments to build collaborative interfaces that provide intuitive and efficient access to text, document, and image digital libraries. Spatio-temporally referenced visualizations of user activity are generated to assist users in making sense of the world, its information resources, and collaboration possibilities; to aid designers with the organization and layout of world content and the selection of interaction possibilities; and to enable researchers to study evolving communities in 3-D virtual worlds.

Kevin Boyack holds an appointment as Principal Member of Technical Staff in the Computation, Computers, and Mathematics Center at Sandia National Laboratories. His Ph.D. in chemical engineering is from Brigham Young University. Dr. Boyack's main responsibility is analysis using Sandia's VxInsight knowledge visualization tool with various types of data sets (e.g., literature, patent, genomic). He has produced and analyzed science maps or domain visualizations from literature and patent sources on many topics of interest to Sandia for competitive intelligence purposes. He is also interested in semantics, augmented cognition, and the application of mathematical tools to information spaces.

Ewa Callahan is an adjunct lecturer and doctoral student in information science at Indiana University. She earned her M.A. in history with specialization in archives at Jagiellonian University, Cracow, Poland in 1993 and M.I.S. at Indiana University in 1998. Her research and teaching interests are in the areas of international issues in information science, scholarly communication, human-computer interaction, information visualization, and development and use of information technologies in post-communist countries.

Rafael Capurro holds a Licentiate in Philosophy from Salvador University, Buenos Aires, Argentina. He was awarded a Diploma in Documentation from the Lehrinstitut für Dokumentation, Frankfurt am Main in 1973 and a Ph.D. in Philosophy from Düsseldorf University in 1978. Since 1986, he has been Professor of Information Management and Information Ethics at the Fachhochschule Stuttgart, Hochschule der Medien (University of Applied Sciences), and a Lecturer at the Institute of Philosophy, Stuttgart University since 1987. Dr. Capurro was Founder of the International Center for Information Ethics (ICIE) and is a Member of the European Group on Ethics in Science and New Technologies (EGE).

Chaomei Chen is Associate Professor in the College of Information Science and Technology at Drexel University. His research interests include information visualization, knowledge domain visualization, human-computer interaction, and virtual environments. He is the author of *Information Visualisation and Virtual Environments* (Springer, 1999) and *Mapping Scientific Frontiers* (Springer, 2002). Dr. Chen is the Editor-in-Chief of *Information Visualization* (*IVS*), a peer-reviewed international journal published quarterly by Palgrave Macmillan. He has been principal investigator on several research grants from the British Engineering and Physical Science Research Council (EPSRC), the European Fifth Framework Programme, and the Council for Museums, Archives and Libraries in the U.K. He earned his Ph.D. in Computer Science from the University of Liverpool, his M.Sc. in computation from the University of Oxford, and his B.Sc. in Mathematics from NanKai University in China.

Gobinda G. Chowdhury is currently Senior Lecturer in the Department of Computer and Information Sciences at the University of Strathclyde in Glasgow, U.K. Having earned his first degree in chemistry, he moved on to the field of information science where he completed his Master's and Ph.D. at Indian universities. He obtained his second Ph.D. from the University of Sheffield in the U.K. for his research in natural language processing of chemical patents. Prior to his appointment at Strathclyde, Dr. Chowdhury worked as an associate professor at Nanyang Technological University in Singapore. He has an extensive publishing record that includes seven books and 65 papers in refereed journals and conferences.

Mark R. Dibben is Founding Director of the Chapter for Applied Process Thought at the University of St. Andrews, Scotland, and a member of faculty in the Department of Management. A major focus of his research concerns the role and effect of trust in and between organizations; publications on this topic range from philosophy, medicine and human-computer interaction to marketing, international business and entrepreneurship. Other interests include Whiteheadian metaphysics and the impact of interpersonal dynamics and information technology on organizational emergence. Dr. Dibben is co-editor of *Concrescence: The Australasian Journal of Process Thought* and is a research associate with two leading management consultancies specializing in personal development.

J. Stephen Downie is Assistant Professor at the Graduate School of Library and Information Science, University of Illinois at Urbana-Champaign. He holds a B.A. (music theory and composition), M.L.I.S., and Ph.D. in library and information science, all from the University of Western Ontario. Dr. Downie specializes in the areas of music information retrieval (MIR) system evaluation and informetrics. He has been very active in fostering the growth of the MIR research community through a wide variety of multidisciplinary symposia, workshops, and panels. He is a founding organizer of the International Symposium on Music Information Retrieval (ISMIR).

Sharon E. Farb is the Coordinator for Digital Acquisitions at the University of California, Los Angeles (UCLA) Library. She is also a doctoral student in information studies at UCLA specializing in information policy. Ms. Farb's research focuses on the intersection of information law, policy, and technology and includes the areas of information equity, licensing, digital copyright, privacy, and the long-term preservation of electronic records and cultural property.

Birger Hjørland is Professor of Information Science, Royal School of Library and Information Science, Copenhagen, Denmark. He was formerly Professor of Information Science at University College Borås, Sweden. He holds a Ph.D. in information science from the University of Gothenburg and an M.A. in psychology from the University of Copenhagen. Dr. Hjørland worked at the Royal Library in Copenhagen for 12 years as a subject specialist in psychology and as coordinator of the library's computer-based reference services. He has taught the history and philosophy of psychology at the University of Copenhagen and also taught information retrieval at the Institute of Applied and Mathematical Linguistics.

Rob Kling is Professor of Information Science and Information Systems at Indiana University (IU). He directs the Center for Social Informatics, an interdisciplinary research center at IU. Since the early 1970s, Dr. Kling has studied the social opportunities and dilemmas of computerization for managers, professionals, workers, and the public. He is co-author of *Computers and Politics: High Technology in American*

Local Governments (Columbia University Press, 1982) and the editor of *Computerization and Controversy: Value Conflicts & Social Choices* (Academic Press, 1996), which examined the social controversies about computerization in organizations and social life, regarding productivity, work life, personal privacy, risks of computer systems, and computer ethics. His research has been published in more than 100 journal articles and book chapters.

Leah A. Lievrouw is Professor in the Department of Information Studies at the University of California, Los Angeles, and is affiliated with the UCLA Communication Studies Program. She holds a Ph.D. in communication research from the Annenberg School for Communication at the University of Southern California. Her research examines the relationship between new information and communication technologies, and knowledge and the social and cultural changes associated with these technologies. Currently, she is exploring shifts toward social separatism that have developed alongside the proliferation of new media systems and their implications for communities and systems of knowledge. She is the co-editor of the *Handbook of New Media: Social Shaping and Consequences of ICTs* (Sage, 2002).

Stephen Marsh obtained his B.Sc. in Computing Science in 1990, and Ph.D. in Computing Science for the formalization of the phenomenon of cooperative trust in 1994, both from the University of Stirling in Scotland. Dr. Marsh was a lecturer at the University of Stirling until 1996, when he migrated to Canada and now works for the National Research Council for Canada, Institute for Information Technology, in Ottawa. His current research is focused on what he terms "socially adept technology," the incorporation of human social norms in user interfaces, autonomous agents, and physical human-centered interaction spaces.

Paul F. Marty is Assistant Professor in the School of Information Studies at Florida State University. He has a background in classics and computer science engineering, and his Ph.D. is from the Graduate School of Library and Information Science at the University of Illinois at Urbana-Champaign. From 1996 to 2002, he was Director of Information Technology at the University of Illinois' Spurlock Museum. He studies museums as sociotechnical systems, and is particularly interested in the social implications of introducing new technologies into the museum environment. He has published several articles on various aspects of museum informatics.

Edie M. Rasmussen is Professor in the School of Information Sciences, University of Pittsburgh. She has also held appointments at the School of Library and Information Studies at Dalhousie University, Nova Scotia, Canada; the School of Library Science at the Institiut Teknoloji MARA, Kuala Lumpur, Malaysia; Nanyang Technological University, Singapore; and Victoria University of Wellington, New Zealand. Her research areas include indexing and information retrieval in text and multimedia databases and digital libraries.

W. Boyd Rayward is Research Professor in the Graduate School of Library and Information Science of the University of Illinois at Urbana-Champaign and Professor Emeritus in the School of Information Systems, Technology, and Management of the University of New South Wales in Sydney. He was educated in Australia and the U.S. His Ph.D. is from the University of Chicago. He has published widely on the history of aspects of the organization of information.

Michael B. Twidale is Associate Professor in the Graduate School of Library and Information Science of the University of Illinois at Urbana-Champaign. His Ph.D. in computer science is from Lancaster University in the U.K. His research interests include computer supported cooperative work, computer supported collaborative learning, and human-computer interaction. He is currently studying how people learn how to use computer applications in a variety of settings (including in offices and in museums), in order to design systems that are easier to learn and mesh more closely with the social nature of much work and learning.

Pertti Vakkari is Professor of Information Studies at the University of Tampere, Finland. He is the chairman of the Finnish Doctoral Program for Information and Communication Studies, and chairman of the Nordic Information Studies Research Education Network. He is a member of the editorial boards of journals such as *Information*

Processing & Management, Journal of Documentation, and *Archival Science.* Professor Vakkari's research interests include: (1) studies of information seeking; (2) studies on task performance process, information search tactics, and relevance assessments; (3) investigation of the historical roots of library science; and (4) theoretical and empirical analyses of information science.

About the Editor

Blaise Cronin is the Rudy Professor of Information Science at Indiana University, Bloomington, where he has been Dean of the School of Library and Information Science since 1991. He is concurrently Visiting Professor of Information Science in the Department of Information and Communication at the Manchester Metropolitan University and also Visiting Professor in the School of Computing at Napier University, Edinburgh. From 1985 to 1991 he was Professor of Information Science and Head of the Department of Information Science at the Strathclyde University Business School in Glasgow.

Professor Cronin is the author of numerous research articles, monographs, technical reports, conference papers, and other publications. Much of his research focuses on scholarly communication, citation analysis, and cybermetrics—the intersection of information science and social studies of science. He has also published widely on topics such as information warfare, competitive analysis, and strategic intelligence. Professor Cronin sits on many editorial boards, including the *Journal of the American Society for Information Science and Technology*, *Scientometrics*, *Cybermetrics*, and the *International Journal of Information Management*. He has extensive international experience, having taught, conducted research, or consulted in more than 30 countries; clients have included the World Bank, Asian Development Bank, Unesco, Brazilian Ministry of Science & Technology, U.S. Department of Justice, European Commission, British Council, Her Majesty's Treasury, Hewlett-Packard, British Library, Commonwealth Agricultural Bureaux, and Association for Information Management. Over the years, he has been a keynote or invited speaker at scores of conferences, nationally and internationally. Professor Cronin was a founding director of Crossaig, an electronic publishing start-up in Scotland, which was acquired in 1992 by ISI. For six years he was a member of ISI's strategic advisory board.

Professor Cronin was educated at Trinity College Dublin (M.A.) and the Queen's University of Belfast (Ph.D., D.S.Sc.) In 1997, he was awarded the degree Doctor of Letters (D.Litt., *honoris causa*) by Queen Margaret University College, Edinburgh for his scholarly contributions to information science.

About the Associate Editor

Debora Shaw is Associate Professor and Associate Dean at the School of Library and Information Science, Indiana University Bloomington. Her research focuses on information organization, information seeking and use, and patterns of publication. Her work has been published in the *Journal of the American Society for Information Science*, *Journal of Documentation*, *Online Review*, *Scientometrics*, and *First Monday*, among others. She serves on the editorial boards of the *Journal of Educational Resources in Computing* and *Library & Information Science Research*.

Dr. Shaw served as President of the American Society for Information Science and Technology (1997) and has also served on the Society's Board of Directors. She has been affiliated with *ARIST* as both a chapter author and as indexer for the past 16 years. Dr. Shaw received bachelor's and master's degrees from the University of Michigan and a Ph.D. from Indiana University. She was on the faculty at the University of Illinois before joining Indiana University.

Language and Representation

CHAPTER 1

Information Retrieval and the Philosophy of Language

David C. Blair
University of Michigan

Introduction

Information retrieval—the retrieval, primarily, of documents or textual material—is fundamentally a linguistic process. At the very least we must describe what we want and match that description with descriptions of the information that is available to us. Furthermore, when we describe what we want, we must *mean* something by that description. This is a deceptively simple act, but such linguistic events have been the grist for philosophical analysis since Aristotle. Although there are complexities involved in referring to authors, document types, or other categories of information retrieval context, here I wish to focus on one of the most problematic activities in information retrieval: the description of the intellectual content of information items. And even though I take information retrieval to involve the description and retrieval of written text, what I say here is applicable to any information item whose intellectual content can be described for retrieval—books, documents, images, audio clips, video clips, scientific specimens, engineering schematics, and so forth. For convenience, though, I will refer only to the description and retrieval of documents.

The description of intellectual content can go wrong in many obvious ways. We may describe what we want incorrectly; we may describe it correctly but in such general terms that its description is useless for retrieval; or we may describe what we want correctly, but misinterpret the descriptions of available information, and thereby match our description of what we want incorrectly. From a linguistic point of view, we can be misunderstood in the process of retrieval in many ways. Because the philosophy of language deals specifically with how we are understood and *mis*-understood, it should have some use for understanding the process of description in information retrieval.

First, however, let us examine more closely the kinds of misunderstandings that can occur in information retrieval. We use language in searching for information in two principal ways. We use it to describe what we want and to discriminate what we want from other information that is available to us but that we do not want. Description and discrimination together articulate the goals of the information search process; they also delineate the two principal ways in which language can *fail* us in this process. Van Rijsbergen (1979) was the first to make this distinction, calling them "representation" and "discrimination."

The Retrieval Problem: Failures of Description

A failure of description can occur in a number of ways. The most obvious failure is when an item of information is described incorrectly: a textbook on "economics" is described, for example, as being on "anthropology," or a book by Mark Twain is described as being written by Henry James. But there are more subtle failures of description, too, such as when the description is generally correct but is beyond the comprehension of the typical inquirer who might see it. An example of this is a book described as being about "plate tectonics" when the typical inquirer who is interested in theories of "continental drift" may not realize that "plate tectonics" is the more formal description of the same subject matter. In other situations, opposing views arise as to how a particular literature should be described; for example, some researchers may consider "cold fusion" to be a valid field of scientific research deserving its own category, while others see work on "cold fusion" as more appropriately subsumed under the rubric "crank theories" or "pseudo-science."

When we look at just the reasonably correct or useful descriptions that can represent an item of information, this set of reasonable descriptions may be quite large. It has been shown empirically (Swanson, 1996), and argued theoretically (Blair, 1990), that the number of different descriptions that can represent the intellectual content of even a relatively short document may have no upper bound. This conclusion calls into question the notion of "exhaustive indexing"—the assignment of *all* the index descriptions that could represent the intellectual content of an item of information. Some have argued that information retrieval systems should use *all* possible index terms to represent the intellectual content of a document—a strategy called "unlimited aliasing" (Furnas, Landauer, Gomez, & Dumais, 1987). Such a strategy ignores two things. First, there may be no upper bound to the number of words and phrases that can represent the intellectual content of even a small item of information. Second, some of the many possible index terms will always be more useful for retrieval than others, so the assignment of *any* reasonable index terms to a document may not be the best indexing strategy—some index terms really are better than others, as Brooks (1993) has shown.

The high number of reasonable descriptions is both good and bad. It is good in the sense that it is easy to come up with one or more reasonable index terms. But it is bad in the sense that because so many reasonable descriptions for a document exist, a searcher may have a difficult time anticipating the ones actually assigned to the documents of interest, and further, documents that have the same intellectual content might be described in a number of different ways (e.g., one described as concerning "continental drift" whereas another on the same topic is described as concerning "tectonic plates").

The Retrieval Problem: Failures of Discrimination

Although the process of description is primarily focused on an individual document or category of information, the process of discrimination takes a broader view of the representation problem. It is not concerned only with individual documents or categories of information, but also with the relationship between the desired document(s) and the other documents that are available to the inquirer. The goal of discrimination is to distinguish, by means of description, documents that are likely to be useful to the inquirer from available documents with similar intellectual content that are not likely to be useful. The ability to discriminate between useful and useless information establishes a continuum of description that can be characterized as ranging from specific (highly discriminating) to general (less discriminating) terms. The most obvious failure of discrimination is a description of the intellectual content of the desired document that is too general to distinguish it from the intellectual content of useless documents. For example, if the subject description "computers" were added to all the books and journals in a computer science library, it would have no discriminating power at all within that library. Such failure of discrimination is too obvious to be commonplace, but a more insidious form of discrimination failure can occur with even the most thoughtfully applied indexing descriptions. This failure happens when a description identifies a relatively small number of documents in an information retrieval system, and thus discriminates well, but during the lifetime of the system, more and more documents described in the same way are added. Eventually, the number of documents described in this way reaches a point at which the description, by itself, does not discriminate well enough to be of use to inquirers; that is, when the description is used by itself as a search term, it retrieves more documents than inquirers are willing to look through to find what they want (Blair, 1980).

Of course, the point at which a description fails to discriminate well is not a precise number and can be contingent on many factors, including the persistence of the inquirers using that description and the availability of other descriptions that can reduce the size of the less-discriminating category of information. Some inquirers are significantly more persistent or motivated than others and more willing to browse through large sets of retrieved documents. Such persistence often depends on the importance of finding the desired documents and the time available for the search. On the other hand, using other descriptions may reduce the number of items in a particular category. Time periods are frequently used to qualify a less-discriminating description, such as when one asks for only the most recent items described as being in the broad category of "computer science."

Recall and Precision

Any discussion of failure in information retrieval calls to mind the two complementary measures of retrieval performance: recall, which is the percentage of relevant documents retrieved, and precision, which is the percentage of retrieved documents that are relevant (Blair & Maron, 1985). In general, we can say that failures of description lead to low recall, whereas failures of discrimination tend to lower precision. Recall and precision are known to trade off in a rough and imprecise way— higher levels of recall are achieved at the expense of lower levels of precision, and vice versa. This effect suggests that description and discrimination may trade off in similar ways. Describing what we want in the most inclusive (that is, general) terms may lead to the construction of search queries that will be inclusive, but do not discriminate well (i.e., recall will be high and precision low). On the other hand, making our search queries as discriminating (that is, precise) as possible may lead to queries that do not describe what we want very inclusively (i.e., precision will be high and recall low). As in the case with recall and precision, the trade-off between description and discrimination is rough and imprecise.

The Processes of Description and Discrimination

The proliferation of electronic document collections, in particular the ubiquity of the World Wide Web (WWW, or Web), and the wide availability of Internet search engines have placed the tools of information retrieval in the hands of anyone with access to the Web. Individuals who in the past would have had to consult professional searchers such as librarians can now conduct their own searches. Such wide accessibility to public domain information can only please advocates of a free and open democratic society, but the widespread use of Internet search engines may be changing the way we ask for information. When inquirers asked a professional searcher for help in finding information, they could describe what they wanted using all the subtleties and nuances of natural language expression. The professional searcher, in turn, could clarify the inquirers' requests by asking appropriate questions. Now that typical inquirers conduct their own searches using search engines, much of the subtlety of the interaction between inquirers and professional searchers has been lost. The typical information request submitted to an Internet search engine today is comprised of only a few words—often only one. As a consequence, it is important that we examine exactly what is meant by individual words when they are used to request (that is, to describe) information with a particular intellectual content.

Another change taking place in the information retrieval process is the dramatic growth in size of available document collections. Everyone is aware of how the Web is growing, of course, but even private document collections such as institutional and corporate intranets and document databases continue to grow at a spectacular rate. The reason for this is largely economic. We have reached the point with electronic document collections at which the cost of examining and discarding materials, such as Web pages that have outlived their usefulness, is higher than the cost of simply keeping them. As a result, we have many electronic collections that are never or rarely weeded of obsolete documents. The resulting collections of electronic information are, like the Internet, growing without any clear upper bound. But as document collections grow larger and larger, a subtle change in the information retrieval process is taking place. Instead of the goal of search query formulation being primarily the *description* of what is wanted, the overriding goal of query formulation has become the *discrimination* of small numbers of desirable documents from increasingly large numbers of unwanted documents.

What Do Descriptions Mean?

Because of the dramatic and seemingly inevitable growth in the size of information retrieval systems and the many ways that descriptions of information can go wrong, if we are to improve the complementary processes of describing what we want and describing what is available to us, it is important that we examine as closely as possible the activity of describing the intellectual content of information. At the very beginning of this discussion, I stated the obvious when I said, "when we describe what we want, we *must* mean something by that description." But what exactly *do* we mean when we describe what we want? A decade and a half ago, van Rijsbergen (1986a) wrote that one of the most conspicuously absent components of information retrieval theory had been an explicit, formal notion of meaning. It is here that the philosophy of language may provide us with some guidance. (The complementary nature of the indexing and searching processes was a major theme of Blair [1990]. An earlier attempt to reduce the indeterminacy of these two processes was presented in Blair [1986].)

"Words and Meanings"

Philosophers have pondered the "meaning of meaning" since at least the time of Aristotle, but perhaps no philosopher has had more impact on the philosophy of language than Ludwig Wittgenstein (1889–1951). Wittgenstein's later work was instrumental in bringing about the "linguistic turn" in analytic philosophy during the 20th century. The "linguistic turn" resulted from the realization that philosophers who purported to study "ideas" were actually studying *descriptions of ideas*— not what we are thinking, but what we *say* we are thinking. The only direct access to ideas that we have is to our own ideas, by introspection. But we cannot easily generalize from our own introspection to statements about how others think (Hacker 1996b; Rorty, 1967). Wittgenstein (1953) reinforced this change in his later work, *Philosophical Investigations,* by arguing that many of the philosophical problems that puzzled philosophers were not problems at all, but were merely the result of misuses of language. As he put it so succinctly, "Philosophy is a battle against the bewitchment of our intelligence by means of language" (Wittgenstein, 1953, p. 47). It would be impossible, of course, to provide a complete discussion of Wittgenstein's extensive work in the philosophy of language here. His published works run to 13 volumes, and his *Nachlass,* or literary estate, much of which is still not published, is even larger—more than 30,000 pages (this is in the process of being published in 15 or more volumes as the *Wiener Ausgabe* [Nedo, 1993]). The story of the complications and intrigues of this project are detailed in Toyton (1997). The complete electronic CD-ROM versions of Wittgenstein's *Nachlass,* published writings, lectures, and letters, are each available from InteLex (http://library.nlx.com/). The reader should also understand that Wittgenstein is not the only major philosopher of language; I will discuss some others here. Nor is it the case that every philosopher accepts Wittgenstein's arguments without dispute. My purpose here is not to defend Wittgenstein, but to present relevant portions of his work as clearly as possible because it has been enormously influential in philosophical circles and in related areas of linguistics and psychology. An excellent overview of 20th century philosophy of language is provided by Lycan (2000). Blackburn (1984) provides an introduction to the philosophy of language written specifically for the nonphilosopher. Devitt and Sterelny's (1999) introduction to the philosophy of language includes a section on "language and mind" and a discussion of linguist Noam Chomsky's work. Finally, many of the salient papers in the philosophy of language are collected in Rosenberg and Travis (1971). A more recent collection can be found in Ludlow (1997).

The commentaries on Wittgenstein's work are also extensive. The most detailed commentaries on Wittgenstein's most influential work, *Philosophical Investigations,* are by the co-authors G. P. Baker and P. M. S. Hacker (the first two volumes are by Baker and Hacker [1980, 1985], and volumes 3 and 4 are by Hacker alone [1990, 1996b]). Wittgenstein's discussions on specific topics are frequently scattered throughout his writing, so Garth Hallet's (1977) concordance to *Philosophical Investigations* can often be an extremely useful tool for locating and bringing together his writings on the same subject. Wittgenstein's former student and Cornell philosophy professor, Norman Malcolm, has put together several collections of his own insightful essays on Wittgenstein's work. Of particular note is his *Wittgensteinian Themes: Essays 1978–1989* (Malcolm, 1995). Even Wittgenstein's personal life has a compelling interest because, for Wittgenstein, philosophy was not just a collection of puzzles, but a guide for living; as he once said,

> what is the use of studying philosophy if all that it does for you is to enable you to talk with some plausibility about some abstruse questions of logic, etc., if it does not improve your thinking about the important questions of everyday life? (Malcolm, 1972, p. 39)

The two best biographical works are Norman Malcolm's (1972) short but intimate *Ludwig Wittgenstein: A Memoir,* and Ray Monk's (1990) excellent, detailed biography *Ludwig Wittgenstein: The Duty of Genius.* A third work, Theodore Redpath's (1990) *Ludwig Wittgenstein: A*

Student's Memoir offers an undergraduate's impressions of the philosopher. Several of Wittgenstein's students have published literal transcriptions of his classroom lectures and discussions (Ambrose & Macdonald, 1979; Geach, Shah, & Jackson, 1989; King & Lee, 1978). Finally, Bouwsma published his notes of discussions that he had with Wittgenstein during the last few years of the philosopher's life (Bouwsma, Wittgenstein, Craft, & Hustwit, 1986).

An important characteristic of Wittgenstein's work was his own self-criticism. Early in his career he was strongly influenced by the logic and analytical philosophy of Gottlob Frege and Bertrand Russell. After studying with Russell at Cambridge University, he wrote his first book, *Tractatus Logico-Philosophicus* (Wittgenstein, 1961a, 1961b). This was the only philosophy book by Wittgenstein published during his lifetime; it lays out a rigorous, logical model of language and a "picture theory of meaning" that has clear antecedents in the work of Frege and Russell. Wittgenstein wrote most of the *Tractatus* while serving as a much-decorated soldier in the Austrian army during World War I. After writing the *Tractatus,* Wittgenstein felt that he had solved the major problems of analytic philosophy. But while he was away from academic life, his book was having a major impact on analytic philosophy in England, of course, but also within the newly formed Austrian movement in analytic philosophy, Moritz Schlick's "Der Wiener Kreis" (The Vienna Circle). Wittgenstein began to see that he had not solved all the problems of philosophy and that there were serious problems with some things he said in the *Tractatus.* He spent the remainder of his academic life at Cambridge University. Although Bertrand Russell strongly supported his return to professional philosophy, Wittgenstein was soon to criticize and change much of his earlier philosophy that Russell had found so attractive. Wittgenstein's (1953) reassessment of his early philosophy culminated in the collection of philosophical remarks called *Philosophical Investigations.* Although the *Investigations* was a product of Wittgenstein's extensive editorial efforts over the last years of his life, it was not published until shortly after his death, and the questions it raised, of course, could not be answered by Wittgenstein himself. (Wittgenstein's other books have been put together from selections of his unpublished writings by his former students after his death.) Wittgenstein has left us with two interpretations of his intellectual legacy: *Philosophical Investigations* is either an extensive critique of his earlier work in the *Tractatus,* or, as some commentators insist, the second of two largely separate philosophies. Which of these two views is correct will probably never be answered to everyone's satisfaction, but the best attempts to put Wittgenstein's early and late philosophy into perspective are Norman Malcolm's (1986) *Nothing Is Hidden: Wittgenstein's Criticism of His Early Thought,* and P. M. S. Hacker's (1989) *Insight and Illusion.*

Although Wittgenstein focused his philosophical efforts on many specific themes, the published works themselves do not separate his writings into categories: *Remarks on the Foundations of Mathematics* (1978) contains many remarks on language as well as mathematics, *Philosophical Investigations* (1953) contains remarks on philosophy in addition to mathematics, logic, and psychology, and *Remarks on the Philosophy of Psychology* (1980) contains remarks on language, psychology, and other subjects. Wittgenstein's philosophy on a particular topic is, in some sense, everywhere in his writings, but not collected or summarized in any one place. Successive paragraphs in a given work may deal with a specific topic, but the topic is dropped in favor of another and picked up again, seemingly at random, later in the work, or in another work. Certainly one of the reasons for this patchwork approach to philosophy is that Wittgenstein was continually grappling with very deep and elusive problems, problems that had defied systematic solution by the best analytical minds of the 20th century. So, many of his recorded comments were not solutions to these problems, but the remnants of an intellectual battle that he fought all his life (his published writings go right up to a few days before he died, when he succumbed to a long illness). Those who are interested in specific aspects of Wittgenstein's work and do not have the time to make a study of his extensive writings must rely on secondary sources to bring together his work on particular topics. Fortunately, there are some good works. For those interested in his late philosophy of language, the first 130 pages of Hanna Pitkin's (1972) *Wittgenstein and Justice* is, in this author's opinion, the single best introduction to this aspect of his work. Those interested in Wittgenstein's thought concerning more specific topics such as the determinacy of sense, the rejection of private languages, the denial of psycho-physical parallelism, and the rejection of mind–body dualism, among others, would do well to consult Glock's (1996) *A Wittgenstein Dictionary,* which contains short discussions on, and references for, many major and minor topics in Wittgenstein's writings. Readers who would like to see Wittgenstein's writings on the same topic, but in different works, brought together should consult Anthony Kenny's (1994) *The Wittgenstein Reader.*

Wittgenstein's writings on the philosophy of language were extensive and closely linked to his views on the philosophy of mind. To him, language is not a *product* of thought, as most philosophers accepted; "language," as he put it, "is ... the vehicle of thought."

> When I think in language, there aren't "meanings" going through my mind in addition to the verbal expressions: the language is itself the vehicle of thought. (Wittgenstein, 1953, p. 107)

Or, stated somewhat differently:

> Knowledge is not *translated* into words when it is expressed. The words are not a translation of something else that was there before they were. (Wittgenstein, 1967, p. 32)

The point Wittgenstein is making is not that all thought uses language as a medium, for we can surely "think about" music or visual images without reference to language at all, but that when we use language we usually use it as a means for thinking, not as a product of thought or as an expression of something we "have in mind."

This "Copernican Reversal" in the way that thought and language had traditionally been seen to be related has important implications for information retrieval. The process of information retrieval is often seen as one in which the inquirer has something "in mind"—an "information need"—which he or she then translates into an actual search query, in the same way that people were thought to express in ordinary language what they already had "in mind." But if Wittgenstein is right that our use of language is a form of thinking, then the "language" of retrieval— the search terms that are available to us and the ways in which they can be combined—are the "language" with which we think about, and thereby articulate, what information we want. In short, how we think about our information needs is strongly constrained by the retrieval language that is available to us, and insofar as the language of retrieval is limited, so will be our thinking about what we want. The language of retrieval not only limits how we articulate what we want but can also constrain the very thought process in which we determine what we want. Presumably, we would like to think that we mold our information retrieval systems to serve our need for finding information; but, if Wittgenstein is correct, then it may be the case that our information retrieval systems are molding us to think along their lines. If this is the case, then it may be extremely difficult to design radically different or improved retrieval systems, because we are virtually locked into the way of thinking about retrieval that is embodied by existing systems.

Wittgenstein presented his own view of language in terms of a critique of traditional, widely accepted views. In *Philosophical Investigations* he presents a theory of language based on the writings of the medieval philosopher St. Augustine. The Augustinian model of language is a simple referential model that, although old, has been remarkably persistent, existing in various forms even today. The Augustinian model of language sees linguistic meaning in the following way:

1. Words name objects: the meaning of a word is the object for which it stands.
2. Every word has a meaning.
3. The meaning of a word is independent of context.
4. Sentence meaning is composed of word meanings.

1. Words Name Objects

If we consider examples of words such as "chair," "apple," and "pencil," language does seem to work this way. But if we look at examples such as "rectitude," "charisma," and "the day after tomorrow," it is harder to make the case that words name "objects." Wittgenstein (1953, p. 174) gives us a hint of the complexity he sees in these kinds of statements when he asks rhetorically:

A dog believes his master is at the door. But can he also believe his master will come the day after to-morrow?[sic]—

And *what* can he not do here?—How do I do it?—How am I supposed to answer this?

If "the day after tomorrow" were simply a phrase correlated with an object, or "meaning," of some kind, it would be plausible that even a dog could understand it and could come to expect his master then. A dog, after all, can recognize other kinds of objects: balls, bones, food, leashes, cats, and other dogs, as well as more abstract objects such as friends and enemies, and characteristic situations like his master coming home soon, playing, or being frightened. Further, a dog can "expect" things to happen some short time in the future, such as getting fed. But can a dog expect his master "the day after tomorrow?" Wittgenstein does not answer his question explicitly, but it is clear from his writings that he does not believe that a dog can do this. For Wittgenstein, the "day after tomorrow" is not a phrase that has a meaning, although we sometimes speak of it this way; that is, there are circumstances in which we use the word "meaning" in this way (we can imagine someone who is learning English asking "What does the 'day-after-tomorrow' mean?"). According to Wittgenstein (1953, p. 20), if we really want to understand the "meaning" of the "day after tomorrow" we need to look at its use:

> For a large class of cases—though not for all—in which we employ the word 'meaning' it can be explained thus: the meaning of a word is its use in the language.

Consequently, to understand the "meaning" of the "day after tomorrow," we need to be able to use it in the right circumstances, and to use it in the right circumstances we need experiences of distinguishing one day from another—"today," "tomorrow," "the day after tomorrow"—of observing the succession of one day following another, and of using days as units of time in a variety of activities. Further, these are not independent activities that can be separated from our daily lives and practices. To use the "day after tomorrow" correctly is not just to know a dictionary definition, it is to be able to discern the appropriate circumstances and activities in which it can be used, and this ability is further contingent on our ability to participate in a broad range of human activities in which understanding the "day after tomorrow" is important.

Someone who speaks another language and is learning English asks me, "What does the 'day after tomorrow' mean?" He can get along with this simple question because he already speaks another language and is probably familiar with the kinds of activities in which such a phrase is used. A dog, however, doesn't share with us the activities in which the "day after tomorrow" is important. Wittgenstein (1953, p. 223) brings this out more strikingly with one of his more enigmatic statements:

> If a lion could talk we could not understand him.

The reason we could not understand the speaking lion is that we have no personal experience of the activities in which he is engaged. If we can come to understand the meaning of a word by looking at its use, then meaning is intimately linked to the activities and practices that we have in common with others. If we do not have any activities in common, then there is nothing that we can talk about. In Wittgenstein's words, we have too few "forms of life" in common with the lion on which we could base a common language. For Wittgenstein:

> We don't start from certain words, but from certain occasions or activities. (Wittgenstein, 1972, p. 3)

> Only in the stream of thought and life do words have meaning. (Wittgenstein, 1967, p. 30)

After considering these problems with the Augustinian model of language, we may try to draw some comfort from the fact that language appears to work according to Augustine's model, at least in the cases where actual objects are referred to. But even here the relationship between language and "objects" is not simple. "Words" and "objects" recall the much-debated topic of "reference." Frege was one of the first philosophers to discuss some of the complexities of reference, but these issues reach back at least to the third century B.C. and Eubulides' "paradox of the masked man" (sometimes called "the paradox of the hood"). Suppose, said Eubulides, that you see a masked man. In reality, the masked man is your brother. But you cannot say that you saw your brother. Frege (1952) highlighted one of the important issues of reference with his example of the "Morning Star" and the "Evening Star."

Both the Morning Star and the Evening Star refer to the same celestial object, the planet Venus. Yet the descriptions "Morning Star" and "Evening Star" do not have precisely the same meaning for the simple reason that we cannot use them interchangeably in everyday discourse. That is, in ordinary usage we cannot say, in the morning, that we see the "Evening Star" and, in the evening, that we are looking at the "Morning Star," although neither statement is, technically, false.

In Frege's example we can at least tell what the speaker who refers to the "Morning Star" in the evening, or the "Evening Star" in the morning actually *means*. But Bertrand Russell (1905, p. 485) gave us an example of a problem of reference where it is not at all clear what the speaker means. Consider the following two statements:

"George the IV wished to know if Scott was the author of *Waverley*."

"Scott is the author of *Waverley*."

Now if "Scott" and "the author of *Waverley*" refer to the same person, *and* the meaning of a word is completely explained by its reference, as Augustine claims, then we should be able to use "Scott" and "the author of *Waverley*" interchangeably. If we substitute "Scott" for "the author of *Waverley*" in Russell's first sentence, then we get: "George the IV wished to know if Scott was Scott." Here, in contrast to Frege's example, the substitution of "Scott" for "the author of *Waverley*" leaves us with a sentence that Russell believed was clearly false and whose intended meaning would be impossible to discern. Russell (1905) went on to develop his *Theory of Definite Descriptions*, which was aimed at uncovering the logical form (as opposed to the grammatical form) of statements that refer to a single individual, like "the author of *Waverley*." This was used to address some of the troublesome puzzles about definite descriptions, such as the substitutivity problem, above, and references to nonexistent things (e.g., "There is no place called Shangri-La"). Although such a level of detail is beyond the scope of this review, it still makes engaging reading. (The interested reader should consult chapter 2 of Lycan [2000] for a very readable presentation of Russell's work on definite descriptions and the subsequent debates that he engaged in, principally with Strawson [1950].)

It is clear that even when a word or phrase has an obvious reference such as "Scott" and "the author of *Waverley*" do, the sense, or "meaning" of that word or phrase is more than just its reference. In some cases when we refer to a particular person we may not mean the person at all, but some salient aspect of the person. For example, Wittgenstein's father, Karl, was once referred to as "the Andrew Carnegie of Austria." By this, it was *not* meant that Karl looked like Carnegie, or had Scottish ancestry, but that he, like Carnegie, was a wealthy industrialist who patronized the arts. Finally, it is evident that many words, such as "rectitude" and "unicorn" do not refer to objects at all, yet we still use them regularly and are understood when we do so. Meaning must be something other than simple reference.

Augustine's model of language is a simple model and easy to comprehend, but some subtle aspects of it are not obvious at first. In particular, Augustine's description of how he learned to speak is important. In his words, he "...heard words repeatedly used ... [and] gradually learnt to understand what objects they signified ..." (Wittgenstein, 1953, p. 2). This passage makes the point that we can hear and distinguish words before we understand them. That is, words can exist for us without meaning—as words we don't understand. Further, because we can have words without meaning, it follows that "meaning" can exist independently of words—it appears to be something that can be added to words by a specific act such as looking them up in a dictionary. In some instances we can even have a "sense" or "meaning" without a word. We can see this sometimes when we compare words in two languages. For example, the Japanese have a word that means the point when a sound, such as the single stroke of a large bell, has diminished to a level where the listener cannot tell whether he can still hear it or not. In English, we don't have a word or simple phrase for this "meaning." Augustine's view of language dichotomizes words and meaning and sets up a framework in which they can be considered separately, a framework that exists in various forms to this day, most prominently in the belief in the independence of syntax and meaning that was the cornerstone of Chomsky's (1965) generative grammar.

This dichotomy between words and meaning forces us to deal with questions of meaning in a predictable, almost unavoidable, way. Specifically, when we can no longer maintain the claim that meaning equals some entity such as an "object," we give up the "object" but we inevitably try to keep the framework in which the "meaning" of a word is an entity of *some* kind. We think of a word having a "meaning" in the same way that we think of people having biological parents. The child may not know who his parents are, but their existence at some time is beyond doubt. Wittgenstein, too, believed in the dichotomization of meaning and words or grammar early in his career. But it was one of his major contributions to the philosophy of language to question this fundamental dichotomy; in short, to resist the "compulsion" to separate words and meaning that the Augustinian model of language seems to force on us.

> The questions "What is length?," "What is meaning?," "What is the number one?" etc., produce in us a mental cramp. We feel that we can't point to anything in reply to them and yet ought to point to something. (We are up against one of the great sources of philosophical bewilderment: a substantive makes us look for a thing that corresponds to it.) (Wittgenstein, 1958, p. 1)

Augustine's model of language reinforced the basic dichotomy between words and meaning, leaving to subsequent philosophers the task of trying to get them back together again. The fact that many words and phrases obviously do *not* refer to objects, yet are nonetheless meaningful, compels us to look for another entity that "meaning" could be. John Locke was able to articulate an alternative theory of meaning that preserved Augustine's separation of words and meaning but did not fall prey to its failures. For Locke (1690/1985, p. 114):

> Words in their primary or immediate signification, stand for nothing but the ideas in the mind of him that uses them.

Locke's linking of a word's signification, or "meaning," with an "idea" resolves the problem of words that do not refer to a physical object or type of object. We may not be able to link all words to objects, but it seems evident to some theorists that when we know the meaning of the words "rectitude" or "unicorn" we do have something "in mind." It is then easy to take the next step and assume that what we have "in mind" is what the word *means*. This is the "mentalistic theory of meaning"—a semantic theory that has widespread appeal and is implicit in much information retrieval theory.

Locke's mentalistic theory of meaning has had a long history of support, and various forms of it survive today. But, as appealing as mentalistic theories of meaning are, they suffer from a number of fatal problems. In the first place, if the meaning or sense of a word that I understand is an idea, then that idea, by definition, is something private to me. But if meaning is private, how do I teach you *my* idea of the meaning of a word, or learn the meaning of a word that you understand but I do not—after all, you cannot see what is in my mind. We *do* explain the meaning of words and phrases to each other, but is this explanation really a presentation of our ideas? If the explanation we give turns out to be wrong, what is the source of our error? Did we have the right idea, but explained it incorrectly, or was our original idea incorrect in the first place? There is no way to tell. Yet to teach or learn the meaning of a word or phrase requires clear criteria of correctness, something a purely mentalistic theory of meaning does not—and cannot—have. For Wittgenstein, the criterion for whether you understand the meaning of a word is not whether you have the right idea, but whether you use it correctly in your day-to-day speech and writing. If I want to teach you the "meaning" of a word, I can give you examples of how it is used, or show you how it is used in the appropriate actual or hypothetical circumstances. The question of whether you have the "right idea" doesn't come up in ordinary usage. Thus, if the criterion for correct understanding is correct usage, then ideas are not the foundation of our understanding—usage is. This is not to deny that some "mental phenomena" accompany our language use, it only means that, whatever those "mental phenomena" are, they are not required for teaching or learning a language; they are what epistemologists call "epiphenomena." The problem in semantics is not what the definition of "meaning" is, the problem is the seeming dichotomy between words and meanings that encourages us to think of "meaning" as a separate entity—something that can be linked to words and examined apart from usage. This is an example of what

Wittgenstein (1958, p. 143) called a "disease of thinking." A disease of thinking is a mistaken way of conceptualizing a problem that leads us unavoidably to the wrong conclusion. This is exactly what happens, Wittgenstein says, when we dichotomize our view of language by saying that "words have meanings." As soon as we talk as if there are such things as "meanings" that are linked, somehow, to words, we quite literally force ourselves to grant the independent existence of "meanings." Once we do that, it is a forgone conclusion that we will find something that we will be able to call the "meaning" of a word. Wittgenstein does not discuss the notion of a "disease of thinking" at any length, but the philosopher Gilbert Ryle (1931, p. 139), who admitted to being strongly influenced by Wittgenstein, wrote a classic paper in which he describes and discusses a number of different kinds of linguistic errors like this—what he aptly called "systematically misleading expressions." Note, though, that asking for the "meaning" of a particular word, is a quite ordinary and acceptable kind of request for speakers to make. Wittgenstein felt that it was acceptable for ordinary speakers to talk this way because they weren't concerned about the ultimate status of "meanings." The problem occurs when philosophers try to analyze this statement. For Wittgenstein, many of the "diseases of thinking" about language are only problems for philosophers, not for ordinary native speakers.

But "meanings" are not separate things that can be examined as a geologist examines rock samples. Meanings are not "entities," but rather are emergent phenomena arising from our day-to-day activities and practices (Holland, 1998). They are not solely mental entities, conscious or unconscious, because they are usually contingent on the circumstances and context of their usage. But although Wittgenstein linked meaning and use, he did not intend for meaning to be interpreted solely as behavior, a common misunderstanding of his work. Meaning is not solely behavioral because it often has a mental component, otherwise we would not be able to distinguish between someone who lies but has the same statements and behavior as someone telling the truth. Wittgenstein (1953, p. 220) expressed his attitude toward meaning and use most clearly when he said, "Let the use of words teach you their meaning."

The philosopher Hilary Putnam (1988) identifies several other problems with mentalism in his essay "Three Reasons Why Mentalism Can't

Be Right." Max Black (1968), a contemporary of Wittgenstein, presents an argument for the rejection of mentalism in his *The Labyrinth of Language*.

2. Every Word Has a Meaning

Even if the "meaning" of a word is not an object, there is still a tendency to think of the meaning of a word as a single thing, something that is the same in all applications. This is implicit in the notion that meaning is fixed by definitions, a view with which Wittgenstein explicitly disagrees. Again, if we think of tangible objects—chairs, cars, hammers, and the like—this view has a certain appeal. But on closer examination we can see that, even with common objects, there can be cases in which the definition or meaning is not a single thing. Those who think that a chair is simply a chair, should go to a museum of contemporary art. Here, what an artist may call a chair can vary widely from our accepted notion of what a "chair" is. But even in ordinary usage, what we might call a chair can deviate from our normal expectations. A chair has a function, it is something to sit on. Such a function can give the status of "chair" to a lot of objects. For example, if we need to sit down, but there are no ordinary chairs available, we might use a low table or a box to sit on. In a functional sense, the low table or box becomes a chair for the period of time we use it for this purpose. What is important is that the definition of even an ordinary object like a chair is not fixed. The boundary between what is a chair and what is not a chair may be unclear, and may vary according to circumstances. In a like manner, we can view a hammer as a specific kind of tool with a characteristic shape and heft, but we can also view a hammer as something that can be used in certain ways. In the functional sense, a lot of things can be used as hammers: rocks, iron bars, even fists.

The words "hammer" and "chair" can also be used metaphorically, or as figures of speech, such as when the weatherman says that a storm "hammered Cape Cod" or when a reporter states that Senator X "chaired the Armed Services Committee." These metaphorical or figurative uses of these words stretch our notion of what they mean and where it is appropriate to use them.

Some names of objects find a wide variety of applications. The word "head" is used to denote a particular anatomical feature of most animals, but there are other related uses of "head" that may be only distantly related to this anatomical feature:

> "He went to the **head** of the line."
> "She's the **head** of the executive board."
> "The crisis quickly came to a **head**."
> "They began the canoe trip at the **head** of the river."
> "The outlaws wuz **headin'** North, sheriff!"
> "The sailor's punishment was to keep the **head** clean for the next two weeks."

Such examples do not exhaust the different uses of the word "head," and this variability is typical of many other common words, such as "line" or "pitch." Examples like these should dispel any notion that word meaning is precise or a single thing or can even be limited to the various definitions listed in an unabridged dictionary. Hilary Putnam (1988) goes even further. In the first place, he says, meaning is "holistic." By this he means that the meaning of a word is not fixed once and for all by a definition (as logical positivists insisted it had to be), but is contingent on how it is used in a wide variety of statements and circumstances. No single use is definitional. Further, the meaning remains "nonmonotonic" or "defeasible"—it is always subject to revision or change. For example, when I say that the word "bird" means, in part, feathered bipeds that can fly, I do not mean for my listeners to conclude that a bird with a broken wing can fly, or that a newly hatched bird can fly. Nor do I mean that birds like penguins or ostriches can *ever* fly. It is also the case that there may be future unanticipated circumstances in which the birds will not be able to fly. For example, we might find that if a bird were taken into space aboard the space shuttle, it could not fly in weightless conditions. It is also possible that genetic engineering will produce flightless birds of a new type.

Putnam (1988) goes on to show that even when we agree on the meaning, or usage, of a particular word we still may not all have the same criteria for its use. Meaning, he proposes, is subject to a kind of "division of linguistic labor." By Putnam's account, even when we agree on the "meaning of a word" we may not be using identical criteria for its application. I may recognize an elm tree by the general size and shape of its serrated leaf, while my friend may recognize elms just as reliably as I do by examining the shape of the mature tree, the appearance of the bark, and the characteristics of the leaf buds. An expert botanist might be able to identify an elm by the particular cell structure of the wood, which can be seen under a microscope. Putnam's point is that the ability to use a word—here, "elm"—in the same way does not guarantee that the users possess the same criteria for the word's usage. Language, according to Putnam, is a cooperative activity. We may have useful heuristics that help us identify things like elms, but no one, not even the expert, can identify things like elms in every possible circumstance. For example, a botanist would probably not be able to identify an elm in complete darkness, but a blind person may have touch sensitive enough to do so by handling the bark and leaves. To distinguish an elm from a tree that looks very similar to it, or to identify an elm in the winter when it has no leaves, we would probably rely on expert botanists or a tree identification guide. But if we know very little about elms, we may just rely on our neighbor to help us identify them. This is what Putnam means by the "division of linguistic labor." The expert, according to Putnam, does not know a "more complete" definition of "elm" than we do, he or she simply knows more about elms than we do, and this additional information about elms may be useful for identifying elms in certain circumstances.

Wittgenstein (1953) would say that what accounts for the different criteria that we have, even when we can each identify elms reliably, is that we use the word "elm" in different "forms of life" and "language games." Forms of life are the regular activities and practices we engage in on a day-to-day basis, and language games are the regular patterns of word usage that dictate how we employ language in these activities and practices. Certain language games may be used primarily in specific forms of life. We need only the criteria to identify elms in the forms of life and language games that concern us. If we are not botanists, we may want only to identify the elms that we see in our own yard or neighborhood. The ability to distinguish species of elms, e.g., those that grow in southern latitudes from those that grow in northern latitudes, may not be important to us. For some botanists, distinguishing various species of elm may be important, but understanding the cell structure of elm wood may not be important. For a botanist at a tree farm, understanding the many varieties of cultivated elm species may be important, but understanding how to identify elms in the wild may be unimportant. And a botany student studying for an exam may need only to be able to write down the scientific definition of an "elm," which might include its Latin name and its correct phylum and genus. Some of these language games may pick out the same trees as elms, and some may not. There is no sense of a "complete" definition of an "elm" that would enable us to pick out elms in all conceivable circumstances because a single individual would probably not find himself or herself in "all conceivable circumstances." It also should be clear that there is no single language game that would require such an all-inclusive understanding of what an elm is. The criterion for whether individuals know the meaning of a word like "elm" is not whether they command some arbitrarily "complete" definition of an elm, but whether they can use the word "elm" correctly in the activities and practices in which they wish to participate.

3. The Meaning of a Word Is Independent of Context

Indexicals are good examples of context-dependent words: words like "here," "now," "this," "that," "him," "her," and "it." The references for these words change from context to context. These examples are fairly obvious, but other examples are more subtle and deal with aspects of context beyond the notion of physical presence or absence. Wittgenstein (1969, p. 348) gives the example, "I am here." This sentence has the indexicals "I" and "here," and these would be clarified by ascertaining who spoke the sentence and on what occasion. But if, as Wittgenstein notes, you are sitting before me and are perfectly visible, and you utter, "I am here" you probably mean something else entirely than the simple statement describing where you are; that is, it is obvious to me that you are here, so you must be trying to tell me something else. One can imagine a situation in which one person is distraught over something. A close friend or relative approaches, touches his or her hand, and says, "Don't worry, I am here," meaning, of course, not just that the speaker is physically present, but that the speaker is emotionally supportive. In this utterance the context needed to interpret the meaning of the sentence extends beyond the simple notion of physical presence and includes the relationship between the two individuals and the particular circumstances in which they find themselves.

Context can often indicate which of the many meanings of a word is currently being used. For example, the word "pitch" can mean a lot of things: the slope of a roof, the modulation of voice, a specific action in a baseball game, a tar-based substance, the description of a product that a salesman gives his customer, and so on. But if two individuals are talking while they attend a baseball game and use the word "pitch," it is highly unlikely that it means anything other than a specific action in the game. In fact, if the speaker at the baseball game were to continually remind the listener that he or she was using the word "pitch" to refer to an action in the baseball game and not any of the other uses of "pitch," such explanation would be considered bizarre, irritating, or even insulting.

Sometimes the context of an utterance can be so strong that it completely overrides the meaning of the actual words spoken. President Franklin Roosevelt would often dispel the boredom of a long receiving line before a White House dinner by saying completely inappropriate things to the guests as he greeted them—one of his favorite greetings was "I murdered my grandmother this morning." The guests, of course, would not hear his exact words and would assume that the President had greeted them in a cordial and expected manner (Fadiman & Bernard, 2000). Some individuals can even carry such a strong context with them that it becomes virtually impossible for them to say, or be understood to say, certain things. Could the Dalai Lama make an obscene gesture? Probably not, no matter what his intention actually was.

4. The Meaning of a Sentence Is Composed of the Meanings of Its Words

If we insist on understanding "meanings" as entities that are somehow attached to words, it can lead us into another problem; specifically, we may conclude that sentence meaning is somehow put together from the meanings of the words. If this is the case, then, most fundamentally, understanding the meaning of a sentence means that we must *be aware* of all the words in a sentence. Yet there is ample empirical evidence that, at least with speech, we often do not even hear every word in a sentence.

For example, suppose that you walk into a fast food restaurant and go up to the counter to order what you want. As you approach the counter, a clerk approaches you and says, "Kelp ya?" In spite of the fact that the clerk, strictly speaking, has not said any English words, we generally understand him to have said, "Can I help you?"—a phrase that makes sense. In cases like this, it is clear that we understand the situation or circumstances *before* we understand what is said to us, and our expectations about what is likely to be said may supersede what is actually said. Thus, sentence meaning, in this example, is not built up out of word meanings for the simple reason that we did not hear the words in the sentence.

But what about cases where we *do* hear all the words in a sentence. Are there ever cases in which the meaning of a sentence seems to have nothing to do with the meanings of the individual words? Yes, there are. Consider the following example. I come into my office in the morning, and after greeting a colleague I ask her, "Is Bill back from vacation yet?" She answers, in a perfectly forthright manner, "I saw a yellow Volkswagen in the parking lot this morning." What did she mean? It is not difficult to determine that she is saying that she believes Bill is back from vacation—i.e., that Bill owns a yellow VW, that a yellow VW is uncommon enough that Bill probably has the only one, and if Bill is back from vacation he will have likely driven his car to the office and parked it where it can be seen by others. But no matter how extended and detailed the descriptions are of the meanings of "saw," "yellow," "Volkswagen," "parking lot," and so on, there is no way that we can derive the meaning my colleague intended only from the meanings of her words. To understand what is happening here, we must turn to the work of another philosopher of language, Paul Grice, who distinguished between sentence meaning and speaker meaning.

The idea that words have meanings or definitions and that we come to understand what is said by somehow "looking up" the meanings of what we hear has been called the "Coding Theory of Language" (Eco, 1976). In short, words are codes that we must read or hear and then translate in order to arrive at their meaning. Sometimes language works this way, but, according to Grice, it is often the case that our understanding of what is said or written is *inferential*. Specifically, when we listen to what is said to us we begin with a number of assumptions about the intentions of the person to whom we are listening. Grice called these assumptions "conversational implicatures." In this example, when our colleague tells us "I saw a yellow Volkswagen in the parking lot this morning," she does not answer our question directly, and we must therefore infer what she meant rather than take the literal meaning of what she said to be what she intended. But we can only do this if we make the initial assumption that she is honestly trying to answer our question. This is the "cooperation principle." Whenever we talk to someone, we almost always assume they want to cooperate with us. But we make other assumptions too. Grice's (1989, pp. 26–27) Principle of Cooperation is based on the satisfaction of nine maxims, which fall into four categories: Quantity, Quality, Relation, and Manner:

> There are two maxims of **Quantity:**
> 1. Make your contribution as informative as is required (for the current purposes of the exchange).
> 2. Do not make your contribution more informative than is required.
>
> Two maxims of **Quality:**
> 1. Do not say what you believe to be false.
> 2. Do not say that for which you lack adequate evidence.
>
> One maxim of **Relation:**
> 1. Say only what you believe to be relevant.
>
> Four maxims of **Manner:**
> 1. Avoid obscurity of expression.
> 2. Avoid ambiguity.
> 3. Be brief (avoid unnecessary prolixity).
> 4. Be orderly.

It is my assumption, in this example, that my colleague is answering my question in a cooperative and relevant manner that allows me to make the necessary inferences that lead me to understand what she means. Without this assumption of cooperation, our communication would be far more difficult, and everything we say would have to be taken literally; that is, statements whose literal interpretation did not make sense would have to be considered odd, inappropriate, or meaningless.

In information retrieval, the process of describing what we want and evaluating what we retrieve is a lot like a conversation. We make requests and the retrieval system "answers" with sets of retrieved documents. Thus, we would expect that for successful "communication" to take place, Grice's maxims must be upheld in the search process. It is here that we can get the clearest picture of the difference between using a search engine to find information and asking an experienced searcher, such as a librarian, to help us. For both a search using a search engine and a search in which we ask a professional searcher to help us, we will probably assume, as Grice asserts, that both will be cooperative—they will try to answer our request. The difference between the two situations becomes clearer when the initial search fails to produce useful information. With the professional searcher, we can explain which of Grice's maxims has been violated in the search, and thereby provide guidance to the searcher on how to revise the search. For example, if we don't get enough information (a violation of the first maxim of Quantity) we might say, "That's what I'm looking for, but I need more of the same kind of information." If we get too much information (a violation of the second maxim of Quantity), we might say, "That's way too much detail, can you get me a more concise summary?" In another situation, we might receive information that is on the desired topic, but of questionable veracity (a violation of the first maxim of Quality), so we might say, "The information you got me claims that event X actually occurred, but can you find any documentation that substantiates that claim?" We could give examples for the violation of Grice's other maxims, too. The only kinds of retrieval failure that have been discussed much in the information retrieval literature have been the retrieval of nonrelevant documents (a violation of the maxim of Relation) and the retrieval of too much information (a violation of the second maxim of Quantity). It might be useful to consider the other maxims as additional criteria for successful retrieval (Blair, 1992).

Externalism and the Philosophy of Language

Recent work in the philosophy of language has shown the influence of the trend toward "Externalism" in the philosophy of mind. (A good presentation of the various forms of Externalism can be found in McGinn, 1989. See also McCulloch, 1995, and Rowlands, 1999.) Traditionally, the philosophy of mind has been almost exclusively "internalist"—that is, the workings of the mind, our thought processes, have been seen as acting entirely within the physical boundaries of the brain and skull. Internalism has been an implicit but essential component of the mind–body dualism most strongly associated with Descartes, and is still, in various forms, fundamental to many current models of cognition. Externalism, on the other hand, does not place the boundaries of cognition within the skull, but argues that there are many external facilities or processes that are necessary for cognition. Wittgenstein, who can be said to have had Externalist leanings, gave the example of our using a pencil and paper when we perform calculations. Many of us need such external implements for even simple calculations, but all of us need them for complex calculations. If we do not have a paper and pencil handy, we, quite literally, *cannot think*—the pencil and paper become a *sine qua non* for thought itself. Today, we have many such tools essential for thought: computers, databases, graphical plotters, and so on. None of us remembers everything he or she needs to conduct our daily affairs. Books, databases, and personal computers become necessary extensions of our memories. Without these implements, we would not be able to think the way we do.

The beginnings of Externalism, as a distinct movement in the philosophy of mind, finds its roots in Putnam's (1975) "Twin Earth" thought experiment. Putnam asked us to imagine that there was a "Twin Earth" that was exactly like our own earth, even to the point of having a "twin" of every person on this earth. But there was one aspect of Twin Earth that was different: On Twin Earth they had a substance they called "water," which was exactly like our own water except that instead of having a chemical structure H_2O it had a different structure that Putnam called "XYZ." Except for the different chemical structure, Twin Earth water had exactly the same function there as it does here: Twin Earthers drank it, washed in it, poured it on their plants, and used it in squirt guns for amusement. Twin Earth "water" came out of the sky in the form of rain, and large amounts of it formed rivers, lakes, and oceans, just like ours does. Since the Twin Earthers' use of their "water" was exactly like our own use of water, their conception of water—that is, their idea of what it was and how it was used—was exactly the same as our own idea of what we called "water." In other words, what average Twin Earthers had "in their heads" about water was exactly the same as what we had in our heads about our version of water. Yet, Putnam wrote, Twin Earth water was different from our water because it had a different chemical structure (XYZ vs. H_2O). The ineluctable conclusion of this thought experiment is that semantic meaning is not entirely internal. At least part of the definition of what water is, is external to our skulls because what we and the Twin Earthers have in our heads cannot distinguish our water from Twin Earth water. As Putnam (1975, pp. 144) put it, "Cut the pie any way you like, 'meanings' just ain't in the head!" Tyler Burge (1979) published an article a few years later extending Putnam's externalist interpretation of semantics to include intentional mental states such as beliefs, desires, hopes, and fears. Burge called the internalist interpretation that he and Putnam criticized "individualism."

Although the Twin Earth thought experiment is entirely fanciful, similar phenomena occur every day. In most categories there is a level of generality where different people will call different things by the same name—for example, what I call a "sparrow" and another person calls a "sparrow" might actually be different species of birds, even though they have the same behavior, general appearance, and habitat. The Twin Earth thought experiment has had a profound effect on philosophy over the last three decades. As Pessin and Goldberg (1996, p. xi) observed, "Twin Earth and 'The Meaning of Meaning,' the article in which it became famous, comprise perhaps the most influential single philosophical episode in the past half century." This quotation was taken from the preface of their valuable 20-year retrospective collection of prominent articles written about Putnam's Twin Earth thought experiment.

Externalist theories of cognition have been appearing in areas outside of philosophy, too. Andy Clark (1997), a neuroscientist/philosopher, has extended it to cognitive science with what he calls "scaffolding." Scaffolding is the process in which people intentionally alter their environment in ways that will elicit the kinds of responses that they want. Scaffolding provides external augmentation for intelligent activity, enabling us to achieve outcomes that would be difficult or impossible for a single, unassisted individual. This external assistance can be physical (e.g., a hammer, a truck, a boat, databases), cognitive (e.g., books, methods of estimation, rules of thumb, explicit directions), or social (e.g., creating professional societies or guilds of craftsmen to establish professional standards, to facilitate the dissemination of information, and to monitor professional conduct). Scaffolding contrasts most specifically with the Internalist foundation for intelligent behavior—"mental models." For some Externalists, mental models are not the foundation of understanding at all. As they put it, we don't need internal representations of the world, that is, mental models, because "the world is its own best representation" (Clark, 1997, p. 46).

Clark traces the roots of the idea of scaffolding back to the Soviet psychologist Lev Vygotsky (1986). As Clark (1997, p. 45) describes it: "Vygotsky stressed the way in which experience with external structures (including linguistic ones, such a words and sentences …) might alter and inform an individual's intrinsic modes of processing and understanding." The more general notion of "mind as inextricably interwoven with body, world, and action" (Clark, 1997, p. xvii) has its antecedents in the works of philosophers Martin Heidegger (1961) and Maurice Merleau-Ponty (1962, 1963). This ability to alter our immediate environment in order to augment our abilities and stimulate specific actions gives us the capability to perform exceptionally complex tasks, from building a house, to constructing a dam, to designing the equipment that can take astronauts to the moon and return them safely to Earth. Scaffolding occurs even on a simple level when we make subtle changes in our environment, for example, to help us remember things; that is, we can put an overdue library book on the driver's seat of the car so that when we get into the car next we will see the book and be reminded to return it. Or, we can leave notes to ourselves stuck to prominent places, like the refrigerator, to remind us of things we need to do.

Some of the most interesting scaffolding is that which we erect to enable several individuals to work together to perform a complex task. An exceptionally rich and detailed example of this kind of deliberate scaffolding occurs in Hutchins' (1995) *Cognition in the Wild,* in which the author describes a long and detailed study of the process of navigation on a Navy ship. This example is interesting because it involves the collaboration of several individuals, each of whom brings a different kind of expertise to the activity, and it requires a kind of precision and low fault tolerance that puts significant pressure on the individuals involved to get all the procedures right. As Clark (1997, p. 214), talking about Hutchins' work, put it, "Ship navigation emerges from the well-orchestrated adaptation of an extended complex system comprising individuals, instruments, and practices."

Scaffolding and Information Retrieval

If scaffolding can be considered an often necessary part of our cognitive processes, then it takes no great exercise of insight to see that information retrieval systems can be part of the scaffolding for many of our intelligent activities. An information retrieval system is, most obviously, a kind of external memory that can greatly augment what we remember, allowing us to consider and compare much more information than we could keep in our heads. But, more subtly, it can influence *how* we think as well. The particular searching procedures and the explicit or implicit theory of representation used by an information retrieval system can, quite literally, become extensions of the cognitive processes of inquirers—this can be either good or bad. For example, a simple full-text document retrieval system works by having searchers specify the words and phrases that they believe will occur in the literal text of the documents that have the intellectual content they would find useful, but would not occur in the text of documents they would not find useful. It has been shown, though, that on a reasonably large system, searchers looking for documents with a particular intellectual content are not very good at predicting the words and phrases that would occur in the documents they want, but would not occur in similar documents that they would not want (Blair & Maron, 1985). A simple full-text retrieval system, as scaffolding, extends the cognitive processes of the searcher, but it does so in an unnatural way, forcing the searcher to predict the exact words and phrases that occur in the desired documents, but do not occur in undesirable documents—something that people don't do well on a reasonably large system. Because information retrieval systems are potentially part of the scaffolding of inquirers, and, thus, are extensions of their cognitive processes, it becomes important that the systems provide a good fit between what they do and what people are good at. In the example just discussed (Blair & Maron, 1985), the searchers were lawyers trying to find evidence that supported the defense of a large corporate lawsuit. Full-text retrieval was not a good extension of the lawyers' thought processes in this case because it is hard to predict the exact words and phrases that can be used to discuss a particular topic. But one could imagine situations where full-text retrieval would be a good extension of our cognitive processes: perhaps a system providing access to newspaper articles where most of the searches are for articles discussing specific individuals, companies, institutions, cities or countries, or within certain time frames. People *are* quite good at remembering proper names and approximate time frames. An article discussing Henry Kissinger's 1972 talks with Andrei Gromyko on East Berlin will, almost certainly, have each of these names and the date in the article, and articles that do not discuss this event will almost certainly *not* have all of these names in the literal text. Here, a full-text information retrieval system will extend the cognitive capacities of the searchers in ways that take advantage of how they think; that is, it facilitates, or even improves, their thinking. Naturally, information retrieval systems should augment what we *don't* do well, too, such as having literal recall of gigabytes of written text or images.

If IR systems can be like extensions of our thought processes, then we must take heed of the way that memory works. Human memory is not a faculty in which everything perceived is deposited literally and kept. Psychologists have shown that we are quite selective about what we remember, and time has a natural way of weeding out memories that are less important or less useful to us. In other words, forgetting may be just as important as remembering. "The Russian neuropsychologist Alexander Luria described a much-celebrated mnemonist, Shereshevskii, who ... was overwhelmed by detailed but useless recollections of trivial information and events. He could recount without error long lists of names, numbers, and just about anything else that Luria presented to him. ... Yet when he read a story or listened to other people, he recalled endless details without understanding much of what he read or heard ... he had great difficulty grasping abstract concepts" (Schacter,

1996 referring to Luria, 1968, p. 81). The literal, nonforgetting memory of Luria's mnemonist is probably a close analogy to the way that computer "memory" works, and the difficulties Shereshevskii had with total recall are certainly a caveat of sorts. Thus, if the ranking of memories by their importance and the forgetting of useless ones are significant processes in human recollection, then IR systems, if they are to be adequate scaffolding for intelligent activities, may need to have similar characteristics—records should be continually ranked by their importance and less important ones regularly weeded out and forgotten. IR systems do not always have to mimic the way human memory works, but they should complement its functionality. Sometimes this may mean doing things essentially the same way, but sometimes it may mean doing things very differently. This is one of the main points made by Winograd and Flores (1987).

The only article in the information science literature to make explicit use of Clark's work on scaffolding is Jacob's (2001). In this article, Jacob relates classification theory to the "everyday world of work," a context that is strongly reliant on scaffolding. Scaffolding theory will undoubtedly have an important impact on description and classification in information retrieval, so it is likely that there will be more publications utilizing it in the future.

Implications of the Philosophy of Language for Information Retrieval

The general features of the philosophy of language's theory of meaning that I have presented here can be summarized as follows:

1. "Meanings" are not linked to words (Wittgenstein).
2. "Meanings" are not concepts or any other single *thing* (Wittgenstein, Putnam).
3. To understand the meaning of a word is not to have some definition in your head, but to be able to use the word correctly in the activities and practices in which it is normally used (Wittgenstein). To understand a word means to know *when* to use it—which activities and practices

(Wittgenstein's "forms of life") it is relevant in—and *how* to use it (Wittgenstein's "language games").

4. "Let the use of words teach you their meaning" (Wittgenstein, 1953, p. 220). Meaning is not the same as use, but *emerges* through use.

5. Context is important for language. We often understand the situation in which language is used before we understand the words used (Wittgenstein). Meaning, in part, is an *external* notion—what we have in our heads, our ideas, are neither necessary nor sufficient for determining what we mean: Context and circumstances are often essential determinants of meaning (Putnam, Wittgenstein).

6. We make a variety of assumptions about the intentions of those with whom we talk. In particular, unless given evidence to the contrary, we assume that the individuals with whom we talk will cooperate with us and follow Grice's maxims.

Although I have presented the principal themes of several prominent philosophies of language here, the reader should keep a number of caveats in mind. First of all, these are not the only issues engaged by philosophers of language. The literature of the philosophy of language is both deep and extensive, ranging far beyond the intellectual boundaries of the issues presented here. Secondly, the philosophical conclusions presented here are by no means accepted by all philosophers. Philosophy of language, like most other active intellectual processes, remains very much a dialectic. Nevertheless, the philosophies presented here *are* prominent, and have established themselves as major landmarks in the intellectual landscape of the philosophy of language.

The Significance of the Philosophy of Language for Information Retrieval

Because the thesis of this discussion is that the philosophy of language has some significance for the problem of description in information retrieval, I will briefly sketch some of this significance.

1. If the contexts of activities and practices are important for understanding language, it stands to reason that activities and practices are important for understanding document descriptions, too. As a consequence, it is essential for information retrieval systems to be as close as possible to the activities and practices that they serve. As Wittgenstein (1953, p. 220) said, we need to "let the use of words teach [us] the meaning." If we want to know what the descriptions used to represent a document *mean,* we must examine how these descriptions are used in the activities and practices that use that information—how do people ask for this information and how do they talk about it? One of the consequences of computerizing information retrieval systems is that the information they contain is often separated from these relevant activities and practices. Paper-based information has some obvious disadvantages regarding storage and copying when compared to the same information in electronic form. But paper-based information has one distinct advantage over electronic information: Because a paper document does not need delicate electronic equipment to present it, it can be carried and used almost anywhere—from the office, to the home, to a bus, to a rainy construction site, and so on. It is also easy to mark up, annotate, or highlight, and parts of it can be clipped out or photocopied and distributed. Further, small accidents such as dropping the information or spilling coffee on it do not render paper unreadable, although information on a laptop could not stand such abuse. Consequently, paper-based information can remain close to the activities that produce or use it, and these activities can provide an interpretive context for that information. But when that information is computerized, the very act of computerization may have the effect of removing the information from the activity context that provides much of its meaning and interpretation. The importance of the proximity of information systems to the activities and practices they serve was a major concern of Blair (1990).

2. If information retrieval systems cannot be physically near the activities and practices they support, then it may be useful to bring some of this context into the descriptions of the documents themselves. This enhancement could be done by linking documents to the respective activities and practices in which they might be used,

and weeding out information germane to activities that have concluded. The first step in information retrieval system design, then,
is to develop a detailed taxonomy of the various activities and practices that produce or use the information on the system. Each document on the system must then be explicitly linked to one or more
of these activities or practices. For private industry, documents
could be linked specifically to the value-creating activities and the
core competencies of the firm (Prahalad & Hamel, 1990).

3. If information retrieval can be seen as a kind of conversation
   between the searchers and those who designed the system or represented the documents, then the quality of retrieval is in some
   sense related to the quality of this conversation. But one of the
   characteristics of conversation is that the conversing parties are
   able to respond immediately to each other's expressions. This
   immediate conversational feedback minimizes the number of misunderstandings that can occur, by allowing the conversationalists
   to clarify any confusions or ambiguities of meaning that might
   arise. But one of the principal characteristics of information
   retrieval systems, especially computer-based ones, is that they
   inevitably create a distance between the conversationalists—
   searchers and system designers/indexers—that prevents them
   from getting the immediate feedback so characteristic of normal
   conversation (Blair, 1990). Linguistic meaning emerges through
   the interaction of individuals trying to make themselves understood as they conduct their daily affairs. But because no immediate
   feedback or chance at clarification takes place for searchers using
   an information retrieval system, the local interactions from which
   meanings emerge just don't occur. Looking at the information
   retrieval process as a conversation helps to clarify the role of the
   professional searcher in the search process. The professional
   searcher (for example, a librarian) must assume, primarily, the role
   of an interpreter. He or she must interpret or explain the intended
   meaning of the document descriptions to the searcher, and help the
   searcher express information needs in ways that, when used as
   queries, will retrieve any useful documents that are available on
   the system.

The unnatural conversations between searchers and systems designers/indexers point to important avenues of research and system design. First and foremost, system designers should look into designing information retrieval systems that afford the opportunity for searchers and systems designers/indexers to converse in a more real-time mode. For systems in which this is impossible, it would be useful to develop procedures that use searcher feedback to adapt document descriptions. User feedback has been an area of IR research for decades, but no major commercial systems use these techniques, and, although considerable research into adaptive systems has been conducted, no real consensus has emerged about which techniques are the best or even which techniques are better than others. (For early work in adaptive information retrieval see Salton [1989]. Some of the most interesting work on adaptation uses genetic algorithms. An excellent discussion of its importance in IR can be found in Serich [1999].)

4. Because much of our intelligent activity is heavily scaffolded, it stands to reason that information retrieval systems may often be an integral part of that scaffolding. For scaffolding to work well, though, it must supplement, support, or extend our actual cognitive processes. In other words, information retrieval systems must be designed, at least in part, to work with some specific cognitive ability or process that is endemic to humans and is essential to our ability to search for information. The information retrieval problem will probably not be addressed satisfactorily if it is seen as a purely technical problem—that is, if the retrieval problem is addressed by simply taking advantage of specific technical resources or efficiencies, such as storage capacity or physical access rates. The danger here is that by designing systems that take advantage of certain technical resources or efficiencies, we may actually force searchers to act in unnatural or problematic ways (see our example of using simple full-text retrieval to make fine discriminations of intellectual content in large systems [Blair & Maron, 1985]).

5. Finally, it is becoming increasingly important to understand how the growth in the size of information retrieval systems affects the prospects for designing effective systems. This situation is not a direct consequence of the philosophy of language, but arose in my

initial discussion of the ways in which document descriptions can fail. Because it is cheaper to keep all electronic documents than to regularly weed out those that are no longer useful, most computer-based information retrieval systems will continue to become larger. This increase in size will alter the way that documents and search requests are represented, changing the primary strategy of document representation from description to discrimination. But theories of document representation are primarily oriented toward description and rarely take into consideration how well index terms discriminate. Most existing automatic indexing procedures used by commercial systems operate solely within the textual boundaries of the document they are indexing and make no allowances for how discriminating the assigned index terms are for actual searches on a particular system. The notion of "term discrimination" considered here is not just a comparison of term frequency occurrences, in which a term that occurs in just one document in the collection is considered a good discriminator and a term that appears in all the documents is not. What I mean by a good discriminator is a term that discriminates useful from useless documents for a typical searcher. So term discrimination, the way that I mean it, must take into consideration the searching characteristics, techniques, and judgments of the typical searcher using the system in addition to the frequency of occurrence of the term. For example, if you are looking only at term frequency as a basis for discrimination, then identifying each document in a collection by a unique accession number is an excellent discriminator. But from the searcher's point of view, the unique accession number by itself would not be a very useful discriminator because there may be no simple way to relate it to what the searcher would find useful.

As information retrieval systems grow larger, the pressure to discriminate useful from useless documents will become greater and the ability to discriminate will most likely get worse; mutatis mutandis, it is easier to discriminate, that is, to find, two useful documents among 10 useless ones, than it is to discriminate or find two useful documents among 1,000 useless ones. Thus, as document retrieval systems become larger, retrieval effectiveness will generally get worse (or retrieval effort for the same level of effectiveness will get greater, which amounts to the same thing). Part of this problem can be mitigated by setting up rigorous document retention policies and other procedures for weeding out useless documents from existing systems. But some systems, such as the World Wide Web, will grow without any upper bound, so the exclusion of useless Web sites, even if it could be done systematically, would probably not be enough to mitigate the problems brought on by the growth in the overall number of Web sites. But for those systems for which periodic document weeding would be useful, the criteria for removing documents may be purely pragmatic: Documents should be weeded out of a system when the activities to which they are relevant have concluded.

There is a semantic lesson here, although it is a subtle one. One of the most important claims that Wittgenstein made in his philosophy of language was that questions of meaning in language cannot be adjudicated by appealing to abstract principles of semantics or to dictionary definitions, but can be resolved only by appealing to the ordinary usage of language. In short, whatever meaning there is in language, it is a meaning that emerges only from the day-to-day interactive usage of language—there can be no "better" or "more accurate" meaning in language than the meaning of ordinary discourse (this is why Wittgenstein's philosophy of language is called "ordinary language philosophy"). If the final criterion for semantics is everyday usage, then we can see very quickly that information retrieval systems are forcing us to use language in an unnatural way. Specifically, our language was never intended to be used to discriminate the intellectual content of small numbers of documents from vast numbers of other documents with similar intellectual content. In our typical day-to-day interactions we simply don't make such fine distinctions.

In the majority of information retrieval situations, as has been shown, the strategy for representing intellectual content is oriented almost exclusively toward the description of content rather than the discrimination of content. In one kind of information retrieval, however, discrimination is taken into account in the representation of intellectual content—cases in which the retrieval of information is a prominent part of an established practice. Good examples include some of the scientific disciplines, particularly the natural sciences. Here, the development of a taxonomy, which both describes and discriminates the major topics within the practice, is an important part of the practice itself. Biologists expend a significant amount of time discussing and even arguing about how the plants, animals, and professional activities of their respective fields are to be represented—that is, how they are to be described and discriminated from other, often similar, elements in their field. In fact, the theory behind the development of taxonomies in the life sciences has become a field of study in itself. As document collections grow to unprecedented sizes, perhaps we will need to take a lesson from the taxonomical efforts of the natural sciences and find ways to develop taxonomies of the more mundane information that we deal with on a daily basis. To expect that there will be a simple technical solution to this problem—the development of a particularly fast search engine, for example—is to ignore the complexity of language to which the field of the philosophy of language is a testament.

Writings on the Philosophy of Language and IR

Although the relevance of the philosophy of language to information retrieval is significant, its actual direct impact on the IR literature has been modest. Some of this may be due to the difficulty of the philosophy literature, but it is also the case that the philosophy of language is primarily concerned with puzzles of its own—puzzles such as the boundaries of factual discourse or the supervenience of psychological states on brain states—which are of less obvious value for understanding the problems of document representation and retrieval. Consequently, the reader interested in information retrieval problems might have to read a fairly large body of writings before he or she could distill something useful from it. It is to be hoped that this discussion will have provided the reader with some useful entrées to that literature. Nonetheless, a few authors interested in the problems of information retrieval have found the philosophy of language useful. Frohmann (1990) utilized the philosophy of language's critique of mentalism to point out similar shortcomings in the mentalism of indexing theory. In the same year, Blair (1990) published *Language and Representation in Information Retrieval*, in which he presented an extended argument for the importance of the problem of representation in information retrieval and for the relevance of Wittgenstein's philosophy of language for understanding it better. Two years later, Blair (1992) published a paper in which he gave a brief overview of the relevance of the linguistic philosophies of Austin, Searle, Grice, and Wittgenstein to the problems of information retrieval. In 1998, Hjørland published a paper in which he used the early and late philosophies of Wittgenstein as frameworks through which to examine some of the issues of information retrieval. In particular, he contrasts the early and late theories of meaning articulated by Wittgenstein in his "picture theory of meaning" and his "language games." Blair and Kimbrough (2002) have applied Wittgenstein's notion of "perspicuous examples" ("Übersichtliche Darstellungen") to the description of documents. They propose that in many document collections there are what they call "exemplary documents," which provide a guide to the intellectual content of many of the documents. Finally, there is an indirect link between an article on "relevance" by Harter (1992) and Grice's philosophy of language. Harter discusses the notion of relevance as presented by Sperber and Wilson (1986) who, in turn, base much of their work on Grice's philosophy of language.

One branch of the philosophy of language that has had a clear influence on information system design in general and, to a lesser extent, information retrieval has been the theory of Illocutionary, or Speech, Acts: Austin (1962) called them "Illocutionary Acts," while Searle (1969) gave them their more common name, "Speech Acts." Their biggest impact has been on electronic messaging systems (Kimbrough, 1990; Kimbrough & Lee 1986; Winograd & Flores, 1987), but Blair (1990, 1992) has described how they could be applied to information retrieval. The essence of Illocutionary, or Speech, Acts is that a class of linguistic events (Speech Acts) exists that has predictable structures and processes. I can say:

1. I'll mail you the check tomorrow.
2. I christen this ship the "Norton Sound, AVM-1."
3. Pick me up outside the main gate after the game.
4. Mary is the best copyeditor we have.

When we say such things (make a promise, christen a ship, give an order, or make an evaluation), we aren't so much talking *about* something, or making an assertion, we are actually doing something with our statements. If a reasonable individual in a normal situation promises to do something, then, by virtue of that statement, he or she has made a promise. What makes a Speech Act work is a set of "felicity conditions" that must be satisfied. Felicity conditions are ordinary circumstances or conventions that each Speech Act presupposes. I can promise you that I will lend you my car, if I have a car. But I cannot promise to make you a member of the House of Lords, because I am not the ruling British Monarch. Searle (1969) identifies the following kinds of Speech Acts:

- Directives: In which we order others to do things (e.g., "Get me a Guinness Stout and a bag of chips.")
- Commissives: In which we promise to do something (e.g., "I'll return the book I borrowed tomorrow.")
- Declarations: In which we bring about changes in the world solely by our utterance—in short, "Saying makes it so" (e.g., "I now pronounce you husband and wife.")
- Expressives: In which we express our personal feelings and attitudes (e.g., "You did a terrific job!")
- Assertives: In which we make statements, truly or falsely, about how things are (e.g., "The Sears Tower is the tallest building in Chicago.")

Each of these acts has a predictable structure and felicity conditions that guarantee its success. The best known applications of Speech Acts to electronic messaging is the COORDINATOR system (Flores, Graves, Hartfield, & Winograd, 1988; Winograd, 1988; Winograd & Flores, 1987). In this system, if you send a message making a promise to someone, the COORDINATOR system will prompt you in the future to fulfill your promise (the COORDINATOR cannot tell whether you have made a promise, given an order, or made a declaration; nor can it ascertain whether all the felicity conditions have been satisfied—this information must be provided by the individual sending the message). The idea that a number of messages can be related as parts of the same transaction is an important consequence of Speech Act analysis.

Blair (1990, 1992) has suggested using the different Speech Acts as a way of categorizing messages on an information retrieval system. This would provide another kind of access for retrieving documents. Such a classification system is especially useful for business communication in which the type of document—promise, order, declaration, and so on—can be important in many business processes (e.g., a "promise" in a business context might be a contract, whereas a statement of corporate strategy might be a kind of directive).

Finally, a number of authors in the information retrieval literature have found some use for an area of philosophy that historically has often been part of the philosophy of language—formal logic. Aristotle's syllogistic logic is arguably the first serious philosophy of language, and over the subsequent centuries logic has been primarily used to model formal relationships in language, such as the structure of argument and the nature of propositions. The early work in applying logic to the problems of IR was by Cooper (1971). More recently there has been a contribution by van Rijsbergen (1986a, 1986b, 1989), followed by a compilation by Crestani, Lalmas, and van Rijsbergen (1998). Crestani et al. bring together a nice selection of papers on logic and information retrieval. Cooper's paper defined a logically rigorous notion of relevance in information retrieval. The idea of relevance has been the focus of much concern and extensive writing, but little agreement. For Cooper, a document is relevant to a search query if its text can be used to form a "minimal premise set" that could be used to prove the assertion implicit in the search query. Although such a formal notion of relevance has a fairly narrow application, it does a useful job of establishing the boundaries of logical analysis in information retrieval. Some works, such as Wilson's (1973) writing on what he called "situational relevance" and van Rijsbergen's (1979), acknowledge an explicit debt to Cooper's seminal paper.

Conclusion

This discussion has attempted to provide an overview of some of the main ideas in the philosophy of language that have relevance to the issues of information retrieval. The philosophy of language is a much deeper and broader field of study than could be demonstrated in this chapter. Nevertheless, many of the most obvious connections between the philosophy of language and information retrieval should be apparent, and the relevance of the philosophy of language to the problems of information retrieval should be evident. Much good work applying the insights of the philosophy of language to information retrieval remains to be done.

Bibliography

Ambrose, A., & Macdonald, M. (Eds.). (1979). *Wittgenstein's lectures: Cambridge, 1932–1935*. Chicago: University of Chicago Press.

Austin, J. L. (1962). *How to do things with words*. Oxford, UK: Oxford University Press.

Baker, G. P., & Hacker, P. M. S. (1985). *Analytical commentary on the philosophical investigations: Wittgenstein: Rules, grammar and necessity*, Oxford, UK: Basil Blackwell.

Baker, G. P., & Hacker, P. M. S. (1980). *An analytical commentary on Wittgenstein's Philosophical Investigations: Vol. 1. Wittgenstein, understanding and meaning*. Chicago: University of Chicago Press.

Black, M. (1968). *The labyrinth of language*. New York: New American Library.

Blackburn, S. (1984). *Spreading the word: Groundings in the philosophy of language*. Oxford, UK: Clarendon Press.

Blair, D. C. (1992). Information retrieval and the philosophy of language. *Computer Journal, 35*, 200–207.

Blair, D. C. (1990). *Language and representation in information retrieval*. Amsterdam: Elsevier Science.

Blair, D. C. (1986). Indeterminacy in the subject access to documents. *Information Processing & Management, 22*, 229–241.

Blair, D. C. (1980). Searching biases in large, interactive document retrieval systems. *Journal of the American Society for Information Science, 31*, 271–277.

Blair, D. C., & Kimbrough, S. O. (2002). Exemplary documents: A foundation for information retrieval design. *Information Processing & Management, 38*, 363–379.

Blair, D. C., & Maron, M. E. (1985). An evaluation of retrieval effectiveness for a full-text document retrieval system. *Communications of the ACM, 28*(3), 289–299.

Bouwsma, O. K., Wittgenstein, L., Craft, J. L., & Hustwit, R. E. (1986). *Wittgenstein: Conversations, 1949–1951*. Indianapolis, IN: Hackett Publishing Company.

Brooks, T. A. (1993). All the right descriptors: A test of the strategy of unlimited aliasing. *Journal of the American Society for Information Science, 44*, 137–147.

Burge, T. (1979). Individualism and the mental. In P. A. French, T. E. Uehling, Jr., & H. K. Wettstein (Eds.), *Midwest Studies in Philosophy, 4, Studies in Metaphysics* (pp. 73–122). Minneapolis: University of Minnesota Press.

Chomsky, N. (1965). Aspects of the theory of syntax. Cambridge, MA: MIT Press.

Clark, A. (1997). *Being there: Putting brain, body, and world together again*. Cambridge, MA: MIT Press.

Cooper, W. S. (1971). A definition of relevance for information retrieval. *Information Storage and Retrieval, 7,* 19–37.

Crestani, F., Lalmas, M., & van Rijsbergen, C. J. (1998). *Information retrieval: Uncertainty and logics: Advanced models for the representation and retrieval of information.* Boston: Kluwer Academic.

Devitt, M., & Sterelny, K. (1999). *Language and reality: An introduction to the philosophy of language,* 2nd ed. Cambridge, MA: MIT Press.

Eco, U. (1976). *A theory of semiotics.* Bloomington, IN: Indiana University Press.

Fadiman, C., & Bernard, A. (Eds.). (2000). *Bartlett's book of anecdotes.* New York: Little Brown.

Flores, F., Graves, M., Hartfield, B., & Winograd, T. (1988). Computer systems and the design of organizational interaction. *ACM Transactions on Office Information Systems 6,* 153–172.

Frege, G. (1952). On sense and meaning. In P. Geach & M. Black (Eds.), *Translations from the philosophical writings of Gottlob Frege* (pp. 56–78). Totowa, NJ: Rowman and Littlefield.

Frohmann, B. (1990). Rules of indexing—A Critique of mentalism in information-retrieval research. *Journal of Documentation, 46,* 81–101.

Furnas, G. W., Landauer, T. K., Gomez, L. M., & Dumais, S. T. (1987). The vocabulary problem in human-system communication. *Communications of the ACM, 30*(11), 964–971.

Geach, P. T., Shah, K. J., & Jackson, A. C. (1989). *Wittgenstein's lectures on philosophical psychology, 1946–47.* Chicago: University of Chicago Press.

Glock, H.-J. (1996). *A Wittgenstein dictionary.* Cambridge, MA: Basil Blackwell.

Grice, P. (1989). *Studies in the way of words.* Cambridge, MA: Harvard University Press.

Hacker, P. M. S. (1989). *Insight and illusion: Themes in the philosophy of Wittgenstein.* Oxford, UK: Oxford University Press.

Hacker, P. M. S. (1990). *Analytical commentary on the philosophical investigations: Wittgenstein: Vol. 3. Meaning and mind.* Oxford, UK: Basil Blackwell.

Hacker, P. M. S. (1996a). *Analytical commentary on the philosophical investigations: Vol. 4. Wittgenstein: Mind and will.* Oxford, UK: Basil Blackwell.

Hacker, P. M. S. (1996b). *Wittgenstein's place in twentieth-century analytic philosophy,* Oxford, UK: Basil Blackwell.

Hallett, G. (1977). *A companion to Wittgenstein's Philosophical Investigations,* Ithaca, NY: Cornell University Press.

Harter, S. P. (1992). Psychological relevance and information science. *Journal of the American Society for Information Science, 43,* 602–615.

Heidegger, M. (1961). *Being and time.* (J. Macquarrie & E. Robinson, Trans.). New York: Harper and Row. (Original work published in 1927.)

Hjørland, B. (2000). Library and information science: Practice, theory, and philosophical basis. *Information Processing & Management, 36,* 503–531.

Hjørland, B. (1998). Information retrieval, text composition, and semantics. *Knowledge Organization, 25,* 16–31.

Holland, J. (1998). *Emergence: From chaos to order*. Reading, MA: Addison-Wesley.

Hutchins, E. (1995). *Cognition in the wild*. Cambridge, MA: MIT Press.

Jacob, E. (2001). The everyday world of work: Two approaches to the investigation of classification in context. *Journal of Documentation, 57*, 76–100.

Kenny, A. (1994). *The Wittgenstein reader*. Oxford, UK: Blackwell.

Kimbrough, S. O. (1990). On representing schemes for promising electronically. *Decision Support Systems, 6*, 99–122.

Kimbrough, S. O., & Lee, R. M. (1986). On illocutionary logic as a telecommunications language. *Proceedings of the 7th International Conference on Information Systems*, 15–26.

King, J., & Lee, D. (1978). *Wittgenstein's lectures: Cambridge, 1930–1932*. Chicago: University of Chicago Press.

Locke, J. (1985). An essay concerning human understanding. In A. J. Ayer & R. Winch (Eds.), *British empirical philosophers, (Book III)*. London: Routledge and Kegan Paul. (Original work published in 1690.)

Ludlow, P. (Ed.). (1997). *Readings in the philosophy of language*. Cambridge, MA: MIT Press.

Luria, A. R. (1998). *The mind of a mnemonist: A little book about a vast memory* (L. Solotaroff, Trans.). New York: Basic Books.

Lycan, W. (2000). *Philosophy of language: A contemporary introduction*. London: Routledge.

Malcolm, N. (1972). *Ludwig Wittgenstein: A memoir*. London: Oxford University Press.

Malcolm, N. (1986). *Nothing is hidden: Wittgenstein's criticism of his early thought*. Oxford, UK: Basil Blackwell.

Malcolm, N. (1995). *Wittgensteinian themes: Essays 1978–1989* (G. H. von Wright, Ed.). Ithaca, NY: Cornell University Press.

McCulloch, G. (1995). *The mind and its world*. New York: Routledge.

McGinn, C. (1989). *Mental content*, Oxford, UK: Basil Blackwell.

Merleau-Ponty, M. (1962). *The phenomenology of perception* (C. Smith, Trans.). London: Routledge and Kegan Paul.

Merleau-Ponty, M. (1963). *The structure of behavior* (A. L. Fisher, Trans.). Boston: Beacon Press.

Monk, R. (1990). *Ludwig Wittgenstein: The duty of genius*. New York: The Free Press.

Nedo, M. (Ed.). (1993). *Wiener Ausgabe* [Vienna edition]. Vienna: Springer-Verlag.

Pessin, A. & Goldberg, S. (Eds.). (1996). *The twin earth chronicles: Twenty years of reflections on Hilary Putnam's "The meaning of 'meaning.'"* Armonk, NY: M. E. Sharpe.

Pitkin, H. (1972). *Wittgenstein and justice*. Berkeley, CA: University of California Press.

Prahalad, C. K., & Hamel, G. (1990). The core competencies of the corporation. *Harvard Business Review, 68*(3), 79–91.

Putnam, H. (1975). The meaning of "meaning." In K. Gunderson (Ed.), *Minnesota studies in the philosophy of science*: Vol. 7. Language, mind and knowledge (pp. 131–193). Minneapolis, MN: University of Minnesota Press.

Putnam, H. (1988). *Representation and reality*, Cambridge, MA: MIT Press.

Redpath, T. (1990). *Ludwig Wittgenstein: A student's memoir*. London: Duckworth.

Rorty, R. (Ed.). (1967). *The linguistic turn: Recent essays in philosophical method*. Chicago: University of Chicago Press.

Rosenberg, J. F., & Travis, C. (Eds.). (1971). *Readings in the philosophy of language*. Englewood Cliffs, NJ: Prentice-Hall.

Rowlands, M. (1999). *The body in mind: Understanding cognitive processes*. New York: Cambridge University Press.

Russell, B. (1986). The philosophy of logical atomism and other essays, 1914–19. In J. G. Slater (Ed.), *The collected papers of Bertrand Russell: Vol. 8*. London: Allen & Unwin.

Russell, B. (1905). On denoting. *Mind, 14*, 479–493. [Reprinted in R. Marsh (Ed.). (1956) *Logic and knowledge*. London: Allen & Unwin.].

Ryle, G. (1931). Systematically misleading expressions. *Proceedings of the Aristotelian Society, 32*, 139–170.

Salton, G. (1989). *Automatic text processing: The transformation, analysis, and retrieval of information by computer*. Reading, MA: Addison-Wesley.

Schacter, D. (1996). *Searching for memory: The brain, the mind, and the past*. New York: Basic Books.

Searle, J. (1969). *Speech acts: An essay in the philosophy of language*. Cambridge, UK: Cambridge University Press.

Serich, S. T. (1999). Zipf's law as a necessary condition for mitigating the scaling problem in rule-based agents. (Doctoral dissertation, University of Michigan). (UMI No. 9959857).

Sperber, D. & Wilson, D. (1986). *Relevance: Communication and cognition*. Oxford, UK: Basil Blackwell.

Swanson, D. R. (1996). *Studies of indexing depth and retrieval effectiveness*. Unpublished report, National Science Foundation Grant GN 380.

Strawson, P. F. (1950). On referring. *Mind, 59*, 320–344.

Toyton, E. (1997, June). The Wittgenstein controversy. *Atlantic Monthly, 276*(6), 28–41.

van Rijsbergen, C. J. (1979). *Information retrieval*, 2nd ed., London: Butterworths.

van Rijsbergen, C. J. (1986a). A new theoretical framework for information retrieval. *Proceedings of the Annual International ACM SIGIR Conference on Research and Development in Information Retrieval (SIGIR '86)*, 194–200.

van Rijsbergen, C. J. (1986b). A non-classical logic for information retrieval. *Computer Journal, 29*, 481–485.

van Rijsbergen, C. J., & Lalmas, M. (1996). An information calculus for information retrieval. *Journal for the American Society for Information Science, 47*, 385–398.

Vygotsky, L. (1986). *Thought and language* (A. Kozulin, Trans.). Cambridge, MA: MIT Press.

Wilson, P. (1973). Situational relevance. *Information Storage and Retrieval, 9,* 457–471.

Winograd, T. (1988). Where the action is. *Byte, 13,* 256A–258.

Winograd, T., & Flores, F. (1987). *Understanding computers and cognition: A new foundation for design.* Reading, MA: Addison Wesley.

Wittgenstein, L. (1953). *Philosophical investigations* (G. E. M. Anscombe, Trans.). New York: Macmillan.

Wittgenstein, L. (1958). *The blue and brown books.* New York: Harper.

Wittgenstein, L. (1961a). *Notebooks: 1914–1916* (G. H. von Wright & G. E. M. Anscombe, Eds.; G. E. M. Anscombe, Trans.). New York: Harper.

Wittgenstein, L. (1961b). *Tractatus logico-philosophicus* (D. F. Pears & B. F. McGuinness, Trans.). London: Routledge & Paul. (Original work published in 1921.)

Wittgenstein, L. (1967). *Zettel* (G.E.M. Anscombe & G.H. von Wright, Eds.; G. E. M. Anscombe, Trans.) Oxford, U. K.: Basil Blackwell.

Wittgenstein, L. (1969). *On certainty.* Oxford, U. K.: Basil Blackwell.

Wittgenstein, L. (1972). *Lectures and conversations on aesthetics, psychology, and religious belief* (C. Barrett, Ed.). Berkeley, CA: University of California Press.

Wittgenstein, L. (1974). *Philosophical grammar.* Oxford, U. K.: Basil Blackwell.

Wittgenstein, L. (1975). *Philosophical remarks.* Oxford, U. K.: Basil Blackwell.

Wittgenstein, L. (1978). *Remarks on the foundations of mathematics* (Rev. ed.) (G. H. von Wright, R. Rhees, & G. E. M. Anscombe, Eds; G. E. M. Anscombe, Trans.) Cambridge, MA: MIT Press.

Wittgenstein, L. (1980). *Remarks on the philosophy of psychology* (G.E.M. Anscombe, G.H. von Wright, & H. Nyman, Eds.; G. E. M. Anscombe, C.G. Luckhardt & M. A. E. Aue, Trans.) Chicago: University of Chicago Press.

Wittgenstein, L. (1992). *Last writings on the philosophy of psychology,* Vol. 2. *The inner and the outer, 1949–1951* (G. H. von Wright & H. Nyman, Eds.; C. G. Luckhardt & M. A. E. Aue, Trans.) Oxford, UK: Basil Blackwell.

CHAPTER 2

Natural Language Processing

Gobinda G. Chowdhury
University of Strathclyde

Introduction

Natural Language Processing (NLP) is an area of research and application that explores how computers can be used to understand and manipulate natural language text or speech to do useful things. NLP researchers aim to gather knowledge on how human beings understand and use language so that appropriate tools and techniques can be developed to make computer systems understand and manipulate natural languages to perform desired tasks. The foundations of NLP lie in a number of disciplines, namely, computer and information sciences, linguistics, mathematics, electrical and electronic engineering, artificial intelligence and robotics, and psychology. Applications of NLP include a number of fields of study, such as machine translation, natural language text processing and summarization, user interfaces, multilingual and cross-language information retrieval (CLIR), speech recognition, artificial intelligence, and expert systems.

One important application area that is relatively new and has not been covered in previous *ARIST* chapters on NLP relates to the proliferation of the World Wide Web and digital libraries. Several researchers have pointed out the need for appropriate research in facilitating multi- or cross-lingual information retrieval, including multilingual text processing

and multilingual user interface systems, in order to exploit the full benefit of the Web and digital libraries (see for example, Borgman, 1997; Peters
& Picchi, 1997).

Scope

Several *ARIST* chapters have reviewed the field of NLP (Haas, 1996;
Warner, 1987). Literature reviews on large-scale NLP systems, as well as
related theoretical issues, have also appeared in a number of publications
(see for example, Jurafsky & Martin, 2000; Mani & Maybury, 1999;
Manning & Schutze, 1999; Sparck Jones, 1999; Wilks, 1996). Smeaton
(1999) provides a good overview of past research on the applications of
NLP in various information retrieval tasks. Several *ARIST* chapters
have appeared on areas related to NLP, such as machine-readable dictionaries (Amsler, 1984; Evans, 1989), speech synthesis and recognition
(Lange, 1993), and cross-language information retrieval (Oard &
Diekema, 1998). Research on NLP is regularly published in the annual
proceedings of the Association of Computational Linguistics (ACL) and
its European counterpart EACL, biennial proceedings of the
International Conference on Computational Linguistics (COLING),
annual proceedings of the Message Understanding Conferences (MUCs),
Text REtrieval Conferences (TRECs), and ACM SIGIR (Association for
Computing Machinery, Special Interest Group on Information Retrieval)
conferences. The most prominent journals reporting NLP research are
Computational Linguistics and *Natural Language Engineering*. Articles
reporting NLP research also appear in a number of information science
journals such as *Information Processing & Management, Journal of the
American Society for Information Science and Technology,* and *Journal of
Documentation.* Several researchers have also conducted domain-specific
NLP studies and reported them in journals specifically dealing with the
field in question, such as the *International Journal of Medical
Informatics* and *Journal of Chemical Information and Computer Science.*

Beginning with the basic issues of NLP, this chapter aims to chart the
major research activities in this area since the last *ARIST* chapter in
1996 (Haas, 1996): natural language text processing systems—text summarization, information extraction, information retrieval, and so on,
including domain-specific applications; natural language interfaces;

NLP in the context of the Web and digital libraries; and evaluation of NLP systems.

Linguistic research in information retrieval is not covered; this huge area is dealt with separately in this volume by David Blair. Similarly, NLP issues related to information retrieval tools (e.g., search engines) for Web search are not covered here because indexing and retrieval for the Web are the subjects of Edie Rasmussen's chapter, also in this volume.

Tools and techniques developed for building NLP systems are discussed in this chapter along with the specific areas of application for which they are built. Although machine translation (MT) is an important part, and in fact the origin, of NLP research, this topic is not addressed in great detail because it is a large area and demands separate treatment. Similarly, cross-language information retrieval, although a very important area in NLP research, is not covered in depth. A chapter on CLIR research appeared recently in *ARIST* (Oard & Diekema, 1998). However, MT and CLIR have become two important areas of research in the context of digital libraries. This chapter reviews some works on MT and CLIR in the context of NLP and information retrieval (IR) in digital libraries and the Web. Artificial intelligence techniques, including neural networks, are excluded.

Some Theoretical Developments

Previous *ARIST* chapters (Haas, 1996; Warner, 1987) described a number of theoretical developments that have influenced research in NLP. The most recent can be grouped into four classes: (1) statistical and corpus-based methods in NLP, (2) efforts to use WordNet for NLP research, (3) the resurgence of interest in finite-state and other computationally lean approaches to NLP, and (4) the initiation of collaborative projects to create large grammar and NLP tools.

Statistical methods are used in NLP for a number of purposes, e.g., for word sense disambiguation, for generating grammars and parsing, for determining stylistic evidence of authors and speakers, and so on. Charniak (1995) points out that 90 percent accuracy can be obtained in assigning part-of-speech tags to words by applying simple statistical measures. Jelinek (1999) is a widely cited source on the use of statistical methods in NLP, especially in speech processing. Rosenfield (2000) reviews statistical language models for speech processing and argues for a Bayesian approach to the integration of linguistic theories of data.

Mihalcea and Moldovan (1999) mention that, although statistical approaches have thus far been considered best for word sense disambiguation, they are useful in only a small set of texts. They propose the use of WordNet to improve the results of statistical analyses of natural language texts. WordNet is an online lexical reference system developed at Princeton University. This excellent NLP tool contains English nouns, verbs, adjectives, and adverbs organized into synonym sets, each representing one underlying lexical concept. Details of WordNet are available in Fellbaum (1998) and on the Web (http://www.cogsci.princeton.edu/~wn). WordNet is now used in a number of NLP research and application areas. One of the major applications of WordNet in NLP has been in Europe with the formation of EuroWordNet in 1996. EuroWordNet is a multilingual database with WordNets for several European languages including Dutch, Italian, Spanish, German, French, Czech, and Estonian, structured in the same way as the WordNet for English (http://www.hum.uva.nl/~ewn).

Finite-state automation is the mathematical approach used to implement regular expressions—the standard notation for characterizing text sequences. Variations of automata such as finite-state transducers, Hidden Markov models, and n-gram grammars are important components of speech recognition and speech synthesis, spell checking, and information extraction, which are the principal applications of NLP. Different applications of the finite state methods in NLP have been discussed by Jurafsky and Martin (2000), Kornai (1999), and Roche and Shabes (1997).

The work of NLP researchers has been greatly facilitated by the availability of large-scale grammars for parsing and generation. Researchers can gain access to large-scale grammars and related tools through several Web sites; for example, Lingo (http://lingo.stanford.edu/), Computational Linguistics and Phonetics (http://www.coli.uni-sb.de/software.phtml), and the Parallel Grammar Project (http://www.parc.xerox.com/istl/groups/nltt/pargram/). Another significant recent development is the formation of various national and international consortia and research groups that can help share expertise and facilitate research in NLP. The Linguistic Data Consortium (LDC) (http://www.ldc.upenn.edu/)

at the University of Pennsylvania is a typical example that creates, collects, and distributes speech and text databases, lexicons, and other resources for research and development among universities, companies, and government research laboratories. The Parallel Grammar project is another example of international cooperation. This project is a collaborative effort involving researchers from Xerox PARC in California, the University of Stuttgart and the University of Konstanz in Germany, the University of Bergen in Norway, and Fuji Xerox in Japan. This project aims to produce wide-coverage grammars for English, French, German, Norwegian, Japanese, and Urdu, which are written collaboratively with a commonly agreed upon set of grammatical features (http://www.parc. xerox.com/istl/groups/nltt/pargram/). The recently formed Global WordNet Association is yet another example of cooperation. It is a non-commercial organization that provides a platform for discussing, sharing, and connecting WordNets for all languages in the world. The first international WordNet conference, held in India in January 2002, addressed various problems of NLP faced by researchers from different parts of the world (http://www.ciil.org/gwn/report.html).

Natural Language Understanding

At the core of any NLP task is the important issue of natural language understanding. The process of building computer programs that understand natural language involves three major problems: The first relates to thought processes, the second to the representation and meaning of the linguistic input, and the third to world knowledge. Thus, an NLP system may begin at the word level to determine the morphological structure and nature (such as part-of-speech or meaning) of the word; and then may move on to the sentence level to determine the word order, grammar, and meaning of the entire sentence; and then to the context and the overall environment or domain. A given word or sentence may have a specific meaning or connotation in a given context or domain, and may be related to many other words and/or sentences in the given context.

Liddy (1998) and Feldman (1999) suggest that in order to understand natural languages, it is important to be able to distinguish among the following seven interdependent levels that people use to extract meaning from text or spoken languages:

- Phonetic or phonological level that deals with pronunciation

- Morphological level that deals with the smallest parts of words that carry meaning, and suffixes and prefixes

- Lexical level that deals with lexical meaning of words and parts of speech analyses

- Syntactic level that deals with grammar and structure of sentences

- Semantic level that deals with the meaning of words and sentences

- Discourse level that deals with the structure of different kinds of text using document structures

- Pragmatic level that deals with the knowledge that comes from the outside world, i.e., from outside the content of the document

A natural language processing system may involve all or some of these levels of analysis.

NLP Tools and Techniques

A number of researchers have attempted to improve the technology for performing various activities that form important parts of NLP work. These activities may be categorized as follows:

- Lexical and morphological analysis, noun phrase generation, word segmentation, and so forth (Bangalore & Joshi, 1999; Barker & Cornacchia, 2000; Chen & Chang, 1998; Dogru & Slagle, 1999; Kazakov, Manandhar, & Erjavec, 1999; Lovis, Baud, Rassinoux, Michel, & Scherter, 1998; Tolle & Chen, 2000; Zweigenbaum & Grabar, 1999).

- Semantic and discourse analysis, word meaning, and knowledge representation (Kehler, 1997; Meyer & Dale, 1999; Mihalcea & Moldovan, 1999; Pedersen & Bruce, 1998; Poesio & Vieira, 1998; Tsuda & Nakamura, 1999).

- Knowledge-based approaches and tools for NLP (Argamon, Dagan, & Krymolowski, 1998; Fernandez & Garcia-Serrano, 2000; Martinez

& Garcia-Serrano, 1998; Martinez, de Miguel, Cuadra, Nieto, & Castro, 2000).

Dogru and Slagle (1999) propose a model lexicon that involves automatic acquisition of the words as well as representation of the semantic content of individual lexical entries. Kazakov et al. (1999) report research on word segmentation based on an automatically generated, annotated lexicon of word-tag pairs. Wong et al. (1998) report the features of an NLP tool called Chicon used for word segmentation in Chinese text. Zweigenbaum and Grabar (1999) propose a method for acquiring morphological knowledge about words in the medical literature, which takes advantage of commonly available lists of synonym terms to bootstrap the acquisition process. Although the authors experimented with the method on the SNOMED International Microglossary for Pathology in its French version, they claim that because the method does not rely on a priori linguistic knowledge, it is applicable to other languages such as English. Lovis et al. (1998) propose the design of a lexicon for use in processing medical texts.

Noun phrasing is an important NLP technique used in information retrieval. One of the major research areas is combining traditional keyword and syntactic approaches with semantic approaches to text processing in order to improve the quality of information retrieval. Tolle and Chen (2000) compared four noun phrase generation tools in order to assess their ability to isolate noun phrases from medical journal abstracts databases. The NLP tools evaluated were: Chopper, developed by the Machine Understanding Group at the MIT Media Laboratory; Automatic Indexer and AZ Noun Phraser, developed at the University of Arizona; and NPTool, a commercial NLP tool from LingSoft, a Finnish Company. The National Library of Medicine's SPECIALIST Lexicon was used along with the AZ Noun Phraser. This experiment used a reasonably large test set of 1.1 gigabytes of text, comprising 714,451 abstracts from the CANCERLIT database. This study showed that with the exception of Chopper, the NLP tools were fairly comparable in their performance, measured in terms of recall and precision. The study also showed that the SPECIALIST Lexicon increased the ability of the AZ Noun Phraser to generate relevant noun phrases. Pedersen and Bruce (1998) propose a corpus-based approach to word-sense disambiguation that requires only information that can be automatically extracted from untagged text. Barker and Cornacchia (2000) describe a simple system for choosing noun phrases from a document based on their length, their frequency of occurrence, and the frequency of the head noun, using a base noun phrase skimmer and an off-the-shelf online dictionary. This research revealed some interesting findings: (1) the simple noun-phrase-based system performs roughly as well as a state-of-the-art, corpus-trained keyphrase extractor, (2) ratings for individual keyphrases do not necessarily correlate with ratings for sets of keyphrases for a document, and (3) agreement among unbiased judges on the keyphrase rating task is poor. Silber and McCoy (2000) report research that uses a linear time algorithm for calculating lexical chains, which is a method of capturing the "aboutness" of a document.

Mihalcea and Moldovan (1999) argue that the reduced applicability of statistical methods in word sense disambiguation is due basically to the lack of widely available, semantically tagged corpora. They report research that enables the automatic acquisition of sense tagged corpora, and is based on (1) the information provided in WordNet, and (2) the information gathered from the Internet using existing search engines.

Martinez and Garcia-Serrano (1998) and Martinez et al. (2000) propose a method for the design of structured knowledge models for NLP. The key features of their method comprise the decomposition of linguistic knowledge sources in specialized sub-areas to tackle the complexity problem and a focus on cognitive architectures that allow for modularity, scalability, and reusability. The authors claim that their approach profits from NLP techniques, first-order logic, and some modeling heuristics (Martinez et al. 2000). Fernandez and Garcia-Serrano (2000) comment that knowledge engineering is increasingly regarded as a means to complement traditional formal NLP models by adding symbolic modeling and inference capabilities in a way that facilitates the introduction and maintenance of linguistic experience. They propose an approach that allows the design of linguistic applications to integrate different formalisms, reuse existing language resources, and support the implementation of the required control in a flexible way. Costantino (1999) argues that qualitative data, particularly articles from online news agencies, are not yet successfully processed, and as a result, financial operators, notably traders, suffer from qualitative data overload. IE-Expert is a system that combines the techniques of NLP, information extraction, and expert systems in order to be able to suggest investment decisions from a large volume of texts (Constantino, 1999).

Natural Language Text Processing Systems

Manipulation of texts for knowledge extraction, for automatic indexing and abstracting, or for producing text in a desired format, has been recognized as an important area of research in NLP. This is broadly classified as the area of natural language text processing that allows structuring of large bodies of textual information with a view to retrieving particular information or to deriving knowledge structures that may be used for a specific purpose. Automatic text processing systems generally take some form of text input and transform it into an output of a different form. The central task for natural language text processing systems is the translation of potentially ambiguous natural language queries and texts into unambiguous internal representations on which matching and retrieval can take place (Liddy, 1998). A natural language text processing system may begin with morphological analyses. Stemming of terms, in both the queries and documents, is done in order to derive the morphological variants of the words involved. The lexical and syntactic processing involves the utilization of lexicons for determining the characteristics of the words, recognizing their parts of speech, determining the words and phrases, and parsing of the sentences.

Past research concentrating on natural language text processing systems has been reviewed by Haas (1986), Mani and Maybury (1999), Smeaton (1999), and Warner (1987). Some NLP systems have been built to process texts using particular small sublanguages to reduce the size of the operations and the nature of the complexities. These domain-specific studies are largely known as "sublanguage analyses" (Grishman & Kittredge, 1986). Some of these studies are limited to a particular subject area such as medical science, whereas others deal with a specific type of document, such as patents.

Abstracting

The terms "automatic abstracting" and "text summarization" are now used synonymously. This area of NLP research is becoming more common in the Web and digital library environments. In simple abstracting or summarization systems, parts of text—sentences or paragraphs—are selected automatically, based on some linguistic and/or statistical criteria, to produce the abstract or summary. More sophisticated systems may merge two or more sentences, or parts thereof, to generate one coherent sentence, or may generate simple summaries from discrete items of data.

Recent interest in automatic abstracting and text summarization is reflected in the large volume of research appearing in a number of international, national, and regional conferences and workshops presented by the ACL, the American Association for Artificial Intelligence (AAAI), and the ACM SIGIR. Several techniques are used for automatic abstracting and text summarization. Goldstein, Kantrowitz, Mittal, and Carbonell (1999) use conventional IR methods and linguistic cues for extracting and ranking sentences for generating news article summaries. A number of studies on text summarization have been reported recently. Silber and McCoy (2000) claim that their linear time algorithm for calculating lexical chains is an efficient method for preparing automatic summarization of documents. Chuang and Yang (2000) report a text summarization technique using cue phrases appearing in the texts of U.S. patent abstracts.

Roux and Ledoray (2000) report a project, Aristotle, that aims to build an automatic medical data system capable of producing a semantic representation of a text in a canonical form. Song and Zhao (2000) propose a method of automatic abstracting that integrates the advantages of both linguistic and statistical analysis of a corpus.

Moens and Uyttendaele (1997) describe the SALOMON (Summary and Analysis of Legal Texts for Managing Online Needs) project that automatically summarizes Belgian criminal court cases. The system extracts relevant information from the full texts, such as the name of the court issuing the decision, the decision date, the offenses charged, the relevant statutory provisions disclosed by the court, and the legal principles applied in the case. A text grammar represented as a semantic network is used to determine the category of each case. RAFI (Résumé Automatique à Fragments Indicateurs) is an automatic text summarization system that transforms full-text scientific and technical documents into condensed texts (Lehmam, 1999). RAFI adopts discourse analysis techniques, using a thesaurus for recognition and selection of the most pertinent elements of texts. The system assumes a typical structure of areas from each scientific document, namely, previous knowledge, content, method, and new knowledge.

Most automatic abstracting and text summarization systems work satisfactorily within a small text collection or within a restricted domain. Building robust and domain-independent systems is a complex and resource-intensive task. Arguing that purely automatic abstracting systems do not always produce useful results, Craven (1988, 1993, 2000) proposes a hybrid abstracting system in which some tasks are performed by human abstractors and others by assistance software called TEXNET. However, recent experiments on the usefulness of the automatically extracted keywords and phrases in actual abstracting by human abstractors showed considerable variation among subjects, with only 37 percent of the abstractors finding keywords and phrases useful in writing their abstracts (Craven, 2000).

Information Extraction

Knowledge discovery and data mining have become important areas of research over the past few years, and in addition to *ARIST*, several information science journals have published special issues reporting research on these topics (see, for example, Benoît, 2002; Qin & Norton, 1999; Raghavan, Deogun, & Server, 1998; Trybula, 1997; Vickery, 1997). Knowledge discovery and data mining use a variety of techniques to extract information from source documents. Information extraction (IE) is a subset of knowledge discovery and data mining that aims to extract useful bits of textual information from natural language texts (Gaizauskas & Wilks, 1998). A variety of IE techniques is used and the extracted information can serve a number of purposes: for example, to prepare a summary of texts, populate databases, fill in slots in frames, and identify keywords and phrases for information retrieval. IE techniques are also used for classifying text items according to predefined categories. CONSTRUE, an early categorization system developed for Reuters, classifies news stories (Hayes, 1992). The CONSTRUE software was subsequently generalized into a commercial product called Text Categorization Shell (TCS). Yang and Liu (1999) report an evaluation of five text categorization systems.

Morin (1999) suggests that, although many IE systems can successfully extract terms from documents, revealing relations between terms is still difficult. PROMETHEE is a system that extracts lexico-syntactic patterns relative to a specific conceptual relation from technical corpora (Morin, 1999). Bondale, Maloor, Vaidyanathan, Sengupta, and Rao (1999) suggest that IE systems must operate at many levels, from word recognition to discourse analysis at the level of the complete document. They report an application of the Blank Slate Language Processor (BSLP) for the analysis of a real-life natural language corpus of responses to open-ended questionnaires in the field of advertising.

Glasgow, Mandell, Binney, Ghemri, and Fisher (1998) describe a system called Metlife's Intelligent Text Analyzer (MITA) that extracts information from life insurance applications. Ahonen, Heinonen, Klemettinen, and Verkamo (1998) propose a general framework for text mining using pragmatic and discourse level analyses of text. Sokol, Murphy, Brooks, and Mattox (2000) combine visualization and NLP technologies to perform text mining. Chang, Ko, and Hsu (2000) argue that IE systems are usually event-driven (i.e., based on domain knowledge built on various events) and propose using the neural network paradigm for event detection to drive intelligent information extraction. They employ the back propagation (BP) learning algorithm to train the event detector, and apply NLP technology to aid the selection of nouns as feature words to characterize documents. These nouns are stored in an ontology as a knowledge base and are used for the extraction of useful information from e-mail messages.

Cowie and Lehnert (1996) reviewed research on IE and observed that the NLP research community was ill-prepared to tackle the difficult problems of semantic feature tagging, co-reference resolution, and discourse analysis, all of which are important aspects of IE research. Gaizauskas and Wilks (1998) reviewed IE research from its origin in the artificial intelligence world in the 1960s and 1970s through to the present. They discussed major IE projects undertaken in different sectors, namely, academic research, employment, fault diagnosis, finance, law, medicine, military intelligence, police, software system requirements specification, and technology/product tracking.

Chowdhury (1999a) reviewed research that used template mining techniques in a range of contexts: extracting proper names from full-text documents, extracting facts from press releases, abstracting scientific papers, summarizing new product information, extracting specific information from chemical texts, and so on. He also discussed how some Web search engines use templates to facilitate information retrieval, and recommended that each Web author complete a template to characterize his/her document, to regularize the creation of document surrogates. However, he warns that a single, all-purpose metadata format will not be applicable for all authors in all domains, and further research is necessary to develop appropriate formats for each.

Smeaton (1997) argues that IE has been the subject of much research and development and has been delivering working solutions for many decades, whereas IE is a more recent and emerging technology. He urges the IE community to see how a related task—perhaps the most-related task, information retrieval—has managed to use basic NLP technology in its development. Commenting on the future challenges of IE researchers, Gaizauskas and Wilks (1998) mention that the performance levels of the common IE systems, which lie in the 50 percent range for combined recall and precision, need to improve significantly to satisfy information analysts. Cost is a major stumbling block of IE systems development. CONSTRUE, for example, required 9.5 person years of effort (Hayes & Weinstein, 1991). Portability and scalability are also two big issues for IE systems, which depend heavily on domain knowledge. A given IE system may work satisfactorily in a relatively small text collection, but it may not perform well in a larger collection or in a different domain. Alternative technologies are now being used to overcome these problems. Adams (2001) discusses the merits of NLP and the wrapper induction technology in extracting information from Web documents. In contrast to NLP, wrapper induction operates independently of specific domain knowledge. Instead of analyzing the meaning of discourse at the sentence level, wrapper technology identifies relevant content based on the textual qualities that surround the desired data. Wrappers operate on the surface features that characterize texts of training examples. A number of vendors, such as Jango (purchased by Excite), Junglee (purchased by Amazon), and Mohomine employ wrapper induction technology (Adams, 2001).

Information Retrieval

Information retrieval (IR) has been a major application area of NLP, resulting in a large number of publications. Lewis and Sparck Jones (1996) commented that the generic challenge for NLP in information retrieval was whether the necessary processing of texts and queries was doable; and the specific challenges were whether non-statistical and statistical data could be combined, and whether data about individual documents and whole files could be combined. They further suggested that there were major challenges in making NLP technology operate effectively and efficiently and also in conducting appropriate evaluation tests to assess whether and how far the approach worked in the case of interactive searching of large text files. Feldman (1999) suggested that in order to achieve success in IR, NLP techniques should be applied in conjunction with other technologies such as visualization, intelligent agents, and speech recognition.

Arguing that syntactic phrases were more meaningful than statistically obtained word pairs, and thus more powerful for discriminating among documents, Narita and Ogawa (2000) used shallow syntactic processing instead of statistical processing to identify candidate phrasal terms from query texts. Comparing the performance of Boolean and natural language searches, Paris and Tibbo (1998) found that, in their experiment, Boolean searches had better results than freestyle (natural language) searches. However, they concluded that neither could be considered superior for every query. In other words, different queries demand different techniques.

Pirkola (2001) showed that languages vary significantly in their morphological properties. However, for each language there are two variables that describe the morphological complexity, namely, an index of synthesis (IS) that describes the amount of affixation in an individual language, i.e., the average number of morphemes per word in the language; and an index of fusion (IF) that describes the ease with which two morphemes can be separated in a language. Pirkola (2001) found that calculation of the ISs and IFs in a language is a relatively simple task, and once established, they could be utilized fruitfully in empirical IR research and system development.

Variations in presenting subject matter greatly affect IR, and, hence, the linguistic variation of document texts is one of the field's greatest challenges. In order to investigate how consistently newspapers choose words and concepts to describe an event, Lehtokangas and Järvelin (2001) chose articles on the same news stories from three Finnish newspapers. Their experiment revealed that for short newswire items the consistency was 83 percent and for long articles, 47 percent. The newspapers were very consistent in using concepts to represent events, with a level of consistency varying between 92 and 97 percent.

Khoo, Myaeng, and Oddy (2001) investigated whether information obtained by matching cause–effect relations expressed in documents with the cause–effect relations expressed in user queries improves results in document retrieval when compared with the keywords only, without considering the relations. Their experiment with the *Wall Street Journal* full-text database revealed that searching either the cause or the effect as a wildcard can improve information retrieval effectiveness if the appropriate weight for the type of match can be determined. However, the authors stressed that the results of this study were not as strong as they had expected.

Chandrasekar and Srinivas (1998) suggested that coherent text contains significant latent information, such as syntactic structure and patterns of language use, and that this information could be used to improve the performance of information retrieval systems. They described Glean, a system that uses syntactic information to filter irrelevant documents, thereby improving the precision of information retrieval.

A number of tracks (research groups or themes) in the TREC series of experiments deal directly or indirectly with NLP and information retrieval, such as the cross-language, filtering, interactive, question-answering, and Web tracks. Reports of progress of the Natural Language Information Retrieval (NLIR) project are available in the TREC reports (Perez-Carballo & Strzalkowski, 2000; Strzalkowski, Fang, Perez-Carballo, & Jin, 1997; Strzalkowski et al., 1998; Strzalkowski et al., 1999). The major goal of this project has been to demonstrate that robust NLP techniques used for indexing and searching of text documents perform better than the simple keyword and string-based methods used in statistical full-text retrieval (Strzalkowski et al., 1999). However, results indicated that simple linguistically motivated indexing (LMI) was no more effective than well-executed statistical approaches in English language texts. Nevertheless, it was noted that more detailed search topic statements responded well to LMI, when compared to terse one-sentence search queries. Thus, it was concluded that query expansion, using NLP techniques, leads to sustainable advances in IR effectiveness (Strzalkowski et al., 1999).

Natural Language Interfaces

A natural language interface is one that accepts query statements or commands in natural language and sends data to some system, typically a retrieval system, which then provides appropriate responses to the commands or query statements. A natural language interface should be able to translate the natural language statements into appropriate actions for the system. A large number of natural language interfaces that work reasonably well in narrow domains have been reported in the literature (for a review of such systems see Chowdhury, 1999b, Chapter 19; Haas, 1996; Stock, 2000).

Many of the efforts in natural language interface design to date have focused on handling rather simple natural language queries. Several question-answering systems are now being developed that aim to provide answers to natural language questions, as opposed to documents containing information related to the question. Such systems often use a variety of IE and IR operations employing NLP tools and techniques to derive the correct answer from the source texts. Breck, Burger, House, Light, and Mani (1999) report a question-answering system that uses techniques from knowledge representation, information retrieval, and NLP. The authors claim that this combination promotes domain independence and robustness in the face of text variability, both in the question and in the raw text documents used as knowledge sources. Research reported in the Question Answering (QA) track of TREC shows some interesting results. The basic technology used by the participants in the QA track included several steps. First, cue words and phrases like "who" (as in "Who is the prime minister of Japan?") and "when" (as in "When did the Jurassic period end?") were identified to guess what was needed; and then a small portion of the document collection was retrieved using standard text retrieval technology. This was followed by a shallow parsing of the returned documents, to identify the entities required for an answer. If no appropriate answer type was found, the best matching passage was retrieved. This approach works well as long as the query types recognized by the system have broad coverage, and the system can classify questions reasonably accurately (Voorhees, 1999). In TREC-8, the first QA track of TREC, the most accurate QA systems could answer more than two thirds of the questions correctly. In the second QA track (TREC-9), the best performing QA system, the Falcon system from Southern Methodist University, was able to answer 65 percent of the questions (Voorhees, 2000). These results are quite impressive in a domain-independent, question-answering environment. However, the questions were still simple in the first two QA tracks. In the future more complex questions, requiring answers to be obtained from more than one document, will be handled by QA track researchers.

Owei (2000) argued that the drawbacks of most natural language interfaces to database systems result primarily from their weak interpretative power, which is caused by their inability to deal with the nuances in human use of natural language. The author further argued that the difficulty with NL database query languages (DBQLs) could be overcome by combining concept-based DBQL paradigms with NL approaches to enhance the overall ease-of-use of the query interface.

Zadrozny, Budzikowska, Chai, and Kambhatla (2000) suggested that in an ideal information retrieval environment, users should be able to express their interests or queries directly and naturally, by speaking, typing, and/or pointing; the computer system should then be able to provide intelligent answers or ask relevant questions. However, they commented that even though we build natural language systems, this goal cannot be fully achieved due to limitations of science, technology, business knowledge, and programming environments. The specific problems include the following (Zadrozny et al., 2000):

- Limitations of NL understanding

- Managing the complexities of interaction (for example, when using NL on devices with differing bandwidth)

- Lack of precise user models (for example, knowing how demographics and personal characteristics of a person should be reflected in the type of language and dialogue the system employs to interact with the user)

- Lack of middleware and toolkits

NLP Software

A number of specific NLP software products have been developed over the years, some of which are free, while others are available commercially. Many such NLP software packages and tools have already been mentioned in this chapter. More NLP tools and software are introduced in this section.

Pasero and Sabatier (1998) describe the principles underlying ILLICO, a generic natural language software tool for building larger applications that perform specific linguistic tasks such as analysis, synthesis, and guided composition. Liddy (1998) and Liddy, Diamond, and McKenna (2000) discuss the commercial use of NLP in IR with the example of DR-LINK (Document Retrieval Using LINguistic Knowledge) system demonstrating the capabilities of NLP for IR. Detailed product information and a demo of DR-LINK are available online (http://www. textwise.com/dr-link.html). Nerbonne, Dokter, and Smit (1998) report on GLOSSER, an intelligent assistant for Dutch students learning to read French. Scott (1999) describes the Kana Customer Messaging System that can categorize inbound e-mails and messages, forward them to the right department, and generally streamline the response process. Kana also has an auto-suggestion function that helps a customer service representative answer questions on unfamiliar territory. Scott (1999) describes another system, Brightware, which uses NLP techniques to elicit meaning from groups of words or phrases and reply to some e-mails and messages automatically. NLPWin is an NLP system from Microsoft that accepts sentences and delivers detailed syntactic analyses, together with a logical form representing an abstraction of the meaning (Elworthy, 2000). Scarlett and Szpakowicz (2000) report a diagnostic evaluation of DIPETT, a broad-coverage parser of English sentences.

The Natural Language Processing Laboratory, Center for Intelligent Information Retrieval at the University of Massachusetts (http://www-nlp.cs.umass.edu/nlplic.html), distributes source codes and executables to support IE system development efforts at other sites. Each module is designed to be used in a domain-specific and task-specific customizable IE system. Available software includes:

- MARMOT Text Bracketting Module, a text file translator that segments arbitrary text blocks into sentences, applies low-level specialists such as date recognizers, associates words with part-of-speech tags, and brackets the text into annotated noun phrases, prepositional phrases, and verb phrases
- BADGER Extraction Module, analyzes bracketed text and produces case frame instantiations according to application-specific domain guidelines
- CRYSTAL Dictionary Induction Module, learns text extraction rules, suitable for use by BADGER, from annotated training texts
- ID3-S Inductive Learning Module, a variant on ID3 that induces decision trees on the basis of training examples

Waldrop (2001) briefly describes the features of three NLP software packages:

- Jupiter, a product of the MIT Research Lab that works in the field of weather forecasting
- Movieline, a product of Carnegie Mellon University that talks about local movie schedules
- MindNet from Microsoft Research, a system for automatically extracting a massively hyperlinked Web of concepts, from, say, a standard dictionary

Feldman (1999) mentions a number of NLP software packages:

- ConQuest, a part of Excalibur, that incorporates a lexicon implemented as a semantic network
- InQuery that parses sentences, stems words, and recognizes proper nouns and concepts based on term co-occurrence
- The LinguistX parser from Xerox PARC that extracts syntactic information and is used in InfoSeek
- Text mining systems like NetOwl from SRA and KNOW-IT from TextWise

A recent survey of 68 European university centers in computational linguistics and NLP, carried out under the auspices of the Socrates Working Group on Advanced Computing in the Humanities, revealed that Java has already become the second most commonly taught programming language (Black, Rinaldi, & McNaught, 2000). In addition, Java-based programs are being used to develop interactive instructional materials. Black et al. (2000) review some Java-based courseware and discuss the issues involved in more complex natural language processing applications that use Java.

Internet, Web and Digital Library Applications of NLP

The Internet and the Web have brought significant advances in the way we create, look for, and use information. A huge volume of information is now available through the Internet and digital libraries. However, these developments have made problems related to information processing and retrieval more prominent. According to a recent survey (Global Reach, 2001), 55 percent of Internet users are non-English speakers; this is increasing rapidly, thereby reducing the percentage of Net users who are native English speakers. However, about 80 percent of the Internet and digital library resources available today are in English (Bian & Chen, 2000). This dramatizes the urgent need for multilingual information systems and CLIR facilities. How to manipulate the large volume of multilingual data has become a major research question. At the user interface level, a query translation system must translate from the user's native language to the language of the system. Several approaches have been proposed for query translation. The dictionary-based approach uses a bilingual dictionary to convert terms from the source language to the target language. Coverage and up-to-dateness of the bilingual dictionary are major issues here. The corpus-based approach uses parallel corpora for word selection, where the problem lies with the domain and scale of the corpora. Bian and Chen (2000) proposed MTIR, a Chinese-English CLIR system on the Web that integrated query and document translation. They also addressed a number of issues regarding machine translation on the Web; specifically, the role played by HTML tags in translation, the trade-off between the speed and performance of the translation system, and the form in which the translated material is presented.

Staab et al. (1999) described the features of an intelligent information agent called GETESS that used semantic methods and NLP capabilities to gather tourist information from the Web and present it to the human user in an intuitive, user-friendly way. Ceric (2000) reviewed advances in Web search technology and mentioned that NLP technologies would have a positive impact on the success of search engines. Mock and Vemuri (1997) described the Intelligent News Filtering Organizational System (INFOS) that was designed to filter unwanted news items from a Usenet news group. INFOS built a profile of user interests based on user feedback. After the user browsed each article, INFOS asked the user to rate the article, and used this as a criterion for selection (or rejection) of similar articles next time around. News articles were classified by a simple, quick-pass keyword method, called Global Hill Climbing (GHC). Articles that could not be classified by GHC were passed through a WordNet knowledge base through a case-based reasoning (CBR) module, a slower but more accurate method. Very small-scale evaluation of INFOS suggested that the indexing pattern method, i.e., mapping of the words from the input text into the correct concepts in the WordNet abstraction hierarchy, correctly classified 80 percent of the articles; the major reason for errors was the weakness of the system in disambiguating pronouns.

One of the major stumbling blocks to providing personalized news delivery over the Internet is the difficulty of automatically associating related items from different media. Carrick and Watters (1997) described a system that aimed to determine to what degree any two news items refer to the same news event. This research focused on determining the association between photographs and stories by using names. The algorithm developed was tested against a test data set as well as new data sets, with human experts checking the pairs of news items and photos generated by the system. In terms of recall, precision, and time, the system performed comparably for the new and training sets.

Because of the volume of text available on the Web, many researchers have proposed using it as the testbed for NLP research. Grefenstette (1999) argued that, although noisy, Web text presents language as it is used, and statistics derived from the Web can have practical uses in many NLP applications.

Machine Translation and CLIR

With the proliferation of the Web and digital libraries, multilingual information retrieval has become a major challenge. Two sets of issues are considered here: (1) recognition, manipulation, and display of multiple languages; and (2) cross-language information search and retrieval (Peters & Picchi, 1997). The first set of issues relates to the enabling technology that will allow users to access information in whatever language it is stored, while the second set implies permitting users to specify their information needs in their preferred language while retrieving information in whatever language it is stored. Text translation can take place at two levels: (1) translation of the full text from one language to another for the purpose of search and retrieval; and (2) translation of queries from one language to one or more different languages. The first option is feasible for small collections or for specific applications, as in meteorological reports (Oudet, 1997). Translation of queries is a more practicable approach, and promising results have been reported in the literature.

Oard (1997) commented that seeking information from a digital library could benefit from the ability to query large collections once using a single language. Furthermore, if the retrieved information was not available in a language the user can read, some form of translation would be needed. Multilingual thesauri such as EUROVOC help to address this challenge by facilitating controlled vocabulary searches using terms from several languages, whereas services such as INSPEC produce English abstracts for documents in other languages (Oard, 1997). However, as Oard noted, fully automatic MT was neither sufficiently fast nor sufficiently accurate to adequately support interactive cross-language information seeking in the Web and digital library environments. Fortunately, an active and rapidly growing research community has coalesced around these and related issues, applying techniques drawn from several fields, notably IR and NLP, to provide access to large multilingual collections.

Borgman (1997) commented that we have hundreds (and sometimes thousands) of years' worth of textual materials in hundreds of languages, created long before data encoding standards existed. She illustrated the multilanguage digital language challenge with examples drawn from the research library community, which typically handles collections of materials in about 400 different languages.

Ruiz and Srinivasan (1998) investigated an automatic method for CLIR that utilized the multilingual Unified Medical Language System (UMLS) Metathesaurus to translate Spanish natural language queries into English. They concluded that the UMLS Metathesaurus-based CLIR method was at least equivalent to, if not better than, multilingual-dictionary-based approaches. Yang, Gomez, and Song (2000) observed that there was no reliable guideline as to how large, machine readable corpora should be compiled to develop practical NLP software packages and/or complete dictionaries for humans and computational use. They proposed a new mathematical tool—a piecewise curve-fitting algorithm—and suggested how to determine the tolerance error of the algorithm for good prediction, using a specific corpus.

Two telematics application program projects in the Telematics for Libraries initiative, TRANSLIB and CANAL/LS, were active between 1995 and 1997 (Oard, 1997). Both projects investigated cross-language searching in library catalogs, and each included English, Spanish, and at least one other language; CANAL/LS added German and French, while TRANSLIB added Greek. MULINEX (http://mulinex.dfki.de), another European project, is concerned with the efficient use of multi-lingual online information. The project aims to process multilingual information and present it to the user in a way that facilitates finding and evaluating the desired information quickly and accurately. TwentyOne, started in 1996, is an EU-funded project aiming to develop a tool for efficient dissemination of multimedia information in the field of sustainable development (http://twentyone.tpd.tno.nl/twentyone). Details of these and CLIR research projects in the U.S. and other parts of the world have been reviewed by Oard and Diekema (1998).

Magnini, Not, Stock, and Strapparava (2000) described two projects where NLP had been used for improving performance in the public administration sector. The first project, GIST, was concerned with auto-matic multilingual generation of instructional texts for form filling. The second project, TAMIC, aimed to provide an interface for interactive access to information, centered on NLP and designed to be used by the clerk along with the active participation of the individual citizen.

Powell and Fox (1998) described SearchDB-ML Lite, a federated search system, for searching heterogeneous multilingual collections of theses and dissertations on the Web (the Networked Digital Library of

Theses and Dissertations, NDLTD [www.ndltd.org/]). A markup language, called SearchDB, was developed for describing the characteristics of a search engine and its interface, and a protocol was built for requesting word translations between languages. A review of the results generated from simultaneously querying over 50 sites revealed that in some cases more sophisticated query mapping was necessary to retrieve results sets that truly correspond to the original query. The authors reported that an extended version of the SearchDB markup language was being developed that could reflect the default and available query modifiers for each search engine; work was also underway to implement a mapping system that used this information.

Several companies now provide machine translation services, for example (McMurchie, 1998):

- Berlitz International, Inc. offers professional translation service in 20 countries

- Lernout and Hauspie has an Internet Translation Division

- Orange, California-based Language Force, Inc., has a product called Universal Translator Deluxe

- IBM MT services through its WebSphere Translation Server

Numerous research papers discuss MT and CLIR projects that deal with specific languages; for example, Chinese (Kwok, Grunfeld, Dinstl, & Chan, 2000; Lee, Ng, & Lu, 1999), Japanese (Ma et al. 2000; Ogura, Nakaiwa, Matsuo, Ooyama, & Bond, 2000; Yang & Akahori, 2000), Portugese (Barahona & Alferes, 1999), Sinhalese (Herath & Herath, 1999), Spanish (Marquez, Padro, & Rodriguez, 2000; Weigard & Hoppenbrouwers, 1998), Thai (Isahara, Ma, Sornlertlamvanich, & Takahashi, 2000), and Turkish (Say, 1999). Some studies have considered more than two languages; see, for example, Ide (2000). Various aspects of MT are considered, for example:

- Use of cue phrases in determining relationships among the lexical units in a discourse (Say, 1999)

- Generation of semantic maps of terms (Ma et al., 2000)

- Creation of language-specific semantic dictionaries (Ogura et al., 2000)
- Discourse analysis (Yang & Akahori, 2000)
- Lexical analysis (Ide, 2000; Lee et al., 1999)
- Part-of-speech tagging (Isahara et al., 2000; Marquez et al., 2000)
- Query translation (Kwok et al., 2000)
- Transliteration of foreign words for information retrieval (Jeong, Mayeng, Lee, & Choi, 1999)

Weigard and Hoppenbrouwers (1998) reported how an English/Spanish lexicon, including an ontology, is constructed for NLP tasks in an ESPRIT project called TREVI. Emphasizing the point that there had not been any study of natural language information retrieval in Swedish, Hedlund, Pirkola, and Järvelin (2001) described the features of the language and point out a number of research problems. They stressed that research in NLP in Swedish is required because the research findings and tools for other languages do not quite apply to Swedish because of the language's unique features.

Reviewing the progress of MT research, Jurafsky and Martin (2000, p. 825) commented "machine translation system design is hard work, requiring careful selection of models and algorithms and combination into a useful system." They continued, "despite half a century of research, machine translation is far from solved; human language is a rich and fascinating area whose treasures have only begun to be explored."

Evaluation

Evaluation is an important area in any system development activity, and information science researchers have long been struggling to determine appropriate evaluation mechanisms for large-scale information systems. Similarly, NLP researchers have also been trying to develop reliable methods for evaluating robust NLP systems. However, a single set of evaluation criteria will not be applicable to all NLP tasks. Different evaluation parameters may be required for each task, such as information extraction and automatic abstracting, which are significantly different in nature when compared with other NLP tasks such, as MT, CLIR, or natural language user interfaces.

The Evaluation in Language and Speech Engineering (ELSE) project, under contract from the European Commission, studied the possible implementation of comparative evaluation in NLP systems. Comparative evaluation in language engineering has been used since 1984 in the U.S. Defense Advanced Research Projects Agency (DARPA) research program on human language technology. Comparative evaluation consists of a set of participants who compare the results of their systems using similar tasks and related data with agreed-upon metrics. Usually this evaluation is performed in a number of successive evaluation campaigns with more complex tasks performed at each stage. The ELSE approach departs from the DARPA research program in two ways: first by considering usability criteria in the evaluation, and second by trading competitive aspects for more contrastive and collaborative ones through the use of multidimensional results (Paroubek & Blasband, 1999). The ELSE consortium has identified the following five types of evaluation (Paroubek & Blasband, 1999):

- Basic research evaluation: tries to validate a new idea or assess the amount of improvement it creates in older methods
- Technology evaluation: tries to assess the performance and appropriateness of a technology for solving a problem that is well-defined, simplified, and abstracted
- Usage evaluation: tries to assess the usability of a technology for solving a real problem in the field. It involves the end-users in the environment intended for the deployment of the system under test
- Impact evaluation: tries to measure the socio-economic consequences of a technology
- Program evaluation: attempts to determine how worthwhile a funding program has been for a given technology

The Expert Advisory Group on Language Engineering Standards—Evaluation Workgroup (EAGLES) (Centre for Language Technology, 2000), phase one (1993–1995) and phase two (1997–1998), was a

European initiative that proposed a user-centered evaluation of NLP systems. The EAGLES work took as its starting point an existing standard, ISO 9126, which is concerned primarily with the definition of quality characteristics to be used in the evaluation of software products.

The Diagnostic and Evaluation Tools (DiET) project (1997–1999) was designed to develop data, methods, and tools for the glass-box evaluation of NLP components, building on the results of previous projects covering different aspects of assessment and evaluation. The Web page of the DiET project (http://www.dfki.de.lt/projects/diet-e.html) indicates that the project "will extend and develop test-suites with annotated test items for grammar, morphology, and discourse for English, French, and German. DiET will provide user support in terms of database technology, test-suite construction tools, and graphic interfaces." Further, it "will result in a tool-package for in-house and external quality assurance and evaluation, which will enable the commercial user to assess and compare Language Technology products."

The Message Understanding Conferences, now ceased, pioneered an international platform for sharing research on NLP systems. In particular, MUC researchers were involved in the evaluation of IE systems applied to a common task. The first five MUCs focused on analyzing free text, identifying events of a specified type, and filling a database template with information about each such event (http://www.cs.nyu.edu/cs/faculty/grishman/muc6.html). After MUC-5, a broad set of objectives was defined for subsequent MUCs, such as, to push information extraction systems toward greater portability to new domains, and to encourage evaluations of some basic language analysis technologies. In MUC-7 (the last MUC), the multilingual named entities evaluation was run using training and test articles from comparable domains for all languages (Chinchor, 2001). The MUC-7 papers report some interesting observations by system developers who were not native speakers of the languages of their systems and system developers who were. Results of MUC-3 through MUC-7 have been summarized by Chinchor (2001).

Conclusions

Some NLP experiments reported in this chapter show encouraging results. However, one should not forget that most of these experimental systems remain in the lab; very few experimental systems are converted to real systems or products. One of the major stumbling blocks of NLP research, as in areas like information retrieval research, has been the absence of large test collections and reusable experimental methods and tools. Fortunately, the situation has changed over the past few years. Several national and international research groups are now working together to build and reuse large test collections and experimental tools and techniques. Since the origin of the Message Understanding Conferences, group research efforts have proliferated with regular conferences and workshops; for example, the TREC series and other conferences organized by the North American Chapter of the Association for Computational Linguistics, European ACL, and so on. These group efforts help researchers share their expertise by building reusable NLP tools, test collections, and experimental methodologies. References to some reusable NLP tools and cooperative research groups have already been made in this chapter (see the section "Some Theoretical Developments").

Some recent studies on evaluation are promising. Very small-scale evaluation of INFOS suggests that the indexing pattern method, i.e., mapping of the words from the input text into appropriate concepts in the WordNet abstraction hierarchy, correctly classified 80 percent of the articles (Mock & Vemuri, 1997). Some large-scale experiments with NLP also show encouraging results. For example, Kwok et al. (1999, 2000) report that their PIRCS system can perform the tasks of English-Chinese query translation with an effectiveness of over 80 percent. Strzalkowski et al. (1998) report that by automatically expanding queries using NLP techniques, they obtained an average 37 percent improvement over a baseline where no expansion was used. Conflicting results have arisen, too. For example, Elworthy (2000) reports that the NLP system, using the Microsoft product NLPWin, performed much more poorly in the TREC-9 test set compared with the TREC-8 test set. While trying to find out the reasons for this discrepancy, Elworthy (2000) comments that an important challenge may be figuring out how to build a system that merges definitive, pre-encoded knowledge, with ad hoc documents of unknown reliability.

As already mentioned in the section on "Abstracting," Craven's study with TEXNET (Craven, 1996) resulted in limited success (only

37 percent). Gaizauskas and Wilks (1998) mention that the performance levels of the common IE systems lie in the 50 percent range for combined recall and precision. Such low success rates are not acceptable in large-scale operational information systems.

Smith (1998) suggests that there are two possible scenarios for future relations between computers and humans: (1) in the user-friendliness scenario, computers become smart enough to communicate in natural language; and (2) in the computer friendliness scenario, humans adapt their practices in order to communicate with, and make use of, computers. He further argues that the use of computer-friendly encoding of natural language texts on the Web is symptomatic of a revolutionary trend toward the computerization of human knowledge. Petreley (2000, p. 102) raises a very pertinent question about natural language user interfaces: "Will the natural language interface have to wait until voice recognition becomes more commonplace?" This question appears to be quite legitimate when we see that, although a large number of natural language user interfaces were built—most at the laboratory level and a few at the commercial level (for details of these see Chowdhury, 1999b, [chapters 18–21]; Haas, 1996)—natural language user interfaces are still not common. The impediments to progress lie on several planes, including language issues. Zadrozny et al. (2000) mention that, except for very restricted domains, we do not know how to compute the meaning of a sentence based on the meanings of its words and its context. Another problem is caused by the lack of precise user models. Zadrozny et al. (2000) maintain that, even assuming that we could have any piece of information about a person, we do not know how to use this knowledge to make this person's interaction with a dialogue system most effective and pleasant.

MT involves a number of difficult problems, mainly because human language is at times highly ambiguous, full of special constructions, and replete with exceptions to rules. Nonetheless, there has been steady development, and MT research has now reached a stage where the benefits can be enjoyed. A number of Web search tools—AltaVista, Google, Lycos, and AOL—offer free MT facilities of Web-based information resources. A number of companies also provide MT services commercially. For example, the IBM WebSphere Translation Server for Multiplatforms is a machine translation service available commercially for translating Web documents in a number of languages, such as English, French, Italian, Spanish, Chinese, Japanese, and Korean. In June 2001, Autodesk, a U.S. software company, began to offer MT services to its European customers at a cost that is 50 percent less than human translation services (Schenker, 2001). Although machine translations are not always perfect and do not produce translations as good as those produced by humans, the results and evidence of interest in improving the performance level of MT systems are very encouraging.

One application area that has drawn much research attention, but where the results have yet to provide the general public with an acceptable level of performance, is the natural language question-answering system. While some systems, as already noted, produce acceptable results, there are still many failures and surprises. Results from systems tested under the QA track of TREC (reported in the "Natural Language Interfaces" section) show promising results with some simple types of natural language queries. However, these systems are still in the experimental stage, and much research is needed before robust QA systems can be built that are capable of accepting user queries in any form of natural language and producing natural language answers from distributed information resources. Scalability and portability are the main challenges facing natural language text processing research. Adams (2001) argues that current NLP systems establish patterns that are valid for a specific domain and for a particular task only; as soon as the topic, context, or user changes, entirely new patterns must be established. Sparck Jones (1999) rightly warns that advanced NLP techniques, such as concept extraction, are too expensive for large-scale NLP applications. The research community, however, is making continuous efforts. The reason for not having reliable NLP systems that work at a high level of performance with a high degree of sophistication may have less to do with the inefficiency of the systems or researchers than with the complexities and idiosyncrasies of human behavior and communication patterns.

Bibliography

Adams, K. C. (2001). The Web as a database: New extraction technologies & content management, *Online, 25,* 27–32.

Ahonen, H., Heinonen, O., Klemettinen, M., & Verkamo, A. I. (1998). Applying data mining techniques for descriptive phrase extraction in digital document collections. *IEEE International Forum on Research and Technology. Advances in Digital Libraries—ADL '98*, 2–11.

Amsler, R. A. (1984). Machine-readable dictionaries. *Annual Review of Information Science and Technology, 19*, 161–209.

Argamon, S., Dagan, I., & Krymolowski, Y. (1998). A memory-based approach to learning shallow natural language patterns. *17th International Conference on Computational Linguistics (COLING '98)*, 67–73.

Bangalore, S. & Joshi, A. K. (1999). Supertagging: An approach to almost parsing. *Computational Linguistics, 25*, 237–265.

Barahona, P. & Alferes, J. J. (Eds.). (1999). Progress in artificial intelligence. *9th Portuguese Conference on Artificial Intelligence, EPIA '99*. Berlin: Springer-Verlag.

Barker, K. & Cornacchia, N. (2000). Using noun phrase heads to extract document keyphrases. In H. J. Hamilton (Ed.), *Advances in artificial intelligence. Proceedings of 13th Biennial Conference of the Canadian Society for Computational Studies of Intelligence, AI 2000*, 40–52.

Benoît, G. (2002). Data mining. *Annual Review of Information Science and Technology, 36*, 265–310.

Bian, G.-W. & Chen, H.-H. (2000). Cross-language information access to multilingual collections on the Internet. *Journal of the American Society for Information Science, 51*, 281–296.

Black, W. J., Rinaldi, F., & McNaught, J. (2000). Natural language processing in Java: Applications in education and knowledge management. *Proceedings of the Second International Conference on the Practical Application of Java*, 157–170.

Bondale, N., Maloor, P., Vaidyanathan, A., Sengupta, S. & Rao, P. V. S. (1999). Extraction of information from open-ended questionnaires using natural language processing techniques. *Computer Science and Informatics, 29*, 15–22.

Borgman, C. L. (1997). Multi-media, multi-cultural, and multi-lingual digital libraries: Or how do we exchange data in 400 languages? *D-Lib Magazine.* Retrieved December 5, 2001, from http://www.dlib.org/dlib/june97/06borgman.html.

Breck, E., Burger, J., House, D., Light, M., & Mani, I. (1999). Question answering from large document collections. *Question Answering Systems. Papers from the 1999 AAAI Fall Symposium*, 26–31.

Carrick, C. & Watters, C. (1997). Automatic association of news items. *Information Processing & Management, 33*, 615–632.

Centre for Language Technology. (2000). EAGLES-ll Information Page: Evaluation of NLP Systems. Retrieved December 5, 2001, from http://www.cst.ku.dk/projects/eagles2.html.

Ceric, V. (2000). Advancements and trends in the World Wide Web search. In D. Kalpic & V. H. Dobric (Eds.), *Proceedings of the 22nd International Conference on Information Technology Interfaces* (pp. 211–220). Zagreb: SRCE University Computer Centre.

Chandrasekar, R. & Srinivas, B. (1998). Glean: Using syntactic information in document filtering. *Information Processing & Management, 34*, 623–640.

Chang, H.-H., Ko, Y.-H., & Hsu, J.-P. (2000). An event-driven and ontology-based approach for the delivery and information extraction of e-mails. In *Proceedings/International Symposium on Multimedia Software Engineering* (pp.103–109). Los Alamitos, CA: IEEE Computer Society.

Charniak, E. (1995). Natural language learning. *ACM Computing Surveys, 27*, 317–319.

Chen, J. N. & Chang, J. S. (1998). Topical clustering of MRD senses based on information retrieval techniques. *Computational Linguistics, 24*, 61–96.

Chinchor, N. A. (2001.) Overview of MUC-7/MET-2. Retrieved December 5, 2001, from http://www.itl.nist.gov/iaui/894.02/related_projects/muc/proceedings/muc_7_proceedings/overview.html.

Chowdhury, G. G. (1999a). Template mining for information extraction from digital documents. *Library Trends, 48*, 182–208.

Chowdhury, G. G. (1999b). *Introduction to modern information retrieval.* London: Library Association Publishing.

Chuang, W. & Yang, J. (2000). Extracting sentence segments for text summarization: A machine learning approach. *Proceedings of the 23rd Annual International ACM SIGIR Conference on Research and Development in Information Retrieval*, 152–159.

Costantino, M. (1999). Natural language processing and expert system techniques for equity derivatives trading: The IE-Expert system. In D. Kalpic & V. H. Dobric (Eds.), *Proceedings of the 21st International Conference on Information Technology Interfaces*, (pp. 63–69). Zagreb, Croatia: University of Zagreb.

Cowie, J. & Lehnert, W. (1996). Information extraction. *Communications of the ACM, 39*(1), 80–91.

Craven, T. C. (1988). Text network display editing with special reference to the production of customized abstracts. *Canadian Journal of Information Science, 13*, 59–68.

Craven, T. C. (1993). A computer-aided abstracting tool kit. *Canadian Journal of Information Science, 18*, 19–31.

Craven, T. C. (1996). An experiment in the use of tools for computer-assisted abstracting. *Proceedings of the 59th ASIS Annual Meeting*, 203–208.

Craven, T. C. (2000). Abstracts produced using computer assistance. *Journal of the American Society for Information Science, 51*, 745–756.

Dogru, S., & Slagle, J. R. (1999). Implementing a semantic lexicon. In W. Tepfenhart & W. Cyre (Eds.), *Conceptual Structures: Standards and Practices. 7th International Conference on Conceptual Structures* (pp. 154–167). Berlin: Springer-Verlag.

Elworthy, D. (2000). Question answering using a large NLP system. *The Ninth Text REtrieval Conference (TREC 9)*. Retrieved December 5, 2001, from http://trec. nist.gov/pubs/trec9/papers/msrc-qa.pdf.

Evans, M. (1989). Computer-readable dictionaries. *Annual Review of Information Science and Technology, 24*, 85–117.

Feldman, S. (1999). NLP meets the jabberwocky. *Online, 23,* 62–72.

Fellbaum, C. (Ed.). (1998). WordNet: An electronic lexical database. Cambridge, MA: MIT Press.

Fernandez, P. M. & Garcia-Serrano, A. M. (2000). The role of knowledge-based technology in language applications development. *Expert Systems With Applications, 19,* 31–44.

Gaizauskas, R., & Wilks, Y. (1998). Information extraction: Beyond document retrieval. *Journal of Documentation, 54,* 70–105.

Glasgow, B., Mandell, A., Binney, D., Ghemri, L., & Fisher, D. (1998). MITA: An information-extraction approach to the analysis of free-form text in life insurance applications. *AI Magazine, 19*(1), 59–71.

Global Reach (2001). Global Internet Statistics (by language). Retrieved December 5, 2001, from http://www.euromktg.com/globstats.

Goldstein, J., Kantrowitz, M., Mittal, V., & Carbonell, J. (1999). Summarizing text documents: Sentence selection and evaluation metrics. *Proceeding of the ACM SIGIR 22nd Annual International Conference on Research and Development in Information Retrieval,* 121–128.

Grefenstette, G. (1999). The World Wide Web as a resource for example-based machine translation tasks. *Translating and the Computer 21. Proceedings of the Twenty-first International Conference on Translating and the Computer.* Retrieved April 29, 2002, from: http://www.xcre.xerox.com/competencies/content-analysis/publications/Documents/P49030/content/ggaslib.pdf.

Grishman, R. & Kittredge, R. (Eds.). (1986). *Analyzing language in restricted domains: Sublanguage descriptions and processing.* London: Lawrence Erlbaum.

Haas, S. W. (1996). Natural language processing: Toward large-scale robust systems. *Annual Review of Information Science and Technology, 31,* 83–119.

Hayes, P. (1992). Intelligent high-volume text processing using shallow, domain-specific techniques. In P. S. Jacobs (Ed.), *Text-based intelligent systems,* (pp. 227–241). Hillsdale, NJ: Lawrence Erlbaum.

Hayes, P. & Weinstein, S. (1991). Construe-TIS: A system for content-based indexing of a database of news stories. In A. Rappaport, & R. Smith (Eds.), *Innovative applications of artificial intelligence 2* (pp. 51–64). Cambridge, MA: MIT Press.

Hedlund, T., Pirkola, A., & Järvelin, K. (2001). Aspects of Swedish morphology and semantics from the perspectives of mono- and cross-language information retrieval. *Information Processing & Management, 37,* 147–161.

Herath, S. & Herath, A. (1999). Algorithm to determine the subject in flexible word order language based machine translations: A case study for Sinhalese. *Communications of COLIPS, 9,* 1–17.

Ide, N. (2000). Cross-lingual sense determination: Can it work? *Computers and the Humanities, 34,* 223–234.

Isahara, H., Ma, Q., Sornlertlamvanich, V., & Takahashi, N. (2000). ORCHID: Building linguistic resources in Thai. *Literary & Linguistic Computing, 15,* 465–478.

Jelinek, F. (1999). *Statistical methods for speech recognition*, Cambridge, MA: MIT Press.

Jeong, K. S., Mayeng, S. H., Lee, J. S., & Choi, K. S. (1999). Automatic identification and back-transliteration of foreign words for information retrieval. *Information Processing & Management, 35*, 523–540.

Jurafsky, D. & Martin, J. H. (2000). *Speech and language processing: An introduction to natural language processing, computational linguistics and speech recognition*. Upper Saddle River, NJ: Prentice Hall.

Kazakov, D., Manandhar, S., & Erjavec, T. (1999). Learning word segmentation rules for tag prediction. In S. Dzeroski & P. Flach (Eds.), *Inductive Logic Programming. 9th International Workshop, ILP-99 Proceedings* (pp. 152–161). Berlin: Springer-Verlag.

Kehler, A. (1997). Current theories of centering for pronoun interpretation: A critical evaluation. *Computational Linguistics, 23*, 467–475.

Khoo, C. S. G., Myaeng, S. H., & Oddy, R. N. (2001). Using cause-effect relations in text to improve information retrieval precision. *Information Processing & Management, 37*, 119–145.

Kim, T., Sim, C., Sanghwa, Y., & Jung, H. (1999). From To-CLIR: Web-based natural language interface for cross-language information retrieval. *Information Processing & Management, 35*, 559–586.

King, M. (1996). Evaluating natural language processing systems. *Communications of the ACM, 39*(1), 73–80.

Kornai, A. (Ed.). (1999). *Extended finite state models of language*. Cambridge, UK: Cambridge University Press.

Kwok, K. L., Grunfeld, L., Dinstl, N., & Chan, M. (1999). TREC-8 ad-hoc, query filtering experiments using PIRCS. *The Eighth Text REtrieval Conference (TREC 8)*. Retrieved December 5, 2001, from http://trec.nist.gov/pubs/trec8/papers/ queenst8.pdf.

Kwok, K. L., Grunfeld, L., Dinstl, N., & Chan, M. (2000). TREC-9 cross language, Web and question-answering track experiments using PIRCS. *The Ninth Text REtrieval Conference (TREC 9)*. Retrieved December 5, 2001, from http://trec. nist.gov/pubs/trec9/t9_proceedings.html.

Lange, H. (1993). Speech synthesis and speech recognition: Tomorrow's human-computer interfaces? *Annual Review of Information Science and Technology, 28*, 153–185.

Lee, K. H., Ng, M. K. M., & Lu, Q. (1999). Text segmentation for Chinese spell checking. *Journal of the American Society for Information Science, 50*, 751–759.

Lehmam, A. (1999). Text structuration leading to an automatic summary system: RAFI. *Information Processing & Management, 35*, 181–191.

Lehtokangas, R. & Järvelin, K. (2001). Consistency of textual expression in newspaper articles: An argument for semantically based query expansion. *Journal of Documentation, 57*, 535–548.

Lewis, D. D. & Sparck Jones, K. (1996). Natural language processing for information retrieval. *Communications of the ACM, 39*(1), 92–101.

Liddy, E. (1998). Enhanced text retrieval using natural language processing. *Bulletin of the American Society for Information Science, 24*(4), 14–16.

Liddy, E., Diamond, T., & McKenna, M. (2000). DR-LINK in TIPSTER III. *Information Retrieval, 3,* 291–311.

Lovis, C., Baud, R., Rassinoux, A. M., Michel, P. A., & Scherter, J. R. (1998). Medical dictionaries for patient encoding systems: A methodology. *Artificial Intelligence in Medicine, 14,* 201–214.

Ma, Q., Kanzaki, K., Murata, M., Utiyama, M., Uchimoto, K., & Isahara, H. (2000). Self-organizing semantic maps of Japanese nouns in terms of adnominal constituents. In S. Herath & A. Herath (Eds.), *Proceedings of the IEEE-INNS-ENNS International Joint Conference on Neural Networks. IJCNN 2000. Neural Computing: New Challenges and Perspectives for the New Millennium,* (pp. 91–96). Los Alamitos, CA: IEEE Computer Society.

Magnini, B., Not, E., Stock, O., & Strapparava, C. (2000). Natural language processing for transparent communication between public administration and citizens. *Artificial Intelligence and Law, 8,* 1–34.

Mani, I. & Maybury, M. T. (1999). *Advances in automatic text summarization.* Cambridge, MA: MIT Press.

Manning, C. D. & Schutze, H. (1999). *Foundations of statistical natural language processing.* Cambridge, MA: MIT Press.

Marquez, L., Padro, L., & Rodriguez, H. (2000). A machine learning approach to POS tagging. *Machine Learning, 39,* 59–91.

Martinez, P., De Miguel, A., Cuadra, D., Nieto, C., & Castro, E. (2000). Data conceptual modelling through natural language: Identification and validation of relationship cardinalities. *Challenges of Information Technology Management in the 21st Century. 2000 Information Resources Management Association International Conference* (pp. 500–504). Hershey, PA: Idea Group Publishing.

Martinez, P. & Garcia-Serrano, A. (1998). A knowledge-based methodology applied to linguistic engineering. In R. N. Horspool (Ed.), *Systems Implementation 2000. IFIP TC2 WG2.4 Working Conference on Systems Implementation 2000: Languages, Methods and Tools* (pp. 166–179). London: Chapman & Hall.

McMurchie, L. L (1998). Software speaks user's language. *Computing Canada, 24,* 19–21.

Meyer, J. & Dale, R. (1999). Building hybrid knowledge representations from text. In J. Edwards (Ed.), *Proceedings of the 23rd Australasian Computer Science Conference. ACSC 2000,* (pp. 158–165). Los Alamitos, CA: IEEE Computer Society.

Mihalcea, R. & Moldovan, D. I. (1999). Automatic acquisition of sense tagged corpora. In A. N. Kumar & I. Russell (Eds.), *Proceedings of the Twelfth International Florida AI Research Society Conference,* (pp. 293–297). Menlo Park, CA: AAAI Press.

Mock, K. J. & Vemuri, V. R. (1997). Information filtering via hill climbing, WordNet and index patterns. *Information Processing & Management, 33,* 633–644.

Moens, M.-F. & Uyttendaele, C. (1997). Automatic text structuring and categorization as a first step in summarizing legal cases. *Information Processing & Management, 33*, 727–737.

Morin, E. (1999). Automatic acquisition of semantic relations between terms from technical corpora. In P. Sandrini (Ed.), *TKE '99. Terminology and Knowledge Engineering. Proceedings, Fifth International Congress on Terminology and Knowledge Engineering*, (pp. 268–278). Vienna: TermNet.

Narita, M. & Ogawa, Y. (2000). The use of phrases from query texts in information retrieval. *SIGIR Forum, 34*, 318–320.

Nerbonne, J., Dokter, D., & Smit, P. (1998). Morphological processing and computer-assisted language learning. *Computer Assisted Language Learning, 11*, 543–559.

Oard, D. W. (1997). Serving users in many languages: Cross-language information retrieval for digital libraries. *D-Lib Magazine*. Retrieved December 5, 2001, from http://www.dlib.org/dlib/december97/oard/12oard.html.

Oard, D. W. & Diekema, A. R. (1998). Cross-language information retrieval. *Annual Review of Information Science and Technology, 33*, 223–256.

Ogura, K., Nakaiwa, H., Matsuo, Y., Ooyama, Y., & Bond, F. (2000). The electronic dictionary. Goi-Taikei: A Japanese lexicon and its applications. *NTT Review, 12*, 53–58.

Oudet, B. (1997). Multilingualism on the Internet. *Scientific American, 276*(3), 77–78.

Owei, V. (2000). Natural language querying of databases: An information extraction approach in the conceptual query language. *International Journal of Human-Computer Studies, 53*, 439–492.

Paris, L. A. H. & Tibbo, H. R. (1998). Freestyle vs. Boolean: A comparison of partial and exact match retrieval systems. *Information Processing & Management, 34*, 175–190.

Paroubek, P. & Blasband, M. (1999). Executive summary of a blueprint for a general infrastructure for natural language processing systems evaluation using semi-automatic quantitative black box approach in a multilingual environment. Retrieved December 5, 2001, from http://www.limsi.fr/TLP/ELSE/Preamble XwhyXwhatXrev3.htm.

Pasero, R., & Sabatier, P. (1998). Linguistic games for language learning: A special use of the ILLICO library. *Computer Assisted Language Learning, 11*, 561–585.

Pedersen, T., & Bruce, R. (1998). Knowledge lean word-sense disambiguation. *Proceedings Fifteenth National Conference on Artificial Intelligence (AAAI-98). Tenth Conference on Innovative Applications of Artificial Intelligence* (pp. 800–805). Menlo Park, CA: AAAI Press/MIT Press.

Perez-Carballo, J. & Strzalkowski, T. (2000). Natural language information retrieval: Progress report. *Information Processing & Management, 36*, 155–178.

Peters, C. & Picchi, E. (1997). Across languages, across cultures: Issues in multilinguality and digital libraries, *D-Lib Magazine*. Retrieved December 5, 2001, from http://www.dlib.org/dlib/may97/peters/05peters.html.

Petreley, N. (2000). Waiting for innovations to hit the mainstream: What about natural language? *InfoWorld, 22*(4), 102.

Pirkola, A. (2001). Morphological typology of languages for IR. *Journal of Documentation, 57*, 330–348.

Poesio, M. & Vieira, R. (1998). A corpus-based investigation of definite description use. *Computational Linguistics, 24*, 183–216.

Powell, J. & Fox, E. A. (1998). Multilingual federated searching across heterogeneous collections. *D-Lib Magazine*. Retrieved December 5, 2001, from http://www.dlib.org/dlib/september98/powell/09powell.html.

Qin, J. & Norton, M. J. (Eds.). (1999). Introduction. [Special Issue] Knowledge discovery in bibliographic databases. *Library Trends, 48*, 1–8.

Raghavan, V. V., Deogun, J. S., & Server, H. (Eds.). (1998). Knowledge discovery and data mining [Special topics issue] *Journal of the American Society for Information Science, 49*(5).

Roche, E. & Shabes, Y. (Eds.). (1997). *Finite-state language processing*. Cambridge, MA: MIT Press.

Rosenfield, R. (2000). Two decades of statistical language modeling: Where do we go from here? *Proceedings of the IEEE. 88*(8), 1270–1278.

Roux, M. & Ledoray, V. (2000). Understanding of medico-technical reports. *Artificial Intelligence in Medicine, 18*, 149–172.

Ruiz, M. E., & Srinivasan, P. (1998). Cross-language information retrieval: An analysis of errors. *Proceedings of the 61st ASIS Annual Meeting*, 153–165.

Say, B. (1999). Modeling cue phrases in Turkish: A case study. In V. Matousek et al. (Eds.). *Text, speech and dialogue. Second International Workshop, TDS '99* (pp. 337–340). Berlin: Springer-Verlag.

Scarlett, E., & Szpakowicz, S. (2000). The power of the TSNLP: Lessons from a diagnostic evaluation of a broad-coverage parser. In H. J. Hamilton (Ed.), *Advances in Artificial Intelligence. 13th Biennial Conference of the Canadian Society for Computational Studies of Intelligence* (pp. 138–150). Berlin: Springer-Verlag.

Schenker, J. L., (2001, July 16). The gist of translation: How long will it be before machines make the Web multilingual? *Time, 158*, 54.

Scott, J. (1999, December). E-mail management: The key to regaining control. *Internet Business*, 60–65.

Silber, H. G., & McCoy, K. F. (2000). Efficient text summarization using lexical chains. In H. Lieberman (Ed.), *Proceedings of IUI 2000 International Conference on Intelligent User Interfaces* (pp. 252–255). New York: ACM.

Smeaton, A. F. (1999). Using NLP or NLP resources for information retrieval tasks. In T. Strzalkowski (Ed.), *Natural language information retrieval* (pp. 99–111). Dordrecht, Netherlands: Kluwer Academic.

Smeaton, A. F. (1997). Information retrieval: Still butting heads with natural language processing? In M. T. Pazienza (Ed.), *Information extraction. A multidisciplinary approach to an emerging information technology international summer school, SCIE '97* (pp. 115–138). Berlin: Springer-Verlag.

Smith, D. (1998). Computerizing computer science. *Communications of the ACM, 41* (9), 21–23.

Sokol, L., Murphy, K., Brooks, W., & Mattox, D. (2000). Visualizing text-based data mining. *Proceedings of the Fourth International Conference on the Practical Application of Knowledge Discovery and Data Mining* (pp. 57–61). Blackpool, UK: Practical Application Company.

Song J., & Zhao, D.-Y. (2000). Study of automatic abstracting based on corpus and hierarchical dictionary. *Journal of Software, 11,* 308–314.

Sparck Jones, K. (1999). What is the role for NLP in text retrieval? In T. Strzalkowski (Ed.), *Natural language information retrieval* (pp. 1–25). Dordrecht, Netherlands: Kluwer.

Staab, S., Braun, C., Bruder, I., Dusterhoft, A., Heuer, A., Klettke, M., et al. (1999). GETESS-searching the Web exploiting German texts. *Cooperative Information Agents III. Third International Workshop, CIA '99* (pp. 113–124). Berlin: Springer-Verlag.

Stock, O. (2000). Natural language processing and intelligent interfaces. *Annals of Mathematics and Artificial Intelligence, 28,* 39–41.

Strzalkowski, T., Fang, L., Perez-Carballo, J., & Jin, W. (1997). *Natural language information retrieval TREC-6 Report, NIST Special Publication 500-240.* Retrieved December 5, 2001, from http://trec.nist.gov/pubs/trec6/t6_proceedings.html

Strzalkowski, T., Perez-Carballo, J., Karlgren, J., Hulth, A., Tapanainen, P., & Lahtinen, T. (1999). *Natural language information retrieval: TREC-8 report. NIST Special Publication 500-246.* Retrieved December 5, 2001, from http://trec.nist. gov/pubs/trec8/papers/ge8adhoc2.pdf.

Strzalkowski, T., Stein, G., Wise, G. B., Perez-Carballo, J., Tapanainen, P., Jarvinen, et al. (1998). *Natural language information retrieval: TREC-7 report. NIST Special Publication 500-242.* Retrieved December 5, 2001, from http://trec.nist. gov/pubs/trec7/t7_proceedings.html.

Tolle, K. M. & Chen, H. (2000). Comparing noun phrasing techniques for use with medical digital library tools. *Journal of the American Society for Information Science, 51,* 352–370.

Trybula, W. J. (1997). Data mining and knowledge discovery. *Annual Review of Information Science and Technology, 32,* 197–229.

Tsuda, K., & Nakamura, M. (1999). The extraction method of the word meaning class. In L. C. Jain (Ed.), *Third International Conference on Knowledge-Based Intelligent Information Engineering Systems* (pp. 534–537). Piscataway, NJ: IEEE.

Vickery, B. (1997). Knowledge discovery from databases: An introductory review. *Journal of Documentation, 53,* 107–122.

Voorhees, E. (1999). The TREC-8 question answering track report. Retrieved December 5, 2001, from http://trec.nist.gov/pubs/trec8/papers/qa-report.pdf.

Voorhees, E. (2000). The TREC-9 question answering track report. Retrieved December 5, 2001, from http://trec.nist.gov/pubs/trec9/papers/qa-report.pdf.

Waldrop, M. M. (2001). Natural language processing. *Technology Review*, *104*, 107–108.

Warner, A. J. (1987). Natural language processing. *Annual Review of Information Science and Technology*, *22*, 79–108.

Weigard, H., & Hoppenbrouwers, S. (1998). Experiences with a multilingual ontology-based lexicon for news filtering. In A. M. Tjoa & R. R. Wagner (Eds.), *Proceedings of the Ninth International Workshop on Database and Expert Systems Applications* (pp. 160–165). Los Alamitos, CA: IEEE Computer Society.

Wilks, Y. (1996). Natural language processing. *Communications of the ACM*, *39*(1), 60.

Wong, K.-F., Lum, V. Y. & Lam, W.-I.(1998). Chicon: A Chinese text manipulation language. *Software - Practice and Experience*, *28*, 681–701.

Yang, D. H., Gomez, P. C., & Song, M. (2000). An algorithm for predicting the relationship between lemmas and corpus size. *ETRI Journal*, *22*, 20–31.

Yang, J. C. & Akahori, K. (2000). A discourse structure analysis of technical Japanese texts and its implementation on the WWW. *Computer Assisted Language Learning*, *13*, 119–141.

Yang, Y. & Liu, X. (1999). A re-examination of text categorization methods. In *Proceedings of the 22nd Annual International ACM SIGIR Conference on Research and Development in Information Retrieval*, 42–49.

Zadrozny, W., Budzikowska, M., Chai, J., & Kambhatla, N. (2000). Natural language dialogue for personalized interaction. *Communications of the ACM*, *43*(8), 116–120.

Zweigenbaum, P., & Grabar, N. (1999). Automatic acquisition of morphological knowledge for medical language processing. In W. Horn, et al. (Eds.), *Joint European Conference on Artificial Intelligence in Medicine and Medical Decision Making* (pp. 416–420). Berlin: Springer-Verlag.

CHAPTER 3

Indexing and Retrieval for the Web

Edie M. Rasmussen
University of Pittsburgh

Introduction

The introduction and growth of the World Wide Web (WWW, or Web) have resulted in a profound change in the way individuals and organizations access information. In terms of volume, nature, and accessibility, the characteristics of electronic information are significantly different from those of even five or six years ago. Control of, and access to, this flood of information rely heavily on automated techniques for indexing and retrieval. According to Gudivada, Raghavan, Grosky, and Kasanagottu (1997, p. 58), "The ability to search and retrieve information from the Web efficiently and effectively is an enabling technology for realizing its full potential." Almost 93 percent of those surveyed consider the Web an "indispensable" Internet technology, second only to e-mail (Graphic, Visualization & Usability Center, 1998). Although there are other ways of locating information on the Web (browsing or following directory structures), 85 percent of users identify Web pages by means of a search engine (Graphic, Visualization & Usability Center, 1998). A more recent study conducted by the Stanford Institute for the Quantitative Study of Society confirms the finding that searching for information is second only to e-mail as an Internet activity (Nie & Ebring, 2000, online). In fact, Nie and Ebring conclude, "... the Internet today is a giant public library with a decidedly commercial tilt. The most widespread use of the Internet today is as an information search utility for products, travel, hobbies, and general information. Virtually all users interviewed responded that they engaged in one or more of these information gathering activities."

Techniques for automated indexing and information retrieval (IR) have been developed, tested, and refined over the past 40 years, and are well documented (see, for example, Agosti & Smeaton, 1996; Baeza-Yates & Ribeiro-Neto, 1999a; Frakes & Baeza-Yates, 1992; Korfhage, 1997; Salton, 1989; Witten, Moffat, & Bell, 1999). With the introduction of the Web, and the capability to index and retrieve via search engines, these techniques have been extended to a new environment. They have been adopted, altered, and in some cases extended to include new methods. "In short, search engines are indispensable for searching the Web, they employ a variety of relatively advanced IR techniques, and there are some peculiar aspects of search engines that make searching the Web different than more conventional information retrieval" (Gordon & Pathak, 1999, p. 145).

The environment for information retrieval on the World Wide Web differs from that of "conventional" information retrieval in a number of fundamental ways. The collection is very large and changes continuously, with pages being added, deleted, and altered. Wide variability between the size, structure, focus, quality, and usefulness of documents makes Web documents much more heterogeneous than a typical electronic document collection. The wide variety of document types includes images, video, audio, and scripts, as well as many different document languages. Duplication of documents and sites is common. Documents are interconnected through networks of hyperlinks. Because of the size and dynamic nature of the Web, preprocessing all documents requires considerable resources and is often not feasible, certainly not on the frequent basis required to ensure currency. Query length is usually much shorter than in other environments—only a few words—and user behavior differs from that in other environments. These differences make the Web a novel environment for information retrieval (Baeza-Yates & Ribeiro-Neto, 1999b; Bharat & Henzinger, 1998; Huang, 2000).

Scope

This chapter explores current research on indexing and ranking as retrieval functions of search engines on the Web. While seminal works are included as necessary, the emphasis is on studies reported over the last five years. The focus is on studies that attempt to determine the size and character of the Web as a database and the extent to which it is indexed by search engines, and studies that develop and evaluate indexing and retrieval techniques. The studies discussed have a research component; works that are simply descriptive, discuss how to search using Web search engines, or provide low-level descriptions of how search engines work are not included. Considerable interest in retrieval of non-text media on the Web abounds, but large-scale implementation comparable with text has not been achieved due to problems in indexing and scalability; thus, only text retrieval is considered here. The emphasis is on automated techniques for indexing and retrieval. Initiatives to manually index and/or categorize the Web, and to provide access through directory structures such as Yahoo! (http://www.yahoo.com/) are not covered. Studies on hypertext, navigation, and browsing are also excluded, although the role of hyperlinks as indexing structures is addressed. The research reported focuses on improving retrieval performance; although much important research addresses engineering issues related to scalability and efficiency in Web indexing and retrieval, it is beyond the scope of this discussion.

Sources of Information

Research on indexing and retrieval on the Web is addressed by many communities, including librarians and information scientists, computer scientists, human factors specialists, and Web researchers. This work appears in journals such as *Computer Networks, IEEE Internet Computing, Information Processing & Management, Information Retrieval, Journal of Documentation*, and *Journal of the American Society for Information Science and Technology*. A special issue of *Information Processing & Management* on Web-based information retrieval research addressed both user-focused and systems-focused research issues (Spink & Qin, 2000). Conferences are an important venue for dissemination of Web research results, particularly the International World Wide Web

Conferences (IW3C). Work is also presented at the Association for Computing Machinery (ACM) Special Interest Group on Information Retrieval (SIGIR) Annual International ACM SIGIR Conference on Research and Development in Information Retrieval; the ACM Special Interest Group on Hypertext, Hypermedia and the Web (SIGWEB) Conference on Hypertext and Hypermedia; and the VLDB (Very Large Data Base) Conference. The Text REtrieval Evaluation Conference (TREC) sponsors an annual track in Web retrieval.

Given the nature of the topic, it would be surprising if Web sites were not an important source of information. Web search engines and their characteristics are tabulated and tracked by Search Engine Watch (http://www.searchenginewatch.com/), a major source of current information. Similar information is also available on Search Engine Showdown (http://www.searchengineshowdown.com/). Many Web researchers post preprints or published papers on their Web sites, and these are identified, indexed, and cached by NEC's ResearchIndex (http://www.researchindex.com/) (formerly CiteSeer), which provides document and citation indexing, and in most cases, a copy for download.

A number of reviews or overviews have been published. Molyneux and Williams (1999) comprehensively reviewed the literature that measures characteristics of the Internet, including the Web. Gudivada et al. (1997) provided an overview of the techniques used in indexing and retrieval on the Web. Schatz (1997) brought an historical perspective to networked information retrieval, from Licklider's (1965) early vision of the library of the future, through the evolution of retrieval technology over the past 30 years to today's Web, with a vision of semantic retrieval across large collections in the not-too-distant future. An early review of the history and evaluation of Web search engines was provided by Schwartz (1998). Baeza-Yates and Ribeiro-Neto (1999b) discussed information retrieval techniques as applied to Web searching. Kobayashi and Takeda (2000) reviewed information retrieval on the Web with reference to, and explanations of, traditional IR techniques. Huang (2000) provided a systems perspective. Arasu, Cho, Garcia-Molina, Paepcke, and Raghavan (2000) also provided a design perspective, with emphasis on performance issues.

Characterizing the Web

The Web has been described as a very large distributed information space (Gudivada et al., 1997), a giant public library (Nie & Ebring, 2000), and an "almost ubiquitous information source for millions of people" (Griffiths, 1999, p. 230). Although it may lack the formal characteristics of a library (Griffiths, 1999), and the purpose and direction provided by a rigorous collection policy, it is for many users the largest and most convenient body of information available.

Although its size remains somewhat uncertain, many estimates of the number of hosts and number of Web pages have appeared, as well as predictions of its growth rate (see, for example, Bray, 1996; Lawrence & Giles, 1998b). Bray (1996) used the data extracted from the OpenText index in 1995 to produce three-dimensional visualizations of areas of the Web based on visibility (pointers to a site), size (number of pages in a site), and luminosity (number of pointers from a site). Bharat and Broder (1998b) estimated a Web size of at least 275 million distinct, static pages as of March 1998. A widely quoted estimate by Lawrence and Giles (1999) suggested 800 million pages for the publicly indexable Web as of February 1999, or about 15 terabytes of information or 6 terabytes of text. (Bharat & Broder [1998b] suggested that their count is lower because it includes only distinct pages.) A study by Inktomi and NEC reported finding over a billion unique Web pages in January 2000 (Inktomi, 2000). As of December 2001, Google reported indexing, directly and indirectly, about 2 billion pages, although this includes documents in formats such as PDF and Microsoft Office (Sullivan, 2001a).

The nature of the Web as a corpus has also been characterized. Woodruff, Aoki, Brewer, Gauthier, and Rowe (1996) analyzed over 2.6 million documents collected by the Inktomi Web crawler for attributes such as domain, document size, tags, and links. Grefenstette and Nioche (2000) examined the multilingual nature of the Web, using a method based on word frequencies in various languages. On the basis of the AltaVista index, they found that English was the most common language on the Web, although, based on historical data, non-English languages were growing at a faster pace.

Other researchers have attempted to describe the Web in theoretical terms. Albert, Jeong, and Barabási (1999) explored the topology of the

Web. They defined a parameter d, which they described as the smallest number of URL links needed to navigate between a pair of documents. The average d was 19, which they interpreted as the diameter of the Web, measuring the shortest distance between any two points. Broder et al. (2000, online) studied the Web as a graph with pages as nodes and hyperlinks as arcs. Their diagram of Web connectivity is noteworthy for its "bowtie" shape. It shows a central core—a "giant strongly connected component"—all the pages of which able to reach one another along directed hyperlinks. They compared their results, with a diameter of 16, to those of Albert et al.; however, they found no directed path between two nodes over 75 percent of the time. Huberman and Adamic (1999) used data from Alexa (http://www.alexa.com/) and InfoSeek (http://infoseek.go.com/) to explore the growth dynamics of the Web, finding that the distribution of site sizes followed a power law, appearing linear on a log–log scale. These researchers (Adamic & Huberman, 2001) also showed that the number of visitors to a site and the links pointing to and from a site followed power law distributions as well, and suggested that these regular distributions are useful in predicting the evolution and future behavior of the Web.

The dynamic nature of the Web—in terms of growth, changes to existing pages, and page or site deletions—constitutes a major difference between Web and traditional IR. Knowledge about Web dynamics provides an indicator of how often Web pages should be revisited to maintain currency in search engine indexes. A number of researchers have attempted to quantify the rate of change. Douglis, Feldman, Krishnamurthy, and Mogul (1997) analyzed full-content responses for corporate http requests and found that 16.5 percent of resources accessed at least twice were modified every time they were accessed. Koehler (1999) argued that the Web represents an intermediate form between ephemeral, oral communication, and permanent, recorded information. He examined permanence and constancy (rate of change) for a sample of Web pages and sites and found that about 12 percent of Web sites and 20 percent of Web pages failed to respond after six months, rising to 18 percent and 32 percent after one year. Over six months, 97 percent of Web sites underwent some change, and 99 percent had changed after a year. Lawrence et al. (2001) examined all URLs for over 100,000 articles in the ResearchIndex database (http://researchindex.org/) and found invalid

URLs ranging from a high of 53 percent in 1994 to 23 percent in 1999. The average number of URLs in scientific publications on the Web increased steadily over time.

Brewington and Cybenko (2000) used empirical data and analytic modeling to provide a basis for calculating how often a search engine should re-index Web pages based on two parameters, the (a,b)-currency, where a is the probability that a search engine is current for a randomly selected Web page, relative to a grace period, b.

Measuring Search Engine Stability

Search engines have also been reported to be dynamic in nature, leading to unexpected variations in search results over time and creating a potential problem for retrieval research studies. Selberg and Etzioni (2000) analyzed searches on Web search engines repeated over time, and found a greater variation in results than would be explained by published estimates of Web growth or change. They suggested that results that disappear and reappear in the top 10 ranking may be due to variations in processing, adopted in a quality-for-speed trade-off during peak processing times. Bar-Ilan (2000) found a similar problem with the HotBot search engine (http://www.hotbot.lycos.com/); Snap's Power Search (now NBCi), by comparison, was relatively stable in its results listings. In a study over a six-month period, with a follow-up six months later, she found that URLs disappeared and reappeared (Bar-Ilan, 1998/9). Rousseau (1998/9) performed daily searches over a 12-week period, and found irregularities on AltaVista, and that Northern Light was more stable. He suggested that time series data should be collected in Web characterization research. Bar-Ilan (2001) proposed methods for evaluating search engine performance over time that take into account URLs that are "forgotten" by the search engine.

Measuring the Coverage of Web Search Engines

It would seem logical to assume that a significant portion of Web content is being searched when using a search engine to find information. However, because the Web is distributed and rapidly growing and changing, it is difficult for search engines to keep pace with growth and updates. Bharat and Broder (1998a) developed a method for calculating relative coverage of search engines, rather than absolute values, and found that for four major search engines the relative coverage ranged from 17 percent to 47 percent. Lawrence and Giles (1998b) found that, of six major search engines, none covered more than about a third of the "indexable Web," and the worst covered only three percent. A later study (Lawrence & Giles, 1999) found that coverage had decreased with Web growth, with no engine indexing more than about 16 percent. Sites that were "popular" (having more links to them) were more likely to be indexed, as were U.S. sites compared to non-U.S. sites. Lawrence & Giles (1999) suggested several reasons why search engines index only a small fraction of the Web: cost–benefit, limitations in scalability of indexing and retrieval technology, limitations in bandwidth, and diminishing returns to users. This rationale is supported by interviews with search engine representatives (Brake, 1997).

The above data on search engine size are now dated. More current data are available from the search engines themselves because they self-report the size of their indexes, data that are published (but not audited) by Search Engine Watch (http://www.searchenginewatch.com/). (Notess [2002] provides some estimates of effective size, the size of the database from which a searcher is likely to obtain results, that tend to be somewhat smaller than reported sizes.) As of December 11, 2001, the claim for largest index was Google's (http://www.google.com/), with 1.5 billion Web pages indexed. A number of other large search engines were around the 500 million page mark. Because Google uses anchor text to index linked pages that they do not visit, they claim actual coverage of about 2 billion pages (Sullivan, 2001a).

Henzinger, Heydon, Mitzenmacher, and Najork (1999) suggest that because search engine index growth is not keeping up with the growth rate of the Web, it is important to focus on index quality as a search engine characteristic. They developed and tested a method based on a random walk on the Web, approximating PageRank values (as discussed later in the section on "Hyperlinks for Indexing and Ranking," [Brin & Page, 1998]) and using a method based on that of Bharat and Broder (1998a) to determine whether the pages were covered by each search engine in the study. Lycos (http://www.lycos.com/)

was found to have the highest average page quality based on the PageRank measure.

Evaluation of Indexing and Retrieval on the Web

As a retrieval environment, the Web is particularly complex. Not only does the collection of documents (Web pages) change constantly, but also large variation persists among search engines in the number and instances of Web pages covered. Relevance information is generally not available, and comprehensive information cannot be obtained for such a large collection. However, the proliferation of search engines naturally leads to an interest in the question of which one is "best," and a growing body of literature has appeared that attempts to address this question. Gordon and Pathak (1999) distinguish between two types of study: the "testimonial" and the "shootout." Although many authors base their answers on tabulation of features, anecdotal evidence, or unstructured tests (the testimonial), a number of researchers have attempted to apply more rigorous standards based on the experimental norms of information retrieval (the shootout). Schwartz (1998) provides an early review of research on Web search engine performance. A more recent, comprehensive review of experimental studies is provided by Oppenheim, Morris, and McKnight (2000), who identify the need for a set of benchmarking tests and specify criteria that should be included.

Of course, this leads to the question of what form the evaluation should take. The traditional and most widely used performance measures for information retrieval are recall and precision, in which recall measures the ability of the system to retrieve *all* relevant materials, and precision measures the ability to retrieve *only* relevant material. A classic retrieval experiment uses a laboratory environment in which many variables are controlled: the document collection is static, the queries are provided in a standard form, and the documents that are relevant to the query are known a priori. This control makes it possible to calculate and compare precision and recall for a set of queries across systems, or for the same system while varying internal parameters. Performance measurement in an operational environment is much more complex, because the document collection is constantly changing and the set of all relevant documents is impossible to calculate. If users are involved in the experiment, variations in their background knowledge and search expertise further complicate the results.

As Leighton and Srivastava (1999) have pointed out, results of the earlier studies are primarily of historical interest, because significant changes have been made to the features provided by search engines. More interesting, perhaps, is the ongoing development of evaluation methodologies for the Web, as more rigorous experimental techniques are introduced.

Evaluation in an Operational Environment

A study by Ding and Marchionini (1996) is fairly typical of early work on search engine evaluation. It included a feature comparison as well as an experimental study, used a relatively small number of queries, examined three of the most popular search engines of the time (InfoSeek, Lycos, and OpenText [http://www.opentext.net/]), and examined relevant documents in the first 20 items presented for each query. No one search engine stood out overall, although variations across queries were identified. The authors found the lack of overlap between search engines surprising, and identified indexing quality and speed as limiting factors in search engine performance. A concurrent study (Tomaiuolo & Packer, 1996) attempted to use a more realistic number of queries. Tomaiuolo and Packer based their study on 200 queries searched on each of five search services (Magellan, Point, Lycos, InfoSeek, AltaVista [http://www.altavista.com/]), using precision for the top 10 items retrieved as the evaluation measure. Chu and Rosenthal (1996) evaluated three search engines using queries based on real reference questions, going beyond precision to consider other performance criteria including response time, output options, and user effort. Su (1997), recognizing a need for user-oriented evaluation, proposed a systematic methodology involving real users that captures information on participants' characteristics as well as precision, relevance ranking by users, user satisfaction, and value of search results as a whole. This methodology, employed in a pilot study with faculty and graduate students, found significant differences among search engines (AltaVista, InfoSeek, Lycos, and OpenText) (Su, Chen, & Dong, 1998). Reporting on a study conducted in 1997, Leighton and Srivastava (1999) used 15 queries to study the precision of five search engines (AltaVista, Excite [http://www.excite.com/], HotBot, InfoSeek, and Lycos). Although their search engine ranking may be of limited current value, their evaluation measures are of interest. Their precision measure, based on "first 20," or precision within the first 20 ranked items, was modified to include weights for rank within the first 20. They used binary relevance judgments within five distinct categories (not a linear scale).

Gordon and Pathak (1999) suggested that, in spite of the continuous change in search engines, no dramatic performance improvements in retrieval should be expected in the near future because the results of information retrieval research studies have been available from the outset of search engine development, and new algorithms, if available, may be too resource-intensive to implement. In their study of search engines, they found that absolute retrieval effectiveness is fairly low, and that there are statistical differences among the search engines' performances that seem to be more dependent on a search engine's matching function than its query formulation capabilities. They also observed a marked lack of overlap in the documents located by different search engines, over both relevant documents found and all documents found.

Unlike classic information retrieval evaluation, which measures both precision and recall, most quantitative studies of Web performance measure precision alone, either because of the difficulty in measuring recall in the Web environment or because precision is claimed to be more suited to users' information needs on the Web. An exception is the study by Clarke and Willett (1997), which used 30 queries and three search engines to measure recall. They proposed a method using pooled recall in which relevant items from each query on all three search engines, adjusted for inclusion in the index of the individual search engines, would form the basis for the recall calculation. Their method also allowed them to calculate another measure: coverage, the percentage of relevant items actually included in the search engine's index.

A recurrent theme in search engine evaluation is movement toward quality standards for evaluation, a topic that is addressed more comprehensively in recent papers. Leighton and Srivastava (1999) discussed the issues of methodological rigor in search engine evaluation, such as using sufficient queries for valid statistical analyses, avoiding bias in query selection, randomizing the order of search engines, and blinding of results to ensure impartiality in making relevance judgments. They evaluated earlier studies on the extent to which they adhered to these principles. Gordon and Pathak (1999) provided a list of seven criteria an experimental study should meet in order to be considered accurate and informative, including using "real" queries, employing a large number of searchers, studying most major search engines, having relevance judgments made by the user rather than surrogate judges, and conducting experiments rigorously. This list was debated by Hawking, Craswell, Bailey, and Griffiths (2001), who took issue with several of Gordon and Pathak's requirements; for example, that the user perform the relevance assessments, and that queries should be optimized for each search engine. They provided a revised and augmented list of desirable features for future Web search evaluation.

Evaluation in a Laboratory Environment

A significant problem in evaluating retrieval in the Web environment is the changing content of the database and variation in coverage among search engines. Creating a test collection of static Web pages and making it available to researchers would allow comparisons to be made between search engines on the basis of the same underlying data, although, as Hawking et al. (2001) pointed out, this requires the willingness of search engine companies to use it. More realistically, a static Web collection also allows researchers to isolate specific retrieval algorithms or system components in order to measure their impact on retrieval performance. Landoni and Bell (2000) suggested that a greater degree of collaboration between the information retrieval (IR) and Web research communities would lead to an enhanced evaluation platform.

Recently, a Web track was introduced into the TREC (http://trec.nist.gov/) experiments with the goal of building a test collection that mimics the Web retrieval environment (Hawking, Craswell, Thistlewaite, & Harman, 1999). This annual conference, hosted by the National Institute of Standards and Technology (NIST) is intended to encourage research in text retrieval based on large test collections, encourage the development of new evaluation techniques, and promote the exchange and implementation of research ideas (Voorhees, 2000b). TREC participants are provided with test collections and queries, and results are pooled prior to relevance judgments by TREC assessors. Standardized evaluation measures are used. For the Web track, a 1997 snapshot of the Web was obtained, and several test collections were produced. In TREC-8, a 2-gigabyte subset (WT2g) was used for the Small Web Task, with performance tested on the TREC ad hoc topics (Hawking, Voorhees, Craswell, & Bailey, 2000). This was increased to 10 gigabytes (WT10g) in TREC-9 (Voorhees, 2000b). In both cases a 100-gigabyte (VLC2/WT100g) set was used for the Large Web Task employing queries adapted from search engine query logs. Overall goals in the Web track were an assessment of how well the best methods in non-Web TREC data performed on the Web collections, and data gathering on the impact of link information. Individual participants had goals related to their own interests, such as Boolean-ranked output comparisons, issues related to speed of retrieval, and the role of parallelism (Hawking et al., 2000).

Using a static Web test collection eliminates problems inherent in experimentation on the dynamic Web, removing the impact of the Web crawler from the assessment of the text retrieval system. It also allows the evaluation of individual retrieval techniques in isolation from specific search engines. Specific examples of this type of evaluation will be given in the context of indexing and ranking techniques.

Indexing the Web

Given the size, breadth, and rate of change of the Web, it is not surprising that automated techniques for indexing its content dominate. Lynch (1997, online) described the need for both human and automated indexing: "the librarian's classification and selection skills must be complemented by the computer scientist's ability to automate the task of indexing and storing information. Only a synthesis of the different perspectives brought by both professions will allow this new medium to remain viable." However, despite the democratic nature of Web publishing and the potential for manual indexing of their documents by Web publishers, the practice is not widespread, as documented in the following section.

Indexing by Web Publishers

Individuals or organizations posting pages on the Web can self-index their sites by providing significant keywords in contexts that are specifically indexed or even preferentially treated by search engines. In theory, at least, this provides a mechanism for an individual or organization to provide direction to search engines, which extract indexing information from their sites. Many articles and commercial services advise on valid (and sometimes less than ethical) ways for Web publishers to optimize their rankings by providing indexing information; see, for example, Stanley (1997b). The HTML META tags in particular provide an opportunity for Web publishers to specify their own metadata indicating the content of their pages, especially with the KEYWORDS and DESCRIPTION tags. This information is stored with the Web page without being viewed on screen, and is available to search engines for indexing. It should be noted, however, that not all search engines index the META tags; for example, FAST, Google, and Northern Light, specifically exclude this information (Sullivan, 2001b). Turner & Brackbill (1998) evaluated the impact of META tag content by evaluating the rankings of a small set of documents created with different combinations of tags (no META tags, keyword only, description only, and both keyword and description). They found that only the keyword content significantly improved document ranking on the two search engines they examined (AltaVista and InfoSeek).

To what extent are Web publishers making use of the opportunity to index their sites by incorporating metadata in their Web pages? Data on this issue are difficult to interpret because studies differ in their selection of source documents and their treatment of metatags automatically generated by page creation software. Examining over a thousand Web documents in polymer science, Qin and Wesley (1998) found that only 24 percent used one or more HTML META fields and, where included, the meta attributes were often misused. Lawrence and Giles (1999) observed relatively low metadata use on the sites they sampled, with 34 percent using simple keyword and description metatags, and only 0.3 percent of sites used the Dublin Core Metadata Standard (http://www.dublincore. org/). On a random sample of Web pages generated by Yahoo!, Craven (2000) found that 57 percent used metatags and 26 percent used the DESCRIPTION metatag; however, only five of 628 sites used Dublin Core metadata elements.

An often mentioned, although not well documented, problem with the indexing of Web pages is the ability of Web publishers to manipulate rankings by providing spurious or repeated keywords (referred to as "search engine persuasion," "stuffing," "spamdexing," or "keyword spamming" [Stanley, 1997a]). Because term frequency is a factor in the ranking algorithm used by many search engines, repeating significant words or phrases, either in the metatags or in "invisible" text (using a very small font size in the background color) so that it is present in the source code but not viewed on the screen, can potentially raise the ranking of a Web page for a particular search. This manipulative indexing may be done to gain a commercial advantage by making a product more visible than its competitors, or to bring users to a site that does not match their topic. The most famous instance of keyword spamming was found at the Heaven's Gate Web site, which used both metatags and black on black text to attract visitors (Liberatore, 1997). To counteract these practices, search engines modify their ranking algorithms to ignore repeated terms, and many search engines do not index metatags. It is unfortunate that misuse of the opportunity to provide clear and accurate indicators of Web page content, and a potential improvement in retrieval performance, often results in this information being discarded altogether.

Many Web documents may warrant indexing of a higher quality than that provided by Web search engines, but the evidence cited here suggests that human indexing of Web documents is relatively rare, at least in the publicly indexable Web, although the situation may be different in the "hidden Web" (that portion of the Web that is dynamic, stored in local databases, and created on demand). The remaining discussion focuses on automatic indexing as it is performed in the Web search environment.

Deconstructing a Search Engine

Descriptions of search engines and their methods and algorithms at the implementation level are scarce, although nonproprietary details are available or discernable. According to Gordon and Pathak (1999, p. 144), "the precise algorithms that search engines use for retrieval are not publicized, but one can infer their approximate workings by reading the Help, Hint or FAQ pages that accompany them as well as by being familiar with the field of IR." One exception is the Google search engine, for which some details have been provided (Brin & Page, 1998), as well as details of Google's PageRank algorithm, discussed in the section on

"Hyperlinks for Indexing and Ranking" (Page, Brin, Motwani, & Winograd, 1998). More detailed descriptions are also found for experimental, noncommercial search engines (see, for example, Lawrence & Giles, 1998a). A general description of search engine architecture was given by Baeza-Yates and Ribeiro-Neto (1999b); Huang (2000) provided more detail, and Arasu et al. (2000) described the architecture of a noncommercial search engine.

Most major search engines have a centralized architecture, with the index and retrieval engines located on a single site. Search engines have a number of necessary components: the crawler (or robot) is a program that traverses the Web, following links and retrieving pages for indexing. The indexer module extracts the words (or some subset of words) and (in some cases) hyperlinks from each page and creates indexes to them. (Arasu et al. [2000] distinguish a collection analysis module that creates additional indexes.) The retrieval engine consists of a query module that receives and fills users' queries and a ranking module that compares queries to information in the indexes, producing a ranked list of the results. The design of these components raises research questions related to optimizing the performance of the search engine.

Crawling

Crawlers treat the Web as a graph and, using a set of known URLs as a seed set, usually traverse the graph either breadth first or depth first. Research on crawlers addresses both effectiveness and efficiency issues, although they may be interrelated because a more efficient crawling algorithm may save resources while improving the quality of the database. Research issues include how to prioritize URLs to obtain the best pages (due to resource limits on the proportion of Web pages that can be indexed). Cho, Garcia-Molina, and Page (1998) presented a number of URL-ordering schemes based on metrics of page importance, showing that a good ordering strategy makes it possible to efficiently obtain a significant proportion of important pages. Najork and Wiener (2001), using PageRank as a quality metric, found that a breadth-first crawling strategy tends to deliver high-quality pages early in the crawl.

A related problem involves determining the best schedule for revisiting pages; Coffman, Liu, and Weber (1998) provided a theoretical analysis of optimal scheduling based on individual page-change rates. The order and frequency of Web site visits are issues that will affect the quality of information that can be offered. Arasu et al. (2000) reviewed work at Stanford on crawler page selection and page refresh. Two additional issues, minimizing load on the servers visited and coordinating multiple crawlers operating simultaneously, were addressed with a queuing model by Talim, Liu, Nain, and Coffman (2001). Most crawlers deliver indexing information to a central repository; an alternative model allows distributed indexing and caching of results, as, for example, in the Harvest system (Bowman, Danzig, Hardy, Manber, & Schwartz, 1995).

Instead of attempting to crawl all or a significant portion of the Web, crawlers can also be focused to deliver information on specific topics. A focused crawler selectively finds and returns pages relevant to a set of topics as specified using sample documents, making relevance and priority judgments to direct the crawl (Chakrabarti et al., 1998). Anecdotal evidence based on the topics of cycling and mutual funds demonstrated their viability. In general, evaluation of topic-specific crawlers is difficult because the set of relevant pages is unknown. Menczer, Pant, and Srinivasan (2001) proposed three metrics by which the performance could be evaluated: via classifiers, ranking with an IR system, and calculation of mean topic similarity. O'Meara and Patel (2001) proposed a solution for building and maintaining topic-specific indexes appropriate for a distributed system, based on what they call the restless bandit model. Diligenti, Coetzee, Lawrence, Giles, and Gori (2000) suggested that with performance improvements gained by adding a context graph and allowing partial reverse crawling, crawling is moving toward implementation as a personal tool in the PC environment.

Indexing and Ranking

Information retrieval research has examined a number of approaches, notably the Boolean, vector space, and probabilistic models. Techniques such as keyword stemming, use of stop lists to eliminate common terms, term weighting schemes, such as the common *tf*idf* (term frequency*inverse document frequency), and use of similarity coefficients to calculate document–query similarity are well known (Baeza-Yates &

Ribeiro-Neto, 1999a; Frakes & Baeza-Yates, 1992; Korfhage, 1997; Salton, 1989; Witten et al., 1999).

A number of shortcomings of IR as performed by search engines have been identified; these include the large answer set and low precision of the search results, an inability to preserve hypertext structure for matching documents, and a lack of effectiveness for general-concept queries (Kao, Lee, Ng, & Cheung, 2000). The long-standing tradition of performance evaluation in IR research is being carried over to the Web retrieval environment. In recent years, these IR techniques have been tested and refined on large test collections in the TREC experiments, most recently in the context of a Web-like environment (Hawking et al., 2000; Voorhees, 2000b).

Early search engines returned and indexed only components of each Web page, but, increasingly, the full text of Web pages is being indexed. General details of search engine characteristics are reported by Search Engine Watch and elsewhere, but specific information on the form and weight of index terms, and the means by which relevance rankings are calculated, are generally proprietary. However, several studies have suggested ranking techniques that are adapted to Web queries. Yuwono and Lee (1996) evaluated four ranking algorithms based on keyword matching and hyperlinks: Boolean Spreading Activation; Most-cited; the tf^*idf vector space model; and vector spreading activation, which combines tf^*idf with spreading activation. They found that term-based approaches worked better than link-based ones. Adaptation to short queries has also been suggested. Standard similarity measures are usually used with queries that are longer than those typically found in the Web environment, leading to an interest in developing ranking metrics better adapted to Web queries of only a few words (Clarke, Cormack, & Tudhope, 2000).

Because of the size of the indexable Web, significant scalability issues arise in creating efficiently organized and accessible indexes for the Web (Arasu et al., 2000; see also Witten et al., 1999), which will not be addressed here.

A critical question asks whether IR techniques found to improve retrieval effectiveness on standard IR test collections perform in the same way on the Web. Savoy and Picard (2001) used the 2-gigabyte Web collection provided through TREC to evaluate the effectiveness of established IR techniques. These techniques included a variety of term weighting schemes such as binary, term frequency, term frequency* inverse document frequency, and normalization for document length. They also evaluated use of a stopword list, stemming of index terms, and query expansion in the Web test collection. Savoy and Picard (2001, p. 556) concluded, "We may infer that search strategies having a good overall retrieval effectiveness on classical test collections will also produce good average precision on the Web."

Hawking et al. (1999, 2001) examined ways to combine the features of an operational and a laboratory experiment to overcome the problem of comparing traditional IR techniques with those used by Web search engines. They compared TREC retrieval systems used in the TREC-7 Very Large Collection track with Web search engines by submitting TREC-7 short queries to five search engines searching the Web and comparing the results to TREC retrieval using the VLC2/WT2g collection (Hawking et al., 1999). They found that all five search engines performed below the median for the TREC search engines. In a later study (Hawking et al., 2001), they searched 54 queries extracted from search engine logs on 20 public search engines, comparing the results with previous studies as well as with TREC Web track results for the same measures. They found a high correlation with Gordon and Pathak's (1999) study. As a group, the search engines were inferior to participants in the TREC-8 Web track, although the best approached the effectiveness achieved by TREC Large Web task participants. Singhal and Kaszkiel (2001), however, found search engines to be superior for some tasks, as discussed in the next section.

Hyperlinks for Indexing and Ranking

A defining characteristic of the Web is the presence of hyperlinks between Web pages, which are primarily seen as navigational devices. However, hyperlinks also carry information that can be used in indexing and retrieval and related tasks, as reviewed by Chakrabarti, van den Berg, and Dom (1999) and Henzinger (2001). Information in hyperlinks is found not only in the fact of the link itself, but also in the importance of the linking document and the overall popularity of the linked document. In a seminal paper, Kleinberg (1998) developed a theory of "hubs" (pages that have links to multiple relevant authoritative pages) and "authorities" (pages that are pointed to by many good hubs). For broad queries with many relevant pages (the "Abundance Problem"), it is desirable to retrieve documents that are both relevant and authoritative. Kleinberg proposed an iterative algorithm (HITS) for identifying authoritative pages based on the link structure, and for identifying distinct communities among relevant pages. Lempel and Moran (2000) explored a method based on random walks on graphs derived from link structure, which is computationally more efficient than Kleinberg's algorithm. The best known use of hyperlinks for ranking is in the PageRank algorithm, developed by Page et al. (1998), which operates iteratively to calculate a PageRank value for each page, normalized by the number of links on each page. The PageRank algorithm is a major feature of the Google search engine (Brin & Page, 1998).

Kleinberg's work has been extended to incorporate text as well as link information. Chakrabarti et al. (1998) developed ARC (Automatic Resource Compiler) to compile lists of Web resources on broad topics. Bharat and Henzinger (1998) identified several problems with Kleinberg's initial algorithm, including "topic drift," in which well-connected hubs and authorities are not about the original topic. They proposed and tested algorithms to address these problems, including the addition of content analysis using traditional IR techniques. Borodin, Roberts, Rosenthal, and Tsaparas (2001) examined several known and new algorithms (including modifications to the Kleinberg algorithm and two algorithms based on a Bayesian statistical approach) and began to develop a theoretical framework for exploration of these algorithms.

Another use of hyperlinks in retrieval involves the implementation of constrained spreading activation (Crestani & Lee, 2000). This method begins with a relevant Web page, or pages, and fans out through the network of linked pages, calculating a similarity for each page, subject to experimentally determined constraints, which direct the process and determine at what point the pages are ranked and presented to the user. The WebSCSA (Web Search by Constrained Spreading Activation) system was intended to be an adjunct to a search engine, and experimental results suggested it could enhance precision of results by about 30 percent.

Kao et al. (2000) proposed using hyperlink information in a somewhat different way, to support anchor point indexing. They define anchor points as a small set of key pages from which a set of matching pages can be accessed easily and logically, thus preserving the structure of hyperdocuments in the Web.

Singhal and Kaszkiel (2001) questioned findings from the TREC Web track showing that link-based methods provide no advantage over methods based on keyword indexing alone. This result, they contended, was counter-intuitive and contrary to general wisdom within the Web search community. They suggested several reasons why the TREC Web track environment might favor keyword indexing techniques over linkage ones, including a dated (by Web standards) test collection and relevance judgments that favored pages over sites. They demonstrated that for some tasks, such as finding the Web page or site for an organization or individual, commercial Web search engines were better than current TREC algorithms. Craswell, Hawking, and Robertson (2001) also examined the Web site-finding task in the TREC environment, and found that a retrieval method based on anchor text from incoming links had a strong advantage over one based on textual content of the document.

Ranking for Metasearch

A long-standing information retrieval problem is that of data fusion, or merging into a single ranked list the output from multiple sources (Voorhees & Tong, 1997). This is the problem faced by metasearch engines on the Web, which submit a user query to multiple search engines and integrate the results for the user. Dwork, Kumar, Naor, and Sivakumar (2001) proposed a method of rank aggregation, which is effective in combating spam indexing.

Inquiris is a metasearch engine that downloads Web pages from individual search engines and analyzes them for the context of query terms. Display order depends on both speed of return and document ranking, based on number and proximity of query terms (Lawrence & Giles, 1998a).

Document Structure as Indexing Information on the Web

Web documents typically have structural components identified by HTML tags, such as title, headings, and anchors, and this information can be used to advantage by search engines in assigning value to index terms. Cutler, Shih, and Meng (1997) proposed an extension of the vector space model that weights terms according to their presence in these components, deriving the importance factors experimentally. Davison (2000, p. 272) explored two fundamental Web ideas: "Most Web pages are linked to others with related content" and "text in, and possibly around, HTML anchors describe[s] the pages to which they point." He found empirical evidence that topical locality mirrored spatial locality on the Web, both between and within pages. Web pages were typically linked to pages with similar textual content, and sibling pages (those linked from the same page) were more similar when the links from the parent were closer together.

Other Research Issues Related to Indexing and Ranking

Many other research issues related to the indexing and retrieval of Web pages have been explored. These include citation indexing, the adaptation of relevance feedback and query expansion techniques to the Web, the "more like this" problem of finding pages related to known relevant pages, and the use of the Web as a basis for question answering. Due to space limitations discussion of these topics will be limited to a few representative studies.

Citation Indexing on the Web

Citation indexing has a long tradition in print resources and through the Institute for Scientific Information's (ISI's) citation indexes, now available as the Web of Science (Atkins, 1999). Posting of scholarly papers on the Web has become commonplace, particularly in technical fields. This provides a ready source of material for citation indexing, as well as for bibliometric analysis (Cronin, 2001). These papers may be electronic versions of print publications (often expanded or including additional data), preliminary versions for comment, or electronic-only versions. Lawrence (2001) found a clear correlation between the number of times an article is cited and the probability that it is freely available online. This may be because online articles are easier to access and more likely to be read (and hence cited) or because articles made available online are of a higher quality. The ResearchIndex system (Lawrence, Giles, & Bollacker, 1999) identifies research papers posted to the Web and downloads them, caches them, and extracts and indexes citations. The system offers keyword search and co-citation search as well as search by cited document.

Relevance Feedback and Query Evaluation

Relevance feedback and query expansion have a long tradition of use in information retrieval systems, reflecting the demonstrable improvement in retrieval performance, which they provide. Relevance feedback uses information about known relevant items to refine a user's query, while the related technique of query expansion uses a variety of methods to add terms to a user's query. Smeaton and Crimmins (1997) proposed a metasearch algorithm and architecture to add this functionality to Web searching. Moldovan and Mihalcea (2000) use WordNet, a machine-readable dictionary, to expand query terms following word–sense disambiguation, increasing precision, and percentage of queries answered correctly.

Finding Related Pages

A classic retrieval problem is to identify related documents, using query by example, or "more like this," in which the searcher identifies a passage or document of interest and wants to retrieve similar documents. This retrieval problem is also of interest in the Web environment, and can be extended to another problem: finding Web pages or sites that are replicas or near-replicas (mirrored hosts) to improve the quality of the Web crawl and ranking of results. Shivakumar and Garcia-Molina (1998) demonstrated a method to calculate the overlap between pairs of Web documents based on 32-bit fingerprints for segments of text. In their sample they found that 22 percent of pages were exact copies, and 33 percent shared significant overlap (25 or more two-line segments of text). Cho, Shivakumar, and Garcia-Molina (2000) addressed the problem of finding similar collections based on a Web graph and demonstrated its usefulness in data crawled by Google, showing a 40 percent reduction in crawl effort and improvement in presentation of results.

Dean and Henzinger (1999) examined two algorithms for finding related pages based only on connectivity (hyperlink) information. The Companion algorithm was derived from Kleinberg's HITS algorithm, while the Cocitation algorithm looked for pages that are frequently pointed to by pages that also point to the query page. Bharat, Broder, Dean, and Henzinger (2000) used information from URLs, IP addresses, and host and document connectivity to find mirrored hosts on the Web. By combining these approaches they achieved a precision of 57 percent and 86 percent recall when tested on a collection of 140 million URLs.

Question Answering on the Web

Question answering, in which a user presents a query to a system in natural language and receives a specific piece of text that contains the answer rather than a pointer to a document, is a long-standing goal in information retrieval. This area is represented in the TREC experiments by the Question-Answering Track, and TREC-9 results suggested that significant performance improvements are being made in this environment (Voorhees, 2000a). Retrieval from the Web, with its large base of users who are untrained in structuring queries, is an obvious arena for question-answering systems. A recent vision statement for the question-answering task posed the challenge of providing responses to complex questions by searching multiple sources, formats, and languages; integrating information; resolving conflicting information and alternatives; adding interpretation; and drawing conclusions (Burger, Cardie, Chaudhri, Gaizauskas, Harabagiu, Israel et al., 2000). The Web as an information source certainly poses all of these problems for question answering. Kwok et al. (2001) explored the problem of scaling question-answering techniques to the Web environment. They developed MULDER, a general-purpose, fully automated question-answering system for the Web, and tested its performance using TREC-8 queries, showing that it provided recall significantly better than AskJeeves (www.askjeeves.com) and entailed much less user effort than Google.

User Issues in Indexing and Retrieval on the Web

Although search engines are becoming more and more technically advanced, there is ample evidence that they are not meeting the needs of all users (Pollock & Hockley, 1997). Many researchers have examined the techniques and performance of Web search engines; however, a smaller but growing body of research is examining how users search— that is, the nature and subject of their queries, number of search terms, sequence of steps followed, and success of the outcome. Jansen and Pooch (2001, p. 236) defined a Web-searching study as one that "focuses on isolating searching characteristic of searchers using a Web IR system via analysis of data, typically gathered from transaction logs." They reviewed three primary studies and a variety of others that were more limited in terms of data, number of users, or sites. They also provided a meta analysis of nine previously reported studies of searching in the traditional IR, library online catalog, and Web environments, concluding that Web searching differs from the other two. Their observation of the difference in definitions and metrics led them to suggest a common framework to improve comparability across such studies in the future.

Search engine transaction logs provide a large and rich resource for analysis of search patterns. A study of the AltaVista transaction log for a six-week period showed almost a billion requests, with an average query size of 2.35 terms (Silverstein, Henzinger, Marais, & Moricz, 1998). Most sessions were short. In 77 percent of the sessions, only a single query was submitted. In 63.7 percent of sessions, there was only one request; that is, one query was entered and one result screen viewed. The data suggest that Web users differ in their search patterns from those using non-Web IR systems. Two studies of transaction logs from the Excite search engine, the first containing about 50,000 queries (Jansen, Spink, & Saracevic, 2000) and the second containing more than a million queries (Spink, Wolfram, Jansen, & Saracevic, 2001), showed similarly short queries (2.21 and 2.4 terms, respectively). In general, queries were short, simple, not often modified, and rarely used any advanced features. The need for Web search engines to adapt to and work with users is clear.

A growing body of research is also addressing the search patterns and behavior of Web searchers. Primary school students (Large & Beheshti,

2000) and high school students (Fidel et al., 1999) have been observed doing class projects and homework. Other researchers have examined cognitive style (Navarro-Prieto, Scaife, & Rogers, 1999; Palmquist & Kim, 2000) and Web experience (Hölscher & Strube, 2000; Lazonder, Biemans, & Wopereis, 2000). A full discussion of research on user issues related to Web retrieval is beyond the scope of this review, although more information is needed to provide a framework for research on indexing and retrieval on the Web. It is, however, important to go beyond simple data on query formulation because information on user needs, behavior, and preferences is needed to guide the evaluation process. A clearer picture of Web retrieval tasks will guide researchers in building improved retrieval engines.

Conclusion

Resource discovery or information retrieval on the Web is an active area for research and development. Like the Web itself, the field has both public and hidden components, and the proprietary nature of much of the work hinders progress in some areas. Research groups closely linked with search engine development are clearly in an advantageous position to provide realistic evidence of the success of their methods. Progress over the five-year span of this review has been remarkable, and due to space constraints many topics within the area of indexing and retrieval on the Web have not been addressed. These topics include the role of categorization and metadata generation for Web documents, current status and potential of multimedia information retrieval on the Web, and the active areas relating to the presentation of Web documents: document summarization, clustering, and visualization. The intention here has been to characterize the Web as an environment for information retrieval, to highlight progress in the evaluation of Web retrieval, and to show the direction and breadth of research on indexing and retrieval topics.

Bibliography

Adamic, L. A. & Huberman, B. A. (2001). The Web's hidden order. *Communications of the ACM, 44* (9), 51–59. Retrieved December 20, 2001, from http://www.hpl.hp. com/research/papers/hiddenweb.html.

Agosti, M., & Smeaton, A. (Eds.). (1996). *Information retrieval and hypertext.* Boston: Kluwer Academic.

Albert, R., Jeong, H., & Barabási, A.-L. (1999). Diameter of the World-Wide Web. *Nature, 401*(6749), 130–131.

Arasu, A., Cho, J., Garcia-Molina, H., Paepcke, A., & Raghavan, S. (2000). Searching the Web. Stanford University Technical Report 2000-37. Retrieved December 20, 2001, from http://dbpubs.stanford.edu/pub/2000-37.

Atkins, H. (1999, September). The ISI® *Web of Science®*—Links and electronic journals. *D-Lib Magazine, 5*(9). Retrieved December 20, 2001, from http://www.dlib.org/dlib/september99/atkins/09atkins.html.

Baeza-Yates, R. & Ribeiro-Neto, B. (Eds.). (1999a). *Modern information retrieval.* New York: ACM.

Baeza-Yates, R. & Ribeiro-Neto, B. (1999b). Searching the Web. In R. Baeza-Yates & B. Ribeiro-Neto (Eds.), *Modern information retrieval* (pp. 367–395). New York: ACM.

Bar-Ilan, J. (1998/9). Search engine results over time: A case study on search engine stability. *Cybermetrics, 2/3* (1), Paper 1. Retrieved December 20, 2001, from http://www.cindoc.csic.es/cybermetrics/articles/v2i1p1.html.

Bar-Ilan, J. (2000). Evaluating the stability of the search tools Hotbot and Snap: A case study. *Online Information Review, 24*, 439–449.

Bar-Ilan, J. (2001). Methods for measuring search engine performance over time. *10th International World Wide Web Conference (WWW10).* Retrieved December 20, 2001, from http://www10.org/cdrom/posters/1018.pdf.

Bharat, K., & Broder, A. (1998a). A technique for measuring the relative size and overlap of public Web search engines. *Computer Networks and ISDN Systems, 30*, 379–388.

Bharat, K., & Broder, A. (1998b, April 24). Measuring the Web. Retrieved December 20, 2001, from http://www.research.compaq.com/SRC/whatsnew/sem.html.

Bharat, K., Broder, A., Dean, J., & Henzinger, M. R. (2000). A comparison of techniques to find mirrored hosts on the WWW. *Journal of the American Society for Information Science, 51*, 1114–1122.

Bharat, K., & Henzinger, M. R. (1998). Improved algorithms for topic distillation in a hyperlinked environment. In W. B. Croft, A. Moffat, C. J. van Rijsbergen, R. Wilkinson & J. Zobel (Eds.), *Proceedings of the 21st Annual International ACM SIGIR Conference on Research and Development in Information Retrieval (SIGIR '98)* (pp. 104–111). New York: ACM.

Borodin, A., Roberts, G. O., Rosenthal, J. S., & Tsaparas, P. (2001). Finding authorities and hubs from link structures on the World Wide Web. *10th International World Wide Web Conference (WWW10)*, 415–429. Retrieved December 20, 2001, from http://www10.org/cdrom/start.htm.

Bowman, C. M., Danzig, P. B., Hardy, D. R, Manber, U., & Schwartz, M. F. (1995). The Harvest information discovery and access system. *Computer Networks and ISDN Systems 28*, 119–125.

Brake, D. (1997). Lost in cyberspace. *New Scientist, 154*, 12–13. Retrieved December 20, 2001, from http://www.newscientist.com/keysites/networld/lost.html.

Bray, T. (1996). Measuring the Web. *5th International World Wide Web Conference (WWW5).* Retrieved December 20, 2001, from http://www5conf.inria.fr/fich_html/papers/P9/Overview.html. (Also published as a special issue of *Computer Networks and ISDN Systems, 28*(7–11), 993–1005.)

Brewington, B. E., & Cybenko, G. (2000). How dynamic is the Web? *Computer Networks, 33* (1–6), 257–276.

Brin, S., & Page, L. (1998). The anatomy of a large-scale hypertextual Web search engine. *Proceedings of the Seventh International World-Wide Web Conference (WWW7)*, published as *Computer Networks and ISDN Systems, 30*, 107–117. (Longer version available at http://decweb.ethz.ch/WWW7/1921/com1921.htm.)

Broder, A., Kumar, R., Maghoul, F., Raghavan, P., Rajagopalan, S., Stat, R. et al. (2000). Graph structure in the Web. *Computer Networks, 33*, 309–320. Retrieved December 20, 2001, from http://www.almaden.ibm.com/cs/k53/ www9.final/.

Burger, J., Cardie, C., Chaudhri, V., Gaizauskas, R., Harabagiu, S., Israel, D. et al. (2000). Issues, tasks and program structures to roadmap research in question & answering (Q&A). Retrieved December 20, 2001, from http://www-nlpir.nist.gov/projects/duc/papers/qa.Roadmap-paper_v2.doc.

Chakrabarti, S., Dom, B., Kumar, S. R., Raghavan, P., Rajagopalan, S., Tomkins, A. et al. (1999). Hypersearching the Web. *Scientific American, 280*(6), 54–60. Retrieved December 20, 2001, from http://www.sciam.com/1999/0699issue/0699raghavan.html.

Chakrabarti, S., Dom, B., Raghavan, P., Rajagopalan, S., Gibson, D., & Kleinberg, J. (1998). Automatic resource compilation by analyzing hyperlink structure and associated text. *Proceedings of the Seventh International World-Wide Web Conference (WWW7)*, published as *Computer Networks and ISDN Systems, 30*, 65–74.

Chakrabarti, S., van den Berg, M., & Dom, B. (1999). Focused crawling: A new approach to topic-specific Web resource discovery. *Proceedings of the 8th International World Wide Web Conference (WWW8)*. Retrieved December 20, 2001, from http:www8.org/w8-papers/51-search-query/crawling/index.html.

Cho, J., Garcia-Molina, H., & Page, L. (1998). Efficient crawling through URL ordering. *Proceedings of the Seventh International World-Wide Web Conference (WWW7)*, published as *Computer Networks and ISDN Systems, 30*(1–7), 161–172.

Cho, J., Shivakumar, N., & Garcia-Molina, H. (2000). Finding replicated Web collections. *Proceedings of 2000 ACM SIGMOD International Conference on Management of Data*. Retrieved December 20, 2001, from http://www.acm.org/sigmod/sigmod00/eproceedings/index.html.

Chu, H., & Rosenthal, M. (1996). Search engines for the World Wide Web: A comparative study and evaluation methodology. In S. Hardin (Ed.), *Proceedings of the 59th Annual Meeting of the American Society for Information Science* (pp. 127–135). Medford, NJ: Information Today for the American Society for Information Science.

Clarke, C. L. A., Cormack, G. V., & Tudhope, E. A. (2000). Relevance ranking for one to three term queries. *Information Processing & Management, 36*, 291–311.

Clarke, S. J., & Willett, P. (1997). Estimating the recall performance of Web search engines. *Aslib Proceedings, 49*(7), 184–189.

Coffman, E. G. Jr., Liu, Z., & Weber, R. R. (1998). Optimal robot scheduling for Web search engines. *Journal of Scheduling, 1*(1), 15–29.

Craswell, N., Hawking, D., & Robertson, S. (2001). Effective site finding using link anchor information. In W. B. Croft, D. J. Harper, D. H. Kraft, & J. Zobel (Eds.), *SIGIR 2001: Proceedings of the 24th Annual International ACM SIGIR Conference on Research and Development in Information Retrieval* (p. 250–257). New York: ACM.

Craven, T. C. (2000). Features of DESCRIPTION META tags in public home pages. *Journal of Information Science, 26*, 303–311.

Crestani, F., & Lee, P. L. (2000). Searching the Web by constrained spreading activation. *Information Processing & Management, 36*, 585–605.

Cronin, B. (2001). Bibliometrics and beyond: Some thoughts on Web-based citation analysis. *Journal of Information Science, 27*, 1–7.

Cutler, M., Shih, Y., & Meng, W. (1997). Using the structure of HTML documents to improve retrieval. *Proceedings of the USENIX Symposium on Internet Technologies and Systems*. Retrieved December 20, 2001, from http://www.usenix. org/publications/library/proceedings/usits97/full_papers/cutler/cutler.pdf.

Davison, B. (2000). Topical locality in the Web. In N. J. Belkin, P. Ingwersen, & M. K. Leong (Eds.), *Proceedings of the 23rd Annual International ACM SIGIR Conference on Research and Development in Information Retrieval (SIGIR 2000)* (pp. 272–279). New York: ACM.

Dean, J., & Henzinger, M. R. (1999). Finding related pages in the World Wide Web. *Proceedings of the 8th International World Wide Web Conference (WWW8)*. Retrieved December 20, 2001, from http://www8.org/w8-papers/4a-search-mining/finding/finding.html.

Diligenti, M., Coetzee, F. M., Lawrence, S., Giles, C. L., & Gori, M. (2000). Focused crawling using context graphs. *Proceedings of the 26th VLDB Conference*, 527–534.

Ding, W., & Marchionini, G. (1996). A comparative study of Web search service performance. In S. Hardin (Ed.), *Proceedings of the 59th Annual Meeting of the American Society for Information Science* (pp. 136–142). Medford, NJ: Information Today for the American Society for Information Science.

Douglis, F., Feldmann, A., Krishnamurthy, B., & Mogul, J. (1997). Rate of change and other metrics: A live study of the World Wide Web. *Proceedings of the USENIX Symposium on Internet Technologies and Systems*. Retrieved December 20, 2001, from http://www.usenix.org/publications/library/proceedings/ usits97/douglis_rate.html.

Dwork, C., Kumar, R., Naor, M., & Sivakumar, D. (2001). Rank aggregation methods for the Web. *10th International World Wide Web Conference (WWW10)*, 613–622. Retrieved December 20, 2001, from http://www10.org/cdrom/start. htm.

Fidel, R., Davies, R. K., Douglass, M. H., Holder, J. K., Hopkins, C. J., Kushner, E. J. et al. (1999). A visit to the information mall: Web searching behavior of high school students. *Journal of the American Society for Information Science, 50*, 24–37.

Frakes, W. B., & Baeza-Yates, R. (Eds.). (1992). *Information retrieval: Data structures & algorithms*. Englewood Cliffs, NJ: Prentice-Hall.

Gordon, M., & Pathak, P. (1999). Finding information on the World Wide Web: The retrieval effectiveness of search engines. *Information Processing & Management, 35*, 141–180.

Graphic, Visualization, & Usability Center. (1998). GVU's 10th WWW User Survey. Retrieved December 20, 2001, from http://www.cc.gatech.edu/gvu/user_surveys/survey-1998-10.

Grefenstette, G., & Nioche, J. (2000). Estimation of English and non-English language use on the WWW. *Proceedings of the RIAO'2000 Conference*. Paris: C.I.D. Retrieved December 20, 2001, from http://133.23.229.11/~ysuzuki/Proceedingsall/RIAO2000/Wednesday/20plenary2.pdf.

Griffiths, J.-M. (1999). Why the Web is not a library. *FID Review, 1*(1), 229–246.

Gudivada, V. N., Raghavan, V. V., Grosky, W. I., & Kasanagottu, R. (1997). Information retrieval on the World Wide Web. *IEEE Internet Computing, 1*(5), 58–68.

Hawking, D., Craswell, N., Bailey, P., & Griffiths, K. (2001). Measuring search engine quality. *Information Retrieval, 4*, 33–59.

Hawking, D., Craswell, N., Thistlewaite, P., & Harman, D. (1999). Results and challenges in Web search evaluation. *Proceedings of the 8th International World Wide Web Conference (WWW8)*. Retrieved December 20, 2001, from http://www8.org/w8-papers/2c-search-discover/results/results.html.

Hawking, D., Voorhees, E., Craswell, N., & Bailey, P. (2000). Overview of the TREC-8 Web track. In E. M. Voorhees, & D. Harman (Eds.), *Proceedings of the Eighth Text REtrieval Conference (TREC-8)*. (NIST Special Publication 500-246). Retrieved December 20, 2001, from http://trec.nist.gov/pubs/trec8/papers/web_overview.pdf.

Henzinger, M. R. (2001). Hyperlink analysis for the Web. *IEEE Internet Computing, 5*(1), 45–50.

Henzinger, M. R., Heydon, A., Mitzenmacher, M., & Najork, M. (1999). Measuring index quality using random walks on the Web. *Proceedings of the 8th International World Wide Web Conference*. Retrieved December 20, 2001, from http://www8.org/w8-papers/2c-search-discover/measuring/measuring.html.

Hölscher, C., & Strube, G. (2000). Web search behavior of Internet experts and newbies. *9th International World Wide Web Conference (WWW9)*. Retrieved December 20, 2001, from http://www9.org/w9cdrom/81.81.html.

Huang, L. (2000). A survey on Web information retrieval technologies. RPE Report. Retrieved December 20, 2001, from http://www.ecsl.cs.sunysb.edu/tr/rpe8.ps.Z.

Huberman, B. A., & Adamic, L. A. (1999). Growth dynamics of the World-Wide Web. *Nature, 401*, 131.

Inktomi (2000). Web surpasses one billion documents. Retrieved December 20, 2001, from http://www.inktomi.com/new/press/2000/billion.html.

Jansen, B. J., & Pooch, U. (2001). A review of Web searching studies and a framework for future research. *Journal of the American Society for Information Science and Technology, 52*, 235–46.

Jansen, B. J., Spink, A., & Saracevic, T. (2000). Real life, real users, and real needs: A study and analysis of user queries on the Web. *Information Processing & Management 36*, 207–227.

Kao, B., Lee, J., Ng, C., & Cheung, D. (2000). Anchor point indexing in Web document retrieval. *IEEE Transactions on Systems, Man, and Cybernetics: Part C: Applications and Reviews, 30,* 364–373.

Kleinberg, J. M. (1998). Authoritative sources in a hyperlinked environment. *Proceedings of the 9th Annual ACM-SIAM Symposium on Discrete Algorithms,* 668–677. (A full version of the paper is available at http://www.cs. cornell.edu/home/kleinber/.)

Kobayashi, M., & Takeda, K., (2000). Information retrieval on the Web. *ACM Computing Surveys, 32*(2), 144–173.

Koehler, W. (1999). An analysis of Web page and Web site constancy and permanence. *Journal of the American Society for Information Science, 50,* 162–180.

Korfhage, R. R. (1997). *Information storage and retrieval.* New York: Wiley.

Kwok, C. C. T., Etzioni, O., & Weld, D. S. (2001). *Scaling question answering to the Web. 10th International World Wide Web Conference (WWW10),* 150–161. Retrieved December 20, 2001, from http://www10.org/cdrom/start.htm.

Landoni, M., & Bell, S. (2000). Information retrieval techniques for evaluating search engines: A critical overview. *Aslib Proceedings, 52* (3), 124–129.

Large, A., & Beheshti, J. (2000). The Web as a classroom resource: Reactions from the users. *Journal of the American Society for Information Science, 51,* 1069–1080.

Lawrence, S. (2001). Online or invisible? *Nature, 411,* 521.

Lawrence, S., Coetzee, F., Glover, E., Pennock, D., Flake, G., Nielsen, F. et al. (2001). Persistence of Web references in scientific research. *IEEE Computer, 34* (2), 26–31.

Lawrence, S., & Giles, C. L. (1998a). Inquirus, the NECI meta search engine. *Computer Networks and ISDN Systems, 30,* 95–105.

Lawrence, S., & Giles, C. L. (1998b). Searching the World Wide Web. *Science, 280* (3), 98–100.

Lawrence, S., & Giles, C. L. (1999). Accessibility of information on the Web. *Nature, 400,* 107–109.

Lawrence, S., Giles, C. L., & Bollacker, K. (1999). Digital libraries and autonomous citation indexing. *IEEE Computer, 32* (6), 67–71.

Lazonder, A. W., Biemans, H. J. A., & Wopereis, G. J. H. (2000). Differences between novice and experienced users in searching information on the World Wide Web. *Journal of the American Society for Information Science, 51,* 576–581.

Leighton, H. V., & Srivastava, J. (1999). First 20 precision among World Wide Web search services (search engines). *Journal of the American Society for Information Science, 50,* 870–881.

Lempel, R., & Moran, S. (2000). The stochastic approach for link-structure analysis (SALSA) and the TKC effect. *9th International World Wide Web Conference (WWW9).* Retrieved December 20, 2001, from http://www9.org/w9cdrom/ start.html.

Liberatore, K. (1997, July 2). Getting to the source: Is it real or spam, ma'am? *Macworld.* Retrieved December 20, 2001, from http://www.macworld.com/features/ pov.4.4.html

Licklider, J. C. R. (1965). *Libraries of the future*. Cambridge, MA: MIT Press.

Lynch, C. (1997, March). Searching the Internet. *Scientific American*. Retrieved December 20, 2001, from http://www.sciam.com/0397issue/0397lynch.html.

Menczer, F., Pant, G., & Srinivasan, P. (2001). Evaluating topic-driven Web crawlers. In W. B. Croft, D. J. Harper, D. H. Kraft, & J. Zobel (Eds.), *SIGIR 2001: Proceedings of the 24th Annual International ACM SIGIR Conference on Research and Development in Information Retrieval* (p. 241–249). New York: ACM.

Moldovan, D. I., & Mihalcea, R. (2000). Using WordNet and lexical operators to improve Internet searches. *IEEE Internet Computing, 4* (1), 34–43.

Molyneux, R. E., & Williams, R. V. (1999). Measuring the Internet. *Annual Review of Information Science and Technology, 34,* 287–339.

Najork, M., & Wiener, J. L. (2001). Breadth-first search crawling yields high-quality pages. *10th International World Wide Web Conference (WWW10)*. Retrieved December 20, 2001, from http://www10.org/cdrom/papers/208.

Navarro-Prieto, R., Scaife, M., & Rogers, Y. (1999). Cognitive strategies in Web search. *Proceedings of the 5th Conference on Human Factors and the Web*. Retrieved December 20, 2001, from http://zing.ncsl.nist.gov/hfweb/proceedings/navarro-prieto/index.html.

Nie, N. H., & Erbring, L. (2000). *Internet and society: A preliminary report*. Stanford, CA: Stanford University, Institute for the Quantitative Study of Society. Retrieved December 20, 2001, from http://www.stanford.edu/group/siqss/Press_Release/Preliminary_Report.pdf.

Notess, G. R. (2002). *Search engine statistics*. Retrieved December 20, 2002, from http://www.searchengineshowdown.com/stats/.

O'Meara, T., & Patel, A. (2001). A topic-specific Web robot model based on restless bandits. *IEEE Internet Computing, 5* (2), 27–35.

Oppenheim, C., Morris, A., & McKnight, C. (2000). The evaluation of WWW search engines. *Journal of Documentation, 56,* 190–211.

Page, L., Brin, S., Motwani, R., & Winograd, T. (1998). The PageRank citation ranking: Bringing order to the Web. Retrieved December 20, 2001, from http://www-diglib.stanford.edu/diglib/WP/PUBLIC/DOC312.pdf.

Palmquist, R. A., & Kim, K.-S. (2000). The effect of cognitive style and online search experience on Web search performance. *Journal of the American Society for Information Science, 51,* 558–566.

Pollock, A., & Hockley, A. (1997, March). What's wrong with Internet searching. *D-Lib Magazine*. Retrieved December 20, 2001, from http://www.dlib.org/dlib/march97/bt/03pollock.html.

Qin, J., & Wesley, K. (1998). Web indexing with meta fields: A survey of Web objects in polymer chemistry. *Information Technology and Libraries, 17,* 149–156.

Rousseau, R. (1998/9). Daily time series of common single word searches in AltaVista and NorthernLight. *Cybermetrics, 2/3*. Issue 1, Paper 2. Retrieved December 20, 2001, from http://www.cindoc.csic.es/cybermetrics/articles/v2i1p2.pdf.

Salton, G. (1989). *Automatic text processing: The transformation, analysis, and retrieval of information by computer*. Reading, MA: Addison-Wesley.

Savoy, J., & Picard, J. (2001). Retrieval effectiveness on the Web. *Information Processing & Management, 37*, 543–569.

Schatz, B. (1997). Information retrieval in digital libraries: Bringing search to the Net. *Science, 275*, 327–334.

Schwartz, C. (1998). Web search engines. *Journal of the American Society for Information Science, 49*, 973–982.

Selberg, E., & Etzioni, O. (2000). On the instability of Web search engines. *Proceedings of the RIAO'2000 Conference.* Paris: C.I.D. Retrieved December 20, 2001, from http://133.23.229.11/~ysuzuki/Proceedingsall/RIAO2000/Wednesday/19plenary2.pdf.

Shivakumar, N., & Garcia-Molina, H. (1998). Finding near-replicas of documents on the Web. *Proceedings of Workshop on Web Databases (WebDB'98).* Retrieved December 20, 2001, from http://dbpubs.stanford.edu/pub/1998-31.

Silverstein, C., Henzinger, M., Marais, H., & Moricz, M. (1998). Analysis of a very large Web search engine query log. Digital SRC Technical Note #1998-014. Retrieved December 20, 2001, from http://www-cs-students.stanford.edu/~csilvers.

Singhal, A., & Kaszkiel, M. (2001). A case study in Web search using TREC algorithms. *10th International World Wide Web Conference (WWW10), 708–716.* Retrieved December 20, 2001, from http://www10.org/cdrom/start.htm.

Smeaton, A. F., & Crimmins, F. (1997). Relevance feedback and query expansion for searching the Web: A model for searching a digital library. In C. Peters & C. Thanos (Eds.), *Research and Advanced Technology for Digital Libraries, First European Conference, ECDL '97* (pp. 99–112). Berlin, Germany: Springer Verlag.

Spink, A., & Qin, J. (2000). Introduction to the special issue on Web-based information retrieval research. *Information Processing & Management, 36*, 205–206.

Spink, A., Wolfram, D., Jansen, B. J., & Saracevic, T. (2001). Searching the Web: The public and their queries. *Journal of the American Society for Information Science and Technology, 52*, 226–234.

Stanley, T. (1997a). Keyword spamming: Cheat your way to the top. *Ariadne, 10.* Retrieved December 20, 2001, from http://www.ariadne.ac.uk/issue10/search-engines/.

Stanley, T. (1997b). Moving up the ranks. *Ariadne, 12.* Retrieved December 20, 2001, from http://www.ariadne.ac.uk/issue12/search-engines.

Su, L. (1997). Developing a comprehensive and systemic model of user evaluation of Web-based search engines. *Proceedings of the 18th National Online Meeting,* 335–344.

Su, L. T., Chen, H., & Dong, X. (1998). Evaluation of Web-based search engines from the end-user's perspective: A pilot study. In C. M. Preston (Ed.), *Proceedings of the 61st ASIS Annual Meeting (ASIS 1998)* (pp. 348–361). Medford, NJ: Information Today for the American Society for Information Science.

Sullivan, D. (2001a, December 11). Search engine sizes. Retrieved December 20, 2001, from http://www.searchenginewatch.com/reports/sizes.html.

Sullivan, D. (2001b, July 2). Search engine features for Webmasters. Retrieved December 20, 2001, from http://www.searchenginewatch.com/webmasters/features.html.

Talim, J., Liu, Z., Nain, P., & Coffman, E. G., Jr. (2001). Optimizing the number of robots for Web search engines. *Telecommunications Systems, 17*, 243–264.

Tomaiuolo, N. G., & Packer, J. G. (1996). An analysis of Internet search engines: Assessment of over 200 search queries. *Computers in Libraries, 16* (6), 58–62.

Turner, T. P., & Brackbill, L. (1998). Rising to the top: Evaluating the use of the HTML meta tag to improve retrieval of World Wide Web documents through Internet search engines. *Library Resources and Technical Services, 42*, 258–271.

Voorhees, E. M. (2000a). Overview of the TREC-9 question answering track. *The Ninth Text REtrieval Conference: TREC-9.* (NIST Special Publication 500-249). Retrieved December 20, 2001, from http://trec.nist.gov/pubs/trec9/papers/qa_overview.pdf.

Voorhees, E. M. (2000b). Report on TREC-9. *SIGIR Forum, 34* (2), 1–8.

Voorhees, E. M., & Tong, R. M. (1997). Multiple search engines in database merging. In R. B. Allen & E. Rasmussen (Eds.), *Proceedings of the 2nd ACM International Conference on Digital Libraries* (pp. 93–102). New York: ACM.

Witten, I. H., Moffat, A., & Bell, T. C. (1999). *Managing gigabytes: Compressing and indexing documents and images* (2nd ed.). San Francisco, CA: Morgan Kaufmann.

Woodruff, A., Aoki, P. M., Brewer, E., Gauthier, P., & Rowe, L. A. (1996). An investigation of documents from the World Wide Web. *Fifth International World Wide Web Conference (WWW5).* Retrieved December 20, 2001, from http://www5conf.inria.fr/fich_html/papers/P7/Overview.html. [Also published as a special issue of *Computer Networks and ISDN Systems, 28*(7–11), 963–980.]

Yuwono, B., & Lee, D. L. (1996). Search and ranking algorithms for locating resources on the World Wide Web. *Proceedings of the 12th International Conference on Data Engineering,* 164–171. Retrieved December 20, 2001, from http://www.cs.ust.hk/~dlee.

Dynamics of Scholarly Communication

CHAPTER 4

Electronic Journals, the Internet, and Scholarly Communication

Rob Kling
Ewa Callahan
Indiana University, Bloomington

Introduction

We are currently in a period of substantial debate about the character of scholarly publishing systems. Some of the issues—such as the cost of journals, speed of publication, and the fairness of blind reviewing practices—predate the Internet. There has been an economic crisis in scholarly publishing since the late 1980s, with the cost of scientific journals rising much faster than both inflation and library budgets (Kirkpatrick, 2000; Miller, 2000; Tenopir & King, 2000, pp. 274–300). During the 1990s, research libraries canceled subscriptions to numerous journals across many disciplines. Many scholars suspected that the cost of publishing electronic journals would be substantially lower than the costs associated with publishing paper journals. Further, some argued that electronic publishing would enable not-for-profit organizations, such as universities, to assume the responsibilies of publishing a substantial fraction of the corpus of scholarly journals at lower cost than "for profit" (trade) publishers.

Concerns about the integrity of peer review processes in traditional scholarly publishing have also arisen.[1] Some analysts hope that new electronic journals (e-journals) will enable review processes to be fairer or clearer, whereas others see electronic publishing offering opportunities for more rapid communication, broader access to scholarly literature, new documentary forms (hypertext), and richer modes of scholarly communication (e.g., the addition of extensive appendices of data, executable algorithms, photographs, and audio/video clips). These debates are fueled by a combination of problems with aspects of existing publication regimes and the beliefs (of some) that various forms of electronic communication may significantly resolve these problems.

Many working scholars in a wide variety of fields, as well as some librarians and others concerned with scholarly publishing, have articulated potential solutions to these problems (and others) in scholarly publishing, solutions in which electronic publishing (and easy access to the Internet and the World Wide Web [WWW, or Web]) is now a central element. It is worth remembering that less than 15 years ago, the leading experiments with e-journals used other media (such as CD-ROMs) and interfaces (e.g., X-Windows for Unix) that were much less commonplace than today's Web browsers. Scholarly communities have undertaken numerous and varied efforts to use the Internet to improve the communication of research articles through the use of e-journals in a variety of formats.

Scholarly communication can take place via a number of documentary genres (as well as conversational genres) including letters, memos, conference papers, technical reports, dissertations, primary articles, review essays, monographs, and edited books. However, the primary scholarly literature is composed of articles (usually published in journals or disseminated at conferences) and books. The vast majority of attempts to use the Internet in enhancing scholarly communication have focused on articles. In addition, most of the research about scholars' experiences with electronic media has emphasized articles; especially those packaged as peer-reviewed e-journals.

In this chapter we will examine the role of the Internet in supporting documentary communication via e-journals. Although this topic may appear rather banal, it has been the subject of substantial controversy among scholars, librarians, publishers, and research sponsors. At the extremes, some analysts have argued that scholars should "free the literature" for broad access by publishing their articles on their own Web sites, making their work available without charge to readers (Harnad,

1995), while others have argued for electronic extensions of publisher-controlled versions of peer-reviewed journals that are sold by subscription to readers. Between these extreme positions lie many proposals and a few empirical studies of scholarly communication via e-journals.

Peer review seems to be one pivotal criterion that many scientists employ in evaluating the legitimacy of publication venues (Kling & Covi, 1995; Weller, 2001). Although we carefully examine the behavior of authors, readers, and other stakeholders regarding (peer-reviewed) scholarly e-journals, we note the outstanding need to examine the electronic distribution of articles that have not been peer reviewed, such as self-published manuscripts or articles in working paper and technical report series.

This chapter emphasizes the contributions of the social and sociotechnical research literatures to our understanding of developments in scholarly communication. However, the literature of other fields will be included as well because it provides important context for the research questions and studies. We will discuss e-journal publication strategies and challenges, and examine how they are shaped by sociotechnical relationships. Our time and expertise have limited our ability to examine some important economic and legal issues, such as the pricing of e-journals and shifts in intellectual property regimes. Most of the reviewed studies concentrate on North American approaches.

We identified relevant research literature for this chapter by starting with studies on scholarly electronic publishing that we knew from our earlier research. We also conducted searches in bibliographies such as the *Scholarly Electronic Publishing Bibliography* compiled by Bailey (2002), *Collection Management and Scholarly Electronic Publishing Resource* by Armstrong (2001), and *Electronic Journals: A Selected Guide* posted online by Harrassowitz (2000). We also examined the bibliographies of monographs such as *Toward Electronic Journals* by Tenopir and King (2000), and *Communicating Research* by Meadows (1998). Other sources were brought to our attention by our colleagues and reviewers of this chapter.

Several previous *ARIST* chapters examined different aspects of scholarly electronic communication. Peek and Pomerantz (1998) reviewed the history of e-journals, and compared various models, scenarios, experiments, and projects. They also discussed acceptance of e-journals in scholarly communities. However, they focused primarily upon the architecture of specific publishing formats and venues. In contrast, we emphasize what can be learned from systematic empirical research about scholars' behavior with regard to the distribution of e-journals, especially via Internet forums.

Dalton (1995) examined early discussions of peer review in electronic publishing. King and Tenopir (1999) reviewed studies of scholars' reading, use, and perception of journals. They emphasized paper journals and a historical comparison of empirical studies conducted from the 1970s to the 1990s. Their chapter briefly examines the use and legitimacy of e-journals. In the most recent *ARIST* chapter on this broad topic, Borgman and Furner (2002) examined authors' citing and linking practices in electronic publications.

This chapter concentrates on empirical, behavioral studies about the role of e-journals in supporting scholarly communication. Some readers may wonder whether such a chapter is needed, given the recent *ARIST* chapters that examined scholarly electronic publishing. In fact, Borgman (2000, pp. 83–84), writing in 1998–1999, noted that the "debates about electronic publishing involve the interaction of technological, psychological, sociological, economic, political, and cultural factors that influence how people create, use, seek, and acquire information." She believed that the debates among the analysts who were advancing different scenarios rested on so many complex evaluations, that "only time will tell whose assumptions and choices of supporting data are most accurate" (Borgman, 2000, p. 84). We are writing in 2002 and believe that some of the sociotechnical reconfigurations of research journals that have taken place since the advent of e-journals in the early 1990s are now sufficiently clear, such that certain widely held assumptions are no longer supportable. This chapter's review of key empirical research studies can help us refine ways of conceptualizing the roles of e-journals and the Internet in scholarly communication.

Before we examine the behavior of readers, authors, and others with e-journals, we want to clarify some important conceptual issues, including the authors and audiences for the literatures about these topics, the relationships between publishing and communication, and the different kinds of e-journals.

Literatures about Scholarly Electronic Communication

Scholarly electronic communication refers to the distribution of scholarly articles, papers, and messages by electronic means as opposed to their distribution by paper media. The vast literature on this subject ranges from research studies to popular writing. In existing bibliographies, research papers, professional articles, and popular works are indiscriminately mixed. Further, only a small fraction of these works report behavioral research about e-journals. In the 41st edition of the most comprehensive and up-to-date bibliography about scholarly electronic publishing, Bailey (2002), only 71 articles (section 3.6) of more than 1,200 are classified explicitly as "research" about electronic serials. We find it helpful to segment the literature about scholarly electronic communication into the following categories on the basis of their authors and likely audiences:

1. *Social and sociotechnical research literature* includes journals such as the *Journal of the American Society for Information Science and Technology,* research monographs (e.g., Tenopir and King, 2000), and specialized research conferences.

2. *Technological research literature* includes analytical examinations of technological standards and design strategies. It is co-extensive with the technological research literature about digital libraries. It includes a *developer literature,* which provides technical details on the structure of various electronic forums.

3. *Practitioner literature (professional writing)* where primary audiences include publishers, librarians, academic administrators, and faculty who may publish in e-media, organize electronic collections, or evaluate such electronic publications. It includes an *enthusiast literature* that advocates and/or predicts an inevitable switch to electronic publishing as the most efficient means of scholarly communication. It also includes a *literature of possibilities,* that is less partisan than the enthusiast literature, and

which acknowledges both the advantages and difficulties associated with electronic publishing.

4. *Popular accounts of scholarly electronic communication forums* are written for the public (for example, in newspapers).

5. *Marketing descriptions of scholarly electronic communication forums* are provided by their organizers to prospective authors.

In this chapter, we will emphasize the social and sociotechnical research literature, drawing upon other accounts for contextual information.

Scholars have many kinds of forums and media for communication about their research. They can participate in face-to-face seminars and meet at conferences. They can use paper mail to send articles to their colleagues. They can publish their articles in journals, books, and conference proceedings. The mix of these forums and their relative importance vary from field to field. For example, peer-reviewed conference proceedings are more important in computer science than in information science. Journals tend to be more important as a medium for communicating original research in the natural sciences than in the humanities. In some fields, such as economics, every major research institute seems to have a working paper series, while research institutes that study humanities topics rarely organize such series.

The use of electronic media expands these traditional opportunities. Scholars can send e-mail or post their manuscripts to scholarly mailing lists asking for comments and suggestions, post their manuscripts in online series of research manuscripts, publish in (electronic) journals, or publish monographic works, some of which may appear in online collections and repositories. The academic community also produces many supporting materials such as conference announcements, Web sites, and bibliographies that facilitate scholarly communication.

The roles and opportunities presented by the various electronic forums are discussed often in the scholarly literature, professional writing, specialized online forums, and in news stories for academics (as in the *Chronicle of Higher Education*). But little systematic, empirically grounded research about the development and use of most of these communication forums has been conducted. Scholars' behavior with scholarly e-journals has attracted the attention of empirically oriented social and behavioral researchers. Our own work on this chapter was expedited by our access to the electronic versions of articles from many different kinds of publishing venues, including authors' own online archives, the Web sites of e-journals, and the electronic versions of paper journals through collections that are site licensed to Indiana University. Before we discuss research about these topics in detail, we must clarify the concept of the e-journal.

A Typology of Electronic Journals

Most discussions of e-journals conflate a number of different formats into one overarching, and sometimes misleading, category: electronic journals. Much of the enthusiasm for e-journals in the early 1990s was based on specific assumptions: They would be electronic only, they could be peer reviewed, and there would be no charges to their authors and readers. Concerns about the long-term archiving of e-journals and their academic legitimacy hinged on similar assumptions (Kling & Covi, 1995). Today, the major scientific, technical, and medical (STM) publishers that offer electronic versions of their paper journals rely on a subscription model in which they allow electronic access to individual subscribers or to members of organizations that purchase more expensive institutional (library) subscriptions.

Okerson (2000) reviewed the history of electronic journals and discussed a few examples from the early 1990s. She also counted the number of electronic journals listed in two directories from 1991 to 1999. The number of titles grew from 27 in 1991, to 3,634 in 1997, and to 8,000 in 1999. She briefly discussed the move by major STM publishers to provide Web-based access to their journals in the period 1996–2000. Unfortunately, Okerson does not carefully distinguish the relatively few journals that were published only in electronic editions in 1999 from the majority that were published in parallel paper and electronic editions. As we discuss here, these distinctions have important consequences.

Observations about the early "pure" e-journals do not necessarily apply to paper-based journals with established reputations and readerships that also provide parallel electronic editions. The distinction between an e-journal without a paper version and a paper journal with an electronic version matters when trying to address such issues as the legitimacy of e-journals or their costs. For example, we know of no evidence that prestigious paper journals, such as *Science*, lost legitimacy after they established online versions alongside their printed publications. The question of legitimacy seems to affect only journals that are completely or primarily distributed in electronic form. Similarly, questions of cost hinge on the number of printed copies a journal produces as well as the character of its electronic form. Finally, questions about a journal's accessibility and readership can also hinge on the extent to which it allows readers free access to electronic versions.

Following Kling and McKim (1997) we find it useful to distinguish at least four kinds of e-journals:

1. Pure e-journals are originally distributed only in digital form. Examples include the *Electronic Journal of Communication*, the *Journal of Digital Information*, the *Internet Journal of Archaeology*, and the *Journal of Electronic Publishing*.

2. E-p-journals are primarily distributed electronically, but may have very limited distribution in paper form. Examples include the *Journal of Artificial Intelligence Research* and the *Electronic Transactions on Artificial Intelligence*.

3. P-e-journals are primarily distributed in paper form, but are also distributed electronically. Examples include *Science*, *Physical Review*, and thousands of other scientific journals.

4. P+e-journals are initiated with parallel paper and electronic editions that may be widely distributed. The American Chemical Society's *Organic Letters* is an example.

There are many published discussions of the possible benefits of pure e-journals and their advantages over traditional "pure paper" journals (p-journals). However, those discussions often ignore three points: First, although beneficial changes may be possible from a technical perspective, the social structure of online publishing does not change as rapidly as the technical structure. Second, possible changes are often discussed without distinguishing the type of e-journal to which they apply. Third, possible advantages are often analyzed separately, without taking into account how one advantage may trade off with another (for example, an e-journal's cost versus the variety of features offered).

Models of Electronic Documents and Scholarly Communication Forums

The literatures about scholarly electronic publishing are primarily informed by two conceptual models. One model, which Kling, McKim, and King (2001) refer to as the "Standard Model," emphasizes the conventional information processing properties of different media, such as paper and digital. An alternative kind of model, a Socio-Technical Network Model (Kling et al., 2001), characterizes the complex interplay between the information processing features of artifacts (such as e-journals) and social behavior at many levels of analysis, including operations/production. A third kind of model, a Socio-Technical Systems Model, examines communication forums in the context of some of the relevant social systems that shape their characters and participants (e.g., copyright systems). The Socio-Technical Systems Model shares the Standard Model's conception of media differences, but examines how organizations and other actors may structure electronic media for different purposes. In these models, the ways that (electronic) media are socially structured will play a major role in determining which of their features will be emphasized (see, for example, Sosteric, 1996, online). Sosteric examines "how individual electronic scholarly publication projects have challenged the traditional publishing houses by offering alternative models of scholarly publication that more closely fit with the needs of the academy." He also examines commercial publishers' countermoves, especially their efforts to create electronic versions of their printed journals rapidly and to sell these in ways that maintain their prices to libraries and individuals. Sosteric conceptualizes electronic media as relatively plastic, and the form of e-journals (including fee-driven subscription-based access) as being shaped by publishers' business interests.

Socio-Technical Systems Models separate those artifacts and relationships that are viewed as technological from the actors and relationships that are deemed to be social. These models emphasize the importance of understanding technological artifacts in relation to social behavior.

These Socio-Technical Systems Models are similar to the sociotechnical systems theories gaining popularity in fields such as human-computer interaction (Eason, 1988) and computer-supported cooperative work (Bannon & Schmidt, 1991). These approaches are major advances over technologically focused alternatives because they encourage designers to actively engage with the people who are likely to use their systems, and to carefully examine the relationships between information technology design and subtle work and communicative practices. But they do maintain sharp boundaries between what is technological and what is social.

According to the Standard Model, an e-journal has distinctive information properties when compared with a p-journal: Its articles can be reviewed more rapidly, it can be distributed more speedily, it is much easier to update or keep current, it is not limited by high per-unit production costs, it can be more easily searched, it can include articles that are much richer in their representations (e.g., more pictures and sound recordings), it should be much less expensive for readers, and it should be more readily available to a wider readership (see, for example, Amiran, Orr, & Unsworth, 1991). Some analysts also identify systematic disadvantages of electronic media, such as perishability and the ease of plagiarism (Wells, 1999).

Kling, McKim, and King (2001) characterize a Socio-Technical Network Model that represents media-in-use as collections of social groups and artifacts that are brought together in intricate and interpenetrating social and technological relationships. Their model treats electronic media-in-use as a sociotechnical network that brings together participants with different roles, rights, responsibilities, resource flows, legitimacies, and taboo behaviors. In this model, differently structured electronic forums inscribe some of these relationships and behaviors into parts of the medium; for instance, a peer-reviewed e-journal is not just a set of documents online. If subscription is limited, unauthorized readers can be excluded by methods such as requiring passwords or access from specific Internet domains. Parts of the electronic spaces that represent the journal may be structured in different ways; for example, articles are normally write-protected in ways that prevent readers from arbitrarily editing their texts. Other parts of the journal's electronic space may be structured so that editors may privately comment about articles that are under review, while allowing readers to comment on articles that have been accepted for publication. This example illustrates how different sets of roles, rights, and responsibilities could be inscribed in software, hardware, and data files.

Socio-Technical Network Models do not just characterize the internal structures and relationships of an electronic forum, but also their relationships with other groups, technologies, and forums. For example, a specific e-journal may gain a level of legitimacy from the status of the organization that publishes it, from its editorial board, or from the quality of articles that it has published recently. Authors and readers of a specific e-journal may also try to publish in, or read, competing journals. Readers also rely upon the bibliographic and search systems that they use to locate journal articles. (Note that the editors of indexing services such as the *Social Sciences Citation Index* or *Sociological Abstracts* select which journals they will cover.)

Socio-Technical Network Models are ecological in that they locate a specific forum in relationship to an extended network of participants, alternative resources, locations, and competing activities.[2] Later in this chapter we examine scholarly journals in terms of Socio-Technical Network Models, and analyze how these models change our understanding of the processes of scholarly communication.

Table 4.1 summarizes some key aspects of both the Standard and Socio-Technical Network Models of e-journals. It is important to note that these models refer to ontologies; i.e., the kinds of objects, relationships, and processes that should be included in characterizing some part of the world—in our case, e-journals. These models must be coupled with some additional theories of social behavior in order to develop various explanations, scenarios, and predictions about topics such as the future role of e-journals in scholarly communication.

Scholarly Communication via Journals

The current journal form developed over several centuries. Henry Oldenburg produced the first issue of a scientific journal, the *Philosophical Transactions of the Royal Society of London*, in 1665 (Schaffner, 1994). In 2001, *Ulrich's International Periodicals Directory* (2001) listed over 160,000 periodicals and serials published throughout

Table 4.1 Models of electronic journals.

Dimension	Standard Model of an e-journal	Socio-Technical Network Model of an e-journal
Analytical focus	E-forum, users' interactions	Ecological: e-forum, participation, participants' interactions in the e-forums and with other socio-technical networks and settings
Actors	Users	Individual participants plus diverse groups and organizations that influence behavior in the e-forum
Conceptions of actors	Individuals	Interactors, participating in multiple overlapping social and socio-technical networks and perhaps in different social settings
Treatment of information technology	Cheap, easy, and "standardized"	Configured socially and by technical inscription
Information technology infrastructure	Taken for granted	Variable, sometimes can be problematic
Social behavior	Can be easily reformed to take advantage of new conveniences, efficiencies, and values	• Influenced strongly by interactions outside the e-forums as well as within • E-forum resources considered relative to other opportunities elsewhere
Resource flows and business models	Taken for granted	Examined (includes money flows, regulatory regimes)
E-forum legitimacies	Taken for granted	Journal's legitimacy treated as an accomplishment

the world; this included the proceedings of annual conferences and annual reviews, as well as journals. The number of scientific and abstract journals published worldwide is usually estimated at over 100,000, having grown steadily and rapidly during the second half of the 20th century (Tenopir & King, 2000, p. 58).

Much of the debate on the future of electronic publishing concentrates on opportunities for readers, writers, and publishers. The accessibility of scholarly e-journals, their potentially lower production costs, the possibility of multimedia publication, and reference linking are treated as compelling features of the medium that will enable them to thrive.

Relative Advantages of E-Journals and P-Journals

Many visible enthusiasts of e-journals, such as Okerson (1991, 2000) and Odlyzko (1995, 2002), rely upon a Standard Model of e-journals and portray the transition of journals from paper to electronic media as a relatively straightforward process. The Internet is seen as a medium that will be able to solve many of the difficulties associated with traditional publishing. The Standard Model of scholarly communication often does not take into account the variety of social changes or the many sets of institutionalized norms that are involved, with effects beyond information technology infrastructures and applications. Sociotechnical change can be challenging, but such adjustments will be essential to the successful transition of scholarly communication from a purely print-based model. Tenopir and King (2000) carefully studied scientists' journal use and journal costs since the late 1970s. They advanced a rich sociotechnical model of journal publishing (Tenopir & King, 2000, pp. 83–104) and concluded that shifting to scientific communication based solely on e-journals would be uneven and relatively slow.

The issues involved in publishing scholarly e-journals have been summarized by Buckley, Burright, Prendergast, Sapon-White, and Taylor (1999), Tenopir and King (2000), and Wells (1999), among others. Buckley et al. briefly examine six major issues from the point of view of librarians: access, cataloging, indexing, pricing, archiving, and licensing. Wells lists a set of eight potential advantages and six potential disadvantages of e-journals and provides citations for specific claims about them. In the next sections we analyze the most commonly discussed issues from the perspectives of the Standard and Socio-Technical Network Models of e-journals.

Publication Speed

A common belief that switching from paper to electronic distribution will improve the speed of publication persists. This result would be especially beneficial in fields where the publication process takes years rather than a few months. According to Walsh and Bayma (1996), the median publication lags for some top biology and physics journals was six months in 1990. In contrast, a top chemistry journal took eight months and a top mathematics journal took 19 months. The extreme case was a mathematics journal, which took as long as 42 months to publish some articles. Overall, the lag in each field ranged from three to four months for the most rapid publication.

After a manuscript is submitted by an author, it goes through a peer review process, which could be comparably long for p-journals and e-journals. Some (e.g., Harnad, 1996; Nadasdy, 1997) have advocated alternative forms of review, but we have not found systematic studies that show how much those forms actually improve the speed or quality of publication. We analyze manuscript review processes later in this chapter.

Regardless of journal medium, each accepted manuscript goes through an electronic typesetting process. This can take longer for p-e-journals because each version must be formatted separately. The time needed for typesetting pure e-journals depends upon the complexity of the text formatting; an ASCII file can be prepared quickly whereas SGML coding requires much more work. This process also varies from discipline to discipline; those in which articles are predominantly text, such as many humanities disciplines, require less time than those disciplines in which articles contain graphs or color photography, such as some natural sciences.

Another reason for publication delay of printed journals is the so-called "backlog effect." Paper journals are budgeted to publish a certain number of pages per year. If the manuscripts accepted for publication in a given year exceed this number, they will be published in the next year, thus extending the queue of the articles to be published. E-journals need not experience this type of delay.

An accepted manuscript can be posted rapidly on an e-journal's Web site (after typesetting). Thus, an e-journal could significantly decrease its publication time if the publisher decided to post each article as it was accepted and typeset. The actual practices of posting on the Web vary from journal to journal. For example, the *Astrophysical Journal* posts the titles, authors, and texts of articles soon after they are accepted for publication. The American Chemical Society (ACS) also posts individual electronic manuscripts on its journal Web site soon after they are accepted for publication, a format that the ACS calls "As Soon As Publishable (ASAP)." This can lead to electronic access being 11 weeks faster than the print publication (Wilkinson, 1998). The p-e-journals published by European publishers and scientific societies tend to distribute both paper and electronic versions almost simultaneously. In contrast, articles available at the PubMedCentral service (http://www.pubmedcentral.nih.gov/), sponsored by the U.S. National Institutes of Health, may appear two months after their initial print publication.[3]

Publishers of pure e-journals can post accepted electronic manuscripts on their Web sites soon after they are delivered to the editor, especially since many e-journals request that authors properly format their articles. But editors may wait until they receive more electronic manuscripts to bundle them together as an issue; thus some potential publishing speed is lost. (For example, the pure e-journal, the *Journal of Computer Mediated Communication*, publishes quarterly issues, while the pure e-journal, the *Journal of Artificial Intelligence Research*, publishes individual articles soon after they are accepted.)

The claim that electronic publishing substantially decreases publication time is based on the Standard Model of electronic publishing, with the belief that it is possible to publish an article soon after it is received. However, if we analyze the publishing process from the perspective of the Socio-Technical Network Model, we can observe that the process is influenced by media-independent forces such as editorial review times, author revision times, and the strategy and timing of posting articles individually or as a package.

Cost of Producing E-Journals

Variations in the design and maintenance of e-journals can cause their production costs to differ. Harnad (1995) claims that electronic publishing may be 70 to 90 percent less costly than paper because pure electronic publishing incurs only the costs associated with peer review and copyediting. However, the cost of an e-journal may depend on the type of document coding used. Formatting manuscripts in ASCII or HTML is relatively inexpensive, while SGML tagging can be much more costly (Holoviak & Seitter, 1997). Many e-journals distribute their articles in multiple formats to ensure that potential readers have access to a format that their computers can support or that they prefer. Some costs may be shifted from editors to authors by requesting that they provide articles in specific formats, such as TeX or Adobe PDF.

The inclusion of additional features such as multimedia presentations or lengthy data sets can readily increase an e-journal's cost. Whisler and Rosenblatt (1997) estimate that an electronic version of a journal may be about 20 percent less costly, but that those savings will be outstripped by the costs of new features. For p-e-journals and e-p-journals, the costs will be even greater, as some costs of printed and electronic versions must be added, even if one version is based on the other.

The administrative costs of e-journals may be affected, depending on whether they are free to all readers or available only by subscription. One of largest costs (for fee-based e-journals) is the cost of installing and maintaining authentication software and subscriber data. The subscribers to printed journals are responsible for storing and archiving their own journal issues, while the e-journal publisher assumes responsibility for organizing, storing, and maintaining electronic archives.

Estimating the costs of the technology needed to create and maintain an e-journal in future decades can be difficult because price and price–performance improvements do not translate linearly into lower costs. For example, a PC today may perform over 300 times faster than the first IBM PC/XTs, but it costs much more than 1/300 the price of the original PC/XT because of minimum costs for keyboards, monitors, packaging, marketing, software, and sales (Crawford, 1998).

Bot, Burgemeester, and Roes (2000) calculated the costs of the pure e-journal *Electronic Journal of Comparative Law (EJCL)* and compared these calculations to their cost estimates for printed law journals. They based their cost estimates on each journal's subscription price minus a hypothetical 30 percent profit margin. They concluded that the cost of the e-journal was considerably less than the cost of producing p-journals; but because their findings are based on estimates, it is difficult to compare their data with other e-journal cost studies.

Different conclusions were reached by Fisher (1997), who calculated the costs to the MIT Press of publishing the *Chicago Journal of Theoretical Computer Science (CJTCS)* as a pure e-journal. She compared these costs with those of publishing the print journal *Neural Computation (NC)*. Fisher reports that the production costs were considerably lower for the e-journal (291 percent less). However, the overhead costs were 1,240 percent higher for *CJTCS*. The overhead costs (per article) consisted of staff labor costs and the costs of hardware and software. The journals' relative overhead costs (per article) were strongly influenced by the much smaller number of articles published in *CJTCS*. Although reaching different conclusions, the authors of these two cost analyses agree that estimating the costs of pure e-journals is difficult at this time. Fisher bases her judgments on the relative cost per article, whereas Bot, Burgemeester, and Roes base theirs on the size of readership and subscriptions. In the 1990s both the submission rates and subscription rates for pure e-journals were relatively low.

Cost analyses that are based upon the Standard Model assume that printed and online journals have the same features. A direct comparison based on those features suggests that e-journals are considerably less expensive because of the reductions in printing and mailing costs (Okerson, 1991). But maintaining an e-journal may require the use of other features, such as subscriber authentication software, which increases production costs. The addition of features such as internal links to other e-journal articles, multimedia, and various kinds of subscriber notification services[4] can add substantial value while increasing costs as well.

Thus the cost of producing a journal is based not only on basic production and marketing cost, but also on the set of features the publisher chooses to include. The inclusion of additional features and the choice of coding types will probably be a compromise between readers' preferences and available resources. The marketing of the journal may also be conducted through various means, such as mailing journal announcements to prospective readers, offering free access to the site for a limited time, or providing free sample issues. Each of these options carries a different cost. Thus, the cost-consuming activities of an e-journal's production and promotion are not eliminated; rather they are reconfigured (Fisher, 1997).

Pricing of E-Journals

The price of journals is closely related to their production costs. However, critics of scientific journal prices have observed that some commercial publishers seem to add a substantial profit element when setting subscription prices. Journals with annual institutional subscription costs that exceed $5,000 (such as *Tetrahedron Letters* and *Brain Research*) have been highly visible targets. The extensive literature on journal pricing goes far beyond the scope of this chapter (McCabe, 1998, 1999; Noll, 1996). However, the suggestions by some analysts that a shift from paper to electronic media can dramatically reduce a journal's production costs, and thus its price, do come within our scope. Okerson (1991, p. 9) expected that the savings in printing and mailing costs of pure e-journals would "eventually relieve the 'serials crisis.'" More recently, Walker's (1998) article in *The American Scientist* advocated establishing pure e-journals sponsored by scientific societies, which could be published very inexpensively and help to solve the serials cost crisis.

In the case of printed journals, the subscriber pays for a copy of an issue, receives it, and can store it, lend it, and read the articles for an unlimited period of time. In the case of e-journals, subscribers are paying for access; after their subscriptions expire, their access to the original articles is lost unless they print copies of articles or download and archive them. Libraries may be precluded from printing and/or archiving articles from pure e-journals by their license agreements. Rather, they may simply facilitate access to these journals for their patrons by linking to their Web sites or offering Internet services such as Catchword (http://www.catchword.com/).

Various licensing configurations and pricing schemes are available; publishers may allow access to e-journals only through a limited number of computers, or limit the number of library patrons simultaneously accessing the site. Each arrangement may be priced differently. In addition, publishers of p-e-journals may offer the electronic version only to those who subscribe to the printed version, offer a special price or combined price for both versions, or price each of them separately.

The American Chemical Society's p+e-journal, *Organic Letters,* is an interesting example. During the 1990s, considerable criticism arose of Elsevier's pricing of *Tetrahedron Letters,* which was heading toward $10,000 per year. The Scholarly Publishing and Academic Resources Coalition (SPARC, http://www.arl.org/sparc/), which is sponsored by the Association of Research Libraries (ARL), sought projects that could help lower journal prices. SPARC worked with the ACS to develop the new p+e-journal, *Organic Letters,* in 1998. The ACS's endorsement of *Organic Letters* helped it to attract high-quality articles and to be viewed as a significant chemistry journal. The ACS offers several kinds of institutional subscriptions to *Organic Letters.* In 2002, these ranged in price from about $2,400 for a copy of the print edition, through about $4,000 for a site license to the electronic edition, to about $4,600 for both editions (see http://pubs.acs.org/orglett). *Organic Letters* is not an inexpensive journal, except in relationship to *Tetrahedron Letters*. Its electronic edition is more expensive than its print edition! And it was developed in a concerted effort by two relatively prestigious organizations, rather than by the actions of a few chemists with an inexpensive Web server.

Publishers may also apply different pricing polices to different groups of subscribers, such as individuals and libraries. In addition, scholarly societies usually sell journal subscriptions at lower prices to their members and to students. In some cases, such as the ACS, access to electronic versions of their journals is available only to the society's members and to institutional subscribers. Individual ACS members can subscribe to the electronic edition of *Organic Letters* for $25 per year.

Access and Searching Capabilities

Readers' easy access to articles is perceived to be one of the major advantages of e-journals (Okerson, 1991; Tomney & Burton, 1998). However, perceptions that e-journals are uniformly simple to access and search are based on the Standard Model rather than on a Socio-Technical Network analysis. For example, Okerson (2000) notes that the American Association for the Advancement of Science developed one of the first pure e-journals, the *Online Journal of Current Clinical Trials*. It was launched in 1992, but was discontinued soon afterward because it had trouble attracting authors and readers. Okerson attributes this failure to the journal's newness. Unfortunately, she does not note that this journal was distributed on CD-ROMs with special PC-DOS software, and was typically available through a medical library. The journal's relatively cumbersome sociotechnical accessibility must have played some role in its difficulty in attracting readers (and thus authors).

Today, many scholars in first world countries work in university offices where high-speed Internet connections enable the rapid transmission of networked e-journals. Those working from home or from universities that do not have high-speed Internet connections may have more difficulty accessing the same e-journals, especially if their articles include graphic files or are stored as large PDF files. In addition, some e-journals are site-licensed to universities and authenticate legitimate readers by their IP addresses. Although IP address authentication schemes reduce a reader's dependence on remembering or managing a set of distinctive passwords, they can also block access to legitimate readers who log in from off-campus locations using an Internet service provider other than their institution. Thus, complex sociotechnical contingencies can limit a reader's legitimate access to e-journals, even though she or he has "Internet access."

The disparities in network access may actually widen "the digital divide" rather than bridge it, as some enthusiasts have postulated. The electronic versions of p-e-journals may be especially attractive for individual subscribers in countries where the cost of air freight is high, but these versions will not help many scholars in countries where networks are slow and Internet access is limited. Even in the more developed countries, access to U.S. sites is best during the hours in which most Americans are asleep.

For an article to be read, it first has to be located. Analysts who rely upon the Standard Model sometimes assume that the availability and ease of use of various Web search engines make searching for research articles straightforward. Although articles in free, pure e-journals may be found by search engines, a reader must be willing to spend time distinguishing research articles from other electronic documents. In addition, many p-e-journals try to limit access through registration or subscription, and do not allow search engines to access their sites or index their articles.

Further, searching with common search engines does not guarantee that a desired electronic manuscript will be found. Cronin, Snyder, Rosenbaum, Martinson, and Callahan (1998) compared various search engines and their abilities to find information about noted scholars in information science. They found dramatic differences among search engines in their abilities to locate references to these scholars and to their publications: from one to 73 articles and from four to 136 conference proceedings were retrieved, depending on the engine.

Ford and Harter's (1998) attempts to locate pure e-journals through online directories and catalogs provide a useful perspective on the difficulties of Web access. They examined four online directories and two online union catalogs, noting their coverage, accuracy, currency, and agreement on entries for 36 pure e-journals. The Association of Research

Libraries' *Directory of Electronic Journals, Newsletters, and Academic Discussion Lists* included the largest number of the titles (33). The Research Libraries Information Network (RLIN) and OCLC, Inc. listed 31 and 32 journals, respectively, and included URLs to the mirror sites of many journals. The Committee on Institutional Cooperation (CIC) directory included 26 titles, the University of Houston Libraries' listing of *Scholarly Journals Distributed via the World Wide Web* returned 21, and Ejournal, the WWW Virtual Library electronic journals list, found 25 e-journals.

The numbers of functioning and current URLs revealed the difficulty of maintaining accuracy in these databases. The highest percentage of working URLs was at the University of Houston site (95.2 percent), followed by the CIC Index (71.7 percent), and Ejournal (61.5 percent); other databases fell below 60 percent. The least accurate databases also listed gopher and ftp URLs that had expired by 1998. The total percentage of unique http URLs that were functioning and current was 66.7 percent, compared to 50 percent current and functioning URLs overall. The number of different URLs per journal is also interesting. *Psycoloquy* and *Postmodern Culture* had 16 and nine different URLs, respectively. Furthermore, the researchers found an additional 17 (!) URLs to *Psycoloquy* through online searches and correspondence—including multiple spellings of the journal's name at an ftp site.

In 2001, Crawford (2002) examined the current status of 104 scholarly pure e-journals that were indexed in the 1995 edition of the ARL's *Directory of Electronic Journals, Newsletters, and Academic Discussion Lists*. Fifty-seven of these had URLs for their gopher sites or Web sites. Only 17 of these 57 URLs worked in early 2001. After considerable effort, Crawford found the URLs of 49 of 104 e-journals that were still publishing and were free to readers, as well as the URLs of 22 others that had ceased publication.

Potential journal readers may be frustrated when they encounter expired links. Librarians face the difficulty of deciding which Web page should be considered a home page, as the variety of pages can make it difficult to determine which page is most current and should be cited. In short, the path between a potential reader and an e-journal may not simply be a "link and a click away," but rather be the product of a complex sociotechnical network.

The question remains: Why are most pure e-journals not indexed by publicly available databases? Because pure e-journals and electronic databases are based on the same medium, the transition from one to the other may seem automatic. However, sociotechnical networks do not reconfigure themselves instantaneously. First, pure e-journals are not automatically indexed into directories; their citations are identified, selected, organized, and then indexed with some human mediation. Second, decisions about which journals to include may be based on the preferences of a database's maintainers and a journal's perceived reputation. Third, the medium that is presumed to facilitate access to journals may actually impair access to some information; for example, if some of the links do not work or if multiple URLs complicate locating the most recent versions.

Existing databases of articles (print or electronic) allow users to search authors, titles, abstracts, and, sometimes, full text. However, the relevance of retrieved results depends on three things: the search engine, database construction, and search strategy employed. Various databases provide different search mechanisms (e.g., simple search, advanced search, or search with thesaurus extension). Most journals and publishers implement much simpler e-searching (by keyword) than do aggregators such as Dialog, LexisNexis, and Academic Search Elite (Smith, 2000). The variety of search options is a feature of the medium, but implementation alone does not necessarily mean that a desirable article will be retrieved. Researchers must use appropriate search strategies. Because searching mechanisms vary from journal to journal, this necessitates some learning time on the part of readers.

Citations to E-Journals

Another potential advantage of e-journals over p-journals is their ability to include active hyperlinks to bibliographic citations. This function is not yet routine, however, because the Web environment is somewhat unstable and the location of files can be changed over time. In addition, pure e-journals, as well as the electronic editions of printed journals, may disappear. For example, out of 35 publicly accessible pure e-journals Harter (1996) studied, five did not appear in the locations provided in his article in the summer of 2001. A more recent study (Zhang, 1998) found that authors who publish in pure e-journals are more willing to cite articles from other pure e-journals than are the authors who publish in pure p-journals. This tendency may result in internal hyperlinking, with the articles in the same pure e-journal hyperlinked to each other. Although links to other articles in other journals are common, over time many links will become outdated, and the journal providers face the choice of maintaining accurate links or allowing their articles' bibliographies to be contaminated with link rot.

The publication of p-e-journals and e-p-journals raises a question about which version of an article should be cited. Some journals, such as the *Journal of Artificial Intelligence Research*, try to avoid this possible confusion by suggesting how to cite their articles. One definite advantage of e-journals over pure p-journals is the ability to download citations into citation management programs, such as EndNote or ProCite.

Interactivity

One form of interactivity between authors and readers is to allow readers to comment on articles that appear in a journal. P-journals vary in the extent to which they include "letters to the editor." Traditional p-journals may print comments about an article in the next issue. In pure e-journals and e-p-journals, comments can be submitted and posted more rapidly after the article is published and attached directly to the online version of the article, and/or can appear in discussion lists made available by the publisher. However, adding comments to the electronic versions of print journals after they are electronically received and before the printed versions appear may create confusion—the comments may be available only to some members of the audience, authors of comments may prefer to have their comments included in the print version of the journal, and readers may see greater value in comments that are reviewed before they are made publicly available.

E-journals vary in their practices for publishing readers' comments on their articles. For example, *D-Lib Magazine* (a pure e-journal) does not publish comments. *First Monday* (a pure e-journal) publishes comments as "letters to the editor" in the next issue. The *British Medical Journal (BMJ)* (a p-e-journal) takes advantage of the electronic options by allowing readers to e-mail comments about an article, and to have them rapidly linked to the relevant article. In addition, the *BMJ* provides a customized alert service, posts citations to related articles that they have published, and offers a citation alert service.

Analyzing interactivity features through the prism of the Standard Model shows them to be very powerful instruments to facilitate communication between authors and readers. However, interactors reside in different social settings, and their communication is moderated not only by the Internet, but also by editors and publishers. The network of readers and authors develops on many levels—citations, reviews, personal communications—and the interactive features of e-journals are only one part of this network. For example, free comment posting creates the possibility of spam and unprofessional remarks, which can require setting up a socially accepted authority to maintain professional decorum.

Additional E-Journal Features

E-journals offer the ability to include links to raw data, to attach multimedia files, or to include algorithms. In practice, few p-e-journals include these features. Most p-e-journals publish their electronic manuscripts as an electronic copy of the printed article. Including new features in different file formats in documents requires readers to have the tools necessary to decode them. Publishers need to ensure that their files can be viewed using publicly accessible software and generally provide access to such software from the publisher's Web site.

Many of the opportunities the medium offers are not used, or are deliberately suppressed, in order to give the look and feel of an article in a print-based journal (e.g., using vertical flow of pages and consecutive page numbering). An example of such a journal (e-p), *Journal of Artificial Intelligence Research (JAIR)*, was analyzed by Kling and Covi (1995). *JAIR* publishes its articles in PostScript and PDF formats on its Web site. Each article is formatted and paginated as it would appear in a printed journal. By design, an article printed from *JAIR* looks exactly like a photocopy of an article from a traditional p-journal. Although access to the electronic version is free of charge, the publishing house, Morgan-Kaufman, also sells a printed version of *JAIR* as an annual volume. This strategy has probably facilitated *JAIR*'s success. The authors cite their articles without revealing that they were published in an e-p-journal, thus avoiding any prejudice against the electronic medium. The existence of the printed volume ensures that articles will be accessible regardless of what happens with electronic versions in the future, and provides access for those who prefer traditional paper-based issues or do not have easy access to the Internet.[5]

An additional advantage of pure e-journals is the possibility that their articles need not be limited in length in consideration of printing and mailing costs. However, this space advantage cannot be exploited in those p-e-journals that require the online version to be identical with the printed version.

Summary of the Relative Advantages of E-Journals and P-Journals

Tables 4.2, 4.3, and 4.4 summarize the discussion in this subsection. They contrast pure e-journals with p-e-journals, using the Standard and Socio-Technical Network Models.

Complexities of E-Journals

While e-journals offer many advantages, they also present librarians with new archiving problems, and authors may suffer from more frequent plagiarism. We examine these issues next.

Archiving and Cataloging

Printed journals are usually retained in libraries and in private collections even after the journals cease publication or subscriptions expire. A fear persists that pure e-journals may cease and that previously published and cited articles will no longer be available. Publishers of e-p-journals try to overcome this fear by printing a limited version of the journal for libraries so that the articles are always available in print.

Long-term archiving is a concern to many. Arms (1999) presented three case studies of different approaches to long-term storage of electronic articles, analyzing how the Association for Computing Machinery (ACM) Digital Library, the Internet RFC (Requests for Comments) series, and *D-Lib Magazine* archived electronic resources. He examined several factors that might predict how archiving would be handled. The ACM is an association with over 50 years of tradition, more than 80,000 members, and significant financial resources. The ACM Digital Library is perceived by the ACM's publishing staff to be one of its biggest assets. The

Table 4.2 Models of electronic journals' speed of publication, cost, and pricing.

	Model	Pure e-journal	P-e-journal
Speed of publication	Standard Model	May be technically faster by speeding delivery time	Publication time may be longer, since creating two versions of the journal may consume more time
	Socio-Technical Network Model	Publication of individual articles may be faster, but publishing a complete issue may be prolonged by editorial decisions to include more articles or to maintain a predictable publishing schedule	Speed of publication depends on editorial decisions. If the electronic version is published before the print version it may be faster
Cost	Standard Model	• The costs of paper, printing, binding, delivery, etc. are eliminated • Depends on type of coding used and number of additional features	Same as printed journal plus cost of creating and maintaining electronic versions
	Socio-Technical Network Model	• Cost may be higher as some journals publish in multiple formats to ensure that all subscribers have access to formats they can support • Cost may also be elevated by price of security software and site maintenance • Readers may be forced to acquire/purchase additional software to be able to retrieve multimedia files; cost is shifted to the users	Even if the electronic version is a copy of the printed one, the costs may be higher due to the need for security and site maintenance
Price	Standard Model	Eliminating printing and mailing costs should result in lowered prices	Same as printed journal
	Socio-Technical Network Model	Depends upon the business model (i.e., whether authentication is required) and features offered	Each of a journal's versions can be priced separately

academic community may be reasonably confident that this collection will be maintained. The prospects are less certain for the Internet RFC series. Currently, the Internet Engineering Task Force maintains it, but the informal status of the organization does not guarantee that the

Table 4.3 Models of electronic journals' accessibility, searchability, and inclusion in abstracting and indexing services.

	Model	Pure e-journal	P-e-journal
Accessibility	Standard Model	• May be limited by poor Internet connection and lack of necessary software • Assumes that all readers are comfortable with electronic format	• Does not depend entirely on Internet connection • Readers may select the medium they prefer
	Socio-Technical Network Model	• Some journals have copies in multiple locations, which can create confusion • Access *may* be restricted by site licensing or subscription	• Articles can be more easily found in databases if the print version was already indexed • Access *often* restricted by site licensing or subscription
Searching	Standard Model	Full-text articles can be searched by keyword	Full-text articles can be searched by keyword
	Socio-Technical Network Model	Readers are required to learn new ways of searching and browsing documents, especially if journals and databases vary in their search options	Electronic edition may require readers to learn new ways of searching
Inclusion in abstracting and indexing services	Standard Model	E-journals can be easily connected to electronic databases	
	Socio-Technical Network Model	Indexing services may not include e-journals; inclusion is based on social judgments, and is not automatic	Printed versions may be included in indexing services, depending on the journal's reputation

series will be available in the long term. The Corporation for National Research Initiatives (CNRI), which publishes *D-Lib Magazine*, depends on U.S. Defense Advanced Research Projects Agency (DARPA) grants. If the funding ceases, CNRI may stop publishing *D-Lib Magazine*. With no funds for maintaining the Web site, the collection could be lost after some years.

Other complexities are associated with managing and reading e-journals, such as the possibility that they can be stored in multiple locations. Mirroring a journal's Web site speeds access from different corners of the world, but also increases costs, as it requires the maintenance of separate servers and access software. In addition, some publishers allow

Table 4.4 Models of electronic journals' interactivity and flexibility.

	Model	Pure e-journal	P-e-journal
Interactivity	Standard Model	• Easy feedback on articles through e-mail and discussion lists • Comments may be attached directly to an article	After the electronic version is created the comments may be attached directly to an article
	Socio-Technical Network Model	• Comments in discussion lists not reviewed, although discussion lists may be moderated • Spam protection necessary	In cases when p- and e-versions are different, commentators may prefer to have their remarks included in the printed version
Additional features and flexibility	Standard Model	• Able to include raw data, animation, movies, mathematical codes, etc. • Length of the articles and enhancements unlimited	• Able to include links to raw data, animation, movies, mathematical codes, etc. • Able to include additional lengthy articles in the online version
	Socio-Technical Network Model	• Reader has to have appropriate tools to be able • Many use only ASCII or HTML because of cost and accessibility concerns	• Adding features to only one version of the journal requires editorial decisions on prices and privileges for different groups of subscribers • Currently most electronic editions do not take advantage of available options, are just copies of the printed versions; PDF or proprietary formats are most common

authors to "publish" their electronic manuscripts on their personal Web sites, which increases the number of copies (and, potentially, versions) available.

Libraries have to tackle the issues of cataloging e-journals and deciding the kinds of access to pure e-journals to include in their online catalogs. The p-e-journals are even more complicated because libraries' policies vary, with some cataloging each version separately and some cataloging them together. Wilkins (1997) surveyed British libraries and learning centers about their practices for cataloging p-e-journals. Twelve university libraries responded to her survey; one institution had not yet faced the issue, and three were held back by lack of resources and still debating what to do. Some respondents were concerned about temporary

Table 4.5 Comparison of archiving and cataloging pure e-journals with p-e-journals.

	Model	Pure e-journal	P-e-journal
Archiving and cataloging	Standard Model	If the journal ceases publication, there is no guaranteed access to what has been published	Printed copies available in libraries and on private shelves, even if the journal ceases publication
	Socio-Technical Network Model	• Archiving responsibility moved from libraries to publishers • Libraries shift from ownership to access, depending on subscription options	Different library cataloging practices—both versions can be cataloged as one or they can be cataloged separately

pilot site license agreements that would require a substantial amount of work in terms of cataloging and updating records, and then having to restructure them if funding for these projects from sources such as the Higher Education Funding Council for England (HEFCE) were terminated. Most of the libraries surveyed cataloged one entry per title. In addition, Wilkins' respondents preferred to provide the "real" URL for each journal title, rather than providing a link to the p-e-journal publisher's Web site. In some universities, e-journals were accessible only from the library's home page; some universities reported plans to include journal records in a Web-based library catalog. Dual journal versions created additional difficulties because librarians wanted to add information about access to electronic copies on each printed journal's record. Table 4.5 summarizes some of the complexities of archiving e-journals, as they are viewed through the lenses of the Standard Model and the Socio-Technical Network Model.

Possibility of Direct Plagiarism

E-journals are considered easy targets for plagiarism, as they enable the direct copying and pasting of sections of one document into another (although some journals try to prevent this by posting their articles in Adobe Acrobat or Postscript formats, which many people would find much more difficult to copy). At the same time, current technology also allows easier copying from printed journals, through the use of scanners and character recognition software.

The electronic technologies that simplify plagiarism also may make it easier to detect the practice. The posting of files on the Web can often be traced back to the person who downloaded them, and text fragments can be compared for similarity. Initiatives are already in place to use specialized software for detecting copies and very similar documents in digital libraries, such as SCAM (Stanford Copy Analysis Mechanism [Denning, 1995; Shivakumar & Garcia-Molina, 1995]). However, because it is impossible to compare each document against thousands of others, it remains easier to copy an article than to identify plagiarism. For example, Kock (1999) *accidentally* discovered that one of his articles had been plagiarized. The chances for successful plagiarism are relatively low in fields where research projects are highly visible to participating scholars (e.g., experimental high energy physics, where research data are collected at a few major laboratories). In contrast, a plagiarist may have greater chances of success in fields where the invisible colleges are not tightly knit and where the research could have been conducted almost anywhere and by any of many competent investigators. Kock works in the field of information systems, which has this less tight-knit structure—a "low visibility" field (Kling & McKim, 2000).

Legitimacy of E-Journals

One of the most important issues in electronic publishing is the legitimacy of pure e- journals and e-p-journals. The legitimacy of e-journals can be understood differently by different players in the scholarly communication process: authors, journal editors, and those who conduct academic career reviews, such as the members of promotion and tenure (P&T) committees. Several studies have tried to evaluate the legitimacy of e-journals in specific scholarly communities by examining different aspects of the issue: faculty perceptions, use of e-journal articles, citing behavior, P&T written guidelines, and so forth.

Usefulness of E-Journals

Studies of the perception of e-journals have changed their focus over time. The older studies concentrated on possible benefits of e-journals, whereas more recent studies ask questions about legitimacy. Cornell University chemists reported that they expected their access to e-journals would allow them to read more complete articles, spend their reading time more efficiently, and read articles sooner after publication (Stewart, 1996). For these survey respondents, the most important features of e-journals were the ability to create printed copies and to browse text and graphics. They believed that e-journals would soon adopt all the functions of p-journals (e.g., browsing text, graphics capability, flipping through pages, annotating and highlighting text). But one-third did not expect that p-journals would ever be replaced by some form of e-journal.

In the spring of 1994, Butler (1995) studied approximately 500 natural and social scientists who had either published in at least one of 10 peer-reviewed pure e-journals or who had served on their editorial boards. She reported that 63 percent of her respondents felt many of their colleagues did not perceive their e-journal publications as "real," and 43 percent felt that their colleagues viewed pure e-journals as less important than pure p-journals.

Brown (1999) reported that less than 50 percent of the faculty in science fields at the University of Oklahoma obtained journal articles electronically, and 62 to 65 percent preferred print versions. Between 23 percent and 31 percent of her respondents favored an electronic version (depending on their field). Those who desired access to both versions wanted to be able to print copied articles from the electronic version.

According to a survey conducted by Björk and Turk (2000), researchers in the area of construction information technology and construction management downloaded half of the materials that they read from Internet sites.[6] Lenares (1999) studied a diverse but small (500 subjects) sample of faculty at 20 research universities in 1998 and 1999. She found that the number of faculty who reported using e-journals increased (from 48 percent in 1998 to 61 percent in 1999), with the biggest increase, from 60 to 90 percent, in the physical sciences. However, pure p-journal usage still predominated—only 14 percent of respondents to the survey reported using e-journals frequently, compared with 65 percent for print journals. While Lenares noted that a large fraction of the "e-journals" listed in the most recent edition of the Association of Research Libraries' *Directory of Electronic Journals* were p-e-journals rather than pure e-journals, her article does not clearly report how much of the increase in e-journal readership is of pure e-journals versus p-e-journals (or both).

Speier, Palmer, Wren, and Hahn (1999) surveyed a sample of the business school faculty of 95 universities whose libraries belong to the Association of Research Libraries. The results of their study differ from those conducted in the sciences. Less than one-third of their sample of 300 scholars reported a "general awareness of electronic publishing" (Speier et al., 1999, p. 540); approximately 16 percent read articles in some kind of e-journal, and only seven percent had submitted manuscripts to some kind of e-journal (or intended to do so). Business faculty did not perceive e-journals to be of as high quality as p-journals, which suggests that they were reporting their beliefs about "electronic journals" based on pure e-journals and e-p-journals. The younger faculty and the more prolific faculty reported higher levels of awareness of e-journals. Tenured faculty reported more willingness to submit their manuscripts to e-journals. Of special interest is the finding that faculty who served on P&T committees were more likely to report greater awareness of e-journals and to read electronic manuscripts. Faculty in more technical disciplines, such as finance, accounting, and information systems, were more willing to integrate e-journals into their scholarly work. These results are similar to those of Tomney and Burton (1998). Faculty from more technically oriented fields, such as science and engineering, were more likely to read e-journals, while faculty from the fields of history and education reported no use of e-journals. However, of the survey respondents who had read e-journals, the overwhelming majority (71 percent) considered the quality of the articles in e-journals to be the same as in p-journals.

These studies focused primarily on the process of receiving articles (electronically) and ignored the differences between p-e-journals and pure e-journals. Of these studies, only Butler (1995) distinguished between these two types of journals by selecting pure e-journals for study. Today, when the majority of e-journals are p-e-journals, researchers must be careful to learn which version(s) of an article their informants obtain. Moreover, in some cases, such as when a scholar receives a copy of an article from a colleague, he or she may be unsure whether it came from some form of e-journal.

Citations to E-Journals

A few researchers have used citation analysis to determine the scholarly impact of e-journals. Harter (1996) examined citations to articles in 39 peer-reviewed pure e-journals and p-e-journals. His results suggest that the majority of scholarly, peer-reviewed pure e-journals had negligible influence on scholarly communication in their respective fields in the mid-1990s. Only eight of the 28 pure e-journals had been cited 10 or more times over the course of their lifetimes. However, the most cited (and now defunct) pure e-journal, *The Public-Access Computer Systems Review,* was highly cited relative to other journals in library and information science. Unfortunately, Harter combined citations to articles in pure e-journals and p-e-journals in some of his analyses. It is difficult to determine which citations should be associated with the electronic edition of the 11 p-e-journals. A similar study of e-journals in the library and information sciences by Zhang (1998) found that during the years 1994–1996, the impact of e-journals increased, although not to a statistically significant extent.

One of the most interesting examples of differences among print journals, p-e-journals and pure e-journals is evident in the journal *Pediatrics* (Anderson, Sack, Krauss, & O'Keefe, 2001). This journal has been published in print since 1948. In January 1997, the editors added an online-only section, named *Pediatrics Electronic Pages.* Articles published online were chosen by an editor from accepted papers, with preference given to those of broader international interest. Abstracts of those articles were published in the printed version of the journal. In July 1998, the editors started publishing the print content online (by subscription), while still maintaining the *Pediatrics Electronic Pages* free of charge. Anderson et al. studied articles published from 1997 through 1999 in order to determine how successful the articles published online were. They examined Web usage statistics, citations within the biomedical literature, and author perceptions. Interviews with the authors revealed that they perceived online-only publications as second-tier publishing compared to print, and felt that they were not as highly regarded as print publications by P&T committees and the academic community.

Authors' fears that articles published in pure e-journals will be devalued is consistent with findings from other studies (for example, Schauder, 1994). In contrast with this perception are the results of

Andersen et al.'s citation analysis and P&T committees' opinions. Sixteen percent of the *Pediatrics* survey respondents (44) reported that they had applied for tenure since their articles were published in *Pediatrics Electronic Pages* and that they included those articles in their portfolios. In all cases these articles were accepted by their institutions. All of these authors included their *Pediatrics Electronic Pages* articles on their résumés, even if they considered them inferior to their publications in p-journals. Articles in *Pediatrics Electronic Pages* were cited in a manner similar to articles in *Pediatrics*, the print journal, and there were no differences in how quickly the articles were cited after publication. The articles that were published in *Pediatrics Electronic Pages* were accessed four times as often as the *Pediatrics* print edition articles on the Web site. This difference may be due to the fact that the *Pediatrics Electronic Pages* are free of charge. One caveat: only 21 percent of the readership of *Pediatrics* is actively engaged in research, and the other readers are primarily practicing pediatricians.

Perception of E-Journals in Academic Career Reviews

Presenting one's results to peers (and sometimes the public) is an important part of a researcher's job. The quality, and to some extent the quantity, of one's publications in recognized scholarly journals are the measures typically used in a variety of academic career reviews—for initial appointments, for research grants, for promotion and tenure, and for periodic salary reviews. Faculty seeking promotion may be under special pressure to publish their scholarship. However, publishing is important at every stage in an active scholar's career, especially at research universities. But not all publications are considered to be of equal value. Many scholars compete to have their work published in the more prestigious journals, which attract larger audiences of their peers.

Publishing in pure e-journals may be especially appealing to untenured faculty, who are often advised to produce numerous publications rapidly. However, there is a common assumption that publications in pure e-journals will not be regarded as equal in quality to publications in p-journals. For this reason, some faculty may not want to publish their best work in pure e-journals or e-p-journals, fearing that review committees will not consider it to be as valuable. The presumed lesser value of e-journals (other than p-e-journals) may result from unfamiliarity with their peer-review processes as well as the fact that many of them are new titles that have yet to establish a reputation for quality.

Only a few studies examine promotion and tenure procedures with regard to e-journals and the attitudes of P&T committee members toward the legitimacy of pure electronic publications. Cronin and Overfelt (1995) examined 49 sets of P&T guidelines from various universities. They found only one mention of electronic publishing media; and it seemed to refer to nonrefereed electronic bulletins. The other guidelines did not mention electronic publishing, but emphasized the quality of the research rather than its quantity. Quality was assessed by whether an article was peer reviewed and by the perceived quality or status of the journal in which it was published. Journals were also evaluated on the basis of rejection rates, editorial board membership, and refereeing policies. One of the most important aspects was longevity of the journal, which may help explain why (new) e-journals are felt to be of lesser scholarly value.

Formal guidelines are only one element in academic career reviews. The people who serve on review committees, such as P&T committees, play a critical role when they interpret and apply their guidelines to specific cases. The analysis of unsolicited comments from provosts, deans, chairs, and others, which accompanied the guidelines examined in Cronin and Overfelt's study, suggests that what is taken into consideration most while reviewing a scholarly portfolio is not the publishing medium but the refereeing process. E-journal articles that have gone through the same peer-review process as p-journal articles were likely to be treated in the same manner. However, some respondents stated that in many fields evaluating articles from pure e-journals was not an active issue as their colleagues did not publish in them and thus their P&T committees did not evaluate pure e-journals.

Despite a modest growth in the number of pure e-journals since 1995, the situation may not have changed appreciably. Sweeney (2000) surveyed the administrators and faculty of Florida State University about their perceptions of the acceptability of e-journals for promotion and tenure. The survey did not distinguish between pure e-journals and p-e-journals (which was pointed out by some respondents); thus, the responses to these questions are problematic. However, Sweeney included comments by the administrators and faculty, which constitute a rich source of information about the attitudes of the scholarly community toward electronic publishing. The results of the survey are consistent with the findings of Cronin and Overfelt (1995). The respondents were not aware of P&T guidelines with specific regard to electronic publishing, but pointed out that the refereeing process was a key issue. Because many of the pure e-journals and e-p-journals were then relatively new, the respondents suggested that researchers should be required to attach a description of a pure e-journal's reviewing process to articles they included in their portfolios. However, faculty seeking a promotion review submitted relatively few articles published in pure e-journals.

The findings of these studies suggest that in the 1990s many scholars were unwilling to submit their work to pure e-journals and e-p-journals because they feared that those publications would be less valued in academic reviews than are publications in p-journals (or p-e-journals). On the other hand, designers of P&T guidelines did not see the need to address the value of pure e-journals because relatively few scholars published in them. The small number of publications in pure e-journals and e-p-journals may also be a byproduct of their relatively small number today. In any case, publication medium does not seem to be an important factor in P&T review processes.

Peer-Review Processes of E-Journals

Peer review is perceived to be the primary factor in legitimizing scholarly journals, including e-journals. The stereotypical peer review of a manuscript requires that it be evaluated by outside specialists for its relevance to the journal, its likely importance, and its scholarly quality. In practice, journals vary in terms of the number of peer reviews they solicit, the specific processes they use for selecting reviewers, the effort to shield identities of authors and reviewers, and so on (Weller, 2001, pp. 15–27).

Although the concept of peer review is more than 200 years old, it was widely adopted only after World War II. Weller's (2001) superb integrated review of research about peer-review practices identifies some of the key variations, as well as the few studies that examine the impact of peer review. These studies found that authors felt that peer review generally did not result in substantive changes in their manuscripts, but that it helped them to improve the structure and clarity of their analyses and conclusions.

The peer-review process has been criticized for being both lengthy and undemocratic. One of the proposed changes to the status quo was to replace reviews with readers' comments (signed or anonymous) on articles. The comments would help authors make necessary changes, and would inform other readers about the quality of the articles. In traditional scholarly publishing, readers do not usually know the names of the reviewers of a particular article, but may know the members of the editorial board and/or they trust that an editor will select reviewers with appropriate expertise. When readers can comment on articles in open peer commentary (such as for the *ETAI* [*Electronic Transactions on Artificial Intelligence*] or *Cogprints*), readers evaluate both the posted articles and the comments about them. The names and electronic signatures of the commentators may give readers some sense of their relevant expertise. (If these review processes were completely anonymous, some less-than-honest authors could post their own positive comments.)

Some new initiatives are attempting to restructure peer review by enabling a journal's readers to participate in the process. The differences between these more open processes and traditional peer review lie in the way that the public's comments are treated in the process (Weller, 2001). Also, different practices in different disciplines may reflect the nature of the research studies conducted. Weller (2001, p. 303) suggests that public comments may be more useful in disciplines that rely on wide discussion than in those that base analyses on very specialized empirical data.

Let us examine some examples of e-journals and their peer-review processes. Wood and Hurst (2000) describe an experiment conducted in 1996 by the Royal Society with the journal *Proceedings: Biological Sciences*. This experiment applied the traditional model of peer review, while utilizing a Web site to facilitate the process through the Electronic Submission and Peer Review (ESPERE) service. Authors would post their articles in PDF format in password-protected personal workspaces. The editor would then e-mail the referees the papers' URLs, and the referees would submit their comments through a Web-based report form.

The experiment had promising results—almost half the authors contacted (23) took advantage of the offer. After the study, authors were asked to evaluate the service. They seemed to be satisfied with this form of submission, once they had mastered the approach. However, they expressed concern that exclusive use of this method would restrict submissions and referees to countries with high-quality Internet access.

Reviewers chosen for the experiment were experienced computer users, who worked on the Internet daily. Their comments were also positive. Eighty-nine percent of reviewers (39) reported that they would like to receive papers for review electronically. The majority reported that their electronic review took less time (60 percent) or the same time (29 percent) as a traditional review of a paper manuscript, and was less (46 percent) or equally (43 percent) difficult. The results of this experiment encouraged the editors to change their submission policy. After August 2001, *Proceedings: Biological Sciences* stopped accepting paper submission of manuscripts; only electronic manuscripts can now be submitted for review and possible publication in this p-e-journal.

A similar approach was tested by the p-e-journal *Medical Journal of Australia (MJA)* (Protocol for Internet peer review study II, 1998). Articles submitted for publication were circulated among reviewers via the Web (with password-protected entry) and the review process was conducted as an online discussion (which took three to four weeks) among the journal's editors, reviewers, authors, and a small number of consultants who represented the journal's readership. After acceptance, articles and records of the review process were published on the Internet, for open review by the readers. After four weeks of open review the articles were published in print form.

The standard reviewing procedure for the *MJA* is double blind. For the Internet study reviewers were asked for permission to publish their reviews for an open review period on the journal's Web site. Almost two-thirds of the 90 percent who agreed to participate signed their reviews; the rest posted anonymously (with their identities known to the editor). In the second stage of the review, anonymous comments were e-mailed to the editor, who judged their merit. In this study most of the participants in both stages of the process did identify themselves by name.

A similar system is used by the editors of *Journal for Interactive Media in Education* (Sumner & Shum, 1996). After submission, an article is placed on a Web site and reviewers use a computer-supported collaborative argumentation (CSCA) environment to develop their comments. The software allows them to work in two windows: one displays the article text and the second is used for their comments for each section of the article. The editor pulls together all the comments, and the article and reviewers' comments are then posted on the Web site. The process moves into an open discussion phase, during which authors, reviewers, and readers can engage in debate. The editor decides if the article is to be accepted and which changes are necessary. The discussion can continue even after publication.

Nadasdy (1997), the editor of the now defunct pure e-journal *Electronic Journal of Cognitive and Brain Sciences*, suggested another approach to the peer-review process, which he calls "Interactive Publishing." In this system, the process of submission and review was highly automated. Submitted articles were posted on the journal's Web site and readers could rate the quality of the papers. They could fill out a Likert-style form containing questions such as: How significant is the problem discussed in the paper? (not significant–extremely significant); How appropriate is the method used to investigate the problem? (inappropriate–quite appropriate); How well founded is the conclusion based on the empirical evidence? (not founded–well founded); How original are the findings? (not original–absolute original); What is the expected future impact? (no impact–strong impact). The process was completely anonymous. Articles that received a score of 80 percent or higher were to be transferred to an archive of accepted papers. Between 1997 and 1999, the *EJCBS* had only six articles posted for review, and none accepted. By 2001, the journal's Web site had been removed.

Conclusion

This review has examined analytical and empirical research on the roles and uses of e-journals in scholarly communication. Such research is especially sensitive to how issues are framed at the time the work is conceived and conducted. The 1990s saw the emergence of e-journals, which by the turn of the century numbered over 8,000 (Okerson, 2000). However, the dominant form of e-journal changed three times in the 1990s, and some of the research was not sufficiently sensitive to these rapid and important shifts. In the early 1990s, pure e-journals that were circulated by mailing lists were dominant. In the mid-1990s, pure e-journals that were stored on searchable gopher and Web sites were dominant. By 1998, p-e-journals were by far the most numerous.

Tenopir and King (2000, pp. 61–65) trace discussions of scholarly e-journals back to the 1930s, identifying the topic as one of active federally sponsored research in the U.S. in the 1970s and 1980s, and in the U.K. in the 1980s. Tenopir and King note that researchers in this era studied scientific communication, and emphasized the role of e-journals in improving its efficiency and reducing costs. In particular, they envisioned centralized article and bibliographic databases reducing the number of communication channels and also reducing redundant communication (i.e., multiple publication of the same study).

Since 1990 a tremendous transformation has taken place in the discourses about e-journals, as well as related practice. Okerson (1991) contrasts conservative and revolutionary visions of e-journals. In her view, a conservative approach to electronic manuscripts has them paralleling the format of the traditional pure p-journal, except that the articles might be made available individually, rather than packaged in issues. She praised Stevan Harnad as an "electronic seer" (Okerson, 1991, p. 9), who envisioned the Internet as a medium to support new forms of publishing, including articles enriched with sound and images, as well as forums that would support open peer commentary.

In the early 1990s, a number of peer-reviewed pure e-journals were launched that were free to authors and readers. Some, such as *Psycoloquy* (established in 1990), *Postmodern Culture* (established in 1990), and the *Journal of Artificial Intelligence Research* (established in 1993) seem to be thriving in 2002. Regrettably, a number of the earliest pure e-journals have ceased publication. These include the *EJournal*, the *Public-Access Computer Systems Review (PACS-Review)*, the *Interpersonal Computing and Technology Journal (IPCT)*, and the *Electronic Journal on Virtual Culture (EJVC)*. Nevertheless, continuous growth in the number of peer-reviewed pure e-journals and e-p-journals has persisted through the late 1990s. Crawford (2002) identified 50 such journals that were publishing in 1995 and were still alive in 2001. In the early 1990s, the term "electronic journal" was synonymous with the idea of pure e-journals, free to readers. Even so, there were some important shifts in the e-journal's format. Until about the mid-1990s, e-journals that were based in ASCII text were initially distributed by electronic mailing lists. Some pure e-journals soon added access via searchable sites (such as gopher and the Veronica search engine) in the mid-1990s.

And many of these pure e-journals were reorganized on Web sites between 1995 and 1997. These technological shifts generally expanded potential access to pure e-journals and their archives.

Some analysts hoped that new e-journals would provide important new functions, such as enriched media, discussions of articles, cross-linking articles, and so on (Borgman, 2000, p. 90). Relatively few of these pure e-journals added the new affordances that some had hoped would be integral to the new breed of e-journals. *Psycoloquy* did create a forum for open peer commentary, while *JAIR* utilized a Usenet newsgroup, comp.ai, for the discussion of published articles. The *Electronic Transactions on Artificial Intelligence* developed a process whereby an article could be discussed in an electronic forum before it was formally submitted for peer review and potential publication. *Internet Archaeology* allowed authors to include large numbers of photographs with their articles, and a few of their articles contain well over 100 photographs. However, these examples illustrate a relatively small number of exceptions. An intriguing example is *JAIR*, which instructed its authors to format their articles so that when they were printed they would be indistinguishable from those that were photocopied from traditional p-journals, and thus their legitimacy would be less likely to be questioned.

The mid-1990s marked a transition from a time when this easy equation of e-journals with pure e-journals that were free of charge to readers was valid to a period in which p-e-journals that were often site licensed to institutional subscribers became dominant. For example, the Johns Hopkins University Press initiated Project Muse in 1995 as a way to make several dozen of its p-journals available as p-e-journals. Project Muse rapidly acquired the pure e-journal *Postmodern Culture*, and shifted its access model to one that required a paid subscription. Although Project Muse currently allows individual subscriptions to its two pure e-journals, subscriptions to various subsets of its collection of over 100 p-e-journals are restricted to institutions. Furthermore, it authenticates readers with an IP address-checking scheme that limits off-campus access through an Internet service provider other than the subscribing institution.

By 1996, several large STM publishers had created electronic editions of some of their p-journals (Brown & Duda, 1996). By 1998, these new p-e-journal editions numbered in the thousands. Unfortunately, they are uncritically mixed with pure e-journals and e-p-journals by writers such as Okerson (2000) and Tenopir and King (2001). As we have shown in this chapter, this uncritical mixing complicates the already vexing issues of assessing the relative costs, quality, accessibility, legitimacy, and uses of electronic and paper media for journal publication. Thus, we have introduced a typology to help differentiate the various e-journal formats and make our analyses more precise.

The transition in the late 1990s that introduced thousands of p-e-journals has important control dimensions as well. In particular, some of the early enthusiasts for pure electronic journals had hoped that they would be sufficiently simple and inexpensive to produce and distribute so that they could be organized by scholars rather than by professional publishers. Borgman (2000, pp. 84–90) provides a detailed and balanced critique of these visions. Some of the earliest pure e-journals seemed to fulfill this promise. However, the flood of p-e-journals from large STM publishers and scientific societies in the late 1990s enabled traditional scholarly publishers to retain editorial control (and profit) from the vast majority of e-journals.

Even though the current scholarly e-journal system is primarily publisher-driven, p-e-journals do offer some important conveniences to readers. Unfortunately, the recent empirical research about e-journal usage has been conducted with closed-form surveys that seem not to be very sensitive to the different types of e-journals and the different conditions under which scholars may access and read them. As we noted in Tables 4.2, 4.3, and 4.4, as well as in the text, pure e-journals and p-e-journals are often quite different when viewed from a socio-technical perspective.

We do not know how scholars actually differentiate between pure e-journals, e-p-journals, p-e-journals, pure p-journals, and p+e-journals. We can speculate that they evaluate their relative accessibility and also rely upon traditional indicators of scholarly merit, which may not relate to the distribution medium.

Some potential virtues of pure e-journals, such as price competitiveness, have resulted from substantial organizational initiatives rather than from a few scholars organizing a pure e-journal with an inexpensive Web server. The example of SPARC and the ACS collaborating to produce the p+e-journal *Organic Letters* illustrates this observation.

As traditional scholarly publishers have become the dominant developers and providers of e-journals, increasing attention is being given to radical innovations such as publication venues other than e-journals for manuscripts that have not yet been peer reviewed. The electronic manuscript repository (arXiv.org) created by Paul Ginsparg for physics, mathematics, and computer science has excited the idea of possible extensions to other disciplines, as well as substantial controversy (Kling & McKim, 2000).

Walker's (1998) article about the role of pure e-journals in solving the serials crisis was the stimulus for *The American Scientist* to sponsor a lively online forum about scholarly electronic publishing, moderated by Stevan Harnad. That forum continues to be active into early 2002. However, under Harnad's moderation, the discussion shifted its emphasis to issues related to centralized electronic manuscript repositories, such as their costs, quality control, copyright, and long-term archiving.

These topics are not completely separate, since many journal editors are unwilling to publish articles that may have been readily available as unrefereed electronic manuscripts. Thus, the behavior of journal editors can influence scholars' willingness to circulate unrefereed electronic manuscripts. Conversely, there are interesting speculations that the availability of articles in freely available electronic manuscript form (even after they have been published in a peer-reviewed venue) may increase the extent to which they are read and cited. In some fields, such as particle physics, mathematics, and computer science, it is common for unrefereed electronic manuscripts, as written before editorial review, to be freely available, even after they are published as peer-reviewed articles. Scholarly communication via unrefereed electronic manuscripts is a sufficiently complex topic to warrant its own review. We suspect that the widespread availability of articles on special Web sites prior to their acceptance by journals will probably do more to improve scholarly communication than will the development of yet more new e-journals. Even so, we do not believe that e-journals are unimportant. In fact, much remains to be learned about their roles in scholarly communication. In closing, we suggest some new lines of research about e-journals.

Tenopir and King (2000, pp. 83–104) try to characterize the scholarly journal system in ways that do not clearly identify different versions of journals, access points, workplaces, and discriminating features. In our view, the various forms of e-journals and the variety of ways that readers can access them so complicate "the system" that it is much less orderly than their account suggests. It is more a constellation of resources than an easily described system. Further, this e-journal constellation is situated within a galaxy of heterogeneous scholarly communication resources that includes the informal collegial sharing of manuscripts, research manuscript series, disciplinary electronic manuscript repositories, conference proceedings, p-journals, monographs, and edited collections. These galaxies provide scholars with a range of publication options (Kling & McKim, 1999).

The structure of an e-journal constellation and its larger galaxy of communication resources varies from one discipline to another. Particle physicists are renowned for their reliance on electronic manuscripts that have not yet been peer reviewed, whereas American Chemical Society journal editors continue to exclude such manuscripts from their journals. However, a chemist's informational galaxy may be "electron rich" if she or he has access to *Chemical Abstracts* and the ACS's e-journal collections and new services, such as ASAP. It also may be "paper rich" if she or he continues to subscribe to some paper editions of chemistry p-e-journals or to print out and retain paper copies of electronic manuscripts.

Tenopir and King's map of a "scholarly journal system" was probably more accurate for the 1970s and 1980s than for this century. It is also probably more accurate for disciplines, such as history, that have not invested deeply in e-journals and/or electronic archives than it is for disciplines, such as economics, that have invested more heavily in publishing electronic manuscripts.

Where do different kinds of e-journals fit within scholars' information galaxies? Literature about e-journals is loaded with intriguing speculations; these can be sorted out with careful empirical research that is sensitive to the disciplinary galaxy of scholarly resources as well as to the institutional location and activities of authors, editors, readers, and other key participants.

Consider the speculation that the use of electronic manuscript repositories is reducing the amount of journal reading. Of course, this is more likely in fields where such repositories are well established. How does access to electronic archives of any kind, whether e-journals or agglomerations of journals—such as EBSCO's Academic Search Premier or Dow Jones Interactive—alter scholars' information galaxies?

Relatively few e-journals have experimented with new formats, such as open peer review or extensive multimedia supplements to articles. It would help to know how much scholars in disciplines with these enriched journals value these extensions and how they use them. For example, how much do artificial intelligence specialists read the *Electronic Transactions on Artificial Intelligence,* which supports an open peer-review period; and what encourages them to participate or not in the open discussions? How much do archaeologists track *Internet Archaeology* because its articles are often richly documented with photographs?

Some prestigious scholarly societies have started new p+e-journals (such as *Organic Letters*) that have rapidly become important in their fields. However, other societies have initiated pure e-journals. For example, the Association for Information Systems (AIS) started two peer-reviewed pure e-journals: *Communications of the AIS* (1999) and the *Journal of the AIS* (2000). Where do these journals fit in the constellation of information systems journals? Who publishes in them? Who reads them? How do information systems scholars use them? What kind of legitimacy do they have relative to other information systems journals? Most seriously, we need to learn about the ways that the reading of, writing for, and citation of pure e-journals such as these fit into the complex mix of socio-technical access and career issues.

Most of the behavioral studies of e-journal use have been conducted at research-intensive institutions, and either focus on primary research use or do not distinguish between the ways that scholars use journals (for teaching, for review articles, and so forth). It would help to learn whether electronic access to journals—via e-journals or via agglomerations—increases their accessibility to faculty and students at less-research-intensive universities.

Many studies of e-journal use are based on closed-form surveys. Some of these studies have been very useful, although we noted that most of them fail to make sufficiently refined distinctions between types of e-journals in their questions. However, closed-form surveys are likely to be too blunt an instrument to answer some of these questions about the roles of e-journals in the more complicated scholarly journal constellations. As we discussed in the section on access to e-journals, research must be sensitive to the sociotechnical networks that link readers and e-journal articles. Further, constellation mapping requires that researchers be able to learn where and how scholars position specific e-journals relative to others in their constellation, and—most importantly—*why*. If the constellation of e-journals is rapidly changing, we need to develop a theoretical understanding of its dynamics as well as an understanding of its time-dependent cartography.

Acknowledgments

Funding was provided in part by NSF Grant #SBR-9872961 and with support from the School of Library and Information Science at Indiana University. This chapter benefited from helpful discussions about electronic scholarly communication with a number of colleagues, including Ingemar Bohlin, David Cheney, Blaise Cronin, Noriko Hara, and Geoff McKim. Sharon Ross provided important editorial assistance. The anonymous referees provided useful guidance.

Endnotes

1. Many aspects of peer review—including reviewer biases—have been systematically examined in medicine. See the Fourth International Congress on Peer Review in Biomedical Publication, 2001, http://www.amaassn. org/public/peer/peerhome.htm. Also, see Weller's (2001) comprehensive monograph about peer review in a variety of disciplines.

2. For example, an analysis of an astronomer's use of articles that are published in *The Astrophysical Journal* based on the Standard Model might focus on its special information processing features, such as hyperlinks between articles and the availability of new articles soon after they are accepted for publication. A Socio-Technical Network analysis might examine how the astronomer working at a campus facility can access some of these features via a site-licensed version of *The Astrophysical Journal*. However, when she works from home and uses another Internet service provider (ISP), she would be unable to use her university's site license to the journal. Instead she might search for recent articles in an alternative location—such as the "open access" astrophysics database on arXiv.org.

3. The length of the "blackout period" depends upon the journal that is publishing an e-version on PubMedCentral.

4. Many e-journals offer to send tables of contents regularly to their subscribers. However, some journals, such as *Science Online*, offer to send

their subscribers an e-mail note when a new article cites an article that the subscriber specifies.

5. While it is unlikely that anyone who is interested in AI research does not have good Internet access, this observation is applicable to many other e-p-journals.

6. The results of this survey must be interpreted with caution, as the survey was conducted through the Web, thus introducing self-selection, which limits the generalizability of their results.

Bibliography

Amiran, E., Orr, E., & Unsworth, J. (1991). Refereed electronic journals and the future of scholarly publishing. In J. A. Hewitt (Ed.), *Advances in library automation and networking* (pp. 25–53). Greenwich, CT: JAI Press.

Anderson, K., Sack, J., Krauss, L., & O'Keefe, L. (2001, March). Publishing online-only peer-reviewed biomedical literature: Three years of citation, author perception, and usage experience. *The Journal of Electronic Publishing, 6*. Retrieved April 24, 2001, from http://www.press.umich.edu/jep/06-03/anderson.html.

Arms, W. Y. (1999, December). Preservation of scientific serials: Three current examples. *The Journal of Electronic Publishing, 5*. Retrieved May 1, 2001, from http://www.press.umich.edu/jep/05-02/arms.html.

Armstrong, C. J. (2001, April 2). Collection management and scholarly electronic publishing resource. Retrieved July 19, 2001, from http://www.i-a-l.co.uk/CM_SEP1.htm.

Bailey, C. W. Jr. (2002, February 22). Scholarly electronic publishing bibliography. Retrieved April 10, 2002, from http://info.lib.uh.edu/sepb/sepb.html.

Bannon, L. J., & Schmidt, K. (1991). CSCW: Four characters in search of a context. In J. Bowers & S. Benford (Eds.), *Studies in computer supported cooperative work: Theory, practice and design* (pp. 3–16). Amsterdam: North-Holland.

Björk, B.-C., & Turk, Z. (2000). A survey of the impact of the Internet on scientific publishing in construction IT and construction management. *Electronic Journal of Information Technology in Construction, 5*. Retrieved May 1, 2001, from http://www.itcon.org/2000/5.

Borgman, C. L. (2000). *From Gutenberg to the global information infrastructure: Access to information in the networked world*. Cambridge, MA: MIT Press.

Borgman, C. L. & Furner, J. (2002). Scholarly communication and bibliometrics. *Annual Review of Information Science and Technology, 36*, 3–72.

Bot, M., Burgemeester, J., & Roes, H. (2000, November). The cost of publishing an electronic journal: A general model and a case study. *D-Lib Magazine, 11*. Retrieved November 16, 2001, from http://www.dlib.org/dlib/november98/11roes.html.

Brown, C. M. (1999). Information seeking behavior of scientists in the electronic information age: Astronomers, chemists, mathematicians, and physicists. *Journal of the American Society for Information Science, 50,* 929–943.

Brown, E. W., & Duda, A. L. (1996, Fall). Electronic publishing programs in science and technology part 1: The journals. *Issues in Science and Technology Librarianship.* Retrieved April 11, 2002, from http://www.library.ucsb.edu/istl/96-fall/brown-duda.html.

Buckley, C., Burright, M., Prendergast, A., Sapon-White, R., & Taylor, A. (1999, Spring). Electronic publishing of scholarly journals: A bibliographic essay of current issues. *Issues in Science and Technology Librarianship, 22.* Retrieved November 16, 2001, from http://www.library.ucsb.edu/istl/99-spring/article4.html.

Butler, H. J. (1995). Research into the reward system of scholarship: Where does scholarly electronic publishing get you? In A. Okerson (Ed.), *Filling the Pipeline and Paying the Piper: Proceedings of the Fourth Symposium* (pp. 167–177). Washington, DC: Office of Scientific and Academic Publishing, Association of Research Libraries.

Crawford, W. (1998, January). Paper persists: Why physical library collections still matter. *Online, 22.* Retrieved July 17, 2001, from http://www.onlinemag.net/OL1998/crawford1.html.

Crawford, W. (2002). Free electronic refereed journals: Getting past the arc of enthusiasm. *Learned Publishing, 15,* 117–123.

Cronin, B., & Overfelt, K. (1995). E-journals and tenure. *Journal of the American Society for Information Science, 46,* 700–703.

Cronin, B., Snyder, H. W., Rosenbaum, H., Martinson, A., & Callahan, E. (1998). Invoked on the Web. *Journal of the American Society for Information Science, 49,* 1319–1328.

Dalton, M. S. (1995). Refereeing of scholarly works for primary publishing. *Annual Review of Information Science and Technology, 30,* 213–250.

Denning, P. J. (1995). Plagiarism in the Web. *Communications of the ACM, 38,* 29.

Eason, K. (1988). *Information technology and organizational change.* London: Taylor & Francis.

Fisher, J. (1997). *Comparing electronic journals to print journals: Are there savings?* Paper presented at Scholarly Communication and Technology Conference organized by The Andrew W. Mellon Foundation at Emory University, April 24–25, 1997. Retrieved November 17, 2000, from http://www.arl.org/scomm/scat/fisher.html.

Ford, C. E., & Harter, S. P. (1998). The downside of scholarly electronic publishing: Problems in accessing electronic journals through online directories and catalogs. *College & Research Libraries, 59,* 335–346.

Harnad, S. (1995). The postGutenberg galaxy: How to get there from here. *Information Society, 11,* 285–292.

Harnad, S. (1996). Implementing peer review on the Net: Scientific quality control in scholarly electronic journals. In R. P. Peek & G. B. Newby (Eds.), *Scholarly publishing: The electronic frontier* (pp. 103–108). Cambridge MA: MIT Press.

Harrassowitz. (2000, May 4). *Electronic journals: A selected resource guide.* Retrieved February 20, 2001, from http://www.harrassowitz.de/top_resources/ejresguide.html.

Harter, S. P. (1996). The impact of electronic journals on scholarly communication: A citation analysis. *The Public-Access Computer Systems Review, 7.* Retrieved January 16, 2001, from http://info.lib.uh.edu/pr/v7/n5/hart7n5.html.

Holoviak, J., & Seitter, K. L. (1997, September). Transcending the limitations of the printed page. *The Journal of Electronic Publishing, 3.* Retrieved September 5, 2000, from http://www.press.umich.edu/jep/03-01/EI.html.

King, D. W., & Tenopir, C. (1999). Using and reading scholarly literature. *Annual Review of Information Science and Technology, 34,* 423–477.

Kirkpatrick, D. D. (2000, November 3). As publishers perish, libraries feel the pain: Mergers keep pushing up journal costs. *The New York Times,* pp. C1, C5.

Kling, R., & Covi, L. (1995). Electronic journals and legitimate media in the systems of scholarly communication. *The Information Society, 11,* 261–271.

Kling, R., & McKim, G. (1997). *A typology for electronic journals: Characterizing scholarly journals by their distribution forms.* (Working Paper No.WP-97-07) Indiana University, Bloomington, Center for Social Informatics. Retrieved November 16, 2001, from http://www.slis.indiana.edu/csi/wp97-07.html.

Kling, R., & McKim, G. (1999). Scholarly communication and the continuum of electronic publishing. *Journal of the American Society for Information Science, 50,* 890–906.

Kling, R., & McKim, G. (2000). Not just a matter of time: Field differences and the shaping of electronic media in supporting scientific communication. *Journal of the American Society for Information Science, 51,* 1306–1320.

Kling, R., McKim, G., & King, A. (2001). *A bit more to IT: Scholarly communication forums as socio-technical interaction networks.* (Working Paper No.WP-01-02) Indiana University, Bloomington, Center for Social Informatics. Retrieved November 16, 2001, from http://www.slis.indiana.edu/csi/wp01-02.html.

Kock, N. (1999). A case of academic plagiarism. *Communications of the ACM, 42*(7), 96–104.

Lenares, D. (1999). *Faculty use of electronic journals at research institutions.* Paper presented at Racing Toward Tomorrow, ACRL Ninth National Conference, April 8–11, 1999, Detroit, Michigan. Retrieved November 16, 2001, from http://www.ala.org/acrl/lenares.pdf.

McCabe, M. J. (1998). The impact of publisher mergers on journal prices: A preliminary report. ARL: *A Bimonthly Report on Research Library Issues and Actions from ARL, CNI, and SPARC, 200.* Retrieved April 19, 2002, from http://www.arl.org/newsltr/200/mccabe.html.

McCabe, M. J. (1999). The impact of publisher mergers on journal prices: An update. *ARL: A Bimonthly Report on Research Library Issues and Actions from ARL, CNI, and SPARC, 207.* Retrieved April 19, 2002, from http://www.arl.org/newsletr/207/mccabe.html.

Meadows, A. J. (1998). *Communicating research.* London: Academic Press.

Miller, R. H. (2000). Electronic resources and academic libraries, 1980–2000: A historical perspective. *Library Trends, 48,* 645–671.

Nadasdy, Z. (1997, September). A truly all-electronic journal: Let democracy replace peer review. *The Journal of Electronic Publishing, 3.* Retrieved April 24, 2001, from http://www.press.umich.edu/jep/03-01/EJCBS.html.

Noll, R. G. (1996). *The economics of scholarly publications and the information superhighway* (Brookings Discussion Papers in Domestic Economics). Washington, DC: The Brookings Institution. Retrieved April 24, 2001, from http://www.brook.edu/Views/Papers/Domestic/003.htm.

Odlyzko, A. M. (1995). Tragic loss or good riddance: The impending demise of traditional scholarly journals. *International Journal of Human-Computer Studies, 42,* 71–122. Retrieved August 31, 1997, from http://www.dtc.umn.edu/~odlyzko/doc/eworld.html.

Odlyzko, A. M. (2002). The rapid evolution of scholarly communication. *Learned Publishing, 15,* 7–19. Retrieved January 18, 2002, from http://www.dtc.umn.edu/~odlyzko/doc/eworld.html.

Okerson, A. (1991). The electronic journal: What, whence, and when? *The Public-Access Computer Systems Review, 2.* Retrieved April 2, 2002, from http://www.library.yale.edu/~okerson/pacs.html.

Okerson, A. (2000). Are we there yet? Online e-resources ten years after. *Library Trends, 48,* 671–694.

Peek, R. P. & Pomerantz, J. P. (1998). Electronic scholarly journal publishing. *Annual Review of Information Science and Technology, 33,* 321–356.

Protocol for Internet peer review study II (1998). Retrieved April 29, 2001, from http://www.mja.com.au/public/information/iprs2bod.html.

Schaffner, A. C. (1994). The future of scientific journals: Lessons from the past. *Information Technology and Libraries, 13,* 239–247.

Schauder, D. (1994). Electronic publishing of professional articles: Attitudes of academics and implications for the scholarly communication industry. *Journal of the American Society for Information Science, 45,* 73–100.

Shivakumar, N. & Garcia-Molina, H. (1995, November). The SCAM approach to copy detection in digital libraries. *D-Lib Magazine, 11.* Retrieved July 17, 2001, from http://www.dlib.org/dlib/november95/scam/11shivakumar.html.

Smith, A. G. (2000, April). Search features of digital libraries. *Information Research, 5.* Retrieved November 16, 2001, from http://informationr.net/ir/5-3/paper73.html.

Sosteric, M. (1996). Electronic journals: The grand information future? *Electronic Journal of Sociology, 2.* Retrieved May 15, 2001, from http://www.sociology.org/vol002.002/Sosteric.article.1996.html.

Speier, C., Palmer, J., Wren, D., & Hahn, S. (1999). Faculty perceptions of electronic journals as scholarly communication: A question of prestige and legitimacy. *Journal of the American Society for Information Science, 50,* 537–543.

Stewart, L. (1996). User acceptance of electronic journals: Interviews with chemists at Cornell University. *College & Research Libraries, 57,* 339–349.

Sumner, T., & Shum, S. B. (1996). Open peer review and argumentation: Loosening the paper chains on journals. *Ariadne, 5.* Retrieved April 29, 2001, from http://www.ariadne.ac.uk/issue5/jime/.

Sweeney, A. E. (2000). Tenure and promotion: Should you publish in electronic journals? *The Journal of Electronic Publishing, 6.* Retrieved February 20, 2001, from http://www.press.umich.edu/jep/06-02/sweeney.html.

Tenopir, C., & King, D. W. (2000). *Towards electronic journals: Realities for scientists, librarians and publishers.* Washington, D.C.: Special Libraries Association.

Tenopir, C., & King, D. W. (2001). Lessons for the future of journals [Electronic edition]. *Nature, 413,* 672–674.

Tomney, H., & Burton, P. F. (1998). Electronic journals: A study of usage and attitudes among academics. *Journal of Information Science, 24,* 419–429.

Ulrich's international periodicals directory (2001). New Providence, NJ: Bowker.

Walker, T. J. (1998). Free Internet access to traditional journals [Electronic edition]. *American Scientist, 86,* 463–471.

Walsh, J. P., & Bayma, T. (1996). Computer networks and scientific work. *Social Studies of Science, 26,* 661–703.

Weller, A. C. (2001). *Editorial peer review: Its strengths and weaknesses.* Medford, NJ: Information Today, Inc.

Wells, A. (1999). Advantages and disadvantages of electronic journals. In *Exploring the development of the independent, electronic, scholarly journal.* Unpublished master's thesis, University of Sheffield, UK. Retrieved May 15, 2001, from http://panizzi.shef.ac.uk/elecdiss/edl0001/ch0402.html.

Whisler, S. & Rosenblatt, S. F. (1997, April). *The library and the university press: Two views of the current system of scholarly publishing.* Paper presented at Scholarly Communication and Technology Conference organized by The Andrew W. Mellon Foundation at Emory University. Retrieved November 16, 2001, from http://www.arl.org/scomm/scat/rosenblatt.html.

Wilkins, V. (1997). Cataloguing e-journals: Where are we now? *Ariadne, 11.* Retrieved November 25, 2000, from http://www.ariadne.ac.uk/issue11/survey.

Wilkinson, S. L. (1998, May 18). Electronic publishing takes journals into a new realm. *Chemical & Engineering News.* Retrieved November 16, 2001, from http://pubs.acs.org/hotartcl/cenear/980518/elec.html.

Wood, D., & Hurst, P. (2000). Online peer review: Perception in biological science. *Learned Publishing, 13,* 95–100.

Zhang, Y. (1998). The impact of Internet-based electronic resources on formal scholarly communication in the area of library and information science: A citation analysis. *Journal of Information Science, 24,* 241–254.

CHAPTER 5

Visualizing Knowledge Domains

Katy Börner
Indiana University, Bloomington

Chaomei Chen
Drexel University, Philadelphia

Kevin W. Boyack
Sandia National Laboratories, Albuquerque

Introduction

This chapter reviews visualization techniques that can be used to map the ever-growing domain structure of scientific disciplines and to support information retrieval and classification. In contrast to the comprehensive surveys conducted in traditional fashion by Howard White and Katherine McCain (1997, 1998), this survey not only reviews emerging techniques in interactive data analysis and information visualization, but also depicts the bibliographical structure of the field itself. The chapter starts by reviewing the history of knowledge domain visualization. We then present a general process flow for the visualization of knowledge domains and explain commonly used techniques. In order to visualize the domain reviewed by this chapter, we introduce a bibliographic data set of considerable size, which includes articles from the citation analysis, bibliometrics, semantics, and visualization literatures. Using tutorial style, we then apply various algorithms to demonstrate the visualization effects[1] produced by different approaches and compare the results. The domain visualizations reveal the relationships within and between the four fields that together constitute the focus of this chapter. We conclude with a general discussion of research possibilities.

Painting a "big picture" of scientific knowledge has long been desirable for a variety of reasons. Traditional approaches are brute force—scholars must sort through mountains of literature to perceive the outlines of their field. Obviously, this is time-consuming, difficult to replicate, and entails subjective judgments. The task is enormously complex. Sifting through recently published documents to find those that will later be recognized as important is labor intensive. Traditional approaches struggle to keep up with the pace of information growth. In multidisciplinary fields of study it is especially difficult to maintain an overview of literature dynamics. Painting the big picture of an ever-evolving scientific discipline is akin to the situation described in the widely known Indian legend about the blind men and the elephant. As the story goes, six blind men were trying to find out what an elephant looked like. They touched different parts of the elephant and quickly jumped to their conclusions. The one touching the body said it must be like a wall; the one touching the tail said it was like a snake; the one touching the legs said it was like a tree trunk, and so forth. But science does not stand still; the steady stream of new scientific literature creates a continuously changing structure. The resulting disappearance, fusion, and emergence of research areas add another twist to the tale—it is as if the elephant is running and dynamically changing its shape.

Domain visualization, an emerging field of study, is in a similar situation. Relevant literature is spread across disciplines that have traditionally had few connections. Researchers examining the domain from a particular discipline cannot possibly have an adequate understanding of the whole. As noted by White and McCain (1997), the new generation of information scientists is technically driven in its efforts to visualize scientific disciplines. However, limited progress has been made in terms of connecting pioneers' theories and practices with the potentialities of today's enabling technologies. If the difference between past and present generations lies in the power of available technologies, what they have in common is the ultimate goal—to reveal the development of scientific knowledge. Application areas include studies of scholarly communities and networks, the growth and evolution of fields, the diffusion of research topics, and the relationships among individual authors and institutions.

White and McCain's 1997 review was done in the traditional way, in other words, using manual and intellectual analysis. Since then the size and the scope of the field have exploded, and it is now well beyond the reach of traditional survey methods. The techniques needed to undertake analyses quickly and effectively are precisely those that belong to the domain visualization toolkit. These new techniques allow us to streamline the practice with unprecedented scalability and repeatability. Forming the big picture itself is a typical problem in domain visualization. How to choose the source of data, how to analyze and visualize the data, and how to make sense of what is in the picture—these are decisions to be made by the new generation of information cartographers.

This review does not attempt to update earlier work by providing an extensive bibliography with commentary on the field of literature mapping and visualization, but instead provides an overview of the many techniques used in the process of mapping and visualizing knowledge domains. It also offers an opportunity to compare and contrast different visualizations of the same data in order to illustrate characteristics of particular mapping techniques. The chapter does not cover some potentially relevant and important issues such as user and task analysis, alternative input/output devices, visual perception principles, or evaluation of map relevance.

The first section sketches the history of research on visualizing knowledge domains, which is rooted in fields like scientometrics, bibliometrics, citation analysis, and information visualization. The second explains the general process flow of visualizing knowledge domains and the overall structure of the chapter. We then review measures and approaches to determine bibliographic, linguistic, co-word, co-term, co-classification, content, or semantic similarities. The next section provides an overview of the different mathematical techniques commonly used to analyze and visualize bibliographic data. Appropriate visualization and interaction metaphors ensuring that resulting maps can be intuitively and effectively used are also described. We then introduce a bibliographic data set of considerable size that is used to map research on the visualization of knowledge domains. We conclude with a discussion of promising new avenues of research.

History

Narin and Moll (1977) and White and McCain (1997) compiled the first *ARIST* chapters on bibliometrics. White and McCain (1998) give vivid accounts of the history of citation analysis, which is a key element in domain visualization. Borgman (1990; 2000; Borgman & Furner, 2002) provides a comprehensive overview of bibliometric methods that can be used to describe, explain, predict, and evaluate scholarly communication. Wilson's (1999/2000) recent *ARIST* chapter is a comprehensive review of informetrics, covering bibliometrics as well as other areas. An in-depth account of theories and practices in the endeavor of mapping scientific frontiers is also the central topic of a recent book (C. Chen, 2002).

Scientometrics, Bibliometrics, and Citation Analysis

The wide commercial availability of citation indexes dates from the 1950s. Indexing in the 1950s was inconsistent and uncoordinated. Dissatisfaction with the array of traditional discipline-oriented indexing and abstracting services was widespread (Garfield, 1955). Eugene Garfield's (1955) seminal paper in *Science* laid the foundation for citation analysis today. As the founder of the Institute for Scientific Information (ISI), he initiated development of the *Science Citation Index*—a unique multidisciplinary database representing scholarly communication. In addition, he was instrumental in designing a sophisticated set of conceptual tools for studying the dynamics of science. The concept of citation analysis today forms the basis of much of what is known variously as scientometrics, bibliometrics, infometrics, cybermetrics, and webometrics. Garfield's invention continues to have a profound impact on the way we think about and study scholarly communication.

One of the pioneering domain visualization studies based on citation data was the creation of the historical map of DNA research, which was done manually almost 40 years ago, in the early 1960s (Garfield, Sher, & Torpie, 1964). Soon thereafter, Derek Price studied the same data in his classic work on mapping scientific networks (Price, 1961, 1963, 1965). In domain visualization, interrelationships between research fronts are spatially represented. Such spatial representations allow users to navigate the scientific literature based on the patterns depicted.

Domain visualization aims to reveal realms of scientific communication as reflected in the scientific literature and the citation paths woven by individual scientists in their publications. There is indeed an important connection between domain visualization and what Hjørland (1997) called domain analysis. Domain visualization can provide enabling techniques for domain analysis, especially in multidisciplinary and fast-moving knowledge domains. The field of domain visualization has also been called "scientography" (Garfield, 1994), although this term does not seem to be widely used.

Garfield (1994) also introduced the concept of longitudinal mapping. In longitudinal mapping, a series of chronologically sequential maps can be used to detect advances in scientific knowledge. Analysts and domain experts can use longitudinal maps to forecast emerging trends in a subject domain. Since domain visualizations typically identify key works, they enable the novice to become familiar with a field through easy location of landmark articles and books, as well as members of invisible colleges or specialties. *The Web of Knowledge,* published in 2000 to commemorate Eugene Garfield's 75th birthday, comprehensively addresses the history, theory, and practical applications of citation indexing and analysis (Cronin & Atkins, 2000).

Scientometrics is a distinct discipline that has emerged from citation-based domain visualization. Scientometrics is the quantitative study of scientific communication, which applies bibliometrics, inter alia, to scientific literature. Robert Merton and Eugene Garfield (1986, p. vii) regard the late Derek De Solla Price (1922–1983) as the "father of scientometrics." Price made profound contributions to information science through his seminal work on networks of scientific papers (Price, 1965) as well as his landmark book *Little Science, Big Science, and Beyond* (Price, 1986).

In 1981, ISI published the pioneering *Atlas of Science in Biochemistry and Molecular Biology.* The *Atlas* was based on a co-citation index associated with publications in the field over a one-year period. It featured 102 distinct clusters of articles. These clusters, representing research front specialties, formed a snapshot of significant research activities in biochemistry and molecular biology. The construction of this pioneering *Atlas* took several months. Garfield and Small (1989) explained the role of citation structures in identifying the changing frontiers of science.

More recently, ISI has developed the SCI-Map software, which enables users to navigate a citation network. It has been used in numerous subject domains, including physics, chemistry, and quantum systems. For example, Henry Small (1994) used SCI-Map to map AIDS research. SCI-Map creates maps of individual research areas specified by the user. Given an author, paper, or keyword as a starting point, one can seed a map and then grow it by specifying various desired connections at different thresholds of co-citation strength or distance. The network of connected nodes is formed by a series of iterations of clustering, including additional core papers with each successive node. The nodes are selected according to the strength of their links, and positioning is determined by the *geometric triangulation method* (see subsection on "Triangulation" in the "Spatial Configuration" section).

In his more recent work, Small has explored the notion of a passage through science (Small, 1999a, 2000). Passages linking the literature of different disciplines help to import or export a method established in one discipline from or to another. This is known as cross-disciplinary fertilization. As Small has noted, this reaching out or stretching can result in the import or export of methods, ideas, models, or empirical results between fields. This requires scientists to have not only a broad awareness of the literature, but also the creative imagination to foresee how outside information fits with the problem at hand. He developed algorithms to blaze a magnificent trail of more than 300 articles across the literatures of different scientific disciplines. Eugene Garfield (2001) has described an historiography program, named Histcomp Software, which semi-automatically creates a chronological file of milestone papers, patents, and books. (Note that Garfield [1963] had outlined a critical path method for measuring the impact of a primordial paper 38 years earlier.) Starting with a collection of papers, each represented by its ISI source record, the algorithm determines the list of cited references to create a mini-citation index of the field. It then creates a chronological matrix of the bibliography and generates listings of most-cited papers inside and outside the main network. The resulting historiography visualizes the genealogical flow from primordial papers to the present. An historical map of research in DNA is given as an example.

Another application of citation indexing is the Web-based citation database system ResearchIndex (formerly CiteSeer), developed by researchers at the NEC Research Institute (Lawrence, Giles, & Bollacker, 1999). ResearchIndex allows users to search for various citation details of scientific documents available on the Web. This service provides a valuable complementary resource to ISI's citation databases. ResearchIndex takes advantage of the ability to access full-text versions of scientific documents on the Web by introducing a functionality called *citation context*. Not only can users search the database for various bibliographic attributes such as author, article title, and journal title, but they can also use the *citation context* function to retrieve a list of highlighted excerpts from citing documents and access detailed statements of their perceived value. This function provides an invaluable tool for researchers to judge the nature of an influential article.

Typically, the act of referencing another author's work in a scholarly or research paper is assumed to reflect a direct semantic relationship between the citing and cited works. However, a macroanalysis of cited and citing documents in terms of broad subject dispersion and a microanalysis that examined the subject relationship between citing and cited documents (Harter, Nisonger, & Weng, 1993; Nisonger, Harter, & Weng, 1992) suggested that the subject similarity among pairs of cited and citing documents is typically very small, supporting a subjective, psychological view of relevance and a trial-and-error, heuristic understanding of the information search process.

The notion of bibliometric mapping has been further developed by researchers in the Netherlands, in particular Noyons and van Raan (Noyons, Moed, & Luwel, 1999; Noyons & van Raan, 1998a, 1998b; van Raan, 2000). They have developed special mathematical techniques for bibliometric mapping. The basic assumption is that each research field can be characterized by a list of the most important keywords. Each publication in the field can in turn be characterized by a sublist of these keywords. Such sublists are like DNA fingerprints of published articles. By matching keyword-based fingerprints, one can measure the similarity between a pair of publications. The more keywords two documents have in common, the more similar the two publications are, and the more likely it is that they come from the same research area or research specialty at a higher level. Following the DNA metaphor, if two publications' fingerprints are sufficiently similar, they are bound to come from the same species. In their 1999 paper, (Noyons, Moed, & Luwel, 1999), these researchers incorporate performance assessment into the creation of bibliometric maps in order to measure the impact level of different subfields and themes and to address strategic questions such as: "Who is where in the subject domain, and how strong is their research?"

Map Generation and Visualization

In 1987, a National Science Foundation (NSF) panel report (McCormick, DeFanti, & Brown, 1987) recommended that the NSF fund immediate and longer-term research in what is now known as the field of scientific visualization. At that time, there were about 200 supercomputers in the U.S. These supercomputers generated a vast amount of numerical data, mainly through computationally intensive simulation of physical processes. Virtual wind tunnels and high-resolution predictive weather models are typical examples of scientific calculations that require visualization to present their output in an understandable form.

Scientific visualizations map physical phenomena onto two-dimensional (2-D) or three-dimensional (3-D) representations that are typically not very interactive. In contrast, Information Visualization (IV) aims at an interactive visualization of abstract, nonspatial phenomena such as bibliographic data sets or Web access patterns.

Advances in information visualization have been significantly driven by information retrieval research. A central problem for information retrieval researchers is how to improve efficiency and effectiveness. Generally speaking, the more a user knows about her search space, the more likely that her search will be effective. Many information visualization systems depict the overall semantic structure of a collection of documents. Users can use this structural visualization as the basis for subsequent browsing and searching. Card (1996) and Hearst (1999) have surveyed visualizing retrieval results.

Edward Tufte has contributed three seminal books on display and visualization (Tufte, 1983, 1990, 1997). Although his 1983 and 1990 books appeared prior to the emergence of information visualization as a distinct field, they are highly regarded in the information visualization community. In particular, Tufte's detailed case study of information display for the fateful launch of the space shuttle Challenger is a thought-provoking example.

Research in hypertext began to emerge as a distinct field of study in the late 1980s, following a number of pioneering hypertext systems, notably HyperCard from Apple and NoteCards from Xerox PARC (Halasz, 1988; Halasz, Moran, & Trigg, 1987). The thinking-by-association approach of hypertext and the World Wide Web has been widely attributed to the Memex conceived by Vannevar Bush (1945). A central topic in hypertext research is user navigation in hypertextual space (Conklin, 1987). Researchers have studied a variety of navigation cues to help users move around. One of the most popular recommendations is to have an overview map of the entire hypertext structure (Halasz, 1988). Advances have been made in automatically generating overview maps that can help users navigate. The mid-1990s saw the widespread use of the World Wide Web. The sheer size of the Web has posed an unprecedented challenge for mapping.

Geographic information systems (GIS) represent a gray area between information visualization and traditional cartography. Geographic coordinates provide a convenient and natural organizing framework, and a geographic framework can accommodate a wide variety of information. Thematic maps provide a rich metaphor for a class of information visualization known as information landscape. Notable examples include SPIRE/Themescape (Wise et al., 1995) and BEAD (Chalmers, 1992). Dodge and Kitchin (2000) provide a good source of examples of how geography influences the mapping of cyberspace.

The number of review and survey articles on information visualization is steadily increasing (Card, 1996; Hearst, 1999; Herman, Melançon, & Marshall, 2000; Hollan, Bederson, & Helfman, 1997; Mukherjea, 1999). The first edited volume (Card, Mackinlay, & Shneiderman, 1999) and the first authored monograph (C. Chen, 1999a) both appeared in 1999. Currently about a half-dozen books on the market are on information visualization (Card et al., 1999; C. Chen, 1999a; Spence, 2000, 2001; Ware, 2000), as well as a related book on algorithms for graph visualization (Battista, Eades, Tamassia, & Tollis, 1999). In March 2002, Palgrave launched a new, peer-reviewed, international journal, *Information Visualization*. Today, numerous workshops and journal special issues are devoted to information visualization.

Journals such as the *Journal of the American Society for Information Science and Technology (JASIST)* and *Scientometrics* have provided the principal fora for domain visualization. These journals traditionally have their main readership in library and information science (LIS) rather than other potentially relevant disciplines, such as computer science, information visualization, and geographic information systems. In the past 15 years, information retrieval has enjoyed a prominent position in the mainstream information visualization research, but other research areas such as citation analysis and domain analysis remain tied to a relatively focused scientific community. Major information visualization and interaction design techniques, as they pertain to the visualization of knowledge domains, are discussed in the section on "Visualization and Interaction Design."

Process Flow of Visualizing Knowledge Domains

White and McCain (1997) defined five models of literatures: bibliographic, editorial, bibliometric, user, and synthetic. With the computerized tools and techniques available today, the lines between these traditional models can become blurred. The model used by many researchers today might be described as a user meta model. It is first a *user model* in that it is a reduction of the literature based on a user's searches, queries, profiles, or filters, often generated quickly from computerized access to literature data sources and formulated to provide answers to specific questions. It fulfills the role of the *bibliographic* or *meta model* in that it contains metadata—authors, titles, descriptive terms, dates, and so on—that can be used to define relationships pertinent to mapping, and also to display attributes of the data in modern visualizations. These data also often contain, or can easily be used to generate, *bibliometric* data—citation counts, term distributions, attributes by year, impact factors, and so on—that can be easily displayed by visualizations and that enhance map interpretation. Bibliometric attributes also allow for thresholds and rankings, which can be used to limit data to those deemed most pertinent or important by the user.

The *user meta model* is closely related to the process by which domain maps or visualizations are produced. An overview of this process, with many of its possible perturbations, is shown in Figure 5.1. The general steps in this sequence are: (1) data extraction, (2) definition of unit of

DATA EXTRACTION	UNIT OF ANALYSIS	MEASURES	LAYOUT (often one code does both similarity and ordination steps)		DISPLAY
			SIMILARITY	ORDINATION	
SEARCHES ISI INSPEC Eng Index Medline Research Index Patents etc. BROADENING By citation By terms	COMMON CHOICES Journal Document Author Term	COUNTS/FREQUENCIES Attributes (e.g. terms) Author citations Co-citations By year THRESHOLDS By counts	SCALAR (unit by unit matrix) Direct citation Co-citation Combined linkage Co-word/co-term Co-classification VECTOR (unit by attribute matrix) Vector space model (words/terms) Latent Semantic Analysis (words/terms) incl. Singular Value Decomp (SVD) CORRELATION (if desired) Pearson's R on any of the above	DIMENSIONALITY REDUCTION Eigenvect/Eigenvalue solutions Factor Analysis (FA) and Principal Components Analysis (PCA) Multi-dimensional scaling (MDS) Pathfinder networks (PFnet) Self-organizing maps (SOM) includes SOM, ET-maps, etc. CLUSTER ANALYSIS SCALAR Triangulation Force-directed placement (FDP)	INTERACTION Browse Pan Zoom Query Filter Detail on demand ANALYSIS

Figure 5.1 Process flow for mapping knowledge domains.

analysis, (3) selection of measures, (4) calculation of a similarity between units, (5) ordination, or the assignment of coordinates to each unit, and (6) use of the resulting visualization for analysis and interpretation. Steps four and five of this process are often distilled into one operation, which can be described as data layout.

The next few sections of this chapter will address the process described in Figure 5.1. First we review units of analysis, measures, and simple approaches to determine appropriate similarities between units. Then we examine both the Figure 5.1 process and two major problems in communicating information: (1) multivariate data need to be displayed on the two-dimensional surface of either paper or a computer screen, and (2) large amounts of data must be displayed in a limited space with limited resolution. The first problem is tackled by applying mathematical dimensionality reduction algorithms to map n-dimensional data into a 2-D or 3-D space. The purpose of these algorithms is to place objects that are similar to one another in n-dimensions close to each other and to place dissimilar objects far apart. This process is also called ordination. Cluster techniques can be used to further group similar objects together. Commonly used techniques are presented later. The second problem is typically minimized by applying interaction (panning, filtering) and distortion techniques (fisheye views) discussed in the section on "Interaction Design."

The general consensus in relevant fields such as information visualization and geographic cartography is that multiple maps are preferable to a single map whenever possible. This is because each map may provide different insights into the same data set. Therefore, we introduce a bibliographic data set of the subject domain that will be utilized to demonstrate several similarity measures, data mining techniques, and visualization approaches. We then present multiple maps and comparisons of the bibliographic data set, focusing on the key issues and components uncovered through this multiperspective approach.

Units of Analysis

The first step in any mapping process is the extraction of appropriate data. We will not deal further with the extraction issue, search strategies, or the like, but simply note that the quality of any mapping or visualization is necessarily constrained by the quality of the underlying data. The number of documents retrieved to generate a domain map can range from several hundred to tens of thousands.

Selection of a unit of analysis, relevant to the questions one desires to answer, is the second step. The most common units in literature mapping are journals, documents, authors, and descriptive terms or words. Each presents different facets of a domain and facilitates different types of analysis. For instance, a map of journals can be used to obtain a macro view of science (Bassecoulard & Zitt, 1999), showing the relative positions and relationships between major disciplines. Journal maps are also used on a much smaller scale (Ding, Chowdhury, & Foo, 2000; Leydesdorff, 1994; McCain, 1998) to show fine distinctions within a discipline.

Documents (articles, patents, and the like) are the most common unit used to map or visualize a knowledge domain. These maps are used for a variety of purposes, including document retrieval, domain analysis (Small, 1999a, 2000), informing policy decisions, assessing research performance (Noyons, 2001; Noyons, Moed, & Luwel, 1999; Noyons, Moed, & van Raan, 1999; Noyons & van Raan, 1998a, 1998b), science and technology management, and competitive intelligence (Boyack, Wylie, & Davidson, 2002).

Author-based maps are also relatively common and occur in two main forms. Author co-citation maps (C. Chen, 1999b; C. M. Chen, Paul, & O'Keefe, 2001; Ding, Chowdhury, & Foo, 1999; Lin & Kaid, 2000; White & McCain, 1998) are typically used to infer the intellectual structure of a field. By contrast, co-authorship maps are used to show the social network of a discipline or community (Mahlck & Persson, 2000). Co-authorship maps have been used by Glänzel and co-workers at the Hungarian Academy of Sciences for a series of studies designed to reveal international collaborations (Glänzel, 2001; Glänzel & DeLange, 1997).

Newman has studied the structure of scientific networks from a statistical point of view (Newman, 2001a, 2001b). His techniques, while not undertaken from a mapping or visualization standpoint, are relevant and scale to very large systems (e.g., 1.5 million authors from Medline).

Semantic maps, often known as co-word analyses, are used to understand the cognitive structure of a field (Bhattacharya & Basu, 1998; Cahlik, 2000; DeLooze & Lemarie, 1997; He, 1999; Salvador & Lopez-Martinez, 2000). These maps are generated from different textual sources including single words extracted from titles of articles, descriptive terms, or publisher-assigned descriptors supplied by a database vendor (e.g., ISI keywords). Earlier maps were made possible by the popularization and use of the Leximappe software (Callon, Courtial, Turner, & Bauin, 1983). However, Leximappe never really reached the U.S., where researchers tended to use standard bibliographic retrieval software (e.g., Dialog searching) to collect co-descriptor or co-classification data. Ron Kostoff at the Office of Naval Research even wrote his own programs for co-word extraction and analysis. Many users today have computational tools (for example, WordStat, available at http://www.simstat.com/wordstat.htm) that allow them to do their own term extraction and mapping. Kostoff and co-workers have developed the Database Tomography technique, which they use to create science and technology roadmaps (Kostoff, Eberhart, & Toothman, 1998). Some confusion can be caused by reference to "semantic space," which most often refers not to co-word maps, but to document maps using words or terms as labeling features.

No compelling reason prevents multiple units (e.g., journals and authors) from being used in the same map, but it is not commonly done. One example of multiple units is the work by White and Griffith (1982), an author co-citation study in which useful phrases were extracted to "self-label" factors.

Measures and Similarity Calculation

Measures

Measures have been defined very succinctly by White and McCain (1997, p. 103), and rather than muddy the waters, we simply choose to quote their work here for completeness:

> We use certain technical terms such as intercitation, inter-document, co-assignment, co-classification, co-citation, and

co-word. The prefix "inter" implies relationships between documents [or units]. The prefix "co" implies joint occurrences within a single document or unit. Thus, intercitation data for journals are counts of the times that any journal cites any other journal, as well as itself, in a matrix. (The citations appear in articles, of course.) The converse is the number of times any journal is cited by any other journal. The same sort of matrix can be formed with authors replacing journals. Interdocument similarity can be measured by counting indicators of content that two different documents have in common, such as descriptors or references to other writings (the latter is known as bibliographic coupling strength).

Co-assignment means the assignment of two indexing terms to the same document by an indexer (the terms themselves might be called co-terms, co-descriptors, or co-classifications). Co-citation occurs when any two works appear in the references of a third work. The authors of the two co-cited works are co-cited authors. If the co-cited works appeared in two different journals, the latter are co-cited journals. Co-words are words that appear together in some piece of natural language, such as a title or abstract. Both "inter" and "co" relationships are explicit and potentially countable by computer. Thus, both might yield raw data for visualization of literatures.

To this we add a few definitions. A "citation" is the referencing of a document by a more recently published document. The document making the citation is the "citing" document, and the one receiving the citation is the "cited" document. Citations may be counted and used as a threshold (e.g., keep only the documents that have been cited more than five times) in a mapping exercise. Other terms used to describe citing and cited numbers are "in-degree," or the number of times cited, and "out-degree," or the number of items in a document's reference list. Journal impact factors calculated from citation counts are published by ISI, and can be used to enhance visualizations, as can the raw citation counts themselves. Nederhof and Zwaan (1991) collected peer judgments on the quality of journals by means of a worldwide survey and probed the quality of the coverage by the *Social Sciences Citation Index* and the

Arts and Humanities Citation Index of both core and noncore journals. Results showed convergence with those based on journal impact factors. An excellent review of bibliometric and other science indicators has been provided by King (1987).

Simple Similarities

Similarity between units is typically based on one of the following:

- Citation linkages—These include direct citation linkage, co-citation linkage,[2] bibliographic coupling (Kessler, 1963), longitudinal coupling (Small, 1995), and Small's combined linkage method (Small, 1997). Citation linkage similarities are naturally constrained to use with data derived from citation databases, such as the *Science Citation Index* or a patent database.

- Co-occurrence similarities—The most common co-occurrence similarities include co-term, co-classification, author co-citation, and paper co-citation. Two of the more common similarity formulas used with co-occurrence are the simple cosine and Jaccard indices. Each counts the number of attributes common between two units (e.g., the number of terms in common between two articles), but they differ in their normalization. H. C. Chen and Lynch (1992) developed an asymmetric cluster function and showed that it better represents term associations than the popular cosine function. Chung and Lee (2001) recently compared six different co-term association measures and discussed their relative behavior on a set of documents. Rorvig (1999) explored multiple similarity measurements on Text REtrieval Conference (TREC) document sets, finding that cosine and overlap measures best preserved relationships between documents. Co-word similarity uses the same types of associations as co-term, but is commonly based on words extracted from the titles and/or abstracts of articles by counting the number of times any two words appear in the same text segment.

Vector Space Model

The Vector Space Model (VSM) was developed by Gerard Salton (Salton, Yang, & Wong, 1975). It is an influential and powerful framework for storing, analyzing, and structuring documents. Originally developed for information retrieval, the model is a widely used framework for indexing documents based on term frequencies. Its three stages are document indexing, term weighting, and computation of similarity coefficients:

1. *Document indexing:* Each document (or query) is represented as a vector in a high-dimensional space. Dimensionality is determined by the number of unique terms in a document corpus. Non-significant words are removed from the document vector. A stop list, which holds common words, is used to remove high frequency words. (In general, 40–50 percent of the total number of words in a document is removed.)

2. *Term weighting:* Terms are weighted to indicate their importance for document representation. Most of the weighting schemes such as the inverse document frequency (see later discussion) assume that the importance of a term is proportional to the number of documents in which the term appears. Long documents usually have much larger term sets than short documents, which makes long documents more likely to be retrieved than short documents. Therefore, document length normalization is employed.

3. *Computation of similarity coefficients:* The similarity between any two documents (or between a query and a document) can subsequently be determined by the distance between vectors in a high-dimensional space. Word overlap indicates similarity. The most popular similarity measure is the cosine coefficient, which defines the similarity between two documents by the cosine of the angle between their two vectors. It resembles the inner product of the two vectors, normalized (divided) by the products of the vector lengths (square root of the sums of squares).

The discriminatory power of a term is determined by the well-known *tf*idf* model, in which *tf* denotes the term frequency and *idf* represents the inverse document frequency. Each document can be represented by an array of terms T and each term is associated with a weight determined by the *tf*idf* model. In general, the weight of term T_k in document D_i is estimated as follows:

$$w_{ik} = \frac{tf_{ik} \times log\left(\dfrac{N}{n_k}\right)}{\sqrt{\displaystyle\sum_{j=1}^{T} \left(tf_{ij}\right)^2 \times log\left(\dfrac{N}{n_j}\right)^2}}$$

where tf_{ik} is the number of occurrences of term T_k in D_i, N is the number of documents in a given collection, and n_k represents the number of documents containing term T_k. The document similarity is computed as follows based on corresponding vectors $D_i = (w_{i1}, w_{i2}, ..., w_{iT})$ and $D_j = (w_{j1}, w_{j2}, ..., w_{jT})$:

$$sim_{ij}^{content} = \sum_{k=1}^{T} w_{ik} \times w_{jk}$$

Document similarity can be used to group a large collection of documents into a number of smaller clusters such that documents within a cluster are more similar than documents in different clusters.

The vector space model provides an easy way to assess document similarities based on word matches. Note that homographs—for example, the bird "crane" and the "crane" on a construction site—cannot be detected. This shortcoming is known as the "vocabulary mismatch problem," the solution of which requires methods that examine the context of words such as latent semantic analysis (LSA) (Deerwester, Dumais, Landauer, Furnas, & Harshman, 1990); lexical chaining, a notion derived from work in the area of textual cohesion in linguistics (Halliday & Hasan, 1976); or the automatic discovery of vocabulary and thesauri (Mostafa, Quiroga, & Palakal, 1998).

Different applications of the vector space model have been presented (Salton, Allan, & Buckley, 1994; Salton, Allan, Buckley, & Singhal, 1994; Salton & Buckley, 1988, 1991; Salton et al., 1975). For a critical analysis of the vector space model for information retrieval, consult Raghavan and Wong (1986).

Enabling Technologies

This section describes enabling techniques with regard to the analysis and visualization of knowledge. In particular, we describe methods that are generally used to create (interactive) visualizations of knowledge domains.

We introduce dimensionality-reduction techniques that can be applied to represent n-dimensional data by a small number of salient dimensions, and, thus, to display multivariate data on the two-dimensional surface of either paper or computer screen. Several of these algorithms produce a 2-D or 3-D spatial layout in which similar objects are close to one another. This process is also called *ordination*. Cluster analysis can be used to further group similar objects together, and to determine category boundaries and labels. Some of the algorithms presented here generate a document-by-document similarity matrix that can be visualized by spatial configuration algorithms. Last but not least, we present the application of interaction and distortion techniques that aim to solve the second information communication problem—displaying large amounts of data in a limited space with limited resolution. For each technique we give a general description, discuss its value for visualizing knowledge domains, and give references to further reading and code, if available. We conclude with a general comparison of different techniques.

Dimensionality Reduction Techniques

Dimensionality reduction is an effective way to derive useful representations of high-dimensional data. This section reviews a range of techniques that have been used for dimensionality reduction, including eigenvalue/eigenvector decomposition, factor analysis (FA), multidimensional scaling (MDS), Pathfinder network scaling (PF), and self-organizing maps (SOMs).[3]

Eigenvalue/Eigenvector Decomposition

Eigenvalue/eigenvector decomposition is a technique that has been widely used in scientific computation. Given an $N \times N$ matrix A, if there exist a vector v and a scalar value l such that $Av = lv$, the vector v is an eigenvector, and the scalar value l is a corresponding eigenvalue. Eigenvalue/eigenvector decomposition is commonly used to reduce the dimensionality of a high-dimensional space while its internal structure is preserved. A related technique is called *singular value decomposition* (SVD), which is used in latent semantic analysis.

Given a collection of points in a high-dimensional space, the eigenvalues of the covariance matrix reveal the underlying dimensionality of the space. Eigenvector analysis techniques encompass Principal Components Analysis and Empirical Orthogonal Functional Analysis. Common problems of these eigenvalue decompositions include the following: the number of eigenvalues required is small relative to the size of the matrices, and the matrix systems are often very sparse or poorly structured.

Sandia's VxInsight has the option of using an eigenvalue solver (Davidson, Hendrickson, Johnson, Meyers, & Wylie, 1998). However, in practice, this solution, while mathematically robust, does not necessarily place dissimilar objects far apart and tends not to produce discrete clusters.

Factor Analysis and Principal Components Analysis

The term "factor analysis" was introduced by Thurstone (1931). Factor analysis is a multivariate exploratory technique that can be used to examine a wide range of data sets. Primary applications of factor analytic techniques are to reduce the number of variables and to detect structure in the relationships between variables or to classify variables. Therefore, factor analysis is applied as a data reduction or structure detection method. Unlike other methods, such as LSA, the factors can often be interpreted.

A key method in factor analysis is Principal Component Analysis (PCA), which can transform a number of (possibly) correlated variables into a (smaller) number of uncorrelated variables called principal components. The first principal component accounts for as much of the variability in the data as possible, and each succeeding component accounts for as much of the remaining variability as possible. An advantage of using factor analysis over traditional clustering techniques is that it does not force each object into a cluster. Objects can be classified into multiple factors, supporting the frequent observation that truly important work is often universal.

There are many excellent books on factor analysis (e.g., Basilevsky, 1994; Gorsuch, 1983; Harman, 1976). PCA has been routinely used by information scientists, especially in author co-citation analysis (C. Chen & Carr, 1999; McCain, 1990, 1995; Raghupathi & Nerur, 1999; White & McCain, 1998). PCA was also employed in Spatial Paradigm for Information Retrieval (SPIRE) (Hetzler, Whitney, Martucci, & Thomas, 1998; Wise, 1999; Wise et al., 1995), using a context vector similar to those constructed in LSA.

Multidimensional Scaling

Multidimensional scaling (MDS) attempts to find the structure in a set of proximity measures between objects (Kruskal, 1977). This is accomplished by solving a minimization problem such that the distances between points in the conceptual low-dimensional space match the given (dis)similarities as closely as possible.

The result is a least-squares representation of the objects in a lower (often two-dimensional) space. The MDS procedure is as follows:

- All objects and their distances are determined.

- A goodness-of-fit measure called "stress" is maximized to produce a scatterplot of the objects in a low-dimensional space.

- The dimensions are interpreted, keeping in mind that the actual orientations of the axes from the MDS analysis are arbitrary, and can be rotated in any direction. In addition, one can look for clusters of points or particular patterns and configurations (such as circles or manifolds).

The real value of MDS is that it can be used to analyze any kind of distance or similarity matrix. These similarities can represent people's ratings of similarities between documents, similarity between objects based on co-citations, and so on. Due to computational requirements, only small data sets can be processed with MDS. Additionally, no relationship data (links) can be displayed. Numerous texts are available for further reading (e.g., Borg & Groenen, 1996; Kruskal, 1964a, 1964b; Kruskal & Wish, 1984). KYST is a flexible Fortran program developed by Kruskal, Young, and Seery for MDS, which is available on the Internet (http://elib.zib.de/netlib/mds/ˆkyst.f., http://elib.zib.de/netlib/mds/kyst2a_manual.txt).

A long-acknowledged major weakness of MDS is that there are no firm rules to interpret the nature of the resulting dimensions. In addition, analysts often need more local details and more explicit representations of structures. An MDS configuration is limited in meeting these needs. The use of the Pathfinder network scaling technique and Pathfinder networks provide users with increased local detail and explicit representations of structures than MDS configurations (see section on "Pathfinder Network Scaling").

MDS has been one of the most widely used mapping techniques in information science, especially for document visualization (Chalmers, 1992), author co-citation analysis (White & McCain, 1998), document analysis (Hetzler et al., 1998), science mapping (Small, 1999b), and visualizing group memories (McQuaid, Ong, Chen, & Nunamaker, 1999 [see http://ai.bpa.arizona.edu/go/viz/mds.html for an online demo]), and performance assessment (Noyons, Moed, & van Raan, 1999) to name just a few.

Recently, nonlinear MDS approaches have been proposed that promise to handle larger data sets. Examples are the global geometric framework for nonlinear dimensionality reduction named Isomap (http://isomap.stanford.edu) proposed in Tenenbaum, de Silva, and Langford (2000) and nonlinear dimensionality reduction by locally linear embedding proposed by Roweis and Saul (2000). Neither technique has yet been applied to the visualization of knowledge domains.

Latent Semantic Analysis

Latent Semantic Analysis, also called Latent Semantic Indexing (LSI), was developed to resolve the so-called vocabulary mismatch problem (Deerwester et al., 1990; Landauer, Foltz, & Laham, 1998). LSA handles *synonymy* (variability in human word choice) and *polysemy* (the same word with different meanings) by considering the context of words. It uses an advanced statistical technique, singular value decomposition (SVD), to extract latent terms. A latent term may correspond to a salient concept that may be described by several keywords, for example, the concept of human-computer interaction. The procedure is as follows:

- Representative samples of documents are converted to a matrix of title/authors/abstract words by articles. Cell entries are word frequencies in the title/authors/abstract of a given document.

- After an information theoretic weighting of cell entries, the matrix is submitted to singular value decomposition.

- SVD constructs an n-dimensional abstract semantic space in which each original word is presented as a vector.

- LSA's representation of a document is the average of the vectors of the words it contains, independent of their order.

Construction of the SVD matrix is computationally expensive. Cases exist in which the matrix size cannot be reduced effectively. Yet, an effective dimensionality reduction helps to minimize noise and automatically organizes documents into a semantic structure more appropriate for information retrieval. This capability is a prime strength of LSA—once the matrix has been calculated, retrieval based on a user's query is highly efficient. Relevant documents are retrieved, even if they did not literally contain the query words. The LSA matrix can also be used to calculate term-by-term or document-by-document similarities for use in other layout routines.

Numerous LSA Web resources are available, including the Telcordia (formerly BellCore) LSI page (http://lsi.research.telcordia.com), and Web sites at the University of Colorado (http://lsa.colorado.edu), and the University of Tennessee (http://www.cs.utk.edu/~lsi). SVDPACKC (http://www.netlib.org/svdpack) (Version 1.0) developed by Michael Berry comprises four numerical (iterative) methods for computing the singular value decomposition of large sparse matrices using double precision ANSI Fortran-77. The General Text Parser (http://www.cs.utk.edu/~lsi/soft.html) (GTP), developed by Howard, Tang, Berry, and Martin at the University of Tennessee, is an object-oriented (C++) integrated software package for creating data structures and encoding needed by information retrieval models.

LSA has been used in Generalized Similarity Analysis (C. Chen, 1997b, 1999b), StarWalker (C. M. Chen & Paul, 2001), and the LVis— Digital Library Visualizer (Börner, 2000a; Börner, Dillon, & Dolinsky, 2000) visualizations, among others. LSA has also been used by Porter and colleagues for technology forecasting (Zhu & Porter, 2002).

Pathfinder Network Scaling

Pathfinder network scaling is a structural and procedural modeling technique, which extracts underlying patterns in proximity data and represents them spatially in a class of networks called Pathfinder networks (PFnets) (Schvaneveldt, 1990). Pathfinder algorithms take estimates of the proximities between pairs of items as input and define a network representation of the items that preserves only the most important links. The resulting Pathfinder network consists of the items as nodes and a set of links (which may be either directed or undirected for symmetrical or nonsymmetrical proximity estimates) connecting pairs of the nodes. Software for Pathfinder network scaling is available for purchase (http://www.geocities.com/ interlink/home.html).

The essential concept underlying Pathfinder networks is pairwise similarity. Similarities can be obtained based on a subjective estimation or a numerical computation. Pathfinder provides a more accurate representation of local relationships than techniques such as MDS. The topology of a PFnet is determined by two parameters q and r and the corresponding network is denoted as PFnet(r,q). The q-parameter constrains the scope of minimum-cost paths to be considered. The r-parameter defines the Minkowski metric used for computing the distance of a path. The weight of a path with k links is determined by weights w_1, w_2, ..., w_k of each individual link as follows:

$$W(P) = \left[\sum_{i=1}^{k} w_i^r \right]^{\frac{1}{r}}$$

The q-parameter specifies that triangle inequalities must be satisfied for paths with $k \leq q$ links:

$$W_{n_i n_k} = \left[\sum_{i=1}^{k-1} W_{n_i n_k}^r \right]^{\frac{1}{r}} \quad \forall \, k \leq q$$

When a PFnet satisfies the following three conditions, the distance of a path is the same as the weight of the path:

1. The distance from a document to itself is zero.

2. The proximity matrix for the documents is symmetric; thus the distance is independent of direction.

3. The triangle inequality is satisfied for all paths with up to q links. If q is set to the total number of nodes less one, then the triangle inequality is universally satisfied over the entire network.

The number of links in a network can be reduced by increasing the value of the r or q parameter. The geodesic distance between two nodes in a network is the length of the minimum-cost path connecting the nodes. A minimum-cost network (MCN), PFnet ($r = \infty$, $q = n$-1), has the least number of links.

AuthorLink and ConceptLink (http://cite.cis.drexel.edu) (developed by Xia Lin and colleagues), enable one to create interactive author co-citation analysis maps based on PFnet or Self Organizing Maps (White, Buzydlowski, & Lin, 2000).

Pathfinder network scaling is used in generalized similarity analysis (GSA), a generic framework for structuring and visualizing distributed information resources (C. Chen, 1997a, 1998a, 1998b, 1999a). The original version of the framework was designed to handle a number of intrinsic interrelationships in hypertext documents; namely hypertext linkage, content similarity, and browsing patterns. GSA uses the notion of virtual link structures to organize its structural modeling and visualization functionality. Virtual link structures are, in turn, determined by similarity measurements defined between a variety of entity types; for example, document-to-document similarity, author-to-author similarity, and image-to-image similarity. Not only can one extend similarity measurements to new entity–entity relationships, but one can also integrate different similarity measurements to form a new network of entities. For example, interrelationships between hypertext documents can be defined based on a combination of hypertext connectivity, word-occurrence-based similarity, and traversal-based similarity. The generic framework of GSA led to several subsequent extensions to deal with a diverse range of data, including co-citation networks and image networks.

The use of Pathfinder networks in GSA reduces the excessive number of links in a typical proximity network and therefore improves the clarity of the graphical representations of such networks. The extensibility and flexibility of Pathfinder networks have been demonstrated in a series of studies along with a range of other techniques. Some recent examples include StarWalker for social navigation (C. Chen, Thomas, Cole, & Chennawasin, 1999), trailblazing the literature of hypertext (C. Chen & Carr, 1999), author co-citation analysis (C. Chen, 1999b), and visualizations of knowledge domains (C. M. Chen & Paul, 2001).

Self-Organizing Maps

One of the most profound contributions made by artificial neural networks to information visualization is the paradigm of self-organizing maps (SOMs) developed by Kohonen (Kaski, Honkela, Lagus, & Kohonen, 1998; Kohonen, 1985; Kohonen et al., 2000). During the learning phase, a self-organizing map algorithm iteratively modifies weight vectors to produce a typically two-dimensional map in the output layer that will exhibit as effectively as possible the relationship of the input layer.

SOMs appear to be among the most promising algorithms for organizing large volumes of information. However, they have some significant deficiencies, many of which are discussed by Kohonen (1995). These deficiencies comprise the absence of a cost function, and the lack of a theoretical basis for choosing learning rate parameter schedules and neighborhood parameters to ensure topographic ordering. No general proofs of convergence are available, and the model does not define a probability density. A self-organizing map program is available from the Kohonen Neural Networks Research Centre, Helsinki University of Technology (http://www.cis.hut.fi/research/som_pak).

SOM maps have been used to map millions of documents from over 80 Usenet newsgroups (http://websom.hut.fi/websom) and to map the World Wide Web. Xia Lin was the first to adopt the Kohonen SOM for information visualization (Lin, 1997; Lin, Soergel, & Marchionini, 1991) to document spaces. His Visual SiteMaps (http://faculty.cis.drexel.edu/sitemap) visualized clusters of important concepts drawn from a database.

ET-Maps were developed in 1995 by Hsinchun Chen and his colleagues in the Artificial Intelligence (AI) Lab at the University of Arizona (http://ai.bpa.arizona.edu). They constitute a scalable, multilayered, graphical SOM approach to automatic categorization of large numbers of documents or Web sites (C. Chen & Rada, 1996; H. Chen, Schuffels, & Orwig, 1996). The prototype was developed using the Yahoo! Entertainment subcategory (about 110,000 home pages); hence, the name ET-Map.

ET-Maps are category maps that group documents that share many noun phrase terms together in a neighborhood on a 2-D map. Each colored region represents a unique topic that contains similar documents. The size of a subject region is related to the number of documents in that category such that more important topics (if importance can be correlated with counts) occupy larger regions. Neighborhood proximity is applied to plot "subject regions" that are closely related in terms of content, close to each other on the map. ET-Maps show an "up-button" view of an information space to provide the user with a sense of the organization of the information landscape; for example, what is where, the location of clusters and hotspots, and what is related to what. ET-Maps are multilayer maps, with submaps showing greater informational resolution through a finer degree of categorization.

Focus+context techniques have been used to display a large SOM effectively within a limited screen area (Yang, Chen, & Hong, 1999). Usability studies indicate that users tend to get lost when browsing multi-level SOM maps and prefer to use a conventional text-based alphabetic hierarchy (H. Chen, Houston, Sewell, & Schatz, 1998). Today, ET-Maps come with two panels. The left panel is a Windows Explorer-like interface that presents an alphabetic display of the topic hierarchy generated, and the right panel is the graphical display of the SOM output. On the left panel, a user can click on any category of interest and the system displays its subcategories beneath. At the same time, those subcategories are also displayed on the right panel, where the spatial proximity equals the semantic proximity. In addition, colors are employed to indicate how many layers a user can go down within a certain category. A working demo of ET-Maps can be explored at the AI Lab's Web site (http://ai3.bpa.arizona.edu/ent/entertain1). ET-Maps and Cartographic SOM Maps are discussed further and exemplified later in this chapter.

Multi-SOMs are a multimap extension of SOMs. Polanco, Francois, and Lamirel (2001) introduce an automatic way of naming the clusters to divide the map into logical areas, and a map generalization mechanism. They also discuss the application potential of multi-SOMs for visualization, exploration or browsing, and scientific and technical information analysis.

Cluster Analysis

The term "cluster analysis" (CA) was first used by Tryon (1939). Cluster analysis encompasses a number of different classification algorithms that aim to organize a "mountain" of information into manageable, meaningful piles, called clusters.

A clustering problem can be defined by a set of objects (e.g., documents) and a vague description of a set, A. The goal of clustering is to divide the object set into objects belonging to A and a second set not in A. In this clustering problem, one needs first to determine what features are relevant in describing objects in A (intra-cluster similarity) and second, what features distinguish objects in A from objects not belonging to A (inter-cluster similarity).

Alternatively, a cluster problem can be formulated by a set of objects and a similarity or distance function. Here, the goal is to divide the object set into a number of subsets (clusters) that best reveal the structure of the object set. These subdivisions can take the form of partitions or a hierarchically organized taxonomy.

Clusters should be highly internally homogenous (members are similar to one another) and highly externally heterogeneous (members are not like members of other clusters). Thus, the aim is to maximize intra-cluster similarity and minimize inter-cluster similarity. This outcome can be formulated in terms of a *utility measure* that contrasts the sum of within-cluster similarities (*wSim*) with the sum of between-cluster similarities (*bSim*):

$$utility = wSim / (wSim + bSim).$$

Given alternative partitions, the one that shows the highest utility is selected.

Clustering algorithms can be distinguished based on a number of features such as: unsupervised or supervised; divisive or agglomerative; incremental or nonincremental; deterministic or nondeterministic; hierarchical or partitioning; iterative or noniterative; single link, grouped average, or complete link clustering. Interestingly, no clustering algorithm has been shown to be notably better than others when producing the same number of clusters (Hearst, 1999). However, experience demonstrates that some choices seem to fit some kinds of data better than others (e.g., correlation and complete linkage work very well for our sample data set, as described later in this chapter) and there have been "bakeoffs" between clustering approaches (comparing single link, complete link, Ward's trace, centroid, and so forth) that suggest that some approaches are more reliable than others for generic data sets. An excellent review of clustering algorithms can be found in Han and Kamber (2000).

In information visualization, clustering techniques are frequently applied to group semantically similar objects so that object set boundaries can be presented. The automatic assignment of cluster labels is yet another topic of high relevance for IV. For example, work by Pirolli, Schank, Hearst, and Diehl (1996) automatically computes summaries of the contents of clusters of similar documents, providing a method for navigating through these summaries at different levels of granularity.

Spatial Configuration

Attributes of a data set can often be cast in the form of a similarity or distance matrix. Ordination techniques such as triangulation or force-directed placement take a set of documents, their similarities/distances and parameters, and generate a typically two-dimensional layout that places similar documents closer together and dissimilar ones farther apart.

Triangulation

Triangulation is an ordination technique that maps points from an n-dimensional space into a typically two-dimensional one (Lee, Slagle, & Blum, 1977). It starts by placing a randomly selected node at the origin of the coordinate system. Next, the most similar node is determined and the second node is placed at a specified distance from the first. The location of the third node is determined by its distance from the previous two (triangulation). Subsequently, the notion of repulsion from the origin is used to select the quadratic solution placing each node in turn farthest from the origin, and the spatial layout grows outward.

Compared to classical ordination methods, triangulation is computationally inexpensive. The resulting layouts exactly represent the distances between single data points, but lack global optimization. Henry Small (1999b) employed triangulation in the context of information visualization. His *Map of Science* is a series of nested maps showing the multi-dimensional landscape of science at five levels of aggregation.

Force Directed Placement

Force Directed Placement (FDP) can be used to sort randomly placed objects into a desirable layout that satisfies the given similarity relations among objects as well as aesthetics for visual presentation (symmetry, nonoverlapping, minimized edge crossings, and so on) (Battista, Eades, Tamassia, & Tollis, 1994; Fruchterman & Reingold, 1991). FDP views nodes as physical bodies and edges as springs (or weighted arcs) connected to the nodes and providing forces between them. Nodes move according to the forces on them until a local energy minimum is achieved. In addition to the imaginary springs, other forces can be added to the system in order to produce different effects. Many visual examples of these force models can be found in Battista et al. (1994).

The FDP method is easy to understand and implement. However, it can be very slow for large graphs, since the forces between all nodes have to be computed and considered in each iteration step. Modifications to a traditional force-directed approach have been made in the VxInsight ordination algorithm VxOrd, (Davidson, Wylie, & Boyack, 2001), and have resulted in a dramatic increase in computational speed. VxOrd accepts pairwise scalar similarity values as the arc weights, employs barrier jumping to avoid trapping of clusters in local minima, and uses a density grid in place of pairwise repulsive forces to speed up execution. Computation times are thus on the order of $O(N)$ rather than $O(N^2)$. Another advantage of the VxOrd algorithm is that it determines the number and size of clusters automatically, based on the data. Plus, rather than placing objects in discrete (round) clusters, VxOrd often gives elongated or continuous structures (which look like ridges in a landscape visualization) that bridge multiple fields. The VxOrd FDP does not accommodate a continuous stream of updated data, as do some other FDPs.

Semantic tree maps, recently proposed by Feng and Börner (2002), are another option for applying FDP to handle large data sets. Semantic tree maps apply clustering techniques to organize documents into clusters of semantically similar documents. The tree map approach (Shneiderman, 1992) has also been used to determine the size (dependent on the number of documents) and layout of clusters. Finally, FDP is applied to the documents in each cluster to place them based on their semantic similarity. By breaking the data set into smaller chunks, the computational complexity of FDP is reduced, although at the cost of global optimality.

HyperSpace, formerly Narcissus, used FDP to visualize hyperlinks among Web pages (Hendley, Drew, Wood, & Beale, 1995). FDP has been used on small data sets by Börner (Börner, 2000a; Börner et al., 2000). Much larger literature (Boyack, Wylie, & Davidson, 2002), patent (Boyack, Wylie, Davidson, & Johnson, 2000), and even genomic (Kim et al., 2001) data sets have been clustered using the VxOrd FDP.

Visualization and Interaction Design

Given data objects and their spatial positions, visualizations that can be intuitively understood and effectively and accurately explored by a human user need to be designed. However, nobody should expect to understand a complex visualization in a few seconds. "The first response should be content related, not layout" (Tufte, quoted by Isdale, 1998, online).

Different frameworks and taxonomies to characterize information visualization techniques have been proposed. Most commonly used is Shneiderman's (1996, online) framework characterizing IV in terms of data types and user tasks to "sort out the prototypes [that currently exist] and guide researchers to new opportunities." The framework defines:

- Data types comprising linear, planar, volumetric, temporal, multi-dimensional, tree, network, and workspace (added in his textbook [Shneiderman, 1997])

- A typology of tasks such as overview, zoom, filter, details-on-demand, relate, history, and extract

- Visualizations resemble landscapes, circle plots, term plots, spot-fires, starfields, and so on

- Necessary features comprise interaction, navigation, detail on demand, and so on

We now move on to review visualization as well as interaction design techniques and approaches.

Visualization

Visualization refers to the design of the visual appearance of data objects and their relationships. Well-designed domain visualizations offer the following:

- An ability to comprehend huge amounts of data on a large scale as well as a small scale

- A reduction in visual search time (e.g., by exploiting low-level visual perception)

- A better understanding of a complex data set (e.g., by exploiting data landscape metaphors)

- Illumination of relationships otherwise not noticed (e.g., by exploiting perception of emergent properties)

- A data set that can be seen from several perspectives simultaneously

• Facilitation of hypothesis formulation

• Effective sources of communication

Information visualization—the process of analyzing and transforming nonspatial data into an effective visual form—is believed to improve our interaction with large volumes of data (Card et al., 1999; C. Chen, 1999a; Gershon, Eick, & Card, 1998; Spence, 2000, 2001). One key element of any successful visualization is effective exploitation of visual perception principles. Books by Ware (2000) and Palmer (1999) provide excellent introductions to the subject. Visualizations help an increasingly diverse and potentially nontechnical community to gain overviews of general patterns and trends and to discover hidden (semantic) structures. In addition, complex visualizations of different viewpoints of thousands of data objects can greatly benefit from storytelling (Gershon & Ward, 2001). Storytelling and sharing are powerful human strategies to teach effectively, to stimulate critical and creative thinking, and to increase awareness and understanding. Last but not least, the design and presentation of meaningful visualization are arts that require years of expertise and diverse skills. Discussion of the visual perception, storytelling, and artistic aspects of visualization design are beyond the scope of this chapter, however.

Interaction Design

Interaction design refers to the implementation of techniques such as filtering, panning, zooming, and distortion to efficiently search and browse large information spaces.

Ben Shneiderman (1996, p. 336) at the University of Maryland proposed a mantra to characterize how users interact with the visualization of a large amount of information: Overview, Zoom-in (Filter), and Details-on-Demand. Users would start from an overview of the information space and zoom in to the part that seemed to be of interest, then call for more details, and so on. The term "drill down" is also used to refer to processes equivalent to the "zoom in" part of the mantra. As for where to zoom in, theories such as optimal information foraging (Pirolli & Card, 1999) may be a promising route to pursue.

To issue meaningful queries, or to exploit labeling of maps, users need a working knowledge of the subject domain vocabulary. Given the imprecise nature of human language, users frequently encounter the vocabulary mismatch problem (H. Chen et al., 1998; Deerwester et al., 1990).

Although domain maps might provide searching facilities, for example by highlighting documents matching a query, one of their main purposes is to support browsing—the exploration of an information space in order to become familiar with it and to locate information of interest. "Browsing explores both the organization or structure of the information space *and* its content" (H. Chen et al., 1998, p. 583). It requires a working understanding of the applied knowledge organization (typically alphabetical, categorical, or hierarchical) and how to navigate in it. To ease navigation, numerous (real-world) visualization metaphors have been proposed and applied to help improve the understanding of abstract data spaces. Among them are 2-D "cartographic maps," 2-D/3-D "category maps," "desktop," and 3-D "landscape" or "star field" visualizations.

Paul Dourish and Matthew Chalmers (1994) identified three major navigation paradigms: spatial navigation—mimicking our experiences in the physical world; semantic navigation—driven by semantic relationships or underlying logic; and social navigation—taking advantage of the behavior of like-minded people. Ideally information visualization facilitates and supports all three.

Focus+Context

The desire to examine large information spaces on small displays with limited resolution leads to the development of different focus and context techniques that enable users to examine local details without losing the global structure. Distortion-based techniques keep a steady overview. They enlarge some objects while simultaneously shrinking others. Ideally, the total amount of information displayed can be set flexibly and is constant even when users change the focus of their attention over several magnitudes.

Hyperbolic trees, developed at Xerox PARC, were among the very first focus and context techniques (Lamping, Rao, & Pirolli, 1995). Based on Poincaré's model of the (hyperbolic) non-Euclidean plane, the technique assigns more display space to a portion of the hierarchy while still embedding it in the context of the entire hierarchy. A 3-D hyperbolic viewer was developed by Munzner (1997, 1998).

Hyperbolic trees are valuable for visualizing hierarchical structures such as file directories, Web sites, classification hierarchies, organization hierarchies, and newsgroup structures. Traditional methods such as paging (dividing data into several pages and displaying one page at a time), zooming, or panning show only part of the information at a certain granularity, but hyperbolic trees show detail and context at once. Although hyperbolic trees have not been used to visualize knowledge domains, they are commonly used with patent trees and might be well suited to visualization of other hierarchical data.

Fisheye views, developed by Furnas (1986), show a distorted view of a data set in an attempt to reveal local detail while maintaining global context. They mimic the effect of a wide-range fisheye camera that shows the entire scene, but has higher magnification in the center of focus and shrinks objects in relation to their distance from that point.

Two transformation options can be applied to the fisheye view: Cartesian and polar. For Cartesian transformations, all the regions are rectangular; polar transformation regions can be arbitrarily shaped. The technique was improved by Sarkar and Brown (1994) with respect to layout considerations. Fisheye views have also been applied to improve ET-maps (Yang et al., 1999).

Fractal views, based on Mandelbrot's (1988) fractal theory, were first applied to the design of information displays by Koike (1993). They can abstract displayed objects and control the amount of information displayed based on semantic relevance by removing less important information automatically.[4] The fractal dimension, a measure of complexity, is used to control the total number of displayed nodes. Fractal views have been applied to visualize huge hierarchies (Koike & Yoshihara, 1993) and to control the amount of information displayed in ET-Maps (Yang et al., 1999).

Semantic zoom was also introduced by Furnas, and provides multiple levels of resolution. The view changes depending on the "distance" the viewer is from the object. Semantic zoom was implemented in the MuSE multiscale editor (Furnas & Zhang, 1998). It was also used in the Galaxy of News system that visualizes large quantities of independently authored pieces of information, such as news stories (Rennison, 1994).

Zoomable user interfaces, also called ZUIs, incorporate zooming as a fundamental aspect of their design. They place documents at absolute positions within a large zoomable space. Combined with animated navigation, this helps to give users a sense of structure and a sense of where they are within a large information space.

Pad++ is an environment for exploring zooming techniques for interfaces (Bederson et al., 1996). Jazz is a Java 2 toolkit (http://www.cs.umd.edu/hcil/jazz) developed by Bederson and his colleagues at the University of Maryland. It supports the development of 2-D structured graphics programs in general, and ZUIs in particular.

Discussion

Table 5.1 provides an overview of the main features of dimensionality reduction and ordination techniques. Among the features are scalability, computational cost,[5] interpretability of dimensions, dynamic or static layout, and the scale (global or local) to which it can optimally be applied.

One exception to Table 5.1 is noted here. Although VxOrd is classified as an FDP algorithm, it does not act like FDPs as characterized in the table. Rather, it can scale to very large data sets (millions of similarity pairs, limited only by memory constraints), has very fast run times, and provides a static layout. Some ordination techniques have a very high computational complexity for large data sets. This complexity can be reduced at the cost of global optimality by breaking the data set into smaller chunks, ordinating each cluster, and compiling all clusters into a single map.

Incrementally updated visualizations of domains based on incremental data updates, or perhaps continually updated visualizations based on

Table 5.1 Comparison of techniques.

Technique	Scalability	Computation costs	Interpret. of dim.	Layout	Optimality scale
Eigenvalue	high	high	often	static	global
FA/PCA	limited	medium	often	static	global
MDS	limited	medium	often	static	global
LSA	high	high	no		global
PFnet	medium	medium	no	static	Local or global - depends on parameter setting
SOM	high	high	no	static	global
Triangulation					
FDP	limited	high	--	dynamic	local

sequential streaming of previously extracted data, are highly desirable for domain analysis (see the section on "Promising Avenues of Research"). However, few current techniques (only some FDPs) can accommodate this type of data.

The *ARIST* Data Set

Data Retrieval

To demonstrate the literature mapping process and to show the different measurements, layout routines, and visualization metaphors that may be used to visualize a knowledge domain in action, we have developed a data set—the so-called *ARIST* data set—congruent with the subject of this chapter.

First, data were retrieved from the *Science Citation Index (SCI)* and *Social Sciences Citation Index (SSCI)* by querying the titles, abstracts, and terms (ISI keywords and keywords plus) fields for the years 1977–July 27, 2001. Query terms and the number of records retrieved for each query are shown in Table 5.2.

Table 5.2 Search terms used to generate the *ARIST* bibliographic data set. Search terms included terms relevant to *citation analysis, semantics, bibliometrics*, and *visualization* to allow overlaps between those terms and fields to be shown. These four fields will be referred to extensively in the domain analyses that follow. Of the 2,764 unique articles retrieved, 287 were retrieved by more than one of the query terms.

SEARCH TERM	Number
Topic Citation Analysis:	
citation analysis	596
cocitation OR co-citation	177
co-occurrence AND (term OR word)	77
co-term OR co-word	52
science map[ping] OR mapping science OR map[ping] of science	32
Topic Semantics:	
semantic analysis OR semantic index OR semantic map	331
Topic Bibliometrics:	
bibliometric	818
scientometric	327
Topic Visualization:	
data visualization OR visualization of data	275
information visualization OR visualization of information	113
scientific visualization	268

Coverage

It is extremely important to choose an appropriate data source for retrieval, one whose data are likely to provide answers to the questions one wishes to explore using domain visualization. As an example, we discuss some limitations associated with the data for our *ARIST* data set. Numbers of articles retrieved by year are shown in Figure 5.2 for two categories: articles with terms (ISI keywords) and articles without terms. As is well known, ISI's databases did not include either abstracts or terms prior to 1991. Thus, any maps based on either abstracts or terms will naturally exclude articles prior to 1991. In addition, as shown in Figure 5.2, terms are available for only 71 percent of the articles published since 1991. (The lack of terms may be due, for instance, to the journals not requiring index terms from the authors, journals not supplying the terms to the database vendor, or the database vendor choosing not to index an article.) This makes the use of terms a less-than-optimal basis for mapping of these data. By contrast, abstracts are available for 84 percent of the post-1991 *ARIST* data set, making this a richer source of information. The percentages listed here apply

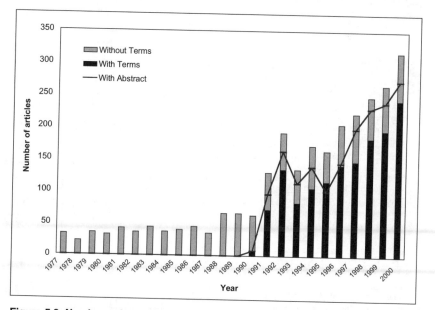

Figure 5.2 Numbers of articles in the *ARIST* data set by year with terms (ISI keywords) of abstracts.

only to this data set; we do not know the overall percentages of ISI records containing abstracts or terms.

Book, journal, and/or conference coverage can also be an issue. For instance, the *Journal of the American Society for Information Science and Technology (JASIST)*, *Scientometrics*, *Journal of Information Science*, *Information Processing & Management*, and the *Journal of Documentation* are key sources for visualization of science or knowledge domains (see Table 5.3), yet the *Science Citation Index (SCI)* did not include these journals until the 1990s. Queries to the *SCI* alone would not have provided sufficient coverage of the intended fields for this time period due to the absence of key journals. Thus, we queried the *SSCI* as well, which covered those journals over the entire time period under investigation. Users of ISI's Web of Science can conduct a search across the combined *SCI, SSCI,* and *AHCI* databases.

Table 5.3 Number of articles by journal in the *ARIST* set (for journals contributing 10 or more articles).

Journal	Categories	# Papers
Scientometrics	ILS, CS	482
JASIS(T)	ILS, CS	139
Journal of Information Science	ILS, CS	51
Information Processing & Management	ILS, CS	45
Lecture Notes in Computer Science	CS	39
Research Policy	Other	32
Journal of Documentation	ILS, CS	31
Current Contents	Other	30
Computers & Graphics	CS	27
IEEE Transactions on Visualization and Computer Graphics	CS	25
Bulletin of the Medical Library Association	ILS	25
IEEE Computer Graphics and Applications	CS	20
Medicina Clinica	Other	20
Library & Information Science Research	ILS	19
Social Studies of Science	Other	18
Computer	CS	16
Computer Graphics Forum	CS	16
Libri	ILS	16
Lecture Notes in Artificial Intelligence	CS	15
Future Generation Computer Systems	CS	15
International Forum on Information and Documentation	ILS	15
Landscape and Urban Planning	Other	14
Proceedings of the ASIS Annual Meeting	ILS, CS	14
Nachrichten für Dokumentation	ILS	14
Library Trends	ILS	13
Library Quarterly	ILS	12
Science Technology & Human Values	Other	12
Scientist	ILS	12
Library and Information Science	ILS	12
Omega-International Journal of Management Science	Other	11
Computers & Geosciences	CS	10
Zentralblatt für Bibliothekswesen	ILS	10

Table 5.3 also shows that the data were dominated by journals jointly classified in the "Information & Library Science" and "Computer Science" (CS) categories. Journals classified as "Other" in Table 5.3 come from a variety of categories, and this suggests that the fields covered by our original queries are accessed by many other disciplines.

For completeness, we include a distribution of the number of articles per field per year, along with average citation counts, for the *ARIST* data set (see Figure 5.3). These additional data show the dramatic increase in work on citation analysis and bibliometrics starting in the late 1980s, and the birth of the visualization field around the same time. It also shows that citation analysis articles were more highly cited than bibliometrics articles in the 1970s and 1980s, and that citation counts for all four fields have generally dropped throughout the 1990s. The most recent articles have, of course, been cited infrequently due to their youthfulness.

Data coverage issues also raise other questions such as the following:

- Does lack of appropriate coverage cause significant distortions of domain visualizations?

- If so, to what extent are the levels of quality of the final domain visualization and the analysis results undermined?

- Can methods to compensate for missing data be obtained?

We have no ready answers to these questions, but suggest that they are important topics for discussion and further research.

The Structure of the Subject Domain

As described earlier, there are many mapping techniques that can be applied to the same data to produce images of a domain from different perspectives. This allows us to stitch different pictures together to create a larger one, which will reveal more insights about a domain than reliance on a single technique. Multiple tools enhance the utility of domain visualization.

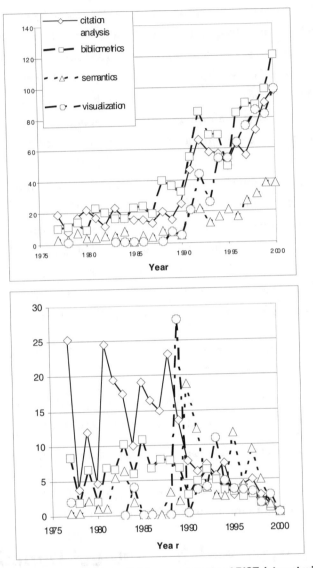

Figure 5.3 Numbers of articles by field per year in the *ARIST* data set with average citation counts.

Multiple Maps of the Domain

The overall organization of the field of domain visualization (the subject of the *ARIST* data set) takes advantage of several emerging techniques. These techniques make it possible not only to decompose the domain according to a range of quantitative measures, but also to compare and contrast different pictures of the same domain. For example, in GSA and StarWalker, the use of factor analysis allows us to break down a domain network into components. A long-recognized advantage of factor analysis over traditional clustering techniques is that factor analysis does not force us to classify an object into only one cluster; instead, it allows multiple classifications for an object. As stated earlier, this helps to support the frequent observation that truly important work is often universal. In SOM, the overall structure is depicted in forms of adjacent regions. Therefore, matches and mismatches between various versions of the domain maps will provide insights. VxInsight uses a landscape metaphor and portrays the structure of a literature space as mountain ridges of document clusters. The size of a cluster and its relative position in the layout provide valuable clues to the role of the cluster in the overall structure. Many different snapshots of the *ARIST* domain are explained in the remainder of this section.

ARIST-GSA/StarWalker

We generated an author co-citation analysis (ACA) map and a document co-citation analysis (DCA) map based on the *ARIST* data set using the four-step procedure described in C. M. Chen and Paul (2001).

Data Preparation

First, we selected authors whose work had received citations above a determined threshold for the author co-citation visualization. This selection was on the first-author-only basis due to the easy availability of the information.[6] Documents were selected similarly for the document co-citation visualization. The threshold parameter can be increased or decreased to control the number of authors or documents to be analyzed. Conventionally, the author citation threshold is set at 10. The intellectual groupings of these authors provide snapshots of the underlying knowledge domain. We computed the co-citation frequencies for these authors from ISI's *SCI* and *SSCI* databases. ACA uses a matrix of co-citation frequencies to compute a correlation matrix of Pearson correlation coefficients. Some researchers believe that such correlation coefficients best capture an author's citation profile.

Author Co-Citation Analysis

Second, we applied Pathfinder network scaling to the network that the correlation matrix defined. Although factor analysis is a standard practice in traditional author co-citation analysis, MDS and factor analysis rarely appear in the same graphical representations. We then overlaid the intellectual groupings that factor analysis identified with the interconnectivity structure of a Pathfinder network. Authors with similar shades/colors essentially belong to the same specialty and should appear as a closely connected group in the network. Therefore, we can expect to see the two perspectives converge in the visualization.

Finally, we displayed the citation impact of each author atop the intellectual groupings. The height of a citation bar—which consists of a stack of shade/color-coded annual citation sections—represents the magnitude of the impact. Sample author co-citation analysis maps are displayed in Figures 5.4 and 5.5.

Figure 5.4 An overview of the author co-citation map (1977–2001), consisting of 380 authors with nine or more citations. The map is dominated by the largest specialty of citation indexing. No strong concentration of other specialties is found, which indicates the diversity of the domain.

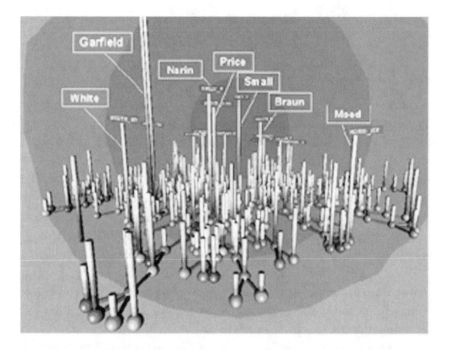

Figure 5.5 A landscape view of the ACA map displayed in Figure 5.4. The height of a bar indicates the number of citations to the author. Lighter shading indicates more recent citations. Authors with more than 50 citations are displayed with semi-transparent labels.

The factor analysis identified 10 factors whose eigenvalues were greater than one. These factors explain 90 percent of variance in the data. Each factor corresponds to a specialty in domain visualization. The three largest factors cumulatively explain 63 percent of variance. The next four specialties can be identified in the map, although the Pathfinder structure and the overlay factor analysis color scheme did not converge in this case—a sign of a heterogeneous subject domain:

- Mapping science: fundamentals

- Social studies of science

- Bibliometrics: quantitative analysis and evaluation

- Scholarly communication and co-citation analysis

The top three specialties correspond to shade/color-coded factors in the map: mapping science in light gray (red in the color version available online), social studies of science in dark gray (green), and bibliometrics in black (blue). Remaining specialties are likely to be a combination of all the colors, and readers can cross-reference between factor analysis results and the map.

The resultant author co-citation map contains 380 authors who have nine or more citations over the entire period between 1977 and 2001. Pathfinder network scaling limited the number of "salient" connections among these authors to 384. As usual, each author's node is shaded/colored by the factor loadings in the three largest specialties. An author co-citation map of a focused, coherent subject domain should demonstrate a considerable degree of conformance between the Pathfinder network structure and the factor analysis shading color patterns. However, this is not the case here, suggesting that science mapping constitutes a number of largely independent disciplines: as Leydesdorff and Wouters (1999) say of scientometrics, it is pre-paradigmatic.

It is interesting to note that none of the four largest factors is centered in either visualization or semantics, which were two of the four groups comprising the *ARIST* data set. These two fields are relatively new and are not highly cited (see Figure 5.3). Thus, they are unlikely to be strong factors in an ACA-type analysis.

Document Co-Citation Analysis

Given the flexibility of GSA, we also generated a document co-citation map based on the top-sliced set of documents (see Figures 5.6 and 5.7). As expected, as many as 15 factors generate eigenvalues greater than one. These 15 factors cumulatively explain 90 percent of variance in the *ARIST* data. The four largest factors explain 56 percent.

As with the author co-citation maps, the top three specialties in document co-citation maps also correspond to color-coded factors in the map: mapping science in light gray (red), social studies of science in dark gray (green), and bibliometrics in black (blue). Remaining specialties are likely to be a combination of all the shades/colors, and readers can cross-reference between factor analysis results and the map.

In this network, a number of tight clusters are connected to an artery-like chain. Documents on the artery chain tend to be seminal works in

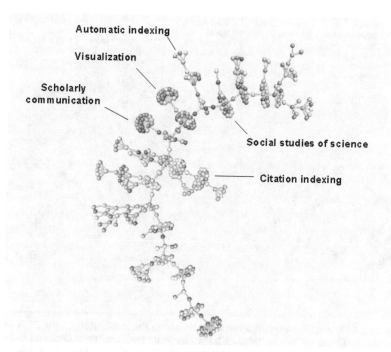

Figure 5.6 **An overview of the document co-citation map of 394 articles with 10 or more citations.**

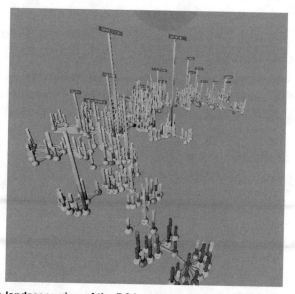

Figure 5.7 **A landscape view of the DCA map displayed in Figure 5.6 at a distance.**

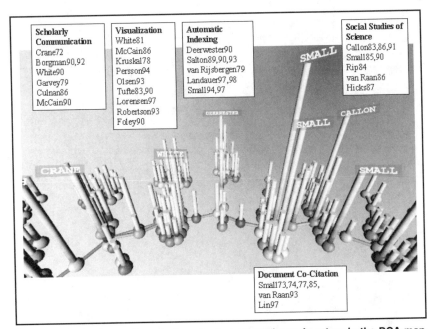

Figure 5.8 A close-up view of a few clusters along the main artery in the DCA map (Figure 5.6). The height a bar represents the number of citations to a publication. Labels indicate articles in a cluster, for example Small73 for an article by Henry Small published in 1973. Multiple publications in the same year are not distinguished at this level, so Small73 includes all his publications in that year.

connected clusters. Diana Crane's (1972) *Invisible Colleges: Diffusion of Knowledge in Scientific Communities* in the scholarly communication cluster is an example of an "outer node," a document that was not included in the original dataset. Because it has been cited by documents in our dataset, her book found its way into our document co-citation map.

ARIST-*ET-Map*

Bin Zhu and Hsinchun Chen of the University of Arizona visualized the *ARIST* data set using ET-Maps. They trained 10*10 nodes using the ID/keyword data. At the end of the map creation process, each node is associated with a list of documents that are semantically similar to each other. In addition, a phrase is assigned to each node as its label, and adjacent nodes with the same labels are grouped into one region or category. Thus, spatial proximity on the map indicates semantic proximity,

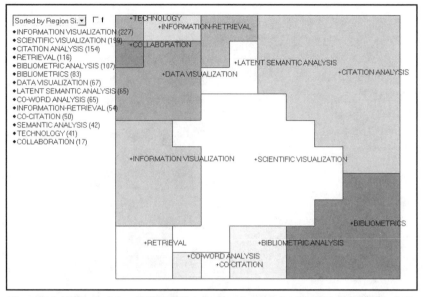

Figure 5.9 ET-Map of the *ARIST* data set using keywords. On the left is a list of all categories. A user can select a category of interest and the interface will display documents in that category.

meaning that if two categories are close together on the SOM map, they are also semantically similar to each other.

A screenshot of the resulting ET-Map utilizing different visual encasings is shown in Figure 5.9. The top-level map shows 14 subject regions represented by regularly shaped tiles. Each tile is a visual summary of a group of documents with similar keywords. The tiles are shaded to differentiate them and labels identify the subject of the tiles. The subjects are also listed on the left-hand side, together with a number in brackets indicating how many individual documents each category contains. In a typical browsing session, a user will first see an overview, then zoom in on areas of interest, and finally access a particular document. Alternatively, a user can select a category of interest and the interface will display documents within that category.

Note that subject area *citation analysis* appears to be much larger than *information visualization* even though the former has fewer documents. The size of the subject area is not necessarily related to the number of documents in an ET-map, but rather denotes the amount of space

Figure 5.10 Cartographic SOM map of *ARIST* data set.

between areas based on the number of nodes used to generate the map (see Figure 5.14b).

ARIST-Cartographic-SOM Maps

André Skupin, a geographer at the University of New Orleans, uses SOMs to generate domain visualizations in a cartographic fashion (Skupin, 2000; Skupin & Buttenfield, 1996). He used SOM_PAK to train a SOM based on the ID/keyword list of the *ARIST* data set and ArcGIS, to generate the visualization. Labeling of clusters was done automatically within ArcGIS based on rules that were given to it regarding the links between attributes and label characteristics.

The map shown in Figure 5.10 aims to facilitate the use of the same skills traditionally associated with geographic maps. The underlying SOM consists of 2,200 neurons (i.e., 40 × 55 nodes).[7] A hierarchical clustering tree was computed for these neurons in order to allow scale-dependent exploration of the data set in a zoomable interface. In this particular visualization, only the 25-cluster solution is shown.

For each cluster, three label terms were computed, to better convey cluster content. Because the clusters were computed from the SOM itself, these labels indicate the potential topic or theme that one would expect to find in articles assigned to a particular cluster. In order to show the relative prominence of topics in the data set, the clusters were ranked by the number of articles assigned to their data sets. Clusters containing more articles appear larger and more prominent.

The terrain visualization expresses the degree to which the three highest-ranked components of each neuron dominate the neuron's n-dimensional term vector, which allows some judgment regarding the relative merits of the clustering solution that is overlaid. Higher elevation (percentage) indicates a very organized, focused, and coherent portion of the information space. These areas tend to be recognized and preserved by the cluster routine, which shows up nicely in this map. At the other extreme, low-lying areas occur, especially at the bottom right of the map. This area indicates a lack of strong organization, an absence of distinct themes that would be recognized by the clustering routine but does not necessarily imply a lack of "meaning" to this area. Rather, clusters containing it should be interpreted more cautiously. In this case, the main reason for the lack of organization is that most of the articles with one or two keywords are congregated here. In the 25-cluster solution, this area is contained in a cluster whose labels ("Volume-Rendering"—"Information-Retrieval"—"Impact") indicate a lack of coherence. Labels for this cluster are scaled correctly but are de-emphasized by using a lighter shading. The clustering solution and terrain visualization also indicate areas of transition and overlap between different major topics. For example, note the cluster labeled "Information-Visualization"—"Pattern"—"Science" located between the larger clusters that are dominated by "Information Visualization" and "Science."

Skupin (2000) discusses various ways in which cartographic techniques could be used to further improve information visualization.

ARIST-VxInsight

Sandia's VxInsight was used to generate a number of document-based views of the *ARIST* data set using several different similarity functions. Four separate maps were created, all using the VxOrd FDP algorithm:

1. A citation-based map using direct and co-citation linkages after the combined linkage method of Small (1997) using a direct:co-citation weighting factor of 20:1. Four different time segments are shown in Figure 5.11.

2. A co-term map based on a cosine similarity using the ISI keywords (see Figure 5.12, left).

3. A map based on LSA over words extracted from the titles of articles. LSA was performed using SVDPACK to generate a document-by-document similarity matrix. Only similarity values > 0.9 were used in the VxOrd FDP to generate the map shown in Figure 5.12, right.

4. A co-classification map based on a cosine similarity from the ISI journal classifications for each article (see Figure 5.13).

In all three figures, we used the following shading/color scheme to indicate the various query terms that have been used to retrieve articles: white for citation analysis, co-citation, co-word, and so forth; light gray (green in color version available online) for bibliometrics and scientometrics; dark gray (blue) for semantics; and black (magenta) for visualization. Articles that match multiple query terms show multiple shadings/color markers.

A quick perusal of the landscapes in Figures 5.11–5.13 shows that each reveals different information about the domain. The citation-based map in Figure 5.11 shows the relationships among the four fields for four different time segments. The growth is easy to see in the four fields—citation analysis, bibliometrics, semantics, and visualization—from a comparison of the figures. Citation analysis and bibliometrics (white and light gray dots) both have roughly equal numbers of papers during the first time segment (1977–1982). More detailed analysis reveals that citation analysis was stronger in the late 1970s, with bibliometrics picking up steam in the early 1980s.

The second segment (1983–1988) shows bibliometrics as the larger field with some well-defined clusters near the top of the map (labeled A). The semantics and visualization fields have not yet appeared (see Figure 5.3 as well). The third segment (1989–1994) shows the formation of the visualization field in three clusters (labeled B). The fact that these visualization clusters are formed at the edges of a citation map indicates

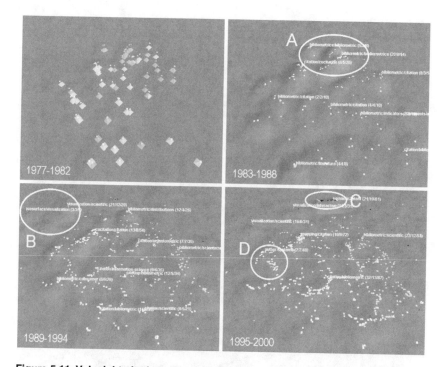

Figure 5.11 VxInsight citation maps of *ARIST* data for four different time segments; circles indicate areas highlighted in the text. Dot legend—white: citation analysis, light gray: bibliometrics, dark gray: semantics, black: visualization.

that they are not well linked to the main body of citation and bibliometric work in the center of the map. Pictures showing the citation links (not included here) confirm this and indicate that the visualization papers are not as highly cited as the citation and bibliometrics papers. This may be due to their relative youth or perhaps may indicate that visualization researchers tend to cite other work less frequently.

The fourth segment (1995–2000) shows semantic analysis as a new field (labeled C), which, like the visualization clusters, is not well linked to the main body of work. The citation analysis and bibliometrics fields each seem to be well defined, with some mixing of the two in certain clusters. Although bibliometrics seemed to be growing faster than citation analysis in the middle two segments (late 1980s and early 1990s), comparison of the numbers of papers in the late 1990s shows citation analysis to be gaining strength. One interesting cluster (labeled D) illustrates a mixture of citation analysis, bibliometrics, and visualization (see also Figure 5.14).

Figure 5.12 shows both co-term and LSA maps. In the co-term map, citation analysis and bibliometrics articles are found mainly in the two large peaks at the right edge of the map, and seem to be more mixed

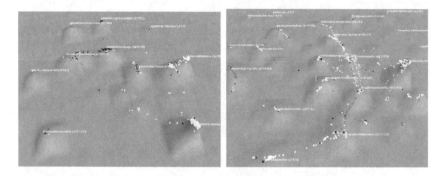

Figure 5.12 VxInsight co-term (left) and LSA (right) maps of *ARIST* data.

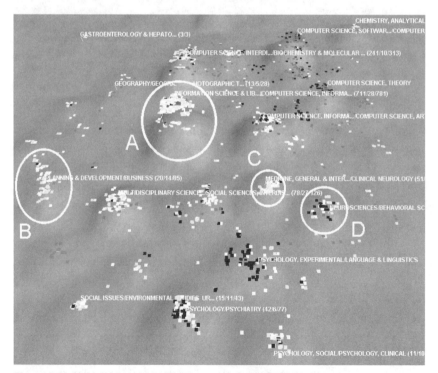

Figure 5.13 VxInsight co-classification map of *ARIST* data.

than in the citation map of Figure 5.11. This result could be simply because there are fewer clusters in the co-term map than in the citation map. However, it could also indicate a lack of specificity in using a term-based similarity, which leads to fewer clusters. The visualization and semantics papers form clusters of their own. A couple of peaks form where the four fields are mingled in the center of the landscape.

The map based on LSA over article titles shows some different features. The titles contained 4,802 unique words, the abstracts, 14,494 unique words. Here, the semantics papers are spread throughout the landscape. The visualization papers are also more mixed, and in several cases, they seem to bridge groups of citation analysis and bibliometrics articles. Bibliometrics and citation analysis articles, although appearing in the same clusters, are segregated within the clusters.

The co-classification map in Figure 5.13 gives completely different information about the domain. This type clearly shows the fields in which various groups of articles were published. The large peak with white and light gray dots (labeled A) is dominated by information and library sciences, which is where one would expect citation analysis and bibliometrics articles to be published. However, the white/light gray combination is also found in peaks comprised mainly of planning and development journals (labeled B), and general medicine (labeled C). Interestingly, a peak comprised mainly of articles in neuroscience-related journals (labeled D) contains articles from all four main areas of the *ARIST* data.

Note that the VxInsight tool is not simply a way to take pictures of a domain visualization, but is a dynamic tool with which one can browse the information. Zoom, rotation, dynamic labeling (updated at each zoom step) based on different attributes such as titles, or terms, showing of citation or other linkages, filtering by date, detail-on-demand for individual articles, the ability to import different layouts, and a query facility are all features that enable a highly interactive exploration of the information space.

Comparison of Maps

The several layouts based on terms or words are compared here (Cartographic SOM map, ET map, VxInsight co-term map, and LSA map). Three of the maps were generated from an ID/term list, as shown in Table 5.4, and one was generated from LSA on article titles using

Table 5.4 Comparison of document maps.

	A: Carto-SOM	B: ET-map	C: Co-term	D: LSA	Citation
Basis	id/term	id/term	cosine	id/title words	direct/cocite
Years	1991–2001	1991–2001	1991–2001	1977–2001	1977–2001
# papers	1446	1286	1446	2702	1626
# ID/term pairs	5202	5202	5202		
# citations					4632
# sim pairs			72664	48435	18258

VxOrd. Information about the citation map is also given in Table 5.4 for completeness. Numbers of articles appearing in each map, along with the number of ID/term pairs, citations, and/or similarity pairs (where known) that were used to generate the map, are also provided.

Some issues surround the use of terms to generate domain maps, two of which we address here. First is the distinction between the use of words (single words), compound terms (typically noun phrases parsed from titles or abstracts and consisting of multiple words), and specific terms (terms as they appear in lists from bibliographic sources). In this analysis, we have used specific terms, which can be either single words or multi-word phrases. For instance, in the *ARIST* data, the terms "scientometrics," "scientometric indicators," and "stationary scientometric indicators" all occur multiple times. Multiword terms, such as "domain visualization" tend to be more specific than, for example, "domain" and "visualization." Consequently, if multiword terms are used for co-term analysis and clustering, they tend to produce more specific clusters. Parsing to single words from the small number of specific compound terms is an option that leads to a large number of more general terms that can be used to index documents.

A second issue concerns the number of terms associated with each article. For the *ARIST* data, 34 percent of the articles with terms have one to three terms, 42 percent have four to seven, 17 percent have eight to ten, and the remaining 7 percent have 11 or more. Chung and Lee

(2001) showed that cosine measures tend to emphasize high-frequency terms. Skupin's experience with SOM is that articles with only one or two terms tend to either congregate in less dense areas of the SOM or in the middle of clusters, rather than at their edges. Boyack's experience using a cosine co-term similarity with FDP is that articles with only one or two terms tend to be evenly distributed if the associated terms are specific, multi-word terms, but lie in the middle of large clusters if the associated terms are single-word, general terms (e.g., "science"). Different results may arise from different layout routines; nevertheless, a definitive study on the effects of term types, the generality of terms, and term distributions is needed.

The term-based maps all show only a portion (around 50 percent) of the 2,767 articles in the *ARIST* set. This is due to the lack of keywords for papers published prior to 1991, and to the lack of terms in 26 percent of the papers published since. A total of 872 unique terms occurred more than once in the list of 5,202 ID/term pairs.

The citation map retained a few more papers (1,626, over 58 percent), but missed 1,141 because there were no citation links between them and any other member of the set. The LSA map, if the entire document-by-document matrix were used (3.83 million similarity values above the matrix diagonal), would have retained all 2,767 articles. However, due to the size of the matrix, only similarities of 0.9 or greater were used in ordination, and thus 65 articles were not retained in the map.

Figure 5.14 compares the layouts of the four term- or word-based maps. Much is similar between these four layouts. In all four, citation analysis and bibliometrics (light and medium gray dots) are found together, while visualization (black) and semantics (dark gray) are mostly by themselves. Some areas in each map contain some overlap between semantics and visualization, and some very small regions contain overlap among all four areas. Thus, at a macro level, the different layout techniques seem to give similar groupings from the term or word expressions. We have not done a neighborhood analysis to verify this statistically, but leave that to another time and study.

Figure 5.14 also makes clear the obvious visual differences among the layouts. The Cartographic SOM and ET-Maps each have more clusters than the co-term map (likely due to the parameters under which they were generated), while the LSA map shows more continuous structures.

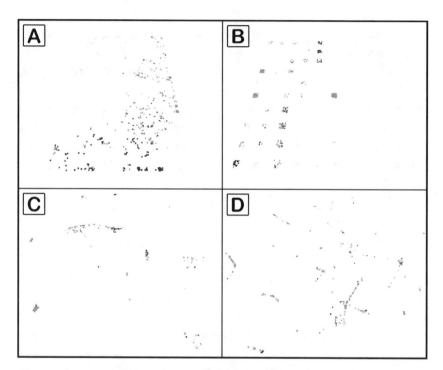

Figure 5.14 Comparison of layouts of four different document maps based on terms or words. A: Cartographic-SOM (compare Figure 5.10), B: ET-Map (compare Figure 5.9), C: Co-term (compare Figure 5.12, left), D: LSA (compare Figure 5.12, right). Dot legend—light gray (yellow in color version available online): citation analysis, medium gray (green): bibliometrics, dark gray (blue): semantics, black (magenta): visualization.

The three term-based layouts are shown in Figure 5.15 with strong co-term linkages (based on the cosine similarity) represented as lines. This view highlights more differences among the layouts. Intracluster linkages criss-cross the maps for the Cartographic-SOM and ET-Map, whereas few intercluster linkage trails occur on the co-term map. This pattern suggests that, although the SOM-based methods break the data into more clusters, and tend to fill the space much more uniformly, perhaps fewer clusters and less efficient space-filling can be justified. The LSA map is not compared here because title words and terms give different levels of information (Qin, 2000).

We now provide a comparison of reference-based citation maps with maps based on similarities between terms or words. The area around cluster D of Figure 5.11 seemed to be of interest due to the overlap

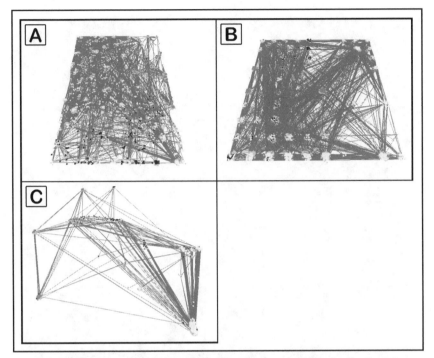

Figure 5.15 Strong co-term linkages based on cosine similarity for the three term-based document maps of Figure 5.14.

between citation analysis, bibliometrics, and visualization. Browsing of that cluster showed that the visualization papers were all related to visualization of neural networks, and that they appeared in that cluster with a large number of citation and bibliometrics studies on decision-support systems. Browsing near the cluster also revealed that different types of citation analysis seemed to be clustered by analysis type.

The first panel of Figure 5.16 (citation map) shows the results of three queries to abstracts: author co-citation, co-word, and co-citation (*not* author co-citation). The results of those queries lie in the clusters labeled A, B, and C, respectively, with very little scatter. Indeed the citation map portion of Figure 5.16 shows only a small section of the overall citation map (compare Figure 5.11). Browsing of individual articles confirmed that each cluster was composed of articles in which researchers used the technique central to the cluster. Identical queries were made to the Cartographic-SOM, co-term, and LSA maps, with the results shown in

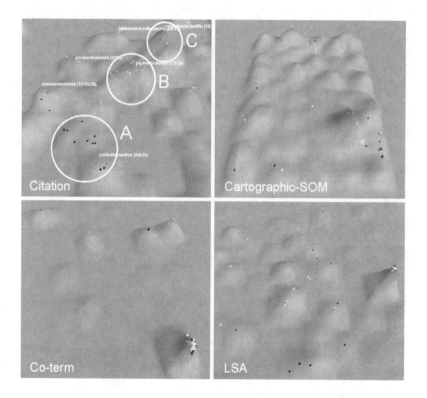

Figure 5.16 **Comparison of distinct fields of the citation map with their counter-parts on the term or title-based maps. Legend—medium gray (blue in color version available online): author co-citation (ACA), light gray (green): co-word analysis and Leximappe, black (magenta): co-citation analysis.**

Figure 5.16. In these three maps, the query results are spread throughout the maps and are not associated with any discrete clusters. Thus, articles are clustered much better by technique when using references than when using term- or title-based similarity measures, which is most likely due to lack of consistent use of terms corresponding to techniques in either keyword lists or titles. We expect that maps based on similarities between words in abstracts would do a much better job of clustering by technique than do any of the measures shown here.

The analysis and layout comparisons presented here do not show that any one type of similarity method and layout is better than any other for producing domain visualizations. Rather, they show that trade-offs are involved and that the researcher should use the combination of similarity and layout techniques that is most likely to aid in answering the questions at hand. Each researcher will, of course, have his or her favorite methods. We encourage all who are involved in domain visualization to broaden their horizons and expand the suite of methods that they use, to the benefit of all who read and rely upon their work. Note also that this survey is largely based on quantitative approaches. It is also important to take into account qualitative views.

Promising Avenues of Research

While working on this chapter, we discussed a large number of diverse ways to potentially improve the generation of domain visualizations and their interpretation. In particular, we find the following to be of great interest:

- Ways to increase the accessibility of domain visualizations for nonexperts

- Employing domain visualization to help answer real-world questions

- Bringing together leading researchers in different fields that contribute to the visualization of knowledge domains to improve the dissemination of results

- Development of more robust, scalable algorithms

Promising avenues of research that address these interests are discussed below.

Increasing the Accessibility of Domain Visualizations for Nonexperts

Despite advances in visualization research, many nonexperts find the use of visualization tools to be alien and nonintuitive. Domain visualizations could greatly benefit from the incorporation of advanced visual perception (Palmer, 1999; Ware, 2000) and cognitive principles into tools to aid the nonexpert.

In addition, it seems both desirable and advantageous to compare existing and novel algorithms on existing data sets and to compare the results with human performance (see Börner, 2000b, for first results). Ultimately, visualizations that best fit users' cognitive models will be easier to understand and use.

Cartographic design considerations and specific techniques can enrich the presentation of domain visualizations in a number of ways. The value of using a geographic metaphor was first discussed in Wise et al. (1995). Today, several geographers are involved in extending past work on geographic metaphors and primitives (Couclelis, 1998; Golledge, 1995) with the aim of developing and testing specific interfaces for spatialized browsing of nongeographic information (Fabrikant, 2000; Fabrikant & Buttenfield, 2001; Skupin & Buttenfield, 1996). Cartographic perspectives on information visualization are presented in Skupin (2000). The relevance of data structures and analytical tools common in geographic information systems is investigated in Skupin (2001).

Using Domain Visualization to Help Answer Real-World Questions

We believe that visualizations of knowledge domains can help assess scientific frontiers, forecast research vitality, identify disruptive events/technologies/changes, and find knowledge carriers. For example, Schwechheimer and Winterhager (1999, 2001) applied a co-citation analysis-based method to identify and analyze highly dynamic, rapidly developing research fronts in climate research. They used journal profiles, co-citation maps, and actor profiles as information elements. Results by Nederhof and Noyons (1992) indicate that bibliometric assessment of research performance is potentially useful in humanities disciplines. Much of the work done with VxInsight has been for competitive intelligence purposes (Boyack et al., 2002). Multi-SOM maps have been proposed for a knowledge-oriented analysis of science and technology via knowledge indicators (Polanco et al., 2001).

New commercial applications are also being devised for domain analysis. VantagePoint (http://www.thevantagepoint.com/ and http://tpac. gatech.edu/) reads bibliographic data files from many different sources and automates such techniques as cross-correlation analyses and factor analyses for purposes of technology assessment and opportunity analysis. Other products, such as SemioMap (http://www.semio.com/) or Knowledg-ist (http://www.invention-machine.com/), use linguistic techniques, semantic analysis, Bayesian models, or ontologies to understand the content of unstructured textual sources, whether in local files or on the Internet. These products seek to replace the "hunt-and-peck" method of keyword searching with the ability to browse the entire search space for relevant documents. Internet Cartographer (http://www.inventix.com/) is Inventix Software's solution to information overload on the Internet. It combines advanced artificial intelligence techniques with sophisticated information visualization techniques to build maps of accessed documents, organized in a hierarchy of more than 500 predefined categories.

Recent work on so called "small world graphs," aiming at a graph theoretic analysis of the Web, may turn out to be applicable to the analysis and visualization of bibliographic data and also research networks. Research by Kleinberg (1999) and colleagues on "hubs" (documents that cite many other documents) and "authorities" (documents that are highly cited) could be used to identify excellent review articles and high-quality papers, respectively. It may also suggest improved measures to identify emerging research fronts and communities based on authors of documents sharing some common theme.

Bringing Together Leading Researchers

We believe that research on visualizing knowledge domains could be sped up considerably if one or two well-understood and expert-verified domain analysis data sets, for example, in the form of a TREC data set (http://trec.nist.gov/data.html), were made available for general use to rate different algorithms and visualization techniques. In addition, a centralized repository of data analysis and visualization software for creating domain visualizations would improve the dissemination of algorithmic knowledge, facilitate comparisons of algorithms, and save the time spent on re-implementing algorithms (Börner & Zhou, 2001). Assuming that ownership and privacy issues can be resolved, we believe that a data set and software repository would also boost creativity by easing access to existing work; foster consultation with others working on related topics; accelerate implementation of new (commercial) applications, which would in turn stimulate the development and improvement of the algorithms; promote exploration of new ideas; and, last but not least, encourage dissemination of results to the wider scientific community (Shneiderman, 2000). The design of collaborative information visualizations that can be explored by multiple, potentially distributed users at the same time is also likely to improve collaborative data collection, access, examination, and management.

Development of More Robust, Scalable Algorithms

More robust semantic similarity measures and highly scalable ordination techniques are needed. Most current similarity generation and layout algorithms require hours or more to produce results. This limitation has not been a deterrent to domain researchers who spend a great deal of time analyzing the results of domain maps, but will discourage future generations of users who want quick answers from small literature sets (500 or fewer articles) that they can download in real time. Examples of this new generation of systems include AuthorLink and ConceptLink (http://cite.cis.drexel.edu/) by Xia Lin and colleagues, JAIR Space (http://www.infoarch.ai.mit.edu/jair/) by Mark Foltz, or StarWalker (http://www.brunel.ac.uk/~cssrccc2/starwalker.htm) by Chaomei Chen.

Layout algorithms that give robust answers are also needed. By robust answers, we mean a layout that does not change significantly with slight or even modest perturbations to the input. Recent work by Davidson (Davidson et al., 2001) using VxOrd showed that some clusters will break up with the introduction of small amounts of noise (random changes to similarities of two percent or less), while other clusters retain their structure with the addition of large amounts of noise (on the order of 10 percent). For cases in which robustness cannot be achieved, analysis to quantify the stability of individual clusters can be done to aid researchers in knowing how much confidence to place in their results.

In the same way that the Web continuously sprouts new pages, a steady stream of new work appears in the scientific literature. Hence, research by Barabási and his colleagues (Barabási & Albert, 1999; Barabási, Albert, & Jeong, 2000) on the development of algorithms that mimic the growth of the Web may be able to model the growth of scientific disciplines as well.

Work on incremental ordination and layout algorithms is essential to visualize continuously changing data. One advantageous feature of such algorithms is that they enable incremental update while preserving the main topology of the layout. Organic information design was first proposed by Mackinlay, Rao, and Card (1995) and applied recently by Fry (2000). It borrows ideas such as growth, atrophy, responsiveness, homeostasis, and metabolism, and it applies them to design information visualization that one "can 'feed' data to, and watch how the data is digested" (Fry, quoted by Dodge, 2001, online).

Generative Topographic Mapping (GTM) (Bishop, Svensen, & Williams, 1998) is an alternative to SOMs in that it generates topographic maps. The model was developed at the Neural Computing Research Group, Aston University, U. K. (http://www.ncrg.aston.ac.uk/GTM/) and is a novel form of latent variable modeling, which allows general nonlinear transformations from latent space to data space. For the purposes of data visualization, the mapping is then inverted using Bayes' theorem, resulting in a posterior distribution in latent space. GTPs overcome most limitations of the self-organizing maps and might turn out to be a valuable method for the visualization of knowledge domains.

The genomics and bioinformatics world has been home to many algorithmic innovations in recent years, several of which could be applied to data analysis, clustering, and visualization. The research focuses on matching algorithms, scalability of clustering methods, effectiveness of methods for clustering complex shapes and types of data, high-dimensional clustering techniques, and methods for clustering mixed numerical and categorical data in large databases. Continuing research into eigenvector and matrix techniques, and parallel algorithms may also lead to advances in information science.

In the 1960s and early 1970s Belver Griffith used bibliometrics and behavioral measures to reveal disciplinary communication structures (Griffith & Garvey, 1966; Griffith & Mullins, 1972). Recent work by Sandstrom (2001) shows that universal principles such as prey-choice models from optimal foraging theory (developed by biologists in the 1970s) can be successfully applied in the bibliographic microhabitat to explain information seeking and use behavior. Sandstrom (1994) was among the very first to see scholars as subsistence foragers in a socioecological framework. Research by Pirolli and Card (1999) supports the claim that foraging theory can be extended to understand information foraging and the evolution of knowledge domains, and to improve their visualizations.

Lastly we agree with Hjørland and Albrechtsen (1995) that information science in general, and the visualization of knowledge domains in particular, should be seen as a social rather than purely abstract research area (see also Capurro & Hjørland in this volume). This new view stresses the social, ecological, and purpose-oriented production and usage of knowledge.

Conclusion

We have covered some history, the general process of generating domain maps, commonly used units and measures, specific techniques, and the application of several techniques to generate and compare diverse maps of the focal subject domain. These maps make clear that this research field is currently divided into a few major islands, some of which are isolated (e.g., the information visualization and semantics islands). However, some interesting connecting points could be exploited in future work.

We hope that our review provides a starting point for researchers and practitioners to appreciate the richness and complexity of this rapidly evolving field, determine their own positions, identify related work in other research areas, and plan (interdisciplinary) collaborations and future work on promising applications. We believe that research aimed at visualizing knowledge domains can benefit by incorporating findings from other fields to improve the readability and effectiveness of domain visualizations. It can also contribute to the development of science in general by exporting methods and approaches to identify related work by experts in relevant research areas, assess research vitality, and identify emerging research fronts. We hope that the various snapshots and our interpretations of this dynamic and interdisciplinary field of study can lead to insights about the field as a whole and its future.

Acknowledgments

We greatly appreciate the time and effort Bin Zhu, Hsinchun Chen, and André Skupin put into the generation, discussion, and comparison of the ET-Map and Cartographic SOM map. The section on SOM maps benefited from André Skupin's detailed feedback. We wish to thank Katherine W. McCain, Blaise Cronin, Henry Small, Pamela Sandstrom, and the anonymous reviewers for their very insightful comments. Ben Shneiderman and Alan Porter commented on an earlier version of this chapter. We also gratefully acknowledge support for this work by The Council for Museums Archives and Libraries in the U.K. (RE/089), Laboratory Directed Research and Development, Sandia National Laboratories, U.S. Department of Energy (DE-AC04-94AL85000), and an NIH/NIA demonstration fund for Mapping Aging Research.

Sandia is a multiprogram laboratory operated by Sandia Corporation, a Lockheed Martin Company, for the United States Department of Energy under Contract DE-AC04-94AL85000.

Endnotes

1. The figures in this chapter are available in color at http://www.asis.org/Publications/ARIST/Vol37/BornerFigures.html.

2. Co-citation is known to have a low "recall" of clusters because only papers that have citation links within the data set and the defined time window can be classified. Co-citation and bibliographical coupling offer cross-sectional views given narrow, one-year citing periods. Longitudinal coupling becomes effective only when wider periods are used. At the end of a time period, documents will be linked through their references to earlier items, whereas at the beginning, linking will be through citations received (Small, 1997, pp. 278–279).

3. Principal component analysis is used in eigenvalue and factor analysis. However, eigen solutions can give coordinates for each document, whereas a factor analysis does not.

4. A linear clustering algorithm that groups objects according to the effects they have on the fractal dimension of the clusters was proposed in (Barbará & Chen, 2000).

5. Most data analysis techniques are computationally expensive and are applied in a batch job. During run time, the results of the data-mining step are used to interactively visualize a data set with a certain point of view.

6. This way of gathering data has the effect of privileging sole or first authors. Researchers who publish frequently in non-first-author positions are thus not included even though they should be. Research has shown that first-author citation studies distort the picture in terms of most

influential researchers. All-author citation counts should be preferred when visualizing the structure of research fields. The subfield structure tends to be just about the same for both methods (Persson, 2001; van Dalen & Henkens, 2001).

7. Note that SOMs use a raster data model instead of a vector data model.

Bibliography

Barabási, A.-L., & Albert, R. (1999). Emergence of scaling in random networks. *Science, 286,* 509–512.

Barabási, A.-L., Albert, R., & Jeong, H. (2000). Scale-free characteristics of random networks: The topology of the World Wide Web. *Physica, 281,* 69–77.

Barbará, D., & Chen, P. (2000). Using the fractal dimension to cluster datasets. *Proceedings of Sixth ACM SIGKDD Conference on Knowledge Discovery in Data Mining,* 260–264.

Basilevsky, A. (1994). *Statistical factor analysis and related methods: Theory and applications.* New York: Wiley.

Bassecoulard, E., & Zitt, M. (1999). Indicators in a research institute: A multi-level classification of journals. *Scientometrics, 44,* 323–345.

Battista, G., Eades, P., Tamassia, R., & Tollis, I. G. (1994). Algorithms for drawing graphs: An annotated bibliography. *Computational Geometry: Theory and Applications, 4,* 235–282.

Battista, G. D., Eades, P., Tamassia, R., & Tollis, I. G. (1999). *Graph drawing: Algorithms for the visualization of graphs.* Upper Saddle River, NJ: Prentice Hall.

Bederson, B. B., Hollan, J. D., Perlin, K., Meyer, J., Bacon, D., & Furnas, G. (1996). Pad++: A zoomable graphical sketchpad for exploring alternate interface physics. *Journal of Visual Languages and Computing, 7*(1), 3–31.

Bhattacharya, S., & Basu, P. K. (1998). Mapping a research area at the micro level using co-word analysis. *Scientometrics, 43,* 359–372.

Bishop, C. M., Svensen, M., & Williams, C. K. I. (1998). GTM: The generative topographic mapping. *Neural Computation, 10*(1), 215–234.

Borg, I., & Groenen, P. (1996). *Modern multidimensional scaling.* New York: Springer.

Borgman, C. L. (2000). Scholarly communication and bibliometrics revisited. In B. Cronin & H. B. Atkins (Eds.), *The web of knowledge: A Festschrift in honor of Eugene Garfield* (pp. 143–162). Medford, NJ: Information Today.

Borgman, C. L. (Ed.). (1990). *Scholarly communication and bibliometrics.* Newbury Park, CA: Sage.

Borgman, C. L. (2000). Scholarly communication and bibliometrics revisited. In B. Cronin & H. B. Atkins (Eds.), *The web of knowledge: A Festschrift in honor of Eugene Garfield.* Medford, NJ: Information Today.

Borgman, C. L., & Furner, J. (2002). Scholarly communication and bibliometrics. *Annual Review of Information Science and Technology, 36,* 3–72.

Börner, K. (2000a). Extracting and visualizing semantic structures in retrieval results for browsing. *Proceedings of the 2000 ACM / IEEE Joint Conference on Digital Libraries*, 234–235.

Börner, K. (2000b). Searching for the perfect match: A comparison of free sorting results for images by human subjects and by latent semantic analysis. *Proceedings of Information Visualisation 2000, Symposium on Digital Libraries*, 192–197.

Börner, K., Dillon, A., & Dolinsky, M. (2000). LVis—digital library visualizer. *Proceedings of Information Visualisation 2000, Symposium on Digital Libraries*, 77–81.

Börner, K., & Zhou, Y. (2001). A software repository for education and research in information visualization. *Proceedings of 5th International Conference on Information Visualization (IV 2001)*, 257–262.

Boyack, K. W., Wylie, B. N., & Davidson, G. S. (2002). Domain visualization using VxInsight for science and technology management. *Journal of the American Society for Information Science and Technology*, *53*, 764–774.

Boyack, K. W., Wylie, B. N., Davidson, G. S., & Johnson, D. K. (2000). Analysis of patent databases using VxInsight. *Proceedings of New Paradigms in Information Visualization and Manipulation '00*. Retrieved February 3, 2002, from http://www.cs.sandia.gov/projects/VxInsight/pubs/npivm00.pdf.

Bush, V. (1945). As we may think. *The Atlantic Monthly*, *176*(1), 101–108.

Cahlik, T. (2000). Comparison of the maps of science. *Scientometrics*, *49*, 373–387.

Callon, M., Courtial, J. P., Turner, W. A., & Bauin, S. (1983). From translation to network: The co-word analysis. *Scientometrics*, *5*, 78–78.

Card, S., Mackinlay, J., & Shneiderman, B. (Eds.). (1999). *Readings in information visualization: Using vision to think*. San Francisco: Morgan Kaufmann.

Card, S. K. (1996). Visualizing retrieved information: A survey. *IEEE Computer Graphics and Applications*, *16*(2), 63–67.

Chalmers, M. (1992). BEAD: Explorations in information visualisation. *Proceedings of the 1992 ACM SIGIR Annual International Conference on Research and Development in Information Retrieval*, 330–337.

Chen, C. (1997a). Structuring and visualizing the WWW with Generalized Similarity Analysis. *Proceedings of the 8th ACM Conference on Hypertext (Hypertext '97)*, 177–186. Retrieved January 20, 2002, from http://www.brunel.ac.uk/~cssrccc2/papers/ht97.pdf.

Chen, C. (1997b). Tracking latent domain structures: An integration of Pathfinder and latent semantic analysis. *AI & Society*, *11*(1–2), 48–62.

Chen, C. (1998a). Bridging the gap: The use of Pathfinder networks in visual navigation. *Journal of Visual Languages and Computing*, *9*, 267–286.

Chen, C. (1998b). Generalised similarity analysis and Pathfinder network scaling. *Interacting with Computers*, *10*, 107–128.

Chen, C. (1999a). *Information visualisation and virtual environments*. London: Springer-Verlag.

Chen, C. (1999b). Visualising semantic spaces and author co-citation networks in digital libraries. *Information Processing & Management*, *35*, 401–420.

Chen, C. (2002). *Mapping scientific frontiers: The quest for knowledge visualization*. London: Springer-Verlag.

Chen, C., & Carr, L. (1999). Trailblazing the literature of hypertext: Author co-citation analysis (1989–1998). *Proceedings of the 10th ACM Conference on Hypertext (Hypertext '99)*, 51–60.

Chen, C., & Rada, R. (1996). Modelling situated actions in collaborative hypertext databases. *Journal of Computer-Mediated Communication*, *2*(3), 125–156. Retrieved March 7, 2002, from www.ascusc.org/jcmc/vol2/issue3/chen.html.

Chen, C., Thomas, L., Cole, J., & Chennawasin, C. (1999). Representing the semantics of virtual spaces. *IEEE Multimedia*, *6*(2), 54–63.

Chen, C. M., & Paul, R. J. (2001). Visualizing a knowledge domain's intellectual structure. *Computer*, *34*(3), 65–71.

Chen, C. M., Paul, R. J., & O'Keefe, B. (2001). Fitting the jigsaw of citation: Information visualization in domain analysis. *Journal of the American Society for Information Science and Technology*, *52*, 315–330.

Chen, H. C., Houston, A. L., Sewell, R. R., & Schatz, B. R. (1998). Internet browsing and searching: User evaluations of category map and concept space techniques. *Journal of the American Society for Information Science*, *49*, 582–603.

Chen, H. C., & Lynch, K. J. (1992). Automatic construction of networks of concepts characterizing document databases. *IEEE Transactions on Systems Man and Cybernetics*, *22*, 885–902.

Chen, H. C., Schuffels, C., & Orwig, R. (1996). Internet categorization and search: A self-organizing approach. *Journal of Visual Communication and Image Representation*, *7*(1), 88–102.

Chung, Y. M., & Lee, J. Y. (2001). A corpus-based approach to comparative evaluation of statistical term association measures. *Journal of the American Society for Information Science and Technology*, *52*, 283–296.

Conklin, J. (1987, September). Hypertext: An introduction and survey. *IEEE Computer*, *20* (9), 17–41.

Couclelis, H. (1998). Worlds of information: The geographic metaphor in the visualization of complex information. *Cartography and Geographic Information Science*, *25*, 209–220.

Crane, D. (1972). *Invisible colleges: Diffusion of knowledge in scientific communities*. Chicago: University of Chicago Press.

Cronin, B., & Atkins, H. B. (Eds.) (2000). *The web of knowledge: A Festschrift in honor of Eugene Garfield*. Medford, NJ: Information Today, Inc.

Davidson, G. S., Hendrickson, B., Johnson, D. K., Meyers, C. E., & Wylie, B. N. (1998). Knowledge mining with VxInsight: Discovery through interaction. *Journal of Intelligent Information Systems*, *11*, 259–285.

Davidson, G. S., Wylie, B. N., & Boyack, K. W. (2001). Cluster stability and the use of noise in interpretation of clustering. *IEEE Proceedings on Information Visualization 2001*, 23–30.

Deerwester, S., Dumais, S. T., Landauer, T. K., Furnas, G. W., & Harshman, R. A. (1990). Indexing by latent semantic analysis. *Journal of the American Society for Information Science*, *41*, 391–407.

DeLooze, M. A., & Lemarie, J. (1997). Corpus relevance through co-word analysis: An application to plant proteins. *Scientometrics, 39*, 267–280.

Ding, Y., Chowdhury, G., & Foo, S. (1999). Mapping the intellectual structure of information retrieval studies: An author co-citation analysis; 1987–1997. *Journal of Information Science, 25*, 67–78.

Ding, Y., Chowdhury, G. G., & Foo, S. (2000). Journal as markers of intellectual space: Journal co-citation analysis of information retrieval area; 1987–1997. *Scientometrics, 47*, 55–73.

Dodge, M. (2001). Mapping how people use a Website. *Mappa Mundi Magazine.* Retrieved January 20, 2002, from http://mappa.mundi.net/maps/maps_022 /#ref_4.

Dodge, M., & Kitchin, R. (2000). *Mapping cyberspace.* New York: Routledge.

Dourish, P., & Chalmers, M. (1994). Running out of space: Models of information navigation. *Proceedings of HCI '94.* Retrieved January 20, 2002 from ftp:// parcftp.xerox.com/pub/europarc/jpd/hci94-navigation.ps.

Fabrikant, S. I. (2000). Spatialized browsing in large data archives. *Transactions in GIS, 4*(1), 65–78.

Fabrikant, S. I., & Buttenfield, B. P. (2001). Formalizing semantic spaces for information access. *Annals of the Association of American Geographers, 91*, 263–280.

Feng, Y., & Börner, K. (2002). Using semantic treemaps to categorize and visualize bookmark files. *SPIE 2002 Conference on Visualization and Data Analysis, 4665*, 24.

Fruchterman, T. M. J., & Reingold, E. M. (1991). Graph drawing by force-directed placement. *Software—Practice & Experience, 21*, 1129–1164.

Fry, B. (2000). *Organic information design.* Unpublished master's thesis, Massachusetts Institute of Technology, Cambridge, MA.

Furnas, G. W. (1986). Generalized fisheye views. *Proceedings of the Conference on Human Factors in Computing Systems (CHI '86)*, 16–23.

Furnas, G. W., & Zhang, X. (1998). MuSE: A multiscale editor. *Proceedings of the 11th Annual ACM Symposium on User Interface Software and Technology*, 107–116.

Garfield, E. (1955). Citation indexes for science: A new dimension in documentation through association of ideas. *Science, 122*,108–111.

Garfield, E. (1963). Citation indexes in sociological and historical research. *American Documentation, 14*, 289–291.

Garfield, E. (1994). Scientography: Mapping the tracks of science. *Current Contents: Social & Behavioral Sciences, 7*(45), 5–10.

Garfield, E. (2001). From bibliographic coupling to co-citation analysis via algorithmic historio-bibliography. A citationist's tribute to Belver C. Griffith. Presented November 27, 2001 at Drexel University, Philadelphia, PA. Retrieved March 5, 2002 from http://garfield.library.upenn.edu/papers/drexelbelvergrif fith92001.pdf.

Garfield, E., Sher, I. H., & Torpie, R. J. (1964). *The use of citation data in writing the history of science.* Philadelphia: Institute for Scientific Information.

Garfield, E., & Small, H. (1989). Identifying the changing frontiers of science. In M. Kranzberg, Y. Elkana, & Z. Tadmor (Eds.), *Innovation: At the crossroads between science and technology* (pp. 51–65). Haifa, Israel: The S. Neaman Press. Retrieved June 26, 2000, from http://www.garfield.library.upenn.edu/papers/362/362.html.

Gershon, N., Eick, S. G., & Card, S. (1998). Design: Information visualization. *Interactions, 5* (2), 9–15.

Gershon, N., & Ward, P. (2001). What storytelling can do for information visualization. *Communications of the ACM, 44*(8). Retrieved January 20, 2002, from http://www.acm.org/cacm/0801/0801toc.html.

Glänzel, W. (2001). National characteristics in international scientific co-authorship relations. *Scientometrics, 51*, 69–115.

Glänzel, W., & DeLange, C. (1997). Modelling and measuring multilateral co-authorship in international scientific collaboration. Part II. A comparative study on the extent and change of international scientific collaboration links. *Scientometrics, 40*, 605–626.

Golledge, R. G. (1995). Primitives of spatial knowledge. In T. L. Nyerges, D. M. Mark, R. Laurini, & M. J. Egenhofer (Eds.), *Cognitive aspects of human-computer interaction for geographic information systems* (pp. 29–44). Dordrecht, The Netherlands: Kluwer.

Gorsuch, R. L. (1983). *Factor analysis* (2nd. ed.). Hillsdale, NJ: Erlbaum.

Griffith, B. C., & Garvey, W. D. (1966). The national scientific meeting in psychology as a changing social system. *American Behavioral Scientist, 9*, 3–8.

Griffith, B. C., & Mullins, N. C. (1972). Coherent social groups in scientific change. *Science, 177*, 959–964.

Halasz, F. (1988). Reflections on NoteCards: Seven issues for the next generation of hypermedia systems. *Communications of the ACM, 31*(7), 836–852.

Halasz, F., Moran, T., & Trigg, R. (1987). NoteCards in a nutshell. *Proceedings of the ACM CHI+GI Conference, 1987*, 45–52.

Halliday, M. A. K., & Hasan, R. (1976). *Cohesion in English*. London: Longman.

Han, J., & Kamber, M. (2000). *Data mining: Concepts and techniques*. San Francisco: Morgan Kaufmann.

Harman, H. H. (1976). *Modern factor analysis*. Chicago: University of Chicago Press.

Harter, S. P., Nisonger, T. E., & Weng, A. W. (1993). Semantic relationships between cited and citing articles in library and information science journals. *Journal of the American Society for Information Science, 44*, 543–552.

He, Q. (1999). Knowledge discovery through co-word analysis. *Library Trends, 48*, 133–159.

Hearst, M. A. (1999). User interfaces and visualization. In R. Baeza-Yates & B. Ribeiro-Neto (Eds.), *Modern information retrieval* (pp. 257–224). New York: ACM Press.

Hendley, R. J., Drew, N. S., Wood, A. M., & Beale, R. (1995). Narcissus: Visualizing information. *Proceedings of IEEE Information Visualization '95 Symposium*, 90–96.

Herman, I., Melançon, G., & Marshall, M. S. (2000). Graph visualization and navigation in information visualization: A survey. *IEEE Transactions on Visualization and Computer Graphics 6*(1), 24–44. Retrieved January 20, 2002, from http://www.cwi.nl/~ivan/AboutMe/CV/RecentReferences.html.

Hetzler, B., Whitney, P., Martucci, L., & Thomas, J. (1998). Multi-faceted insight through interoperable visual information analysis paradigms. *Proceedings of IEEE Information Visualization '98.* Retrieved January 20, 2002, from http://multimedia.pnl.gov:2080/infoviz/ieee98.pdf.

Hjørland, B. (1997). *Information seeking and subject representation: An activity-theoretical approach to information science.* Westport, CT: Greenwood Press.

Hjørland, B., & Albrechtsen, H. (1995). Toward a new horizon in information science: Domain analysis. *Journal of the American Society for Information Science, 46,* 400–425.

Hollan, J. D., Bederson, B. B., & Helfman, J. (1997). Information visualization. In M. G. Helander, T. K. Landauer, & P. Prabhu (Eds.), *The handbook of human-computer interaction* (pp. 33–48). Amsterdam: Elsevier Science.

Institute for Scientific Information. (1981). *ISI atlas of science: Biochemistry and molecular biology,* 1978/80. Philadelphia: Institute for Scientific Information.

Isdale, J. (1998). Info Vis 98 Capstone: Edward Tufte, Yale University. In *IEEE Information Visualization 98 Symposium and Visualization Toolkit Tutorial.* Retrieved May 3, 2002, from http://www.isdale.com/jerry/InfoVis/noframes/IEEE_InfoVis98-Info-2.html.

Kaski, S., Honkela, T., Lagus, K., & Kohonen, T. (1998). WEBSOM—Self-organizing maps of document collections. *Neurocomputing, 21*(1–3), 101–117.

Kessler, M. M. (1963). Bibliographic coupling between scientific papers. *American Documentation, 14,* 10–25.

Kim, S. K., Lund, J., Kiraly, M., Duke, K., Jiang, M., Stuart, J. M., et al. (2001). A gene expression map for Caenorhabditis elegans. *Science, 293,* 2087–2092.

King, J. (1987). A review of bibliometric and other science indicators and their role in research evaluation. *Journal of Information Science, 13,* 261–276.

Kleinberg, J. (1999). Authoritative sources in a hyperlinked environment. *Journal of the ACM, 46,* 604–632.

Kohonen, T. (1985). The self-organizing map. *Proceedings of the IEEE, 73,* 1551–1558.

Kohonen, T. (1995). *Self-organizing maps.* New York: Springer.

Kohonen, T., Kaski, S., Lagus, K., Salojarvi, J., Honkela, J., Paatero, V., et al. (2000). Self organization of a massive document collection. *IEEE Transactions on Neural Networks, 11,* 574–585.

Koike, H. (1993). The role of another spatial dimension in software visualization. *ACM Transactions on Information Systems, 11,* 266–286.

Koike, H., & Yoshihara, H. (1993). Fractal approaches for visualizing huge hierarchies. *Proceedings of the 1993 IEEE Symposium on Visual Languages,* 55–60.

Kostoff, R. N., Eberhart, H. J., & Toothman, D. R. (1998). Database tomography for technical intelligence: A roadmap of the near-earth space science and technology literature. *Information Processing & Management, 34,* 69–85.

Kruskal, J. B. (1964a). Multidimensional scaling by optimizing goodness of fit to a nonmetric hypothesis. *Psychometrika, 29,* 1–27.

Kruskal, J. B. (1964b). Nonmetric multidimensional scaling: A numerical method. *Psychometrika, 29,* 115–129.

Kruskal, J. B. (1977). Multidimensional scaling and other methods for discovering structure. In K. Enslein, A. Ralston, & H. Wilf (Eds.), *Statistical methods for digital computers.* New York: Wiley.

Kruskal, J. B., & Wish, M. (1984). *Multidimensional scaling.* Beverly Hills, CA: Sage.

Lamping, J., Rao, R., & Pirolli, P. (1995). A focus+context technique based on hyperbolic geometry for visualizing large hierarchies. *Proceedings of ACM CHI '95 Conference on Human Factors in Computing Systems,* 401–408. Retrieved January 20, 2002, from http://www.acm.org/sigchi/chi95/proceedings/papers/jl_bdy.htm.

Landauer, T. K., Foltz, P. W., & Laham, D. (1998). Introduction to latent semantic analysis. *Discourse Processes, 25,* 259–284. Retrieved January 20, 2002, from http://lsa.colorado.edu/.

Lawrence, S., Giles, C. L., & Bollacker, K. (1999). Digital libraries and autonomous citation indexing. *IEEE Computer, 32*(6), 67–71. Retrieved January 20, 2002, from http://www.neci.nj.nec.com/home/.

Lee, R. C. T., Slagle, J. R., & Blum, H. (1977). A triangulation method for the sequential mapping of points from N-space to two-space. *IEEE Transactions on Computers, 26,* 288–292.

Leydesdorff, L. (1994). The generation of aggregated journal-journal citation maps on the basis of the CD-ROM version of the Science Citation Index. *Scientometrics, 47,* 143–164.

Leydesdorff, L., & Wouters, P. (1999). Between texts and contexts: Advances in theories of citation. *Scientometrics, 44,* 169–182. Retrieved April 9, 2002, from http://home.pscw.uva.nl/lleydesdorff/citation/rejoin.htm.

Lin, X. (1997). Map displays for information retrieval. *Journal of the American Society for Information Science, 48,* 40–54.

Lin, X., Soergel, D., & Marchionini, G. (1991). A self-organizing semantic map for information retrieval. *Proceedings of the 14th Annual International ACM SIGIR Conference on Research and Development in Information Retrieval,* 262–269.

Lin, Y., & Kaid, L. L. (2000). Fragmentation of the intellectual structure of political communication study: Some empirical evidence. *Scientometrics, 47,* 143–164.

Mackinlay, J. D., Rao, R., & Card, S. K. (1995). An organic user interface for searching citation links. *Proceedings of the Conference on Human Factors in Computing Systems (CHI '95).* Retrieved January 20, 2002, from http://www.acm.org/sigchi/chi95/Electronic/documnts/papers/jdm_bdy.htm.

Mahlck, P., & Persson, O. (2000). Socio-bibliometric mapping of intra-departmental networks. *Scientometrics, 49,* 81–91.

Mandelbrot, B. B. (1988). *Fractal geometry of nature.* San Francisco: W. H. Freeman.

McCain, K. W. (1990). Mapping authors in intellectual space: A technical overview. *Journal of the American Society for Information Science, 41*, 433–443.

McCain, K. W. (1995). The structure of biotechnology research and development. *Scientometrics, 32*, 153–175.

McCain, K. W. (1998). Neural networks research in context: A longitudinal journal cogitation analysis of an emerging interdisciplinary field. *Scientometrics, 41*, 389–410.

McCormick, B. H., DeFanti, T. A., & Brown, M. D. (Eds.). (1987). Visualization in scientific computing [special issue]. *Computer Graphics, 21*(6).

McQuaid, M. J., Ong, T. H., Chen, H. C., & Nunamaker, J. F. (1999). Multidimensional scaling for group memory visualization. *Decision Support Systems, 27*(1–2), 163–176.

Merton, R. K., & Garfield, E. (1986). Forward. In D. J. D. Price, Little science, big science, and beyond (pp. vii–xiii). New York: Columbia University Press.

Mostafa, J., Quiroga, L. M., & Palakal, M. (1998). Filtering medical documents using automated and human classification methods. *Journal of the American Society for Information Science, 49*, 1304–1318.

Mukherjea, S. (1999). Information visualization for hypermedia systems. *ACM Computing Surveys, 31*(4). Retrieved March 7, 2002, from http://doi.acm.org/10.1145/345966.345984.

Munzner, T. (1997). H3: Laying out large directed graphs in 3D hyperbolic space. *Proceedings of the 1997 IEEE Symposium on Information Visualization*, 2–10.

Munzner, T. (1998). Exploring large graphs in 3D hyperbolic space. *IEEE Computer Graphics and Applications, 18*(4), 18–23. Retrieved January 20, 2002, from http://graphics.stanford.edu/papers/h3cga/html/.

Narin, F. & Moll, J. K. (1977). Bibliometrics. *Annual Review of Information Science and Technology, 12*, 35–58.

Nederhof, A. J., & Noyons, E. C. M. (1992). International comparison of departments, research performance in the humanities. *Journal of the American Society for Information Science, 43*, 249–256.

Nederhof, A. J., & Zwaan, R. A. (1991). Quality judgments of journals as indicators of research performance in the humanities and the social and behavioral sciences. *Journal of the American Society for Information Science, 42*, 332–340.

Newman, M. E. J. (2001a). Scientific collaboration networks I: Network construction and fundamental results. *Physical Review E, 64*, 016131:1–016131:8.

Newman, M. E. J. (2001b). Scientific collaboration networks II: Shortest paths, weighted networks, and centrality. *Physical Review E, 64*, 016132:1–016132:7.

Nisonger, T. E., Harter, S. P., & Weng, A. (1992). Subject relationships between cited and citing documents in library and information science. *Proceedings of the Annual Meeting of the American Society for Information Science, 29*, 13–19.

Noyons, E. C. M. (2001). Bibliometric mapping of science in a science policy context. *Scientometrics, 50*, 83–98.

Noyons, E. C. M., Moed, H. F., & Luwel, M. (1999). Combining mapping and citation analysis for evaluative bibliometric purposes: A bibliometric study. *Journal of the American Society for Information Science, 50*, 115–131.

Noyons, E. C. M., Moed, H. F., & van Raan, A. F. J. (1999). Integrating research performance analysis and science mapping. *Scientometrics, 46*, 591–604.

Noyons, E. C. M., & van Raan, A. F. J. (1998a). Advanced mapping of science and technology. *Scientometrics, 41*, 61–67.

Noyons, E. C. M., & van Raan, A. F. J. (1998b). Monitoring scientific developments from a dynamic perspective: Self-organized structuring to map neural network research. *Journal of the American Society for Information Science, 49*, 68–81.

Palmer, S. E. (1999). Vision science: *From photons to phenomenology*. Cambridge, MA: Bradford Books/MIT Press.

Persson, O. (2001). All author citations versus first author citations. *Scientometrics, 50*, 339–344.

Pirolli, P., & Card, S. (1999). Information foraging. *Psychological Review, 106*, 643–675.

Pirolli, P., Schank, P., Hearst, M., & Diehl, C. (1996). Scatter/gather browsing communicates the topic structure of a very large text collection. *Proceedings of the Conference on Human Factors in Computing Systems (CHI '96)*. Retrieved January 20, 2002, from http://www.acm.org/sigchi/chi96/proceedings/papers/Pirolli/pp_txt.htm.

Polanco, X., Francois, C., & Lamirel, J. C. (2001). Using artificial neural networks for mapping of science and technology: A multi-self-organizing-maps approach. *Scientometrics, 51*, 267–292.

Price, D. J. D. (1961). *Science since Babylon*. New Haven, CT: Yale University Press.

Price, D. J. D. (1963). *Little science, big science*. New York: Columbia University Press.

Price, D. J. D. (1965). Networks of scientific papers. *Science, 149*, 510–515.

Price, D. J. D. (1986). *Little science, big science, and beyond*. New York: Columbia University Press.

Qin, J. (2000). Semantic similarities between a keyword database and a controlled vocabulary database: An investigation in the antibiotic resistance literature. *Journal of the American Society for Information Science, 51*, 166–180.

Raghavan, V. V., & Wong, S. K. M. (1986). A critical analysis of vector space model for information retrieval. *Journal of the American Society for Information Science, 37*, 279–287.

Raghupathi, W., & Nerur, S. P. (1999). Research themes and trends in artificial intelligence: An author co-citation analysis. *Intelligence, 10*(2), 18–28. Retrieved March 7, 2002, from http://doi.acm.org/10.1145/309697.309703.

Rennison, E. (1994). Galaxy of news: An approach to visualizing and understanding expansive news landscapes. *Proceedings of ACM Symposium on User Interface Software and Technology, 1994*, 3–12.

Rorvig, M. (1999). Images of similarity: A visual exploration of optimal similarity metrics and scaling properties of TREC topic-document sets. *Journal of the American Society for Information Science, 50*, 639–651.

Roweis, S. T., & Saul, L. K. (2000). Nonlinear dimensionality reduction by locally linear embedding. *Science, 290*(5500), 2323–2326.

Salton, G., Allan, J., & Buckley, C. (1994). Automatic structuring and retrieval of large text files. *Communications of the ACM, 37*(2), 97–108.

Salton, G., Allan, J., Buckley, C., & Singhal, A. (1994). Automatic-analysis, theme generation, and summary of machine-readable texts. *Science, 264*(5164), 1421–1426.

Salton, G., & Buckley, C. (1988). Parallel text search methods. *Communications of the ACM, 31*, 202–215.

Salton, G., & Buckley, C. (1991). Global text matching for information retrieval. *Science, 253*(5023), 1012–1015.

Salton, G., Yang, C., & Wong, A. (1975). A vector space model for automatic indexing. *Communications of the ACM, 18*, 613–620.

Salvador, M. R., & Lopez-Martinez, R. E. (2000). Cognitive structure of research: Scientometric mapping in sintered materials. *Research Evaluation, 9*, 189–200.

Sandstrom, P. E. (1994). An optimal foraging approach to information-seeking and use. *Library Quarterly, 64*, 414–449.

Sandstrom, P. E. (2001). Scholarly communication as a socioecological system. *Scientometrics, 51*, 573–605.

Sarkar, M., & Brown, M. H. (1994). Graphical fisheye views. *Communications of the ACM, 37*(12), 73–84.

Schvaneveldt, R. W. (1990). *Pathfinder associative networks: Studies in knowledge organization*. Norwood, NJ: Ablex.

Schwechheimer, H., & Winterhager, M. (1999). Highly dynamic specialities in climate research. *Scientometrics, 44*, 547–560.

Schwechheimer, H., & Winterhager, M. (2001). Mapping interdisciplinary research fronts in neuroscience: A bibliometric view to retrograde amnesia. *Scientometrics, 51*, 311–318.

Shneiderman, B. (1992). Tree visualization with tree-maps: A 2-D space filling approach. *ACM Transactions on Graphics, 11*, 92–99.

Shneiderman, B. (1996). The eyes have it: A task by data type taxonomy for information visualizations. *Proceedings of IEEE Symposium on Visual Languages*, 336–343. Retrieved April 26, 2002, from http://lemming.uvm.edu/~sjc/colloquia/eyes.html.

Shneiderman, B. (1997). *Designing the user interface: Strategies for effective human-computer interaction* (3rd ed.). Reading, MA: Addison-Wesley.

Shneiderman, B. (2000). Creating creativity: User interfaces for supporting innovation. *ACM Transactions on Computer-Human Interaction, 7*(1), 114–138.

Skupin, A. (2000). From metaphor to method: Cartographic perspectives on information visualization. *IEEE Symposium on Information Visualization 2000*, 91–97.

Skupin, A. (2001). Information visualization, human computer interaction, and cognitive psychology: Domain visualizations. *Proceedings of Visual Interfaces to Digital Libraries—Its Past, Present, and Future, JCDL Workshop*. Retrieved January 20, 2002, from http://vw.indiana.edu/visual01/jcdl.html.

Skupin, A., & Buttenfield, B. P. (1996). Spatial metaphors for visualizing very large data archives. *Proceedings of GIS/LIS '96*, 607–617.

Small, H. (1994). A SCI-MAP case study: Building a map of AIDS research. *Scientometrics, 30,* 229–241.

Small, H. (1995). Navigating the citation network. *Proceedings of the Annual Meeting of the American Society for Information Science, 32,* 118–126.

Small, H. (1997). Update on science mapping: Creating large document spaces. *Scientometrics, 38,* 275–293.

Small, H. (1999a). A passage through science: Crossing disciplinary boundaries. *Library Trends, 48,* 72–108.

Small, H. (1999b). Visualizing science by citation mapping. *Journal of the American Society for Information Science, 50,* 799–813.

Small, H. (2000). Charting pathways through science: Exploring Garfield's vision of a unified index to science. In B. Cronin & H. B. Atkins (Eds.), *The web of knowledge: A Festschrift in honor of Eugene Garfield* (pp. 449–473). Medford, NJ: Information Today, Inc.

Spence, B. (2001). *Information visualization.* Reading, MA: Addison-Wesley.

Tenenbaum, J. B., de Silva, V., & Langford, J. C. (2000). A global geometric framework for nonlinear dimensionality reduction. *Science, 290*(5500), 2319–2323.

Thurstone, L. L. (1931). Multiple factor analysis. *Psychological Review, 38,* 406–427.

Tryon, R. C. (1939). *Cluster analysis.* New York: McGraw-Hill.

Tufte, E. R. (1983). *The visual display of quantitative information.* Cheshire, CT: Graphics Press.

Tufte, E. R. (1990). *Envisioning information.* Cheshire, CT: Graphics Press.

Tufte, E. R. (1997). *Visual explanations.* Cheshire, CT: Graphics Press.

van Dalen, H. P., & Henkens, K. (2001). What makes a scientific article influential? The case of demographers. *Scientometrics, 50,* 455–482.

van Raan, A. (2000). The Pandora's box of citation analysis: Measuring scientific excellence—The last evil? In B. Cronin & H. B. Atkins (Eds.), *The web of knowledge: A Festschrift in honor of Eugene Garfield* (pp. 301–319). Medford, NJ: Information Today, Inc.

Ware, C. (2000). *Information visualization: Perception for design.* San Francisco: Morgan Kaufmann.

White, H. D., Buzydlowski, J., & Lin, X. (2000). Co-cited author maps as interfaces to digital libraries. *Proceedings of IEEE Information Visualization Conference,* 25–30.

White, H. D., & Griffith, B. C. (1982). Authors and markers of intellectual space: Co-citation studies of science, technology and society. *Journal of Documentation, 38,* 255–272.

White, H. D., & McCain, K. W. (1989). Bibliometrics. *Annual Review of Information Science and Technology, 24,* 119–186.

White, H. D., & McCain, K. W. (1997). Visualization of literatures. *Annual Review of Information Science and Technology, 32,* 99–168.

White, H. D., & McCain, K. W. (1998). Visualizing a discipline: An author co-citation analysis of information science, 1972–1995. *Journal of the American Society for Information Science, 49,* 327–356.

Wilson, C. S. (1999/2000). Informetrics. *Annual Review of Information Science and Technology, 34,* 107–286.

Wise, J. A. (1999). The ecological approach to text visualization. *Journal of the American Society for Information Science, 50,* 1224–1233.

Wise, J. A., Thomas, J. J., Pennock, K., Lantrip, D., Pottier, M., Schur, A., et al. (1995). Visualizing the non-visual: Spatial analysis and interaction with information from text documents. *Proceedings of IEEE Symposium on Information Visualization '95.* Retrieved January 20, 2002, from http://multimedia.pnl.gov: 2080/ showcase/?it_content/spire.node/.

Yang, C. C., Chen, H., & Hong, K. K. (1999). Visualization tools for self-organizing maps. *Proceedings of Fourth International ACM Conference on Digital Libraries,* 258–259.

Zhu, D., & Porter, A. L. (2002). Automated extraction and visualization of information for technological intelligence and forecasting. *Technological Forecasting and Social Change, 69,* 495–506.

Information Systems

CHAPTER 6

Museum Informatics

Paul F. Marty
Florida State University

W. Boyd Rayward
Michael B. Twidale
University of Illinois at Urbana-Champaign

Introduction

Museum informatics is the study of how information science and technology affect the museum environment. This kind of study can be undertaken from multiple perspectives, including those of museum professionals and museum visitors. Over the past few decades, new information technologies have dramatically changed museums' capabilities. These changes have influenced how people think about museums and they have had a profound impact on the social interactions that take place in museums. Museum professionals and visitors alike have developed new conceptions of why museums exist and new expectations of what they should offer.

An extensive literature on museums and information technology exists (Keene, 1998; Morrissey & Worts, 1998; Orna & Pettitt, 1998; Thomas & Mintz, 1998). Several recent books, including *The Wired Museum* (Jones-Garmil, 1997, published by the American Association of Museums), cover the many ways museums have been influenced by technology. Proceedings from a variety of conferences deal with topics in museum informatics, including the Museum Computer Network Conference, the Museum Documentation Association Conference, the Conference of the International Committee for Documentation of the

International Council of Museums, the International Cultural Heritage Informatics Meeting (formerly the International Conference on Hypermedia and Interactivity in Museums), and Museums and the Web. Journals such as *Archives and Museum Informatics* (recently incorporated into *Archival Science*) and newsletters such as *Spectra*, a publication of the Museum Computer Network, regularly touch upon issues of museum informatics. A special issue of the *Journal of the American Society for Information Science* (Bearman & Trant, 2000) was devoted to museum informatics.

This material is very idiosyncratic in nature, in part because the literature covers different types of museums, with different collections, audiences, capabilities, and needs. Nevertheless, it is possible to find within this literature underlying commonalties that bridge the concerns of disparate museum professionals. One basic issue, for example, is the search for shared data standards to be used in museum automation. The majority of these commonalties, however, are more general and wide-ranging in their implications. Museum professionals have found that information technologies provide a new range of functionalities to enhance what can be done within the museum environment. The possibilities go well beyond simple computer automation, raising fundamental questions about the job of the museum professional, the experience of visiting a museum, and the very definition of what a museum is.

These questions constitute a new field of study, a field called museum informatics; this contribution is the first *ARIST* chapter on the subject. Like most new fields, museum informatics draws upon many related areas, from social informatics (Kling, 1999) to research into digital libraries (Bishop & Star, 1996). Until recently, most authors writing about museums and technology were more concerned with a narrow and systems-driven approach to how information technology should be used in museums than with how new technologies would change the social relationships that take place both within and outside museum walls. However, given recent developments, it is now virtually impossible to discuss museum technologies in the abstract without touching in some way on the changing role of the museum in the information society.

This chapter examines the nature and status of the technical issues museum professionals face as they take advantage of modern information technologies, while acknowledging that these technical issues are nested within complex and interlocking organizational and social contexts that affect both the nature of museum work and the expectations of the museum's clientele. It is an attempt to take different threads from the existing literature on information technology in museums and spin them into a systematic study of museum informatics. In doing so, it attempts to draw from the literature a coherent account of an emerging field, identifying the main areas of concern and topics of study for researchers interested in the changing sociotechnical nature of museums.

The chapter is organized into three sections. The first part provides an historical perspective covering the use of new technologies in museums over the past few decades and identifying the technological challenges faced by modern, digital museums. The second examines the social effects of computerization on the museum environment from the perspective of all who use museum resources—from the museum professional to the museum visitor. The third explores how these changes are bringing about a redefinition of the museum as part of the information society.

Museums and the Digital Revolution

This section explores the historical progression of the use of computers in museums. It begins by examining the nature of information resources in museums and the traditional ways in which museum professionals have organized these resources. It then explores the changes brought about by advances in computer technologies, the challenges of digitizing museum collections, and the difficulties of developing standards for data sharing.

Museum professionals started using computers for information management in the 1960s. Early advocates of computerization in museums, like those who were advocating the use of computers in libraries at the time, emphasized the computer's value for automating repetitive and time-consuming tasks: sorting records, searching for information, and tabulating results (Varveris, 1979). These functions were tasks of the museum registrar, familiar to every museum professional; organizations such as the Museum Computer Network (http://www.mcn.edu/), established in 1967, could rely on this familiarity when they encouraged museums to use computers (Vance, 1975). However, museum professionals soon realized that the use of computers in museums would involve more than just automating existing tasks. The digital revolution would change not just *how* they managed their records but *why* they managed records in the first place.

Information Resources in Museums

Whether they work in a museum of art, natural history, cultural history, or science and technology, museum professionals must manage a wide variety of information about their collections. This information is needed to identify and describe museum objects and integrate them into particular collections. These extremely complex tasks involve different kinds and levels of information. From the moment an artifact enters a museum, registrars, curators, and other museum professionals examine it and assemble information to be recorded. The object must be accessioned, weighed and measured, photographed, marked with a unique identification number, and so on. Information about how the museum received the object, how long it will be in the museum's collections (if it is on loan), and where it will be stored or displayed must be recorded. Details of the object's provenance, historical importance, and cultural significance must be researched. The specific information generated about any one object becomes part of a vast array of information about the museum's collections, exhibits, and educational potential as a whole. Information about a museum's exhibits forms part of a broader spectrum of knowledge about art, culture, and history.

The identification and gathering of this information are driven by the requirements of different museum professionals as they assess what is needed for their own use and for the use of potential museum visitors. These needs often vary from institution to institution and from visitor to visitor. Students in an art history class, for example, come to a museum searching for appropriate examples to use in their papers. Scholars researching a particular topic need to know how many prints by a given artist exist in the museum's collection or how many paintings deal with a certain subject. Museum curators planning a new exhibit require information about each object's historical significance, in order to select the best artifacts for a given display. The museum's information resources can respond to this variety of needs only if the necessary information has already been gathered, properly organized, and made accessible.

Information Organization and Access

The organization of information about museum artifacts has always been an important topic for museum professionals (Buck & Gilmore, 1998; Dudley & Wilkenson, 1979). Traditionally, museum information resources have been organized into card and ledger files. Such files have a necessarily limited number of access points; information was typically arranged by accession number, donor name, and object name. However, few organizational standards existed for recording and managing this information that held true across different museums. Some museums might use different or additional kinds of card files, organizing objects by material type, for example. A number of methods of assigning accession numbers were available, although most museums now use the tripartite numbering scheme recommended by the American Association of Museums, and a variety of different schemes were in use for classifying museum artifacts.

The traditional card and ledger files and the information they organized, as primitive systems for information storage and retrieval, could answer only a few types of questions about objects in a museum's collections: "How many objects has any one particular donor provided to the museum?" "How many objects were accessioned in the year 1973?" Such questions could be answered easily. However, answering even relatively straightforward questions like "How many lamps does the museum have in its collection?" depended greatly on whether objects were consistently classified when they were accessioned. Questions of a more complex nature were nearly impossible to answer: "How many Attic Red-Figure vases does the museum have from the late fourth century B.C.?" "How many paintings depict the labors of Herakles?" Even the most skilled museum professional would be unable to answer such questions without reading each card entry individually.

Potential and Pitfalls of Automation

When museum professionals began automation projects, they expected computers to provide better organization of records and faster access to information (Rush & Chenhall, 1979). Electronic databases had the potential to provide more access points, faster searching and sorting, and the ability to compile and print lists more quickly (Abell-Seddon,

1988; Vance & Chenhall, 1988). For these reasons, there were many early attempts to computerize museum collections, most notably in the late 1960s at the Smithsonian Institution. Soon, museum professionals around the world were beginning the complicated task of taking data about artifacts from their card or ledger files, converting them into electronic format, and storing them in large, mainframe, networked systems (Chenhall, 1975). Within a few years, organizations such as the Museum Computer Network were experimenting with data collection standards and formats that would enable museum professionals to share data across multiple institutions (Vance, 1975).

Despite this promising beginning, however, computer automation in museums quickly bogged down in a morass of technical problems that undermined even the best attempts to create uniform standards for automation within museums. The inherent uniqueness of museum artifacts meant that there was and could be no organization equivalent to the library world's Ohio College Library Cooperative (now the Online Computer Library Center, http://www.oclc.org/) to help museums develop a shared database of museum records; each institution had to tackle the task of cataloging its collections individually. Additionally, museum professionals, primarily curators, wanted their records to contain extensive data about artifacts that went far beyond the essentially inventory data typical of library catalogs. What these data were, however, often varied from curator to curator, and the creation of a database system that could satisfy the needs of individual institutions was extremely complex and expensive. For these reasons, most museums in this period remained stuck in a world in which automation was considered difficult if not impossible (Doty, 1990; Williams, 1987). Throughout the 1970s, advocates of museum automation saw their efforts rapidly fall behind and diverge from the field of library automation.

Nevertheless, some important general developments occurred at this time in the field of museum automation. The first conference about computers and their potential application in museums was held at the Metropolitan Museum of Art in New York in 1968 (Metropolitan Museum of Art, 1968). The Museum Documentation Association (http://www.mda.org.uk/), established in 1977, drew up and attempted to promulgate minimum information standards in the form of SPEC-TRUM, a guide to electronic collections management (Cowton, 1997).

Meanwhile, other organizations, such as the International Committee of Museums and the Getty Information Institute (formerly the Getty Art History Information Program) joined the Museum Documentation Association in exploring more general models for knowledge sharing (Bower & Roberts, 1995). Such efforts, however, were few and far between. Most museum professionals found themselves in a difficult situation where they were (a) unable to solve the problems involved in automating their collections cooperatively, and (b) unable to afford the high expense incurred in doing it on their own. A possible solution to this dilemma was not found until the 1980s, with the widespread use of the personal computer.

Digitization, Personal Computers, and the Internet Revolution

After two decades of struggle, museum professionals finally had a practical, inexpensive, and easy-to-use tool for digitizing information about their collections: a stand-alone database on a personal computer. As a result, during the late 1980s, the number of museums using computers to store information about their collections began to grow rapidly (Jones-Garmil, 1997). As personal computers became cheaper and easier to use, they were deployed more widely and for more tasks in the museum environment (Hooper-Greenhill, 1995; Thomas & Mintz, 1998). New technologies allowed for the digital imaging of museum artifacts. Multimedia kiosks were used in exhibit galleries to present more detailed information about museum collections. With the arrival of CD-ROM technology, museums began to create multimedia CD-ROMs about their collections to distribute to educational organizations.

Despite these technological advances, however, digitizing information about artifacts remained a stubbornly difficult task. Digitizing an artifact requires much more than simply creating a digital image of the object. A great many fields are needed to describe an artifact completely and thoroughly, and different kinds of artifacts may well need different fields. Thus, most off-the-shelf database systems for museums use relational records with hundreds of fields to describe each artifact. The inherent uniqueness of museum artifacts remained a problem. No two museums can possess exactly the same historical object or work of art;

even reproductions vary greatly in such crucial identifying features as size, material composition, and provenance. These factors not only make describing each object a time-consuming and individual task, they also make it very difficult to share this task among institutions.

Despite advances in digitization technologies, and despite advances in the parallel world of library automation, the problems of inter-museum cooperation remained mostly unsolved. Little coordination of work or sharing of information existed; only limited consideration was given to either standards or accessibility issues (Jones-Garmil, 1997). The same problems that made museum automation virtually impossible in the 1960s and 1970s caused individual museums in the 1980s and 1990s to develop their own, unique solutions to these previously unsolvable problems. It was in this environment that the Internet revolution occurred in the mid-1990s.

Museum professionals quickly began exploring the potential of the Internet for providing greater access to information about their collections than had hitherto been possible. By the time of the first Museums and the Web conference in 1997, many museum professionals were already online—bringing information about their institutions, their collections, and their exhibits to the public as fast as possible over the Internet (Bearman & Trant, 1997). They dreamed of a world in which researchers were able to access online databases of museum collections from their homes or offices over the Internet, where visitors could access additional information about the artifacts on display, and where online educational outreach programs would allow museum professionals to reach wider audiences than ever before (Besser, 1997b; Blackaby, 1997; Frost, 2001). Many museum professionals soon realized that they could provide greater and more useful information online if they shared information about their collections electronically (Hickerson, 1997; Hoopes, 1997; Keene, 1998). Without common, shared standards to draw upon, however, providing access to information in an organized and useful fashion has proven to be very difficult.

Data Sharing and the Search for Standards

The lack of acceptable standards in the museum community was recognized as a serious obstacle for museum professionals who wished to create a shared repository of digital information about their collections

(Bearman, 1994; Dunn, 2000; Fox & Wilkerson, 1998). Developing a common standard for documenting museum artifacts was considered extremely valuable because of its potential to improve (a) communication among institutions, (b) the quality of museum data, and (c) access to museum information resources worldwide. Therefore, museum professionals turned again to the problem of standards, despite the fact that the problems of inherent uniqueness and the difficulty of describing artifacts had not been satisfactorily resolved. This time, however, the focus was on developing standards that could help museum professionals share data among institutions, even if those institutions used different information systems internally. Instead of requiring all museums to use one standard for data entry, many organizations now encourage museums to use their own individual systems as long as their records are exportable to a common standard (Perkins, 2001).

To this end, many professional associations have been actively involved in creating potential standards for data sharing. Object ID (http://www.object-id.com/), for example, developed by the Getty Museum (http://www.getty.edu/) and administered by the Council for the Prevention of Art Theft (http://www.copat.co.uk/), was created to provide guidelines for descriptions that could be useful in recovering lost or stolen museum artifacts (Thornes, 1999). The Research Libraries Group (http://www.rlg.org/) was responsible for a number of efforts, including the Cultural Materials Initiative begun in January 2000. The Visual Resources Association (http://www.vraweb.org/) developed their Core Categories for describing information about collections and their visual representations. The Consortium for the Computer Interchange of Museum Information (http://www.cimi.org/) has explored the possibilities of using a variety of established standards, including XML and the Dublin Core, when describing museum artifacts (Perkins & Spinazze, 1999). The International Committee for Documentation of the International Council of Museums (http://www.cidoc.icom.org/) has promoted the development of standards for museums internationally.

Many attempts have also been made to develop standardized terminologies and controlled vocabularies for museum professionals to draw upon when documenting collections. Such standards would make it even easier for museums to share information about their artifacts. Many cultural heritage institutions, for example, classify their collections of fabricated objects using a standard called Nomenclature (Blackaby & Greeno, 1988; Chenhall, 1978). The Getty Research Institute has developed a series of structured vocabularies, such as the *Art and Architecture Thesaurus* (Petersen, 1990), specifically for the use of museum professionals at a variety of institutions (Lanzi, 1998). Nevertheless, despite this activity and effort, it has proven difficult for museum professionals not only to agree on standards for inter-museum communication, but even to use those standards consistently in their own institutions.

Toward the Wired Museum

Now, in the early 21st century, museum professionals realize that being a "wired museum" involves far more than simply gathering electronic information about artifacts into a digital collection; new technologies can revolutionize information management in museums. The volume of scholarly research that often takes place in museums provides a good example. Many museums hold extensive research files, which usually are not integrated into their collections management databases. Valuable data about the importance of a museum's collections, not just what the museum has, is often lurking just beneath the surface. One challenge facing museum professionals lies in integrating as much related information as possible so that museums can better serve the needs of all their constituents (Blackaby, 1997). Rayward and Twidale (2000), for example, explore the idea of using new technologies to add a user-managed virtual layer of information onto pre-existing artifact descriptions.

Attempts to deploy rapidly evolving information technologies in museums have begun to change the way museum professionals work, and have also gradually fostered new initiatives that open up opportunities for reconceptualizing the role and function of museums in society (Besser, 1997b). It has become clear that museums are complex social environments, in which new information technologies have the potential to affect much more than the ways museums manage their collections. The next section of this chapter explores the wider, sociotechnical impact of information technology on museums, museum professionals, and museum visitors.

The Social Impacts of New Museum Technologies

Information technology has changed the way museum professionals work in-house, from collections management to exhibit design. It has changed the way museum professionals work online, from inter-institutional collaboration to educational outreach. It has changed the way museum visitors approach the museum, its holdings, and educational potential. It has changed what museum visitors expect from a museum, both in real life and online. This section examines the impact of museum informatics on both the museum professional and the museum visitor, exploring information management in museums, collaborations between different museum institutions, educational outreach from museums to schools, interactions between museum professionals and scholarly researchers, multimedia exhibits in museum galleries, virtual museums on the Web, and new methods of personalizing the museum-going experience.

Managing Information within the Museum

New information technologies have meant new methods of performing the various jobs of the museum professional. Registrars can organize and access artifact records more effectively and efficiently with electronic databases. Curators can have immediate access to information about artifacts—information that can help them research their collections and plan exhibits without having to bring artifacts out of storage or off display. Collections managers can have access to state-of-the-art storage and climate control systems to help keep artifacts in good condition. Conservators have new tools that help them analyze and restore artifacts that are in poor condition or damaged. New communication systems and computer-assisted design tools can help exhibit designers plan exhibits and casework, integrating information about artifacts, label copy, and graphics in formats that can be easily shared with curators and collections managers. Educators have access to new tools for informing museum visitors and new opportunities for educational outreach over the Internet.

These possibilities require a new approach to information management, and museum professionals have sought ways to improve their deployment of information resources. Orna and Pettitt (1998), for example, discuss the meaning of information in the museum context, identify the different users of information resources in museums, and explore ways of making information in museums more accessible. They cover a variety of topics from strategies for implementing information policies in museums to the technical details of purchasing and installing collections management systems for tracking information about museum artifacts. They also provide a series of case studies about how different museums around the world have employed information technologies to achieve various goals.

Marty (2000) examines how information and communication technologies changed the social dynamics in a university museum. At the University of Illinois, museum professionals, curators, and exhibit designers collaborated in designing a new museum facility. As part of this process, a new information system was developed to help museum curators communicate their proposed designs more efficiently to the exhibit designers. The new system allowed exhibit designers, working remotely, to access online information about museum artifacts and their proposed placement in museum exhibits. In response to these new information systems the social dynamic that had previously existed between museum professionals, museum curators, and exhibit designers changed significantly. The technology fostered greater collaboration among the participants. Now that it was possible for them to communicate dynamically, exchanging information about artifacts in real time, they found themselves collaborating more frequently and more intensively.

Collaborations and Consortia

One immediately positive outcome of standards development as discussed here has been the number of efforts to encourage data sharing across organizations by building centralized repositories of museum information resources. The Canadian Heritage Information Network (http://www.chin.gc.ca/) and the Art Museum Image Consortium (http://www.amico.org/) provide good examples of organizations that encourage participating institutions to contribute to a centralized database accessible to all members. The Canadian Heritage Information

Network (CHIN), for example, has developed a centralized repository to store information about Canadian cultural heritage. CHIN offers a searchable index, called "Artefacts Canada," that provides access to over 2 million artifacts from hundreds of Canadian museums. Member museums individually submit and update information, including images, about their artifacts using CHIN's own software; guidelines are provided for standardized terminology as well as instructions for converting each museum's records to CHIN's data structure format. In addition, CHIN has used information about its member museums to build a guide to Canadian museums called the "Virtual Museum of Canada."

The Art Museum Image Consortium (AMICO), which documents information about more than 65,000 works of art from over 30 art museums, has been able to use its resources to develop guides for institutions creating digital libraries of museum artwork. AMICO has served as a model for collaboration; helping museum professionals understand why collaboration is important; developing standards to aid museum professionals document and distribute information about their collections; and tackling difficult questions of intellectual property, information access, and economic benefits for participating organizations (Trant, Bearman, & Richmond, 2000).

Many other projects have explored how museums could share data and images. One of the most significant was the Museum Educational Site Licensing Project (MESL), which was initiated by the Getty Art History Information Program and ran from 1994 to 1998 (Trant, 1996). Although this project was primarily concerned with the issues of licensing involved in distributing content from museums and libraries to educational institutions (McClung & Stephenson, 1998), it also broke new ground in exploring technical standards for sharing images and textual data among different institutions (Besser & Stephenson, 1996).

The formation of museum information repositories offers the potential to learn more about inter-institutional collaboration. These consortia have the opportunity to test the suitability of standards for sharing museum information resources and recommend best organizational practices to others. The members of Australian Museums and Galleries Online (http://amol.org.au/) have integrated data for hundreds of thousands of Australian artifacts into one searchable collection. Researchers at the University of Sydney have been studying the efforts of these museum professionals to learn how the implementation of the AMOL project has affected the distribution, access to, and use of museum information resources across Australia (Mack & Llewellyn, 1998).

Research on how museums collaborate can produce useful models for museums and other institutions, such as schools or libraries. The Digital Cultural Heritage Community project (Bennett & Sandore, 2001), at the University of Illinois, studied how museums, libraries, and schools collaborated to achieve specific educational goals. Project participants explored how museums and libraries could take primary source material, digitize it, and deliver it directly to the classroom. In this project, researchers were able to evaluate different standards for information organization and access, assess intellectual property concerns, and determine the suitability of primary source material in digital format for educational purposes.

Other researchers have focused on building a theoretical understanding of how diverse museum groups negotiate different interests when collaborating on a common project. Martin, Rieger, and Gay (1999) analyzed the interactions among a research lab, a human-computer interaction lab, and two museums as they collaborated to build a prototype "Global Digital Museum." Each group approached the project from a different perspective and with different beliefs about the content, format, and educational potential of the proposed design. The researchers developed their own theories about the creation of collaborative online learning environments, culminating in a framework for designing and developing virtual museums based on the social construction of technology model (Gay, 2001). In these ways, museum informatics researchers have been able to help museum consortia collaborate more effectively, setting and achieving goals for the mutual benefit of consortia members.

Educational Outreach from Museums to Schools

New information technologies have enabled museums and schools to connect in innovative ways. The Internet has offered museum educators the ability to bring the resources of the museum directly to students who may be unable to travel to the museum itself. Teachers, no longer limited to one or two field trips to museums each year, can integrate digital museum resources into their lesson plans regularly, even from museums halfway around the world. Yet how effectively do these new technologies support educational goals? It is not enough simply to place a digital photograph of a museum artifact on the museum's Web site and expect students to find it educational. Online museum resources must be explicitly designed for educational purposes and carefully integrated into school curricula. Sumption (2001) critically evaluates several different approaches to Web-based museum education, offering strategies to help museum educators create more effective educational resources online.

As museum educators continue to create new programs, it is important for museum informatics researchers to devise models capable of evaluating these new resources and activities so that they can assist museum educators in their development efforts. Milekic (2000) has discussed the potential of "digital environments" for enhancing art education and exploration in museums. Arguing against technologically focused design concepts, he proposes a human-centered approach to the development of educational technologies for museums. Researchers at the University of Michigan have explored how museums and schools can work together to enhance the online museum experience, placing digital museum artifacts in context and promoting a greater awareness of different cultures among K-12 students (Frost, 1999). They have formulated a model program that engages students through active learning, encourages greater community involvement, and fosters a closer relationship between museums and schools. This initiative has also helped create a better understanding of how museum professionals, content specialists, K-12 teachers, and information specialists can collaborate to produce educational materials (Frost, 2001).

Research Activities Involving Museums and Scholars

As museum professionals use new technologies to improve access to their collections, they are often better able to assist researchers interested in the museum's artifacts. The Internet allows scholars, academics, and other researchers to access detailed information about a museum's collection in a fraction of the time it would have taken them to visit the museum in person. Moreover, since only a small percentage of a museum's collection is ever on display at any one time, access to electronic records describing the museum's entire holdings is of great benefit to scholars who may not otherwise have known the full extent of the collection. As Hickerson (1997) recognizes, these new electronic possibilities have created a different understanding of the value of research collections and the nature of research. He describes many early projects dedicated to improving online access to research collections and considers the challenges and implications for both individual researchers and research institutions. Similarly, Hoopes (1997) explores the potential of the Internet to change the way archaeologists and anthropologists conduct research. He describes many different ways in which the World Wide Web has helped these researchers obtain improved access to information about museum collections, and identifies the challenges that remain if online museum resources are to be truly integrated into the research process.

The Opales project of the French Ministry of the Economy is an example of an innovative use of the Internet for research activities, including the potential for online collaborative knowledge sharing (Betaille, Nanard, & Nanard, 2001). Opales provides a mechanism for external experts to annotate digital records maintained at a centralized location and then to share these annotations with other experts. With this project, researchers are attempting to build a collaborative environment that encourages scholars to add value to databases as they use them. Currently, Opales is operating on a multimedia archive of video and audio records; the technology, however, has the potential to be applied to collections of digital artifacts of all types. It raises the possibility that it may soon be commonplace for remote scholars and researchers to access collections information online and also to add their own expertise to a museum's databases.

Multimedia Exhibits in Museums

The use of interactive multimedia is popular with museum professionals as well as the general public, and several studies have been conducted about the effectiveness of hypermedia applications in attracting and educating museum visitors (Bearman, 1991; Thomas & Mintz, 1998). It is common for museums to install multimedia applications—often computers with touch screens located in standalone kiosks—in their exhibits.

These applications have the potential to convey much more information than can be placed on display in gallery text labels, and so allow museum visitors to explore topics in greater detail, according to their own particular interests, and at their own pace. Some visitors approach an interactive kiosk or multimedia display in a cursory way for brief, top-level information, while others remain with the application for considerable time, reading in-depth material about the exhibit. Carefully designed multimedia applications allow digital representations of artifacts to be placed in context, showing the visitor how a particular historical object, for example, might have been used or why a given work of art might have been created.

Many museum professionals have expressed concern about the effectiveness of multimedia exhibits for education, as well as the possibility that interactive multimedia might distract the museum visitor from the objects on display (Economou, 1998). Some argue that, once the decision has been made to integrate multimedia into an exhibit setting, it is important that the interactive components be developed as part of the normal design process; if they are not properly integrated into the exhibit, such applications may detract from the visitor's experience (Semper, 1998). The suitability of interactive applications on the exhibit floor is something that needs to be researched, and all multimedia applications should be evaluated (Sayre, 1998). Thomas (1998) tells the story of a nine-year-old girl who approached an interactive video application in the National Museum of American History. The application used the story of "Goldilocks and the Three Bears" to illustrate a lesson on materials testing. Just as the girl was about to watch Goldilocks test the suitability of a chair, her mother pulled her away, saying, "This is a museum. We did not come here to watch cartoons." The success or failure of multimedia applications in museums depends heavily on the expectations and preconceptions of the museum visitor.

Virtual Museums on the Web

Once museum professionals discovered the potential of the World Wide Web for attracting visitors to their facilities and distributing information about their collections, they quickly seized the opportunities offered; by the time of the first Museums and the Web conference, thousands of museums had developed Web sites (Bowen, 1997). However, for many museum professionals, Internet presence for their museums was initially problematic. It was relatively simple to put basic information online about an institution, its location, hours of operation, and the nature of its collections; but what about placing information about artifacts online and using the Web for educational purposes or multimedia presentations? Some decisions led to surprising results. The French Ministry of Culture provides a good example of how museums initially approached the Internet and the early problems they faced when bringing their institutions online (Mannoni, 1996). When the discovery of a new cave with 30,000 year old paintings was announced in January 1995, the Ministry of Culture was the first institution to post four pictures of the just-discovered artwork on its Web site; within 24 hours, Internet traffic to the site had increased 22-fold. Astonished by the unexpected interest, the museum had to purchase a new server and a faster Internet connection to keep up with demand to see the four pictures.

Today, museums are well aware of the Internet's potential to attract students, scholars, and the general public. Online visitors can take interactive tours that mimic the experience of visiting a museum in person, with various degrees of completeness. They can browse virtual exhibits on a variety of topics illustrated with museum artifacts. They can access databases, complete with text and images that document millions of artifacts of cultural heritage or great works of art. Museum Web sites offer everything from virtual galleries to three-dimensional representations of artifacts—for any number of examples of how museum professionals make use of the Internet see the conference proceedings from the Museums and the Web conferences (e.g., Bearman, & Trant, 2001).

Museum professionals are able to do many new things online that are impossible in traditional museum settings (Schweibenz, 1998). Connections can be made online that are difficult to make in the physical museum gallery (Hoptman, 1992). Objects not normally on display together, for instance, can be displayed side-by-side on the screen in a virtual gallery (Besser, 1997a). New connections can also be made between museum staff and museum visitors, increasing the potential for educational outreach. The Exploratorium (http://www.exploratorium. edu/) in San Francisco uses Webcasting to connect museum audience members, both in-house and online, with live events worldwide; in 1999, the Exploratorium Webcast the total solar eclipse from Turkey

(Spadaccinni, 2001). In all these ways, the virtual museum offers new possibilities for changing the experience of the museum visit.

Personalizing the Museum Experience

New information technologies can revolutionize the experience of visiting a museum by personalizing it for each visitor. Traditionally, museum visitors see the same objects, read the same label copy, follow the same tour guides, and hear the same information from museum docents. Today, it is common for visitors to be offered some kind of handheld device—typically audio devices, anything from headphones connected to a CD player to a handheld wand-like device that plays MP3s—designed to augment and personalize the museum-going experience. As museum visitors wander the galleries with these devices in hand, they can stop in front of a particular item, enter an identification number, and listen to a recorded message about the artifact in question. Such devices allow exhibit designers to provide museum visitors with more detailed information than could reasonably be placed on exhibit label copy.

Many museums have begun exploring the potential of Personal Digital Assistants (PDAs). These handheld computers allow visitors to retrieve extensive information about a variety of artifacts and exhibits by accessing a wireless network built into the museum itself. An early experiment with PDAs was performed at the Berkeley Art Museum in 1995 when Apple Newtons, loaded with text and images relating to select museum artifacts, were distributed to museum visitors as they entered. However, the difficulty of updating information (combined with the subsequent obsolescence of the hardware itself) caused this, and other similar experiments, to fail (Schwarzer, 2001). Recent studies have focused on determining the factors that contribute to the success or failure of PDAs in museums. Researchers at Xerox PARC have developed a task-oriented model for analyzing how museum visitors make use of handheld devices in museum galleries (Aoki & Woodruff, 2000). Other researchers have investigated the educational potential and use of PDAs in museum galleries, the design and development of applications for PDAs, and the evaluation of these applications from the perspective of museum staff and visitors (Evans & Sterry, 1999).

Museum professionals are only now beginning to realize the full potential of handheld devices. PDAs have the potential to revolutionize the museum visit. Some museums, for example, have integrated the use of handheld computers with their Web sites. The Experience Music Project in Seattle (http://www.emplive.com/) distributes handheld devices to visitors that allow them to "bookmark" artifacts they find interesting while in the museum. After their visit, they can log on to the museum's Web site and download additional information about those selected artifacts. It is possible to envisage a time in the near future when museum visitors will be able to plan out an entire visit ahead of time using the museum's Web site and then download this information to a PDA upon entering the museum itself. There is so much interest in the subject that the Consortium for the Interchange of Museum Information (http://www.cimi.org/) has recently launched a project called Handscape to explore the potential uses of handheld devices in museums. These devices instantiate what Rayward and Twidale (2000) call the Cyberdocent; and they raise questions about the impact of such devices on the social experience of visiting a museum. How does use of handheld devices affect the experience of visiting a museum with other people? How does it affect the way museum visitors access and interpret information about museum artifacts? How does this change the educational mission of the museum? These sorts of questions need to be addressed as more museums integrate handheld devices into their exhibits.

Equally revolutionary trends in personalization are occurring in the online museum environment. Many museums with digital collections have offered their virtual visitors the ability to mark selected records and save them online, creating their own set of personal favorites. Visitors can return to view them whenever they wish, add or remove artifacts at will, and even share their favorites with other online visitors. The Metropolitan Museum of Art (http://www.metmuseum.org/) offers a feature called "My Met Gallery," which allows visitors to build their own collections from the set of artifacts available online. ArtsConnectEd (http://www.artsconnected.org/), a joint project of the Minneapolis Institute of Arts and the Walker Art Center, offers a more advanced option called "Art Collector," in which visitors can group records of digital artifacts into multiple sets, annotate them with textual descriptions, and then distribute them to other individuals. The Fine Arts Museums of San

Francisco (http://www.thinker.org/), for instance, allow online visitors to choose from over 70,000 works of art and arrange them into their own private galleries.

The popularity of such activities raises a variety of questions about the consequences of allowing virtual visitors to access and manipulate information about museum artifacts. Some researchers have focused on the educational potential of allowing museum visitors to build their own virtual collections. Educators at the Seattle Art Museum (http://www.seattleartmuseum.org/), for example, have investigated the effect of allowing middle school students to act as virtual curators of an online art gallery using the a feature called "My Art Gallery" (Adams, Cole, DePaolo, & Edwards, 2001). These individualizing capabilities have led some museums to explore the potential of building dynamic, adaptive virtual museum environments based on user profiling. The Marble Museum in Carrara, Italy, offers visitors a virtual tour that varies in content according to a user-definable profile selected by the virtual visitor (Paterno & Mancini, 2000).

New information technologies, it is clear, have radically altered not only the experience of working in a museum, but also the experience of visiting. For museum professionals and museum visitors alike, museum informatics—the information systems and technologies, and the professional practices in which they are embedded—has redefined the common conception of what a museum is in almost every respect.

Museums as Information Environments

Museum professionals and information scientists have begun to explore the broad implications of viewing the museum as an information environment. This section explores how new information technologies have redefined the role of the museum in the information age. It examines issues of significance to both the museum professional and the information scientist, including the changing notion of the museum's identity in the online world, intellectual property and copyright concerns, and the development of integrated information infrastructures, information storage and retrieval, and human-computer interaction.

The Changing Identity of the Museum

The most important information resource any museum possesses is its collection of artifacts. For thousands of years museums have been collecting a wide variety of objects that document and preserve the record of the past (Pearce, 1992). These objects can be works of artistic achievement, cultural heritage, natural history, or scientific endeavor; they represent the history of human society and the natural world. However, the purpose of museums is not merely to house collections of objects; rather, museum professionals collect objects for the purposes of preservation, research, and education (Burkaw, 1995). To accomplish these goals, they must gather extensive information about the objects in their care. For many museum professionals, this information is at least as important as the objects themselves (Pearce, 1986; Washburn, 1984).

The past few decades have seen a shift away from the idea that museums are repositories of objects to the notion that they are repositories of knowledge (Cannon-Brookes, 1992; Hooper-Greenhill, 1992). The museum is now seen as an information utility (MacDonald, 1991), and the information contained in museums has become a resource that must be maintained and managed in order to be useful. Simultaneously, new information technologies have helped to make the organization of and access to museum information resources faster and easier. It is perhaps ironic that the new technology has helped re-create a view of the information-intensive modern museum that harks back to the idea put forward at the end of the nineteenth century by G. Brown Goode, namely, that a well-arranged museum is actually no more than "a collection of instructive labels illustrated by well-selected specimens" (quoted in Bennett, 1995, p. 42).

Information technology-driven changes in museum practice have important implications for both the purpose and the identity of the modern museum. As the amount of information about museum artifacts available online—including high quality digital images—continues to grow, important questions are being raised that concern museum professionals. How will the availability of online information change the way the general public feels about the museum artifact, let alone the museum? Will electronic visitors confuse the digital representation of a work of art with the real thing? Will they consider an online visit to a museum equivalent to visiting the museum in person? Will the physical object itself become less significant? Will the differences between reproduction and original, surrogate record and authentic artifact, fade away? These, and many similar concerns, continue to remain vital areas for further research (Besser, 1997; Rayward, 1998; Weil, 1996).

Additionally, museum professionals continue to struggle with establishing an online identity. They worry that the virtual museum will take away from what Benjamin (1968) calls the "aura" of the object, the special feeling that makes seeing a museum artifact in person different from seeing a photograph of it. Accustomed to controlling every aspect of in-house exhibits, museum professionals fear losing control over the context in which museum artifacts are viewed in the online world. They worry that if potential visitors can find everything they want online, they will be less likely to visit the museum in person (McKenzie, 1997). Despite the potential problems, many museum professionals have faced these concerns head on, working to build an identity for the virtual museum. Recent studies have explored how museum professionals can best keep the interest of their online audiences (Karat et al., 2001). Growing evidence suggests that an online presence actually increases in-person museum visits, since it raises awareness of the museum and its collections for the general public (Bowen, 1999). In addition, museum professionals, as a group responsible for a distinctive aspect of the Web, took a major step in establishing their own online identity in 2001 when they received their own top level Internet domain, dot museum (http://www.musedoma.org/). Some writers are beginning to explore the notion of a "virtual aura" for the museum itself, taking the first steps to creating a new, more powerful identity for the online museum community (Hazan, 2001).

Intellectual Property and Copyright

Increased access to museum information resources online has meant new concerns about intellectual property and copyright for many museum professionals (Steiner, 2000). These issues invariably arise whenever museum professionals begin a project to digitize their collections and make this information available online. How can they ensure that their intellectual property is properly protected? How can they be certain that their resources, particularly digital images, will not be illegally copied and distributed? Many institutions have sought technological solutions to these problems, such as embedding watermarks in digital images. As a basis for dealing effectively with intellectual property issues and copyright, museum professionals are re-evaluating traditional approaches to content distribution and rights administration and are developing new models for managing their information resources (Bearman, 1997; Zorich, 1999).

Museum professionals are also struggling to identify the potential economic benefits of making information about their artifacts available online. This involves identifying potential markets for online museum resources and developing new economic models, such as site licensing, for distributing their intellectual property. Even the traditional museum gift shop has found a new role in the online world as museum professionals explore e-commerce initiatives and forge alliances with e-commerce vendors (Tellis & Moore, 2000).

Integrated Information Systems and Information Infrastructures

Most of the technology-driven changes in museum information management have occurred piecemeal, affecting some museum departments more than others. The museum registrar, for example, may find that a new information system affects his or her job more than it does the museum curator, even though they may both make use of the same data. For this reason, many researchers now argue that it is necessary to take an holistic approach to information management in museums, building integrated systems that manage all aspects of a museum's information resources (Blackaby, 1997; Zorich, 1997). Such systems would allow museum professionals to access all available information on any given topic no matter where in their institution such information was located (Blackaby & Sandore, 1997). Designers of such a system would face many technical problems. However, the desire for an integrated information system reflects the museum world's evolving perspective on information.

As indicated above, new communication tools have changed the way museum professionals interact with scholars, educate students and visitors, and manage their information resources. These changes are reflected in museum work practices and the ways in which museum professionals collaborate among themselves to achieve common goals.

Researchers have already begun to analyze the sociotechnical information infrastructures of museums to understand how information objects are created, handled, and used from a variety of perspectives. Star and Griesemer (1989), for example, developed their influential concept of the "boundary object" at the Berkeley Museum of Vertebrate Zoology to show how such objects were used to mediate different needs and the viewpoints of different groups within the institution. Marty (1999b) studied how the development of a new information infrastructure at the University of Illinois' Spurlock Museum affected the way different museum professionals within the institution collaborated to achieve a common goal.

As museum professionals come to rely on information technologies in the operations of their organizations, the museum itself becomes an interesting site to study how the collaborative activities of the museum staff are influenced by new technologies (Marty, 1999a). Several researchers have begun to explore the notion of the museum as a complex, sociotechnical environment. Hemmings, Randall, Francis et al. (1997) conducted an ethnographic study of the work practices of museum staff members in two English museums: the Museum of Science and Industry in Manchester and the National Railway Museum in York. They analyzed the nature of museum classification work and the way in which these activities were influenced by new technologies, such as database systems (Hemmings, Randall, Marr et al., 1998). Twidale and Marty (2000), similarly, conducted an ethnographic evaluation of how museum professionals at the University of Illinois developed a collaborative system to inventory, pack, and ship a collection of 30,000 museum artifacts. They stressed the need to develop a robust, sociotechnical system that was flexible enough to adapt to new situations, allowing for the possibility of continuous process improvement. Such studies are only beginning to explore the complicated processes of information management and the evolution of sociotechnical systems in museums.

Information Storage and Retrieval

The problems of providing access to information about museum artifacts are of growing interest to researchers studying information storage and retrieval. Researchers at the University of Bologna explored the potential for mobile agents to access distributed sets of heterogeneous data about museum artifacts (Bellavista, Caorradi, & Tomasi, 2000).

They have programmed a set of information agents that dynamically creates a "virtual museum" to the specifications of the user, querying thousands of museum information records remotely and consolidating the results. Their system accommodates a variety of user profiles and usage patterns, from simple database searches to the automatic updating of pre-specified queries. Researchers at the University of Pennsylvania have explored the possibilities of pattern-directed searches of museum information systems (Dworman, Kimbrough, & Patch, 2000). Unlike traditional record-oriented searches that query a database for records that meet a certain condition, pattern-oriented searches derive from questions that seek relationships between variables in records: for example, how does the production of glassware in Italy vary over the life of the Roman Empire? The researchers have developed a prototype system to find and test patterns in collections of text; they are currently testing this system using textual descriptions from a collection of historic New Orleans photographs.

The problems associated with developing a digital image library for museum collections have intrigued researchers interested in information storage and retrieval (Gladney, Mintzer, Schiattarella, Bescos, & Treu, 1998). Given the visual nature of museum exhibits and collections, it is not surprising that museum professionals are interested in digital imaging (Besser & Trant, 1996; Johnston, 1997). This research has the potential to benefit museums, as well as other organizations conducting advanced research into digital imaging technologies. IBM, for example, has been working with museums since the mid-1990s to develop digital imaging technologies (Gladney et al., 1998; Mintzer et al., 2001). By collaborating with the Vatican Library and the Hermitage Museum in St. Petersburg, for example, IBM has developed new techniques for embedding digital watermarks (visible and invisible) into digital images. Tools such as IBM's Query by Image Content (http://wwwqbic.almaden.ibm.com/) or the University of California Berkeley's BlobWorld (http://elib.cs.berkeley.edu/photos/blobworld) have also contributed to digital image search and retrieval technologies.

Researchers continue to investigate the lack of standards for documenting and sharing information about artifacts. Rinehart (2001), for example, describes the Online Archive of California, an initiative begun in 1995 to test the suitability of the Encoded Archival Description (EAD) standard for describing archival collections. Over the past few years, this initiative has expanded so that it now aims to connect the collections of every library, archive, and historical society in the state of California. In 1999, project participants began a new collaboration (Museums and the Online Archive of California) with the intention of testing the suitability of EAD for use in museums. The Consortium for the Computer Interchange of Museum Information (CIMI) has conducted research into standards for accessing distributed collections of museum information resources. For example, CIMI explored the potential use of the Z39.50 standard, creating an application profile to connect multiple sources of museum data while accounting for different data types, query terms, and record structures (Moen, 1998). Along the same lines, CIMI recently studied the suitability of the Dublin Core for describing museum artifacts and for sharing these data among different institutions (Perkins & Spinazze, 1999). After a two-year study of over 200,000 artifact records, CIMI concluded that the Dublin Core provides a useful framework for museum professionals seeking general guidelines in organizing information about collections, but may prove problematic when applied to the specific needs of individual institutions (Consortium for the Computer Interchange of Museum Information, 2000). Currently, CIMI is investigating the use of XML for describing museum artifacts and exploring the potential of the Open Archives Initiative (Perkins, 2001).

Human-Computer Interaction

Museum applications have proven to be extremely fertile grounds for researchers interested in human-computer interaction. From interactive exhibits in the galleries to online virtual environments, multimedia developers have been able to explore a variety of issues. Researchers have emphasized the importance of usability engineering and user testing when designing museum Web sites (Harms & Schweibenz, 2001). Other researchers have explored the requirements involved in building museum applications, in an effort to streamline the design process. Researchers at the Vienna University of Technology have developed a reusable framework for authoring online museum exhibits (Breiteneder & Platzer, 2001). By separating issues of context creation, data structures, and interface design, they were able to create a system that allowed museum professionals to focus on developing content for the virtual exhibit.

Some museums have experimented with three-dimensional, interactive, virtual environments; these can be electronic representations of existing museum installations or exhibits that have no real-world equivalent. Some researchers have wondered if the virtual environment might offer online visitors more than static online exhibits. Paolini et al. (2000) explored the potential for online collaborative visits to virtual museum environments. They developed a virtual version of the Museum of Science and Technology in Milan, Italy. When online visitors enter the virtual museum, they are represented on screen as avatars and see the museum through the eyes of their own avatars. They can move around the virtual museum at will, see and communicate with the other avatars, and go on a virtual tour by following the avatar of a tour guide. The researchers are currently analyzing the impact of these interactions on the virtual visitor to determine whether collaborative visits to virtual worlds are more effective than individual visits. Other researchers have explored the capabilities of dynamic three-dimensional environments that adapt to the user's needs and requirements automatically. Shiode and Kanoshima (1999) developed a prototype system that allows virtual visitors to enter their preferences and explore a three-dimensional art gallery custom-designed for them. Such research underscores the novel possibilities of the online environment, where visitors can interact with museum artifacts in ways impossible in real life.

Information Science and the Future of Museums

This chapter has shown how, over the past few decades, the museum environment has been radically changed by new information technologies. Perhaps the greatest change has been the realization that the museum is an environment where information about artifacts is as important as the collections themselves. Museum professionals have developed new methods of organizing and accessing information about their collections. They have digitized information about millions of artifacts and made this information available over the Internet to scholars, students, and the general public. They have integrated new technologies into their exhibits and galleries, in-house and online. They have even begun to explore the possibilities afforded by virtual environments, personally tailored to each individual museum visitor.

The future, one may be sure, will bring even more innovation as new technologies are developed and implemented in the museum environment. Three-dimensional representations of museum artifacts will become more common. Once information about museum artifacts has been digitized for one purpose, it can easily be used for many others. Integration of information, both within and among museums, offers many new possibilities. Searching across distributed sets of heterogeneous museum data will become easier. The boundaries of distance and time will continue to erode as museum collections around the world are increasingly integrated, providing new ways for scholars and students to interact with the information. The linking and cross-linking of ideas embodied in museum artifacts has been at the core of collection development and exhibit design, regardless of computer use. With increasing digitization, it is possible for such links to become more explicit (in the form of hypertext and hypermedia) and to accommodate more narrative and interpretation than the limitations of physical space allow. This opens new areas of research for exhibit design, tours, education, research and visitor experiences, and contributes to ongoing research in understanding hypermedia design and use. The physicality of museums is a reminder that one should explore the incorporation of virtual information into a physical world, and not merely seek to replace the physical with the virtual. In ways such as this, work in museums can both inform and draw upon research in information science.

These possibilities are dramatically changing the experience of working in, or visiting, a museum, and they are altering our conception of what a museum is. It is tempting to believe that the groundwork has been laid for the functional integration of libraries, museums, and archives, as foreshadowed by Rayward (1998). Museum informatics research and development ought to consider not only what can be built with new technologies but also what should be built. We can learn from earlier computerization efforts, from traditional information use in museums, and from other disciplines. The education of new museum personnel with information expertise (Hermann, 1997) is needed to handle the flood of new hardware and software possibilities. The aim of museum informatics researchers and practitioners should be to guide the selection and use of these technologies to serve the numerous and evolving purposes of museums.

Bibliography

Abell-Seddon, B. (1988). *Museum catalogues: A foundation for computer processing*. London: Bingley.

Adams, C., Cole, T., DePaolo, C., & Edwards, S. (2001). Bringing the curatorial process to the Web. In D. Bearman & J. Trant (Eds.), *Museums and the Web 2001* (pp. 11–22). Pittsburgh, PA: Archives and Museum Informatics.

Aoki, P., & Woodruff, A. (2000). Improving electronic guidebook interfaces using a task-oriented design approach. In W. A. Kellogg & D. Boyarski (Eds.), *Designing interactive systems: Processes, practices, methods, and techniques* (pp. 319–325). New York: ACM Press.

Bearman, D. (Ed.). (1991). *Hypermedia & Interactivity in Museums: Proceedings of an International Conference*. Pittsburgh, PA: Archives and Museum Informatics.

Bearman, D. (1994). Strategies for cultural heritage information standards in a networked world. *Archives & Museum Informatics, 8*, 93–106.

Bearman, D. (1997). New economic models for administering cultural intellectual property. In K. Jones-Garmil (Ed.), *The wired museum: Emerging technology and changing paradigms* (pp. 231–266). Washington, DC: American Association of Museums.

Bearman, D., & Trant, J. (Eds.). (1997). *Museums and the Web 1997*. Pittsburgh, PA: Archives and Museum Informatics.

Bearman, D., & Trant, J. (Eds.). (1999). *Cultural heritage informatics*. Pittsburgh, PA: Archives and Museum Informatics.

Bearman, D., & Trant, J. (2000). When museum informatics meets the World Wide Web. *Journal of the American Society for Information Science, 51*, 3–4.

Bearman, D., & Trant, J. (Eds.). (2001). *Museums and the Web 2001*. Pittsburgh, PA: Archives and Museum Informatics.

Bellavista, P., Caorradi, A., & Tomasi, A. (2000). The mobile agent technology to support and to access museum information. *Proceedings of the 2000 ACM Symposium on Applied Computing*, 1006–1013.

Benjamin, W. (1968). The work of art in the age of mechanical reproduction. In H. Arendt (Ed.), *Illuminations* (pp. 211–244). New York: Schocken Books.

Bennet, N., & Sandore, B. (2001). The Illinois digital cultural heritage community: Museums and libraries collaborate to build a database for the elementary school classroom. *Spectra, 29*(1), 48–55.

Bennett, T. (1995). *The birth of the museum: History, theory, politics*. London: Routledge.

Besser, H. (1997a). The changing role of photographic collections with the advent of digitization. In K. Jones-Garmil (Ed.), *The wired museum: Emerging technology and changing paradigms* (pp. 115–128). Washington, DC: American Association of Museums.

Besser, H. (1997b). The transformation of the museum and the way it's perceived. In K. Jones-Garmil (Ed.), *The wired museum: Emerging technology and changing paradigms* (pp. 153–170). Washington, DC: American Association of Museums.

Besser, H., & Stephenson, C. (1996). The museum educational site licensing project: Technical issues in the distribution of museum images and textual data to universities. In J. Hemsley (Ed.), *Eva 96 London (Electronic Imaging and the Visual Arts)* (pp. 5:1–5:15). Hampshire, UK: Vasari Ltd.

Besser, H., & Trant, J. (1996). *Introduction to imaging: Issues in constructing an image database*. Los Angeles: Getty Trust Publications.

Betaille, H., Nanard, M., & Nanard, J. (2001). Opales: An environment for sharing knowledge among experts working on multimedia archives. In D. Bearman & J. Trant (Eds.), *Museums and the Web 2001* (pp. 145–154). Pittsburgh, PA: Archives and Museum Informatics.

Bishop, A., & Star, S. L. (1996). Social informatics of digital library use and infrastructure. *Annual Review of Information Science and Technology, 31*, 301–401.

Blackaby, J. (1997). Integrated information systems. In K. Jones-Garmil (Ed.), *The wired museum: Emerging technology and changing paradigms* (pp. 203–230). Washington, D.C.: American Association of Museums.

Blackaby, J., & Greeno, P. (1988). *The revised nomenclature for museum cataloging: A revised and expanded version of Robert G. Chenhall's system for classifying man-made objects*. Walnut Creek, CA: Alta Mira.

Blackaby, J., & Sandore, B. (1997). Building integrated museum information retrieval systems: Practical approaches to data organization. *Archives & Museum Informatics, 11*, 117–146.

Bowen, J. (1997). The virtual library museums page (VLMP): Whence and whither? In D. Bearman & J. Trant (Eds.), *Museums and the Web 1997* (pp. 9–26). Pittsburgh, PA: Archives and Museum Informatics.

Bowen, J. (1999). Time for renovations: A survey of museum Websites. In D. Bearman & J. Trant (Eds.), *Museums and the Web 1999* (pp. 163–174). Pittsburgh, PA: Archives and Museum Informatics.

Bower, J., & Roberts, A. (1995). *Developments in museum and cultural heritage information standards*. Los Angeles: Getty Trust Publications.

Breiteneder, C., & Platzer, H. (2001). A re-usable software framework for authoring and managing Web exhibitions. In D. Bearman & J. Trant (Eds.), *Museums and the Web 2001* (pp. 55–64). Pittsburgh, PA: Archives and Museum Informatics.

Buck, R., & Gilmore, J. (1998). *The new museum registration methods*. Washington, DC: American Association of Museums.

Burkaw, G. E. (1995). *Introduction to museum work*. Walnut Creek, CA: AltaMira Press.

Cannon-Brookes, P. (1992). The nature of museum collections. In J. Thompson (Ed.), *Manual of curatorship* (pp. 500–512). London: Butterworth.

Chenhall, R. (1975). *Museum cataloguing in the computer age*. Nashville, TN: American Association for State and Local History.

Chenhall, R. (1978). *Nomenclature for museum cataloging: A system for classifying man-made objects*. Nashville, TN: American Association for State and Local History.

Consortium for the Computer Interchange of Museum Information. (2000). *Guide to best practice: Dublin core*. Retrieved February 10, 2002, from http://www.cimi.org/.

Cowton, J. (Ed.). (1997). *SPECTRUM: The UK museum documentation standard*. Cambridge, UK: Museum Documentation Association.

Doty, P. (1990). Automating the documentation of museum collections. *Museum Management and Curatorship, 9*, 73–83.

Dudley, D., & Wilkenson, I. (Eds.). (1979). *Museum registration methods* (3rd ed.). Washington, DC: American Association of Museums.

Dunn, H. (2000, September). Collection level description: The museum perspective. *D-Lib Magazine, 6*(9). Retrieved February 12, 2002, from http://www.dlib.org/dlib/september00/dunn/09dunn.html.

Dworman, G., Kimbrough, S., & Patch, C. (2000). On pattern-directed search of archives and collections. *Journal of the American Society for Information Science, 51*, 14–23.

Economou, M. (1998). The evaluation of museum multimedia applications: Lessons from research. *Museum Management and Curatorship, 17*, 173–187.

Evans, J., & Sterry, P. (1999). Portable computers and interactive multimedia: A new paradigm for interpreting museum collections. *Archives & Museum Informatics, 13*, 113–126.

Fox, M., & Wilkerson, P. (1998). *Introduction to archival organization and description: Access to cultural heritage*. Los Angeles: Getty Trust Publications.

Frost, C. O. (1999). Cultural heritage outreach and museum/school partnerships: Initiatives at the School of Information, University of Michigan. In D. Bearman & J. Trant (Eds.), *Museums and the Web 1999* (pp. 223–229). Pittsburgh, PA: Archives and Museum Informatics.

Frost, C. O. (2001). Engaging museums, content specialists, educators, and information specialists: A model and examples. In D. Bearman & J. Trant (Eds.), *Museums and the Web 2001* (pp. 177–188). Pittsburgh, PA: Archives and Museum Informatics.

Gay, G. (2001). Co-construction of digital museums. *Spectra, 29*(1), 12–14.

Gladney, H., Mintzer, F., Schiattarella, F., Bescos, J., & Treu, M. (1998). Digital access to antiquities. *Communications of the ACM, 41*(4), 49–57.

Harms, I., & Schweibenz, W. (2001). Evaluating the usability of a museum Web site. In D. Bearman & J. Trant (Eds.), *Museums and the Web 2001* (pp. 43–54). Pittsburgh, PA: Archives and Museum Informatics.

Hazan, S. (2001). The virtual aura: Is there space for enchantment in a technological world? In D. Bearman & J. Trant (Eds.), *Museums and the Web 2001* (pp. 209–220). Pittsburgh, PA: Archives and Museum Informatics.

Hemmings, T., Randall, D., Francis, D., Marr, L., Divall, C., & Porter, G. (1997). Situated knowledge and the virtual science and industry museum: Problems in social and technical interface. *Archives & Museum Informatics, 11*, 147–164.

Hemmings, T., Randall, D., Marr, L., & Francis, D. (1998). *Scrotum daggers and kidney daggers: An ethnography of classification work in museums* (KORG Research Paper, No. 2). Manchester, UK: Manchester Metropolitan University, Department of Sociology.

Hermann, J. (1997). Shortcuts to Oz: Strategies and tactics for getting museums to the Emerald City. In K. Jones-Garmil (Ed.), *The wired museum: Emerging technology and changing paradigms* (pp. 65–91). Washington, DC: American Association of Museums.

Hickerson, H. T. (1997). Realizing new means: Networked access to research collections. In D. Bearman & J. Trant (Eds.), *Museums and the Web* (pp. 151–160). Pittsburgh, PA: Archives and Museum Informatics.

Hooper-Greenhill, E. (1992). *Museums and the shaping of knowledge*. London: Routledge.

Hooper-Greenhill, E. (1995). *Museum, media, and message*. London: Routledge.

Hoopes, J. (1997). The future of the past: Archaeology and anthropology on the Web. *Archives & Museum Informatics, 11*, 87–105.

Hoptman, G. (1992). The virtual museum and related epistemological concerns. In E. Barrett (Ed.), *Sociomedia: Multimedia, hypermedia, and the social construction of knowledge* (pp. 141–159). Cambridge, MA: MIT Press.

Johnston, L. (1997). Imaging in museums: Issues in resource development. In K. Jones-Garmil (Ed.), *The wired museum: Emerging technology and changing paradigms* (pp. 93–114). Washington, DC: American Association of Museums.

Jones-Garmil, K. (Ed.). (1997). *The wired museum: Emerging technology and changing paradigms*. Washington, DC: American Association of Museums.

Karat, C.-M., Karat, J., Pinhanez, C., Podlaseck, M., Vergo, J., Riecken, D., et al. (2001). "Less clicking, more watching": Results from the user-centered design of a multi-institutional Web site for arts and culture. In D. Bearman & J. Trant (Eds.), *Museums and the Web 2001* (pp. 23–32). Pittsburgh, PA: Archives and Museum Informatics.

Keene, S. (1998). *Digital collections, museums and the information age*. London: Butterworth-Heinemann.

Kling, R. (1999). What is social informatics, and why does it matter? *D-Lib Magazine, 5*(1). Retrieved February 12, 2002 from: http://www.dlib.org:80/dlib/january99/kling/01kling.html.

Lanzi, E. (1998). *Introduction to vocabularies: Enhancing access to cultural heritage information*. Los Angeles: Getty Trust Publications.

MacDonald, G. F. (1991). The museum as information utility. *Museum Management and Curatorship, 10*, 305–311.

Mack, V., & Llewellyn, R. (1998). Australian university museums online. *Archives & Museum Informatics, 12*, 81–88.

Mannoni, B. (1996). Bringing museums online. *Communications of the ACM, 39*(6), 100–106.

Martin, W., Rieger, R., & Gay, G. (1999). Designing across disciplines: Negotiating collaborator interests in a digital museum project. In D. Bearman & J. Trant

(Eds.), *Cultural heritage informatics* (pp. 83–90). Pittsburgh, PA: Archives and Museum Informatics.

Marty, P. F. (1999a). Museum informatics and collaborative technologies: The emerging socio-technical dimension of information science in museum environments. *Journal of the American Society for Information Science, 50,* 1083–1091.

Marty, P. F. (1999b). Museum informatics and information infrastructures: Supporting collaboration across intra-museum boundaries. *Archives & Museum Informatics, 13,* 169–179.

Marty, P. F. (2000). On-line exhibit design: The sociotechnical impact of building a museum over the World Wide Web. *Journal of the American Society for Information Science, 51,* 24–32.

McClung, P., & Stephenson, C. (Eds.). (1998). *Images online: Perspectives on the Museum Education Site Licensing Project.* Los Angeles: Getty Trust Publications.

McKenzie, J. (1997). Building a virtual museum community. In D. Bearman & J. Trant (Eds.), *Museums and the Web* (pp. 77–86). Pittsburgh, PA: Archives and Museum Informatics.

Metropolitan Museum of Art. (1968). *Computers and their potential applications in museums.* New York: Arno Press.

Milekic, S. (2000). Designing digital environments for art education/exploration. *Journal of the American Society for Information Science, 51,* 49–56.

Mintzer, F., Braudaway, G., Giordano, F., Lee, J., Magerlein, K., D'Auria, S., et al., (2001). Populating the Hermitage Museum's new Web site. *Communications of the ACM, 44*(8), 52–60.

Moen, W. (1998). Accessing distributed cultural heritage information. *Communications of the ACM, 41*(4), 45–48.

Morrissey, K., & Worts, D. (1998). A place for the muses? Negotiating the role of technology in museums. In S. Thomas & A. Mintz (Eds.), *The virtual and the real: Media in the museum* (pp. 147–172). Washington, DC: American Association of Museums.

Orna, E., & Pettitt, C. (1998). *Information management in museums.* Aldershot, UK: Gower.

Paolini, P., Barbieri, T., Loiudice, P., Alonzo, F., Zanti, M., & Gaia, G. (2000). Visiting a museum together? How to share a visit to a virtual world. *Journal of the American Society for Information Science, 51,* 33–38.

Paterno, F., & Mancini, C. (2000). Effective levels of adaptation to different types of users in interactive museum systems. *Journal of the American Society for Information Science, 51,* 5–13.

Pearce, S. (1986). Thinking about things: Approaches to the study of artefacts. *Museum Journal, 85,* 198–201.

Pearce, S. (1992). *Museums, objects, and collections: A cultural study.* Leicester, UK: Leicester University Press.

Perkins, J. (2001). A new way of making cultural information resources visible on the Web: Museums and the Open Archive Initiative. In D. Bearman & J. Trant

(Eds.), *Museums and the Web 2001* (pp. 87–92). Pittsburgh, PA: Archives and Museum Informatics.

Perkins, J., & Spinazze, A. (1999). Finding museum information in the Internet commons: A report on the CIMI Dublin Core metadata testbed project. In D. Bearman & J. Trant (Eds.), *Cultural heritage informatics 1999: Selected papers from ICHIM99* (pp. 175–177). Pittsburgh, PA: Archives and Museum Informatics.

Petersen, T. (1990). Developing a new thesaurus for art and architecture. *Library Trends, 38*, 644–658.

Rayward, W. B. (1998). Electronic information and the functional integration of libraries, museums and archives. In E. Higgs (Ed.), *History and electronic artefacts* (pp. 207–224). Oxford, UK: Oxford University Press.

Rayward, W. B., & Twidale, M. B. (2000). From docent to cyberdocent: Education and guidance in the virtual museum. *Archives & Museum Informatics, 13*, 23–53.

Rinehart, R. (2001). Museums and the online archive of California. *Spectra, 29*(1), 20–27.

Rush, C., & Chenhall, R. (1979). Computer and registration: Principles of information management. In D. Dudley & I. Wilkenson (Eds.), *Museum registration methods* (pp. 319–339). Washington, DC: American Association of Museums.

Sayre, S. (1998). Assuring the successful integration of multimedia technology in an art museum environment. In S. Thomas & A. Mintz (Eds.), *The virtual and the real: Media in the museum* (pp. 129–146). Washington, DC: American Association of Museums.

Schwarzer, M. (2001, July/August). Art and gadgetry: The future of the museum visit. *Museum News*, 36–41.

Schweibenz, W. (1998). The virtual museum: New perspective for museums to present objects and information using the Internet as a knowledge base and communication system. In H. Zimmerman & V. Schramm (Eds.), *Knowledge Management und Kommunikationssysteme* (pp. 185–200). Konstanz, Germany: UKV.

Semper, R. (1998). Designing hybrid environments: Integrating media into exhibition space. In S. Thomas & A. Mintz (Eds.), *The virtual and the real: Media in the museum* (pp. 119–128). Washington, DC: American Association of Museums.

Shiode, N., & Kanoshima, T. (1999). Utilising the spatial features of cyberspace for generating a dynamic museum environment. *Proceedings of the fourth symposium on the virtual reality modeling language* (pp. 79–84). New York: ACM Press.

Spadaccini, J. (2001). Streaming audio and video: New challenges and opportunities for museums. In D. Bearman & J. Trant (Eds.), *Museums and the Web 2001* (pp. 105–114). Pittsburgh, PA: Archives and Museum Informatics.

Star, S. L., & Griesemer, J. R. (1989). Institutional ecology, transitions, and boundary objects: Amateurs and professionals in Berkeley's Museum of Vertebrate Zoology. *Social Studies of Science, 19*, 387–420.

Steiner, C. (Ed.). (2000). *A museum guide to copyright and trademark*. Washington, DC: American Association of Museums.

Sumption, K. (2001). "Beyond museum walls": A critical analysis of emerging approaches to museum Web-based education. In D. Bearman & J. Trant (Eds.), *Museums and the Web 2001* (pp. 155–162). Pittsburgh, PA: Archives and Museum Informatics.

Tellis, C., & Moore, R. (2000). Building the next generation collaborative museum shopping site: Merging e-commerce, e-museums, and entrepreneurs. In D. Bearman & J. Trant (Eds.), *Museums and the Web 2000* (pp. 113–118). Pittsburgh, PA: Archives and Museum Informatics.

Thomas, S. (1998). Mediated realities: A media perspective. In S. Thomas & A. Mintz (Eds.), *The virtual and the real: Media in the museum* (pp. 1–17). Washington, DC: American Association of Museums.

Thomas, S., & Mintz, A. (Eds.). (1998). *The virtual and the real: Media in the museum*. Washington, DC: American Association of Museums.

Thornes, R. (1999). *Introduction to object ID: Guidelines for making records that describe art, antiques, and antiquities*. Los Angeles: Getty Research Institute.

Trant, J. (1996). The Museum Educational Site Licensing (MESL) project. *Spectra, 23*(3), 32–34.

Trant, J., Bearman, D., & Richmond, K. (2000). Collaborative cultural resource creation: The example of the Art Museum Image Consortium. In D. Bearman & J. Trant (Eds.), *Museums and the Web 2000* (pp. 39–50). Pittsburgh, PA: Archives and Museum Informatics.

Twidale, M. B., & Marty, P. F. (2000). Coping with errors: The importance of process data in robust sociotechnical systems. *Proceedings of the ACM 2000 Conference on Computer Supported Cooperative Work*, 269–278.

Vance, D. (1975). Museum computer network: Progress report. *Museologist, 135*, 3–10.

Vance, D., & Chenhall, R. (1988). *Museum collections and today's computers*. Westport, CT: Greenwood Press.

Varveris, T. (1979). Computers and registration: Practical applications. In D. Dudley & I. Wilkenson (Eds.), *Museum registration methods* (3rd ed., pp. 340–354). Washington, DC: American Association of Museums.

Washburn, W. (1984). Collecting information, not objects. *Museum News, 62*, 5–15.

Weil, S. (Ed.). (1996). *Museums for the new millennium: A symposium for the museum community*. Washington, DC: American Association of Museums.

Williams, D. (1987). A brief history of museum computerization. *Museum Studies Journal, 3*(1), 58–65.

Zorich, D. (1997). Beyond bitslag: Integrating museum resources on the Internet. In K. Jones-Garmil (Ed.), *The wired museum: Emerging technology and changing paradigms* (pp. 171–202). Washington, DC: American Association of Museums.

Zorich, D. (1999). *Introduction to managing digital assets: Options for cultural and educational organizations*. Los Angeles: Getty Trust.

CHAPTER 7

Music Information Retrieval

J. Stephen Downie
University of Illinois at Urbana-Champaign

Introduction

Imagine a world where you walk up to a computer and sing the song fragment that has been plaguing you since breakfast. The computer accepts your off-key singing, corrects your request, and promptly suggests to you that "Camptown Races" is the cause of your irritation. You confirm the computer's suggestion by listening to one of the many MP3 files it has found. Satisfied, you kindly decline the offer to retrieve all extant versions of the song, including a recently released Italian rap rendition and an orchestral score featuring a bagpipe duet.

Does such a system exist today? No. Will it in the future? Yes. Will such a system be easy to produce? Most decidedly not.

Myriad difficulties remain to be overcome before the creation, deployment, and evaluation of robust, large-scale, and content-based Music Information Retrieval (MIR) systems become reality. The dizzyingly complex interaction of music's pitch, temporal, harmonic, timbral, editorial, textual, and bibliographic "facets," for example, demonstrates just one of MIR's perplexing problems. The choice of music representation—whether symbol-based, audio-based, or both—further compounds matters, as each choice determines bandwidth, computation, storage, retrieval, and interface requirements and capabilities. Overlay the

295

multicultural, multiexperiential, and multidisciplinary aspects of music and it becomes apparent that the challenges facing MIR research and development are far from trivial.

Consider the sheer magnitude of available music facing MIR researchers: 10,000 new albums are released and 100,000 works registered for copyright each year (Uitdenbogerd & Zobel, 1999). Notwithstanding the intrinsic intellectual merits of MIR research problems, the successful development of robust, large-scale MIR systems will also have important social and commercial implications. According to Wordspot (2001), an Internet consulting company that tracks queries submitted to Internet search engines, the search for music—specifically, the now-ubiquitous MP3 format—has displaced the search for sex-related materials as the most popular retrieval request. Yet at this moment, not one of the so-called "MP3 search engines" is doing anything more than indexing the textual metadata supplied by the creators of the files. It is not an exaggeration to claim that a successful, commercially based, MIR system has the potential to generate vast revenue. In the U.S. alone, 1.08 billion units of recorded music (e.g., CDs, cassettes, music videos, and so forth), valued at $14.3 billion, were shipped to retailers in 2000 (Recording Industry Association of America, 2001). Vivendi Universal, parent company of Universal Music Group, recently bought MP3.com, a popular Internet-based distributor of MP3 files, for $372 million (Welte, 2001). Beyond the commercial implications, the emergence of robust MIR systems will create significant added value to the huge collections of underused music currently warehoused in the world's libraries by making the entire corpus of music readily accessible. This accessibility will be highly beneficial to musicians, scholars, students, and members of the general public alike.

A growing international MIR research community is being formed, drawing upon multidisciplinary expertise from library science, information science, musicology, music theory, audio engineering, computer science, law, and business. Through an examination of the multidisciplinary approach to MIR, this chapter identifies and explicates the MIR problem spaces, historic influences, current state-of-the art, and future MIR solutions. The chapter also outlines some of the major difficulties that the MIR community faces as MIR research and development grows and matures into a discipline in its own right.

Facets of Music Information: The Multifaceted Challenge

Over the years, I have found it useful to conceive of music information as consisting of seven facets, each of which plays a variety of roles in defining the MIR domain. These facets are the pitch, temporal, harmonic, timbral, editorial, textual, and bibliographic facets. Due to the intricacies inherent in the representation of music information, what follows is not a facet analysis in the strict sense because the facets are not mutually exclusive. For example, the term *adagio* when found in a score could be placed within both the temporal and editorial facets, depending on context. The harmonic facet, likewise, chiefly derives from the interplay of the pitch and temporal facets. The difficulties that arise from the complex interaction of the different music information facets can be labeled the "multifaceted challenge."

Pitch Facet

Pitch is "the perceived quality of a sound that is chiefly a function of its fundamental frequency in—the number of oscillations per second" (Randel, 1986, p. 638). The graphical representation (e.g., ♪, ♩, ω, ǀ, etc.) in which pitch is represented by the vertical position of a note on the staff is familiar to most. Note names (e.g., A, B, C#), scale degrees (e.g., I, II, III ...VII), solfège (e.g., do, ré, mi ... ti) and pitch-class numbers (e.g., 0, 1, 2, 3 ... 11) are also among the many methods of representing pitch.

The difference between two pitches is called an interval. Intervals can be represented by the signed difference between two pitches as measured in semitones (e.g., -8, -7 ... -1, 0, +1 ... +7, +8, etc.) or by its tonal quality as determined by the location of the two pitches within the syntax of the Western theoretical tradition. For example, the interval between A and C# is called a Major 3rd, whereas the aurally equivalent distance between A and D♭ is a Diminished 4th. Melodies can be considered sets of either pitches or intervals perceived as being sequentially ordered through time.

The notion of key is included here as a subfacet of pitch. The melodic fragment EDCEDC (e.g., "Three Blind Mice") in the key of C Major is considered to be musically equivalent to BAGBAG in the key of G Major.

That is to say, their melodic contours (i.e., the pattern of intervals) are perceived by listeners to be equivalent despite the fact that their absolute pitches are different.

Temporal Facet

Information concerning the duration of musical events falls under the temporal facet. This includes tempo indicators, meter, pitch duration, harmonic duration, and accents. Taken together these five elements make up the rhythmic component of a musical work. Rests in their various forms can be considered indicators of the duration of musical events that contain no pitch information. Temporal information poses significant representational and access problems. Temporal information can be absolute (e.g., a metronome indication of MM=80), general (e.g., *adagio*, *presto*, *fermata*), or relative (e.g., *schneller*, *langsamer*). Temporal distortions are sometimes encountered (e.g., *rubato*, *accelerando*, *rallentando*). Because the rhythmic aspects of a work are determined by the complex interaction of tempo, meter, pitch, and harmonic durations, and accent (whether denoted or implied), it is possible to represent a given rhythmic pattern many different ways, all of which yield aurally identical results. Some performance practices, in which it is expected that the player(s) will deviate from the strict rhythmic values noted in the score (e.g., in Baroque, Jazz), give rise to added complexities, similar to those caused by the temporal distortions mentioned above. Thus, representing temporal information for retrieval purposes is quite difficult indeed.

Harmonic Facet

When two or more pitches sound at the same time, a simultaneity, or harmony, is said to have occurred. This is also known as polyphony. The absence of polyphony is called monophony (i.e., only one pitch sounding at a time). Pitches that align vertically in a standard Western score are creating harmony. The interaction of the pitch and temporal facets to create polyphony is a central feature of Western music. Over the centuries music theorists have codified the most common simultaneities into several comprehensive representational systems, based upon their constituent intervals or pitches and the perceived function of those intervals or pitches within contexts of the works in which they appear. Theorists have also codified the common sequential patterns of simultaneities found within Western tonal music. Although it is beyond the scope of this chapter to examine in detail the complex realm of Western harmonic theory and praxis, it is important to note that an individual harmonic event can be denoted by a combination of the pitches or interval(s) it contains and the scale position of its "root," or fundamental, pitch. A chord, like that sounded when a guitar is strummed, is an example of an harmonic event. Sequences of chords, or harmonic events, can be represented by chord names. The very common harmonic sequence, or progression, in the key of C Major, [C+ F+ G+ C+] is here represented by the note name of the fundamental pitch of each chord. The "+" denotes that each chord contains the intervals of Major 3rd and Perfect 5th as measured from the fundamental note. Another method of representing this harmonic progression, that generalizes it to all major keys, is to indicate the scale degree of the root of the chord using Roman numeral notation: I-IV-V-I.

Simple access to the codified aspects of a work's harmonic information can be problematic because its harmonic events, although present in the score, are not usually denoted explicitly in one of the ways described above. Exceptions to this are the inclusion of chord names or chord symbols in most popular sheet music, and the harmonic shorthand, called *basso continuo*, or figured bass, commonly found in music of the Baroque period. The matter is further complicated by the fact that the human mind can perceive and consistently name one of the codified simultaneities, despite the presence of extra pitches called non-chord tones. Even with the absence, or delay, of one or more of the chord's constituent pitches, most members of Western societies can still consistently classify the chord.

Timbral Facet

The timbral facet comprises all aspects of tone color. The aural distinction between a note played upon a flute and upon a clarinet is caused by the differences in timbre. Thus, orchestration information, that is, the designation of specific instruments to perform all, or part, of a work, falls under this facet. In practice orchestration information, although really part of the timbral facet, is sometimes considered part of the bibliographic facet. The simple enumeration of the instruments used in a composition is usually included as part of a standard bibliographic record. This information has been found to assist in the description, and thus the identification, of musical works.

A wide range of performance methods also affects the timbre of music (e.g., *pizzicatti*, mutings, pedalings, bowings). Here the border between timbral and editorial information becomes blurred, as these performance methods can also be placed within the editorial facet. The act of designating a performance method that affects timbre is editorial; the aural effect of the performance of the chosen method is timbral. Timbral information is best conveyed in an audio, or signal-based, representation of a work. Accessing timbral information through a timbral query (e.g., playing a muted trumpet and asking for matches) requires advanced signal processing capabilities. A simpler, yet less precise, method would be to access timbral information through some type of interpretation of the editorial markings. This possible solution would, of course, be subject to the same difficulties associated with representing editorial information, which are discussed next.

Editorial Facet

Performance instructions make up the majority of the editorial facet. These include fingerings, ornamentation, dynamic instructions (e.g., *ppp, p, ...f, fff*), slurs, articulations, *staccati*, bowings, and so on. The vagaries of the editorial facet pose numerous difficulties. One difficulty associated with editorial information is that it can be either iconic (e.g., -, 3, !), or textual (e.g., crescendo, diminuendo), or both. Furthermore, editorial information can also include the parts of the music itself. The writing out of the harmonies from the *basso continuo*, also known as the "realization of the figured-bass," is an editorial act. *Cadenzi* and other solos, originally intended by many composers to be improvised, are frequently realized by the editor. Lack of editorial information is yet another problem to be considered. Like the *basso continuo*, where the harmonies are implied, nearly all composers prior to Beethoven—and many since—have simply assumed that the performers were competent to render the work in the proper manner without aid of editorial information. In many cases, the editorial discrepancies between editions of the same work make the choice of a "definitive" version of a work for inclusion in a MIR system very problematic.

Textual Facet

The lyrics of songs, arias, chorales, hymns, symphonies, and so on, are included in the textual facet. Libretti, the text of operas, are also included. It is important to note that the textual facet of music information is more independent of the melodies and arrangements that are associated with it than one would generally believe. A given lyric fragment is sometimes not informative enough to identify and retrieve a desired melody and vice versa (Temperley, 1993). Freely interchanging lyrics and music is a strong tradition in Western music. A good example of this phenomenon is the tune, "God Save the Queen." Known to citizens of the British Commonwealth as their royal anthem, this simple tune is also known to Americans as their republican song, "America," or "My Country 'tis of Thee." Many songs have also undergone translation into many different languages. Simply put, one must be aware that a given melody might have multiple texts and that a given text might have multiple musical settings. It is also important to remember the existence of an enormous corpus of music without any text whatsoever.

Bibliographic Facet

Information concerning a work's title, composer, arranger, editor, lyric author, publisher, edition, catalogue number, publication date, discography, performer(s), and so on, are all aspects of the bibliographic facet. This is the only facet of music information that is not derived *from* the content of a composition; it is, rather, information, in the descriptive sense, *about* a musical work. It is music metadata. All of the difficulties associated with traditional bibliographic description and access also apply here. Howard and Schlichte (1988) outline these problems along with some of their proposed solutions. Temperley (1993) is another important work tackling this difficult subject.

Why Is MIR Development So Challenging?

The multifaceted challenge, unfortunately, is not the only problem facing MIR research. Developers and evaluators must constantly take into account the many different ways music can be represented (i.e., the "multirepresentational challenge"). Music transcends time and cultural boundaries, yet each historic epoch, culture, and subculture has created its own unique way of expressing itself musically. This wide variety of expression gives rise to the "multicultural challenge." Comprehending and responding to the many different ways individuals interact with music and MIR systems constitutes the "multiexperiential challenge." Maximizing the benefits of having a multidisciplinary research community while minimizing its inherent drawbacks represents MIR's "multidisciplinarity challenge." For another informative overview of the difficulties facing MIR research, I recommend Byrd and Crawford (2002).

The Multirepresentational Challenge

With the exception of the bibliographic facet, each of the aforementioned facets can be represented as symbols, as audio, or both. Symbolic representations include printed notes, scores, text, and myriad discrete computer encodings, including Musical Instrument Digital Interface (MIDI), GUIDO Music Notation Format, Kern, and Notation Interchange File Format (NIFF). Audio representations include live performances and recordings, both analog and digital (e.g., LPs, MP3 files, CDs, and tapes). The choice of representations, whether they be symbolic or audio, is predicated on a mixture of factors including desired uses of the systems, computational resources, and bandwidth. Symbolic representations tend to draw upon fewer computational and bandwidth resources than do audio representations. For example, a 10-second snippet of music represented in stereophonic CD-quality digital audio requires approximately 14 megabits of data to be processed, transmitted, or stored. Under the simplest of symbolic representations, the same musical event could be represented in as few as eight to 16 bits. However, because the vast majority of listeners understand music solely as an auditory art form, many MIR developers see the inclusion of audio representations, despite their inherent consumption of resources, as absolutely necessary.

The pragmatics of simple availability (or nonavailability) of particular representations is also influencing design decisions. For example, many researchers limit themselves to using music in the MIDI, CD, and/or MP3 formats because it is relatively easy to build collections of these types using Web spidering techniques. Intellectual property issues also create availability difficulties for system developers. The 1998

Sonny Bono Copyright Term Extension Act has created a situation where "virtually all sound recordings are protected until the year 2067" (Haven Sound, 2001). Under the terms of this law, building a multirepresentational database that integrates royalty-free public domain scores (e.g., Bach, Beethoven) and MIDI files with readily accessible audio recordings (e.g., CD or MP3 files) might become impossible for all but the very well financed. An academic developer might, for example, have a collection of public domain MIDI files and scores representing the keyboard works of the Baroque period but cannot provide a more robust, multirepresentational set of access methods because of the financial and administrative costs associated with obtaining copyright clearances for the requisite MP3 representations. Levering (2000) provides a summary of intellectual property law as it pertains to the development of digital music libraries and MIR systems. Extensive information about locating and using public domain music can be found at http://www. pdinfo.com/.

The Multicultural Challenge

Music information is, of course, multicultural. However, a cursory review of the extant MIR literature could lead one to the erroneous conclusion that the only music worth retrieving is tonal Western classical and popular music of the last four centuries (i.e., music based on what is known as "Common Practice"). I believe the bias toward Western Common Practice (CP) music has three causes. First, there are many styles of music for which symbolic and audio encodings are not available, nonstandard, or incomplete. Improvised jazz, electronic art music, music of Asia, and performances of Indian ragas all are examples. Likewise, we do not yet have comprehensive recording sets of African tribal songs nor Inuit throat music. Acquiring, recording, transcribing, and encoding music are all time-consuming and expensive activities. For some musics, whole new encoding schemes will also have to be developed. Thus, it is pragmatically more expedient to build systems based upon easier-to-obtain, easier-to-manipulate, CP music. Second, developers are more familiar with CP music than with other styles, and thus are working with that which they understand. Third, I believe that developers wish to maximize the size of their potential user base and therefore have focused their efforts on CP music because it arguably has the largest transcultural audience. Bonardi (2000) provides an informative overview of the shortcomings of CP representations and the problems musicologists experience as they work with non-CP materials.

The Multiexperiential Challenge

Music ultimately exists in the mind of its perceiver. Therefore, the perception, appreciation, and experience of music will vary not only across the multitudes of minds that apprehend it, but will also vary within each mind as the individual's mood, situation, and circumstances change. Music can be experienced as an object of study, either through scores or through the deliberate audition of recordings, as is the case with many music students, music lovers, and musicologists. Sometimes these same music experts will relegate their objects of study to the background during housework and "listen" to them only at a subconscious level. Soundtrack recordings are listened to by many as an *aide memoire* to reinvoke the pleasurable experience of going to the cinema or theater. Music can be experienced as a continuation of familiar traditions with the singing of nursery songs, hymns, camp songs, and holiday carols being prime examples. Music is experienced by some as a means of religious expression, sublime or ecstatic, through such genres as plainsong, chants, hymns, masses, and requiems. David Huron (2000) suggests that music has drug-like qualities. He contends that users seek out not specific melodic or harmonic experiences, but actual physical and emotional alterations. The seeking out of a certain kind of energetic euphoria that one might associate with hip-hop or acid-house music is a case in point.

The seemingly infinite variety of music experience poses two significant hurdles for MIR developers. First, it raises the problems of intended audience and intended use. Which set of users will be privileged and which set of uses addressed? Even if it were possible to somehow encode, query, and retrieve the drug-like effects of the various pieces of music within an MIR database, would such a system also support the analytic needs of the musicologist?

Second, the multiexperiential problem prompts questions about the very nature of music similarity and relevance. For the most part, the notion of similarity for the purposes of retrieval has been confined to the codified, and relatively limited, areas of music's melodic, rhythmic, harmonic, and timbral aspects. Thus, music objects that have some intervals, beats, chords, and/or orchestration in common are deemed to be "similar" to some extent, and hence are also deemed to be potentially "relevant" for the purposes of evaluation. For background information on the importance of, and the controversies surrounding, the notion of relevance in the traditional IR literature, Schamber (1994) is an excellent resource. For an explication of relevance issues as they pertain to MIR, Byrd and Crawford (2002) is highly recommended.

Computing in Musicology (Hewlett & Selfridge-Field, 1998) has devoted an entire volume to issues surrounding melodic similarity. For those interested, I recommend the complete volume. Several of the articles stand out as exemplary explorations of some of the fundamental concepts in MIR research. Selfridge-Field (1997) provides an excellent overview of the myriad problems associated with MIR development. Crawford, Iliopoulos, and Raman (1998) review the amazing variety of string-matching techniques that can be used in MIR. Howard (1998) discusses an interesting procedure for sorting music *incipits*. Cronin (1998) examines U.S. case law pertaining to copyright infringement suits along with analyses and explications for the decisions made by the courts on what constitutes music similarity.

In what ways, however, do we assess the similarity of a user's *experience* of one piece with others in a collection? How is a desired mood or physiological effect to be considered "similar" to a particular musical work? How would we modify an "experiential" similarity measure as the mood and perceptions of the individual users change over time? How do we adjust our relevance judgments under this scenario of ever-shifting moods and perceptions? Perhaps some combinations of melodic, rhythmic, harmonic, and timbral similarities do play a significant role in the similarity of experiences, and further research will uncover how this is so. Given the undeniable importance of music's experiential component, it is possible that future MIR systems will need to incorporate some type of biofeedback mechanism designed to assess the physiological responses of users as retrieval options are presented to them. Although the idea of having users biometrically "plugged in" to MIR systems sounds fanciful, we must remember that the experiential component of music directly shapes our internal conception of similarity and our internal conception of similarity, in turn, determines our relevance judgments. In short, to ignore the experiential aspect of the music retrieval process is to diminish the very core of the MIR endeavor; namely, the retrieval of relevant music objects for each query submitted. The creation of rigorous and practicable theories concerning the nature of experiential similarity and relevance is the single most important challenge facing MIR researchers today.

The Multidisciplinarity Challenge

The rich intellectual diversity of the MIR research community is both a blessing and a curse. MIR research and development are much stronger for having a wide range of expertise being brought to bear on the problems: audio engineers working on signal processing, musicologists on symbolic representation issues, computer scientists on pattern matching techniques, librarians on bibliographic description concerns, and so on. However, this diversity presents some serious difficulties that threaten to hinder MIR research and development.

The heterogeneity of disciplinary worldviews is particularly problematic. Each contributing discipline brings to the MIR community its own set of goals, accepted practices, valid research questions, and generalizable evaluation paradigms. Of these, the variance in evaluation paradigms is most troubling. To compare and contrast the contributions of the different MIR projects being reported in the literature is difficult at present because the research teams are evaluating their approaches using such a wide variety of formal and ad hoc evaluation methods. Complexity analyses, empirical time-space analyses, informetric analyses, traditional information retrieval (IR) evaluations, and algorithmic validations are but a few of the evaluation techniques employed.

It is worth noting that, for a research area that contains "information retrieval" in its name, the number of published works actually drawing upon any of the formal IR evaluation techniques is strikingly low. By "formal IR evaluation" is meant studies of the kind usually performed within the discipline of information retrieval as described by Keen (1992), Korfhage (1997), Tague-Sutcliffe (1992), and most definitively by Harter and Hert (1997). Projects described in Downie (1999), Foote (1997), and Uitdenbogerd and Zobel (1999) are among the very few that report results using the traditional IR metrics of precision and recall. Even among these three, each has taken a slightly different analytic approach: Foote uses average precision, Downie uses normalized-precision and normalized-recall, whereas Uitdengoberd and Zobel use 11-point recall-precision averages and precision-at-20 measures.

Why are the IR evaluation techniques not being widely accepted, and when they are applied, why not in a consistent manner? The lack of familiarity among members of the various domains with traditional IR evaluation techniques, and their associated metrics, is one reason. Another reason is the lack of standardized, multirepresentational test collections: intellectual property issues are one of the serious problems inhibiting their creation. Notwithstanding the absence of test collections, no standardized sets of queries, or relevance judgments, exist either: the MIR community has yet to arrive at a consensus concerning what constitutes a typical set of queries, and, as explained previously, the relevance question remains unresolved.

Communications are also problematic in MIR's multidisciplinary environment. Language and knowledge-base problems abound, making it difficult for members of one discipline to truly appreciate the efforts of the others. For example, when signal processing experts present their works replete with such abbreviations as FFT (Fast Fourier Transform), STFT (Short Time Fourier Transform), and MFCC (Mel-Frequency Cepstral Coefficients), their fellow experts will have no difficulty in understanding them for these are, in fact, rather rudimentary signal processing concepts. However, for most musicologists, comprehending these terms and the underlying concepts they represent will require hours of extra study. Similarly, to a signal processing expert, the enharmonic equivalence of $G^{\#}$ and $A^{\flat}$ is generally seen as a distinction without a difference. To a musicologist, however, it is common knowledge that this equivalence is not necessarily one of absolute equality for the choice of note name can imply the contextual function of the pitch in question. Communication matters are made worse because the MIR literature has no disciplinary "home base": no official MIR society, journal, or foundational textbook exists through which interested persons can acquire the basics of MIR. With the exception of a handful of small panels, workshops, and symposia (discussed later), most researchers are presenting their MIR results to members of their own disciplines (i.e., through discipline-specific conferences and publications). The MIR literature is thus difficult to locate and difficult to read. A fragmented and basically incomprehensible literature is not something upon which a nascent research community can expect to build and sustain a thriving, unified, and respected discipline.

Representational Completeness and MIR Systems

McLane's chapter in the 1996 *Annual Review of Information Science and Technology,* entitled "Music as Information," is a superlative review of the many Music Representation Languages (MRLs) that have been developed or proposed for use in MIR systems (McLane, 1996). A thorough technical comparison of the attributes of five of the historically most important MRLs can be found in Selfridge-Field (1993–1994). Selfridge-Field describes, in easy-to-understand tabular form, how the facets of music information are (or are not) represented in the MuseData, Digital Alternative Representation of Music Scores (DARMS), SCORE, MIDI, and Kern MRLs. *Beyond MIDI: The Handbook of Musical Codes* (Selfridge-Field, 1997) is an excellent resource for deeper exploration of MRL issues.

It is not the purpose of this chapter to evaluate the relative merits of individual MRLs. What is of interest, however, is the role "representational completeness" plays in the creation of various MIR systems. Inspired by McLane (1996), I define the degree of "representational completeness" by the number of music information facets (and their subfacets) included in the representation of a musical work, or corpus of works. A system that includes all the music information facets (and their subfacets), in both audio and symbolic forms, is "representationally complete."

In general, MIR systems can be grouped into two categories: *Analytic/Production* MIR systems and *Locating* MIR systems. The two types of MIR systems can, in general, be distinguished by (1) their intended uses, and (2) their levels of representational completeness. Of the two, Analytic/Production systems usually contain the more complete representation of music information. If one considers a high degree of representational completeness to be *depth,* and the number of musical works included to be *breadth,* then Analytic/Production MIR systems tend toward depth at the expense of breadth, whereas Locating

MIR systems tend toward breadth at the expense of depth. Working descriptions of the two types of MIR systems are given next.

Analytic/Production MIR Systems

Intended users of Analytic/Production MIR systems include such experts as musicologists, music theorists, music engravers, and composers. These MIR systems have been designed with the goal of being as representationally complete as possible, especially with regard to the symbolic aspects of music. For the most part, designers of such systems wish to afford fine-grained access to all the aforementioned facets of music information, with the possible downplaying of the bibliographic facet. Fine-grained access to music information is required by musicologists to perform detailed theoretical analyses of, for example, the melodic, harmonic, or rhythmic structures of a given work, or body of works. Engravers need fine-grained access to assist them in the efficient production of publication-quality musical scores and parts. Composers make use of fine-grained access to manipulate the myriad musical elements that make up a composition. Because of the storage and computational requirements associated with high degrees of representational completeness, Analytic/Production systems usually contain far fewer musical works than Locating MIR systems.

Locating MIR Systems

Locating MIR systems have been designed to assist in the identification, location, and retrieval of musical works. Text-based analogs include online public access catalogs (OPACs); full-text, bibliographic information retrieval (FBIR) systems, like those provided by the Dialog collection of databases; and the various World Wide Web search engines. Intended users are expected to have a wide range of musical knowledge, ranging from the musically naïve to expert musicologists and other musically sophisticated professionals. For the most part, users wish to make use of the musical works retrieved, either for performance or audition, rather than analyzing or manipulating the various facets of the music information contained within the system. Thus, the objects of retrieval can be considered to be more coarsely grained than those associated with Analytic/Production MIR systems. Because the objects of retrieval are more coarsely grained, access points to music information have been traditionally limited to various combinations of select aspects of the pitch, temporal, textual, and bibliographic facets. Recent research advances, however, suggest that access to the timbral and harmonic (i.e., polyphony) facets should become more common in the near future. The following section will help clarify the principal characteristics of a Locating MIR system.

Uses of a Locating MIR System

Some queries in the field of music are text-based and parallel those in other fields. The bibliographic and textual facets of music information can be used[1] to answer the following queries:

- List all compositions, or all compositions of a certain form, by a specified composer

- List all recordings of a specified composition, or composer

- List all recordings of a specified performer

- Identify a song title given a line of lyrics, or vice versa

A good review of the role the computer has played in improving retrieval from textual catalogs of musical scores and discographies is found in Duggan (1992). She points out, for example, that the Online Computer Library Center (OCLC) contains catalog records for 606,000 scores and 719,000 sound recordings, and the Music Library CD-ROM published by SilverPlatter contains more than 408,000 records for sound recordings. However, the ability to store some searchable representation of the music itself provides the user with the capability of answering queries beyond those served by a Machine Readable Cataloging (MARC) format bibliographic catalog:

- Given a composer, identify by the first few bars each of his or her compositions, or compositions of a certain type

This type of query has traditionally been answered by means of printed *incipit* indexes, typically simple listings of the beginning bars of the scores in a particular collection. Edson (1970) is a good example of a printed *incipit* index. Composer-specific thematic catalogues, such as *Bach-Werke-Verzeichnis* (J. S. Bach) (Schmieder, 1990) or *The Schubert Thematic Catalogue* (Deutsch & Wakeling, 1995), also have a rich tradition of use.

- Given a melody, for example the tune of a song or the theme of a symphony, identify the composition or work

This type of query has traditionally been answered by thematic indexes to musical compositions. Barlow and Morgenstern (1949) is an example; their book contains a few bars of one or more themes from 10,000 musical compositions, arranged by composer. A "Notation Index" in the back of the book permits the user to look up a sequence of six to eight notes, transposed into the key of C, as an alphabetical listing of transposed "themes" to identify the composition in which it occurs. Consider just how incomplete a representation of a given work is provided by the "Notation Index"; it contains only a minimalist representation of the pitch facet. Missing from this representation is all key, harmonic, temporal, editorial, textual, timbral, and bibliographic information. The *National Tune Index* (Keller & Rabson, 1980) offers two similarly minimalist representations of musical *incipits*: scale degree (represented by number) and interval-only sequence (represented by signed integers). Lincoln's (1989) index of Italian madrigals also contains an interval-only (signed integers) representation of the *incipits* it contains. The index developed by Parsons (1975) reduces the degree of representational completeness to an extreme. His index represents musical *incipits* as strings of intervals using text strings containing only four symbols—*, R, U, and D—where "*" indicates *incipit* beginning, "R" for note Repeats (interval of 0 semitones), "U" for Up (any positive interval), and "D" for Down (any negative interval).

Representational Incompleteness and Locating MIR Systems

Obviously, such incomplete representations would have very limited use in an Analytic/Production MIR system. However, as locating tools, these minimal representations have shown themselves to have surprising merit. In fact, it is the incompleteness of their music representations that makes them effective as access tools. By limiting the amount of information contained in the representation of the *incipits*, these indexes also reduce the need for the user to come up with more representationally complete queries. Thus, the musically naïve information seeker can use these representations with relatively few opportunities for introducing query errors. Furthermore, should an error be introduced, it is less likely to result in an identification or retrieval failure. So, for the purposes of identification, location, and retrieval, that is to say, for the essential functions of Locating MIR systems, it is not necessary, nor desirable, to have representational completeness.

This conclusion is supported by McLane (1996, p. 240), who commented on Locating MIR systems:

> Both the choice of view from a representation of music and the degree of completeness of a work's representation depend on the user's information needs. Information retrieval is an interactive process that depends on the knowledge of the user and the level of complexity of the desired information. In the case of the need for the simple identification of a musical work where bibliographic information is not unique enough, one may limit the view to a subjective one involving a relatively small subset of the notated elements of the work, often the pitches of an opening melodic phrase. The representation of pitches will be in a form that the user is likely to expect and be able to formulate a query using the same terminology, or at least one that is translatable into the form of the representation.

I have concluded that representational completeness is not a prerequisite for the creation of a useful Locating MIR system. However, why is it that music information tends to be reduced to simplistic representations of the pitch facet for retrieval purposes? Why not use simple representations of the rhythm facet, or perhaps, the timbral facet? McLane's (1996) comments and the decisions by Barlow and Morgenstern (1949), Parsons (1975), Keller and Rabson (1980), and Lincoln (1989) to represent only the pitch facet, and that only simplistically, were not arbitrary. Pyschoacoustic research has shown the contour, or shape, of a melody to be its most memorable feature (Dowling, 1978; Kruhmhansl & Bharucha, 1986). Thus, any representation that highlights a work's melodic contour (i.e., sequences of intervals) while filtering out extraneous information (e.g., exact pitches, rhythmic patterns) should, in theory, increase the chances for the successful identification, location, and retrieval of a musical work.

More Uses of Locating MIR Systems

Some Locating MIR systems are best considered automated replications of *incipit* and thematic indexes: The *RISM* (1997) database and Prechelt and Typke's (2001) *Tuneserver* are good examples. Other systems, like the *MELDEX* systems discussed by McNab and colleagues exploit the information found in some machine-readable "full-text" representation of the music to overcome the limitations of *incipit* and thematic indexes (McNab, Smith, Bainbridge, & Witten, 1997; McNab, Smith, Witten, Henderson, & Cunningham, 1996). Here "full-text" is used in the sense that melodic information is not arbitrarily truncated (as it is in *incipit* and thematic indexes). For example, Parsons' (1975) index contains no melodic string longer than fifteen notes. The greatest advantage to extending the traditional *incipit* and thematic indexes to include full-text information is that memorable music events can occur anywhere within a work and many potential queries will reflect this fact (McNab, Smith, Witten et al. 1996; Byrd & Crawford, 2002). Thus, when full-text access is made possible, a Locating MIR system should also satisfy the following queries:

- In which compositions can we find the following melodic sequence anywhere in the composition?

- Which composers have used the following combination of instruments in the orchestration of a passage?

- What pieces use the following sequence of simultaneities? Which pieces use the following chord progression?

As MIR research progresses, and issues of aural and experiential similarity are addressed, we should add two important types of queries to this list:

- Which compositions "sound" like, or are in the same style as, this piece?

- Which compositions will induce happiness (or sadness, or stimulation, or relaxation)?

Development and Influence of Analytic/Production MIR Systems

Although this review focuses primarily on Locating systems, it is important to acknowledge the valuable contributions that Analytic/ Production research has made to their development. Many early MIR researchers saw the development of Analytic/Production MIR systems as a computer programming language problem; their work laid the foundation for much of present-day MIR research. I believe the honor of the earliest published study in the domain of MIR research in its modern sense belongs to Kassler for his 1966 article, noteworthy for its title, "Toward Musical Information Retrieval." Kassler (1970) describes the MIR language he and others developed to analyze the works of Josquin des Prez. Another early work in the field (Lincoln, 1967) has been credited by Lemström (2000) for laying out the general framework of modern computerized music input, indexing, and printing.

Over the years, many others have contributed to the retrieval language aspect of MIR system research and development. Sutton (1988) developed a PROLOG-based language called MIRA (Music Information Retrieval and Analysis) to analyze Primitive Baptist hymns. A Pascal-like language called SML (Structured Music Language) was developed by Prather and Elliot (1988). McLane (1996) reports, however, that none of these languages has found general acceptance. He provides an explanation for this development, citing Sutton (1988, pp. 246–247), "the literature seems to show ... that scholars interested in specific musical topics have found it more useful to develop their own systems."

The late 1980s saw some important doctoral theses completed. Rubenstein (1987) extended the classic entity-relation model to include two novel features: hierarchical ordering and attribute inheritance. These features allowed Rubenstein to propose the creation of representationally complete databases of music using the relational database model. The extraordinary number of entities required to realize his model meant that an operational system was never implemented. Rubenstien's proposal to exploit the performance-enhancing characteristics of A-tree indexes to speed up searching is worth noting, for it is one of the first instances in the early literature in which the use of indexes instead of linear scanning is explicitly suggested for music.

McLean's (1988) doctoral research attempted to improve retrieval performance by creating a representationally complete encoding of the score. He concluded that a variety of sequential and indexed-based searches would be part of the necessary set of database-level services required for the creation of useful Analytic/Production MIR systems. Other than a brief discussion of the usefulness of doubly linked lists, how he would implement such indexing schemes is unclear.

Page (1988) implemented an experimental system that afforded access to both rhythmic and melodic information. Although he also mentioned that some type of indexing would improve retrieval performance, his system used a query language based on regular expressions. The musical data were searched using specially designed Finite State Automata. Items of interest were retrieved via a single-pass, linear traversal of the database.

An important goal of Page's doctoral thesis was to map out the necessary components of a musical research toolkit. Many of today's Analytic/Production systems are best thought of as suites of computer tools. Each tool is designed to address one of the many processes involved in the creation and use of an MIR system. Tools include encoding computer programs, extraction, pattern matching, display, data conversion, analysis, and so on.

David Huron's *Humdrum Toolkit* is an exemplar of this type of work (http://www.music-cog.ohio-state.edu/Humdrum/). His collection of more than 50 interrelated programs is designed to exploit the many information-processing capabilities found in the UNIX operating system. Taken together, these tools create a very powerful MIR system in which "queries of arbitrary complexity can be constructed" (Huron, 1991, p. 66). Interest in his system is high, and courses on its use are regularly offered. Huron (1991, p. 66) best describes *Humdrum's* flexibilities:

> The generality of the tools may be illustrated through the *Humdrum pattern* command. The pattern command supports

full UNIX regular-expression syntax. Pattern searches can involve pitch, diatonic/chromatic interval, duration, meter, metrical placement, rhythmic feet, articulation, sonorities/chords, dynamic markings, lyrics, or any combination of the preceding as well as other user-defined symbols. Moreover, patterns may be horizontal, vertical, or diagonal (*i.e.*, threaded across voices).

Like most things in life, all of this power comes at a price. Kornstädt (1996, pp. 110–111) provides a fine example of how *Humdrum*'s Unix-style command-line interface

> minimizes the number of potential users. For example, in order to search for occurrences of a given motive and to annotate the score with corresponding tags, the user has to construct the following command:
>
> extract –i'**kern' HG.kern I semits -x I xdelta -s = I patt -t Motive1 -s = -f Motiv1.pat I extract —i**'patt' I assemble HG.krn
>
> The construction of such a command requires a substantial facility in the use of UNIX tools.

The naïve user ever managing to formulate such a search statement is hard to imagine. That *Humdrum* in its original incarnation was intended for use by musically sophisticated users who needed analytic power more than they needed syntactic simplicity must be stressed. Such users would be motivated to take the time to learn its methods. However, Kornstädt (1998) and his colleagues have gone on to develop a Web-based, user-friendly, Locating system, built upon *Humdrum* technology, called *Themefinder* (http://www.themefinder.org/).

MAPPET (Music Analysis Package for Ethnomusicology) was another collection of programs designed to assist in the encoding, retrieval, and analysis of monophonic music (Schaffrath, 1992b). The ESsen Associative Code (ESAC), a simple alpha-numeric scheme containing pitch and duration information, is used to represent the melodies. Melodies were first manually parsed into their constituent phrases; phrase determination in vocal music is not ambiguous, this process was relatively easy and consistent (Schaffrath, 1992a). The phrases were then ESAC encoded; and each encoded phrase was placed "on its own line in one field of a relational (AskSam) database" (Schaffrath, 1992a, p. 66). There were fields containing title, key, meter, and text information, as well as fields derived from the melodic information, such as mode, pitch profiles, and rhythmic profiles. MAPPET's ANA(lysis) and PAT(tern) software subcomponents could be used to translate an analyst's complex search criteria (e.g., intervallic, scale degrees, and rhythmic patterns) into AskSam queries. Detailed explanations of *MAPPET* and its use in the retrieval of monophonic information can be found in Schaffrath (1992b). Camilleri (1992) used MAPPET to analyze the melodic structures of the *Lieder* of Karl Collan.

The Essen databases of ESAC-encoded melodies are the primary source for the "McNab" collection, which forms the heart of the original MELDEX system (McNab, Smith, Bainbridge, et al., 1997; McNab, Smith, Witten, et al., 1996). Some 7,700 of McNab's 9,400 melodies come from Schaffrath's Essen collection and the remaining 1,700 were taken from the Digital Tradition collection (Greenhaus, 1999). The "McNab" collection was used for our own evaluations (Downie, 1999; Downie & Nelson, 2000; Nelson & Downie, 2001). Pickens (2000) and Södring and Smeaton (2002) have also made use of this collection.

Other examples of the many researcher toolkits available include MODE (Musical Object Development System) (Pope, 1992), the LIM Intelligent Music Workstation (Haus, 1994), and *Apollo* (Pool, 1996).

Revisiting the Facets of Music Information: Affording Access

Pitch and Temporal Access

The *Répetoire International des Sources Musicales*, Series A/II, *Music Manuscripts after 1600* database is the official title of what is generally known as the RISM database. The RISM database is one of the oldest and most ambitious of all MIR systems (McLean, 1988; Howard & Schlichte, 1988). It is an automated thematic index of gargantuan proportions. Originally conceived in the late 1940s as an attempt to catalog more than 1.5 million works, the RISM developers were quick to realize the need for automation (Howard & Schlichte, 1988). Now in its fourth edition, the database contains bibliographic records for more than 200,000 compositions by more than 8,000 composers (RISM, 1997). The RISM database is available on CD-ROM and via the Internet (http://www. RISM.harvard.edu/RISM/Welcome.html). The number of indexed access points is remarkable. The "Music Incipit" index is of most interest, as it contains pitch and duration information. *Incipits* are encoded using Brook's alpha-numeric *Plaine and Easie Code* (Brook & Gould, 1964). This is a very simple encoding scheme originally designed for use on typewriters with pitch denoted alphabetically and duration numerically. Howard and Schlichte (1988, p. 23) provide the following example of the *Plaine and Easie Code incipit* for Mozart's *Il core vi dono* from *Cosi fan tutte*:

%F-4$bB@3/8#'8C.6.3§, B'C&/,8A'D6(-)D/,8G'8.C,6B/8F

The ability afforded by the RISM database to search the *incipits* moved "music bibliography into a new realm" (Duggan, 1992, p. 770). Significant problems remain, however, with accessing the *incipit* information found within the RISM database. First, the *incipits* are entered into the MARC records exactly as shown above. This means that each *incipit* is indexed as one long, rather incomprehensible, "word." Second, because of the way the *incipit* is represented in the index, queries must also be posed using *Plaine and Easie*. Third, bringing together works that contain the same melody transposed into different keys is impossible because exact pitch names are used, not intervals. Fourth, searching on pitch or rhythm exclusively is impossible for one would have to know exactly which values to wildcard along with their exact locations. Fifth, and finally, an *incipit* can be represented in several, equally valid, ways, which puts the onus on users to frame their melodic queries in multiple ways (RISM, 1997).

The advent of multimedia personal computing prompted rising interest in the development of prototype Locating MIR systems. Fenske (1988) briefly describes a project at OCLC, led by Drone, called *HyperBach, a Hypermedia Reference System*. This system is also described by Duggan (1989, p. 88) as having "search access from Schmieder number and music entered through a MIDI interface and keyboard synthesizers." These descriptions represent the extent of information available about the *HyperBach* system. Hawley (1990) also developed a limited system that used a MIDI keyboard as the query interface to find tunes whose beginnings exactly matched the queries. Ghias, Logan, Chamberlin, and Smith (1995) developed a more sophisticated prototype system that incorporated autocorrelation methods for pitch tracking and where input was converted to melodic contours for matching against a 183-song database.

Any discussion of accessing the pitch and temporal (i.e., rhythm) facets of music must include the MELDEX system developed at the University of Waikato, New Zealand (McNab, Smith, Bainbridge, et al., 1997; McNab, Smith, Witten, et al., 1997; Bainbridge, Nevill-Manning, Witten, Smith, & McNab, 1999). Now part of the New Zealand Digital Library, MELDEX represents the clearest picture of how a large-scale, robust, and comprehensive Locating MIR system will look in the future (http://www.nzdl.org/musiclib/). The original collection of roughly 10,000 folksongs (based upon a combination of the Essen and Digital Traditional collections) has been enhanced with a second collection of roughly 100,000 MIDI files pulled from the World Wide Web by a spider. Of the monophonic, symbol-based, Locating retrieval systems currently in use, the MELDEX system is the gold standard.

Listing some of the central research and design features of the MELDEX project provides an overview of this project in particular and elucidates the central research and development trends of the MIR literature in general:

- Search modes, which include "query-by-humming"

- Application of Mongeau and Sankoff's (1990) string matching framework in recognition of the need for fault tolerance

- Related to the previous point, the conception of melodic retrieval as a contiguous-string retrieval problem and not a traditional IR indexing problem

- Search options, which range from basic intervallic contour, such as Parsons (1975), to exact match with or without the use of rhythm

- Recognition of scalability issues: that dynamic programming techniques increase search accuracy but at considerable computation cost when compared with the special modification of dynamic programming by Wu and Manber (1992).

- Implementation of browsing capabilities including the automatic creation of thematic thumbnails

- Use of multiple representations including graphic scores, audio files, and MIDI for both browsing and feedback purposes

Three projects, Downie (1999), Pickens (2000), and Uidenbogerd and Zobel (1998, 1999) have two interesting features in common. First, all three evaluated the retrieval effectiveness of interval-only, monophonic representations using melodic substrings, called n-grams (see Downie and Nelson [2000] for a description of the n-gramming process). Second, each project was influenced by the techniques and evaluation methods of traditional text-based IR. A number of factors limit the comparability of these projects, however. For example, Pickens evaluated probabilistic and language-based models; Downie, a vector-space model; and Uitdenbogerd and Zobel, a variety of methods. Tseng (1999), Doraisamy and Rüger (2001), and Södring and Smeaton (2002) present three additional projects using n-grams. Because the tokens created by n-gramming have many properties in common with word tokens, the use of n-grams allows traditional IR techniques to be employed. Notwithstanding the differences in techniques, it is important to note that all six of these teams have found intervallic n-grams to have significant merit as a retrieval approach. Melucci and Orio's (1999) melodic segmentation research is also inspired by the idea of applying traditional IR text retrieval methods.

Rolland, Raskinis, and Ganascia (1999) provide an overview of Rolland's Melodiscov approach to pitch and rhythm searching. Rolland's research is noteworthy as he tested his methods on a *corpus* that included transcriptions of improvised jazz, a particularly difficult genre with which to work. Jang, Lee, and Kao (2001) continue to develop their SuperMBox system, which provides fault tolerant searches via microphone input. Sonoda's ECHO system (Sonoda & Muraoka, 2000) is also designed to accept sung inputs and is tolerant of errors in rhythm and pitch. Related to this line of research is Smith,

Chiu, and Scott (2000), who are developing an interface that takes spoken input to construct more accurate rhythm queries. Byrd (2001) reports on work that applies the pitch contour ideas of Parsons (1975) to rhythm. This work was done to allow the same kind of flexibility to rhythm searches as contours afford melodic searches.

Researchers at National Tsing Hua University in Taiwan have an impressive record investigating melodic, chordal, and "query-by-rhythm" approaches along with various indexing schemes (Chen & Chen, 1998). Chen (2000) briefly outlines the work of this productive group. It has implemented an evaluation platform called Ultima with an eye toward establishing consistent comparisons between retrieval techniques, both theirs and those of others (Hsu & Chen, 2001).

Harmonic Access

The harmonic facet of music information provides several challenges for MIR. One problem is the automatic disambiguation of melodic material from the harmonies that underpin it (e.g., accompaniment) or of which it is a part (e.g., contrapuntal music). The identification or extraction of melody from polyphonic sources is a classic figure and ground problem (Byrd & Crawford, 2002). Early, yet still important, work in this area comes from research into the creation of automatic accompaniment programs to allow a computer to "accompany" the performances of live musicians in real time (Bloch & Dannenberg, 1985; Dannenberg, 1984).

Uitdenbogerd and Zobel (1998, 1999) explored a variety of techniques to extract the melody from a collection of roughly 10,000 polyphonic MIDI files. The most notable aspect of this research was the use of listeners to assess the output of the different methods. Bello, Monti, and Sandler (2000) are developing a set of methods that can take audio input and extract monophonic melodic information as well as transcribe polyphonic sources. Durey and Clements (2001) apply audio retrieval "wordspotting" techniques to the problem of melody extraction from collections of audio files. Von Schroeter, Doraisamy, and Rüger (2000) examine polyphonic audio input and polyphonic Humdrum encodings to locate recurring themes. Meek and Birmingham (2001) have developed a Melodic Motive Extractor (MME) designed to locate and extract recurring themes from collections of MIDI files; they compared the test results with those indexed by Barlow and Morgenstern (1949). Barthelemy and Bonardi

(2001) are attempting to extract harmonic and tonal information automatically from scores through the information contained in the figured bass.

The second problem in dealing with the polyphonic aspect of the harmonic facet is searching. Polyphonic searching is particularly difficult because the search space is multidimensional, but the query can be either monophonic or polyphonic. Lemström's MonoPoly algorithm (Lemström & Perttu, 2000; Lemström & Tarhio, 2000) uses bit-parallel techniques to locate monophonic sequences efficiently in polyphonic databases. Huron's (1991) Humdrum system can be used to perform monophonic, polyphonic, and harmonic progression searches. Dovey (1999) developed an algorithm capable of either monophonic or polyphonic searches through polyphonic music. He has extended his work by formalizing his polyphonic search methods as a regular expression language (Dovey, 2001a). Meredith, Wiggins, and Lemström (2001) also deal with pattern matching and induction in polyphonic music. Pickens (2000) explores techniques for both monophonic and "homophonic" (i.e., simultaneity) extraction. Doraisamy and Rüger (2001) use n-grams of both interval and rhythmic information in conjunction with traditional IR techniques to search polyphonic music with promising preliminary results. Clausen, Engelbrecht, Meyer, and Schmitz (2000) have also adapted and extended traditional IR techniques to the polyphonic searching problem, again with promising results.

Timbral Access

Explicit access to timbral information within the context of MIR is not as well developed as other aspects. Musclefish (http://www.musclefish.com/) has developed several commercial products based upon their audio retrieval research. One product, called Soundfisher, can be used over a collection of audio files to locate similar sounds (http://www.soundfisher.com/). Another product, Clango, is designed to identify and then retrieve metadata about music audio files as they are being played (http://www.clango.com/). Cano, Kaltenbunner, Mayor, and Batlle (2001) are working on the identification problem with noisy radio broadcasts as their domain of interest. Foote (2000) has implemented an audio-based identification system called Arthur that performs its identification using the dynamic structure (i.e., loudness and softness) of the input. Foote has also mounted a limited demonstration system that conducts audio similarity searches (http://www. fxpal.com/people/foote/musicr/doc0.html). Nam and Berger (2001) build upon the work of Foote to generate their approach to audio-based genre classification. Fujinaga and MacMillan (2000) use genetic algorithms and a k-NN classifier to perform a real-time recognition of orchestral instruments. Liu and Wan (2001) report satisfactory results using a limited set of timbral features to classify instrument sounds in the traditional categories of brass, woodwind, string, keyboard, and percussion. Tzanetakis, Essl, and Cook (2001) exploit timbral information as part of their automated approach to classification and genre identification of audio files. Batlle and Cano (2000) use Competitive Hidden Markov models to perform automatic segmentation and classification of music audio. Rauber and Frühwirth (2001) employ Self-Organizing Maps (SOMs) to cluster music based on audio similarity.

Although these systems utilize highly sophisticated signal processing technologies, it is important to note that these are holistic approaches to identification. The input audio is treated as an indivisible entity, and access to, or identification of, say, the bassoon part in an orchestral piece is not yet practical. The timbral search engine work at the Institute de Recherche et Coordination Acoustique/Musique (IRCAM) in Paris does illustrate, however, that timbral-specific searches are possible in theory (http://zappa.ircam.fr/php3/php.exe/cuidad/Timbre.html).

For more information on the complexities of timbre identification and searching, consult Martin (1999), which is the seminal work in this area. Another foundational work is Scheirer (2000). Hererra, Amatriain, Batlle, and Serra (2000) provide a comprehensive review of the different techniques being suggested for the automatic classification of instruments from audio files along with discussion of the feasibility of each. Foote (1999), Kostek (1999), and Tzanetakis and Cook (2000) are all excellent introductions to the techniques used in signal processing and audio information retrieval.

Editorial, Textual, and Bibliographic Access

XML and other structural markup languages are being put forward as a means of enhancing MIR (Good, 2000; MacLellan & Boehm, 2000; Roland, 2000; Schimmelpfennig & Kurth, 2000). One implication of this line of work is that the editorial components of music can be explicitly tagged and thus retrieved. Navigation through a piece, or a set of pieces, via the hyperlinks that can be constructed using structural markup languages is another potential benefit of this development stream. For more information on the hypertextual navigation of musical works, consult Blackburn (2000), Blackburn and DeRoure (1998), or Melucci and Orio (2000).

Choudhury et al. (2000) and Droettboom et al. (2001) report on the large-scale digitization project being undertaken on the Lester Levy Collection of Sheet Music at Johns Hopkins University. Using the Optical Music Recognition (OMR) technology they developed for the project, symbolic representations are created in both MIDI and GUIDO formats. Lyrics and metadata information are also captured and stored for eventual retrieval. In conjunction with the Levy project, the developers of GUIDO (Hoos, Renz, & Görg, 2001) are enhancing the system's search capabilities to take advantage of the high level of representational completeness while at the same time exploiting the power of probabilistic search models.

Query-by-singing is starting to supplement the more traditional query-by-humming methods. Milan-based Haus and Pollastri (2001) and the University of Michigan-based Museart project (Mellody, Barstch & Wakefield, 2002; Birmingham et al., 2001) are two groups that suggest the promise of lyric searches based upon singing rather than text input. The Milan team uses the modeling of singer errors to recognize sung input. The Museart work is based on the characteristics of sung vowels.

Pachet and Laigre (2001) developed a set of analytical tools designed to interpret, classify, and identify song titles based upon the names of the files that contain them. This activity is necessary for increasing the automation of bibliographic control because many pieces are inconsistently labeled. Smiraglia (2001) explores epistemological perspectives to outline the need for, and the difficulties associated with, interlinking all extant versions and derivatives of individual musical works. Allamanche et al. (2001) use audio processing techniques to classify and identify input streams of possibly unlabeled music audio so that the appropriate metadata can be associated with the analyzed works.

DiLauro, Choudhury, Patton, Warner, and Brown (2001) have implemented techniques for automating name authority control over the digitized scores of the Levy Collection using XML, Library of Congress authority files, and Bayesian probability methods. Dovey (2001b) aims to integrate his content-based retrieval system with a traditional online music catalog via the Z39.50 protocol. The most ambitious work being done on improving bibliographic access to electronic audio-visual material, and thus music files, is the MPEG-7 (Moving Picture Experts Group) project (http://mpeg.telecomitalialab.com). This ISO/IEC (International Organization for Standardization/International Electrotechnical Commission) standardization project has created a flexible yet comprehensive method of describing the contents of multimedia files. Music-specific components to the standard include melodic contour and timbral descriptions (Allemanche et al., 2001; Lindsay & Kim, 2001). An overview of the standard is available (http://mpeg.telecomitalialab.com/standards/mpeg-7/mpeg-7.htm).

Concluding Remarks on the Future of MIR

In this chapter, I have outlined the many challenges facing MIR research both as an intellectual endeavor and as a newly emerging discipline. These challenges are not insignificant; and it is obvious that much work remains to be done. I am, however, increasingly confident that the future of MIR research and development is bright. The growing number of researchers interested in MIR issues appears to be reaching a critical mass. For example, as of August 2001, the music-ir@ircam.fr mailing list had over 350 subscribers (http://www.ircam.fr/listes/archives/music-ir/maillist.html). Since 1999, at least two symposia, two workshops, and three panel sessions exclusively devoted to MIR issues have been conducted. These meetings represent the first steps in overcoming the disciplinary fragmentation noted earlier. I suggest interested readers take the time to explore the links provided in the following list of recent MIR events, with an eye toward uncovering the many worthwhile papers that space did not permit to be included in this review.

Recent MIR Workshops, Panels, and Symposia

- The Exploratory Workshop on Music Information Retrieval, ACM SIGIR 1999, Berkeley, California, USA
  (http://mir.isrl.uiuc.edu/mir/mir_workshop.pdf)

- Workshop on Music Description, Representation and Information Retrieval, Digital Resources in the Humanities 1999, London, UK (http://www.kcl.ac.uk/humanities/cch/drhahc/drh/abst502.htm)

- Notation and Music Information Retrieval in the Computer Age, International Computer Music Conference 2000, Berlin, Germany (http://www.icmc2000.org/intro/workshops/index.html#boehm)

- Digital Music Libraries—Research and Development, Joint Conference on Digital Libraries 2001, Roanoke, Virginia, USA (http://www.acm.org/jcdl/jcdl01/panels.html)

- New Directions in Music Information Retrieval, International Computer Music Conference 2001, Havana, Cuba, (http://benares.centrotemporeale.it/~icmc2001/papers)

- First International Symposium on Music Information Retrieval (ISMIR 2000) Plymouth, Massachusetts, USA (http://ciir.cs.umass.edu/music2000)

- Second International Symposium on Music Information Retrieval (ISMIR 2001) Bloomington, Indiana, USA (http://ismir2001.indiana.edu)

The recent establishment of large-scale, well-funded, and multidisciplinary MIR research projects is another indication of a promising future for MIR. Within the United States, three national projects and one international cooperative project are under way. In Europe, two multinational music delivery projects with strong MIR components are being conducted. All six are important and influential projects from which significant contributions have been, and will continue to be, made. Many of the authors cited in this review are working in conjunction with one or more of these projects.

Major MIR Research Projects

- Digital Music Library (DML) Project, Indiana University Bloomington, National Science Foundation, National Endowment for the Humanities (http://dml.indiana.edu)

- Online Music Recognition and Searching project (OMRAS), King's College, London, and University of Massachusetts at Amherst, Joint Information Systems Committee (UK), National Science Foundation (http://www.omras.org/)

- MuseArts Project, University of Michigan, National Science Foundation (http://musen.engin.umich.edu/musearts.html)

- Levy Project: Adaptive Optical Music Recognition, National Science Foundation, Institute for Museum and Library Services, Levy family, Johns Hopkins University (http://mambo.peabody.jhu.edu/omr)

- Content-based Unified Interfaces and Descriptors for Audio/music Databases available Online (CUIDADO), IRCAM, Oracle, Sony CSL, Ben Gurion University-Beer Shiva, artspages, creamw@re, Universitad Pompeu Fabra-Barcelona (http://www.cuidado.mu/)

- Web DELivering of MUSIC (WEDELMUSIC) Università degli Studi di Firenze, IRCAM, Fraunhofer Institute for Computer Graphics, Artec Group, and others (http://www.wedelmusic.org/)

I am encouraged that issues pertaining to relevance and experiential similarity are beginning to be addressed by various research teams: Byrd and Crawford (2002), Hofmann-Engl (2001), and Uitdenbogerd and Zobel (1998, 1999). Work by Chai and Vercoe (2000) and Rolland (2001) on the application of user modeling in the retrieval process also indicates a growing awareness of the limitations of current, system-based, matching practices and relevance assessments. On the evaluation front, other indicators of developing strength are evident. Stemming from briefing documents submitted to the participants of ISMIR 2000 and 2001 (Crawford & Byrd, 2000; Downie, 2000, 2001a), the participants of ISMIR 2001 ratified a resolution proposed by Huron, Dovey, Byrd, and Downie (2001) calling for the creation of standardized multirepresentational test collections, queries, and relevance judgments. The resolution and its current list of signatories can be found at http://music-ir.org/mir-bib2/ resolution. The establishment of annual MIR competitions modeled after the Text REtrieval Conferences (TREC) (http://trec.nist.gov) is one proposed mechanism through which evaluations could be standardized.

Whatever shape a formal evaluative framework for MIR takes, it should reflect not only the traditional IR paradigms but also the goals and aspirations of the many other disciplines that comprise MIR research. It is apparent that novel definitions of relevance, new evaluation metrics, and new measures of success will have to be designed to address the needs of MIR research explicitly.

The problems associated with a lack of an intellectual "home base" for MIR research are being addressed. The organizers of ISMIR 2002 (http://ismir2002.ircam.fr) established an exploratory committee to investigate the relative merits of affiliating with one of the large research organizations (e.g., the Association for Computing Machinery [ACM], the Institute of Electrical and Electronics Engineers [IEEE], the American Society for Information Science and Technology [ASIST]) or creating an independent International Society for Music Information Retrieval (ISMIR). The Mellon Foundation has provided funding for the MIR Annotated Bibliography Project (http://music-ir.org), which is striving to bring a level of bibliographic control to the highly fragmented MIR literature (Downie, 2001b).

Much of the research discussed in this review is preliminary and exploratory because MIR is still in its infancy. Many intriguing yet-to-be-investigated questions remain within the MIR domain. For example, no rigorous and comprehensive studies in the MIR literature examine the human factors involved in MIR system use. Other than one exploratory report (Downie, 1994), I know of no literature explicitly investigating the information needs and uses of MIR system users.

To recap the central themes of this review, I see future MIR research as confronting 10 central questions:

- Which facets of music information are essential, which are potentially useful, and which are superfluous to the construction of robust MIR systems?

- How do we integrate non-Western, non-CP music into our systems?

- How do we better conjoin the various symbolic and audio representations into a seamless whole?

- How do we overcome the legal hurdles impeding system development and experimentation?

- How do we capture, represent, and then exploit the experiential aspects of music?

- What does "relevance" mean in the context of MIR?

- How do we maximize the benefits of multidisciplinary research while minimizing its drawbacks?

- What do "real" users of MIR systems actually want the systems to do?

- How will "real" users actually interact with MIR systems?

- How will we know which MIR methods to adopt and which to abandon?

I cannot predict which combinations of present-day and yet-to-be-developed MIR approaches will ultimately form the basis of the MIR systems of the future. I can predict, however, with absolute certainty, that some of these systems will rival the present-day Web search engines, both in size and general success. I can also predict, again with absolute certainty, that these MIR systems will fundamentally alter the way we experience and interact with music.

Endnotes

1. Adapted from Tague-Sutcliffe, Downie, and Dunne (1993).

Bibliography

Allamanche, E., Herre, J., Hellmuth, O., Fröba, B., Kastner, T., & Cremer, M. (2001). Content based identification of audio materials using MPEG-7 low level description. *Proceedings of the 2nd Annual International Symposium on Music Information Retrieval (ISMIR 2001)*, 197–204. Retrieved February 7, 2002, from http://ismir2001.indiana.edu/pdf/allamanche.pdf.

Bainbridge, D., Nevill-Manning, C. G., Witten, I. H., Smith, L. A., & McNab, R. J. (1999). Towards a digital library of popular music. *Proceedings of the 4th ACM International Conference on Digital Libraries*, 161–169.

Barlow, H., & Morgenstern, S. (1949). *A dictionary of musical themes*. London: Ernest Benn.

Barthelemy, J., & Bonardi, A. (2001). Figured bass and tonality recognition. *Proceedings of the 2nd Annual International Symposium on Music Information Retrieval (ISMIR 2001)*, 129–136. Retrieved February 7, 2002, from http://ismir2001.indiana.edu/pdf/barthelemy.pdf.

Batlle, E., & Cano, C. (2000). Automatic segmentation using competitive hidden Markov models. *Proceedings of the 1st Annual International Symposium on Music Information Retrieval (ISMIR 2000)*. Retrieved February 7, 2002, from http://ciir.cs.umass.edu/music2000/posters/batlle.pdf.

Bello, J. P., Monti, G., & Sandler, M. (2000). Techniques for automatic music transcription. *Proceedings of the 1st Annual International Symposium on Music Information Retrieval (ISMIR 2000)*. Retrieved February 7, 2002, from http://ciir.cs.umass.edu/music2000/papers/bello_abs.pdf.

Birmingham, W. P., Dannenberg, R. B., Wakefield, G. H., Bartsch, M., Bykowski, D., Mazzoni, D., et al. (2001). MUSART: Music retrieval via aural queries. *Proceedings of the 2nd Annual International Symposium on Music Information Retrieval (ISMIR 2001)*, 73–81. Retrieved February 7, 2002, from http://ismir2001.indiana.edu/pdf/birmingham.pdf.

Blackburn, S. (2000). *Content based retrieval and navigation of music*. Unpublished doctoral dissertation, University of Southampton, U.K. Retrieved February 7, 2002, from http://www.ecs.soton.ac.uk/~sgb97r/phdthesis.pdf.

Blackburn, S., & DeRoure, D. (1998). A tool for content based navigation of music. *Proceedings of the 6th ACM International Conference on Multimedia*, 361–368. Retrieved February 7, 2002, from http://www.mmrg.ecs.soton.ac.uk/publications/archive/blackburn1998/html.

Bloch, J. B., & Dannenberg, R. B. (1985). Real-time accompaniment of polyphonic keyboard performance. *Proceedings of the 1985 International Computer Music Conference (ICMC 1985)*, 279–290.

Bonardi, A. (2000). IR for contemporary music: What the musicologist needs. *Proceedings of the 1st Annual International Symposium on Music Information Retrieval (ISMIR 2000)*. Retrieved February 7, 2002, from http://ciir.cs.umass.edu/music2000/papers/invites/bonardi_invite.pdf.

Brook, B. S., & Gould, M. J. (1964). Notating music with ordinary typewriter characters (a plaine and easie code system for music). *Fontes Artis Musicae, 11*, 142–159.

Byrd, D. (2001). Music notation searching and digital libraries. *Proceedings of the 1st ACM / IEEE Joint Conference on Digital Libraries*, 239–246.

Byrd, D., & Crawford, T. (2002). Problems of music information retrieval in the real world. *Information Processing & Management, 38*, 249–272.

Camilleri, L. (1992). The *Lieder* of Karl Collan. *Computing in Musicology, 8*, 67–68.

Cano, P., Kaltenbunner, M., Mayor, O., & Batlle, E. (2001). Statistical significance in song-spotting in audio. *Proceedings of the 2nd Annual International Symposium on Music Information Retrieval (ISMIR 2001)*, 3–5. Retrieved February 7, 2002, from http://ismir2001.indiana.edu/posters/cano.pdf.

Chai, W., & Vercoe, B. (2000). Using user models in music information retrieval systems. *Proceedings of the 1st Annual International Symposium on Music*

Information Retrieval (ISMIR 2000). Retrieved February 7, 2002, from http://ciir.cs.umass.edu/music2000/posters/chai.pdf.

Chen, A. L. P. (2000). Music representation, indexing and retrieval at NTHU. *Proceedings of the 1st Annual International Symposium on Music Information Retrieval (ISMIR 2000)*. Retrieved February 7, 2002, from http://ciir.cs.umass.edu/music2000/papers/invites/chen_invite.pdf.

Chen, J. C. C., & Chen, A. L. P. (1998). Query-by-rhythm: An approach for song retrieval in music databases. *Proceedings of the 8th International Workshop on Research Issues in Data Engineering: Continuous-Media Databases and Applications*, 139–146.

Choudhury, G. S., DiLauro, T., Droettboom, M., Fujinaga, I., Harrington, B., & MacMillan, K. (2000). Optical music recognition within a large-scale digitization project. *Proceedings of the 1st Annual International Symposium on Music Information Retrieval (ISMIR 2000)*. Retrieved February 7, 2002, from http://ciir.cs.umass.edu/music2000/papers/choudhury_paper.pdf.

Clausen, M., Engelbrecht, R., Meyer, D., & Schmitz, J. (2000). PROMS: A Web-based tool for searching in polyphonic music. *Proceedings of the 1st Annual International Symposium on Music Information Retrieval (ISMIR 2000)*. Retrieved February 7, 2002, from http://ciir.cs.umass.edu/music2000/papers/clausen_abs. pdf.

Crawford, T., Iliopoulos, C. S., & Raman, R. (1998). String-matching techniques for musical similarity and melodic recognition. In W. B. Hewlett & E. Selfridge-Field (Eds.), *Computing in Musicology: Vol. 11. Melodic similarity: Concepts, procedures, and applications* (pp. 73–100). Cambridge, MA: MIT Press.

Crawford, T., & Byrd, D. (2000). Background document for ISMIR 2000 on music information retrieval evaluation. *Proceedings of the 1st Annual International Symposium on Music Information Retrieval (ISMIR 2000)*. Retrieved February 7, 2002, from http://ciir.cs.umass.edu/music2000/evaluation.html.

Cronin, C. (1998). Concepts of similarity in music-copyright infringement suits. In W. B. Hewlett & E. Selfridge-Field (Eds.), *Computing in musicology, vol. 11: Melodic similarity: Concepts, procedures, and applications* (pp. 187–209). Cambridge, MA: MIT Press.

Dannenberg, R. (1984). An on-line algorithm for real-time accompaniment. *Proceedings of the 1984 International Computer Music Conference*, 193–198. Retrieved February 7, 2002, from http://www-2.cs.cmu.edu/~rbd/papers/icmc84accomp.pdf.

Deutsch, O. E., & Wakeling, D. R. (1995). *The Schubert thematic catalogue*. New York: Dover.

DiLauro, T., Choudhury, G. S., Patton M., Warner, J. W., & Brown, E. W. (2001). Automated name authority control and enhanced searching in the Levy Collection. *D-Lib Magazine, 7*(4). Retrieved February 7, 2002, from http://www.dlib.org/dlib/april01/dilauro/04dilauro.html.

Doraisamy, S., & Rüger, S. (2001). An approach towards a polyphonic music retrieval system. *Proceedings of the 2nd Annual International Symposium on*

Music Information Retrieval (ISMIR 2001), 187–193. Retrieved February 7, 2002, from http://ismir2001.indiana.edu/pdf/doraisamy.pdf.

Dovey, M. (1999). An algorithm for locating polyphonic phrases within a polyphonic musical piece. *Proceedings of the AISB'99 [Artificial Intelligence and Simulation of Behaviour] Symposium on Musical Creativity*, 48–53.

Dovey, M. (2001a). A technique for regular expression style searching in polyphonic music. *Proceedings of the 2nd Annual International Symposium on Music Information Retrieval (ISMIR 2001)*, 187–193. Retrieved February 7, 2002, from http://ismir2001.indiana.edu/pdf/dovey.pdf.

Dovey, M. (2001b). Adding content-based searching to a traditional music library catalogue server. *Proceedings of the 1st ACM / IEEE Joint Conference on Digital Libraries*, 249–250.

Dowling, W. J. (1978). Scale and contour: Two components of a theory of memory for melodies. *Psychological Review, 85*, 341–354.

Downie, J. S. (1994). The MusiFind musical information retrieval project, phase II: User assessment survey. *Proceedings of the 22nd Annual Conference of the Canadian Association for Information Science*, 149–166.

Downie, J. S. (1999). *Evaluating a simple approach to music information retrieval: Conceiving melodic n-grams as text.* Unpublished doctoral dissertation, University of Western Ontario, London, Ontario, Canada. Retrieved February 7, 2002, from http://music-ir.org/~jdownie/downie_thesis.pdf.

Downie, J. S. (2000). Thinking about formal MIR system evaluation: Some prompting thoughts. *Proceedings of the 1st Annual International Symposium on Music Information Retrieval (ISMIR2000)*. Retrieved February 7, 2002, from http://music-ir.org/~jdownie/downie_mir_eval.html.

Downie, J. S. (2001a). The music information retrieval annotated bibliography project, phase I. *Proceedings of the 2nd Annual International Symposium on Music Information Retrieval (ISMIR 2001)*, 5–7. Retrieved February 7, 2002, from http://ismir2001.indiana.edu/posters/downie.pdf.

Downie, J. S. (2001b). Whither music information retrieval: Ten suggestions to strengthen the MIR research community. *Proceedings of the 2nd Annual International Symposium on Music Information Retrieval (ISMIR 2001)*, 219–222. Retrieved February 7, 2002, from http://music-ir.org/~jdownie/mir_suggestions.pdf.

Downie, J. S., & Nelson, M. (2000). Evaluation of a simple and effective music information retrieval method. *Proceedings of the 23rd Annual International ACM SIGIR Conference on Research and Development in Information Retrieval*, 73–80.

Droettboom, M., Fujianga, I., MacMillan, K., Patton, M., Warner, J., Choudhury, G. S., et al. (2001). Expressive and efficient retrieval of symbolic music data. *Proceedings of the 2nd Annual International Symposium on Music Information Retrieval (ISMIR 2001)*, 173–178. Retrieved February 7, 2002, from http://ismir2001.indiana.edu/pdf/droettboom.pdf.

Duggan, M. K. (1989). CD-ROM, music libraries, present and future. *Fontes Artis Musicae, 36*, 84–89.

Duggan, M. K. (1992). Electronic information and applications in musicology and music theory. *Library Trends, 40,* 756–780.

Durey, A. S., & Clements, M. A. (2001). Melody spotting using hidden Markov models. *Proceedings of the 2nd Annual International Symposium on Music Information Retrieval (ISMIR 2001),* 109–117. Retrieved February 7, 2002, from http://ismir2001.indiana.edu/pdf/durey.pdf.

Edson, J. S. (1970). *Organ-preludes: An index to compositions on hymn tunes, chorales, plainsong melodies, Gregorian tunes and carols.* Metuchen, NJ: Scarecrow Press.

Fenske, D. (1988). Online Computer Library Center. *Directory of computer assisted research in musicology 1988,* 30–31. Menlo Park, CA: Center for Computer Assisted Research in the Humanities.

Foote, J. (1997). Content-based retrieval of music and audio. In C.-C. J. Kuo, S. F. Chang, & V. N. Gudivada (Eds.), *Proceedings of SPIE Vol. 3229. Multimedia storage and archiving systems II* (pp.138–147). Bellingham, WA: SPIE Press. Retrieved February 7, 2002, from http://www.fxpal.com/people/foote/papers/spie97.pdf.

Foote, J. (1999). An overview of audio information retrieval. *Multimedia Systems,* 7(1), 2–11. Retrieved February 7, 2002, from http://www.fxpal.com/people/foote/papers/acm98.pdf.

Foote, J. (2000). Arthur: Retrieving orchestral music by long-term structure. *Proceedings of the 1st Annual International Symposium on Music Information Retrieval (ISMIR 2000).* Retrieved February 7, 2002, from http://ciir.cs.umass.edu/music2000/papers/foote_paper.pdf.

Fujinaga, I., & MacMillan, K. (2000). Realtime recognition of orchestral instruments. *Proceedings of the International Computer Music Conference (ICMC 2000),* 141–143. Retrieved February 7, 2002, from http://gigue.peabody.jhu.edu/~ich/research/icmc00/icmc00.timbre.pdf.

Ghias, A., Logan, J., Chamberlin, D., & Smith, B. C. (1995). Query by humming: Musical information retrieval in an audio database. *Proceedings of the ACM International Multimedia Conference & Exhibition 1995,* 231–236.

Good, M. (2000). Representing music using XML. *Proceedings of the 1st Annual International Symposium on Music Information Retrieval (ISMIR 2000).* Retrieved February 7, 2002, from http://ciir.cs.umass.edu/music2000/posters/good.pdf.

Harter, S. P., & Hert, C. A. (1997). Evaluation of information retrieval systems: Approaches, issues, and methods. *Annual Review of Information Science and Technology, 32,* 3–91.

Haus, G. (1994). The LIM intelligent music workstation. *Computing in Musicology, 9,* 70–73.

Haus, G., & Pollastri, E. (2001). An audio front-end for query-by-humming systems. *Proceedings of the 2nd Annual International Symposium on Music Information Retrieval (ISMIR 2001),* 65–72. Retrieved February 7, 2002, from http://ismir2001.indiana.edu/pdf/haus.pdf.

Haven Sound. (2001). *Music recordings and public domain.* Retrieved February 7, 2002, from http://www.pdinfo.com/record.htm.

Hawley, M. (1990). The personal orchestra, or audio data compression by 10000:1. *Computing Systems, 3,* 289–329.

Herrera, P., Amatriain, X., Batlle, E., & Serra, X. (2000). Towards instrument segmentation for music content description: A critical review of instrument classification techniques. *Proceedings of the 1st Annual International Symposium on Music Information Retrieval (ISMIR 2000).* Retrieved February 7, 2002, from http://ciir.cs.umass.edu/music2000/papers/herrera_paper.pdf.

Hewlett, W. B., & Selfridge-Field, E. (Eds.). (1998). *Computing in musicology: Vol. 11. Melodic similarity: Concepts, procedures, and applications.* Cambridge, MA: MIT Press.

Hofmann-Engl, L. (2001). Towards a cognitive model of melodic similarity. *Proceedings of the 2nd Annual International Symposium on Music Information Retrieval (ISMIR 2001),* 143–151. Retrieved February 7, 2002, from http://ismir2001.indiana.edu/pdf/hofmann-engl.pdf.

Hoos, H., Renz, K., & Görg, M. (2001). GUIDO/MIR—An experimental musical information retrieval system based on GUIDO music notation. *Proceedings of the 2nd Annual International Symposium on Music Information Retrieval (ISMIR 2001),* 41–50. Retrieved February 7, 2002, from http://ismir2001.indiana.edu/pdf/hoos.pdf.

Howard, J. B. (1998). Strategies for sorting melodic incipits. In W. B. Hewlett & E. Selfridge-Field (Eds.), *Computing in musicology: Vol. 11. Melodic similarity: Concepts, procedures, and applications* (pp. 119–128). Cambridge, MA: MIT Press.

Howard, J., & Schlichte, J. (1988). Repertoire international des sources musicales (RISM). In W. B. Hewlett & E. Selfridge-Field (Eds.), *Directory of computer assisted research in musicology 1988* (pp. 11–24). Menlo Park, CA: Center for Computer Assisted Research in the Humanities.

Hsu, J.-L., & Chen, A. L. P. (2001). Building a platform for performance study of various music information retrieval approaches. *Proceedings of the 2nd Annual International Symposium on Music Information Retrieval (ISMIR 2001),* 153–162. Retrieved February 7, 2002, from http://ismir2001.indiana.edu/pdf/hsu.pdf.

Huron, D. (1991). Humdrum: Music tools for UNIX systems. *Computing in Musicology, 7,* 66–67.

Huron, D. (2000). Perceptual and cognitive applications in music information retrieval. *Proceedings of the 1st Annual International Symposium on Music Information Retrieval (ISMIR 2000).* Retrieved February 7, 2002, from http://ciir.cs.umass.edu/music2000/papers/invites/HuronAbstract.pdf.

Huron, D., Dovey, M., Byrd, D., & Downie, J. S. (2001). *Indicate your support for the ISMIR 2001 resolution on the need to create standardized MIR test collections, tasks, and evaluation metrics for MIR research and development.* Retrieved February 7, 2002, from http://music-ir.org/mirbib2/resolution.

Greenhaus, D. (1999, Spring). About the digitial tradition. *The Mudcat Café.* Retrieved February 7, 2002, from http://www.mudcat.org/DigiTrad-blurb.cfm.

Jang, R. J.-S., Lee, H.-R., & Kao, M.-K. (2001). Content-based music retrieval using linear scaling and branch-and-bound tree search. *Proceedings of IEEE International Conference on Multimedia and Expo (ICME 2001).* Retrieved February 7, 2002, from http://neural.cs.nthu.edu.tw/jang/research/paper/2001icme/2001icme-linearScaling.pdf.

Kassler, M. (1966 Spring-Summer). Toward musical information retrieval. *Perspectives of New Music, 4,* 59–67.

Kassler, M. (1970). MIR: A simple programming language for musical information retrieval. In H. B. Lincoln (Ed.), *The computer and music* (pp. 299–327). Ithaca, NY: Cornell University Press.

Keen, E. M. (1992). Presenting results of experimental retrieval comparisons. *Information Processing & Management, 28,* 491–502.

Keller, K., & Rabson, C. (1980). National tune index: 18th century secular music. New York: University Music Edition.

Korfhage, R. R. (1997). *Information storage and retrieval.* New York: John Wiley and Sons.

Kornstädt, A. (1996). SCORE-to-*Humdrum*: A graphical environment for musicological analysis. *Computing in Musicology, 10,* 105–130.

Kornstädt, A. (1998). THEMFINDER: A Web-based melodic search tool. In W. B. Hewlett & E. Selfridge-Field (Eds.), *Computing in musicology: Vol. 11. Melodic similarity: Concepts, procedures, and applications,* 231–236. Cambridge, MA: MIT Press.

Kostek, B. (1999). *Soft computing in acoustics: Applications of neural networks, fuzzy logic and rough sets to musical acoustics: Studies in fuzziness and soft computing.* New York: Physica-Verlag.

Kruhmhansl, C., & Bharucha, J. (1986). Psychology of music. In D. M. Randel (Ed.), *The new Harvard dictionary of music* (pp. 669–670). Cambridge, MA: Belknap Press.

Lemström, K. (2000). *String matching techniques for music retrieval.* Helsinki, Finland: University of Helsinki.

Lemström, K., & Perttu, S. (2000). SEMEX: An efficient retrieval prototype. *Proceedings of the 1st Annual International Symposium on Music Information Retrieval (ISMIR 2000).* Retrieved February 7, 2002, from http://ciir.cs.umass.edu/music2000/papers/lemstrom_paper.pdf.

Lemström, K., & Tarhio, J. (2000). Searching monophonic patterns within polyphonic sources. *Proceedings of the 6th Conference on Content-based Multimedia Information Access (RIAO 2000),* 1261–1279. Retrieved February 7, 2002, from: http://www.cs.helsinki.fi/u/klemstro/publications/RIAO00.ps.

Levering, M. (2000). Intellectual property rights in musical works: Overview, digital library issues and related initiatives. *Proceedings of the 1st Annual International Symposium on Music Information Retrieval (ISMIR 2000).* Retrieved February 7, 2002, from http://ciir.cs.umass.edu/music2000/papers/invites/levering_invite.pdf.

Lincoln, H. B. (1967). Some criteria and techniques for developing computerized thematic indices. In H. Heckmann (Ed.), *Elektronische Datenverarbeitung in der Musikwissenschaft* (pp. 57–62). Regensburg, Germany: Gustave Bosse Verlag.

Lincoln, H. B. (1989). *The Italian madrigal and related repertories: Indexes to printed collections, 1500–1600*. New Haven, CT: Yale University Press.

Lindsay, A., & Kim, Y. (2001). Adventures in standardization, or how we learned to stop worrying and love MPEG-7. *Proceedings of the 2nd Annual International Symposium on Music Information Retrieval (ISMIR 2001)*, 195–196. Retrieved February 7, 2002, from http://music-ir.org/~jdownie/lindsay-kim.pdf.

Liu, M., & Wan, C. (2001). Feature selection for automatic classification of musical instrument sounds. *Proceedings of the 1st ACM / IEEE Joint Conference on Digital Libraries*, 247–248.

MacLellan, D., & Boehm, C. (2000). MuTaTeD'll: A system for music information retrieval of encoded music. *Proceedings of the 1st Annual International Symposium on Music Information Retrieval (ISMIR 2000)*. Retrieved February 7, 2002, from http://ciir.cs.umass.edu/music2000/posters/boehm.pdf.

Martin, K. D. (1999). *Sound-source recognition: A theory and computational model*. Unpublished doctoral dissertation, Massachusetts Institute of Technology, Cambridge, MA. Retrieved February 7, 2002, from http://sound.media.mit.edu/~kdm/research/papers/kdm-phdthesis.pdf.

McLane, A. (1996). Music as information. *Annual Review of Information Science and Technology 31*, 225–262.

McLean, B. A. (1988). The representation of musical scores as data for applications in musical computing. Unpublished doctoral dissertation, State University of New York at Binghamton.

McNab, R. J., Smith, L. A., Bainbridge, D., & Witten, I. H. (1997, May). The New Zealand Digital Library MELody inDEX. *D-Lib Magazine*. Retrieved February 7, 2002, from http://www.dlib.org/dlib/may97/meldex/05witten.html.

McNab, R. J., Smith, L. A., Witten, I. H., Henderson, C., & Cunningham, S. J. (1996). Towards the digital music library: Tune retrieval from acoustic input. *Digital Libraries '96, Proceedings of the ACM Digital Libraries Conference*, 11–18.

Meek, C., & Birmingham, W. P. (2001). Thematic extractor. *Proceedings of the 2nd Annual International Symposium on Music Information Retrieval (ISMIR 2001)*, 119–128. Retrieved February 7, 2002, from http://ismir2001.indiana.edu/pdf/meek.pdf.

Mellody, M., Barstch, M. A., & Wakefield, G. H. (2002). *Analysis of vowels in sung queries for a music information retrieval system*. Manuscript submitted for publication.

Melucci, M., & Orio, N. (1999). Music information retrieval using melodic surface. *Proceedings of the 4th ACM Conference on Digital Libraries*, 152–160.

Melucci, M., & Orio, N. (2000). SMILE: A system for content-based musical information retrieval environments. *Proceedings of the 6th Conference on Content-based Multimedia Information Access (RIAO 2000)*, 1261–1279. Retrieved

February 7, 2002, from http://133.23.229.11/~ysuzuki/Proceedingsall/RIAO2000/ Friday/103CO2.pdf.

Meredith, D., Wiggins, G. A., & Lemström, K. (2001). Pattern induction and matching in polyphonic music and other multi-dimensional datasets. *Proceedings of the 5th World Multi-Conference on Systemics, Cybernetics and Informatics (SCI2001)*, *10*, 61–66. Retrieved February 7, 2002, from http://www.cs.helsinki. fi/u/klemstro/publications/SCI2001-final.ps.

Mongeau, M., & Sankoff, D. (1990). Comparison of musical sequences. *Computers and the Humanities*, *24*, 161–175.

Nam, U., & Berger, J. (2001). Addressing the "same but different—different but similar" problem in automatic music classification. *Proceedings of the 2nd Annual International Symposium on Music Information Retrieval (ISMIR 2001)*. Retrieved March 9, 2002, from http://ismir2001.indiana.edu/posters/ nam.pdf.

Nelson, M., & Downie, J. S. (2001). Informetric analysis of a music database: Distribution of intervals. In M. Davis & C. S. Wilson (Eds.), *Proceedings of the 8th International Conference on Scientometrics and Informetrics (ISSI 2001)*, Vol. 2 (pp. 477–484). Sydney, Australia: Bibliometrics and Informetrics Research Group.

Pachet, F., & Laigre, D. (2001). A naturalist approach to music file name analysis. *Proceedings of the 2nd Annual International Symposium on Music Information Retrieval (ISMIR 2001)*, 51–58. Retrieved February 7, 2002, from http:// ismir2001.indiana.edu/pdf/pachet.pdf.

Page, S. D. (1988). *Computer tools for music information retrieval*. Unpublished doctoral dissertation, Oxford University, UK.

Parsons, D. (1975). *The directory of tunes and musical themes*. New York: Spencer Brown.

Pickens, J. (2000). A comparison of language modeling and probabilistic text information retrieval approaches to monophonic music retrieval. *Proceedings of the 1st Annual International Symposium on Music Information Retrieval (ISMIR 2000)*. Retrieved February 7, 2002, from http://ciir.cs.umass.edu/music2000/ papers/pickens_paper.pdf.

Pool, O. E. (1996). The *Apollo* project: Software for musical analysis using DARMS. *Computers in Musicology*, *10*, 123–128.

Pope, S. T. (1992). MODE and SMOKE. *Computing in Musicology*, *8*, 130–134.

Prather, R. E., & Elliot, R. S. (1988). SML: A structured musical language. *Computers and the Humanities*, *24*, 137–151.

Prechelt, L., & Typke, R. (2001). An interface for melody input. *ACM Transactions on Computer-Human Interaction*, *8*(2), 133–149. Retrieved February 7, 2002, from http://wwwipd.ira.uka.de/~prechelt/Biblio/Biblio/tuneserver_tochi2001 .pdf.

Randel, D. M. (ed.). (1986). *The new Harvard dictionary of music*. Cambridge, MA: Belknap Press.

Rauber, A. & Frühwirth, M. (2001). Automatically analyzing and organizing music archives. *Research and Advanced Technology for Digital Libraries, Proceedings of the 5th European Conference on Research and Advanced Technology for Digital Libraries (ECDL 2001)*, 402–414. Retrieved February 7, 2002, from http://www.ifs.tuwien.ac.at/ifs/research/pub_pdf/rau_ecdl01.pdf.

Recording Industry Association of America. (2001). *Recording Industry Association of America's 2000 yearend statistics*. Washington, DC: RIAA. Retrieved February 7, 2002, from http://www.riaa.com/pdf/year_end_2000.pdf.

RISM. (1997). *Répertoire international des sources musicales: International inventory of musical sources. Series A / II, Music manuscripts after 1600* [CD-ROM database]. Munich, Germany: K. G. Saur Verlag.

Roland, P. (2000). XML4MIR: Extensible markup language for music information retrieval. *Proceedings of the 1st Annual International Symposium on Music Information Retrieval (ISMIR 2000)*. Retrieved February 7, 2002, from http://ciir.cs.umass.edu/music2000/papers/roland_paper.pdf.

Rolland, P.-Y., (2001). Adaptive user-modeling in a content-based music retrieval system. *Proceedings of the 2nd Annual International Symposium on Music Information Retrieval (ISMIR 2001)*. Retrieved February 7, 2002, from http://ismir2001.indiana.edu/posters/rolland.pdf.

Rolland, P.-Y., Raskinis, G., & Ganascia, J.-G. (1999). Musical content-based retrieval: An overview of the Melodiscov approach and system. *Proceedings of the 7th ACM International Multimedia Conference*, 81–84.

Rubenstein, W. B. (1987). *Data management of musical information*. Unpublished doctoral dissertation, University of California, Berkeley.

Schaffrath, H. (1992a). The *ESAC* databases and *MAPPET* software. *Computing in Musicology, 8*, 66.

Schaffrath, H. (1992b). The retrieval of monophonic melodies and their variants: Concepts and strategies in computer-aided analysis. In A. Marsden & A. Pople (Eds.), *Computer representations and models in music* (pp. 95–105). London: Academic Press.

Schamber, L. (1994). Relevance and information behavior. *Annual Review of Information Science and Technology, 29*, 3–48.

Scheirer, E. D. (2000). *Music-listening systems*. Unpublished doctoral dissertation, Massachusetts Institute of Technology, Cambridge. Retrieved February 7, 2002, from http://sound.media.mit.edu/~eds/thesis/.

Schimmelpfennig, J., & Kurth, F. (2000). MCML: Music contents markup language. *Proceedings of the 1st Annual International Symposium on Music Information Retrieval (ISMIR 2000)*. Retrieved February 7, 2002, from http://ciir.cs.umass. edu/music2000/posters/schimmelpfennig.pdf.

Schmieder, W. (1990). *Bach-Werke-Verzeichnis*. Wiesbaden, Germany: Breitkopf & Härtel.

Selfridge-Field, E. (1993–1994). Optical recognition of music notation: A survey of current work. *Computing in Musicology, 9*, 109–145.

Selfridge-Field, E. (Ed.). (1997). *Beyond MIDI: The handbook of musical codes*. Cambridge, MA: MIT Press.

Smiraglia, R. (2001). Musical works as information retrieval entities: Epistemological perspectives. *Proceedings of the 2nd Annual International Symposium* on *Music Information Retrieval (ISMIR 2001)*, 85–92. Retrieved February 7, 2002, from http://ismir2001.indiana.edu/pdf/smiraglia.pdf.

Smith, L. A., Chiu, E. F., & Scott, B. L. (2000). A speech interface for building musical score collections. *Proceedings of the 5th ACM Conference on Digital Libraries*, 165–173.

Södring, T., & Smeaton, A. (2002). Evaluating a melody extraction engine. *Proceedings of the 24th BCS-IRSG European Colloquium on IR Research*. Retrieved February 7, 2002, from http://www.compapp.dcu.ie/~tsodring/ research/papers.

Sonoda, T., & Muraoka, Y. (2000). A WWW-based music retrieval system: An indexing method for a large melody database. *Proceedings of the International Computer Music Conference (ICMC 2000)*, 170–173. Retrieved February 7, 2002, from http://www.sonoda.net/papers/sonoda-icmc2000.pdf.

Sutton, J. B. (1988). *MIRA: A PROLOG-based system for musical information retrieval and analysis*. Unpublished master's thesis, University of North Carolina, Chapel Hill.

Tague-Sutcliffe, J. (1992). The pragmatics of information retrieval experimentation, revisited. *Information Processing & Management, 28*, 467–490.

Tague-Sutcliffe, J., Downie, J. S., & Dunne, S. (1993). Name that tune: An introduction to musical information retrieval. *Proceedings of the 21st Annual Conference of the Canadian Association for Information Science*, 204–216.

Temperley, N. (1993). The problem of definitive identification in the indexing of hymn tunes. In R. D. Green (Ed.), *Foundations of music bibliography* (pp. 227–239). Binghamton, NY: Haworth Press.

Tseng, Y.-H. (1999). Content-based retrieval for music collectors. *Proceedings of the 22nd Annual International ACM SIGIR Conference on Research and Development in Information Retrieval (SIGIR '99)* 176–182.

Tzanetakis, G., & Cook, P. (2000). Audio information retrieval (AIR) tools. *Proceedings of the 1st Annual International Symposium on Music Information Retrieval (ISMIR 2000)*. Retrieved February 7, 2002, from http://ciir.cs. umass.edu/music2000/papers/tzanetakis_paper.pdf.

Tzanetakis, G., Essl, G., & Cook, P. (2001). Automatic musical genre classification of audio signals. *Proceedings of the 2nd Annual International Symposium on Music Information Retrieval (ISMIR 2001)*, 205–210. Retrieved February 7, 2002, from http://ismir2001.indiana.edu/pdf/tzanetakis.pdf.

Uitdenbogerd, A. L., & Zobel, J. (1998). Manipulation of music for melody matching. *Proceedings of the 6th ACM International Conference on Multimedia*, 235–240. Retrieved February 7, 2002, from http://www.acm.org/sigmm/MM98/electronic_proceedings/uitdenbogerd/index.html.

Uitdenbogerd, A. L., & Zobel, J. (1999). Matching techniques for large music databases. *Proceedings of the 7th ACM International Multimedia Conference*, 57–66.

Von Schroeter, T., Doraisamy, S., & Rüger, S. (2000). From raw polyphonic audio to locating recurring themes. *Proceedings of the 1st Annual International Symposium on Music Information Retrieval (ISMIR 2000)*. Retrieved February 7, 2002, from http://ciir.cs.umass.edu/music2000/posters/shroeter_ruger.pdf.

Welte, J. (2001, May 23). MP3.com: A dream deferred. *Business 2.0*. Retrieved February 7, 2002, from http://www.business2.com/articles/web/0,1653,15733,FF. html.

Wordspot. (2001). *WordSpot search engine word usage covering August 27th through September 3rd, 2001*. Retrieved February 7, 2002, from http://www.wordspot.com.

Wu, S., & Manber, U. (1992). Fast text searching allowing errors. *Communications of the ACM, 35*(10), 83–91.

Theorizing Information and Information Use

CHAPTER 8

The Concept of Information

Rafael Capurro
University of Applied Sciences, Stuttgart
Birger Hjørland
Royal School of Library and Information Science, Copenhagen

Introduction

The concept of information as we use it in everyday English, in the sense of knowledge communicated, plays a central role in contemporary society. The development and widespread use of computer networks since the end of World War II, and the emergence of information science as a discipline in the 1950s, are evidence of this focus. Although knowledge and its communication are basic phenomena of every human society, it is the rise of information technology and its global impacts that characterize ours as an information society. It is commonplace to consider information as a basic condition for economic development together with capital, labor, and raw material; but what makes information especially significant at present is its digital nature. The impact of information technology on the natural and social sciences in particular has made this everyday notion a highly controversial concept. Claude Shannon's (1948) "A Mathematical Theory of Communication" is a landmark work, referring to the common use of information with its semantic and pragmatic dimensions, while at the same time redefining the concept within an engineering framework. The fact that the concept of knowledge communication has been designated by the word *information* seems, prima facie, a linguistic happenstance.

For a science like information science (IS), it is of course important how fundamental terms are defined; and in IS, as in other fields, the question of how to define information is often raised. This chapter is an attempt to review the status of the concept of information in IS, with reference also to interdisciplinary trends. In scientific discourse, theoretical concepts are not true or false elements or glimpses of some element of reality; rather, they are constructions designed to do a job in the best possible way. Different conceptions of fundamental terms like *information* are thus more or less fruitful, depending on the theories (and in the end, the practical actions) they are expected to support. In the opening section, we discuss the problem of defining terms from the perspective of the philosophy of science.

The history of a word provides us with anecdotes that are tangential to the concept itself. But in our case, the use of the word information points to a specific perspective from which the concept of knowledge communication has been defined. This perspective includes such characteristics as novelty and relevance; i.e., it refers to the process of knowledge transformation, and particularly to selection and interpretation within a specific context. The discussion leads to the questions of why and when this meaning was designated with the word *information*. We will explore this history, and we believe that our results may help readers better understand the complexity of the concept with regard to its scientific definitions.

Discussions about the concept of information in other disciplines are very important for IS because many theories and approaches in IS have their origins elsewhere (see the section "Information as an Interdisciplinary Concept" in this chapter). The epistemological concept of information brings into play nonhuman information processes, particularly in physics and biology. And vice versa: the psychic and sociological processes of selection and interpretation may be considered using objective parameters, leaving aside the semantic dimension, or more precisely, by considering objective or situational parameters of interpretation. This concept can be illustrated also in physical terms with regard to release mechanisms, as we suggest. Our overview of the concept of information in the natural sciences as well as in the humanities and social sciences cannot hope to be comprehensive. In most cases, we can refer only to fragments of theories. However, the reader may wish to follow the leads provided in the bibliography.

Readers interested primarily in information science may derive most benefit from the section on "Information in Information Science," in which we offer a detailed explanation of diverse views and theories of information within our field; supplementing the recent *ARIST* chapter by Cornelius (2002). We show that the introduction of the concept of information circa 1950 to the domain of special librarianship and documentation has in itself had serious consequences for the types of knowledge and theories developed in our field. The important question is not only what meaning we give the term in IS, but also how it relates to other basic terms, such as documents, texts, and knowledge.

Starting with an objectivist view from the world of information theory and cybernetics, information science has turned to the phenomena of relevance and interpretation as basic aspects of the concept of information. This change is in no way a turn to a subjectivist theory, but an appraisal of different perspectives that may determine in a particular context what is being considered as informative, be it a "thing" (Buckland, 1991b) or a document. Different concepts of information within information science reflect tensions between a subjective and an objective approach. The concept of interpretation or selection may be considered to be the bridge between these two poles. It is important, however, to consider the different professions involved with the interpretation and selection of knowledge. The most important thing in IS (as in information policy) is to consider information as a constitutive force in society and, thus, recognize the teleological nature of information systems and services (Braman, 1989).

How to Define a Scientific Term
Definition and Meaning Theory

It is well known that definitions are not true or false, but more or less fruitful. In a way, people are free to define terms as they like, but in reality their definitions may encounter problems. In children's play, a chair can be defined as a table and vice versa. This works as long as the children remember and obey their own decisions and do not apply their own conventions in communication with outsiders. However, when somebody defines a term in such an idiosyncratic way, that definition will be neglected and will not contribute to understanding, communication, or the advance of practice.

Knowing how different people apply the terms they use is helpful. Wittgenstein's (1958a) famous use theory of meaning emphasizes this aspect, defining terms by finding out how people actually use them (see Blair's chapter in this volume). This aspect also applies to the term *information*. Dictionaries such as *The Oxford English Dictionary* (1989) provide valuable insights about the etymology of a word and how different authors have used it throughout the centuries (see Appendix). This etymology should be supplemented by more detailed descriptions of how the word has been used in different disciplines. The actual use of terms may differ from their more formal definitions. The ordinary use of a term like *information* may carry meanings other than formal definitions, implying that conflicting theoretical views may arise between the explicit scientific definitions and the implicit definitions of ordinary use. Because of this tendency, we must not only compare different formal definitions, but also consider the meaning of a word like *information* as it is used in relation to, for example, information seeking, information systems, and information services.

Studies of how a term has been used cannot, however, help us to decide how we should define it. When we use language and terms, we perform a type of act, with the intention of accomplishing something. The different meanings of the terms we use are more or less efficient tools to help us accomplish what we want to accomplish. In this way, according to pragmatic philosophers such as Charles Sanders Peirce (1905), the meaning of a term is determined by not just the past, but also the future.

We also cite Braman (1989), pointing out how important it is for information policy to define information adequately, thus applying this pragmatic principle of definition to practical policy.

Theory Dependency of Scientific Terms

The kind of activity performed in the sciences is the production of knowledge and the development of scientific theories. In this respect, the meaning of terms must be considered in the framework of the theories they are supposed to serve. In the philosophy of science, Chalmers (1999, pp. 104–105) has provided an important analysis of the meaning of scientific concepts:

> Observation statements must be expressed in the language of some theory. Consequently, it is argued, the statements, and the concepts figuring in them, will be as precise and informative as the theory in whose language they are formed is precise and informative. For instance, I think it will be agreed that the Newtonian concept of mass has a more precise meaning than the concept of democracy, say. It is plausible to suggest that the reason for the relatively precise meaning of the former stems from the fact that the concept plays a specific, well-defined role in a precise, closely-knit theory, Newtonian mechanics. By contrast, the social theories in which the concept *democracy* occurs are vague and multifarious. If this suggested close connection between precision of meaning of a term or statement and the role played by that term or statement in a theory is valid, then the need for coherently structured theories would seem to follow directly from it.

Chalmers also considers alternative ways of defining scientific terms, by, for example, lexical or ostensive definitions. The main problem with lexical definitions is that concepts can be defined only in terms of other concepts, the meanings of which are given. If the meanings of these latter concepts are themselves established by definition, it is clear that an infinite regress will result, unless the meanings of some concepts are known by other means. A dictionary is useless unless we already know the meanings of many words. Newton could not define mass or force in terms of previously available concepts. It was necessary for him to transcend the limits of the old conceptual framework by developing a new one. The main problem with ostensive definitions is that they are difficult to sustain, even in the case of an elementary notion like *apple*.

Defining something like *mass* in mechanics, *electrical field* in electromagnetism, or *information*, *subject*, or *topicality* in information science is even more challenging. The dependence of the meaning of concepts on the structure of the theory in which they occur—and the dependence of the precision of the former on the precision and degree of coherence of the latter—is thus made plausible by noting the limitations of some of the alternative ways in which a concept might be thought to acquire meaning.

Chalmers also points out that the history of a concept, whether it be *chemical element*, *atom*, *the unconscious*, and so forth, typically involves the emergence of the concept as a vague idea, followed by its gradual clarification as the theory in which it plays a part takes on a more precise and coherent form. He argues that Galileo was in the process of making a major contribution to the building of a new mechanics that was to prove capable of supporting detailed experimentation at a later stage. It is hardly surprising that—contrary to popular myth—his efforts involved thought experiments, analogies, and illustrative metaphors rather than detailed experimentation. This situation is understandable if it is accepted that experimentation can only be carried out if one has a theory capable of yielding predictions in the form of precise observations.

Following Chalmers, we propose that the scientific definitions of terms like *information* depend on the roles we give them in our theories; in other words, the type of methodological work they must do for us. With regard to the term *information*, Spang-Hanssen (2001, online) remarks:

> In fact, we are not obliged to accept the word information as a professional term at all. It might be that this word is most useful when left without any formal definition, like e.g., the word *discussion,* or the word *difficulty,* or the word *literature.* It might be that the word information is useful in particular when we try to raise our professional status in relation to other professions; it sounds smart and imposing and gives an air of technicality. I find no moral objections to this sort of use of words; language is certainly not only for informative uses ("informative" here refers to the so-called intellectual or factual meaning of a text or an utterance). However, we must

realize that the status-raising effect of a word may depend precisely on its being used in other fields as well, preferably in fields having a high status, like engineering and nowadays sociology. The uses in such other fields actually makes [*sic*] it impossible at the same time to keep this word as a formally defined professional term in our field without some risk of confusion; the words force, energy and effect—used both generally and in physics as formally defined terms—illustrate this situation.

The word information—and combinations like information retrieval, information center—have definitely contributed to raise the public perception of library and documentation work, which is generally held to be a little dull, dusty and distant from what is actually going on in society. Maybe it would be wise to leave the word information there, were it not for the fact—already mentioned—that several attempts have been made to define information as a formal term relative to documentation and information work, and even to define it as some measurable quantity, corresponding to questions of the type: How much information was retrieved by the search?

The Danger of Applying Persuasive Definitions

Many kinds of definitions exist (Yagisawa, 1999). The tendency to use and define terms in order to impress other people has been called persuasive definition. The definition provided by Brookes (1977) $K(S) + \delta I \rightarrow K(S + \delta S)$ seems to us to serve only such a persuasive function. If we agree with Spang-Hanssen that definitions are legitimate ways to boost the status of a profession or research field, we must face the fact that such use can cause internal confusion and lack of self-respect in the discipline. Schrader, among others, has demonstrated this outcome. He studied about 700 definitions of *information science* and its antecedents from 1900 to 1981 and found that:

[T]he literature of information science is characterized by conceptual chaos. This conceptual chaos issues from a variety of problems in the definitional literature of information science: uncritical citing of previous definitions; conflating of study and practice; obsessive claims to scientific status; a narrow view of technology; disregard for literature without the science or technology label; inappropriate analogies; circular definition; and, the multiplicity of vague, contradictory, and sometimes bizarre notions of the nature of the term "information." (Schrader, 1983, p. 99)

As we can see, the cost of applying persuasive definitions in IS has been extremely high; this approach should no longer be accepted by journals and authorities in the field. We have to ask more seriously: What role—if any—should the concept of information play in IS? In order to answer this question, one must clarify the role and nature of scientific theories in IS. We suggest that focusing on the concept of information may have misdirected our field, and that closer attention to concepts such as signs, texts, and knowledge may provide more satisfactory conceptual frameworks for the kind of problems that IS is trying to answer. When we use the term *information* in IS, we should always keep in mind that information is what is informative for a given person. What is informative depends on the interpretative needs and skills of the individual (although these are often shared with members of a discourse community).

Studies and Sources of the Word Information

[A] word never—well, hardly ever—shakes off its etymology and its formation. In spite of all changes in the extensions of and additions to its meanings, and indeed rather pervading and governing these, there will still persist the old idea … Going back into the history of a word, very often into Latin, we come back pretty commonly to pictures or models of how things happen or are done. (Austin 1961, pp. 149–150)

The study of the history of a word, its etymology, is not concerned, as the word etymology itself prima facie suggests, with a true meaning (Greek, *étymon*) that apparently may be the basis of its formation and use; but rather with the interrelation of its different uses (particularly its translation into other languages and contexts), including its metaphors and metonyms. By examining the history of word uses, we find some of the primitive forms or contexts that underlie higher-level scientific practices. This lessens the expectations we may have with regard to univocal higher-level concepts, and may help us better manage vagueness and ambiguity. To question modern terminology, to look more closely at the relation between signs, meanings, and references, and to pay attention to historic context shifts help us understand how present and future uses are interwoven.

The word *information* has Latin roots *(informatio)*. Before we explore this thread we should examine its entry in *The Oxford English Dictionary* (1989, see Appendix). We shall consider two basic contexts in which *information* is used; namely, the act of molding the mind and the act of communicating knowledge. These two activities are, obviously, intimately related. But when and how do information and molding come together? Based on studies by Seiffert (1968) and Schnelle (1976), Capurro (1978) explores the Greek origins of the Latin word *informatio* as well as its subsequent development. This historico-critical background makes possible a better understanding of the higher-level concepts of information in the Hellenistic period as well as in the Middle Ages and in modern times. Peters' (1988) view is highly supportive of these analyses.

Latin Roots and Greek Origins

The *Thesaurus Linguae Latinae*[2] (1900) gives detailed references to the uses of *informatio* and *informo* in Latin from Virgil (70–19 B.C.) until the eighth century. There are two basic contexts, namely a tangible *(corporaliter)* and an intangible *(incorporaliter)* one. The prefix *in* may have the meaning of negation as in *informis* or *informitas,* but in our case it strengthens the act of giving a form to something, as in Virgil's verses on Vulcan and the Cyclops hammering out *(informatum)* lightening bolts for Zeus *(Aen.* 8, 426) or a huge shield for Aeneas *(Aen.* 8, 447). Early references to the use of *informo* are in a biological context, for instance by Varro (116–27 B.C.) who describes how the fetus is being "informed" *(informatur)* by head and backbone *(Frg.* Gell. 3, 10, 7). The intangible or spiritual context concerns moral and pedagogical uses since the second century A.D. that reveal not only the influence of Christianity—Tertullian (ca. 160–220 A.D.) calls Moses *populi informatory;* that is, people's educator or molder—but in several cases also an explicit reference to Greek philosophy, particularly to Plato (427–348/7 B.C.) and Aristotle (384–322 B.C.). Several Greek words were translated with *informatio* or *informo,* such as *hypotyposis* (which means *model,* especially in a moral context) and *prolepsis* (representation), but most higher-level uses are explicitly related to *eidos, idea, typos,* and *morphe;* that is, to key concepts of Greek ontology and epistemology (Capurro, 1978). This relationship is clearly the case with prominent thinkers such as, for instance, Cicero (106–43 B.C.) and Augustine (354–430 A.D.). Nevertheless, these higher-level concepts have their roots in the low-level use of these words, particularly in the primitive context of pottery as well as in the Greek experience of limitation and shining-forth of what we perceive sensually *(phainonemon).*

Cicero explicitly translates in *De Natura Deorum* Epicure's (341–270 B.C.) concept of *prolepsis*—i.e., the representations of the gods or of things impressed in our souls before any experience (a priori, as Kant would say) as *informatio rei* (*nat. deor.* 1, 43). At the same time he uses this word in a rhetorical context—for instance in *De Oratore* (2, 358) as well as in *Orator,* where he explicitly points to Plato's ideas (*orat.* 10)—in order to describe the active and a posteriori action of the mind depicting something unknown or helping memory, as part of the *ars memoriae,* to better remember a past situation through the pictorial representation of a sentence *(sententiae informatio).* Several references are to the use of *informo* in a biological as well as in a pedagogical and moral context. A particularly interesting one can be found in his speech *Pro Archia.*

In Augustine, we have the influence of Greek ontology and epistemology on the one hand, and of Christian tradition on the other. In *De Trinitate,* Augustine calls the process of visual perception *informatio sensus* (*trin.* 11, 2, 3) and he uses the famous Platonic (*Theaet.* 191d) and Aristotelian (*De an.* 424 a 17) metaphor of the impression *(imprimitur)* of a ring seal into wax (*trin.* 11, 2, 3). According to Augustine, the images or representations of the perceived objects are stored in memory. These images do not inform, following the Platonic view, the soul *(mens)* or the rational intellect *(intelligentia rationalis),* but only reflection *(cogitatio)*; that is, the faculty dealing with internal representations *(informatio cogitationis)* *(trin.* 14, 8, 11). Augustine uses *informatio* also in a pedagogical context: Christ is God's form *(forma dei)*. His deeds instruct and educate us *(ad eruditionem informationemque nostram)* *(epist.* 12). In *De civitate dei*, he describes the process of illumination of the heavenly community *(informatio civitatis sanctae)* *(civ.* 11, 24).

Throughout the Middle Ages, *informatio* and *informo* are commonly used in the aforementioned epistemological, ontological, and pedagogical senses by several authors (see Capurro, 1978 for details). The Aristotelian influence on the higher-level philosophical concept of *informatio* is shown best in the work of Thomas Aquinas (1225–1274). Bussa (1975) lists in his *Index Thomisticus* 66 references to *informatio*—15 of them in nominative—and 454 references to *informo*. Schütz (1958) distinguishes in his *Thomas-Lexikon* between *informatio* in the sense of "providing something with a form" in an epistemological or ontological context and the pedagogical sense of education or instruction.

Modern and Postmodern Uses of Information

"The action of 'informing' with some active or essential quality" had, according to the *Oxford English Dictionary* "a quite restrictive use" not only in English, but also in other modern European languages, and references to "formation or molding of the mind or character, training, instruction, teaching" date from the 14th century. Probably the most intriguing question from the point of view of the history of ideas concerns the ontological use of *informatio*—both in the lower-level sense of "molding matter" as well as in the higher-level sense used by the Scholastics as *informatio materiae*—which became obsolete not only in modern languages that, like English, inherited the Latin word and slightly transformed it into *information*, retaining the epistemological meaning, but also, for instance, in German where the word *Information* has actually been used in the sense of education and communication since the 15th century. *Informatio* was translated literally—first in a mystical context as *in-Bildunge or in-Formunge*; later on in a general pedagogical sense, such as used by Christoph Martin Wieland (1733–1813)—with *Bildung*, a term heavily charged with higher-level meaning (Capurro 1978, p. 176). A plausible explanation for the loss of the ontological higher-level sense is the decline of

Scholastic philosophy caused by the rise of modern empirical science. As Peters (1988, p. 12) states:

> In the feverish demolition of medieval institutions in the seventeenth and eighteenth centuries, the notion that information consisted in the activity or process of endowing some material entity with form remained largely unchanged. But the notion that the universe was ordered by forms fell into disrepute, and the context of this in-forming shifted from matter to mind. Both changes inaugurated a massive inversion in the meaning of information.

This transition from Middle Ages to Modernity in the use of the concept of information—from "giving a (substantial) form to matter" to "communicating something to someone"—can be detected in the natural philosophy of René Descartes (1596–1650), who calls ideas the "forms of thought," not in the sense that these are "pictured" *("depictae")* in some part of the brain, but "as far as they inform the spirit itself oriented to this part of the brain" (Descartes, 1996, VII, p. 161). As Peters (1988, p. 13) states:

> The "doctrine of ideas," developed initially by Descartes, was central to early modern philosophy, both rationalist and empiricist. Abandoning the "direct perception" of the scholastics—the immediate communion of Intellect and Nature—Descartes interposed "ideas" between the two. An "idea" was something present to the mind, an image, copy, or representation, with a problematic relation to real things in the world. For empiricists (like Locke), the stream of ideas was the raw material from which genuine knowledge could be built; for rationalists (like Descartes), it was a veil of illusion, to be pierced by logic and reason.

Nevertheless, the concept of information ceases to be a higher-level concept until the rise of information theory in the 20th century. Philosophers such as Francis Bacon (1561–1626), John Locke (1632–1704), George Berkeley (1685–1753), David Hume (1711–1776), and Thomas Reid (1711–1796) criticize scholastic hylomorphism and particularly the theory of abstraction. Peters (1988, p. 12) asserts that Bacon's (1967) "Great Instauration":

> criticizes the logicians of his day for receiving "as conclusive the immediate informations of the sense ..." Instead, those "informations" must be subjected, according to Bacon, to a sure plan that will sort the true from the false. Though Bacon's usage may not appear irreconcilable with our own, the inverted pluralization should tip us off that he does not completely share our prejudices (we should say "the information of the senses"). In fact, this locution exemplifies a perfectly hylomorphic notion of the workings of the senses: they are a kind of matter (wax being a favorite empiricist instance) on which objects of the world may leave their shapes or stamps. What is interesting here is that the site of information is being shifted from the world at large to the human mind and senses. This shift requires no break with scholastic notions of mind or nature.

Indeed this epistemological notion of information(s), particularly the wax metaphor, was a key higher-level concept throughout the Middle Ages. Consider Locke's (1995, p. 373) statement: "No existence of anything without us, but only of GOD, can certainly be known further than our senses inform us." Peters (1988, pp. 12–13) concludes:

> Information was readily deployed in empiricist philosophy (though it played a less important role than other words such as impression or idea) because it seemed to describe the mechanics of sensation: objects in the world in-form the senses. But sensation is entirely different from "form" —the one is sensual, the other intellectual; the one is subjective, the other objective. My sensation of things is fleeting, elusive, and idiosynchratic [sic]. For Hume, especially, sensory experience is a swirl of impressions cut off from any sure link to the real world ... In any case, the empiricist problematic was how the mind is informed by sensations of the world. At first informed meant shaped by; later it came to mean received reports

from. As its site of action drifted from cosmos to consciousness, the term's sense shifted from unities (Aristotle's forms) to units (of sensation). Information came less and less to refer to internal ordering or formation, since empiricism allowed for no preexisting intellectual forms outside of sensation itself. Instead, information came to refer to the fragmentary, fluctuating, haphazard stuff of sense. Information, like the early modern worldview more generally, shifted from a divinely ordered cosmos to a system governed by the motion of corpuscles. Under the tutelage of empiricism, information gradually moved from structure to stuff, from form to substance, from intellectual order to sensory impulses.

Later developments in etymology are partly covered in the next section. Here we will conclude that the modern uses of information show a transition period in which the medieval ontological concept of "molding matter" is not just abandoned but reshaped under empirical and epistemological premises. It has been extremely interesting to observe how the concept of information is closely connected to views of knowledge. This conclusion is important when we later analyze the concept of information in information science, because it indicates a severely neglected connection between theories of information and theories of knowledge.

Information as an Interdisciplinary Concept

Almost every scientific discipline uses the concept of information within its own context and with regard to specific phenomena. Can a common meaning for this term be derived, or do we have to agree with the skeptical view expressed by Bogdan (1994, p. 53)?

My skepticism about a definitive analysis of information acknowledges the infamous versatility of information. The notion of information has been taken to characterize a measure of physical organization (or decrease in entropy), a pattern of communication between source and receiver, a form of control and feedback, the probability of a message being transmitted over a communication channel, the content of a cognitive state, the meaning of a linguistic form, or the reduction of an uncertainty. These concepts of information are defined in various theories such as physics, thermodynamics, communication theory, cybernetics, statistical information theory, psychology, inductive logic, and so on. There seems to be no unique idea of information upon which these various concepts converge and hence no proprietary theory of information.[3]

A broad philosophical debate continues as to whether the concept should address a knowledge process including, as a necessary condition, a human knower or, at the very least, an interpretative system, or whether it should exclude mental states and user-related intentions (Pérez Gutiérrez, 2000; Ropohl, 2001). Between these two positions are different kinds of mediating theories, including the quest for a unified theory of information (Hofkirchner, 1999). This controversy reflects the complex history of the term.

In their seminal book *The Study of Information: Interdisciplinary Messages,* Machlup and Mansfield (1983) collected key views on the interdisciplinarity controversy in computer science, artificial intelligence, library and information science, linguistics, psychology, and physics, as well as in the social sciences. Machlup (1983, p. 660) himself disagrees with the use of the concept of information in the context of signal transmission, the basic senses of information in his view all referring "to telling something or to the something that is being told. Information is addressed to human minds and is received by human minds." All other senses, including its use with regard to nonhuman organisms as well to society as a whole, are, according to Machlup, metaphoric and, as in the case of cybernetics, anthropomorphic. The confusion started with the abstraction of meaning in information theory (Shannon & Weaver, 1972). Machlup (1983, p. 660) found that human sciences like psychology, economics, decision theory, and linguistics had adopted the basic human-related meaning, asserting it with some restrictions:

> The requirement of truth or correctness should exclude false
> or incorrect messages; the requirement of value or usefulness
> should exclude messages not helpful in decisions and actions;
> the requirement of novelty should exclude repeated or redun-
> dant messages; the requirement of surprise should exclude
> messages that the recipient expected; the requirement of
> uncertainty-reduction should exclude messages that leave
> the recipient's state of uncertainty unchanged or increased;
> and so forth. No exhaustive enumeration of persuasive or dic-
> tatorial restrictions is here intended.

In short, for Machlup, information is a human phenomenon. It
involves individuals transmitting and receiving messages in the context
of possible actions.

More than 10 years later, Kornwachs and Jacoby (1996) edited
Information. New Questions to a Multidisciplinary Concept. This volume
displays a general tendency toward what we might call the naturalization of information. In his contribution "Can Information Be
Naturalized?," Zoglauer responds in the negative with regard to semantic and pragmatic information, which is different from syntactic information; that is, from any kind of mind-dependent semiotic units as well as
functional information whose interpreter can be a Turing machine and/or
any kind of living organism processing neural and genetic information.
Also in this volume Capurro (1996) defines information as an anthropological category concerning the phenomenon of human messages, whose
vertical and horizontal structures are related to the Greek concept of
message *(angelia)* as well as to philosophical discourse *(logos)*. The controversy surrounding the naturalization of information goes back to the
work of physicists and engineers such as L. Boltzmann, J. von Neumann,
L. Szilard, H. Nyquist, N. Wiener, and particularly to R. V. L. Hartley
(1928, p. 536), who in his article "Transmission of Information," argued
that, because electrical transmission systems have to do with machines
and not with human beings, "it is desirable therefore to eliminate the
psychological factors involved and to establish a measure of information
in terms of purely physical quantities."

Warren Weaver discussed the elimination of meaning from the concept
of information, within the engineering context of signal transmission, in

a similar way with regard to Shannon's "Mathematical Theory of Communication:"

> The word information, in this theory, is used in a special sense that must not be confused with its ordinary usage. In particular, information must not be confused with meaning. In fact, two messages, one of which is heavily loaded with meaning and the other of which is pure nonsense, can be exactly equivalent, from the present viewpoint, as regards information. It is this, undoubtedly, that Shannon means when he says, "the semantic aspects of communication are irrelevant to the engineering aspects." But this does not mean that the engineering aspects are necessarily irrelevant to the semantic aspects. (Shannon & Weaver, 1972, p. 8)

The philosophical controversy about the concept of information in the 20th century had its origin in cybernetics, because the concepts of communication and information were conceived at a higher level of abstraction and not reduced to the communication of human knowledge as expressed by Norbert Wiener's (1961, p. 132) famous dictum: "Information is information, not matter or energy. No materialism which does not admit this can survive at the present day." This was of course a challenge to dialectical materialism. Studies of the concept of information from a materialistic point of view followed (Karpatschof, 2000; Kirschenmann, 1969; Klaus, 1963; Ursul, 1970). Wiener's idea of information as a third metaphysical principle was developed by Günther (1963), while, according to Titze (1971), information is not a substantial or metaphysical principle but expresses a tendency for order and evolution. In his seminal work, Oeser (1976) places information within the context of epistemology as a key concept concerning the creation of scientific knowledge. He explicitly refers to the Latin and Greek roots of the term *information* as well as to its central role in medieval epistemology and ontology. Weizsäcker (1974) also follows this path, as we shall show in the next section. But, with some exceptions, the concept of information is not at the core of philosophical research until the end of the century. The historical review of the concept by Schnelle (1976) refers to linguistics and cybernetics. Weizsäcker develops his views on the relationship between language and information particularly in dialog with Heidegger (1959). In a seminar with Eugen Fink on Heraclitus, Heidegger also points to the naturalization of the concept of information in biology; that is, to genetic information (Heidegger & Fink, 1970, pp. 25–26; Capurro, 1981). Conceptions of information within the philosophy of science and analytic philosophy, particularly since the late 1970s, are related to specific sciences, particularly physics, biology, and linguistics. As a result of this development the tendency has been to re-humanize the concept of information; that is, to place it within a cultural context. But at the same time, a search continues for a higher level of reflection in which information and communication, whether human or not, are seen with their corresponding *differentia specifica* from the viewpoint of the genus of interpretation or selection. This higher level of reflection means, on the one hand, a renaissance of the ontological dimension of the Greek roots of *informatio* beyond a restrictive humanistic view, while, on the other, the modern, but now de-humanized, perspective of information as knowledge communicated, gives rise to what we could call a communicative ontology where not only living beings (other than humans) but also all kinds of systems are said to produce, process, and exchange information. This perspective may also explain the rise of information science as a science that is supposed to be related to (computer) systems as well as to human beings.

The Concept of Information in the Natural Sciences

Information is prima facie something that flows between a sender and a receiver. But Shannon's definition of information is quantitative concerning possible selections from a repertoire of physical symbols. It is, in fact, as Underwood (2001) remarks, a theory of signal or message, not of information, transmission. Shannon's model of communication (see Figure 8.1) includes six elements: a source, an encoder, a message, a channel, a decoder, and a receiver (Shannon, 1948).

Strictly speaking no information could be communicated between a sender and receiver, because this theory is not concerned with the communication of a meaningful message, but rather with the reproduction of a selection process. Shannon correlates information—that is, the number of possible choices in order to create a message—and uncertainty. The

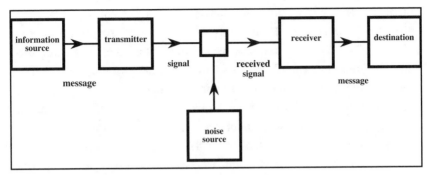

Figure 8.1 Shannon's model of communication.

greater the freedom of choice, the greater the uncertainty; that is, the information. This concept of information seems, as Weaver remarks, "disappointing and bizarre—disappointing because it has nothing to do with meaning, and bizarre because it deals not with a single message but rather with the statistical character of a whole ensemble of messages, bizarre also because in these statistical terms the two words information and uncertainty find themselves to be partners" (Shannon & Weaver, 1972, p. 27).

Völz (1982–1983) gives an overview of the different approaches to the concept of information in the natural sciences. According to Mahler (1996), information is a "contextual concept;" in other words, the question: "What is information?" cannot be stated without reference to a situation. In the case of quantum physics, this situation is a dynamic scenario in which "decisions" are carried out by a system that gives rise to an "information flow." Such decision making, although arranged by human beings, does not require conscious observers. Quantum mechanical systems are embedded within a classical environment. The theoretical model must combine system dynamics and information dynamics, which are separated within the classical world of observation, where information can be copied at will. Given the incompatibility of observables like location and impact, there is no transmission of encoded information in the individual photons between A and B, local information coming into being only after measurement. Mahler shows that this fundamental contextuality can be exploited in communication scenarios, particularly with regard to cryptography. According to Mahler (1996, p. 117), "information can only be defined within the scenario, it is not just out there." In other words, information is not a pure observable, but a theoretical construct. It is "interpreted data." As Bennett and DiVincenzo (2000) show, an information theory based on quantum principles extends and completes classical information theory. A quantum theory of information offers benefits not only to cryptography but also to quantum information processing. A quantum bit or "qubit" is a microscopic system, such as an atom, or nuclear spin, or photon.

The physicist and philosopher Carl-Friedrich von Weizsäcker conceives of information as a twofold category: (1) information is only that which is understood; (2) information is only that which generates information (Weizsäcker, 1974). Weizsäcker points to the Aristotelian and Platonic origins of the term to show that the concept of information is related to form or structure (definition 2). Information means, at the human level, the concept; not the thinking process itself. In order for a concept to be information, two conditions are necessary; namely, it must be a linguistic entity and it must be univocal. A circular movement between language and information serves as a precondition of scientific thinking (Weizsäcker, 1974). Weizsäcker (1974, p. 347) stresses that a biological structure, or more generally, information as "a measure for the amount of form," is something that can be potentially known (definition 1). At the same time, an entire organism is the product of genetic information (definition 2). Weizsäcker (1974, p. 351) calls generating forms "objectivized semantics." Information is a property of material entities: "matter has form, consciousness knows form." (Weizsäcker, 1974, p. 167). At the level of thermodynamics, actual information means the opposite of entropy; at the level of consciousness it has syntactic, semantic, and pragmatic dimensions. Evolution is the increase of form. Weizsäcker translates the information concept within signal transmission into the context of thermodynamics and biological evolution. The macro state of, say, the Latin alphabet used to send a message, makes possible the choice of a specific letter at the micro level. The same can be said with regard to chromosomes and a DNA sequence. Thermodynamic entropy measures the distance between knowledge of the macro and ignorance at the micro level. The probability of possible events always takes place within specific conditions. No absolute concept of information exists (Weizsäcker, 1985). Contrary to Plato, information should not be conceived as a perennial form, but as changing over time (Weizsäcker, 1992).

Finally, Weizsäcker (1974, p. 60) points to the "unavoidable circle" between language and information; that is, between word plurivocity and conceptual univocity, as a characteristic of exact thinking. The reason is that we are finite observers and actors within language as well as within evolution. We cannot, in Kantian terms, understand things as they are in themselves and therefore we never have fully univocal concepts (Weizsäcker 1992). On the basis of Weizsäcker's twofold concept of information, Lyre (1998, p. 76) develops "a quantum theory of information" *(Ur-Theorie)* with "basic alternatives" *(Ur-Alternativen)* representing the information content of a yes/no decision or one bit of quantum-theoretic potential information *(Ur)*. *Urs* are potential information (Lyre, 1998). This idea of information units is prima facie similar to Stonier's theory of objective information. According to Stonier (1990, p. 21), "information exists;" that is, information exists independently of human thinking (Stonier, 1997). Stonier follows Norbert Wiener's (1961, p. 132) famous dictum:

> The mechanical brain does not secrete thought "as the liver does bile," as the earlier materialists claimed, nor does it put it out in the form of energy, as the muscle puts out its activity. Information is information, not matter or energy. No materialism which does not admit this can survive at the present day.

Structural and kinetic information is an intrinsic component of the universe. It is independent of whether or not any form of intelligence can perceive it (Stonier, 1991). Information may exist in particular form, comparable to photons, as "infons" (Stonier, 1996, 138). The term "infon" was coined by Keith Devlin (1991) and refers to parameters corresponding to individuals and locations (Israel & Perry, 1990). Stonier's view is orthogonal to Weizsäcker's twofold conception of information and Lyre's quantum theory of information with its Kantian background. *Urs* are not infons; that is, they are not particles in space and time. Finally, Stonier separates the syntactic from the semantic aspects of information, whereas Lyre (1998, pp. 155–156) looks for a "complete concept of information." Stonier's (1999) evolutionary view foresees the emergence of a global brain similar to Teilhard de Chardin's (1964) "noosphere."

According to Stonier, it is important to distinguish between information and meaning. Information is, say, the letters of a written alphabet or the nucleotides of a strand of DNA. Two moles of sodium chloride contain twice as much information as one mole. It may yield a message if and only if it has been processed. If the nucleotide in the second sequence is identical to the first, its message is merely redundant. The message may acquire a meaning if and only if it has been information-processed by a recipient. The meaning of two identical messages would not double "although it might be increased somewhat as a result of being repeated" (Stonier, 1996, p. 137). This evolutionary approach to information within the natural (and social) sciences has been discussed at international conferences on the foundations of information science (Conrad & Marijuan, 1996; Hofkirchner, 1999). Information science is seen in this context as an interdisciplinary or multidisciplinary science:

> As a putative vertical science it creates its own spattering of subdisciplines in the overlapping with the other existing sciences: information physics, information chemistry (molecular computing), bioinformation (artificial life), informational neuroscience (artificial intelligence), and socioinformation. (Marijuan, 1996, p. 91)

Biological systems are treated as networks in which information processes at all levels participate (Loewenstein,1999). The features of this autopoietic universe are collapse, irreversibility, and self-regulation, where higher levels act downwardly on the lower levels. This circularity remains imperfect. The physics of biological life recapitulates the underlying physics of the universe (Conrad, 1996). According to Matsuno (1996), information is intrinsically ambivalent with regard to temporality. Shannon's information theory refers to synchronic information; that is, to a process existing in a finite time period and ignoring historical antecedents. Matsuno (1996, p. 111) quotes Weizsäcker: Information is only that which produces information. In evolutionary processes we are concerned only with diachronic information. The historicity of events does not allow participants to claim a global perspective in an atemporal manner. Within this internalist perspective conflicts among the participants inevitably arise as there is no possibility of attaining simultaneous communication among the participants. The duration of time in production contrasts with the static configuration within products. Products constitute boundary conditions for subsequent production. Measurement of products by an external observer is opposed to internal measurement of production. Internal measurement remains local; external measurement is global. In other words, an external perspective is possible only with regard to what has been accomplished and frozen in the record. Matsuno's question is, then, how an external description of internal measurement is possible. The introspective and the extrospective boundary conditions must coincide "otherwise, the integrity of the notion of boundary conditions would collapse." The local-to-global activity of information becomes crystallized in a product in global time while the global-to-local activity makes synchronization skewed in locally asynchronous time. "Information is intrinsically a conceptual device connecting the local to the global." (Matsuno 1998, p. 66). Matsuno (2000) formulates this connection between local and global information in linguistic terms: How could the present progressive tense be related to the present perfect tense, and how could this relationship be addressed in the present tense?

According to Fleissner and Hofkirchner (1995), the concept of information should not be restricted to a particular level of reality. But, due to qualitative changes at different levels of reality, the concept of information may have:

- The same reference in all contexts, such that qualitative changes are not grasped.

- Similar aspects between the references. In this case a question arises about the primary or basic reference to which analogical concepts refer.

- Finally, qualitatively distinct references may exist. In this case the concepts of information are equivocal.

Fleissner and Hofkirchner call this problem "Capurro's trilemma," which is indeed an Aristotelian one (Capurro 1995; Capurro, Fleissner, & Hofkirchner 1999; Fleissner & Hofkirchner 1995). The view of evolution as self-organization offers, according to Fleissner and Hofkirchner, a paradigm for dealing with this problem. In the process of evolution, different kinds of low structures generate higher-level structures, starting with physical systems through biological systems to social systems. Evolution is an autopoietic process in which these systems select possible ways of reaction, and forms are transformed. It is a nondeterministic process that is not merely ruled by the classic concept of causality (*actio est reactio,* or, "every action has a reaction"), but by the principle: *causa non aequat effectum, actio non est reactio,* or, "equal causes do not have equal effects, every action does not have an equal reaction" (Fleissner & Hofkirchner 1999, p. 209). This second type of self-organized causality is based on informational relations. This information concept is related to its Latin origins as *information,* meaning a dynamic process of formation and not just the meaning of a message (Fleissner & Hofkirchner, 1995). A unified theory of information should give an account of the dynamic process of evolution that embraces the whole of reality (Hofkirchner, 1999). Laszlo (1999, p. 6) asks for "invariant patterns appearing in diverse transformation" during the evolutionary process. Brier (1999) conceives of cybersemiotics as an ontological and epistemological framework for a universal information science. The evolutionary dissolution of the trilemma has, in our opinion, a metaphysical rather than a scientific status insofar as it presupposes a view of the whole of reality that is not possible for a finite observer.

Some philosophers explicitly criticize the use of the concept of information in the natural sciences. As Küppers (1996, p. 140) remarks:

> The majority of biologists, especially molecular biologists, appear to accept that biological information is indeed a natural entity, which expresses itself in the specific structures of biological macromolecules. However, this attitude has recently been the target of strong criticism from the constructivistic philosophers of science (Janich, 1992). Their main attack has been directed against the application of the concept of information in non-human areas that are governed entirely by natural laws.

According to Küppers, human language can be understood as a higher evolutionary development of the molecular-genetic language, which is the opposite of Janich's view of biological information as analogous with human information. The use of the concept of information in the natural sciences is a redundant description of the concept of causality (Janich, 1996).

The Concept of Information in the Humanities and Social Sciences

Psychology as a field bridges the natural sciences on one hand and the humanities and social sciences on the other. In psychology, the concept of information has had a central role, with the so-called cognitive revolution from 1956 onward, also called the information-processing paradigm in psychology. (This development gave birth to a whole new interdisciplinary field, named cognitive science, from about 1975. Gärdenfors [1999] reviews the development of this field.) In spite of early disappointments with information theory (see Quastler, 1956; Rapoport, 1956), the dominant trend in psychology has been a kind of functionalism in which human cognitive processes are seen as analogous with information processing by computers. There has not been much explicit discussion of the concept of information in psychology. (Some exceptions are Golu [1981], Hamlyn [1977], Harary & Batell [1978], Harrah [1958], Miller [1953], Miller [1988], Nørretranders [1998], Peterfreund & Schwartz [1971], Rapoport [1953], and Rogers [2000].) The trend has been reductionistic in the sense that human beings are seen as extracting information from the physical and chemical properties of sensory stimuli. Such reductionism stands in contrast to more hermeneutic and historical understandings in which perception is also informed by cultural factors, and information is not defined or processed according to mechanisms in the brain, but by historically developed criteria and mechanisms. (Problems relating to psychological conceptions of information are also important for other human and social sciences, and for the proper understanding of users in library and information science. See Karpatschof [2000] for a culturally informed conception of human cognition.)

Information may refer, as Qvortrup (1993) remarks, to a change in the external world, and in this case it has been defined as "a difference which makes a difference" (Bateson 1972, p. 459); that is, an operational change brought about by the external world in an observing system. It may also refer, inverting the order of this relation, to the process of finding differences—information as a difference which finds a difference—in which case the system is stimulated by a difference in the external world. On one hand, information is a thing, on the other, a psychic construction. Information as a difference in reality—as something existing independent of an observer—seems to be the view of information in engineering and the natural sciences, although, as we have seen, this is not always the case. This view was one implication of Shannon's exclusion of the semantic and pragmatic aspects of the everyday use of the word *information*. According to Qvortrup (1993), Shannon and Weaver are unclear as to whether they conceive information as a substance or as a sign.

Nevertheless, we note that Shannon retains a basic aspect of the modern concept of information in the sense of knowledge communication, namely selection. When dealing with the meaning of a message we discuss interpretation; that is, the selection between a message's semantic and pragmatic possibilities. To interpret a message means, in other words, to introduce the receiver's perspective—her or his beliefs and desires; to make her or him an active partner in the information process. We would like to suggest a difference between motivational (or anthropological) and causal (or natural) theories of information. Shannon develops a perspective, as we shall show, on causal theories of information with different kinds of "family resemblance" (Wittgenstein, 1958a). One important resemblance between the two kinds of theories is the role of selection in each. Even in the extreme case in which any interpretation is supposedly excluded—as in the engineering perspective of the conduit metaphor—we can still recognize a process of selection. In other words, we state a resemblance between interpreting meaning and selecting signals. The concept of information makes this resemblance possible. Bar-Hillel pointed to the "semantic traps" of Shannon's terminology, particularly with regard to the analogies between the psychological and the engineering fields. Bar-Hillel and Carnap (1953) developed a semantic theory of information in which they distinguish between information and amount of information within a linguistic framework. Dretske's (1981, p. 63–64) theory of semantic information is based on the distinction between information and meaning. Information does not require an interpretive process, although it is a necessary condition for acquiring knowledge. He states three conditions that a definition of information must satisfy, namely:

"(A) The signal carries as much information about s as would be generated by s's being F."

"(B) s is F"

"(C) The quantity of information the signal carries about s is (or includes) that quantity generated by s's being F (and not, say, by s's being G)."

On one hand, information is not an absolute concept, because we can acquire varying degrees of information about a source. On the other hand, however, "the information that s is F does not come in degrees. It is an all or nothing affair" (Dretske, 1981, p. 108). According to Dretske (1981, pp. 80–81), information is always relative to "a receiver's background knowledge" (k); it is "something that is required for knowledge." It is indeed a "harmless fiction" to think about a number of possibilities existing at the source "independently of what anyone happened to know." There is no false information but there is meaning without truth (Dretske, 1981, pp. 171–235). Indeed, "information is what is capable of yielding knowledge, and since knowledge requires truth, information requires it also" (Dretske, 1981, p. 45). The flow of information is based on the following Xerox principle: "If A carries the information that B, and B carries the information that C, then A carries the information that C" (Dretske, 1981, p. 57). Dretske's information concept is different from meaning, but basically related to cognitive systems. The relation between knowledge and information is a recursive but not a circular one. In order to learn that s is F, a person should know about s, without knowing that s is F. On the other hand, the information that s is F "causes K's belief that s is F." "Knowledge is information-produced belief" (Dretske, 1981, pp. 91–92). Thus, in the case of "genuine cognitive systems," as distinct from "mere processors of information," knowledge is specified with regard to information, meaning, and belief; or, in other words, with regard to interpretation during the learning process. Computers have, at least so far, no capability of using information. It means nothing to them. They can only manipulate symbols (Dretske, 1986).

Dretske's definition of information does not initially include k (that is, the receiver's background knowledge). This cognitivistic limitation seems illegitimate if we consider other kinds of receivers or, more precisely, other kinds of situations. Becoming aware of this contradiction, Barwise and Perry (1983) developed situation theory and situation semantics (STASS). This theory is based on the idea of regularities between types of situations, which allow information flow to take place (Barwise & Seligman, 1997). Linguistic regularities, as considered by Dretske, are a special case of this flow.

Information is not a property of facts but it is context or constraint dependent. A difference exists between "pure information" and "incremental information." "Pure information" is illustrated as follows:

> Whenever there is a state of affairs consisting of some x-ray's having such and such a pattern at some time t, then there is a state of affairs involving a dog's leg having been the object of that x-ray and that leg's being broken at t. So the indicated proposition is that there is a dog of which this is the x-ray, and it has a broken leg. The pure information is about the x-ray, but not about Jackie, or her leg. (Israel & Perry, 1990, p. 10)

"Incremental information" concerns more specific information that may result at the terminus of "information flow architectures" (Israel & Perry, 1991). A distinction is made between "informational content" and "information": "Informational content is only information when the constraints and connecting facts are actual" (Israel & Perry, 1991, p. 147). The causal relations among the contents of an "information system" are called "architectural" (Israel & Perry, 1991, pp. 147–148).

Dretske's Xerox principle becomes a regulative one: the point is to develop information flow architectures whose signals at the terminus will contain incremental information with regard to the earlier ones (Israel & Perry, 1991). In contrast to Dretske's concept of information, the theory of situation semantics defines information within a realistic and not just cognitivistic framework. Information contents are not dependent on the knowledge of the receiver, Dretske's k, but on types of situations. Two different receivers may extract, due to different constraints and facts, different information content from the same signal. According to Pérez Gutiérrez's (2000), further development of this theory—he was inspired by the formalization of the information flow through Barwise and Seligman (1997)—the incremental information content may be defined only with regard to "classifications" or clusters of situations connected through channels by which the information is transmitted without any reference to a receiver's interpretation. Based on Wittgenstein's (1958b) notion of language games as specified by the formal notion of situations as well as on Gregory Bateson's (1979) ecological paradigm, Rieger (1996, p. 292) analyzes the linear (or syntagmatic) and selective (or paradigmatic) constraints that natural language structure imposes on the formation of strings of linguistic entities:

> The regularities of word-usage may serve as an access to and a representational format for those elastic constraints which underlay [sic] and condition any word-type's meaning, the interpretations it allows within possible contexts of use, and the information its actual word-token employment on a particular occasion may convey.

We conclude this analysis of the semantic concept of information by stating that even if information is seen as something existing independently of a receiver's knowledge, this does not necessarily imply that information is something absolute. The situation theory conceives information in relation to situations with their constraints and contingencies. Oeser (1976) remarks that the objectivity of scientific knowledge is not attained through the elimination of the knower, but on the basis of the intersubjective information process. Information is a "system-relative concept" (Oeser, 1976, II, p. 86). Some classical theories of information define it with regard to the change in the receiver's model of reality; that is, as a pragmatic concept (MacKay, 1969; Morris, 1955). This is particularly the case with definitions based on system theory, second-order cybernetics, and semiotics (Qvortrup, 1993). Kornwachs (1996) defines pragmatic information as an impinging entity, one that is able to change the structure and the behavior of systems. According to biologists like Humberto Maturana and Francisco Varela (1980), as well as cyberneticians like Heinz von Foerster (1980, 1984), information is the observer's construction of a mental difference that makes and/or finds a difference in the external world. For Flückiger (1999), information is an individual's brain construct. According to Qvortrup (1993, p. 12), the conception of information as a mental difference "doesn't necessarily imply that the difference in reality that triggered the mental difference called information is a mental construction." The German sociologist Niklas Luhmann has developed an information concept based on the theory of self-referential systems. Luhmann (1987) distinguishes between biological and social (and psychic) systems. Social (and psychic) systems are constituted by meaning (*Sinn*). In the case of biological systems, self-reference means self-reproduction. Meaning is produced through processing differences, and this is possible because there is a meaning offer (*Mitteilung*) out of which a selection can be made. Information (*Information*) is, then, an event that produces a connection between differences or—Luhmann cites Bateson's (1972, p. 459) famous definition—"a difference that makes a difference." "Understanding" (*Verstehen*) is the difference between "meaning offer" (*Mitteilung*) and "selection" (*Information*). Communication is the unity of meaning offer, information, and understanding. According to this theory, no transmission of information occurs between a sender and a receiver. This thing-oriented metaphor implies that there is something the sender has and loses when she or he sends it. The sender, in fact, makes a suggestion for selection. Information is not something identical for both sender and receiver, but it has to be constituted through the communication process (Luhmann 1987, pp. 193–194). Janich (1998) develops a theory of information that is exclusively related to purpose-oriented human actions. Information is defined as a predicate that qualifies standard request dialogues where linguistic utterances are speaker-, listener-, and form-invariant. Such invariances make it possible to reproduce these situations on the basis of anthropomorphic artificial devices.

Information is a key concept in sociology, political science, and the economics of the so-called information society. According to Webster (1995, 1996), definitions of information society can be analyzed with regard to five criteria: technological, economic, occupational, spatial, and cultural (Webster, 1995, p. 6). The technological definition is concerned with applications of information technologies in society. The economic definition goes back to the pioneering work of Machlup (1962), Boulding (1966), Arrow (1979), and Porat (1977). The occupational definition is at the heart of Porat's (1977) and Bell's (1973) theories. The spatial definition concerns information networks and the emergence of a "network marketplace" (Castells, 1989). The cultural definition is related to the influence of media in society. Classic theoreticians of the information society are, according to Webster: Bell, Giddens, Schiller, Habermas, Baudrillard, Vattimo, Poster, Lyotard, and Castells.

According to Bougnoux (1993, 1995) the concepts of information and communication are inversely related: Communication is concerned with forecasting and redundancy; information with the new and the unforeseen. There is no pure information or "information-in-itself" (that is, information is always related to some kind of redundancy or "noise"). To inform (others or oneself) means to select and to evaluate. This concept is particularly relevant in the field of journalism and mass media, but also, of course, in information science. The action of bringing a message and the message itself were designated in Greek by the terms *angellein* and *angelia* (Capurro, 1978). The modern concept of information as knowledge communication is not related just to a secular view of messages and messengers but includes also a modern view of empirical knowledge shared by a (scientific) community. Postmodernity opens this concept to all kinds of messages, particularly within the perspective of a digital environment. We may call a science of knowledge (better: message) communication information science or *angeletics* (Capurro, 2000). Flusser (1996) has developed a "communicology" in which "discursive media" are concerned with the distribution of information whereas "dialogical media" deal with the creation of new information. Flusser fears that mass media may swallow up dialogical media into a hierarchical model. He did not foresee the Internet as a communication structure in which both media would merge beyond a central or panoptic power. It is, of course, an open question how far this is, or will be, the case. Krippendorff (1994) has explored different information and communication metaphors such as message transmission, the container metaphor, the metaphor of sharing common views, the argument metaphor, the canal metaphor, and the control metaphor. These metaphors originate within different cultural environments. The phenomena they address are intimately related to the metaphors themselves. We must learn to use them creatively; that is, to see their limits and to learn how to apply them accurately in different theoretical and practical situations.

Braman (1989) provides an important discussion of approaches to defining information for policy makers. Four major views are identified: (1) information as a resource, (2) information as a commodity, (3) information as a perception of patterns, and (4) information as a constitutive force in society. The relative benefits and problems with each of these four conceptions are discussed. Her article points out that the selection of one definition over another has important consequences, and also that the tendency to neglect this problem results in conflicts rather than cooperation. Defining information is thus also a political decision.

The information age is also called "the age of access" (Rifkin, 2000). Information production, distribution, and access are at the heart of the new economy. The terminological shift from information society to knowledge society signals that content, and not information technology, is the main challenge for the economy as well as for society in general. From the perspective of knowledge management, information is used to designate isolated pieces of meaningful data that, when integrated within a context, constitute knowledge (Gundry 2001; Probst, Raub, & Romhard, 1999). This semantic concept of information, located between data and knowledge, is not consistent with the view that equates information (management) with information technology. According to Nonaka and Takeuchi (1995)—who follow Polanyi's (1966) distinction between tacit and explicit knowledge—only explicit knowledge (information) can be managed. Correctly speaking, knowledge cannot be managed, only enabled (von Krogh, Ichijo, & Nonaka, 2000). For Cornella (2000), companies are information. Castells (1996–1998) gives a comprehensive and critical analysis of the information age, including its social, economic, and cultural dimensions. For Hobart and Schiffman (2000), information is not a phenomenon that appears with modern technology but rather the product of complex interactions between technology and culture. They distinguish among classical, modern, and contemporary information ages, the meaning of information being specific to each age.

> The fundamental fact of information's historicity liberates us from the conceit that ours is the information age, a conceit that underlies Kauffmanesque inferences from "computer-simulation movies" to history. It allows us to stand outside our contemporary information idiom, to see where it comes from, what it does, and how it shapes our thought. (Hobart & Schiffman, 2000, p. 264)

Brown and Duguid (2000) question "the myth of information" and information technologies that would be able to shape social organization by themselves. For it is not shared information but shared interpretation that binds people together. Borgmann's (1999, p. 57) critical appraisal of the nature of information is a plea for a new cultural and ethical balance between what he calls technological, natural, and cultural information: "Natural information pivots on natural signs—clouds, smoke, tracks. Cultural information centers on conventional signs—letters and texts, lines and graphs, notes and scores."

Borgmann (1999, pp. 218–219) sees technological information as the product of developments that began a century ago:

> Based on information technology, our omniscience and omnipotence have achieved such transparency and control of information that there are not things any more to be discovered beyond the signs. Nothing is any longer buried beneath information. Behind the virtual self-representations there are no real persons left to be acknowledged.

We close this by no means exhaustive analysis of the concept of information in the humanities and social sciences with Eliot's (1969, p. 147) famous quotation:

> Where is the Life we have lost in living?
> Where is the wisdom we have lost in knowledge?
> Where is the knowledge we have lost in information?

We started this presentation of interdisciplinary theories by asking whether a common core can be found in the concept of information. According to Karpatschof (2000, pp. 131–132):

> Information
> The quality of a certain *signal* in relation to
> a *certain release mechanism,* the signal being
> a low-energy phenomenon fulfilling some
> release specifications.

The *signal* is thus the indirect cause, and the process of the *release mechanism* the direct cause of the resulting high-energy reaction.

The release mechanism itself is, of course, an emergent entity, when it is seen from a cosmological position. This is the precise agenda, for biogony and biogenesis to furnish theories with an analysis of this emergence. We can thus more precisely define:

Release Mechanisms
Systems having at their disposal a store of potential energy, the system being "designed" to let this energy out in a specific way, whenever trigged by a signal fulfilling the specifications of the release mechanism

It is now clear why there has been this tendency to consider information to be an obscure category that is in addition to the classical categories of physics. Information is indeed a new category, but it cannot be placed, eclectically, beside the prior physical categories. Information is a category, not beside, but indeed above the classical categories of physics. Therefore, information is neither directly reducible to these classical categories, nor is it a radically different category of another nature than mass and energy. Information is, in fact, the causal result of existing physical components and processes. Moreover, it is an *emergent* result of such physical entities. This is revealed in the systemic definition of information. It is a relational concept that includes the *source,* the *signal,* the *release mechanism* and the reaction as its relatants. One might ask where I place the category of *information* in my system of ontology.

> Should it be placed in the object field of cosmology, just
> as mass, energy and causality? Or, should it be placed
> in the object field of biology? My answer to this question
> will be the latter position. (all emphasis in original)

In our opinion, Karpatschof's explanation identifies a key perspective
of the concept of information that most interdisciplinary discussions can
agree upon. It seems to be a reductionistic and indeed mechanical perspective, antithetical to a humanistic understanding. However, this is
not the case. Karpatschof does not explain psychological or sociological
phenomena by physical or biological principles. He does not consider
information as a thing or as something objective. He forces us to look at
the many different kinds of mechanisms at different levels in evolution
and culture that have evolved to discriminate certain kinds of signals. In
other words, he forces us to shift the perspective from information as an
object to the subjective mechanisms that account for discrimination,
interpretation, or selection. What distinguishes different theories of
information is, thus, not so much the concept of information itself. It is,
to a much higher degree, the nature of the "release mechanism" (or "information processing mechanisms"), the selectors or interpreters. To ask
about the nature of this mechanism means, for instance, to ask about the
nature of living organisms, the nature of human beings, human language, society, and technology. Because there are many kinds of release
mechanisms developed in biology, in the human mind, in cultures, and in
technologies, different sciences tend to work with different concepts and
theoretical frames of reference. Information can and should thus be studied within a network of different disciplines, not just by "information science" (Capurro, 2001). No wonder, then, that the mechanisms of
information—and information itself—have been so difficult to tackle.

Information in Information Science
Relationship with Librarianship and Scientific Documentation

As we have seen, the word *information* has a much richer history than
the fields of inquiry known as library science, documentation, and information science, which are largely products of the 20th century. Tracing the

influence of this term and the very complex net of disciplines connected with it is indeed difficult. Machlup and Mansfield (1983, p. 22) suggested that "in the broad sense information science is a rather shapeless assemblage of chunks picked from a variety of disciplines that happen to talk about information in one of its many meanings." In this chapter only a few important points will be illuminated.

Some key events can be taken as signposts for our orientation in this complex area.

> Information desk appeared as an alternate to reference desk by 1891. Information bureau was in use by 1909 to denote an office where reference service was provided; in 1924 the Association of Special Libraries and Information Bureaux (Aslib) was founded in Britain. In the *Aslib Proceedings* for 1932, information work was introduced to describe reference assistance. Use of information as an equivalent of reference began to give way, under the influence of developments in computing, to more sophisticated usage. (Shapiro, 1995, p. 384)

The term *information* was also used in 1915 by the American special librarian, Ethel Johnson, who noted, "before everything else, it [the special library] is an information bureau. The main function of the general library is to make books available. The function of the special library is to make information available" (quoted by Williams, 1998, p. 174).

According to Williams (1998), special librarians were the first documentalists in the U.S.; and, according to Rayward (1998), documentalists can be seen as the first information scientists. We are thus able to trace one line of development from special librarianship via documentation to information science in both the U.K. and the U.S. The line of development from Paul Otlet (1934) and Suzanne Briet (1951) is discussed by Day (2001) in critical fashion.

In 1968, the American Documentation Institute (founded in 1937) changed its name to the American Society for Information Science. From that time, "information" gradually replaced "documentation" as a name for a profession and field of study (at least until a recent tendency to reintroduce the concept of documents by Buckland, 1997; Hjørland, 2000; Lund, 1997; White & McCain, 1998; and others). Only a few institutions have preserved the term *documentation* (e.g., *Journal of Documentation;* Féderation Internationale de Documentation). One notable exception is in Tromsø, Norway, where "Documentation Science" has recently been chosen as the name for a newly founded institute. It is far more common to do as the Royal School of Library and Information Science in Copenhagen did in 1997: namely, add *information* to its name (although only to the English version). The important question is, of course, what kinds of theoretical influences lie behind such choices? How is the term *information* theoretically related to what is studied (if at all)?

According to Hjørland (2000) the increasing trend toward using the term *information* in institutions of librarianship and documentation is mainly related to: (1) an increasing interest in computer applications (or "information technology"), and (2) an indirect, theoretical influence from information theory (Shannon & Weaver, 1972) and the paradigm of information processing in the cognitive sciences.

The same paper also argues that this tendency has serious drawbacks. Theories that are appropriate for computer science are not necessarily adequate for library science, documentation, and scientific communication. A serious risk arises such that concepts and theories related to information theory tend to reduce the study of documentary communication to computer science and cognitive science, thus removing the basis of the field in its own right.

Library science as taught in schools of librarianship has always had public libraries as a major focus simply because public libraries have constituted an important market for professionally trained librarians. This situation has influenced both the focus of the field and its underlying assumptions, preferences, and "paradigms" (for example, the predilection for universal classifications systems and the relative neglect of domain-specific knowledge). Special librarianship and documentation (and later information science), on the other hand, were much more concerned with research libraries, databases, and with activities connected to the seeking and dissemination of scientific literature—and also the application of information technologies. Documentation/information science was originally based more on specific subject knowledge (chemistry has played an especially important role in information science), whereas special librarianship relied more on education and training in schools of librarianship. According to Williams (1998, p. 177) special librarians in the U.S. lost ground to documentalists and information scientists because they lacked the specific subject knowledge to handle complex information (for example, in chemical indexing and retrieval).

> These changes, particularly when confronted with the insistence of the documentalists that a new profession different from librarianship, even special librarianship, needed to be developed, had the effect of making them [the special librarians] more general library oriented and less special library oriented. The overall effect on special librarianship and SLA [Special Libraries Association] is a decline in their domination of new developments in information management. As will be shown in the next section, one of the major reasons special librarians had lost this dominance was because they emphasized general education in librarianship to the neglect of the scientific fields they had to serve. They were now librarians first and foremost, and only knowledgeable about their subject areas second, if at all.

However, since about 1975, information science has been foregrounded in schools of library science. This may be due in part to an increasing interest in being associated with such important fields as computer-based information retrieval and other areas of information science. Although schools of library science are major contributors in the field, as reflected in their contributions to the leading journals in IS; they have also faced challenges, particularly in the U.S. This situation may be connected to what they teach, including the old problem concerning the lack of specific subject knowledge. It may be, however, that the neglect of subject knowledge reflects a privileging of research into users rather than information, and, by implication, a tendency toward psychologism, subjective idealism, and methodological individualism.[4] The terms information and IS became institutionalized in, among other places, schools of library science, which in the process often changed their names and their curricula. The question is how well we have succeeded in developing information science as a healthy field of inquiry.

Information Retrieval and the Concept of Information

The term information retrieval (IR) is possibly one of the most important terms in the field known as information science. A critical question is, thus, why, and in what sense, IR uses the term information. IR can be seen both as a field of study and as one among several research traditions concerned with information storage and retrieval.[5] Although the field is much older, the tradition goes back to the early 1960s and the Cranfield experiments, which introduced measures of recall and precision. Those experiments rank among the most famous in IS and continue today in the TREC experiments (Text REtrieval Conference). This tradition has always been closely connected to document/text retrieval, as stated by van Rijsbergen (1979, p. 1):

> Information retrieval is a wide, often loosely-defined term, but in these pages I shall be concerned only with automatic information retrieval systems. Automatic as opposed to manual and information as opposed to data or fact. Unfortunately the word information can be very misleading. In the context of information retrieval (IR), information, in the technical meaning given in Shannon's theory of communication, is not readily measured (Shannon and Weaver). In fact, in many cases one can adequately describe the kind of retrieval by simply substituting "document" for "information." Nevertheless, "information retrieval" has become accepted as a description of the kind of work published by Cleverdon, Salton, Sparck Jones, Lancaster and others. A perfectly straightforward definition along these lines is given by Lancaster: "Information retrieval is the term conventionally, though somewhat inaccurately, applied to the type of activity discussed in this volume. An information retrieval system does not inform (i.e. change the knowledge of) the user on the subject of his inquiry. It merely informs on the existence (or non-existence) and whereabouts of documents relating to his request." This specifically excludes Question-Answering systems as typified by Winograd and those described by Minsky. It also excludes data retrieval systems such as used by, say, the stock exchange for on-line quotations. [Notes to references omitted].

In 1996, van Rijsbergen and Lalmas (p. 386), however, declared that the situation had changed and that the purpose of an information retrieval system was to provide information about a request. Although some researchers have fantasized about eliminating the concept of document/text and simply storing or retrieving the facts or "information" contained therein, it is our opinion that IR usually means document retrieval and not fact retrieval.[6] We shall return to the difference between documents and facts later, but here we want to show why information (and not, for example, document, text, or literature) was chosen as a central term in this core area.

Ellis (1996, pp. 187–188) describes "an anomaly" in IS:

> Brookes noted the anomaly could be resolved if information retrieval theory were named document retrieval theory which would then be part of library science. However, he commented that those working in the field of information retrieval were making the explicit claim to be working with information not documentation.

What Brookes (1981, p. 2) stated was,

> From an information science point of view, research on IR systems offers only a theoretical cul-de-sac. It leads nowhere. The anomaly I have noted is this: the information-handling processes of the computers used for IR systems, their storage capacities, their input, and internal information transmissions, are measured in terms of *Shannon* theory measures— in bits, megabits per second, and so forth. On the other hand, in the theories of information retrieval effectiveness, information is measured in what I call *physical* measures—that is, the documents (or document surrogates) are counted as relevant or non-relevant and simple ratios of these numbers are used. The subsequent probabilistic calculations are made as though the documents were physical things (as, of course, they are in part), yet the whole enterprise is called information retrieval theory. So why, I ask, are *logarithmic* measures of information used in the theory of the machine and *linear* or physical measures of information in IR theory?

If *information* retrieval theory were called document retrieval theory, the anomaly would disappear. And document retrieval theory would fall into place as a component of *library* science, which is similarly concerned with documents. But that is too simple an idea. Those who work on IR theory explicitly claim to be working on *information,* not *documentation.* I therefore abandon the simple explanation of a misuse of terminology. I have to assume that IR theorists mean what they say—that they are contributing to *information science.* But are they? [emphasis in original]

Ellis and Brookes should not refer to the opinions of researchers in their attempts to solve this problem. Only arguments count. In our view, it is not too simple an idea to claim that information retrieval theory is in reality document retrieval theory and thus closely associated with library science. It is not difficult to disprove Brookes's statement that information retrieval does not deal with documents. A short examination of the literature demonstrates this, and even if the Cranfield experiments spoke about "information retrieval," their modern counterpart, the TREC experiments, speak about "text retrieval." "Text retrieval" and "document retrieval" are often used as synonyms for IR.

If one reads Brookes's statement in the light of the relationship between the early documentalists and information scientists, it becomes clear that information scientists wanted to forge a distinct identity to be both more information technology-oriented and more subject-knowledge oriented. One reason for information scientists to prefer not to be linked to library science might be that important technological improvements were carried out not by people associated with librarianship, but by those affiliated with computer science. This preference is most probably the reason they claimed to work with "information, not documentation." Nevertheless Brookes's statement is flawed, and it has provoked endless speculation about the nature of information, which has not contributed to an understanding of the problems of IR. (Compare the quotation by Schrader, 1983, p. 99, cited earlier.)

The worst thing may be that information scientists have overlooked some of the most important theoretical problems in the field. Van Rijsbergen (1986, p. 194) has pointed out that the concept of meaning has been overlooked in IS. The fundamental basis of all previous work—including his own—is in his opinion wrong because it has been based on the assumption that a formal notion of meaning is not required to solve IR problems. For us it is reasonable to suggest a link between the neglect of the concepts of text and documents on one hand and meaning (or semantics) on the other. Semantics, meaning, text, and documents are much more related to theories about language and literature, whereas information is much more related to theories about computation and control. We do not claim, however, that the statistical methods used in IR have not been efficient. We do claim, however, that semantics and pragmatics, among other things, are essential to better theoretical development in IR, and in the long run also to the improvement of operational systems.

Information and Assemblages of Facts

In spite of our claim that IR is actually document retrieval, there has been throughout the history of the field a problematic tendency to regard information as assemblages of facts or opinions freed from the documents.

In the literature of IS a distinction is made between document retrieval and fact retrieval. As a response to a query, a document retrieval system provides a list of references about the subject, which with a certain probability is supposed to contain the answer to the query, or rather to reveal the present documented knowledge about the problem. Fact retrieval systems, on the other hand, are supposed to provide concrete answers to queries. If the query is: "What is the definition of information science?" a document retrieval system such as *Library and Information Science Abstracts (LISA)* produces a long list of papers discussing this issue, whereas a fact retrieval system provides you with one selected definition.

Some distinguished IS researchers have regarded the creation of fact retrieval systems as the ultimate goal of information science. Karen Sparck Jones (1987, p. 9), for instance, claims that "we are concerned with access and, more materially, indirect access to the information the user wants: he wants the information in the documents, but the system only gives him the documents." This statement represents a rather narrow view with roots back to the foundation of documentation and information science:

Some of Paul Otlet's basic ideas are described by Rayward (1994, p. 247) as "the outmoded paradigm of nineteenth-century positivism:"

Otlet's concern was for the objective knowledge that was both contained in and hidden by documents. His view of knowledge was authoritarian, reductionist, positivist, simplistic—and optimistic! ... It is merely a question of institutionalizing certain processes for analyzing and organizing the content of documents. For him that aspect of the content of documents with which we must be concerned is facts. He speaks almost everywhere of facts.

Rayward (1994, pp. 247–248) finds the same view represented in modern IS:

In describing the Xanadu Project, Nelson (1987) for example, in capital letters, says that it is "just one thing: a new form of interconnection for computer files—CORRESPONDING TO THE TRUE INTERCONNECTION OF IDEAS which can be refined and elaborated into a shared network" (p. 143). These words and the sentiments that they both express and seem to imply could be, except for the term "computer files," Otlet's own. They suggest an atavistic positivist perspective that takes one by surprise.

In practice, document retrieval systems coexist with systems that provide concrete answers. Directories, dictionaries, handbooks of chemical and physical constants, and many other kinds of reference works are examples of factographic works and databases that have important functions and exist side-by-side with bibliographic databases. However, we find it important to argue against the view that bibliographical databases or full-text databases should be less than ideal because "[the user] wants the information in the documents, but the system only gives him the documents" (Sparck Jones, 1987, p. 9).

The idea that bibliographic information systems should be reduced to fact retrieval systems is a problematic assumption. We agree with Rayward that this view is related to a kind of obsolete positivism. We also see this view as one reason for the use of the terms *information* and *information science*. Because it is often desirable to know the source (e.g., in order to compare it with other sources or to evaluate its cognitive authority), document retrieval should not be reduced to fact retrieval systems.

We let Spang-Hanssen (1970/2001, online) have the final word on this issue:

> Moreover, these terms are not seldom confused with a more or less obscure use of the word information to mean something factual or real as opposed to representations of such facts; what is found written in documents—or what is said in a lecture—are according to this view only disguises or at best surrogates of facts. This more or less vague conception seems to be the basis of the distinction sometimes made between "fact retrieval" and "document retrieval."
>
> This distinction I find philosophically unbased; we here touch upon the fundamental problem of the meaning of meaning and of the nature of signs and symbols. What is more essential to us, this distinction seems unhappy in actual documentation work. There will, admittedly, be cases in which a document or information center is set up with the exclusive function of providing information concerning physical data, or statistical figures, or exchange rates of currencies, or stock market prices. But even in such cases it applies that neither the person who requests such information nor the person to deliver it should ignore the reliability of data and forget about the general setting in which the data are acquired. An information about some physical property of a material is actually incomplete without information about the precision of some figure and about the conditions under which this figure was obtained. Moreover, various investigations of a property have often led to different results that cannot be compared and evaluated apart from information about their background. An empirical fact always has a history and a perhaps not too certain future. This history and future can be known only by information from particular documents, i.e. by document retrieval.

> The so-called fact retrieval centers seem to me to be just
> information centers that keep their information sources—i.e.
> their documents—exclusively to themselves.

Romm (1997) shows that serious ethical implications are involved in defining something as factual as opposed to meaningful. To the extent that information is seen or presented and legitimized in terms of its supposed factual content, it authorizes a picture of the world—rather than inviting debate on the construction and relevance of the picture. Conversely, insofar as information is treated as a product of specific world-constructing activities, it invites discursive inquiry as to its meaning and relevance.

Information and the Scientific Division of Labor

Are information scientists the only professionals who are working with the "generation, collection, organization, interpretation, storage, retrieval, dissemination, transformation, and use of information"? (This quote is part of the official definition of information science given by the American Society for Information Science and Technology [Borko, 1968; Griffith, 1980] quoted in full later in this chapter.) We often assume this to be the case. If this is not the case, it seems important to try to specify the special role of information scientists in handling information.

In one sense of the word *information*, astronomers can be seen as experts who identify, process, and interpret information from the universe. The byproducts of their activities they keep as observations in one form or another. They may make photographs of parts of the universe and of single stars, planets, and galaxies. They also publish their empirical and theoretical findings in journals and other publications. Both the photographs and the publications are examples of documents. The library, documentation, and information profession is interested in all kind of documents. Its core interest and expertise is, however, related to the communication of published documents. Our point is that in the sense of the word *information* as it is used about astronomers' activities, information scientists are not experts in interpreting the information from the stars, but at most are experts in handling information documented by astronomers (e.g., indexing and retrieving astronomical documents). In this example, information is defined in a broader sense than is usually implied in information science.

Just as astronomers can be said to handle information professionally, so it is with other groups. Publishers, researchers, historians, lawyers, and teachers can be said to be professional information handlers in some fashion. Defining information in a way other than implied here can solve this problem. Belkin (1978, p. 60) explicitly seeks to solve this problem by demanding that, "in general, any information concept for information science must refer to at least the specific domain of information science, as indicated by its problem. This means purposeful, meaningful, human communication, with the specific requirements as noted above."

But this solution has some disadvantages. In information science we are sometimes interested in studying the researcher's selection of an information channel, including whether he or she prefers to go the library or to make an observation for himself or herself.

This distinction was made in Taylor's (1968) study of question negotiation and information seeking in libraries. If we define *information* in the narrow sense, as something belonging solely to information science (as proposed by Belkin), we are not able to make comparative studies of this sort. Because we find Taylor's questions relevant and consider that he uses the concept of information in a fruitful way, we see a dilemma in using Belkin's (1978) definition in information science.[7]

The role of information specialists may be relatively clear when the target group is, for example, astronomers: information specialists are experts on forms of publications, databases, reference tools, and so forth. In the case of, for example, historians or lawyers, the borders are much less clear because the information that these professions are seeking, interpreting, and using is itself contained in publications and documents. The historian, not the librarian or information specialist, is the expert in seeking, organizing, interpreting, and utilizing the documents needed in his or her professional work. Still, an information specialist has more professional expertise regarding specific matters such as databases and cataloging.

One of the most frequently used definitions of information science is as follows:

> Information science is concerned with the generation, collection, organization, interpretation, storage, retrieval, dissemination, transformation, and use of information, with particular emphasis on the applications of modern technologies in these areas.
>
> As a discipline, it seeks to create and structure a body of scientific, technological, and systems knowledge related to the transfer of information. It has both pure science (theoretical) components, which inquire into the subject without regard to application, and applied science (practical) components, which develop services and products. (Griffith, 1980, p. 5)[8]

In our view, this definition does not contain a good identification of the special focus of information science. No science should be defined by its tools (e.g., modern technologies). All fields are supposed to utilize the most appropriate tools available. A science should be defined by its object of study. As such, the study of information is a better one. We need, however, to identify the specific role of information science in relation to "the generation, collection, organization, interpretation, storage, retrieval, dissemination, transformation and use of information" as distinct from the activities in which other professionals are more qualified. In our view, information professionals usually have a broad overview of information sources, sociological patterns in knowledge production, document types, and so on. They should also have a broader knowledge of the philosophy of science (e.g., paradigms and epistemology), and of the principles of language use for special purposes. We believe that the focus of information professionals (as distinct from the professional groups they are serving) implies a sociological and epistemological approach to "the generation, collection, organization, interpretation, storage, retrieval, dissemination, transformation and use of information."[9] Information scientists—by the very nature of their field—must work in a top-down mode, from the general field of knowledge and information sources to the specific, whereas domain experts must work in a bottom-up mode, from the specific to the general.

With regard to the concept of information, the implication is that what counts as information—what is informative—depends on the question to be answered. The same representation of an object (e.g., a stone in a field) contains different information for, say, an archaeologist or a geologist. The same matter should therefore be represented differently in different subject databases. The concept of information itself can be defined universalistically (e.g., Bateson, 1972). Information is anything that is of importance in answering a question. Anything can be information. In practice, however, information must be defined in relation to the needs of the target groups served by information specialists, not in a universalistic or individualistic, but rather in a collectivist or particularistic fashion. Information is what can answer important questions related to the activities of the target group. The generation, collection, organization, interpretation, storage, retrieval, dissemination, and transformation of information must therefore be based on views/theories about the problems, questions, and goals that the information is going to satisfy. In public libraries, those goals are related to the democratic role of the public library in society. In medicine, they are related to the solving of health problems. In women's studies, they are related to the understanding and emancipation of women. In commercial systems, they are linked to business strategy.

Diverse Views and Theories of Information in IS

Information Theory

Outside documentation and library science, in 1948, important developments occurred in so-called information theory, in cybernetics, and in technological theories as well as in communication (Shannon & Weaver, 1972; Wiener, 1961). These fields built the foundations for subsequent developments in computer science (or information technology).[10] It is widely recognized that information theory is a problematic term, and that even the term *information technology* may be a misleading label for data technology or computer technology. A consequence of Shannon's theory was that the word *information* became extremely influential in all areas of society, and fashionable in English and other languages.

Shannon's information theory has had an impact on many fields, including library and information science and documentation. The history of this impact or reception has yet to be written. There is no doubt, however, that in the 1950s many people found that this theory could be used as a strong conceptual model for research in numerous fields, including psychology, the social sciences, and documentation. Problems with this approach soon appeared (Rapoport, 1953), and the initial optimism disappeared, leaving many fields without an adequate theoretical frame. From an information-theoretical point of view, information can be precisely defined and measured. For example, in February 1999, Lawrence and Giles (1999) found about 15 terabytes of information on the Internet. This is not, however, the same concept of information as that used by information specialists when seeking, selecting, or indexing information sources. These activities relate to the content and meaning of messages, not just to their physical storage and transmission.

Wersig (1996, p. 221) concluded his presentation of information theory with the following remark:

This was not so in human contexts, where neither the assumption of coherent sets of signs nor the assumption of the identity of original message, signs, and reconstructed message were applicable. The very notion of semiotics, which in fact became one of the most important critiques of too simple an application of information theory to human communication, led to the insight that Shannon's mathematical theory was only a theory on the syntactical level (relation of signs to signs), but with no reference to the semantic (relations of signs to meanings) and pragmatic (relation of signs to humans) levels. In consequence, some attempts were made to develop out of Shannon's theory a semantic (e.g., Bar-Hillel & Carnap, 1953) or pragmatic (e.g., Yovits, 1975) information theory. But they remained in the literature with no great success.

In spite of the overall tendency to regard Shannon's information theory as a blind alley in information science, studies are still published from this perspective (e.g., Wong & Yao, 1992; Zachary, Iyengar, & Barhen, 2001).

Dretske's theory originates from philosophy and was outlined earlier. It has been cited 15 times in the literature of library and information science.[11] Patrick Wilson (1983, p. 62) has provided a short but useful review of Dretske (1981). He concludes:

How relevant is all of this to information science? I suspect that most information scientists are not much concerned with information in Dretske's sense of the word; they are concerned with meaning, not information. The documents whose storage and retrieval interests them may or may not carry any information, but they do have semantic content or meaning, which is the main thing. If that is so, and if Dretske's notion of information is the "right" one, then information science is perhaps misnamed. Dretske's idea of information is clearly closer to the "ordinary" idea of information than is the usual information scientist's idea of information; in the ordinary sense, information is contrasted with misinformation, but not so for the information scientist. It would, I think, be beneficial if some information scientists would take the trouble to read this book, with this question in mind: is information science really concerned with information? And if it is not now, could it be in the future?

Wilson's proposal has been heeded. Van Rijsbergen and Lalmas (1996) are the most prominent followers of Dretske's approach. Together with Barwise (1993) and Devlin (1991), van Rijsbergen and Lalmas (1996, p. 385) call their approach DBD: Dretske, Barwise and Devlin. Van Rijsbergen withdraws his former conclusion that information retrieval is actually document retrieval and tries to develop a theory that bases IR on an objective conception of information. The other references to Dretske's theory in IS (e.g., Bonnevie, 2001; Losee, 1997; Mingers, 1995) seem rather unrelated to one another.

The Cognitive View

We have already discussed core definitions of information connected with the cognitive view in information science: Brookes's (1977) pseudomathematical expression: $K(S) + \delta I \rightarrow K(S + \delta S)$ and Belkin's (1978, p. 60) definition, which managed to define information as a phenomenon relatively specific to information science by viewing information as a communicated and transformed knowledge state in the form of a structure.

Through the work of Brookes (1980), Karl Popper's metaphysical pluralism has been connected to the cognitive view. As is well known, Popper's ontology consists of three worlds:

World 1: physical objects or states,
World 2: consciousness or psychical states,
World 3. intellectual contents such as books, documents, scientific theories, etc.

Popper uses the words "knowledge" and "information" interchangeably. In Popper (1974, p. 1051), World 3 explicitly encompasses information:

In my way of looking at World 3, its theories contain essentially the information content which is conveyed by them. And two books which may differ widely as World 1 objects may be identical insofar as they are World 3 objects—say, if they contain the same coded information.

Popper's World 3 has been compared to the concept of signs in the (monist) semiotic tradition from Charles Peirce onward (see Skagestad, 1993):

While Freeman and Skolimowski discuss both Peirce's doctrine of signs and Popper's World 3 epistemology, they do not note that the entities comprising Popper's World 3 are signs in the Peircean sense, or that Peirce's doctrine of signs represents a World 3 epistemology that in many respects is more detailed and developed than Popper's; nor has this been noted by any other writer that we are aware of. Again, we do not mean simply that World 3 consists of objects which Peirce would have classified as signs—that would be a rather trivial observation, given the ambitious scope of Peirce's doctrine of signs. Rather, as we have already seen, Popper's own statement that a World 3 object, such as a book, is constituted by its "dispositional character of being understood or interpreted," is what recapitulates Peirce's definition of a sign as whatever is capable of being interpreted.

The tendency within and beyond IS has been to favor Peirce's semiotic view over Popper's metaphysical pluralism. It makes sense to consider informative objects as signs (as World 1 phenomena) that for some subjects (or "release mechanisms," which are also World 1 phenomena) trigger some responses (interpretation, selection), and thus introduce teleological principles into the material world (World 1). According to Rudd (1983), we simply do not need Popper's World 3 in order to explain informational processes.

The most recent description of the cognitive view is presented by Borlund (2000, p. 16), who is a student of Peter Ingwersen. She finds that Ingwersen adds the concepts of potential information and data "and in a way the modified model becomes the trademark of Ingwersen, as he, in several cases, uses it to present an overview of IR interactions." We see the cognitive view as taking a position between the objective concept of information in both information theory and Dretske's theory on one hand, and the subjective or interpretative view taken by information scientists inspired by hermeneutics, semiotics, domain analysis, and so forth, on the other hand.

Information-as-Thing

Buckland (1991a) analyzes various uses of the term *information* in information science. It can be used in relation to things, processes, and knowledge (see Table 8.1).

Buckland's analysis seems to have two important consequences: On one hand, it reintroduces the concept of document ("information-as-thing"), and on the other hand, it points out the subjective nature of

Table 8.1 Four aspects of information (after Buckland, 1991a. p. 6).

	INTANGIBLE	TANGIBLE
ENTITY	Information-as-knowledge Knowledge	Information-as-thing Data, document, recorded knowledge
PROCESS	Information-as-process Becoming informed	Information processing Data processing, document processing, knowledge engineering ["Fluxed information": telephone calls, TV broadcast hours, etc.]

information. A stump of a tree contains information about its age as well as about the climate during the tree's lifetime. In similar fashion, anything might in some imaginable circumstances be informative: "We conclude that we are unable to say confidently of anything that it could not be information" (Buckland, 1991a, p. 50., underlining in original). Just as anything could/might be symbolic, Buckland maintains that *any* thing could/might be informative/information.

Domain Analysis, Socio-Cognitivism, Hermeneutics, Semiotics, and Related Views

The cognitive view takes a step toward a subjective understanding of information. Buckland goes another step. The domain analytic view sees different objects as being informative relative to the social division of labor in society. In this way, information is a subjective concept, but not primarily in an individual sense. Criteria for what counts as information are formed by sociocultural and scientific processes. Users should be seen as individuals in concrete situations within social organizations and domains of knowledge. A stone in a field could contain different information for different people. It is not possible for information systems to map all possible information values. Nor is any one mapping the only "true" situation. People have different educational backgrounds and play different roles in the division of labor in society. A stone in a field (or, of course, a document about a stone in a field such as a photograph) represents one kind of information for the geologist and another for the archaeologist. The information from the stone can be mapped onto the different collective knowledge structures produced by geology and archaeology. Information can be identified, described, and represented in information systems for different domains of knowledge. Of course, problems arise in determining whether a thing is informative or not for a domain. Some domains have a high degree of consensus and explicit relevance criteria. Other domains have different, conflicting paradigms, each containing its own more or less implicit view of the informativeness of different kinds of information sources.

The domain-analytic view is related to a hermeneutic view because the understanding is determined by the pre-understanding of the observer. An explicit "information hermeneutics" has been developed by

Capurro (e.g., 1986). It is also related to semiotic approaches (e.g., Brier, 1992, 1999) and to the approach known as social constructivism (e.g., Frohmann 1990, 1994; Savolainen, 2000).

Conclusion

We should be aware that library and information science is only one discipline among a network of disciplines and metadisciplines dealing with communication, technology, systems, and related processes. We should try to further clarify our identity and our specific goals, and to strengthen historical continuity in the field. We should not consider the concept of information in isolation, but see it in relation to other concepts such as, for example, documents and media. The concept of information may indeed have had a positive effect as a status booster for professions primarily working with documents. However, this positive effect has had the unfortunate consequence of raising the level of confusion in the discipline. It is worth noting that important books can be written in the field without using the concept of information (e.g., Lancaster, 1998). Thus, researchers should be explicit about how they define this and other theoretical terms. It should either be used for the sake of theoretical clarification, or—as Fairthorne (1965) recommended—not at all.

There are many concepts of information, and they are embedded in more or less explicit theoretical structures. In studying information it is easy to lose one's orientation. Therefore, it is important to state the pragmatic question: "What difference does it make if we use one or another theory, or concept, of information?" This task is difficult because many approaches involve implicit or vague concepts, which must be clarified. (Such a clarification may provoke resistance because information is so often used as a status-enhancing term with little theoretical ambition.) We should also ask ourselves what more we need to know about the concept of information in order to contribute to the further development of information science.

In our view, the most important distinction is that between information as an object or a thing (e.g., number of bits) and information as a subjective concept, information as a sign; that is, as depending on the interpretation of a cognitive agent. The interpretative view shifts attention from the attributes of things to the "release mechanisms" for which those attributes are of importance. This shift may cause frustration because it is inherently difficult and because it implies teleological principles that are foreign to the positivist principles of science. It is relatively easy to count the number of words in a document or describe it in other ways; it is much more difficult to try to figure out for whom that document is of importance, and what the important questions are that the document can answer. Questions of interpretation are also difficult because we often confuse interpretation with an individualist approach. Meaning is, however, determined in social and cultural contexts.

Finally, we want to emphasize the need to explicate the foundations of knowledge claims. When we represent data in our information systems, we do so in order to support certain human activities. We should not simply regard our representations as objective, because that implies that we never fully specify the theoretical, social, and historical assumptions on which we act. All kinds of information systems have policies and more or less explicit goals. What we regard as information should also be a reflection of the social role of the information system.

As information systems become more global and interconnected, implicit information is often lost. This situation challenges information science to be more receptive to the social and cultural impacts of interpretative processes and also the qualitative differences between different contexts and media. This change means including interpretative processes as a *conditio sine qua non* of information processes. As we have shown, this task is an essentially multidisciplinary and interdisciplinary one. Building networks is basically an interpretation process. Building a scientific network as a self-reflective activity presupposes the clarification of common concepts. One such concept is information.

Appendix

The Oxford English Dictionary (1989). Lists the following meanings for "information" [references omitted]:

Information. Forms: a. 4-6 enformacion, (-ioun, -ione, -yon), 6-7 enformation. b. 4-6 informacion, (-ioun, -yon), 6- information. [a. OF. enformacion, informacion (mod. F. information), ad. L. information-em outline, concept, idea, in med.Schol.L.the action of 'informing' matter, n. of action from informare to INFORM. Conformed to the L. spelling in 16th c. The

L. sb. had a very restricted use; the Eng. senses represent all the senses of the verb; but the chronological appearance of these does not accord with the logical order.]

I.1.a. The action of informing (in sense 4 of the verb); formation or moulding of the mind or character, training, instruction, teaching; communication of instructive knowledge. Now rare or Obs. b. with an and pl. An item of training; an instruction. Obs. c. Divine instruction, inspiration. Obs. 2. The action of informing (in sense 5 of the verb); communication of the knowledge or 'news' of some fact or occurrence; the action of telling or fact of being told of something. 3.a. Knowledge communicated concerning some particular fact, subject, or event; that of which one is apprised or told; intelligence, news. spec. contrasted with data. b. with an and pl. An item of information or intelligence; a fact or circumstance of which one is told. In earlier use, An account, relation, narrative (of something). Obs. c. Separated from, or without the implication of, reference to a person informed: that which inheres in one or two or more alternative sequences, arrangements, etc., that produce different responses in something, and which is capable of being stored in, transferred by, and communicated to inanimate things. d. As a mathematically defined quantity (see quots.); now esp. One which represents the degree of choice exercised in the selection or formation of one particular symbol, sequence, message, etc. out of a number of possible ones, and which is defined logarithmically in terms of the statistical probabilities of occurrence of the symbol or the elements of the message. 4. The action of informing against, charging, or accusing (a person). (Originally the general sense whence 5 arises; now Obs., exc. as transf. from 5; cf. also 6). 5. spec. in Eng. Law. a. A complaint or charge against a person lodged with or presented to a court or magistrate, in order to the institution of criminal proceedings without formal indictment. b. A complaint of the Crown in respect of some civil claim, in the form of a statement of the facts by the attorney general or other proper officer, either ex officio, or on the relation or report of a private individual. c. information quo warranto (superseding the ancient Writ of Quo warranto): the step by which proceedings are commenced to remedy the usurpation of an office or franchise. 6. In other legal systems. a. In Civil Law. b. In Scots Law. (a) in Civil Procedure: A written argument upon a case ordered either by a Lord Ordinary in the Court of Session when reporting the case to the

Inner House (obs.), or by the Court of Justiciary in a case where difficult questions of law or relevancy are raised before it (now rare), (b) in Criminal Procedure: A statement or complaint in writing in which a person is specifically charged with a criminal offence, upon which a warrant of commitment to gaol (*sic*) for trial may proceed. c. Applied also to similar proceedings in foreign systems of judicature, ancient or modern.

II. 7. The action of 'informing' with some active or essential quality (see INFORM v. 3); the giving of a form or character to something; inspiration, animation (e.g. of the body by the soul)

III. 8. attrib. and Comb., as information content, desk, explosion [EXPLOSION 4 b], flow, gap [GAP sb. 1 6a], office, service, storage, system, transfer, work; information-carrying, -gathering (so gatherer), -giving, -seeking vbl. Sbs. And ppl. adjs.; information bureau, an office where information is given and questions are answered; also fig.; information officer, a person engaged in the provision of specialized information; information processing, the processing of information so as to yield new or more useful information; data processing; information retrieval, the tracing of information stored in books, computers, or other collections of reference material; information revolution, the increase in the availability of information and the changes in the ways it is stored and disseminated that have occurred through the use of computers; information room (see quot. 1958); information science, (that branch of knowledge which is concerned with) the procedures by which information, esp. that relating to technical or scientific subjects, is stored, retrieved, and disseminated; hence information scientist, a person employed in providing an information service, or one who studies the methods used to do so; information technology, the branch of technology concerned with the dissemination, processing, and storage of information, esp. by means of computers. Also INFORMATION THEORY.

Endnotes

1. The authors have equal responsibility for this chapter.
2. References to Greek and Latin sources are not given in this chapter, but may be found in Capurro (1978).
3. Actually, Bogdan himself develops a general view of information that stands in contrast to this skeptical quotation.
4. Of course, library schools can have a strong focus on subject knowledge. One example is the University of Sheffield's Department of Information Studies

(http://www.shef.ac.uk/uni/academic/I-M/is/home.html), in which strong programs are offered in Chemoinformatics, among other fields. The tendencies within IS are to overcome this problem, for example, by the development of the domain-analytic approach (Hjørland & Albrechtsen, 1995).

5. Other traditions are, for example, the facet analytic tradition founded by S. R. Ranganathan, the cognitive tradition, and the natural language processing (NLP) tradition. Stockwell (2000) in *A History of Information Storage and Retrieval* has a much wider view of the field than the tradition in IS. This book includes, for example, the history of encyclopedias under this concept.

6. Frei (1996, p. 3) express a similar view on this issue: "For years on end, academic researchers studied how to index, store, and retrieve bibliographic references, calling their discipline information retrieval rather than reference retrieval. Thus, for a long time, IR was concerned with finding a very restricted kind of information and the term information retrieval was a real misnomer. Retrieving relevant bibliographic references is certainly a valid problem useful to some people. But it clearly does not reflect the majority of the problems that have to be solved facing today's information explosion. Business analysts, journalists, and scientists hardly ever need bibliographic references for their work. Most of the time they need facts; that is, direct information about the problem area they are working in; oftentimes they have neither the interest nor the time to follow up references, get articles from the library, and read papers."

7. The tendency to define information as an object of study of only one group of experts has an additional disadvantage. Information science is supposed to support the delivery of services to different groups, including astronomers. Of importance to IS is how such groups conceptualize and classify their objects, how their language is designed, what they regard as important and relevant, and so forth. If information scientists isolate themselves from the work of their target groups, they risk becoming superfluous in the eyes of that group. Therefore, we find it very important that information science does not isolate activities such as indexing and retrieving documents from the knowledge-producing activities in discourse communities. These communities produce the knowledge that is to be organized in the information systems, and may be the most important users of the information scientists' services.

8. This definition quoted from Griffith, 1980, is quite similar to a definition given by Borko, 1968. This last reference was explicitly motivated by the name shift ADI made to ASIS in 1968.

9. In our view, the computational aspects of "the generation, collection, organization, interpretation, storage, retrieval, dissemination, transformation, and use of information" are not specific to information science, but are to a large degree part of computer science; but, of course, these two fields overlap.

10. "In Shannon, Weaver, and Wiener's texts the terms 'communication' and 'information' are often used interchangeably, although the term 'information' is also used to signify the content of communication. The relative synonymy of these two terms continues a tendency that was prevalent before the Second World War, as well e.g., in the texts of Paul Otlet and other European documentalists

and social theorists. From a contemporary perspective, we may object that these two terms now signify different events and research fields. This article proposes, however, that they share a common heritage in an epistemological model that is still in use today. Further, the ease by which information technologies converge with communication technologies and visa [sic] versa, today—e.g., in the case of the Internet, which is understood as both a communicational and an informational medium—suggests that the issue of defining the 'real' difference between these two terms is less important than that of accounting for their historical congruence in theory and in practice." (Day, 2000, p. 805).

11. According to the *Social Sciences Citation Index*, July 2001.

Bibliography

Arrow, K. J. (1979). The economics of information. In M. L. Dertouzos, & J. Moses (Eds.), *The computer age: A twenty-year view* (pp. 306–317). Cambridge, MA: MIT Press.

Austin, J. L. (1961). *Philosophical papers.* J. C. Urmson & G. J. Warnock (Eds.). Oxford, UK: Clarendon Press.

Bacon, F. (1967). The great instauration. In E.A. Burtt (Ed.), *The English philosophers from Bacon to Mill.* New York: Random House. (Original work published in 1620)

Bar-Hillel, Y. (1973). *Language and information.* London: Addison-Wesley.

Bar-Hillel, Y., & Carnap, R. (1953). Semantic information. *British Journal of Science, 4,* 147–157.

Barwise, J. (1993). Constraints, channels and the flow of information. In P. Aczel, D. J. Israel, Y. Katagiri, & S. Peters (Eds.), *Situation theory and its application* (pp. 3–27). Stanford, CA: Stanford University Center for the Study of Language and Information.

Barwise, J., & Perry, J. (1983). *Situations and attitudes.* Cambridge, MA: MIT Press.

Barwise, J., & Seligman, J. (1997). *Information flows: The logic of distributed systems.* Cambridge, UK: Cambridge University Press.

Bateson, G. (1972). *Steps to an ecology of mind.* New York: Ballantine Books.

Bateson, G. (1979). *Mind and nature: A necessary unity.* New York: Dutton.

Belkin, N. J. (1978). Information concepts for information science. *Journal of Documentation, 34,* 55–85.

Bell, D. (1973). *The coming of the post-industrial society: A venture in social forecasting.* New York: Basic Books.

Bennett, C. H., & DiVincenzo, D. P. (2000). Quantum information and computation. *Nature, 404,* 247–255.

Berkeley, G. (1901). *The works of George Berkeley.* Oxford, UK: Clarendon Press.

Bogdan, R. J. (1994). *Grounds for cognition: How goal-guided behavior shapes the mind.* Hillsdale, NJ: Lawrence Earlbaum.

Bonnevie, E. (2001). Dretske's semantic information theory and meta-theories in library and information science. *Journal of Documentation, 57,* 519–534.

Borgmann, A. (1999). *Holding on to reality. The nature of information at the turn of the millennium*. Chicago: University of Chicago Press.

Borko, H. (1968). Information science: What is it? *American Documentation, 3*, 5.

Borlund, P. (2000). *Evaluation of interactive information retrieval systems*. Åbo, Finland: Åbo Academy University Press.

Bougnoux, D. (1993). *Sciences de l'information et de la communication* [Information and communication sciences]. Paris: Larousse.

Bougnoux, D. (1995). *La communication contre l'information* [Communication versus information]. Paris: Hachette.

Boulding, K. E. (1966). The economics of knowledge and the knowledge of economics. *American Economic Review, 56*, 1–13.

Braman, S. (1989). Defining information: An approach for policymakers. *Telecommunications Policy, 13*(1), 233–242.

Brier, S. (1992). Information and consciousness: A critique of the mechanistic concept of information. *Cybernetics and Human Knowing, 1*(2/3), 1–24.

Brier, S. (1999). What is a possible ontological and epistemological framework for a true universal "information science?" The suggestion of a cybersemiotics. In W. Hofkirchner (Ed.), *The quest for a unified theory of information. Proceedings of the Second International Conference on the Foundations of Information Science* (pp. 79–99). Amsterdam: Gordon and Breach.

Briet, S. (1951). *Qu'est-ce que la documentation?* (What is documentation?) Paris: Edit.

Brookes, B. C. (1977). The developing cognitive view in information science. *International Workshop on the Cognitive Viewpoint*, CC-77, 195–203.

Brookes, B. C. (1980). The foundations of information science: Part I: Philosophical aspects. *Journal of Information Science, 2*, 125–133.

Brookes, B. C. (1981). Information technology and the science of information. In R. N. Oddy, S. E. Robertson, C. J. van Rijsbergen, & P. W. Williams (Eds.), *Information retrieval research* (pp. 1–8). London: Butterworths.

Brown, J. S., & Duguid, P. (2000). *The social life of information*. Boston: Harvard Business School Press.

Buckland, M. K. (1991a). *Information and information systems*. New York: Praeger.

Buckland, M. K. (1991b). Information as thing. *Journal of the American Society for Information Science, 42*, 351–360.

Buckland, M. K. (1997). What is a "document?" *Journal of the American Society for Information Science, 48*, 804–809.

Bussa, R. (1975). *Index Thomisticus Sancti Thomae Aquinatis operum omnium. Indices et concordantiae* [Index of Saint Thomas Aquinas' complete works]. Stuttgart, Germany: Frommann-Holzboog.

Capurro, R. (1978). *Information. Ein Beitrag zur etymologischen und ideengeschichtlichen Begründung des Informationsbegriffs* [Information: A contribution to the foundation of the concept of information based on its etymology and in the history of ideas]. Munich, Germany: Saur.

Capurro, R. (1981). Heidegger über Sprache und Information [Heidegger on language and information]. *Philosophisches Jahrbuch, 88*, 333–344.

Capurro, R. (1986). *Hermeneutik der Fachinformation* [Hermeneutics of scientific information]. Freiburg, Germany: Alber.

Capurro, R. (1995). *Leben im Informationszeitalter* [Living in the information age]. Berlin, Germany: Akademie Verlag.

Capurro, R. (1996). On the genealogy of information. In K. Kornwachs & K. Jacoby (Eds.), *Information: New questions to a multidisciplinary concept* (pp. 259–270). Berlin, Germany: Akademie Verlag. Retrieved December 18, 2001, from http://www.capurro.de/cottinf.htm.

Capurro, R. (2000). Ethical challenges of the information society in the 21st century. *International Information & Library Review, 32,* 257–276. Retrieved December 18, 2001, from http://www.capurro.de/EEI21.htm.

Capurro, R. (2001). Informationsbegriffe und ihre Bedeutungsnetze [Information concepts and their semantic networks]. *Ethik und Sozialwissenschaften, 1,*(12), 14–17. Retrieved December 18, 2001, from http://www.capurro.de/ropohl.htm.

Capurro, R., Fleissner, P., & Hofkirchner, W. (1999). Is a unified theory of information feasible? A trialogue. In W. Hofkirchner (Ed.), *The quest for a unified theory of information. Proceedings of the Second International Conference on the Foundations of Information Science* (pp. 9–30). Amsterdam: Gordon and Breach. Retrieved December 18, 2001, from http://www.capurro.de/trialog.htm.

Castells, M. (1989). *The informational city: Information technology, economic restructuring and the urban-regional process.* Oxford, UK: Blackwell.

Castells, M. (1996–1998). *The information age: Economy, society and culture.* Oxford UK: Blackwell.

Chalmers, A. F. (1999). *What is this thing called science?* (3rd ed.). Buckingham, UK: Open University Press.

Conrad, M. (1996). Cross-scale information processing in evolution, development and intelligence. *Bio Systems, 38,* 97–109.

Conrad, M., & Marijuan, P. C. (Eds.). (1996). Proceedings of the First Conference on Foundations of Information Science: From Computers and Quantum Physics to Cells, Nervous Systems, and Societies. *Bio Systems, 38,* 87–266.

Cornelius, I. (2002). Theorizing information. *Annual Review of Information Science and Technology, 36,* 393–425.

Cornella, A. (2000). *Infonomia.com. La empresa es información* [Infonomía.com: The company is information]. Bilbao, Spain: Deusto.

Day, R. E. (2000). The "conduit metaphor" and the nature and politics of information studies. *Journal of the American Society for Information Science, 51,* 805–811.

Day, R. E. (2001). *The modern invention of information: Discourse, history, and power.* Carbondale, IL: Southern Illinois University Press.

Descartes, R. (1996). *Oeuvres,* C. Adam & P. Tannery (Eds.). Paris: Vrin.

Devlin, K. J. (1991). *Logic and information.* Cambridge, UK: Cambridge University Press.

Dretske, F. I. (1981). *Knowledge and the flow of information.* Cambridge, MA: MIT Press.

Dretske, F. I. (1986). Minds, machines and meaning. In C. Mitcham, & A. Huning (Eds.), *Philosophy and technology II: Information technology and computers in theory and practice* (pp. 97–109). Dordrecht, The Netherlands: Reidel.

Eliot, T. S. (1969). Choruses from "The Rock." In *T. S. Eliot: The complete poems and plays*. London: St. Edmundsbury Press. (Original work published in 1934)

Ellis, D. (1996). *Progress and problems in information retrieval*. London: Library Association.

Fairthorne, R. A. (1965). "Use" and "mention" in the information sciences. In L. B. Heilprin, B. E. Markuson, & F. L. Goodman (Eds.), *Proceedings of the Symposium for Information Science* (pp. 9–12). Washington, DC: Spartan Books.

Fleissner, P., & Hofkirchner, W. (1995). Informatio revisited. Wider den dinglichen Informationsbegriff [Information revisited: Against the concept of information-as-thing]. *Informatik-Forum, 8*, 126–131.

Fleissner, P., Hofkirchner, W. (1999). Actio non est reactio: An extension of the concept of causality towards phenomena of information. In W. Hofkirchner (Ed.), *The quest for a unified theory of information: Proceedings of the Second International Conference on the Foundations of Information Science* (pp. 197–214). Amsterdam: Gordon and Breach.

Flückiger, F. (1999). Towards a unified concept of information: Presentation of a new approach. In W. Hofkirchner (Ed.), *The quest for a unified theory of information. Proceedings of the Second International Conference on the Foundations of Information Science* (pp. 101–111). Amsterdam: Gordon and Breach.

Flusser, V. (1996). *Kommunikologie*. Mannheim, Germany: Bollmann Verlag.

Frei, H.-P. (1996). Information retrieval: From academic research to practical applications. Retrieved December 18, 2001, from http://www.ubilab.org/publications/print_versions/pdf/fre96.pdf.

Frohmann, B. (1990). Rules of indexing: A critique of mentalism in information retrieval theory. *Journal of Documentation, 46*, 81–101.

Frohmann, B. (1994). Discourse analysis as a research method in library and information science. *Library & Information Science Research, 16*, 119–138.

Gärdenfors, P. (1999). Cognitive science: From computers to anthills as models of human thought. *Human IT, 3*(2), Retrieved December 18, 2001, from http://www.hb.se/bhs/ith/2-99/index.htm.

Golu, M. (1981). The methodological value of the concept of information in psychology. *Revue Roumaine des Sciences Socials: Serie de psychologie, 25*(1), 71–75.

Griffith, B. C. (Ed.). (1980). *Key papers in information science*. New York: Knowledge Industry Publications.

Günther, G. (1963). *Das Bewußtsein der Maschinen: Eine Metaphysik der Kybernetik* [The consciousness of machines: A metaphysics of cybernetics]. Krefeld/Baden-Baden, Germany: Agis Verlag.

Gundry, J. (2001). Knowledge management. Retrieved November 15, 2001, from http://www.knowab.co.uk/kma.html.

Hamlyn, D. W. (1977). The concept of information in Gibson's theory of perception. *Journal for the Theory of Social Behaviour, 7*(1), 5–16.

Harary, F., & Batell, M. F. (1978). The concept of negative information. *Behavioral Science, 23,* 264–270.

Harrah, D. (1958). The psychological concept of information. *Philosophy & Phenomenological Research, 18,* 242–249.

Hartley, R.V.L. (1928). Transmission of information. *Bell System Technical Journal, 7,* 335–363.

Heidegger, M. (1959). Der Weg zur Sprache [The path to language]. In *Martin Heidegger: Unterwegs zur Sprache* [Martin Heidegger: The way to language] (pp. 239–268). Pfullingen, Germany: Neske.

Heidegger, M., & Fink, E.(1970). *Heraklit* [Heraclitus]. Frankfurt am Main, Germany: Klostermann.

Hjørland, B. (2000). Documents, memory institutions, and information science. *Journal of Documentation, 56,* 27–41.

Hjørland, B., & Albrechtsen, H. (1995). Towards a new horizon in information retrieval: Domain analysis. *Journal of the American Society for Information Science, 46,* 400–425.

Hobart, M. E., & Schiffman, Z. S. (2000). Information ages: Literacy, numeracy, and the computer revolution. Baltimore, MD: Johns Hopkins University Press.

Hofkirchner, W. (Ed.). (1999). *The quest for a unified theory of information. Proceedings of the Second International Conference on the Foundations of Information Science.* Amsterdam: Gordon and Breach.

Hume, D. (1962). *On human nature and the understanding.* A. Flew (Ed.). New York: Macmillan. (Original work published in 1748)

Israel, D., & Perry, J. (1990). What is information? In P. Hanson (Ed.), *Information, language and cognition* (pp. 1–19). Vancouver, BC: University of British Columbia Press.

Israel, D., & Perry, J. (1991). Information and architecture. In J. Barwise, J. M. Gawron, G. Plotkin, & S. Tutiya, (Eds.), *Situation theory and its applications* (pp. 147–160). Stanford, CA: Stanford University Center for the Study of Language and Information.

Janich, P. (1992). *Grenzen der Naturwissenschaft* [The limits of natural science]. Munich, Germany: Beck.

Janich, P. (1996). *Konstruktivismus und Naturerkenntnis. Auf dem Weg zum Kulturalismus* [Constructivism and the knowledge of nature: On the path to culturalism]. Frankfurt am Main, Germany: Suhrkamp.

Janich, P. (1998). Informationsbegriff und methodisch-kulturalistische Philosophie [The concept of information and methodologic-culturalist philosophy]. *Ethik und Sozialwissenschaften, 2,* 169–182.

Johnson, E. (1915). The special library and some of its problems. *Special Libraries, 6,* 158–159.

Karpatschof, B. (2000). *Human activity: Contributions to the anthropological sciences from a perspective of activity theory.* Copenhagen, Denmark: Dansk Psykologisk Forlag.

Kirschenmann, P. (1969). *Kybernetik, Information, Widerspiegelung. Darstellung einiger philosophischer Probleme im dialektischen Materialismus* [Cybernetics, information and reflection: An exposition of some philosophical problems of dialectical materialism]. Munich, Germany: Pustet.

Klaus, G. (1963). *Kybernetik in philosophischer Sicht* [Cybernetics from a philosophical viewpoint]. Berlin, Germany: Dietz.

Kornwachs, K. (1996). Pragmatic information and system surface. In K. Kornwachs & K. Jacoby (Eds.), *Information: New questions to a multidisciplinary concept* (pp. 163–185). Berlin, Germany: Akademie Verlag.

Kornwachs, K., & Jacoby, K. (Eds.). (1996). *Information: New questions to a multidisciplinary concept*. Berlin, Germany: Akademie Verlag.

Krippendorff, K. (1994). Der verschwundene Bote [The vanished messenger]. In K. Merten, S. J. Schmidt, & S. Weischenberg (Eds.), *Die Wirklichkeit der Medien* [The reality of media] (pp. 79–113). Opladen, Germany: Westdeutscher Verlag.

Küppers, B.-O. (1996). The context-dependence of biological information. In K. Kornwachs & K. Jacoby (Eds.), *Information. New questions to a multidisciplinary concept* (pp. 137–145). Berlin, Germany: Akademie Verlag.

Lancaster, F. W. (1998). *Indexing and abstracting in theory and practice* (2nd ed.). London: Library Association.

Laszlo, E. (1999). A note on evolution. In W. Hofkirchner (Ed.), *The quest for a unified theory of information: Proceedings of the Second International Conference on the Foundations of Information Science* (pp. 1–7). Amsterdam: Gordon and Breach.

Lawrence, S., & Giles, L. (1999). Accessibility and distribution of information on the Web. *Nature, 400*, 107–109. Retrieved December 18, 2001, from http://www.wwwmetrics.com/.

Leydesdorff, L. (2001). *A sociological theory of communication. The self-organization of the knowledge-based society*. Parkland, FL: Universal Publishers.

Locke, J. (1995). *An essay concerning human understanding*. London: J. M. Dent. (Original work published in 1726)

Loewenstein, W. R. (1999). *Molecular information, cell communication, and the foundations of life*. New York: Oxford University Press.

Losee, R. M. (1990). *The science of information: Measurement and applications*. San Diego, CA: Academic Press.

Losee, R. M. (1997). A discipline independent definition of information. *Journal of the American Society for Information Science, 48*, 254–269.

Losee, R. M. (1999). The beginnings of "Information Theory." Retrieved December 18, 2001, from http://www.ils.unc.edu/~losee/b5/node7.html.

Luhmann, N. (1987). *Soziale Systeme* [Social systems]. Frankfurt am Main, Germany: Suhrkamp.

Lund, N. W. (1997). Institutt for dokumentasjonsvitenskap i Tromsø: En realitet pr. 1.8.1997. [The Institute for Documentation Science in Tromso: A reality as from 1.8.1997]. *Synopsis, 28*, 287–291.

Lyre, H (1998). *Quantentheorie der Information* [Quantum theory of information]. Vienna: Springer.

Machlup, F. (1962). *The production and distribution of knowledge in the United States*. Princeton, NJ: Princeton University Press.

Machlup, F. (1983). Semantic quirks in studies of information. In F. Machlup & U. Mansfield (Eds.), *The study of information: Interdisciplinary messages* (pp. 641–671). New York: Wiley.

Machlup, F., & Mansfield, U. (Eds.). (1983). *The study of information: Interdisciplinary messages*. New York: Wiley.

MacKay, D. M. (1969). *Information, mechanism and meaning*. Cambridge, MA: MIT Press.

Mahler, G. (1996). Quantum information. In K. Kornwachs & K. Jacoby (Eds.), *Information: New questions to a multidisciplinary concept* (pp. 103–118). Berlin, Germany: Akademie Verlag.

Marijuan, P. C. (1996). First conference on foundations of information science. From computers and quantum physics to cells, nervous systems, and societies. *Bio Systems, 38*, 87–96.

Matsuno, K. (1996). Internalist stance and the physics of information. *Bio Systems, 38*, 111–118.

Matsuno, K. (1998). Dynamics of time and information in a dynamic time. *Bio Systems, 46*, 57–71.

Matsuno, K. (2000). The internalist stance: A linguistic practice enclosing dynamics. *Annals of the New York Academy of Sciences, 901*, 332–350.

Maturana, H. R., & Varela, F. J. (1980). *Autopoiesis and cognition*. Dordrecht, The Netherlands: Reidel.

Miller, G. A. (1953). What is information measurement? *American Psychologist, 8*, 3–11.

Miller, G. L. (1988). The concept of information: A historical perspective on modern theory and technology. In B. D. Ruben (Ed.), *Information and behavior* (Vol. 2, pp. 27–53). New Brunswick, NJ: Transaction Publishers.

Mingers, J. C. (1995). Information and meaning: Foundations for an intersubjective account. *Information Systems Journal, 5*, 285–306.

Morris, C. W. (1955). *Signs, language and behavior*. New York: Braziller. (Original work published in 1946)

Nelson, T. (1987). *The Xanadu paradigm* [poster]. San Antonio, TX: Theodor H. Nelson.

Nonaka, I., & Takeuchi, H. (1995). *The knowledge-creating company: How Japanese companies create the dynamics of innovation*. New York: Oxford University Press.

Nyquist, H. (1924). Certain factors affecting telegraph speed. *Bell System Technical Journal, 3*, 324–346.

Nørretranders, T. (1998). *User illusion: Cutting consciousness down to size*. New York: Viking Penguin.

Oeser, E. (1976). *Wissenschaft und Information* [Science and information]. Vienna, Austria: Oldenbourg.

Otlet, P. (1934). *Traité de documentation: Le livre sur le livre, théorie et pratique* [Treatise on documentation: The book on the book, theory and practice]. Brussels, Belgium: Editions Mundaneium.

Oxford English Dictionary (2nd ed.). (1989). Prepared by J. A. Simpson & E. S. C. Weiner, Oxford, UK: Clarendon Press.

Peirce, C. S. (1905). What pragmaticism is. *The Monist, 15,* 161–181.

Pérez Gutiérrez, M. (2000). *El fenómeno de la información: Una aproximación conceptual al flujo informativo* [The phenomenon of information: A conceptual approximation of the flow of information]. Madrid, Spain: Trotta.

Peterfreund, E., & Schwartz, J. T. (1971). The concept of information. *Psychological Issues, 7,* 115–125.

Peters, J. D. (1988). Information: Notes toward a critical history. *Journal of Communication Inquiry, 12,* 10–24.

Polanyi, M. (1966). *The tacit dimension.* Garden City, NY: Doubleday.

Popper, K. R. (1979). *Objective knowledge: An evolutionary approach* (Rev. ed.). New York: Oxford University Press.

Popper, K. R. (1974). Replies to my critics. In P. A. Schlipp (Ed.), *The philosophy of Karl Popper* (pp. 949–1180). La Salle, IL: Open Court.

Porat, M. U. (1977). *The information economy: Definition and measurement.* Washington, DC: U.S. Department of Commerce, Office of Telecommunications.

Probst, G., Raub, S., & Romhard, K. (1999). *Managing knowledge.* London: Wiley.

Quastler, H. (Ed.). (1956). *Information theory in psychology: Problems and methods.* New York: The Free Press.

Qvortrup, L. (1993). The controversy over the concept of information. An overview and a selected and annotated bibliography. *Cybernetics & Human Knowing, 1*(4), 3–24.

Rapoport, A. (1953). What is information? *Etc., 10,* 247–260.

Rapoport, A. (1956). The promise and pitfalls of information theory. *Behavioral Science, 1,* 13–17.

Rayward, W. B. (1994). Visions of Xanadu: Paul Otlet (1868–1944) and hypertext. *Journal of the American Society for Information Science, 45,* 235–250.

Rayward, W. B. (1998). The origins of information science and the International Institute of Bibliography/International Federation for Information and Documentation (FID). In T. B. Hahn & M. Buckland (Eds.), *Historical studies in information science* (pp. 22–33). Medford, NJ: ASIS/Information Today, Inc.

Reid, T. (1967). *Philosophical works.* Hildesheim, Germany: Olms. (Original work published in 1895)

Rieger, B. B. (1996). Situation semantics and computational linguistics: Towards informational ecology: A semiotic perspective for cognitive information processing systems? In K. Kornwachs & K. Jacoby (Eds.), *Information. New questions to a multidisciplinary concept* (pp. 285–315). Berlin, Germany: Akademie Verlag.

Rifkin, J. (2000). *The age of access: The new culture of hypercapitalism where all of life is a paid-for experience.* New York: Tarcher/Putnam.

Rogers, S. (2000). The emerging concept of information. *Ecological Psychology, 12,* 335–343.

Romm, N. (1997). Implications of regarding information as meaningful rather than factual. In R. L. Winder, S. K. Probert, & I. A. Beeson (Eds.), *Philosophical aspects of information systems* (pp. 23–34). London: Taylor & Francis.

Ropohl, G. (2001). Der Informationsbegriff im Kulturstreit [The concept of information in the framework of the culturalist struggle]. *Ethik und Sozialwissenschaften, 1,* 1–12.

Rudd, D. (1983). Do we really need World III? Information science with or without Popper. *Journal of Information Science, 7,* 99–105.

Savolainen, R. (2000). Incorporating small parts and gap-bridging: Two metaphorical approaches to information use. *The New Review of Information Behaviour Research, 1,* 35–50.

Schnelle, H. (1976). Information. In J. Ritter (Ed.), *Historisches Wörterbuch der Philosophie, IV* [Historical dictionary of philosophy, IV] (pp. 116–117). Stuttgart, Germany: Schwabe.

Schrader, A. M. (1983). Toward a theory of library and information science. (Doctoral dissertation, Indiana University, 1983). Dissertation Abstracts International, AAT 8401534.

Schütz, L. (1958). *Thomas-Lexikon* [Thomas lexicon]. Stuttgart, Germany: Frommann-Holzboog. (Original work published in 1895)

Seiffert, H. (1968). *Information über die Information* [Information about information]. Munich, Germany: Beck.

Shannon, C. (1948). A mathematical theory of communication. *Bell System Technical Journal, 27,* 379–423, 623–656.

Shannon, C., & Weaver, W. (1949/1972). *The mathematical theory of communication.* Urbana, IL: University of Illinois Press. (Original work published in 1949)

Shapiro, F. R. (1995). Coinage of the term information science. *Journal of the American Society for Information Science, 46,* 384–385.

Skagestad, P. (1993). Thinking with machines: Intelligence augmentation, evolutionary epistemology, and semiotics. *Journal of Social and Evolutionary Systems, 16,* 157–180. Retrieved December 18, 2001, from http://www.hf.ntnu.no/anv/Finnbo/Skagestad.html%20.

Spang-Hanssen, H. (2001). How to teach about information as related to documentation. *Human IT, 5*(1), 125–143. (Original work published in 1970) Retrieved December 18, 2001, from http://www.hb.se/bhs/ith/1-01/hsh.htm.

Sparck Jones, K. (1987) Architecture problems in the construction of expert systems for document retrieval. In I. Wormell (Ed.), *Knowledge engineering: Expert systems and information retrieval* (pp. 7–33). London: Taylor Graham.

Stockwell, F. (2000). *A history of information storage and retrieval.* Jefferson, NC: McFarland & Company.

Stonier, T. (1990). *Information and the internal structure of the universe: An exploration into information physics.* London: Springer.

Stonier, T. (1991). Towards a new theory of information. *Journal of Information Science 17,* 257–263.

Stonier, T. (1996). Information as a basic property of the universe. *Bio Systems, 38,* 135–140.

Stonier, T. (1997). *Information and meaning: An evolutionary perspective*. London: Springer.

Stonier, T. (1999). The emerging global brain. In W. Hofkirchner (Ed.), *The quest for a unified theory of information: Proceedings of the Second International Conference on the Foundations of Information Science* (pp. 561–578). Amsterdam: Gordon and Breach.

Taylor, R. S. (1968). Question-negotiation and information seeking in libraries. *College & Research Libraries, 29*, 178–194.

Teilhard de Chardin, P. (1964). *The future of man* (Trans. N. Denny). New York: Harper & Row. (Original work published in 1959)

Thesaurus linguae latinae [Thesaurus of the Latin language]. (1900). Leipzig, Germany: Teubner.

Titze, H. (1971). *Ist Information ein Prinzip?* [Is information a principle?]. Meisenheim, Germany: Hain.

Underwood, M. (2001). *Communication, culture & media studies*. Retrieved November 3, 2001, from http://www.cultsock.ndirect.co.uk/MUHome/cshtml.

Ursul, A. D. (1970). *Information: Eine philosophische Studie* [Information: a philosophical study]. Berlin, Germany: Dietz.

van Rijsbergen, C. J. (1979). Information retrieval. (2nd ed.), London: Butterworths. Retrieved December 18, 2001, from http://www.dcs.gla.ac.uk/Keith/Preface. html.

van Rijsbergen, C. J. (1986). A new theoretical framework for information retrieval. *Annual International ACM SIGIR Conference on Research and Development in Information Retrieval (SIGIR '86)*, 194–200.

van Rijsbergen, C. J. (1996). Information, logic, and uncertainty in information science. *CoLIS 2: Second International Conference on Conceptions of Library and Information Science: Integration in Perspective*, 1–10.

van Rijsbergen, C. J., & Lalmas, M. (1996). Information calculus for information retrieval. *Journal of the American Society for Information Science, 47*, 385–398.

Völz, H. (1982–1983). *Information I: Studie zur Vielfalt und Einheit der Information; Information II: Ergänzungsband zur Vielfalt und Einheit der Information - Theorie und Anwendung vor allem in der Biologie, Medizin und Semiotik* [Information I: A study of the variety and unity of information; Information II: Supplementary volume to variety and unity of information: Theory and application, particularly in biology, medicine and semiotics]. Berlin, Germany: Akademie Verlag.

von Foerster, H. (1980). Epistemology of communication. In K. Woodward (Ed.), *The myths of information* (pp. 18–27). Sun Prairie, WI: Baugartner.

von Foerster, H. (1984). *Observing systems*. Seaside, CA: Intersystems Publications.

von Krogh, G., Ichijo, K., & Nonaka, I. (2000). Enabling knowledge creation. *How to unlock the mystery of tacit knowledge and release the power of innovation*. New York: Oxford University Press.

Webster, F. (1995). *Theories of the information society*. London: Routledge.

Webster, F. (1996). The information society: Conceptions and critique. In A. Kent (Ed.) *Encyclopedia of library and information science* (Vol. 58, Suppl. 21, pp. 74–112). New York: Marcel Dekker.

Weizsäcker, C. F. von (1974). *Die Einheit der Natur* [The unity of nature]. Munich, Germany: Deutscher Taschenbuch Verlag.

Weizsäcker, C. F. von (1985). *Aufbau der Physik* [Foundation of physics]. Munich, Germany: Hanser.

Weizsäcker, C.F. von (1992). *Zeit und Wissen* [Time and knowledge]. Munich, Germany: Hanser.

Wersig, G. (1996). Information theory. In J. Feather & P. Sturges (Eds.), *International encyclopedia of library and information science* (pp. 220–227). London: Routledge.

White, H. D., & McCain, K. W. (1988). Visualizing a discipline: An author co-citation analysis of information science, 1972–1995. *Journal of the American Society for Information Science, 49*, 327–355.

Wiener, N. (1961). *Cybernetics or control and communication in the animal and the machine* (2nd ed.). New York: MIT Press.

Williams, R. V. (1998). The documentation and special libraries movements in the United States, 1910–1960. In T. B. Hahn & M. Buckland (Eds.), *Historical studies in information science* (pp. 173–180). Medford, NJ: ASIS/Information Today, Inc.

Wilson, P. (1983). Knowledge and the flow of information [Book review]. *Information Processing & Management, 19*, 61–62.

Wittgenstein, L. (1958a). *Philosophical investigations*. G. E. M. Anscombe (Trans.), Oxford, UK: Blackwell.

Wittgenstein, L. (1958b). *The blue and brown books*. R. Rhees (Ed.). Oxford, UK: Blackwell.

Wong, S. K. M., & Yao, Y. Y. (1992). An information theoretic measure of term specificity. *Journal of the American Society for Information Science, 43*, 54–61.

Yagisawa, T. (1999). Definition. In R. Audi (Ed.), *The Cambridge dictionary of philosophy* (2nd ed.) (pp. 213–115). Cambridge, UK: Cambridge University Press.

Yovits, M. C. (1975). A theoretical framework for the development of information science. In *International Federation for Documentation. Theoretical problems in informatics (FID 530)*, 90–114.

Zachary, J., Iyengar, S. S., & Barhen, J. (2001). Content based image retrieval and information theory: A general approach. *Journal of the American Society for Information Science and Technology, 52*, 840–852.

Zoglauer, T. (1996). Can information be naturalized? In K. Kornwachs & Jacoby, K. (Eds.), *Information. New questions to a multidisciplinary concept* (pp. 187–207). Berlin, Germany: Akademie Verlag.

CHAPTER 9

Task-Based Information Searching

Pertti Vakkari
University of Tampere

Introduction

The rationale for using information systems is to find information that helps us in our daily activities, be they tasks or interests. Systems are expected to support us in searching for and identifying useful information. Although the activities and tasks performed by humans generate information needs and searching, they have attracted little attention in studies of information searching. Such studies have concentrated on search tasks rather than the activities that trigger them. It is obvious that our understanding of information searching is only partial, if we are not able to connect aspects of searching to the related task. The expected contribution of information to the task is reflected in relevance assessments of the information items found, and in the search tactics and use of the system in general. Taking the task into account seems to be a necessary condition for understanding and explaining information searching, and, by extension, for effective systems design.

Scope and Approach

In this chapter, I shall review studies on the relationship between task performance and information searching by end-users. I focus mainly on information searching in electronic environments, especially in information retrieval (IR) systems. The process of information searching is cyclical, but it can be broken down into the following components:

- The kind of information that is needed and searched for

- The query formulation process, including the choice of search terms and operators

- Search tactics

- The use of search support tools

- Relevance and utility judgments regarding the information found

Several approaches to characterizing tasks in the literature are in use. In the studies I have found on information searching, tasks have been either characterized as a process consisting of several stages, or this aspect has been left open. In the latter case, the task has been treated as a given and left without characterization; only its context being described. A typical example is observing university students searching for information for study purposes without explicating those purposes. In these studies, the point of departure is searching, not the work task that produces it.

Only a limited number of studies relate tasks to searching. Because of this, I take into account studies based on natural search goals, insofar as they further our understanding of task-based searching. I also review a few studies based on assigned search goals. In general, the models and findings are scattered and difficult to integrate into the framework of task-based searching.

Ideally, a study should connect the task with the search process in order to analyze their interaction (Belkin, 1990). This sort of study typically requires a longitudinal research design. Due to the rarity of such process analyses, studies that analyze the relation between tasks and searching synchronously are also included. I focus principally on the literature published after 1990 simply because the number of empirical studies has grown since then. I start by introducing different conceptions of tasks in studies of information searching and briefly outline task analysis. I move on to analyze search goals and actions. I then discuss issues of modeling information searching, particularly from a task perspective. I then review models and theories that link task performance to information searching, thereafter introducing results from empirical studies on the relations between task performance and various aspects of information searching. I conclude with some methodological comments and suggestions for further research in the area.

Some texts touch upon the topic of this chapter. Ingwersen's (1992) book provides a good summary of the research on interactive IR, as does Marchionini's (1995) monograph on information searching in electronic environments. Allen (1996) combines results from user studies with ideas from systems design. The chapters in *ARIST* by Harter and Hert (1997) on the evaluation of IR systems, by Ingwersen (2001) on the cognitive approach in IR, by Marchionini and Komlodi (1998) on interfaces for information seeking, and by Sugar (1995) on user-centered perspectives on IR research and analysis methods, contain useful information relating to task-oriented IR.

Background

In studies of information searching, it has been typical to take the characteristics of humans or systems as a starting point and ignore the tasks being carried out. However, some attempts have been made to explain information searching by reference to human actions—mainly theoretically, but also empirically (Belkin, 1980; Dervin, 1992; Kuhlthau, 1993; Spink, Greisdorf, & Bateman, 1998; Spink, Wilson, Ellis, & Ford, 1998; Vakkari, 2001; Wersig & Windel 1985). However, most of those studies do not use the term "action," but conceptualize it in terms of tasks or problem solving. It has been common to study complex and highly intentional work tasks like those performed by scholars, lawyers, or engineers.

The advent of the cognitive approach in IR at the end of the1970s signified a shift in interest from mere document representation to representation of the cognitive structures of humans as well. It was realized that the knowledge structures generated by the documents read did not directly reflect the cognitive structures of texts, but rather were integrated with the cognitive structures of their recipients. The meaning of a text was seen as a function of the prior knowledge of its reader, not as something intrinsic to the text. Thus, one can say that the cognitive approach advocates user orientation in studies of information seeking and retrieval (Ingwersen, 1992). This view has many methodological implications. First, if meaning depends on readers' prior knowledge, relevance is not an objective, but a subjective property of documents. Second, it is evident that prior knowledge changes when subjects acquire new information. Thus, information needs, and consequently information searching and use, are dynamic, not static, and depend on changes in humans' cognitive structures (Belkin, 1980).

In the 1980s, information searching was analyzed from the perspective of problem solving (Belkin, Oddy, & Brookes, 1982a, 1982b; Belkin, Seeger, & Wersig 1983; Wersig & Windel, 1985); tasks as an explanatory factor gained firmer footing from the 1990s onward (Ingwersen, 1992; Järvelin, 1987; Sutcliffe & Ennis, 1998; Vakkari, 1999). The latter approach was inspired by developments in computer science, systems science, and organizational studies, in which task analysis is a central tool in systems design. In this chapter, I analyze information searching in terms of tasks, because it is a broader concept than problem solving, which it subsumes.

Conceptions of Tasks

Task

A task is an activity to be performed in order to accomplish a goal (Hackos & Redish, 1998; Hansen, 1999; Shepherd, 1998). Tasks have been conceptualized in two different ways: first, as an abstract construction, which does not include performance (Byström, 1999; McCormick, 1979; Shepherd, 1998). A task, especially a complex one, may include specifiable, smaller subtasks. In the second definition, a task is viewed from a functional perspective: as a series of actions undertaken in pursuit of a particular goal by an actor. The performance of a task includes physical and cognitive actions. This performance has a recognizable purpose, beginning, and end. It consists of a series of subtasks. A task, when performed, results in a meaningful product (Byström, 1999; Hackos & Redish, 1998; McCormick, 1979).

This characterization of a task does not provide a strict operational definition. Tasks can be analyzed at different levels of granularity (Hackos & Redish, 1998); if we wish to analyze task performance, it is an open question as to which elements constitute the task and which its subtasks. For instance, writing a research proposal can be seen as a subtask of a research project or as an independent task, depending on the point of departure. It is evident that in analyzing information searching, defining a task and its subtasks is a practical matter dictated by the research questions of the study. It is not necessary to give a definition of a task that would be applicable in all situations; it is sufficient to characterize it in a way that helps to identify it for the purpose of the analysis. Subtasks can be labeled in several ways. They can be called actions or operations. Sequences of subtasks are named plans, procedures, or scripts (Hackos & Redish, 1998; Shepherd, 1998).

Task Analysis

In human-computer interaction, task analysis is a set of techniques that can be used to describe and evaluate the interactions between people and their (work) environments in terms of sequences of actions and cognitive processes (Hansen 1999). However, a lack of agreement persists regarding the nature of task analysis (Shepherd, 1998). It seems to depend on how "a task" is understood. Some treat a task more as an abstract construct, whereas others connect it to the way actors perform specific activities. Task analysis can be anywhere along this spectrum depending on the goal (Byström, 1999; Hackos & Redish, 1998; Shepherd, 1998). Hierarchical task analysis (HTA), as defined by Shepherd (1998), represents a more formal approach to task analysis, while task analysis as presented by Hackos and Redish (1998) or Suchman (1995) emphasizes conceptualizing tasks more from the point of view of the actor and the social context of task performance, as do Checkland and Holwell (1998) in their excellent presentation of soft systems methodology. Activity theory is an approach that also emphasizes the social context of activities in terms of their material conditions. Good introductions to activity theory are Engeström, Miettinen, and Punamäki (1999), Nardi (1996), and Spasser (1999). The analysis of users' goals in task performance unifies all these approaches.

HTA is concerned with establishing an accurate description of the steps that are required in order to complete a task; that is, an analytical account of objective task requirements, be they physical or cognitive (Shepherd, 1998). Shepherd includes a good description of a strategy in

HTA. In Richardson, Ormerod, and Shepherd (1998), HTA is used as a tool for analyzing requirements for interface design. Hackos and Redish (1998) distinguish between six variants of task analysis. Critical to each is analyzing goals and understanding what users do to meet those goals. The types of analysis are as follows:

- Workflow analysis: how work gets done when several people are involved

- Job analysis: what a single individual does over a longer period of time

- Task inventories: what tasks are performed by all the people who may use the system

- Process analysis: the order in which users perform tasks

- Task hierarchies: how a larger task is made up of subtasks

- Procedural analysis: what steps and decisions users take to accomplish a task

Naturally, these variants can be combined depending on the goals of task analysis. Hackos and Redish (1998) include a detailed presentation of various types of task analysis and methods and also discuss implementing the findings in interface design. Practical tips in analyzing human activities for systems design can be found in the following: Nielsen (1994), who describes a technique for extending a task analysis based on the goal composition principle; Henderson (2000) who organizes along six dimensions the vast range of human activity that designers must address; Suchman (1995) who considers how to make underlying work practices visible.

Proper task analysis is not common in studies on information searching. This is understandable, because task analysis is a tool for systems design. However, its principles and methods could be used in research designs for information searching. Examples of studies applying task analysis to various degrees in information searching are Belkin, Marchetti, and Cool (1993), Belkin, Cool, Stein, and Theil (1995), Pejtersen (1990), and Stein, Gulla, and Theil (1999).

Characteristics of Tasks

Several ways to characterize and classify tasks are in use. Hansen (1999) gives a comprehensive list of categorizations of tasks, which might be useful in studying information searching. In studies of information seeking, it has been common to analyze difficult, information-intensive tasks. Byström (1999) argues that task complexity is frequently used to differentiate tasks in domains such as organizational studies, psychology, and information science. Complexity has been tied to several factors in the literature (Byström, 1999; Campbell, 1988). Campbell (1988) presents an integrative framework for task complexity. He relates task complexity directly to the task attributes that increase information load, diversity, or rate of change. He claims that complexity can be defined objectively, independent of particular task doers. Conversely, he concludes that these three information-processing factors can also capture the cognitive demands experienced by task doers. The framework consists of four basic task characteristics that meet the requirements of information load, diversity, and change: (1) multiple paths indicate the number of possible ways to arrive at a desired outcome, (2) multiple outcomes, (3) conflicting interdependence among paths, and (4) uncertain linkages between potential path activities and desired outcome. By combining these characteristics, Campbell creates a typology of complex tasks. Based on the typology he classifies tasks into simple, decision, judgment, and problem tasks.

Task complexity has been treated in very few studies of information seeking. Pinelli, Glassman, Affelder, Hecht, and Kennedy (1993) studied the effects of technical uncertainty and project complexity on information use by asking participants to rate both dependent variables on 5-point scales. In the studies by Byström (1999), Byström and Järvelin (1995), and Tiamiyu (1992), task complexity is reduced to the a priori determinability of a task, referring to the degree the input, performance process, and output of a task can be known in advance. In the least complex tasks, the type of task result, the associated work process, and the types of information required can all be described in advance. In the most complex tasks none of these aspects can be determined a priori (Byström 1999). Byström and Järvelin (1995) have created a classification of tasks based on their a priori determinability.

It is evident that the research community in information searching would extend the understanding of these phenomena, if ideas generated in other fields concerning task performance and analysis were taken into account. Several definitions and approaches may be used, depending on the goal of the study. A priori determinability may be a productive way of conceptualizing tasks for studies of information searching because it refers directly to the information requirements, which the actors must satisfy, and it can be related to the process analysis of tasks (Vakkari, 1999). It is evident that actors' abilities to anticipate the information requirements of a task increase as they proceed in its performance; that is, when they learn (Kuhlthau, 1993; Robertson, 2001; Vakkari, 2001).

Search Goals

Goals and Actions

A task is what someone does in order to achieve a goal (Hackos & Redish 1998). The goal of information searching is to find information, which supports task performance when an actor has insufficient knowledge. Thus, the search for information is a subtask in task performance. It is typical in experimental studies on IR to speak about search tasks, which refer to requests or topics (Hancock-Beaulieu, Fieldhouse, & Do, 1995). Occasionally tasks have been confused with the search task. For that reason, some researchers (Borlund & Ingwersen, 1997; Ingwersen, 1996) have begun to refer to it as a work task. The intention of the authors is not to restrict it to the work context, but to include other activities in its scope.

An alternative is to restrict the term "task" to those activities, like work tasks and interests, that trigger information searching. In searching it would be reasonable to distinguish between the search goal and the actions undertaken to achieve that goal. A search goal refers to the information or information items the actor is trying to discover (Xie, 2000). A search goal is here identical with an information problem. The activities for reaching the goal consist of actions the user must perform to find the needed information (Borlund, 2000). The activities could be conceptualized in various ways.

Xie (1997, 2000) suggests dividing search goals into interactive intentions (IIs) and information-seeking strategies (ISSs). IIs are subgoals to achieve the search goal. IIs refer to the interactions between the users and specific information or the system with which the user is interacting. The definition is somewhat vague. It is based on Suchman's (1986) idea of situated actions; that is, actions as responses to situations encountered. ISSs consist of methods and resources. Methods like scanning, searching, selecting, or comparing refer to the techniques users apply to interact with information, information objects, and humans. Resources are information, information objects, or humans with whom users interact, and include meta-information, information items, or databases. Based on empirical data, Xie (2000) was able to identify eight interactive intentions, eight ISSs, and some types of shifts in interactive intentions. Xie's categorizations provide an interesting starting point for conceptualizing the actions users take when searching for information in databases, although the conceptualizations of IIs and of methods of ISSs are too generic. One would have expected her to utilize the rich classifications of search tactics and moves by Bates (1990) or Fidel (1991a), which list actions for reaching a search goal.

Types of Search Goals

At least three types of search goals have been studied: natural, simulated, and assigned. Natural search goals are generated by the task performance process. They reflect users' information needs and consist of looking for information to support task performance. The user can attain these goals by a series of activities, which will result in finding the relevant objects required (Borlund, 2000). The search goals were natural, for example, in the studies by Choo, Detlor, and Turnbull (2000); Hert (1996); Siegfried, Bates, and Wilde (1993); Spink et al. (1998); Vakkari (2000a, 2000b); and Yang (1997).

In IR experiments search goals are assigned. They do not reflect the information needs of the searchers. They are artificial constructs for the purposes of the research design. Assignments may vary from a very short statement on the information needed to a more comprehensive description of the request, depending on the degree the assignment is expected to reflect real information needs or types of information needs. An assigned search goal is met when the user has tried to find as many information items as possible within the given time. The actions required do not differ from the actions required for a natural search goal. In IR experiments, the assigned search goals are also called requests or topics.

The motivation for using assigned search goals is to control the effects of output or process variables on search performance (Hancock-Beaulieu et al., 1996). The challenge to use natural research design, and the results by Saracevic and Kantor (1988) and Hersh (1996), have led to efforts to use search goals that reflect the real information needs of users more closely. They showed that professional searchers with information about clients' problem statements outperformed those whose searching was based solely on clients' questions. They concluded that the user's context (the problem at hand and the intent) is a potentially powerful element in retrieval effectiveness.

Interest in developing simulated search goals as a function of (work) tasks has been growing. Borlund (2000) calls this arrangement a simulated work task situation. The aim of a simulated search goal is to imitate natural search goals by means of a "cover story," which describes a situation that may lead to information searching (Borlund, 2000; Borlund & Ingwersen, 1997; Brajnik, Mizzaro, & Tasso, 1996). The cover story is a description of a problematic situation, which triggers and frames information needs and searching. It permits individual interpretations of the situation, as in real life. On the other hand, by being the same for all subjects it provides experimental control. Borlund's (2000) findings that the users' actions did not differ whether they were searching for their own goals or simulated goals provide evidence that simulated information needs bring realism and control to the research design: realism compared to laboratory IR research and control compared to field studies in IR.

The reason for developing simulated search goals is to bring greater validity into IR system evaluation by overcoming the limitations of traditional laboratory-based, batch-mode studies, such as the lack of real users, unrealistic queries, and unrealistic relevance judgments (Hersh, 1996). It is evident that simulated information needs provide some realism and control in research design. However, control may be compromised because each study participant is likely to interpret the simulated search goal in a somewhat different way.

Modeling Information Searching

Dependent and Independent Variables

User models are explicit representations of various characteristics of the user that are thought to be important in shaping IR interactions as a whole, as well as the search output (Savage-Knepshield & Belkin, 1999). These models aim at describing characteristics of users that are supposed to have a major impact on the IR interaction—that is, on search process variables and on search outcome variables. The methodological rule is to model the features of the searchers from the point of view of search process and outcome. We should identify those factors in users that cause systematic variation in search process and outcome—that is, that are systematically connected to searching and search results. This view implies that user characteristics are independent and search process and outcome are dependent variables.

In IR experiments, the most common variable to be explained, the dependent variable, has been search output, typically in terms of recall and precision. Process variables such as search tactics or term choices can be used either as dependent or independent factors, depending on the problem formulation. Borgman, Hirsh, and Hiller (1996) emphasize the need to manipulate search task variables to study the process of the search rather than the outcome. Their article includes an excellent discussion of the use of search process and product variables as dependent and independent variables in IR research.

How to Model Task-Oriented IR

Studies in information searching commonly aim at understanding IR interaction without relation to systems features or even systems output. Typical independent variables are individuals' traits such as domain knowledge, systems knowledge, or education. Dependent variables might be search tactics and search outcomes. Typically, analyses are field studies. They do not commonly include variables representing systems features, and, thus, they cannot directly inform system design. They provide only indirect clues for improving system performance. However, some field studies examine the usability or features of a system based on natural search goals (e.g., Hancock-Beaulieu et al., 1995;

Hert & Marchionini, 1997) or based on assigned search goals (e.g., Belkin et al., 1999; Brajnik et al., 1996; Fowkes & Beaulieu, 2000; Koenemann & Belkin, 1996; Wildemuth, Friedman, & Downs, 1998).

What would be a relevant and fertile way of modeling information searching by subjects, and subjects' characteristics in relation to searching? The answer naturally depends on the aim of the research. If the aim of information searching is to find information that supports task performance, the natural point of departure in explaining searching and modeling users is how well the information found meets the needs of the task performer. Moreover, if we wish to develop systems to support information needs and searching generated by work tasks, we should model people's tasks and characteristics so that they are connected to those features of systems that can be manipulated to improve the search process and results. These features range from indexing language to the organization of search results.

The role of the search result is crucial because it contains information that is expected to support task performance. Thus, the information in the search results that helps the subject to proceed in his or her task should be the factor to be explained, and those factors with a major impact on the search outcome should be mediating and explanatory factors. Typically, search process variables can be used as mediating factors on the search result, if task and subjects' characteristics are used as explanatory factors.

The starting point in modeling the user as well as the search process is the search result aimed at supporting task performance. The composition of the search result depends mainly on: (1) the activity or task to be supported; (2) individuals' characteristics, including task knowledge (domain knowledge, subject knowledge) and search skills (IR knowledge); (3) system features (Ingwersen, 1996; Marchionini, 1995; Marchionini, Plaisant, & Komlodi, in press; Vakkari, 2001); and (4) current information need (i.e., search goal). These factors can be used as independent and mediating variables in explaining search outcome, and thus in modeling information searching. Together with the search result they constitute the system to be studied in research on IR.

Modeling Tasks

Several options exist for modeling tasks as independent variables. Campbell's (1988) framework presented earlier allows us to classify tasks as simple, decision, judgment, or problem, depending mainly on task attributes that increase information load, diversity, or rate of change. Another approach draws on task complexity as defined by Byström and Järvelin (1995). It is based on the idea of how much an actor knows about the information requirements, process, and the outcome of the task. Kuhlthau's (1993) information search process model can also serve as a starting point for analyzing tasks and their connections to information searching. The latter two are promising in the sense that both make explicit connections between features of tasks and information searching.

Modeling Search Goals and Systems Features

The kind of information needed for proceeding in task performance is crucial (Checkland & Holwell, 1998) and varies according to task complexity as well as the stage of the task performance process (Byström & Järvelin, 1995; Dervin, 1992; Garvey, 1979; Kuhlthau, 1993; Nilan & Fletcher, 1987; Vakkari, 2000b). The search goal is reflected in the choice of information system and the actions taken while using it. The goal can be pursued using various search strategies and means for supporting them, as suggested by Ellis (1989) and Bates (1989). It seems that in modeling tasks for information searching it is important to try to model the type of information needed as perceived by the user (Belkin, 1993) and link this representation of the search goal to the articulation of search terms and consequent tactics and relevance judgments and to those features of the system that support users in various actions directed toward the search goal.

Systems features support goal-directed actions differently. We can divide search actions into two categories: conceptual and instrumental. The former refers to actions that transform the representations of information needs in the search language and in the result sets. Typically this means articulating and selecting search terms and assessing the relevance of the information found. Instrumental actions refer to actions necessary for manipulating the representations of information needs by using systems features (Fidel, 1985). Typically, these actions include combining search terms with operators, using field restrictions, or understanding the relations between retrieved sets and search terms suggested in relevance feedback. In the latter, selection of terms is a conceptual action based on instrumental understanding of a systems feature. In modeling systems features, both types of actions should be taken into account, because each requires different features.

On the conceptual side, the persistent theme in representing users' information needs is how to translate them into the language of potentially relevant documents (Bates, 1986; Blair & Maron, 1985). Various methods have been created for handling this problem, from the thesaurus to other means of query expansion such as local context analysis (LCA) or relevance feedback (RF) (Belkin et al., 1999; Efthimiadis, 1996). A problem with almost all of these approaches is that they do not treat users' information needs holistically, but as consisting of separate conceptual entities. A thesaurus provides clues for enriching terms within a concept, but does not help to relate concepts. LCA or RF, be they used as term suggestion devices or automatically, do not provide structured clues for identifying terms within concepts or between concepts. If used as term suggestion devices, they typically provide a list of terms without grouping them according to concepts in a user's query. Users seem to find this difficult (Belkin et al., 1999; Hancock-Beaulieu et al., 1995). However, some encouraging attempts to develop systems suggest search terms grouped according to their context (Anick & Tipirneni, 1999).

Modeling and developing systems features, like features of interfaces that support users in articulating their information needs by using terms from potentially relevant documents grouped according to the concepts in the users' queries reflecting the task, would enhance retrieval performance. The terms suggested could be presented either as a classified list of terms (Anick & Tipirneni, 1999) or as a semantic net showing the correlations between terms within concepts and between concepts. Presenting terms in the context of search concepts would help users to refine their queries more accurately, and reveal more about the structure of their information problems.

Users' information needs can also be modeled in terms of stages in task performance and their explicitness. Ill-articulated information needs cause users to browse, not to query (Chang & Rice, 1993; Ingwersen, 1996; Marchionini, 1995). Thus, the clarity of the search goal affects selection of search strategies and tactics. The claim by Bates (1990) that IR system interfaces are not designed around search behaviors that promote strategic and tactical goals is still valid. It seems that actions in IR are treated as separate moves, not as a sequences of moves forming various tactics and, finally, strategies. The lists of tactics and moves created by Bates (1990) and Fidel (1991a) could act as a point of departure in modeling sequences of moves in searching. For instance, in Boolean systems the average user does not use the OR operator in expressing search concepts with several terms each, but replaces terms concept by concept (Sutcliffe, Ennis, & Watkinson, 2000; Vakkari 2000a). The system could recognize this tactic of successive replacement of terms and suggest parallel tactics (OR operators). In general, what is needed is to connect typical sequences of moves or tactics (scripts) to typical search goals. The studies by Xie (2000) and Belkin, Cool, Stein, and Theil (1995) have been steps toward that goal using conceptualizations different from those of Bates or Fidel.

It is evident that the impact of task, subjects' characteristics (including task and IR knowledge), and search goal are mediated through the impact of system and process variables on the search result and its informational value (Vakkari, 2001). Search success in terms of useful information items identified for task performance depends crucially on interaction between human (including task as perceived by the actor) and system characteristics. Thus, a necessary condition for assessing how well IR systems support human action is to include both system and human factors in research design.

Models and Frameworks

Next, I present frameworks for mapping the relations between features of tasks and information searching. Their nature varies from analytical, general models to approaches to theories with empirical validation. In addition to the frameworks to be presented, well-known models of information seeking are included (Dervin, 1992; Dervin &

Frenette, 2001; Leckie, Pettigrew, & Sylvain, 1996; Savolainen, 1995; Wilson, 1981, 1999), which do not deal directly with searching in electronic environments, but might be helpful in providing a broader perspective. Pirolli and Card's (1999) information foraging theory may also provide productive ideas for studying task performance and information searching. It aims at understanding how strategies and technologies for information seeking, gathering, and consumption are shaped by the availability of information in the environment.

Early Frames

Since the end of the 1970s, a driving force in focusing IR research on human cognition, goals, and activities has been the conception of the anomalous state of knowledge (ASK) (Belkin, 1980). In ASK, a person becomes aware of a deficiency in his or her knowledge in some situation. Belkin (Belkin et al., 1982a, 1982b) calls this a problematic situation. The user approaches an information system to obtain documents that would resolve the anomaly. Belkin (1980) emphasizes that the user evaluates information obtained from the system in terms of the problem leading to the ASK. The purpose of the system is to provide information for resolving the anomaly. He concludes that representing users' problems, needs, and ASKs is at least as important as representing texts for systems design. He speculates that ASKs will fall into classes that require different sorts of answers and, therefore, different retrieval strategies, each designed to retrieve texts appropriate to the class of anomaly (Belkin, 1980).

Belkin (1980) proposed that research and theory ought to be directed toward trying first to develop classifications of the characteristics of anomalous states of knowledge and secondly toward identifying strategies appropriate for resolving classes of anomalies. "Strategies" here refers to retrieval strategies. Note that independent factors in Belkin's (1980) approach are ASKs and the information needs arising from them, while dependent ones are information (text) types needed and retrieval strategies.

The ASK research program was developed in the 1980s theoretically and empirically, by Belkin, Oddy, Brooks, and Daniels and, theoretically, by Belkin, Wersig and Hennings. Belkin, Oddy, and Brooks (1982a, 1982b) tried, empirically, to determine and classify ASKs based on elicited problem statements of users (researchers). As a result, a list of ASKs was presented based on how well defined the topic and information problem were. Information problem denotes a search goal. They argue that the bibliographic tools one chooses to use and the way one formulates the query depend on the precision of the definition of information need. Oddy, Palmquist, and Crawford (1986) also represented the ASKs of subjects by analyzing problem statements. They compared word associations derived from problem statements to those derived from the retrieved documents based on the problem descriptions. These projects did not contain data on retrieval strategies, thus leaving open the question about the relation between ASKs and strategies.

Brooks, Daniels, and Belkin (1985) developed problem descriptions and user models by analyzing user-intermediary dialogues in search situations. This empirical work was based on the model of expert problem treatment by Belkin, Seeger, and Wersig (1983). The basic idea was that at different stages of a problem treatment process different kinds of information provision are helpful. Stages refer to how structured the problem is. By identifying these stages, particular functions can be created to support information provision.

Similar conceptions of the problematic situation and IR systems in support of human activities were also developed in Germany in the 1970s and 1980s. Kunz and Rittel (1977) analyzed the relation between research and information processes. Wersig (1979) characterized the problematic situation as the basic concept in information science. Wersig and Windel (1985) suggested a theory of information actions for information science, maintaining that the problem-treatment process consists of stages that require various information resources.

These pioneering projects laid the foundation for research on information searching with the problematic situation as starting point. They emphasized that the information needed and the retrieval strategies used depended on the user's understanding of the problem and task at hand, and that problem treatment was a process. Consequently, systems design should incorporate these aspects. A limitation of these efforts was that the models they produced were abstract and focused mainly on modeling users and problematic situations, while overlooking actual searching (Ingwersen, 1992). Thus, the models did not suggest how we might connect stages of problem treatment to retrieval strategies.

Cognitive Work Analysis

Pejtersen (1990) has applied cognitive work analysis to designing a system (Bookhouse) for fiction retrieval. The analysis consists of a framework, which integrates several levels of work activities to be modeled for systems design (Pejtersen & Rasmussen, 1997). The analysis begins by identifying and representing users' work tasks. The design of Bookhouse was based on empirical studies of the problem domain of end-users and intermediaries during their performance of complex fiction retrieval tasks in libraries. In analyzing the problem of domain, Pejtersen identified how users represented (conceptualized) the types of fiction they were looking for. Moreover, she was able to classify typical search strategies by users. Books in the system were indexed using a classification scheme based on users' representations of fiction. The Bookhouse also included mechanisms that supported users' typical fiction search strategies.

Pejtersen studied and developed the Bookhouse during the 1980s. She partially realized the ASK program by modeling and incorporating the system users' representations of their interests (tasks) and their retrieval strategies. She has applied cognitive work analysis in other domains, such as design (Pejtersen, Sonnenwald, Buur, Govindaraj, & Vicente, 1995) and IR on the Web (Pejtersen & Fidel, 1998).

IR as Interaction

Ingwersen (1992) has developed the idea of information retrieval as interaction between users and various elements in the IR system. He takes the ASK approach several steps further, stressing more explicitly the intermediary role of the system and identifying a number of new functionalities that support the user in finding useful texts. Ingwersen emphasizes that tasks in a work domain give rise to problems, which may be solved through information seeking. His book aims at building a framework (the mediator model) for intermediary requirements in IR interaction for systems design. Domain and user models, including the user's understanding of the work task, play a central role in the framework. The framework is productive for systems design, but, like ASK, it leaves the description of users' actual searching on a sidetrack.

In a more recent work, Ingwersen (1996) develops his ideas further, providing a cognitive model of IR interaction. He conceives of interaction as acts of cognition. The starting point in the model is the actual work task or the interests of subjects leading to the problematic situation and subsequent information searching. The elements of the model represent IR interaction on an abstract and general level.

ASK and IR as Information-Seeking Behaviors

Since the early 1990s, Belkin (1993) has shifted the focus of his research from analyzing the structure of ASKs toward analyzing information seeking actions. He developed a view of IR in which the user is the central component in the system, and interaction is the central process. This approach embeds IR within the general context of human interaction with texts, specifically information-seeking behavior. This conception emanates from a problematic situation, in which a dynamic and changing information need leads to changes in interaction with the retrieved information items and, in turn, to varying information behaviors during a search session. The goal of the system is to support the range of information-seeking behaviors. Belkin realized the value in modeling the user's interactions with an IR system as information-seeking behaviors.

Belkin et al. (1993) constructed a typology of information-seeking behaviors, which they call information-seeking strategies (ISS). These are formed by combining four dimensions: (1) method of interaction (scanning-searching), (2) goal of interaction (learning-selecting), (3) mode of retrieval (recognition-specification), and (4) resource considered (information items-meta-information). Belkin et al. characterize information-seeking behavior as moving from one strategy to another when individuals' knowledge and goals change. They call for studies to establish relations between the ISSs and some other characteristics of the user, such as an individual's goals or problematic situation.

The suggestion to include ISSs in analyzing IR interaction is a step forward to approach information searching from the point of view of ASK and task performance. Xie (1997, 2000) and Lin and Belkin (2000) took up the challenge to study the relations between ISSs and users' goals. Lin and Belkin (2000) aimed to model multiple information-seeking episodes. The starting point recognizes that individuals search for information during several sessions, prompted by tasks or problematic situations. The proposed model consists of a problematic situation leading to an information problem, and consequent information-seeking processes, which include several search episodes. The characteristics and elements of the model are discussed. Eight types of information problems leading to multiple searching episodes are proposed. This model is derived from a literature review.

Oddy et al. (1992) studied researchers' problem statements empirically, as reflections of their work situations, intended uses of information, and relevance criteria. They constructed a process model of an empirical research process, which they called a research script. A script provides an outline of the steps needed to complete a particular task. Their script included 28 steps. Interviews showed that a scholar's place in the research script was related to relevance judgments and the type of information needed. Relevance criteria included both aboutness (topicality) and problem-oriented elements. The latter refers to the immediate problem that a researcher has encountered in an attempt to accomplish a particular task in the script. Oddy et al. concluded that IR systems should include search features that relate to variables describing a person's stage in task performance. This study was an elaboration of the work by Belkin et al. (1982a, 1982b) emphasizing more actual searching.

Kuhlthau's Model of the Information Search Process

Kuhlthau's (1993) model of the information search process is based on a series of empirical studies of students' and library users' learning tasks and problem-solving and information-search processes. She divides the task performance into six stages, which differentiate information searched for, ways of searching, and relevance assessments.

At the outset, individuals become aware of their lack of knowledge and understanding. Thoughts center on understanding the task and relating the problem to prior knowledge. During selection, the task is to identify and select a topic to be investigated. In exploration, the task is to investigate information on the general topic in order to extend personal understanding. Thoughts center on becoming oriented and sufficiently informed about the topic to form a focus. At these stages an inability to express precisely what information is needed makes communication between the user and the system awkward. The information encountered rarely fits smoothly with previously held constructs.

In the formulation stage, a focused perspective on the topic is formed. A focus is comparable to an hypothesis. This phase in task completion is critical because it helps a person to focus on relevant information. At this point, the task is to gather information related to the focused topic. Thoughts center on defining, extending and supporting the focus. Collection is the stage of the process at which the interaction between the user and the information system functions most efficiently. The user, with a clear sense of direction, can specify the need for relevant, focused information (Kuhlthau, 1993). In the presentation stage, the task is to complete the search and use the findings. Actions involve a summary search for rechecking sources (Kuhlthau, 1991).

The strength of the model is that it explicates the (sub)tasks associated with stages of the process. Tasks help us to understand what performers try to do in order to move ahead in the process. These tasks regulate the types of information needed, ways of information seeking, and relevance judgments. Recommendations for systems design can also be inferred from the model (Kuhlthau, 1999).

Another strong feature of the model is that it is based on longitudinal research, which is not common in studies of information searching. Moreover, not only have Kuhlthau's (e.g., Kuhlthau & Tama, 2001) own studies in other domains validated the model, but others (Bateman, 1998; Vakkari, 2001; Yang, 1997) have as well.

A Theory of Task-Based Information Retrieval

Vakkari (2001) has extended Kuhlthau's model in the field of IR based on a series of empirical studies. The explanatory factor of the model—stages in task performance—was the same, and some factors to be explained—information types needed, search tactics, term choices, and relevance judgments—were specified and linked to the stages. He showed that stages in task performance were systematically connected to the information searched for, search tactics, and usefulness of the information retrieved. These results are described in more detail later.

A Cognitive Theory of IR

The cognitive model of users' information searching behavior by Sutcliffe and Ennis (1998) is perhaps conceptually the most elaborated in the field. It is a preliminary version of a cognitive theory, which predicts user behavior in different search task stages according to types of information need, facilities provided by the IR system, and knowledge held by the user. The last includes domain knowledge, thus implying that work tasks are triggers of information needs and searching, although the model takes search tasks as its starting point. The model is conceptually sound, covers several central aspects of information searching, and is specific enough to enable prediction and the formulation of hypotheses concerning connections between the elements of the theory, especially tasks, information needs, query formulation, and term choices. The predictions are given in the form of rules for manipulating search elements for query and search result optimization depending on given factors. The authors have tested the theory empirically (Sutcliffe et al., 2000).

Ellis's Behavioral Model and Bates's Berry-Picking Model

Based on interviews, Ellis (1989) has developed a behavioral model of the information-seeking patterns of academic social scientists. The activities were broken down into six categories: starting, chaining, browsing, differentiating, monitoring, and extracting. He presents several subcategories of these activities. Although he did not clearly relate strategies to the research process, he suggests that starting, chaining, and browsing are more common in the early stages. The article contains an excellent analysis of how many of these strategies and substrategies form the core of information seeking. The extent to which these characteristics are available in existing systems is considered and the requirements for implementing these features on an experimental system are laid out. Ellis has subsequently modified his model based on results about information seeking in the physical sciences (Ellis, Cox, & Hall, 1993) and in engineering (Ellis & Haugan, 1997).

Bates (1989) suggests in her berry-picking model that each new piece of information a searcher encounters gives new ideas and direction to follow, and consequently a new conception of the query. She calls this an evolving search. At each stage of the search, the user may identify useful information items. The query is not satisfied by a single final retrieved set, but by a series of selections of individual references, and bits of information at each stage of the ever-modifying search. Based on findings in the literature on information seeking like those by Ellis (1989), Bates suggests several system capabilities that might support users in their various information-seeking strategies.

Summary

The models presented here differ in their level of abstraction, focus on task performance and the consequent information search process. The early frameworks focused on modeling the ASK and the information problem on a fairly abstract level (Belkin, 1980; Belkin, Oddy, & Brookes 1982a, 1982b; Belkin, Seeger, & Wersig, 1983). Information problem denotes the insufficient knowledge of the user about the task at hand, which regulates the search goal. The empirical work inspired by the ASK model was down-to-earth research concentrating on measuring users' information problems. The models included statements linking information problems with searching, but empirical work did not. Later theorizing based on ASK linked information-seeking behaviors with information problems and search goals (Belkin, 1993; Belkin et al., 1993), and recent empirical research has followed these lines (Lin & Belkin, 2000; Xie, 1997, 2000). Ingwersen (1992, 1996) has developed the ASK model more to understand IR as interaction between the user and various elements in the system. These models have been enriched by early German thinking in the field (Kunz & Rittel, 1977; Wersig, 1979; Wersig & Windel, 1985). These models focused on conceptualizing both the information problem and the search goal, and later, elements of the search process.

The empirical models generally describe the whole task-generated information search process, although the focus varies. Kuhlthau (1993) divides the (learning) task into six stages and connects them to searching and relevance assessments on a fairly general level. Vakkari (2001) extends Kuhlthau's (1993) model by using variables such as search terms, tactics, and relevance assessments. The model by Sutcliffe and Ennis (1998) consists of users' domain knowledge and types of information need leading to the use of various search tactics.

Although the models have evolved, better covering the steps in searching from the problematic situation and search goal to relevance assessments, considerable scope remains for integrating into them earlier conceptualizations of searching (e.g., Bates, 1990 or Fidel, 1991a) and refining concepts relating tasks and consequent search goals. Only in the models by Kuhlthau (1993) and Vakkari (2001) have the task stages been explicated.

Tasks, Information Needs, and Search Tactics: Empirical Results

In almost all of the empirical studies on the effects of task on various information-searching activities, task has been conceptualized as a process comprising several stages. The object of these studies has almost always been the research process. Studies of other activities, as well as those that conceptualize tasks differently, have been scarce.

Before I move on to studies focusing more on information searching in systems, I review studies on the relations between tasks and source use.

Task and the Use of Sources and Channels

These studies have analyzed how characteristics of tasks—typically the research process—lead to variation in the use of sources and channels. They do not cover the use of IR systems. Many of these studies have conceptualized task as process, although they have not used a longitudinal research design.

In an early *ARIST* chapter, Menzel (1966) called for studies to ascertain what information sources were used at a given phase of a research project, and then infer the function served by a source from the phase at which it was predominantly used. White (1975) has shown that the research phases of economists have an impact on their information-gathering behavior. Stages of the process generate needs for differing types of information resulting in differing functions (uses) of the information received in the process. She showed that the economists' research stages differentiated their need for, and use of, information, and, consequently, the use of channels and sources. The findings of Garvey (1979) and his colleagues among psychologists are similar. More recently, Ellis and Haugan (1997) have shown that the information-seeking patterns of engineers and research scientists vary in relation to the stage of their project in line with Ellis's (1989) model of information activities. Findings in keeping with the previous studies can be found among literary critics (Chu, 1999), undergraduates (Fister, 1992), industrial R&D researchers (Hirsh, 1999), and researchers preparing research proposals (Nilan & Fletcher, 1987). In these studies, research stage is the independent variable, and type of information needed, use of sources and channels, and the function of information used are dependent variables.

Byström's (1999; Byström & Järvelin, 1995) work is an exception to previous studies in that it takes task complexity as an independent variable for explaining variation in the type of needed information, use of channels and sources, and information types used. Byström was able to show that task complexity has an impact on these independent variables.

Tasks, Search Goals, and Information Needed

Studies show that the information needed at various phases of task performance varies (Dervin, 1992; Garvey, 1979; Kuhlthau, 1993; Spink, 1996; Vakkari & Hakala, 2000). At the beginning of the process, subjects' mental models of the task are vague; they are not aware of the dimensions of the task or how to structure it (Robertson, 2001). In this stage, background information is needed to support understanding of the context and characteristics of the task. When subjects have been able to construct a focus—structure the task—information about procedures and methods to handle the task and facts, as well other more specific information, gains prominence (Kuhlthau, 1993; Vakkari, 2000b; White, 1975). The searchers typically try to find as much information as possible in the beginning, emphasizing recall due to their vague relevance criteria. Precision comes to the forefront when they know more about the task (Vakkari & Hakala, 2000). Thus, it seems that the goals of the search vary in terms of the information expected at different stages of the task.

The previous results suggest that users' search goals change more between search sessions than within sessions. Hert (1996, 1997) has shown that the search goals of students searching a library's online catalog for their own tasks did not change within a search session. She defined a goal as "what the respondent intended to accomplish during the interaction"; that is, what they were looking for (Hert, 1996, p. 508). The findings of Vakkari (2000a) confirm previous claims, but Spink et al. (1998) have found a positive correlation between change in end-users' self-reported personal knowledge or problem definition and the number of items judged partially relevant. They also found that the less users know about the problem, the more items they accept as partially relevant.

Hert (1996) interprets her findings via Harter's (1992) notion of weak relevance. Bibliographic information alone provides insufficient clues for users to assess the utility of the references. Without examining the entire document, it is difficult for them to change their understanding of the (work) task, and, thus, their search goal remains fairly stable. The findings by Spink et al. (1998) suggest, however, that people with less subject knowledge might change their understanding of the problem as a result of the IR interaction within a session. Their study did not indicate whether the understanding changed such that it resulted in a change of search goals; that is, the information searched for.

It seems that if an individual does not learn more about the task so as to change his understanding of it, he is not capable of changing his view of what information is needed; that is, the search goal. Hert (1996) refers to this by stating that when searchers interact with the system, they do not move on in their wider information-seeking process. However, it is possible that users learn something about the topic when reflecting on search concepts and judging the relevance of the information items retrieved. They may learn new expressions for search concepts, for example. However, this learning is not likely to change the conceptual constructs that represent their information needs. I would consider recognizing new concepts, or modifying interrelations between existing ones, as activities implying changes in search goals. This development may lead users to search for different information; that is, to change their search goals. In a typical search session the searcher does not learn new concepts (by reading the documents retrieved) to the extent of having an impact on the search goal; a search interaction may, however, facilitate learning new *expressions* of concepts. A person who does not know much about a topic may have a vague search goal, which may change due to the meager information provided by the search interaction. These hypotheses still require empirical grounding.

Tasks, Term Choices, and Search Tactics

The search goal is connected to the search results by the search strategies; that is, by the choice of search terms, operators, and tactics. Due to the limited number of studies that connect search tactics to task performance (Beaulieu, 2000), some studies on the relation between search goals and strategies are also presented. The criterion for choosing the latter is that the research design is natural and the study contributes to our understanding of the links between tasks and searching.

Terms

Wang (1997) studied how users' information needs changed during the research process by analyzing selections from the documents retrieved. She analyzed users' vocabulary in the request, document selection, and post-project stages, demonstrating that subjects introduced both narrower and related terms as the research proceeded (Wang, 1997). The introduction of narrower terms refers to the specification of the research problem and the construction of a focus in the research process. Wang (1997) also found that the actual vocabulary in each subsequent search stage was substantially larger than in the previous one, both broader and deeper.

Vakkari (2000a) analyzed how the choice of search terms by students of information science was connected to the stages of preparing a research proposal for their master's theses. He applied Kuhlthau's (1993) model, observing their searches in the Library and Information Science Abstracts database at the beginning, middle, and end of the process. In the beginning, when the students selected a topic, they represented it in the queries with few terms. The vocabulary in the subsequent searches included synonyms, narrower terms, and related terms. Broader terms were dropped, particularly in the last session. Thus, the students were able to express the topic with a larger and more specific vocabulary in successive searches because their mental construct of the topic became more focused and discriminating.

Vakkari, Pennanen, and Serola (in press) tested the validity of the previous findings using similar longitudinal research design in studying how undergraduates in psychology searched the PsychINFO database while preparing a research proposal for a small empirical study. They found that the average number of search terms used increased to some extent from the first to the second (final) session. The students tended to change terms and facets used in the first session to narrower and related ones in the second session. They avoided adding broader terms or facets. Thus, their search vocabulary became slightly larger and more specific in the second search session.

Other studies on the effects of search goals show that the growth of knowledge in task performance can be equated with differences in the level of domain knowledge. Allen (1991) found that, among undergraduates searching an assigned topic in space exploration in an online catalog, those with high levels of knowledge on the topic used more search expressions than low-knowledge students. Shute and Smith (1993) compared 24 Chemical Abstracts database searches by two intermediaries. They found that the searcher with more domain knowledge used a greater number of terms, especially parallel terms, in the searches. The only contradictory finding comes from a study by Wildemuth and her colleagues (Wildemuth, de Blieck, Friedman, & File, 1995). They found no relationship between medical students' domain knowledge and their term selection when performing an assigned search task in a factual database.

Operators and Tactics

Most of the studies on search tactics have focused either on analyzing professional searchers (e.g., Fidel, 1991a, 1991b; Saracevic & Kantor, 1988) or assigned search goals performed by nonprofessionals, typically in relation to their search experience (e.g., Borgman, 1986; Sutcliffe et al., 2000; Yuan, 1997). Studies that connect search tactics to task performance are rare. The relationship between search tactics and domain knowledge is likewise unexplored terrain.

Use of operators and search tactics in task performance has been studied in Boolean systems. A search tactic means a set of moves. A move is an identifiable thought or action that is part of information searching (Bates, 1990) for improving search results (Fidel, 1991a). Vakkari (2000a) found that the number and type of Boolean operators used by information science students increased during the process of preparing their research proposals for master's theses. Moreover, the proportion of OR operators in queries increased, and that of AND operators decreased in the course of the work. An analogical research design with psychology students found no differences in the use of operators at different stages of writing the research proposal (Vakkari et al., in press).

Wildemuth and her colleagues (Wildemuth, Jacob, Fullington, de Blieck, & Friedman, 1991) studied medical students' search tactics in a factual database when they were preparing clinical case problems. They found that the simplest tactics were the most common, with single-move tactics accounting for over half of those used. Students almost always used AND and very seldom employed OR operators.

Vakkari (2000a) found that the range of tactics used by students of information science increased as they proceeded with the preparation of their research proposals. Three different types of tactics were commonly used: Intersect—adding terms to a query using the AND operator; Parallel—adding synonyms or conceptually parallel terms in a query; and Vary—substituting an existing query term with another. The increase in the use of Intersect and Parallel tactics was strong, but the use of Vary tactics was modest. Vakkari (2000a) also found that the increase in the use of Parallel tactics was due to the growth of students' knowledge of their topics and, consequently, of their vocabulary. This tactic displaced Vary tactics when the work proceeded. It seems that, in the beginning when their understanding of the topic was vague, students used Vary for exploring the field. Moreover, Vakkari showed that the use of Parallel tactics, compared to use of merely Intersect or Vary, led to a higher share of relevant items in the retrieved set as assessed by the students.

The use of Vary tactics without developing complex query structures seems to be a very common tactic used by novice searchers, as studies on assigned search goals suggest (Sutcliffe et al., 2000). In general, users conduct simple searches using only AND operators and make very little use of the interactive capability of the search system (Sewell & Teitelbaum, 1986; Siegfried et al., 1993; Yuan, 1997). Evidence from other fields (Avrahami & Kareev, 1993; Essens, McCann, & Hartevelt, 1991) also shows that interpreting logical connectives is complicated.

In contrast to Vakkari's (2000a) earlier findings, psychology students did not change their use of operators and tactics in preparing their research proposals (Vakkari et al., in press), although their search vocabularies grew and became more specific. It is possible that the difference in findings is a result of the differences in the IR knowledge of the two study populations. The information science students had mastered the use of Boolean systems, whereas the psychology students were novices.

One concludes that a necessary condition for utilizing growing conceptual understanding of the topic in formulating queries is a sufficient command of the (Boolean) system used. This conclusion is in line with the findings of Hsieh-Yee (1993), who has shown that subject knowledge becomes a factor only after searchers have acquired a certain amount of experience. She compared the search tactics of librarians and students of educational administration when they searched for two assigned tasks in their own, or other, subject domains on the ERIC database. She found that within the same-search-experience group, subject knowledge had no effect on novice searchers, but positively affected experienced searchers' reliance on their own language, use of synonymous terms, and combinations of search terms.

Yang (1997) studied the search strategies of students using the Perseus hypertext system when working on a class exercise requiring the writing of a thematic essay in history. He found that the use of strategies depended on the stage of the writing process. He identified three major strategies. Each state of searching reflected the subjects' current understanding of the tasks. They typically engaged in exploratory searching before coming up with a specific direction. At this stage, they aimed to establish a framework for their tasks. The database was searched without specific criteria or a coordinated plan. Purposeful searching occurred once they could establish more constant points of reference. At this stage they could search for specific information, which they had identified as directly relevant to the current goals. Finally, they demonstrated associative searching when they proactively looked for related and interconnected information to support arguments they had already established. Yang (1997) also found that, as the task became clearer, the proportion of exploratory and purposeful searches decreased and that of associative searches increased.

In sum, these studies suggest that the choice of search tactics and terms depends on the stage of task performance. It seems that a prerequisite of utilizing growing conceptual understanding and topical vocabulary in searching is command of the system.

Relevance and Utility Judgments

When users assess the information retrieved, they try to infer how it will support task accomplishment. Thus, they assess its situational relevance and utility. Here I will concentrate on reviewing studies of situational relevance. More discussion about the nature of relevance can be found in Cosijn and Ingwersen (1999), Harter (1992), Reid (1999), Saracevic (1996), Schamber (1994), and Schamber, Eisenberg, and Nilan (1990). First, I discuss the degree of relevance of the items retrieved; then I consider the role of relevance criteria and the contribution of the information found. Finally, I review studies on the process of choosing documents.

Degrees of Relevance

Spink et al. (1998) studied relevance assessments of mediated and nonmediated searches among students and faculty members for their own research or study purposes at two universities. They demonstrated that users' specific knowledge about the problem at hand were negatively correlated with partially relevant items. The less they knew about the problem they were researching, the more items they judged to be partially relevant. Broader knowledge of the problem and greater focus in retrieval resulted in a higher number of relevant items. These results seem to imply that growth in the understanding of a task results in a diminishing number of items judged to be partially relevant and in an increasing number of relevant items.

Inconsistent with the results above, Vakkari and Hakala (2000) found in their longitudinal study that when the students progressed in writing a research proposal, the proportion of partially relevant references remained constant while the number of relevant references decreased. The difference in results may be due to methodological differences in the studies.

Relevance Criteria

Individuals use relevance criteria for making predictions about the utility of documents based on the surrogates retrieved (Barry, 1994; Wang & Soergel, 1998). Park (1993) studied the factors academics used when evaluating bibliographic records resulting from a search related to their ongoing research. She identified three major groups of variables affecting relevance assessments. The internal context reflects researchers' interpretations of the citations based on their prior experiences in the area of research in general. Variables in this category include, for example, level of expertise in a subject literature, previous research experience, and educational background. External context refers to the factors that stem from the users' search and current research. They include perception of the search quality, search goal, availability of information, stage of research, and end product of research. Problem context refers to the intended use of the information searched for. Such uses included obtaining definitions, background information, methods, frameworks, and analogies.

Barry (1994) analyzed criteria used in selecting relevant items retrieved from a search for a current research project or study assignment of university students and faculty members. She identified 23 categories, which she grouped into seven broad classes. The four most mentioned classes were information content of the documents, users' backgrounds and experiences, users' beliefs and preferences, and other information sources in the environment.

Bateman (1998) used Kuhlthau's (1993) model in her longitudinal study of changes in relevance criteria. University students preparing an assigned research paper evaluated the highly relevant information sources they found according to a list of 40 criteria four times during the process. The mean importance of the criteria changed very little during the information-seeking stages in Kuhlthau's study. However, criteria were more likely to change between the stages of selection and exploration, and, to a slightly lesser degree, between focus finding and collecting. This is consistent with Kuhlthau's model.

Wang and White (1999) studied criteria for selecting documents at different phases of a research project. Topicality was the most frequently used criterion in the stages of selection, reading, and citation of documents by the researchers. The intellectual orientation/level mattered less, but its importance increased markedly in the citation stage.

Sutton (1994) examined the information-seeking and evaluative behavior of attorneys as they searched a corpus for primary authority in order to solve context-sensitive legal issues. First, he analyzed the dynamic mental models attorneys constructed of the law as expressed in its published artifacts. The relevance judgment of the cases was then explicated in terms of these models. He concluded that relevance judgments shift along a knowledge continuum depending on the status of the attorney's mental model. In the formative stages of the mental model, any case was deemed relevant that contributed in any way to the modeling of the space of relevant cases. Toward the end of the process, the attorneys' mental models became more differentiated, leading to stricter selection of relevant cases.

Topicality and Utility of Information

Tang and Solomon (1998) studied a graduate student's relevance assessments of information items retrieved for a term paper. They observed the student twice, when assessing the bibliographic records and documents obtained immediately after the search session, and a month later when she had become acquainted with the texts. The results showed that the student's perception of the information she needed for the task changed when she interacted with the initial search results and when she had read the texts. This was measured by counting terms and topical expressions marked by the student in the two rounds of observation. The study provides evidence of the gradual change in the student's mental model of the task, and consequently of her understanding of what information was useful. During the process the student became more selective and confident in her choices. The study provides an excellent demonstration of how a person's perception of a topic changes when she constructs and reconstructs it in the light of the information encountered.

When studying relevance criteria used by students at different stages in the preparation of their research proposals according to Kuhlthau's (1993) model, Vakkari and Hakala (2000) demonstrated that the students searched for documents not only on the topic in general, but also on specific aspects. Topicality as such was consistently the most important criterion for choosing references throughout the process. Although less frequently mentioned, the required types of information played a systematic role in selecting references. References to general and theoretical information were searched for in the pre-focus stages. Their significance diminished in the post-focus stages. The role of methodological information increased as the process evolved. In some cases, information types proved to be an important criterion. Evidently, full-text facilitates a deeper, differentiated assessment of the items found (Harter, 1992).

Vakkari (2000b) confirms that the topicality of documents refers to different types of information depending on a student's stage in writing the research proposal. From students' descriptions of how documents contributed to the task, Vakkari identified seven categories: background information, theories and models, methods, cases, facts, empirical results, and focused information. At the beginning, the documents were used typically for background information about the topic as well as models and conceptualizations of it. In the focus-formation stage, the texts still supported the process by providing background information and theories, but to a lesser extent. Texts with methodological advice or information about cases became more important. Toward the end of the process, the students used the documents obtained to receive focused information and empirical research results.

Document Selection and Use

Smithson (1994) and Wang and White (1999) demonstrate that, during the research process, the number of retrieved relevant references is much larger than the number of documents actually obtained and read, and the number of cited documents in research papers is smaller still. Wang and White (1999) also found that those who were more familiar with their topics at the time of the search tended to be more discriminating during the selection process: They selected fewer documents, but read more of them and cited more. The opposite pattern was true of those with little or no information about the topic: They selected more documents, but read and cited fewer. This finding supports the idea that insufficient knowledge in the beginning of a task is associated with a poor ability to discriminate among relevant documents, leading to a greater acceptance of sources.

Wang and Soergel (1998) developed a model of document selection and use during a research project by faculty and graduate students in agricultural economics. In their model of decision making in the document selection process, document information elements (DIE) in records retrieved provide the information for judging documents on 11 criteria (including topicality, orientation, quality, novelty, and authority). The judgments are combined in an assessment of document value along five dimensions (epistemic, functional, conditional, social, and emotional) leading to the use decision.

Wang and Soergel (1998) go on to define document value as the user's perception of the desirability or potential utility of a document. They contend that functional value dominates among researchers when they choose documents from a printout of a database search. The functional value is the perceived utility of a document to make a contribution to the specific task at hand. The functional value is correlated with the topicality and orientation/level of the document. Thus, topicality and orientation, interpreted as information types, seem to predict the potential of a document to contribute to the task at hand.

Impact of System and Searching on Task Outcome

Hersh (1994, 1996; Hersch, Pentecost, & Hickam, 1996) suggests that information systems should be evaluated not only by taking topical or situational relevance into account, but also in terms of the system's impact on users. It is crucial to understand how the information found by using a system helps users in the tasks for which they consulted the system. Hersch (1996) proposes outcomes-based methods to assess the impact of the system upon the user for particular tasks (e.g., for answering a question or solving a problem). He lists several outcomes-oriented studies in the field of medicine. The impact is typically assessed under laboratory conditions, not in real-life situations.

An exception to laboratory-based research is Limberg's (1999) study. She investigated how high school seniors used, and what they learned from, the information they retrieved for a class assignment. She interviewed the students three times during the process: in the beginning, in the intense information-seeking phase, and after presentation of the paper for the assignment. The students' perceptions of information seeking and use predicted the learning outcome in terms of their knowledge of the issue studied. The author left open the question of how the students' understanding of the search process or the topic may have influenced the learning process. Another example is Wildemuth et al. (1995), who used medical students' success in problem solving as an outcomes measure. They found that search results and the selection of search terms were related to database-assisted problem solving.

Overall, these studies suggest that relevance criteria based on bibliographic information change to some extent during the task performance process, whereas criteria based on full-text resources change more significantly. The notion of topicality also seems to vary according to the task process.

Supporting Searching

If the aim of IR systems is to help people by providing information for their various activities, tools for supporting searching based on analysis of these activities and consequent searching are necessary. However, it is not easy to connect behavioral or cognitive studies with design decisions due to the various factors involved in human-computer interaction (Bates, 1990; Marchionini, 1995). Integrating task and systems variables in the research design is a promising way to create information that supports systems design.

Only a few works analyze interaction between task performance, searching, and the use of support tools. First, I will discuss tools for supporting both task structuring and term selection, then discuss query expansion and the organization of retrieved documents. I conclude by reflecting on the role of language use in task communities in relation to tools for supporting searching.

Tools for Supporting Searching

Cole and his colleagues (Cole, 1998; Cole, Cantero, & Sauve, 1998; Cole, Cantero, & Ungar, 2000) developed a front-end software tool to be used by undergraduates accessing information from a database for a social sciences term paper. The device helped the students create relations between two or more situations or phenomena. It supported them in structuring the topic and in articulating search terms. Cole et al. (2000) studied the impact of the software on the learning outcomes of undergraduates participating in a remedial English course. Students using the software achieved higher grades than those who did not.

Buckingham Shum, Motta, and Domingue (1999) propose a knowledge-modeling approach to indexing scholarly documents. It is based on representing scholarly claims by categorizing the contribution of a paper and its relationship to earlier work. They suggest that indexing be matched to scholars' work tasks and approaches to information.

Current information-searching practices reflect a division of labor between task-performance context and information-searching context. A user approaches an information system with an information need in mind, formulates queries, executes the search, and then continues the task. Budzik and Hammond (1999) try to integrate these two contexts in their work on Information Management Assistants (IMAs). An IMA analyzes the text of the document a person is handling and combines the result with the knowledge of how to form queries automatically for traditional information retrieval systems. An individual struggling with an unfinished paper could perform a search using IMA to find fresh information. Budzik and Hammond (1999) argue that viewing the search as a part of a larger task grounds explicit queries in a context that is typically inaccessible to traditional IR systems, due to users' inability to express their queries within these systems' constraints. This conclusion is in line with the findings of Saracevic and Kantor (1988), which suggest that information about the task context increases search effectiveness. The initial evaluation of the IMA system has been promising.

Query expansion is a tool to help users in refining the query. Efthimiadis (1996) gives a balanced overview of the topic. Some recent findings deserve attention from the perspective of task performance. Results by Brajnik et al. (1996) and Fowkes and Beaulieu (2000) suggest that query expansion functions differently depending on the problem at hand or search topic. By using simulated search goals in an experimental setting, Brajnik et al. (1996) show that with more difficult problems, where users may fail to achieve a solid conceptualization, automatic query reformulation does not help them to achieve a better search result. Fowkes and Beaulieu (2000) have studied how students benefit from query expansion using the OKAPI system when searching for TREC-8 Interactive Track test topics. The results revealed that the effectiveness of relevance feedback depended on the characteristics of the topic. Interactive query expansion was more productive for topics the searchers perceived as being more difficult and complex, whereas automatic query expansion was more efficient with simple topics. These results suggest that automatic query expansion does not work if users have little domain knowledge of a complex topic: They are not able to conceptualize and articulate information needs exactly; neither are they competent to differentiate clearly between relevant and irrelevant documents. This results in the extraction of terms from less relevant documents.

The tools described above are designed to help users make their queries more specific and reduce the size of the retrieval set. A complementary approach is to develop tools that help users explore and understand their search results. Grouping the items retrieved is one means to that end. Typical automatic approaches to organizing search results are relevance ranking and clustering (Pratt, Hearst, & Fagan, 1999). The problem with these approaches is that they do not explicitly take users' tasks into account. A knowledge-based approach suggested by Pratt et al. (1999) seems to overcome this restriction, at least partially. They developed DynaCat, a tool that categorized search results into a hierarchy by using knowledge of important queries and a model of the domain terminology. Results from the evaluation (Pratt & Fagan, 2000) showed that DynaCat helped users find answers to important questions more quickly and easily than a relevance-ranking system or a clustering system.

Matching Search Goals and Documents in Task Communities

From the perspective of task performance, a major theme in IR is how to represent the user's task or, more specifically, search goal (desired information) and information resources (Belkin, 1993). Matching is a persistent problem in IR (Bates, 1986; Blair & Maron, 1985). Indexing documents based on the task-doer community's understanding of what types of information contribute to typical tasks and not merely on the basis of topicality would be an option (Buckingham Shum et al., 1999). It seems that enriching the thesaurus by relations representing users' typical work problems may improve retrieval performance (Rada & Barlow, 1991). This solution, however, appears to require that task doers or others index the documents. This indexing approach can extend from formulating the query, through its refinement, to the representation of the search results.

An additional option would be to analyze more closely the language of searchers' requests and also of the documents in the database. In cases where a task doer is working with a text in the computer, this analysis could be a basis for query formulation, as Budzik and Hammond (1999) suggest. However, it is common that in representing the search goal of a task doer as a query the language is reduced to a minimum. Linguistic expressions in the query reflect language usage in the task community, albeit in a limited way. The documents relevant to the search goal reflect more comprehensively the linguistic expressions used in the task community (Bates, 1986; Blair & Maron, 1985; Vechtomova & Robertson, 2000). Variant expressions of a concept are limited in the community. A query consists typically of two or more concepts reflecting a conceptual construct, which should be treated as a whole. The ways of expressing a conceptual construct in a given discourse community are even more restricted than expressing a single concept. The number of expressions of a construct is not simply a combination of its constituents. A crucial factor in determining the meaning of the construct, and consequently, the range of expressions, are the relations between the concepts (Hahn & Chater, 1997; Renouf, 1993). Thus, documents relevant to a query incorporate a limited number of expressions for the construct used in the task community.

The major problem is how to identify these variant expressions based on the query terms. This task is demanding (Bates, 1986; Blair & Maron, 1986). Although current probabilistic attempts to use language models in IR show some progress in enhancing retrieval performance (e.g., Mitra, Singhal, & Buckley, 1998; Ponte & Croft, 1998), their conception of language is simplistic. If we suppose that the language use of a discourse community is patterned and regular, these expressive regularities should be observed in the documents. Current research on corpus linguistics (e.g., word co-occurrences) opens interesting perspectives for the IR community (Carter, 1998; Renouf, 1993; Vechtomova & Robertson, 2000). Corpus linguistics may provide ideas for developing tools to capture the vocabulary used in a task community; thereby enriching users' queries.

Conclusion

This review suggests that various aspects of information searching are deeply rooted in the process of task performance. It seems that the information needed, and search tactics used (including the choice of terms and operators, as well as relevance judgments) are systematically linked to the stage of task performance. The use of some search support tools may also vary according to features of the task. However, our understandings of the mechanisms that link characteristics of tasks to search activities are both tentative and limited.

These are some of the limitations:

- There are few studies that take tasks as a starting point
- Almost all research concentrates on task process, neglecting other aspects
- The interaction of domain and systems knowledge as mediating factors between task and searching is neglected
- The populations selected are often limited to university students and faculty members
- Longitudinal research is rare
- Studies focus on certain aspects of searching, not the overall process
- Systems characteristics are ignored
- Explicit and testable theories that integrate tasks, domain, and systems knowledge and searching are lacking

Most studies do not conceptualize task performance as a process. It is typical to observe users at a certain point in time and focus on a search goal without relating it to the task at hand. Thus, it is impossible to show which components of the task co-vary with features of searching. This limitation underscores the need for longitudinal research. Moreover, almost all the studies draw their subjects from academic environments. The prototypical task is the research process.

Stages of task performance have also been analyzed, but not other task characteristics. The task process has been conceptualized either by using Kuhlthau's (1993) model or, if the academic community is the focus, in terms of stages in the research process. The obvious conclusion is to study other features of tasks in domains other than research. The dimensions of task complexity suggested by Campbell (1988) could serve as a point of departure for this.

In the act of information searching, process and outcome variables interact with each other and with task variables. It is obvious that the information requirements of the task as perceived by the user (information need) is the central feature of the task influencing information searching. A person's task (domain) knowledge molds choice of search terms, interim, as well as final relevance assessments; and in some cases the use of system functionalities. IR (systems) knowledge steers the use of operators and other features of the system, such as support tools. Thus, query formulation and reformulation depend on the features of the task, the user's domain and IR knowledge, and system features. This fact calls for studies into the effects of the interaction of task and systems knowledge on information searching.

It is natural in terms of research economy that most of the studies reviewed here have focused on analyzing connections between selected process or outcome variables and task performance. However, as the argument above shows, task-based information searching is a highly complex process in which several factors interact. In order to gain a more comprehensive and nuanced understanding of the process, studies that relate features of the task both to process and outcome variables are needed. Research projects that link several aspects of the search process to the task would be especially useful.

Debate continues between the user studies community and the laboratory-oriented IR community about the application of results from user studies in systems design. Several factors influence the use of these results, ranging from economic interests through relevance of the findings to awareness of them. It is evident that user studies are needed, for example, to identify problems people face when they use systems. It is also evident that some of the findings provide clues for improving systems. However, if studies of search behavior wish to inform systems design directly, system features should be included in the research design. This inclusion could be an effective way of bridging the gap between user studies and laboratory-based studies. Such integrative studies would speak the language of both communities.

The process of information searching is so complicated that covering all its features in a single study is impossible. In empirical studies, the research design is always restricted and a matter of choice: The results give only a partial view of the phenomenon. Theory is an established tool in science to steer the choice of research questions and systematize and integrate findings (Saracevic & Kantor, 1988). By establishing relationships between the central concepts of the research object, in our case task-oriented information searching, theory informs the selection of factors and their interrelations. At the same time, it clarifies the conditions controlling the variation of independent variables and naturally dependent variables. Finally, it provides a means of integrating the findings of a particular study with the results of other studies into a broader frame. Some tentative theories have been proposed on the connections between task performance and IR (e.g., Sutcliffe & Ennis, 1998; Vakkari, 2001), which might serve as vehicles for theory growth in this field. Growth refers both to empirical validation and conceptual innovation.

Due to the complex nature of information searching, it is impossible to control all necessary factors in natural research settings. Considerable room exists for studies based on assigned search goals. In these studies, it should be possible to take into account some task features; for example, by trying to categorize search tasks or topics according to complexity or users' domain knowledge. By combining analysis of searching in the context of assigned search goals and work tasks, we could create fertile conditions for the growth of knowledge about information searching.

Bibliography

Allen, B. (1991). Topic knowledge and online catalog search formulation. *Library Quarterly, 61*, 188–213.

Allen, B. (1996). *Information tasks: Toward a user-centered approach to information systems*. San Diego, CA: Academic Press.

Anick, P., & Tipirneni, S. (1999). The paraphrase search assistant: terminological feedback for iterative information seeking. *Proceedings of the Annual International ACM SIGIR Conference on Research and Development in Informaton (SIGIR '99)*, 153–159.

Avrahami, J., & Kareev, Y. (1993). What do you expect when you ask for "a cup of coffee and a muffin or croissant?" On the interpretation of sentences containing multiple connectives. *International Journal of Man-Machine Studies, 38*, 429–434.

Barry, C. (1994). User-defined relevance criteria: An exploratory study. *Journal of the American Society for Information Science, 45,* 149–159.

Bateman, J. (1998). Changes in relevance criteria: A longitudinal study. In C. Preston (Ed.), *Proceedings of the 61st American Society for Information Science Annual Meeting (ASIS '98)* (pp. 23–32). Medford, NJ: Information Today, Inc.

Bates, M. (1986). Subject access to online catalogs: A design model. *Journal of the American Society for Information Science, 37,* 357–376.

Bates, M. (1989). The design of browsing and berrypicking techniques for the online search interface. *Online Review, 13,* 407–424.

Bates, M. (1990). Where should the person stop and information interface start? *Information Processing & Management, 26,* 575–591.

Beaulieu, M. (2000). Interaction in information retrieval. *Journal of Documentation, 56,* 431–439.

Beaulieu, M., Robertson, S., & Rasmussen, E. (1996). Evaluating interactive systems in TREC. *Journal of the American Society for Information Science, 47,* 85–94.

Belkin, N. J. (1980). Anomalous states of knowledge as a basis for information retrieval. *Canadian Journal of Information Science, 5,* 133–143.

Belkin, N. J. (1990). A methodology for taking account of user tasks, goals and behavior for design of computerized library catalogs. *SIGCHI Bulletin, 23*(1), 61–65.

Belkin, N. J. (1993). Interaction with texts: information retrieval as information-seeking behavior. In *Information Retrieval '93: Von der Modellierung zur Anwendung [From modeling to application]. Proceedings of the First Conference of the Gesellschaft für Informatik Fachgruppe Information Retrieval* (pp. 55–66). Konstanz: Universitatsverlag Konstanz.

Belkin, N., Cool, C., Head, J., Jeng, J., Kelly, D., Lin, S., et al. (1999). Relevance feedback versus local context analysis as term suggestion devices. *Proceedings of the Eighth Text REtrieval Conference (TREC-8).* Retrieved December 18, 2001, from http://trec.nist.gov/pubs/trec8/papers/ruint.pdf.

Belkin, N., Cool, C., Stein, A., & Thiel, U. (1995). Cases, scripts and information seeking strategies. *Expert Systems with Applications, 9,* 379–395.

Belkin, N. J., Marchetti, P. G., & Cool, C. (1993). Braque: Design of an interface to support user interaction in information retrieval. *Information Processing & Management, 29,* 325–344.

Belkin, N. J., Oddy, R. N., & Brooks, H. M. (1982a). ASK for information retrieval I. *Journal of Documentation, 38,* 61–71.

Belkin, N. J., Oddy, R. N., & Brooks, H. M. (1982b). ASK for information retrieval II. *Journal of Documentation, 38,* 145–164.

Belkin, N. J., Seeger, R., & Wersig, G. (1983). Distributed expert problem treatment as a model for information system analysis and design. *Journal of Information Science, 5,* 153–167.

Blair, D., & Maron, M. (1985). An evaluation of retrieval effectiveness for a full-text document retrieval system. *Communications of the ACM, 28,* 289–299.

Borgman, C. L. (1986). Why are online catalogs hard to use? *Journal of the American Society for Information Science, 37*, 387–400.

Borgman, C. L., Hirsh, S. G., & Hiller, J. (1996). Rethinking online monitoring methods for information retrieval systems: From search product to search process. *Journal of the American Society for Information Science, 47*, 568–583.

Borlund, P. (2000). *Evaluation of interactive information retrieval systems.* Åbo, Finland: Åbo Akademi University Press.

Borlund, P., & Ingwersen, P. (1997). The development of a method for the evaluation of interactive information retrieval systems. *Journal of Documentation, 53*, 225–250.

Bradshaw, S., & Hammond, K. (1999). Constructing indices from citations in collections of research papers. In L. Woods (Ed.), *Proceedings of the 62nd Annual Meeting of the American Society for Information Science (ASIS '99)* (pp. 741–750). Medford, NJ: Information Today, Inc.

Brajnik, G., Mizzaro, S., & Tasso, C. (1996). Evaluating user interfaces to information retrieval systems: A case study. *Proceedings of the Annual International ACM SIGIR Conference on Research and Development in Information Retrieval (SIGIR '96)*, 128–136.

Brooks, H., Daniels, P., & Belkin, N. J. (1985). Problem descriptions and user models. *Informatics, 8*, 191–214.

Buckingham Shum, S., Motta, E., & Domingue, J. (1999). Representing scholarly claims in Internet digital libraries: A knowledge modelling approach. In S. Abiteboul & A. M. Vercoustre (Eds.), *Proceedings of the Third European Conference on Research and Advanced Technology for Digital Libraries.* Berlin: Springer. Retrieved December 18, 2001, from http://link.springer.de/link/service/series/0558/bibs/1696/16960423.htm.

Budzik, J., & Hammond, K. J. (1999). Watson: Anticipating and contextualizing information needs. In L. Woods (Ed.), *Proceedings of the 62nd Annual Meeting of the American Society for Information Science (ASIS '99)* (pp. 727–740). Medford, NJ: Information Today, Inc.

Byström, K. (1999). *Task complexity, information types and information sources. Examination of relationships.* Doctoral dissertation. Department of Information Studies, University of Tampere, Finland. Acta Universitatis Tamperensis, 688.

Byström, K., & Järvelin, K. (1995). Task complexity affects information seeking and use. *Information Processing & Management, 31*, 191–213.

Campbell, D. J. (1988). Task complexity: A review and analysis. *Academy of Management Review, 13*, 40–52.

Carter, R. (1998). *Vocabulary. Applied linguistic perspectives.* London: Routledge.

Chang, S., & Rice, R. (1993). Browsing: A multidimensional framework. *Annual Review of Information Science and Technology, 28*, 231–276.

Checkland, P., & Holwell, S. (1998). *Information, systems and information systems: Making sense of the field.* New York: Wiley.

Choo, C. W., Detlor, B., & Turnbull, D. (2000). *Web work: Information seeking and knowledge work on the World Wide Web.* Dordrecht, Netherlands: Kluwer Academic.

Chu, C. M. (1999). Literary critics at work and their information needs: A research-phases model. *Library & Information Science Research, 21,* 247–273.

Cole, C. (1998). Intelligent information retrieval: Diagnosing information need. Part I. The theoretical framework for developing an intelligent IR tool. *Information Processing & Management, 34,* 709–720.

Cole, C., Cantero, P., & Suave, D. (1998). Intelligent information retrieval: Diagnosing information need. Part II. Uncertainty expansion in a prototype of a diagnostic IR tool. *Information Processing & Management, 34,* 721–737.

Cole, C., Cantero P., & Ungar, A. (2000). The development of a diagnostic-prescriptive tool for undergraduates seeking information for social science/humanities assignment. III. Enabling devices. *Information Processing & Management, 36,* 481–500.

Cosijn., E., & Ingwersen, P. (2000). Dimensions of relevance. *Information Processing & Management, 26,* 533–550.

Dervin, B. (1992). *From the mind's eye of the user: The sense-making qualitative methodology.* In J. D. Glazier, & R. R. Powell (Eds.), *Qualitative research in information management* (pp. 61–84). Englewood, CO: Libraries Unlimited.

Dervin, B., & Frenette, M. (2001). Sense-making methodology: Communicating communicatively with campaign audiences. In R. Rice, & C. K. Atkin (Eds.), *Public communications campaigns* (pp.69–87). Thousand Oaks, CA: Sage.

Efthimiadis, E. (1996), Query expansion. *Annual Review of Information Science and Technology, 31,* 121–187.

Ellis, D. (1989). A behavioural approach to information retrieval system design. *Journal of Documentation, 45,* 171–212.

Ellis, D., Cox, D., & Hall, K. (1993). A comparison of the information seeking patterns of researchers in the physical and social sciences. *Journal of Documentation, 49,* 356–369.

Ellis, D., & Haugan, M. (1997). Modelling the information seeking patterns of engineers and research scientists in an industrial environment. *Journal of Documentation, 53,* 384–403.

Engeström, Y., Miettinen, R., & Punamäki, R.-L. (1999). *Perspectives on activity theory.* Cambridge, UK: Cambridge University Press.

Essens, P. J. M. D., McCann, C. A., & Hartevelt, M. A. (1991). An experimental study of the interpretation of logical operators in database querying. *Acta Psychologica, 78,* 201–225.

Fidel, R. (1985). Moves in online searching. *Online Review, 9,* 61–74.

Fidel, R. (1991a). Searchers' selection of search keys: I The selection routine. *Journal of the American Society for Information Science, 42,* 490–500.

Fidel, R. (1991b). Searchers' selection of search keys: III Searching styles. *Journal of the American Society for Information Science, 42,* 515–527.

Fister, B. (1992). The research processes of undergraduate students. *Journal of Academic Librarianship, 18,* 163–169.

Fowkes, H., & Beaulieu, M. (2000). Interactive searching behavior: Okapi experiment for TREC-8. *Proceedings of the BCS-IRSG: 22nd Annual Colloquium on Information Retrieval Research*. Retrieved December 18, 2001, from http://irsg. edu.org/irsg2000online/papers/fowkes.htm.

Garvey, W. D. (1979). *Communication: The essence of science*. Oxford, UK: Pergamon Press.

Hackos, J., & Redish, J. (1998). *User and task analysis for interface design*. New York: Wiley.

Hahn, U., & Chater, N. (1997). Concepts and similarity. In K. Lamberts & D. Shanks (Eds.), *Knowledge, concepts and categories* (pp. 43–92). Hove, UK: Psychology Press.

Hancock-Beaulieu, M., Fieldhouse, M., & Do, T. (1995). An evaluation of interactive query expansion in an online library catalogue with graphical user interface. *Journal of Documentation, 51*, 225–243.

Hansen, P. (1999). User interface design for IR interaction. A task-oriented approach. In T. Aparac, T. Saracevic, P. Ingwersen, & P. Vakkari (Eds.), *Digital Libraries: Interdisciplinary concepts, challenges and opportunities. Proceedings of the Third International Conference on the Conceptions of the Library and Information Science (CoLIS 3)* (pp. 191–205). Lokve, Croatia: Benja.

Harter, S. (1992). Psychological relevance and information science. *Journal of the American Society for Information Science, 43*, 602–615.

Harter, S., & Hert, C. A. (1997). Evaluation of information retrieval systems: Approaches, issues, and methods. *Annual Review of Information Science and Technology, 32*, 3–94.

Henderson, A. (2000). Design for what? Six dimensions of activity (part 2 of 2). *Interactions, 7*(6), 25–30.

Hersh, W. R. (1994). Relevance and retrieval evaluation: Perspectives from medicine. *Journal of the American Society for Information Science, 45*, 201–206.

Hersh, W. R. (1996). *Information retrieval. A health care perspective*. Berlin: Springer.

Hersh, W., Pentecost, J., & Hickam, D. (1996). A task-oriented approach to information retrieval evaluation. *Journal of the American Society for Information Science, 47*, 50–56.

Hert, C. A. (1996). User goals on an online public access catalog. *Journal of the American Society for Information Science, 47*, 504–518.

Hert, C. A. (1997). *Understanding information retrieval interactions: Theoretical and practical implications*. Greenwich, CT: Ablex.

Hert, C. A., & Marchionini, G. (1997). Seeking statistical information in federal Websites: Users, tasks, strategies, and design recommendations (Final Report to the Bureau of Labor Statistics). Retrieved December 18, 2001, from http://ils.unc.edu/~march/blsreport/blsmain.htm.

Hirsh, S. G. (1999). Information seeking at different stages of the R&D search process. *Annual International ACM SIGIR Conference on Research and Development in Information Retrieval (SIGIR '99)*, 285–286.

Hsieh-Yee, I. (1993). Effects of search experience and subject knowledge on the search tactics of novice and experienced searchers. *Journal of the American Society for Information Science, 44,* 161–174.

Ingwersen, P. (1992). *Information retrieval interaction.* London: Taylor Graham.

Ingwersen, P. (1996). Cognitive perspectives of information retrieval interaction: Elements of a cognitive IR theory. *Journal of Documentation, 52,* 3–50.

Ingwersen, P. (2001). Cognitive information retrieval. *Annual Review of Information Science and Technology, 34,* 3–51.

Järvelin, K. (1987). On information, information technology and the development of society: An information science perspective. In P. Ingwersen, L. Kajberg, & A. M. Pejtersen (Eds.), *Information technology and information use* (pp. 35–55). London: Taylor Graham.

Koenemann, J., & Belkin, N. (1996). A case for interaction: A study of interactive information retrieval behavior and effectiveness. *Proceedings of the human factors in computing systems conference (CHI '96),* 205–212.

Kuhlthau, C. (1991). Inside the search process: Information seeking from the user's perspective. *Journal of the American Society for Information Science, 42,* 361–371.

Kuhlthau, C. (1993). *Seeking meaning.* Norwood, NJ: Ablex.

Kuhlthau, C. (1999). Accommodating the user's information search process: Challenges for information retrieval system designers. *Bulletin of the American Society for Information Science, 25,* 12–16.

Kuhlthau, C., & Tama, S. (2001). Information search process of lawyers: A call for "just for me" information services. *Journal of Documentation, 57,* 25–43.

Kunz, W., & Rittel, H. (1977). *A systems analysis of the logic of research and information processes.* Munich, Germany: Verlag Documentation.

Leckie, G. J., Pettigrew, K. E., & Sylvain, C. (1996). Modeling the information seeking of professionals: A general model derived from research on engineers, health care professionals, and lawyers. *Library Quarterly, 66,* 161–93.

Limberg, L. (1999). Three conceptions of information seeking and use. In T. Wilson & D. K. Allen (Eds.), *Exploring the Contexts of Information Behaviour* (pp. 116–135). London: Taylor Graham.

Lin, S., & Belkin, N. J. (2000). Modeling multiple information seeking episodes. In D. H. Kraft (Ed.), *Proceedings of the 63rd Annual Meeting of the American Society for Information Science and Technology* (pp. 133–147). Medford, NJ: Information Today, Inc.

Marchionini, G. (1995). *Information seeking in electronic environments.* Cambridge, UK: Cambridge University Press.

Marchionini, G., & Komlodi, A. (1998). Design of interfaces for information seeking. *Annual Review of Information Science and Technology, 33,* 89–130.

Marchionini, G., Plaisant, C., & Komlodi, A. (in press). The people in digital libraries: Multifaceted approaches to assessing needs and impact. In A. Bishop, B. Buttenfield, & N. VanHouse (Eds.), *Digital library use: Social practice in design and evaluation.* Boston: MIT Press.

McCormick, E. (1979). *Job analysis: Methods and applications*. New York: Amacom.

Menzel, H. (1966). Information needs and uses in science and technology. *Annual Review of Information Science and Technology, 1*, 41–69.

Mitra, M., Singhal, A., & Buckley, C. (1998). Improving automatic query expansion. *Proceedings of the Annual International ACM SIGIR Conference on Research and Development in Information Retrieval (SIGIR '98)*, 206–214.

Nardi, B. (1996). *Context and consciousness: Activity theory and human-computer interaction*. Cambridge, MA: MIT Press.

Nielsen, J. (1994). As they may work. *Interactions, 1*, 19–24.

Nilan, M., & Fletcher, P. (1987). Information behaviors in the preparation of research proposals: A user study. In C.-C. Chen (Ed.), *Proceedings of the 50th Annual Meeting for the American Society of Information Science* (pp. 186–192). Medford, NJ: Learned Information.

Oddy, R., Palmquist, R., & Crawford, M. (1986). Representation of anomalous states of knowledge in information retrieval. In J. M. Hurd (Ed.), *Proceedings of the 49th ASIS Annual Meeting* (pp. 248–254). Medford, NJ: Learned Information.

Oddy, R., Liddy, E. D., Balakrishnan, B., Bishop A., Elewononi J., & Martin E. (1992). Towards the use of situational information in information retrieval. *Journal of Documentation, 48*, 123–171.

Park, T. (1993). The nature of relevance in information retrieval: An empirical study. *Library Quarterly, 63*, 318–351.

Pejtersen, A. M. (1990). Icons for representation of domain knowledge in interfaces. In R. Fugmann (Ed.), *Tools for knowledge organization and human interface. Proceedings 1st International ISKO Conference* (Vol. 2, pp. 175–193). Frankfurt, Germany: Indeks Verlag.

Pejtersen, A. M., & Fidel, R. (1998). A framework for work-centered evaluation and design: A case study of IR on the Web. Working paper for MIRA workshop. Grenoble, France.

Pejtersen, A. M., & Rasmussen, J. (1997). Ecological information systems and support of learning: Coupling work domain information to user characteristics. In M.G. Helander, T. K. Landauer, & P.V. Prabhu (Eds.), *Handbook of human-computer interaction* (pp. 315–345). Amsterdam: Elsevier.

Pejtersen, A. M., Sonnenwald, D. H., Buur, J., Govindaraj, T., & Vicente, K. (1995). The design explorer project: Using a cognitive framework to support knowledge exploration. In *Proceedings of the 10th International Conference in Engineering Design (ICED 95)* (pp. 219–2299). Zurich, Switzerland: Heurista.

Pinelli, T., Glassman, N. A., Affelder, L. O., Hecht, L. M., & Kennedy, J. M. (1993). *Technical uncertainty and project complexity as correlates of information use by U.S. industry-affiliated aerospace engineers and scientists*. (Technical Memo 107693). Hanton, VA: U.S. National Aeronautics and Space Administration.

Pirolli, P., & Card, S. (1999). Information foraging. *Psychological Review, 106*, 643–675.

Ponte, J., & Croft, W. (1998). A language modeling approach to information retrieval. *Annual International ACM SIGIR Conference on Research and Development in Information Retrieval (SIGIR '98)*, 275–281.

Pratt, W., & Fagan, L. M. (2000). The usefulness of dynamically categorizing search results. *Journal of the American Medical Informatics Association*, 7, 605–617.

Pratt W., Hearst M. A., & Fagan L. M. (1999). A knowledge-based approach to organizing retrieved documents. *Proceedings of the Sixteenth National Conference on Artificial Intelligence (AAAI-99)*. Retrieved December 18, 2001, from http://www.ics.uci.edu/~pratt/pubs/AAAI-99.pdf.

Rada, R., & Barlow, J. (1991). Document ranking using an enriched thesaurus. *Journal of Documentation*, 47, 240–253.

Reid, J. (1999). A new, task-oriented paradigm for information retrieval: Implications for evaluation of information retrieval systems. In T. Aparac, T. Saracevic, P. Ingwersen, & P. Vakkari (Eds.), *Digital libraries: Interdisciplinary concepts, challenges and opportunities. Proceedings of the Third International Conference on the Conceptions of Library and Information Science (CoLIS3)* (pp. 97–108). Lokve, Croatia: Benja.

Renouf, A. (1993). What the linguist has to say to the information scientists. *Journal of Document and Text Management*, 1, 173–190.

Richardson, J., Omerod, T., & Shepherd, A. (1998). The role of task analysis in capturing requirements for interface design. *Interacting with computers*, 9, 367–384.

Robertson, S. I. (2001). *Problem solving*. Hove, UK: Psychology Press.

Robertson, S., & Hancock-Beaulieu, M. (1992). On the evaluation of IR systems. *Information Processing & Management*, 28, 457–466.

Saracevic, T. (1996). Relevance reconsidered '96. In P. Ingwersen, & N. Pors (Eds.), *Information science: Integration in perspective* (pp. 201–218). Copenhagen: Royal School of Librarianship.

Saracevic, T., & Kantor, P. (1988). A study of information seeking and retrieving. Part II: Users, questions, and effectiveness. *Journal of the American Society for Information Science*, 39, 177–176.

Savage-Knepshield, P. A., & Belkin, N. J. (1999). Interaction in information retrieval: Trends over time. *Journal of the American Society for Information Science*, 50, 1067–1082.

Savolainen, R. (1995). Everyday life information seeking: Approaching information seeking in the context of "way of life." *Library & Information Science Research*, 17, 259–294.

Schamber, L. (1994). Relevance and information behavior. *Annual Review of Information Science and Technology*, 29, 3–48.

Schamber, L., Eisenberg, M., & Nilan, M. (1990). A re-examination of relevance: Towards a dynamic, situational definition. *Information Processing & Management*, 26, 755–776.

Sewell, W., & Teitelbaum, S. (1986). Observations of end-user on-line searching behavior over eleven years. *Journal of the American Society for Information Science*, 37, 234–245.

Shepherd, A. (1998). HTA as a framework for task analysis. *Ergonomics, 41,* 1537–1552.

Shute, S., & Smith, P. (1993). Knowledge-based search italics. *Information Processing & Management, 29,* 29–45.

Siegfried, S., Bates, M. J., & Wilde, D. N. (1993). A profile of end-user searching behavior by humanities scholars: The Getty Online Searching Project Report No. 2. *Journal of the American Society for Information Science, 44,* 273–291.

Smithson, S. (1994). Information retrieval evaluation practice: A case study approach. *Information Processing & Management, 30,* 205–221.

Spasser, M. A. (1999). Informing information science: The case for activity theory. *Journal of the American Society for Information Science, 50,* 1136–1138.

Spink, A. (1996). Multiple search sessions model of end-user behavior: An exploratory study. *Journal of the American Society for Information Science, 47,* 603–609.

Spink, A., Greisdorf, R., & Bateman, J. (1998). From highly relevant to non-relevant: Examining different regions of relevance. *Information Processing & Management, 34,* 599–622.

Spink, A., Wilson, T., Ellis, D., & Ford, N. (1998, March). Modeling user's successive searches in digital environments. *D-Lib Magazine.* Retrieved December 18, 2001, from http://www.dlib.org/dlib/april98/04spink.html.

Stein, A., Gulla, J., & Thiel, U. (1999). User-tailored planning of mixed initiative information-seeking dialogues. *User Modelling and User-Adapted Interaction, 9,* 133–166.

Suchman, L. (1986). *Plans and situated actions: The problem of human-machine communication.* Cambridge, UK: Cambridge University Press.

Suchman, L. (1995). Making work visible. *Communications of the ACM, 38,* 56–64.

Sugar, W. (1995). User-centered perspectives of IR research and analysis methods. *Annual Review of Information Science and Technology, 30,* 77–110.

Sutcliffe, A., & Ennis, M. (1998). Towards a cognitive theory of IR. *Interacting With Computers, 10,* 321–351.

Sutcliffe, A., Ennis, M., & Watkinson, S. J. (2000). Empirical studies of end-user information searching. *Journal of the American Society for Information Science, 51,* 1211–1231.

Sutton, S. (1994). The role of attorney mental models of law in case relevance determinations: An exploratory analysis. *Journal of the American Society for Information Science, 45,* 186–200.

Tang, R., & Solomon, P. (1998). Toward an understanding of the dynamics of relevance judgment: An analysis of one person's search behavior. *Information Processing & Management, 34,* 237–256.

Tiamiyu, M. (1992). The relation between source use and work complexity, decision-making discretion and activity duration in Nigerian government ministries. *International Journal of Information Management, 12,* 130–141.

Vakkari, P. (1999). Task complexity, problem structure and information actions. Integrating studies on information seeking and retrieval. *Information Processing & Management, 35,* 819–837.

Vakkari, P. (2000a). Cognition and changes of search terms and tactics during task performance: A longitudinal study. *Proceedings of the RIAO 2000 Conference*, 894–907. Retrieved December 18, 2001, from http://www.info.uta.fi/informaatio/vakkari/Vakkari_Tactics_RIAO2000.html.

Vakkari, P. (2000b). Relevance and contributory information types of searched documents in task performance. *Annual International ACM SIGIR Conference on Research and Development in Information Retrieval (SIGIR 2000)*, 2–9.

Vakkari, P. (2001). A theory of the task-based information retrieval process: A summary and generalisation of a longitudinal study. *Journal of Documentation, 57*, 44–60.

Vakkari, P., & Hakala, N. (2000). Changes in relevance criteria and problem stages in task performance. *Journal of Documentation, 56*, 540–562.

Vakkari, P., Pennanen, M., & Serola, S. (in press). Changes of search terms and tactics while writing a research proposal. *Information Processing & Management*.

Vechtomova, O., & Robertson, S. (2000). Integration of collocation statistics into the probabilistic retrieval model. *Proceedings of the BCS-IRSG: 22nd Annual Colloquium on Information Retrieval Research*, 165–177. Retrieved December 18, 2001, from http://irsg.eu.org/irsg2000online/papers/vechtomova.htm.

Wang, P. (1997). Users' information needs at different stages of a research project: A cognitive view. In P. Vakkari, R. Savolainen, & B. Dervin (Eds.), *Information seeking in context* (pp. 307–318). London: Taylor Graham.

Wang, P., & Soergel, D. (1998). A cognitive model of document use during a research project. Study I. Document selection. *Journal of the American Society for Information Science, 49*, 115–133.

Wang, P., & White, M. D. (1999). A cognitive model of document use during a research project. Study II. Decisions at the reading and citing stages. *Journal of the American Society for Information Science, 50*, 98–114.

Wersig, G. (1979). The problematic situation as basic concept of information science in the framework of the social sciences. In *Theoretical problems for informatics: New trends in informatics and its terminology* (pp. 48–57). Moscow: International Federation for Documentation.

Wersig, G., & Windel, G. (1985). Information science needs a theory of information action. *Social Science Information Studies, 5*, 11–23.

White, M. D. (1975). The communications behavior of academic economists in research phases. *Library Quarterly, 45*, 337–354.

Wildemuth, B., de Blieck, R., Friedman, C., & File, D. (1995). Medical students' personal knowledge, searching proficiency, and database use in problem solving. *Journal of the American Society for Information Science, 46*, 590–607.

Wildemuth, B., Friedman, C., & Downs, S. (1998). Hypertext versus Boolean access to biomedical information: A comparison of effectiveness, efficiency and user preferences. *ACM transactions on computer-human interaction, 5*, 156–183.

Wildemuth, B., Jacob, E., Fullington, A., de Blieck, R., & Friedman, C. (1991). A detailed analysis of end-user search behaviors. In J.-M. Griffiths (Ed.), *Proceedings of the 54th Annual Meeting of the American Society for Information Science* (pp. 302–312). Medford, NJ: Learned Information.

Wilson, T. (1981). On user studies and information needs. *Journal of Documentation*, *37*, 3–15.

Wilson, T. (1999). Models in information behaviour research. *Journal of Documentation*, *55*, 249–270.

Xie, H. (1997). Planned and situated aspects in interactive IR: Patterns of user interactive intentions and information seeking strategies. In C. Schwartz, & M. Rorvig (Eds.), *Proceedings of the 60th Annual Meeting of the American Society for Information Science*, (pp. 101–110). Medford, NJ: Information Today, Inc.

Xie, H. (2000). Shifts of interactive intentions and information-seeking strategies in interactive information retrieval. *Journal of the American Society for Information Science*, *51*, 841–857.

Yang, S. (1997). Information seeking as problem-solving using a qualitative approach to uncover the novice learners' information-seeking process in a Perseus hypertext system. *Library & Information Science Research*, *19*, 71–92.

Yuan, W. (1997). End-user searching behavior in information retrieval: A longitudinal study. *Journal of the American Society for Information Science*, *48*, 218–234.

CHAPTER 10

The Role of Trust in Information Science and Technology

Stephen Marsh
National Research Council, Ottawa

Mark R. Dibben
University of St. Andrews

Introduction

This chapter discusses the notion of trust as it relates to information science and technology, specifically user interfaces, autonomous agents, and information systems. We first present an in-depth discussion of the concept of trust in and of itself, moving on to applications and considerations of trust in relation to information technologies. We consider trust from a "soft" perspective—thus, although security concepts such as cryptography, virus protection, authentication, and so forth reinforce (or damage) the feelings of trust we may have in a system, they are not themselves constitutive of "trust." We discuss information technology from a human-centric viewpoint, where trust is a less well-structured but much more powerful phenomenon.

With the proliferation of electronic commerce (e-commerce) and the World Wide Web (WWW, or Web), much has been made of the ability of individuals to explore the vast quantities of information available to them, to purchase goods (as diverse as vacations and cars) online, and to publish information on their personal Web sites. Now that the hyperbole has died down somewhat and the situation is beginning to stabilize, we wish to examine one of the more important aspects of this "information revolution": the concept of trust. Although always simmering in the background of the social sciences literature, especially over the past decade in management, the study of trust has moved center stage in the world of online information and direct interaction (see, for example, Marsh, Meech, & Dabbour, 2000; Palmer, Bailey, & Faraj, 2000; Rosenbloom, 2000b; Urban, Sultan, & Qualls 1999).

Thus, an understanding of trust's role and impact is crucial for information systems practitioners and researchers; the main purpose of this review is to provide such an understanding. The chapter is primarily aimed at management scientists with an interest in social informatics, designers with an interest in social phenomena, and other similar readers. However, they will be disappointed if they expect a study of a broad range of social interactionist influences, such as social capital (e.g., Lesser, 2000), authenticity and credibility (e.g., Council on Library and Information Resources, 2000), authority (e.g., Wilson, 1983), knowledge management (e.g., Davenport & Cronin, 2000), and communities of practice (e.g., Prusak & Cohen, 2000; Wenger, 1998, 2000), to name but a few. Each of these has a quite separate theoretical base, even if they appear ostensibly similar to the lay reader; a review encompassing such a broad range of influences is beyond our scope.

Trust has been the topic of considerable study in the social sciences for many years. As such, the chapter consists of a number of sections designed to enable the reader to acquire (1) a broader understanding of how trust operates as a social and interactional phenomenon and, based on this, (2) a more specific understanding of where trust fits into research and practice in information systems and information technology. How, for instance, do information professionals view trust as a phenomenon and how do they use it in their systems, both as developers of (by definition interactive) information systems and as potential users of these systems?

Our discussion of trust includes developments primarily from the fields of management, sociology, philosophy, and psychology, as well as agent-based technologies. Secondary fields in which studies of relevance and importance have been carried out will also be included. The objective is to reach a reasonably definitive view of the phenomenon from which we can proceed to examine more detailed trust studies in information systems of different types. Our argument is that, in information systems in general and in related areas such as human-computer interaction (HCI) and agent technologies, trust exists whether it is explicitly recognized or not. Thus, it is imperative that we understand, and can exploit, trust in order to achieve more comfortable and ultimately simpler interaction with information and information technologies (Cheskin, 1999, 2000; Karvonen, 2000; Kim & Moon, 1998; Marsh, Meech, & Dabbour, 2000).

Our aim is to point out where, in specific systems such as those mentioned above, trust comes into play and how, if it is recognized, it can be used as a positive force for improving systems. To this end, we will extend the concept of information systems (IS) to include areas of interest such as human-computer interaction, autonomous agents and multi-agent systems, and virtual reality. Our view is that, in order for information systems to work and be used, a deeper understanding of what is meant by "information system" is necessary. Naturally, some of these "systems" and associated research take an explicit view of trust. We wish to address topics such as the extent to which contemporary information systems deal with the concept of trust, how to trust the information that is obtained, and how trust can be extended to enhance the power and credibility of systems. These systems will also be reviewed and their use of trust documented and critiqued.

Moving from general to specific notions of the nature and uses of trust in information systems, a number of specific models of trust that are applicable to the study of information systems and information science will be considered. In particular, we will present models of trust from psychology (Castelfranchi & Falcone, 1999) and agent systems (Dibben, 2000; Marsh, 1994), among others, and discuss their relevance. We will cover trust and its relation within the broad field of information systems and information science to cooperation, information handling, relevance and credibility, the forwarding of information, belief revision, and the user interface. We will cover both trust in people in virtual settings and the engendering of trusting behavior in artificial agents. We conclude with a discussion of the implications for research and development in theory and practice, before, lastly, a consideration of and a general outlook on possible future developments in the area.

Exploring the Concept of Trust

Any study of the uses and impact of trust in IS first requires a detailed grasp of trust as a generic social phenomenon. This is because its use in the virtual world ultimately stems from its role in the real world. The first section therefore provides a brief introductory discussion of the nature of trust and its role in, and impact on, human interactions derived from a range of literatures in the social sciences. We set out a workable understanding of trust that enables meaningful explication of its operation between individuals in social settings. This understanding, some may argue, fails to make a clear distinction between individual human beings and "agents," and indeed seeks to treat agents anthropomorphically. If indeed this is the case, it is because the role and uses of trust in information science are largely premised upon the interactive nature of the human-computer relationship and the consequent predictive modeling of artificial agents to behave in a trustworthy manner, as if they were human. The following rationalist explanation of trust will facilitate a theoretically grounded understanding of these developments.

Theoretical Meanings of Trust

Attempts to uncover the experiences alluded to by the term "trust" have been made in a number of disciplines, ranging from philosophy (e.g., Baier, 1986; Hosmer, 1995) and sociology (e.g., Barber, 1983; Gambetta, 1990), to psychology (e.g., Deutsch, 1962). The subject is inherently obscured, however, by the fact that each discipline focuses on particular elements of the phenomenon (e.g., Worchel, 1979). Psychological approaches to trust, for example, have tended to concentrate on trust as a personality trait developed by (human) agents in varying degrees depending upon their experiences (e.g., Rotter, 1967, 1971, 1980). Sociological approaches, on the other hand, have either interpreted trust from observed behavior of agents in potentially risky situations (Worchel, 1979), or as agent characteristics perceived by others as trustworthy (e.g., Cook & Wall, 1980; Dasgupta, 1990). An extension of this approach has been to focus on trust in human-to-human relationships, but not in agents' psychological states (Lewis & Weigert, 1985).

Thus, it may be seen that trust has been broadly categorized into three layers: *dispositional trust,* the psychological disposition or personality trait of an agent to be trusting or not; *learned trust,* an agent's general tendency to trust, or not to trust, another agent as a result of experience; and *situational trust,* in which basic tendencies are adjusted in response to situational cues (Worchel, 1979). For example, a situational cue may be the amount and quality of communication (Giffin, 1967); that is, although one may trust an agent on the whole, one may not do so in certain situations and under certain circumstances. These trust layers may be seen to operate such that, in the absence of learned trust, for example, an agent's dispositional trust influences his behavior, and where learned trust exists, then an agent's dispositional trust is less important in determining his behavior (e.g., Wrightsman, 1964). Thus, it follows, broadly speaking, that learned trust may be regarded as the experience born of a collection of past situational trusts (Luhmann, 1979; Stack, 1978).

Specific Studies of Trust

Of the levels of trust just described, an understanding of situational trust is consequently most important, because factors influencing learned trust are those factors that influenced the agent in previous situations. To concentrate specifically on situational trust, therefore, a number of quantitative studies have been conducted on trust in different settings. For example, instruments have been developed to measure interpersonal trust at work (Cook & Wall, 1980), organizational trust (Hart et al., 1986), interpersonal trust in families (Larzelere & Huston, 1980), institutional trust (Chun & Campbell, 1974; Kaplan, 1973), and trust in communication processes (e.g., Giffin, 1967). Similarly, qualitative studies of, for example, worker and managerial trust (e.g., Gabarro, 1978; Jennings, 1971; Lorenz, 1992), project teams (Porter & Lilley, 1996), and negotiation settings (Ross & La Croix, 1996) have also addressed the general question of "what generates, maintains, substitutes or collapses trusting relations" (Gambetta, 1990, p. xi).

Similes and Definitions of Trust

A number of so-called situational trust "types" have been identified, and have been summarized by Marsh (1995, pp. 27–28) as follows: trust as despair, trust as social conformity, trust as innocence, trust as impulsiveness, trust as virtue, trust as masochism, trust as faith, trust as risk taking, and trust as confidence. Mayer, Davis, and Schorman (1995) add trust as cooperation, and trust as predictability. Of particular note, perhaps, in a business setting are *trust as despair* (Mayer et al., 1995) (where the agent has no choice but to trust the other party), *trust as social conformity* (where trust is expected by the other party, and not to trust would lead to an irretrievable breakdown of the relationship), *trust as risk taking* (where the possible positive results of trust being well placed are greater than the negative results should the trust be poorly placed), *trust as confidence* (where the element of risk in the decision to trust is far less than in trust as risk taking, consequently one enters into the decision with far greater optimism), *trust as cooperation* (whereby the probability that an agent "will perform an action that is beneficial or at least not detrimental to us is high enough for us to consider engaging in some form of co-operation with him" [Gambetta, 1990, p. 217]), and *trust as predictability* (where the decision to trust an agent is dependent upon his predictable behavior). Although each of these trust similes helps to give an understanding of what situations may lead an agent to trust, they do not bring us any nearer to an explanation of what trust is, however, for trust cannot be described as any or all of these types. Trust is not, for example, despair, cooperation, confidence, or risk taking. A re-examination of these descriptions reveals that each provides a simile for a part of what might be involved in interpersonal trust. A further understanding of trust may be gleaned by an examination of a number of recognized definitions of trust, listed in Table 10.1.

The Adopted Description of Trust, and Other Concerns

These definitions allow us to surmise that *trust concerns a positive expectation regarding the behavior of somebody or something in a situation that entails risk to the trusting party.* This description of the phenomenon

Table 10.1 A range of trust definitions.

- Behavioral trust is "the willingness to increase one's vulnerability to another whose behaviour is not under one's control" (Zand, quoted in Nooteboom et al., 1997, p. 311).
- Trust is "the extent to which one is willing to ascribe good intentions to and have confidence in the words and actions of others" (Cook & Wall, 1980, p. 39).
- Trust is "a state involving confident expectations about another's motives with respect to oneself in situations entailing risk" (Boon & Holmes, 1991, p. 194).
- Trusting behavior consists of "actions that increase one's vulnerability to another whose behavior is not under one's control and takes place in a situation where the future penalty suffered if the trust is abused would lead one to regret the action" (Lorenz, 1992, p. 456).
- Trust is "an agent's behavioral reliance on another person under a condition of risk" (Currall & Judge, 1995, p. 151).
- Trust is "the expectation that transacting parties will not defect, even when it is in their self interest to do so" (Low & Srivatsan, 1995, p. 61).
- Trust "indicates the willingness of an agent to engage in a transaction in the absence of adequate safeguards" (Noorderhaven, 1995, p. 109).
- "Trust is the expectation that arises, within a community of regular, honest, and cooperative behavior, based on commonly shared norms, on the part of other members of that community" (Fukuyama, 1995, p. 26).
- Trust is "the expectation by one person, group or firm of ethically profitable behavior—that is, morally correct decisions and actions based upon ethical principles of analysis—on the part of the other person, group or firm in a joint endeavor, or economic exchange" (Hosmer, 1995, pp. 392-393).
- Trust is "the willingness of a party to be vulnerable to the actions of another party based on the expectation that the other will perform a particular action important to the trustor, irrespective of the ability to monitor or control that other party" (Mayer et al., 1995, p. 712).
- Intentional Trust is "the subjective probability that one assigns to benevolent action by another agent or group of agents" (Nooteboom et al., 1997, p. 311).
- "Trust emerges from the identification of a need that cannot be met without the assistance of another and some assessment of the risk involved in relying on the other to meet this need [and is thus] a willing dependency on another's actions [limited] to the area of need and ... subject to overt and covert testing" (Hupcey, Penrod, Morse, & Mitcham, 2001, p. 290).
- "Trust is a psychological state comprising the intention to accept vulnerability based upon positive expectations of the intentions or behavior of another" (Rousseau et al., 1998, p. 395).
- Self trust is a psychological state of confident expectation concerning one's own abilities in a situation entailing risk to oneself (Dibben, 2000).

is adopted for the work reported in the following pages. A number of problems remain concerning the trust concept, as is clear from the previous discussion. These problems have been summarized by Mayer et al. (1995) as lack of clarity in the relationship between risk and trust; confusion between trust, its antecedents, and outcomes; lack of specificity of trust referents leading to confusion in levels of analysis; and a failure to consider both the trusting party and the party to be trusted.

With regard first to trust and risk, a generally accepted rule, noted by Mayer et al. (1995) and increasingly apparent in the more recent definitions in Table 10.1, is that, for trust to occur, risk must be perceived by the trusting party (Marsh, 1995). This condition implies that risk and trust are subjectively apprehended by the trusting party. Hence, "trust is always for something we can rightfully demand of others: misplaced trust, accordingly, is not a shortcoming on the part of the trustful person, but of the person in which the trust was placed" (Hertzberg, 1988, p. 319). Thus, as Marsh (1995) notes, the decision to trust may be correct—and even inevitable—in and of itself, but the decision to trust *a particular party in a particular situation* may not be.

Next, with regard to antecedents, outcomes, and substitutes and/or complements, an extensive review by Krieger (1997) of the trust literature in the social sciences isolated a large number of each. *Antecedents* to trust include interest, calculation, probability, risk, uncertainty, information, communication, culture, values, third parties, institutions, integrity, benevolence, morality, intentions, competence, ability, time experience, reputation, proximity, familiarity, similarity, guarantees, agreements, and formal contracts. *Outcomes* of trust include risk taking, investment, cooperation, control system, self-enforcing and self-fulfilling phenomena, innovation, non-zero sum games, and performance. *Substitutes* for and/or *complements,* of trust include power, hierarchies, markets, and instantaneous transactions, to which one might also add promises (Atiyah, 1981; Robins, 1984). With regard to problems regarding specificity of trust referents and levels of analysis (i.e., agent, firm, or society in general), recent definitions of trust tend to overcome this to some extent by focusing more on the agent. These issues will be worked out in the following sections, in preparation for a more detailed consideration of trustors (trusting parties), the types of situational trust placed in trust subjects (trusted parties), and trust objects (situations or issues concerning trust that is placed in the trust subject by the trustor).

Trust and Levels of Analysis

We come, now, to the question of what constitutes organizational trust, an important issue in the study of trust in businesses (Mayer et al., 1995; Rousseau, Sitkin, Burt, & Camerer, 1998). A separate definition has been provided by Nooteboom, Berger, and Noorderhaven (1997, p. 312): "the subjective probability held by an individual with respect to the conduct of an organization." Hart et al. (1986), in a study of employees at General Motors, established a number of factors that appeared to influence employee trust in the organization: information sharing, accurate communication, expressions of confidence, and communication of goals and support of employee goals. Yet, as has been seen, similar factors have been found in interpersonal trust studies. So, in what way might interpersonal trust differ from organizational trust?

The difference between interpersonal trust and organizational trust, it is argued, lies in the *locus of trust*, not in the nature of the trust itself. With regard specifically to the trusting organization, the locus of trust resides not in the organization, but in an agent within the organization. Organizations, being inanimate objects, cannot trust; only an individual can trust. Organizational roles (e.g., boss, subordinate, employee) concern certain tasks that the agent performs in certain relationships with other specified agents in the organization, and in which interpersonal trust plays a key enabling role. The situation is more complex where multiple relations are involved (i.e., greater than a dyadic trust relationship). In a situation involving three agents A, B, and C, for example, six interpersonal trust relationships can be described: A's trust of B, A's trust of C, B's trust of A, B's trust of C, C's trust of A, and C's trust of B. A's relationship with C might influence the relationship with B, but only insofar as this would be a situational cue for the development of the particular agent trust relationship between A and B. Burt and Knez (1996) studied the influence of third-party gossip on trust in dyadic relationships. They found (as common sense leads one to expect) that where the trust relationships of the first and the second parties are strong, the influence is limited, and vice versa. A further example of the importance of the locus of trust is a formal contractual relationship between two agents. Although this situation consists of two trust relationships, the locus of trust resides not in each of the agents but in the formal legal contract. It is this contract that ultimately carries the possibility of legal redress if either party fails to carry out its respective role in the relationship. Thus, the parties' separate and individual trust in the contract as a source of remedy replaces the lack of trust each has in the other.

In light of this discussion, it becomes clear that the "trusting organization" may be more accurately considered in terms of the trust held by the organizational representative with the power and authority to act for the organization (Currall & Judge, 1995), such as a bank manager. Such power, however, is not meant in the negative coercive sense or as "every chance within a social relationship to assert one's will against opposition" (Weber, 1925, quoted in Habermas, 1986, p. 75). Rather, it is meant in the more positive sense (as befits the positive connotation of trust itself) of an agent being "empowered by a certain number of people to act in their name ... for as long as the group keeps together" (Arendt, 1986, p. 64). This contrasts with a number of earlier studies (e.g., Coleman, 1990; Gambetta, 1990; Giddens, 1991; Luhmann, 1979), which, in their varied attempts to unpack the relationship between trust, power, and control, appear to rely on a rather more Weberian interpretation—asymmetric dominant and/or expert relations (see Reed, 2001). It follows that the power and authority of the bank manager result from his being trusted by those in the organization to act on their behalf. Thus, an agent's trust of another represents an empowering of the trusted party by the trusting party, with the associated risks that the trusted party may not behave in a trustworthy fashion with the power bestowed upon him.

Yet, this discussion brings with it the difficulty of accounting for the increasing interest in the role of trust as a social reality (societal trust), belonging to groups rather than to agents (e.g., Fox, 1985; Lewis & Weigert, 1985). This conclusion has led to a further sub-categorization of high-trust societies and low-trust societies, to explain observed differences among cultures, with regard to both business behavior (e.g., Casson, 1990; Dodd, 1996; Sako, 1992, 1995) and more general social settings (e.g., Fukuyama, 1995; Giddens, 1991; Sztompka, 1999). Thomas (1997, p.17) has summarized the general conclusion of such studies: "High-trust societies are economically stronger than low-trust societies. But trust [in such high-trust societies] is being created via looser networks thanks to new technology and new lifestyles."

In spite of its increasing popularity as an explanatory framework, however, the concept of societal trust appears to deny that trust is formed by agents. The presence of trust in the group, large or small, does not come about as a result of the existence of the group per se, but rather as a result of a process of formation and continual renegotiation of trust within the agents' interpersonal relationships that, over time (Dodd, 1996), establish the societal group (Child & Keiser, 1979; Cicourel, 1972, pp. 242–246; Hunt, 1986; Shaw, 1971; Thompson & McHugh, 1990). Thus, rather than being owned by the group (a small business, or the society in general), trust is owned by the trusting agents; the process of situational trust development occurs as a result of agents comparing, finding repeatedly, and designating situational cues (or clues) received (Schlick, 1974, p. 82). The impact of societal trust might therefore best be described as a general atmosphere of integrity (Casson, 1990) within the group, which might affect an agent's situational trust, but as only one of the cues received by the agent during the process of developing his situational trust.

It follows that the locus of trust also accounts for notions of trust in cultural and political systems, trust in the environment (safety concerns), or trust in equipment that certain studies have reported (e.g., Casson, 1990; Clark, 1993; Clark & Payne, 1995; Eisenstadt & Roniger, 1984; Fukuyama, 1995; and Hart et al., 1986). Bearing in mind Nooteboom et al.'s (1997) definition of an agent's organizational trust mentioned earlier, such categories of trust can be described as an agent's perception of the behavior of a group of people, a thing, or a set of things as a result of the situational cues perceived by that agent concerning the behavior of either an agent or agents in the group, or of an inanimate object, who/which is/are in a position to be considered by the trusting agent as representative of the group/set in whom/which trust is placed. The agent then considers by "representational slippage" the behavior of the agent, person, or thing to be the behavior of the community or wider set of things to which it belongs. It follows that such trust levels reflect the unit of analysis considered appropriate (e.g., organization, society, environment), and are also more closely equated with learned trust, which, as a situational cue, is then taken into account in the agent's consideration of the situational trust that arises as the gap-filler for explicit knowledge.

From the perspective of interpersonal trust, therefore, it can be argued that conceptualizations of organizational trust, societal trust, and so on are attempts at reducing the complexity of interpersonal trust (Barber, 1983; Bigley & Pearce, 1998; Cvetkovich & Lofstedt, 1999; Eisenstadt & Roniger, 1984; Fukuyama, 1995; Lane & Bachmann, 1998; Shapiro, 1987; Sztompka, 1999). It follows that such conceptualizations can lead to a blurring of the boundaries between different levels of analysis. Although this may ease the development of argument, the corresponding lack of distinction between levels potentially endangers the analysis; accuracy has been sacrificed to facility.

As such, we have purposely concentrated on the reality of interpersonal trust; that trust existing in one (human) agent concerning another. In this sense, and to conclude this section, we suggest that trust may usefully be considered as a processual phenomenon, ever-changing and evolving in the individual with respect to others. It is thus an example of what Mead (1934) called a subjective experience. Trust resides in one individual and is something to which that individual alone has direct access. It requires another individual as a stimulus. It may also be communicated in behavior toward a society of individuals generating an atmosphere to which each responds and upon which the individual may reflect as a separate experience of self-as-was a moment ago (general trust), to which the self-as-is reacts (situational trust).

Trust in Information Science and Technology

As a complex phenomenon, trust has applications and ramifications in all aspects of human activity. In technological domains, unsurprisingly, the concept of trust is mentioned from user interface design through security to the consideration of information itself. We cannot hope to review all aspects of trust in information science and technology. Instead, we opt to focus on two main areas that we feel are important to information professionals. We present these choices as indicative only of our research interests, not as a definitive mapping of trust in the world of information science and technology. Finally, we recall the caveat from our introduction that, although security and all it entails is a worthwhile approach to creating trusting sensations, it is not what we are considering here.

First, we explore trust in interactions between users and technology. This trust is one of the underpinnings of human-computer interaction, because without human trust in a system, efficiency, productivity, and "plain old comfort" will not be maximized (see, for example, Lee & Moray, 1992, 1994; Moray, Hiskes, Lee, & Muir, 1995; Muir, 1987; Muir & Moray, 1996). In fact, the trust users have in the technologies they use is a vital part of the system seen as a whole. Without trust, users will seek to do their tasks in other ways (Muir, 1987; Muir & Moray, 1996). We will examine this trust on different levels, one of which is trust in the technology to be able to do what it is designed to do; a form of trust-as-confidence. Another level is that of trust inspired by the interface, the interaction the user has with it, and the experience that is felt (Bickmore & Cassell, 2001; Cassell & Bickmore, 2002; Cassell, Bickmore, Vilhjálmsson, & Yan, 2000; Koda & Maes, 1996; Lester, Voerman, Towns, & Callaway, 1997). Clearly, interface design and trust inspiration are important for several reasons, not least that trust in the interface will, we believe, lead to more trust in the technology per se (our first level of trust). At this stage, we introduce the models of trust that have been developed, and that may have an impact on the design and facilitation of trust in interactive systems. Trustworthy interfaces will ultimately be enabling technologies because they will lead the user to want to interact with them, will increase productivity, and will, to take a concrete example, lead to more sales. As Shneiderman (2000, p. 57) states, "designers must facilitate the trust that enables collective action."

Our second focus is on information, both as a tool for working and as the subject of that work. Most recently, it has become clear that much more information is available than humans are able to process (Lawrence & Giles, 1998, 1999, and see http://wwwmetrics.com/). In addition, evidence suggests that online articles are more highly cited than printed ones (Lawrence, 2001), thus increasing the pressure on authors to publish online. The processing task, at least in the initial stages, can conceivably be carried out by autonomous systems (or agents) that can search for, filter, classify, rate, and recommend information based on user queries. Naturally, these systems do not replace human recommendation or rating, but simply augment and, to some extent, simplify these tasks. The introduction of human and machine-readable metadata schemata such as the Dublin Core (http://dublincore.org/) has resulted in an even greater simplification of the initial information-handling tasks. However, metadata goes only so far: It can describe a document and its contents, but ultimately the value and trustworthiness of that document and the information it contains are unknown unless the document is examined. Systems exist that can simplify some of this vital work via human and agent recommendations. For examples of such systems, see Kuokka and Harada (1995), Foner and Crabtree (1996), Marsh and Masrour (1997), and the proceedings of the annual conference on Cooperative Information Agents (Kandzia & Klusch, 1997; Klusch & Kerschberg, 2000; Klusch, Shehory, & Weiss, 1999; Klusch & Weiss, 1998; Klusch & Zambonelli, 2001). Clearly, here, trust in the human or agent making the recommendation is of paramount importance and is related to our first level of trust in technology. Consideration of trust in the information itself—its source, its content, and its meaning—is also vital, as Ketelaar (1997) notes. As the information processors described here work with what they are given, how can they rate that information with respect to their prior knowledge, based on origin, content, recommendations, and so forth? It is evident that mechanisms for ensuring the validity of information are available, and many of these are based concretely on trust. Finally, those in information-intensive occupations, such as the military, have to think about trust at many points in their operations—not just trust in terms of security, but also in terms of intent, meaning, and content (Bisantz, Llinas, Seong, Finger, & Jian, 2000).

Trust in the System: E-Commerce, User Interfaces, and Static Trust

A considerable body of literature has developed around the question of people's trust in others when their interactions are mediated by technology, how the medium affects trust, and, consequently, how this can affect human behavior. Such user trust studies tend to argue that "people trust people not technology" (Friedman, Kahn, & Howe, 2000, p. 36; see also Olson & Olson, 2000). Implicit in these studies is the belief that only humans can trust (and be trusted), and, consequently, they concentrate on how trust can be employed by businesses, consumers, and individuals for the sake of their virtually mediated human relationships (Rosenbloom, 2000a). Although it is clear that trust is an interactional phenomenon, much of the trust research in e-commerce has been devoted to relatively simplistic static versions of trust (e.g., Baba, 1999; Coutu, 1998; Jarvenpaa, Knoll, & Leidner, 1998; Jarvenpaa & Leidner, 1998; Knights, Noble, Vurdubakis, & Willmott, 2001; Palmer, Bailey, & Faraj, 2000).

Use of such static conceptualizations is favored by those who, in contrast to Friedman et al. (2000), argue that people can and do trust technology (e.g., Resnick, Zeckhauser, Friedman, & Kuwabara, 2000). Such studies tend to concentrate on the way in which "humans gradually learn to trust embodied interface agents that use the same social cues people use, including interaction rituals" (Cassell & Bickmore, 2000, p. 50), and, subsequently, how agents can be made to behave in trustworthy fashion (Shneiderman, 2000). Studio Archetype/Sapient and Cheskin's reports on trust and trustworthiness in e-commerce (Cheskin 1999, 2000) are excellent early examples of the e-commerce community's outlook on trust. The first study, carried out in 1999 (Cheskin 1999), examines several e-commerce Web sites and proposes various means of designing for trust in these sites. Ultimately, as noted in Philosophe (2000), these findings address not trust, but trustworthiness. This fact is not in itself a weakness, as long as the difference is noted. In addition, because the study focused on one country's users (the U.S.), specific cultural differences that abound in trust and trust-reasoning behavior were not addressed. This focus is more problematic because interface design must now take different cultures and contexts into account (see, for example, Marcus & Gould, 2000; Pemberton, 2001). Cheskin's more recent study (Cheskin, 2000) addresses some of these concerns by extending its coverage to several South American countries (including Brazil), which brings in different languages as well. Interestingly, Jarvenpaa, Tractinsky, and Saarinen's (1999) examinations into cultures found no cross-cultural differences, although it may be that the subjects (young students in Israel, Australia, and to a lesser extent, Finland) constituted a cultural group, thus introducing a further consideration into the study.

Although the Cheskin studies are undoubtedly important, they do not experiment with trust and interfaces; they simply focus on users' reactions and trusting behaviors given a static interface and stable context within their cultural and task-specific domains. Another approach considers aesthetics or simplicity (Karvonen, 2000; Turner & Nowell, 2000) and anthropomorphism (Bickmore & Cassell, 2001; Cassell & Bickmore, 2000, 2002; Marsh & Meech, 2000; Nass, Steuer, & Tauber, 1994). In order to better understand the influences that act on trust, however, more focused studies are needed. The seminal work in this area is that of Kim and Moon (1998), which examines user reactions to different interface styles, layouts, and designs in the context of a banking application.

Further work (Lee, Kim, & Moon, 2000) examines trust as a factor affecting loyalty among e-commerce customers.

Ultimately, however, Kim and Moon's first study runs into problems, as did the first Cheskin study, in not addressing culture in relation to the context and task in which trust is assessed. Although generalization is possible, it is dangerous to conclude that, for example, Europeans will reason and behave as North Americans do, because culture affects trust (Doney, Cannon, & Mullen, 1998; Fukuyama, 1995). Note, for example, that the second Cheskin study found that organizations were trusted differently across countries and cultures (Cheskin, 2000). Jarvenpaa's later work (Jarvenpaa, Tractinsky, & Saarinen, 1999) highlights the need for much more research in this area. Wider studies are possible given the Web's extraordinary geographical scope. In fact, Fogg's team at Stanford's Persuasive Technology Lab is focusing on credibility (or believability, which is another way of looking at one form of trustworthiness) in Web sites in just this fashion, with global experiments and studies (Fogg et al., 2001). The latest work from Fogg and his team aims to produce guidelines for Web design and credibility based on these experiments, and includes recommendations to:

- Design Web sites to convey the "real world" aspect of the organization

- Make Web sites easy to use (which in itself is far too broad a recommendation)

- Include markers of expertise

- Include markers of trustworthiness (much as in the Cheskin studies)

- Tailor the user experience (see section following on Dynamic Trust)

- Avoid overly commercial elements on a Web site

- Avoid the pitfalls of amateurism (including typographical errors and broken links)

Although some of these recommendations seem obvious (ease of use is, for example, a primary goal of the field of human-computer interaction), it is interesting that they carry such weight in a study of credibility, or trustworthiness. The design of interfaces and interaction, therefore, has a significant effect on user trust levels and must be addressed properly. This message is put across forcefully in Nielsen's (1999) AlertBox and the Nielsen Norman Group's set of guidelines (www.nngroup.com/reports/ecommerce/trust.html).

Dynamic Trust: Relationships with Interactive Systems

These studies of trust at the interface and e-commerce levels do not take into account the inherently interactional nature of the trust phenomenon. Thus, as Philosophe (2000, online) states, "Commerce site designers, however, must understand that they cannot code trust into a site, they can only suggest trust. Trust is a property controlled by the consumer." But this statement considers trust only from the point of view of a static suggestion on a Web site. More recently, researchers have begun to appreciate the nature of the relationship that can be developed by users who interact with a system, an interface, or a Web site (see, for example, Fogg et al., 2000; Nass et al., 1994; Nass & Reeves, 1996). With such relationships, trust becomes a two-way street—user judges system via trust (and other measures), and system considers user in terms of trust. This latter is of some importance in e-commerce contexts, where trust should be seen as more than the understandably important considerations of wondering whether credit cards can guarantee payment, or if a site is free of spelling mistakes.

The relationship model of trust—allowing systems to reason with and about trust in a way that enables them to adapt to users' trust levels, and gives systems an additional tool to judge user behavior—depends for its success on active working models of the phenomenon. Although this is a relatively novel research area, we believe it has the potential to produce worthwhile results. In its restricted way, relationship-based dynamic trust in systems is a form of interpersonal trust. Recently, several models and studies of the phenomenon from this point of view have been proposed.

Much has been made of the Internet's capability to increase interaction between participants. Of course, this brings with it its own problems, many of which involve security. Abdul-Rahman and Hailes's (1997) approach to the need for systems security focuses on a distributed trust model, and has been extended further to enable assessments of information (Abdul-Rahman & Hailes, 1999) and the use of trust in virtual communities (Abdul-Rahman & Hailes, 2000). Abdul-Rahman and Hailes's model is implemented through a series of formulae that allow interested agents to reason with and about trust in a given situation, although the considerations are based not only on internal states but also on recommendations from the outside (social) world. Agents can thus reason about how they trust others, and also how they trust others to make recommendations (about third parties) to them. In fact, this very powerful system of trust organization answers at least one of the problems exposed in Marsh's work. Also, the system is computationally implementable. However, problems remain, not least in the use of ad hoc formulae and value judgments (also revealed in Marsh's work), which raises an important point about trust—since we rely on it for our everyday lives, studying it ultimately means using what we know from personal experience. Although this is not altogether satisfactory, it does at least give grounds for experimentation and observation. To enhance their applicability, the models we develop must be implementable in many different situations.

On a more cognitive level, Castelfranchi's model of trust (Castelfranchi & Falcone, 1999; Castelfranchi & Tan, 2001) examines trust as a composition of several mental states. These states include competence (of the other agent to perform a task), disposition (of the other agent), dependence, fulfillment (for this agent), willingness (of the other agent), self-confidence, and persistence (the belief that the other agent will persist until the task is done). Castelfranchi's trust is not a black and white model—there are degrees of trust. However, Castelfranchi argues that there are not degrees of delegation. Thus, when trust reaches a threshold, the decision to delegate becomes black and white—one either trusts someone else to do something or one does not. Unlike the previous models, it is difficult to see how this approach can contribute to information evaluation. In addition, the focus of the model leaves some doubt as to its potential for implementation until the scope of some of its constructs is more properly defined. However, as a model of trust that allows informed discussion of the phenomenon, it does its job admirably.

Florian Egger's work on e-commerce concentrates on usability in e-commerce and how trust is a factor. In particular, Egger addresses user perceptions of trust and trustworthiness from actual Web site experiences. His MoTeC (Model of Trust for Electronic Commerce) focuses on this aspect and has a very strong HCI emphasis (Egger, 2000; Egger & de Groot, 2000). It has several components by which e-commerce sites can be examined, and has been applied extensively through case studies (see http://www.ecommuse.com/).

In a way that corresponds to Abdul-Rahman and Hailes's model, Jøsang's (1997) view of trust is rooted in the security world and the notion that, ultimately, entities in a distributed system such as the Internet must make trusting decisions in one way or another. Jøsang introduces the concept of subjective logic. Whereas standard logic operates on statements that are either true or false, subjective logic operates on individual, subjective opinions of statements' truth or falsity (binary). Given this logic, Jøsang is able to formalize the concept of trust in distributed systems. Jøsang's current work applies this model in e-commerce situations and the development of automatic decision-making tools (Patton & Jøsang, 2001; see also http://security.dstc.edu.au/).

Marsh (1994) carried out one of the earliest studies of trust in autonomous systems (agents). This study viewed trust as a phenomenon of use to agents in cooperative situations. As such, Marsh's view of trust is that of trust-as-confidence, in Deutsch's (1973) terms. This model proposed a set of formulae that could be implemented within simple trust-reasoning agents, and that utilized concepts such as importance, competence, and subjective risk to attain not only an understanding of trust but also a method of objectively studying the notion (such that it became possible to say, for example, "I have this much trust in you" and to understand what that meant). Marsh's work left a lot of room for future refinement. Most recently, this trust formalization has been applied in information agents (Marsh, 2001) and an e-commerce user interface (Marsh, Meech, & Dabbour, 2000).

At first blush, the models seem similar and yield similar results, but one major requirement—that of computational tractability—is not always satisfied. Another failing of almost all of the models is the lack of concern for the trustee—little consideration is given of the role of the trustee on the trusting relationship, an oversight that has only recently been addressed (Bacharach & Gambetta, 2000; Esfandiari & Chandrasekharan, 2000).

Trust in Information

Information is the raw data upon which knowledge can be built. It takes many forms, and each form is of use in its own particular milieu. Information technology, as a tool for handling the many different forms of information, quite often can be confused with information itself. Thus, the way information is presented often affects our perception of both the information and its credibility. Ordinarily, decisions based on information may not result in an international outcry, but, in some situations, the amount of trust one has in information or system can have serious repercussions—consider the case of the U.S.S. Vincennes shooting down an airliner because the commanding officer trusted the system, which identified the airliner as hostile (Bisantz et al., 2000; Hestad, 2001). Even in everyday life, placing too much faith in a piece of seemingly innocuous information may result in problems; for example, when one unintentionally introduces a virus into a computer system.

Several questions arise here. Not only the method of information delivery or provision is important, but also the provider of that information. Information providers can take many forms, from librarians to libraries as institutions; from individuals to societies and governments; from autonomous agents to online repositories. In receiving information from someone or somewhere, we often have little to go on beyond the perceived reputation of the provider of that information—a problem perhaps exacerbated online (Bickmore & Cassell, 2001; Fogg et al., 2001; Ivory, Sinha, & Hearst, 2001). In this sense, the problem is not so much one of trust estimation and reasoning as trust management (Khare & Rifkin, 1998), a topic that has seen much work over the years, mostly in relation to information security (Bisantz et al., 2000; Blaze, Feigenbaum, & Lacy, 1996; Blaze, Feigenbaum, Resnick, & Strauss, 1996; Povey, 1999).

Ketalaar's (1997) arguments are pertinent here: If we are told something in an electronic world, how can we trust it? Previously, a document's credibility was to some extent maintained by knowledge workers such as librarians, editors, and other intermediaries. Today, this front line of information authentication is not always in place. The problem is compounded when one considers that searching for information may be done not by humans but by automated agents (Bhavsar, Ghorbani, & Marsh, 2000; Menczer, Pant, Ruiz, & Srinivasan, 2001; Pant & Menczer, 2001; Theilmann & Rothermel, 1999). Some method for reasoning about the reliability of information is needed. Abdul-Rahman & Hailes (2000) and Jøsang (Jøsang 1997; Jøsang & Tran, 2000) have addressed the problem of recommendation in distributed information systems (where agents can be human or automated) from slightly different angles. In Abdul-Rahman's work, trusting a recommendation is a process whereby an agent must consider not only whether the recommender is trusted, but also if the recommender is trusted to recommend. In Jøsang's work, a subjective logic is used.

The Platform for Internet Content Selection (PICS) information labeling standard (Resnick & Miller, 1996; see also http://www.w3.org/PICS/) enables metadata to be associated with Web pages or information on the Internet. Although originally focused on helping parents and teachers judge and filter information automatically, it has many other strengths, including the capability to sign information (thus ensuring nonrepudiation—see http://www.w3.org/DSig/). Despite obvious dangers in terms of censorship, as a metadata system, PICS alone does nothing—it is up to the tools that use it to define policies. AT&T's PolicyMaker system (Blaze, Feigenbaum, & Lacy, 1996; Blaze, Feigenbaum, Resnick, & Strauss, 1996), a distributed trust management system that uses digital signatures and public key cryptography, has been applied to this problem with some success.

On the human front, the possibility of revealing the amount of trust one actor has in another has been addressed by Schneider, Kortuem, Jager, Fickas, & Segall (2000). In this system, recommendations are disseminated via handheld or wearable computers in order to allow people to make decisions based on what other members of a society think about potential helpers. It is not difficult to extend Schneider et al.'s concept to the broader information domain, particularly with information systems that rely on social structures for recommendation of information. Indeed, it is exactly what such cooperative agent systems require.

The trusting of information is to a large extent a mixture of two distinct trusting questions. The first, addressed by recommender and reputation systems, is whether to trust what the information says, or who recommended it. The second is whether the information comes from whom it is supposed to. In this respect, advances in encryption, public key technology (Adams, Burmeister, Desmedt, Reiter, & Zimmermann, 2000; Ellison & Scheier, 2000; Hu, 2001; Jøsang, Pedersen, & Povey, 2000), digital watermarking (Berghel, 1997, 1998; Yeung, 1998), and digital signatures (Brown, 1993; Gelbord, 2000; Schecter, 1997) have advanced the state-of-the-art considerably in recent years. The advent of a secure public key infrastructure that is available to all Internet users is particularly significant. One way in which this technology helps is through ensuring the principle of nonrepudiation—that if I have said something it is provable that I indeed did say it. This principle is naturally of great use in e-commerce situations in which credit card numbers are handed out, but it is also useful in information management generally. If I can prove that person X said something to me, or authored this document, that goes a long way to enhancing my potential trust in that document. Nonrepudiation and authentication, coupled with the recommender and reputation systems outlined above, constitute an important research avenue for information science and information systems.

However, it must be recognized that ultimately the use of technologies such as digital signatures does nothing more than transfer trust from person to authority—at the end of any digital signature line is a Certificate Authority (CA)—some authority that is ready to support individuals' claims of being who they say they are (Hestad, 2001). The trust we have in CAs must ultimately be unshakeable if this technology is to work. We are not at present convinced that we have reached that state. Among the reasons for this, perhaps the most elusive is that, ultimately, trust is a social factor. For example, we might trust banks or the government to do certain things (like look after our money or our public health), but that trust can be eroded by lack of public confidence (which could result in a run on the bank or the loss of a particular political party's credibility). In order to achieve maximum reach and trust, the CAs must demonstrate to the majority that they are unshakably trustworthy by being completely secure (Jøsang et al., 2000).

The potential lack of trust by users is where voluntary e-commerce trust standards, such as TRUSTe (Benessi, 1999; see also www.truste. org/) are also weak. If the people who guarantee that Web sites and service providers are trustworthy are also subsidized by those service providers, then their claim to be impartial, and thus their efficacy, must be in doubt (McCullagh, 1999; Rafter, 2000; Regan, 2000). At this stage, the privacy laws inherent in the European Union become more appealing: ultimately, privacy and security norms cannot be policed by the industry itself (Bennett, 2000; Dekleva, 2000).

Conclusion: Trust as a Tool for Information Science and Technology

Although the study of trust, particularly in the situations described in this chapter, involves taking a relatively new direction, progress has been remarkably swift. Much of this progress has been driven by the e-commerce explosion, which has finally directed attention toward the user experience in Web browsing. If users are unsatisfied, they will not complete the transaction, and probably will not revisit the site (Cheskin, 1999, 2000; Rehman, 2000).

For all of this, trust remains an elusive phenomenon. One of the reasons is trust's chameleon-like quality—it appears as all things to all people. In any given situation, trust can be utilized in many different ways, and none of these is the "wrong" way. In essence, then, whatever is done with respect to trust in information systems is an advance, regardless of whether this research concerns the interface or the information itself. However, only extensive research will answer questions as to the real efficacy of a particular approach. Unlike more technically oriented phenomena, trust resides within individuals and is inherently subjective. As researchers in the social sciences know, meaningfully quantifying something that is subjective is difficult and, to a large extent, subconscious.

One answer to this problem is to try to move trust from the subjective to the objective, and the various formalizations described here seek to do so. They are as yet imperfect models of trust, each with its own problems to address, but they do give us one thing: a concrete application that we can understand, develop, discuss, and refine based on empirical observation. This benefit, we believe, will further our understanding of trust, not only in information science and technology, but also in life generally.

Future benefits from the study of trust will undoubtedly come in the form of trust allied with systems: either systems that already exist, such as the common Web browser and the browsing experience, or systems yet to be developed. We envision a complete information architecture that can not only route information, but also judge, rate, and classify that information based on social knowledge and norms of trust.

Whatever the application of trust, it is clear to us that the current surge of interest in the phenomenon will continue for some time. Far too much potential benefit to consumers, users, and suppliers of information and information systems is at stake for it to be otherwise.

Acknowledgments

The authors wish to thank Elisabeth Davenport and three anonymous reviewers for their comments on an earlier version of this chapter.

Bibliography

Abdul-Rahman, A., & Hailes, S. (1997). A distributed trust model. In *Proceedings of the new security paradigms workshop*. New York: ACM Press. Retrieved December 9, 2001, from http://www.acm.org/pubs/articles/proceedings/commsec/283699/p48-abdul-rahman/p48-abdul-rahman.pdf.

Abdul-Rahman, A., & Hailes, S. (1999). Relying on trust to find reliable information. In *Proceedings, International Symposium on Database, Web and Cooperative Systems (DWACOS '99)* Baden-Baden, Germany. Retrieved December 9, 2001, from http://www.cs.ucl.ac.uk/staff/F.AbdulRahman/docs/dwacos99.pdf.

Abdul-Rahman, A., & Hailes, S. (2000). Supporting trust in virtual communities. *Proceedings of the 33rd Hawaii International Conference on System Sciences*. Retrieved May 28, 2002, from http://computer.org/proceedings/hicss/0493/04936/04936007.pdf.

Adams, C., Burmeister, M., Desmedt, Y., Reiter, M., & Zimmerman, P. (2000). Which PKI (public key infrastructure) is the right one? [Panel session]. *Proceedings of the 7th ACM Conference on Computer and Communications security*, 98–101.

Arendt, H. (1986). Communicative power. In S. Lukes (Ed.), Power (pp. 59–74). Oxford, UK: Blackwell. (Reprinted from *On violence*, by H. Arendt, 1969, Orlando, FL: Harcourt Brace.)

Atiyah, P. S. (1981). *Promises, morals and laws*. Oxford, UK: Clarendon Press.

Baba, M. (1999). Dangerous liaisons: Trust, distrust, and information technology in American work organisations. *Human Organization, 58*, 331–347.

Bacharach, M., & Gambetta, D. (2000). Trust in signs. In K. Cook (Ed.), *Social structure and trust.* New York: Russell Sage. Retrieved July 10, 2002, from http:// www.economics.ox.ac.uk/Research/Breb/TSI/trust.pdf.

Baier, A. (1986). Trust and antitrust. *Ethics, 96,* 231–260.

Barber, B. (1983). *The logic and limits of trust.* New Brunswick, NJ: Rutgers University Press.

Benessi, P. (1999). TRUSTe: An online privacy seal program. *Communications of the ACM, 42*(2), 56–59.

Bennett, C. J. (2000). An international standard for privacy protection: Objections to the objections. *Proceedings of the Tenth Conference on Computers, Freedom and Privacy: Challenging the Assumptions,* 33–38.

Berghel, H. (1997). Watermarking cyberspace. *Communications of the ACM, 40*(11), 19–24.

Berghel, H. (1998). Digital watermarking makes its mark. *Networker, 2*(4), 31–38.

Bhavsar, V., Ghorbani, A., & Marsh, S. (2000). Keyphrase-based information sharing in the ACORN architecture. In E. Horlait (Ed.), *Proceedings MATA 2000: Mobile Agents for Telecommunications Applications* (pp. 245–258). Berlin: Springer.

Bickmore, T., & Cassell, J. (2001). Relational agents: A model and implementation of building user trust. *Conference on Human Factors in Computing Systems,* 396–403.

Bigley, G., & Pearce, J. (1998). Straining for shared meaning in organization science. *Academy of Management Review, 23,* 405–421.

Bisantz, A., Llinas, J., Seong, Y., Finger, R., & Jian, J-Y. (2000). *Empirical investigations of trust-related systems vulnerabilities in adversarial decision making.* (United States Air Force Research Laboratory Report No. AFRL-HE-WP-TR-2000-0115.)

Blaze, M., Feigenbaum, J., & Lacy, J. (1996). Decentralized trust management. *IEEE Symposium on Security and Privacy,* 164–173.

Blaze, M., Feigenbaum, J., Resnick, P., & Strauss, M. (1996). Managing trust in an information labeling system. (AT&T Research Report 96-15). Retrieved December 9, 2001, from http://www.research.att.com/resources/trs/TRs/96/96. 15/96.15. 1.abs.html.

Boon, S. D., & Holmes, J. G. (1991). The dynamics of interpersonal trust: Resolving uncertainty in the face of risk. In R. A. Hinde & J. Groebel (Eds.), *Co-operation and prosocial behaviour* (pp. 190–211). Cambridge, UK: Cambridge University Press.

Brown, P. W. (1993). Digital signatures: Can they be accepted as legal signatures in EDI? *ACM Conference on Computer and Communications Security,* 86–92.

Burt, R., & Knez, M. (1996). Trust and third-party gossip. In R. M. Kramer & T. R. Tyler (Eds.), *Trust in organizations: Frontiers of theory and research* (pp. 68–89). Thousand Oaks, CA: Sage Publications.

Cassell, J., & Bickmore, T. (2000). External manifestations of trustworthiness in the interface. *Communications of the ACM, 43*(12), 50–56.

Cassell, J., & Bickmore, T. (2002). Negotiated collusion: Modelling social language and its relation effects in intelligent agents. *User modeling and adaptive interfaces.* Retrieved April 11, 2002, from http://web.media.mit.edu/~bickmore/publications/unmail001.pdf.

Cassell, J., Bickmore, T., Vilhjálmsson, H., & Yan, H. (2000). More than just a pretty face: Affordances of embodiment. *Proceedings of the 2000 International Conference on Intelligent User Interfaces, 52–59.*

Casson, M. (1990). *Enterprise and competitiveness: A systems view of international business.* Oxford, UK: Clarendon Press.

Castelfranchi, C., & Falcone, R. (1999). The dynamics of trust: From beliefs to action. In *Proceedings of the '99 Autonomous Agents Workshop on Deception, Fraud and Trust in Agent Societies, 41–54.*

Castelfranchi, C., & Tan, Y. (2001). The role of trust and deception in virtual societies. In *Proceedings of the Hawaii 34th International Conference on System Sciences.* Retrieved December 9, 2001, from http://dlib.computer.org/conferen/hicss/0981/pdf/09817011.pdf.

Cheskin. (1999). *eCommerce trust study.* Retrieved December 9, 2001, from http://www.cheskin.com/think/studies/ecomtrust.html.

Cheskin. (2000). *Trust in the wired Americas.* Retrieved December 9, 2001, from http://www.cheskin.com/think/studies/trust2.html.

Child, J., & Keiser, A. (1979). Organizational and managerial roles in British and West German companies: An examination of the culture-free thesis. In C. J. Hickson & D. J. Lammers (Eds.), *Organizations alike and unlike* (pp. 251–271). London: Routledge.

Chun, K. & Campbell, J. (1974). Dimensionality of the Rotter Interpersonal Trust Scale. *Psychological Reports, 35,* 1059–1070.

Cicourel, A. V. (1972). Basic and normative rules in the negotiation of status and role. In D. Sudnow (Ed.), *Studies in social interaction* (pp. 229–258). New York: The Free Press.

Clark, M. (1993). *Interpersonal trust in the coal mining industry.* Unpublished doctoral dissertation, University of Manchester, UK.

Clark, M. C., & Payne, R. L. (1995). Interpersonal trust: A review and re-conceptualization. *Sheffield University Management School Discussion Paper Series,* No. 95.6.

Coleman, J. S. (1990). *The foundations of social theory.* Cambridge, MA: Belknap.

Cook, J., & Wall, T. (1980). New work attitude measures of trust: Organizational commitment and personal need non-fulfilment. *Journal of Occupational Psychology, 53,* 39–52.

Council on Library and Information Resources. (2000). *Authenticity in a digital environment.* Washington, DC: Council on Library and Information Resources. Retrieved December 9, 2001, from www.clir.org/pubs/reports/pub92/contents.html.

Coutu, D. L. (1998). Trust in virtual teams. *Harvard Business Review, 76*(3), 20–22.

Currall, S., & Judge, T. (1995). Measuring trust between organization boundary role persons. *Organizational Behavior & Human Decision Processes, 64,* 151–170.

Cvetkovich, G., & Lofstedt, R. (1999). *Social trust and the management of risk*. London: Earthscan.

Dasgupta, P. (1990). The role of trust in economic transactions. In D. Gambetta (Ed.), *Trust: Making and breaking co-operative relations* (pp. 49–72). Oxford, UK: Blackwell.

Davenport, E., & Cronin, B. (2000). Knowledge management: Semantic drift or conceptual shift? *Journal of Education for Library and Information Science*, 41, 294–306.

Dekleva, S. (2000). Electronic commerce: A half-empty glass? *Communications of the Association for Information Systems, 3*. Retrieved December 9, 2001, from http://cais.isword.org/articles/default.asp?vol=3&art=18.

Deutsch, M. (1962). Co-operation and trust: Some theoretical notes. In M. R. Jones (Ed.), *Nebraska Symposium on Motivation* (pp. 275–319). Lincoln: University of Nebraska University Press.

Deutsch, M. (1973). *The resolution of conflict*. New Haven, CT: Yale University Press.

Dibben, M., (2000). *Exploring interpersonal trust in the entrepreneurial venture*. London: Macmillan.

Dibben, M. R. (2001). Trust as process: A study in the application of Whiteheadian thinking to emotional experiences. *Concrescence: The Australasian Journal of Process Thought, 2*. Retrieved April 20, 2002, from http://www.alfred.north. whitehead.com/ajpt_papers/vol02/02_dibben.pdf.

Dodd, N. (1996). *The sociology of money*. Cambridge, UK: Polity Press.

Doney, P. M., Cannon, J. P., & Mullen, M. R. (1998). Understanding the influence of national culture on the development of trust. *Academy of Management Review*, 23, 601–620.

Egger, F. (2000). "Trust me, I'm an online vendor": Towards a model of trust for e-commerce system design [Abstract]. *CHI 2000 Conference on Human Factors in Computing Systems*, 101–102.

Egger, F. N., & de Groot, B. (2000). Developing a model of trust for electronic commerce: An application to a permissive marketing Web site. [Poster] *Proceedings of the 9th International World-Wide Web Conference*, 92–93.

Eisenstadt, S. N., & Roniger, L. (1984). *Patrons, clients and friends: Interpersonal relations and the structure of trust in society*. Cambridge, UK: Cambridge University Press.

Ellison, C., & Scheier, B. (2000). Inside risks: Risks of PKI: E-commerce. *Communications of the ACM*, 43(2), 151–152.

Esfandiari, B., & Chandrasekharan, S. (2000). On how agents make friends: Mechanisms for trust acquisition. *MICON 2000 workshop*. Retrieved December 9, 2001, from http://micmac.mitel.com/micon2000.htm.

Fogg, B. J., Marshall, J., Laraki, O., Osipovich, A., Varma, C., Fang, N., Paul, J., Rangnekar, A., Shon, J., Swani, P., & Treinen. M. (2001). What makes Web sites credible? A report on a large quantitative study. *Proceedings CHI 2001: Conference on Human Factors in Computing Systems*, 61–68.

Foner, L., & Crabtree, I. B., (1996). Multi-agent matchmaking. *BT Technology Journal, 14*(4), 115–123.

Fox, A. (1985). *Man mismanagement.* London: Hutchinson.

Friedman, B., Kahn, P., & Howe, D. (2000). Trust online. *Communications of the ACM, 43*(12), 34–40.

Fukuyama, F. (1995). *Trust: The social virtues and the creation of prosperity.* London: Hamish Hamilton.

Gabarro, J. (1978). The development of trust, influence and expectations. In J. Gabarro & A. Athos (Eds.), *Interpersonal Behavior: Communication and Understanding in Relationships* (pp. 290–303). Englewood Cliffs, NJ: Prentice-Hall.

Gambetta, D. (1990). *Trust: Making and breaking co-operative relations.* Oxford, UK: Blackwell.

Gelbord, B. (2000). Viewpoint: Signing your 011001010. *Communications of the ACM, 43*(12), 27–28.

Giddens, A. (1991). *Modernity and self identity: Self and society in the late modern age.* Cambridge, UK: Polity.

Giffin, K. (1967). The contribution of studies of source credibility to a theory of interpersonal trust in the communication process. *Psychological Bulletin, 68,* 104–120.

Habermas, J. (1986). Hannah Arendt's communications concept of power. In S. Lukes (Ed.), *Power* (pp. 75–93). Oxford, UK: Blackwell.

Hart, K. et al. (1986). Exploring interpersonal trust and its multiple dimensions: A case study of General Motors. *Organizational Development Journal, 4*(2), 31–39.

Hertzberg, L. (1988). On the attitude of trust. *Inquiry, 31,* 307–322.

Hestad, D. R. (2001). A discretionary-mandatory model as applied to network centric warfare and information operations. Unpublished master's thesis, Naval Postgraduate School, Monterey, CA.

Hosmer, L. T. (1995). Trust: The connecting link between organization theory and philosophical ethics. *Academy of Management Review, 20,* 379–403.

Hu, Y.-J. (2001). Some thoughts on agent trust and delegation. *Proceedings of the Fifth International Conference on Autonomous Agents,* 489–496.

Hunt, J. (1986). *Managing people at work.* London: McGraw Hill.

Hupcey, J. E., Penrod, J., Morse, J., & Mitcham, C. (2001). An exploration and advancement of the concept of trust. *Journal of Advanced Nursing, 36,* 282–293.

Ivory, M. Y., Sinha, R. R., & Hearst, M. A. (2001). Empirically validated Web page design metrics. *Proceedings CHI 2001: Conference on Human Factors in Computing Systems,* 53–60.

Jarvenpaa, S., Knoll, K., & Leidner, D. (1998). Is anybody out there? Antecedents of trust in global virtual teams. *Journal of Management Information Systems, 14*(4), 29–64.

Jarvenpaa, S., & Leidner, D. (1998). Communications and trust in global virtual teams. *Journal of Computer-Mediated Communication, 3*(4). Retrieved December 9, 2001, from http://www.ascusc.org/jcmc/vol3/issue4/jarvenpaa.html.

Jarvenpaa, S., Tractinsky, N., & Saarinen, L. (1999). Consumer trust in an Internet store: A cross-cultural validation. *Journal of Computer-Mediated Communication, 5*(2). Retrieved December 9, 2001, from http://www.ascusc.org/jcmc/vol5/issue2/jarvenpaa.html.

Jennings, J. (1971). *Routes to the executive suite.* New York: McGraw Hill.

Jøsang, A. (1997). A trust policy framework. In Y. Han, T. Okamoto, S. Qing (Eds.), *International Conference on Information and Communications Security* (pp. 192–202). Berlin: Springer-Verlag.

Jøsang, A., & Tran, N. (2000). Trust management for e-commerce. *Virtual banking, 2000.* Retrieved December 9, 2001, from http://virtualbanking2000.com.

Jøsang, A., Pedersen, I. G., & Povey, D. (2000). PKI seeks a trusting relationship. *Proceedings of the Fifth Australasian Conference on Information Security and Privacy.* Retrieved April 20, 2002, from http://security.dtsc.edu.au/papers/pkitrust.pdf.

Kandzia, P., & Klusch, M. (Eds.). (1997). *Cooperative information agents. First International Workshop* Berlin: Springer.

Kaplan, R. (1973). Components of trust: Notes on the use of Rotter's scale. *Psychological Reports, 33,* 13–14.

Karvonen, K. (2000). The beauty of simplicity. *Proceedings of the ACM Conference on Universal Usability* (CUU 2000), 85–90.

Ketelaar, E. (1997). Can we trust information? *International Information and Library Review, 29,* 333–338.

Khare, R., & Rifkin, A. (1998). Trust management on the World Wide Web. *First Monday, 3*(6). Retrieved December 9, 2001, from http://www.firstmonday.dk/issues/issue3_6/khare/.

Kim, J., & Moon, J. Y. (1998). Designing towards emotional usability in customer interfaces—trustworthiness of cyber-banking system interfaces. *Interacting with Computers, 10,* 1–29.

Klusch, M., & Kerschberg, L. (Eds.). (2000). *Cooperative information agents IV: The future of information agents in cyberspace. Fourth International Workshop.* Berlin: Springer.

Klusch, M., Shehory, O., & Weiss, G. (Eds.). (1999). *Cooperative information agents Third International Workshop.* Berlin: Springer.

Klusch, M., & Weiss, G. (Eds.). (1998). *Cooperative information agents II. Second International Workshop.* Berlin: Springer.

Klusch, M., & Zambonelli, F. (Eds.). (2001). *Cooperative Information Agents V. Fifth International Workshop.* Berlin: Springer.

Knights, D., Noble, F., Vurdubakis, T., & Willmott, H. (2001). Chasing shadows: Control, virtuality and the production of trust. *Organization Studies, 22,* 311–336.

Koda, T., & Maes, P. (1996). Agents with faces: The effects of personification of agents. *Proceedings of the 5th IEEE International Workshop on Robot and Human Communication.* Retrieved December 9, 2001, from http://citeseer.nj.nec.com/article/koda96agents.html.

Krieger, E. (1997, June). Financing new ventures: A question of trust? Paper presented at the 42nd International Council for Small Business World Conference, San Francisco, CA.

Kuokka, D., & Harada, L. (1995). Matchmaking for information agents. *Proceedings of the International Joint Conference on Artificial Intelligence (IJCAI-95)*, 672–768.

Lane, C., & Bachmann, R. (1998). Trust within and between organisations: Conceptual issues and empirical applications. Oxford, UK: Oxford University Press.

Larzelere, R., & Huston, T. (1980). The dyadic trust scale: Towards understanding interpersonal trust in close relationships. *Journal of Marriage and the Family, 42*, 595–604.

Lawrence, S. (2001, May 31). Online or invisible? *Nature, 411*, 521.

Lawrence, S., & Giles, C. L. (1998, April). Searching the World Wide Web. *Science, 280*, 98.

Lawrence, S., & Giles, C. L. (1999, July 9). Accessibility of information on the Web. *Nature, 400*, 107–109.

Lee, J., Kim, J., & Moon, J. Y. (2000). What makes Internet users visit cyber stores again? Key design factors for customer loyalty. *CHI 2000 Conference on Human Factors in Computing Systems*, 305–312.

Lee, J. D., and Moray, N. (1992). Trust and allocation of function in human-machine systems. *Ergonomics, 35*, 1243–1270.

Lee, J. D., & Moray, N. (1994). Trust, self-confidence and operators' adaptation to automation. *International Journal of Human-Computer Studies, 40*, 153–184.

Lesser, E. (2000). *Knowledge and social capital*. London: Butterworth-Heinemann.

Lester, J. C., Voerman, J. L., Towns, S. G., & Callaway, C. B. (1997). Cosmo: A life-like animated pedagogical agent with deictic believability. *International Joint Conference on Artificial Intelligence, Workshop on Animated Interface Agents: Making Them Intelligent*. Retrieved December 9, 2001, from http://citeseer.nj. nec.com/lester97cosmo.html.

Lewis, J., & Weigert, A. (1985). Trust as social reality. *Social Forces, 63*, 967–985.

Lorenz, E. H. (1992). Trust and the flexible firm. *Industrial Relations, 31*, 455–472.

Low, M., & Srivatsan, V. (1995). What does it mean to trust an entrepreneur? In S. Birley & I. C. MacMillan (Eds.), *International entrepreneurship* (pp. 59–78). London: Routledge.

Luhmann, N. (1979). *Trust and power*. London: Wiley.

Marcus, A., & Gould, E. W. (2000). CROSSCURRENTS: Cultural dimensions and global Web-user interface design. *Interactions, 8*(4), 32–46.

Marsh, S. (1994). *Formalising trust as a computational concept*. Unpublished doctoral dissertation, University of Stirling, Scotland.

Marsh, S. (1995). Exploring the socially adept agent. In *Proceedings of the First International Workshop on Decentralized Intelligent Multi Agent Systems*, 301–308.

Marsh, S. (2001). And introducing: Sociaware. A new concept of information sharing utilizing trust. In *Proceedings MICON 2001*. Retrieved December 9, 2001, from http://micmac.mitel.com/micon.

Marsh, S., & Masrour, Y. (1997). Agent-augmented community information: The ACORN architecture. In H. Johnson (Ed.), *Proceedings CASCON'97: Meeting of Minds*, (pp. 72–81). Toronto: IBM Centre for Advanced Studies.

Marsh, S., & Meech, J. F. (2000). Trust in design [Abstract]. In G. Szcoillus & T. Turner (Eds.), *CHI 2000 Conference on Human Factors in Computing Systems*, 45–46.

Marsh, S., Meech, J. F., & Dabbour, A. (2000). Putting trust into e-commerce: One page at a time. *Proceedings of the Fourth International Conference on Autonomous Agents; Workshop on Deception, Fraud and Trust in Agent Societies*, 73–80.

Mayer, R. C., Davis, J. H., & Schoorman, F. D. (1995). An integrative model of organizational trust. *Academy of Management Review, 20*, 709–734.

McCullagh, D. (1999, November 5). Is TRUSTe trustworthy? *Wired News*. Retrieved December 9, 2001, from http://www.wired.com/news/politics/0,1283,32329,00.html.

Mead, G. H. (1934). *Mind, self and society*. Chicago: University of Chicago Press.

Menczer, F., Pant, G., Ruiz, M., & Srinivasan, P. (2001). Evaluating topic-driven Web crawlers. *Proceedings of the Annual ACM International Conference on Research and Development in Information Retrieval, 2001*. Retrieved December 9, 2001, from http://citeseer.nj.nec.com/menczer01evaluating.html.

Moray, N. P., Hiskes, D., Lee, J., & Muir, B. M. (1995). Trust and human interaction in automated systems. In J.-M. Hoc, P. C. Cacciabue, & E. Hollnagel (Eds.), *Expertise and technology: Cognition and human computer interaction* (pp. 183–194). Hillsdale, NJ: Lawrence Erlbaum.

Muir, B. (1987). Trust between humans and machines, and the design of interactive systems. *International Journal of Man-Machine Studies, 27*, 527–539.

Muir, B. M., & Moray, N. (1996). Trust in automation: Part 2. Experimental studies of trust and human intervention in a process control simulation. *Ergonomics, 39*, 429–460.

Nass, C. & Reeves, B. (1996). *The media equation: How people treat computers, television, and new media like real people and places*. Cambridge, UK: Cambridge University Press.

Nass, C., Steuer, J., & Tauber E. R. (1994). Computers are social actors. In *Proceedings of the Conference on Human Factors in Computing Systems*, 72–78.

Nielsen, J. (1999, March). Trust or bust. Retrieved December 9, 2001, from http://www.useit.com/alertbox/990307.html.

Noorderhaven, N. G. (1995). Trust and transactions: Toward transaction cost analysis with a differential behavioural assumption. *Tijdschrift voor Economie en Management, 15*, 5–18.

Nooteboom, B., Berger, H., & Noorderhaven, N. (1997). Effects of trust and governance on relational risk. *Academy of Management Journal, 40*, 308–338.

Olson, J., & Olson, G. (2000). i2i trust in e-commerce. *Communications of the ACM, 43*(12) 41–44.

Palmer, J. W., Bailey, J. P., & Faraj, S. (2000). The role of intermediaries in the development of trust on the WWW: The use and prominence of trusted third parties and privacy statements. *Journal of Computer-Mediated Communication*, 5(3). Retrieved December 9, 2001, from http://www.ascusc.org/jcmc/ vol5/issue3/ palmer.html.

Pant, G., & Menczer, F. (2001). MySpiders: Evolve your own intelligent Web crawlers. Retrieved December 9, 2001, from http://dollar.biz.uiowa.edu/~fil/ Papers/agents.pdf.

Patton, M. A., & Jøsang, A. (2001). Technologies for trust in e-commerce. In *Proceedings of the IFIP Working Conference on E-Commerce*. Retrieved December 9, 2001, from http://security.dstc.edu.au/papers/technotrust.pdf.

Pemberton, S. (2001). Reflections: The culture of uncertainty. *Interactions*, 8(5), 51–52.

Philosophe (2000). Trust and trustworthiness. *philosophe.com*. Retrieved December 9, 2001, from http://www.philosophe.com/commerce/trust.html.

Porter, T., & Lilley, B. (1996). The effects of conflict, trust and task commitment on project team performance. *International Journal of Conflict Management*, 7, 361–376.

Povey, D. (1999). Developing electronic trust policies using a risk management model. In *Proceedings of the 1999 CQRE [Secure] Congress*. Retrieved December 9, 2001, from http://security.dstc.edu.au/staff/povey.papers/CQRE/123/pdf.

Prusak, L., & Cohen, D. (2000). *In good company: How social capital makes organizations work*. Cambridge, MA: Harvard Business School Press.

Rafter, M. V. (2000, March 6). Trust or bust. *The Industry Standard*. Retrieved December 9, 2001, from http://www.thestandard.com/article/0,1902,12445,00. html.

Reed, M. (2001). Organization, trust and control: A realist analysis. *Organization Studies*, 22, 201–228.

Regan, K. (2000, August 25). TRUSTe stung by own privacy gaffe. *E-commerce Times*. Retrieved December 9, 2001, from http://www.ecommercetimes.com/ perl/story/4122.html.

Rehman, A. (2000). Holiday 2000 e-commerce: Avoiding $14 billion in "silent losses." *Creative Good Report*. Retrieved December 9, 2001, from http://www. creativegood.com.

Resnick, P., & Miller, J. (1996). PICS: Internet access controls without censorship. *Communications of the ACM*, 39(10), 87–93.

Resnick, P., Zeckhauser, R., Friedman, E., & Kuwabara, K. (2000). Reputation systems. *Communications of the ACM*, 43(12), 45–48.

Robins, M. H. (1984). *Promising, intending and moral autonomy*. Cambridge, UK: Cambridge University Press.

Rosenbloom, A. (2000a). Trusting technology. *Communications of the ACM*, 43(12), 31–32.

Rosenbloom, A. (Ed.). (2000b). Trust [Special issue]. *Communications of the ACM*, 43(12).

Ross, W., & La Croix, J. (1996). Multiple meanings of trust in negotiation theory and research: A literature review and integrative model. *International Journal of Conflict Management*, 7, 314–360.

Rotter, J. (1967). A new scale for the measurement of interpersonal trust. *Journal of Personality, 35,* 651–665.

Rotter, J. (1971). Generalized expectancies for interpersonal trust. *American Psychologist, 26,* 443–452.

Rotter, J. (1980, October). Trust and gullibility. *Psychology Today, 14,* 35–42.

Rousseau, D., Sitkin, S., Burt, R., & Camerer, C. (1998). Not so different after all: A cross-discipline view of trust. *Academy of Management Review, 23,* 393–404.

Sako, M. (1992). *Prices, quality and trust: Inter-firm relations in Britain and Japan.* Cambridge, UK: Cambridge University Press.

Sako, M. (1995). *The informational requirement of trust in supplier relations: Evidence from Japan, the UK and the USA.* Paper prepared for the Workshop on Trust and Learning, Paris.

Schecter, R. (1997). Security and authentication with digital signatures: How one university uses PGP and digital signatures to make its network secure. *Linux Journal.* Retrieved December 9, 2001, from http://www.linuxjournal.com/article.php?sid=2304.

Schlick, M. (1974). *A general theory of knowledge.* New York: Springer-Verlag.

Schneider, J., Kortuem, G., Jager, J., Fickas, S., & Segall, Z. (2000). Disseminating trust information in wearable communities. *Second International Symposium on Handheld and Ubiquitous Computing (HUC2K).* Retrieved December 9, 2001, from http://www.cs.uoregon.edu/research/wearables/Papers/HUC2K.pdf.

Shapiro, S. (1987). The social control of impersonal trust. *American Journal of Sociology, 93,* 623–658.

Shaw, M. (1971). *Group dynamics.* New York: McGraw Hill.

Shneiderman, B. (2000). Designing trust into online experiences. *Communications of the ACM, 43*(12), 57–59.

Stack, L. (1978). Trust. In H. London & J. Exner (Eds.), *Dimensions of personality* (pp. 561–599). London: Wiley.

Sztompka, P. (1999). Trust: A sociological theory. Cambridge, UK: Cambridge University Press.

Theilmann, W., & Rothermel, K. (1999). Disseminating mobile agents for distributed information filtering. *First International Symposium on Agent Systems and Applications / Third International Symposium on Mobile Agents,* 152–161.

Thomas, R. (1997, August 4). Make friends and profit by them. *Guardian,* p. 17.

Thompson, P., & McHugh, D. (1990). *Work organizations.* London: MacMillan.

Turner, A., & Nowell, L. (2000). Beyond the desktop: Diversity and artistry [Abstract]. In G. Szcoillus & T. Turner (Eds.), *CHI 2000 Conference on Human Factors in Computing Systems,* 35–36.

Urban, G. L., Sultan, F., & Qualls, W. (1999). Design and evaluation of a trust based advisor on the Internet. *MIT E-Commerce Research Forum.* Retrieved December 9, 2001, from http://ecommerce.mit.edu/forum/papers/ERF141.pdf.

Weber, M. (1925). *Wirtschaft und Gesellschaft* [Economy and society]. Tubingen: Mohr.

Wenger, E. (1998). *Communities of practice: Learning, meaning, and identity.* New York: Cambridge University Press.

Wenger, E. (2000). Communities of practice and social learning systems. *Organization, 7,* 225–246.

Wilson, P. (1983). *Second-hand knowledge: An inquiry into cognitive authority.* Westport, CT: Greenwood Press.

Worchel, P. (1979). Trust and distrust. In W. G. Austin & P. Worchel (Eds.), *Social psychology of intergroup relations* (pp. 174–187). Monterey, CA: Brooks/Cole.

Wrightsman, L. (1964). Measurement of philosophies of human nature. *Psychological Reports, 14,* 328–332.

Yeung, M. (Ed.). (1998). Digital watermarking [Special issue]. *Communications of the ACM, 41*(7).

CHAPTER 11

Information and Equity

Leah A. Lievrouw
Sharon E. Farb
University of California, Los Angeles

Background and Definitions

Inequities in information creation, production, distribution, and use are nothing new. Throughout human history some people have been more educated, better connected, more widely traveled, or more well-informed than others. Until recently, relatively few have enjoyed the benefits of literacy, and even fewer could afford to own books. In the age of mass media, societies and social groups have varied dramatically in terms of their access to and uses of print, radio, television, film, telephone, and telegraph.

What is new, however, is the growing attention being given to informational inequities in an increasingly information-driven global economy. Across disciplinary, national, and cultural boundaries, the widespread agreement is that the use of newer information and communication technologies (ICTs), particularly the Internet, has accelerated the production, circulation, and consumption of information in every form. But also a growing sense has arisen that ICTs have helped to exacerbate existing differences in information access and use, and may even have fostered new types of barriers. As Hess and Ostrom (2001, p. 45) point out, "Distributed digital technologies have the dual capacity to increase as well as restrict access to information." Similarly, Stevenson

(2000, p. 10) notes that, "Like other communication technologies, the Internet has the potential to both centralize and decentralize power." Economists, sociologists, politicians, and information professionals are keenly aware of these shifts, and in recent years have produced a raft of studies examining the social, political, cultural, and economic implications of the so-called "digital divide."

Of course, the relationship between information and social equity is not just a matter of technology. Questions of informational equity must be reassessed periodically in light of changing social, political, cultural, and economic conditions. As the social and material conditions of society evolve, old arrangements and understandings may break down or be supplanted by new ones. Notions of equity and inequity are dynamic, and depend on both stated and unstated principles and assumptions. They can be fully understood only within specific contexts, or, to paraphrase Amartya Sen, by addressing the question "equity of what?" (Sen, 1992).

Therefore, in this chapter we review a selection of recent studies from various disciplines on information and social equity, and on the digital divide. Our primary purpose is to use this overview as an opportunity to outline a basic conceptual framework for thinking about information equity. The following discussion has three main parts.

First, we review a long tradition of research, ranging from early studies of the information "rich and poor" through today's explorations of the digital divide, in which information access and use are generally assumed to be functions of individual and/or group demographics (e.g., income, gender, age, language, ethnicity, education level, geographic location) or other traits. We characterize this as the *vertical* or hierarchical perspective because it associates better information access and use with greater social and economic advantages. Historically this has been the prevalent (and often the sole) approach to the study of inequities and the formulation of relevant policy.

From this perspective information tends to be viewed as a kind of private good or commodity; people use their social and economic advantages to acquire more of it, or to obtain scarce or high-quality information. People who are (for example) wealthier, more educated, younger, or who live in affluent neighborhoods are assumed to have greater access to all kinds of information, and are better able to use it, than those who are poorer, less educated, older, live in poor or rural areas, and so on. Therefore, in most studies of information equity, social groups and individuals are compared or classified in terms of their demographics and other socioeconomic characteristics because those characteristics are taken as proxies for information access and use (McCreadie & Rice, 1999).

By the same token, analysts who make these vertical assumptions tend to conceptualize information access and use problems as a straight-forward matter of the distribution of goods, including technological systems, financial support, social services, and information sources. From this perspective, greater equality of information access and use can be achieved by a more even redistribution of these goods among various groups, and indeed, most policy proposals to date have focused almost exclusively on this goods-distribution approach.

But another body of work takes a different view—namely, that people and groups with *similar* social and economic traits may nonetheless vary widely in terms of their information needs, access, and use. We characterize this as the *horizontal* or heterarchical perspective[1] because it focuses on the differences in people's interests, concerns, expertise, experiences, and social contexts that affect their requirements for and uses of information, even within the same community, economic, or ethnic group.

From this perspective, information is seen more as an intangible public good that is highly subjective and context dependent. The quantity of resources available to an individual or group may be less important than the quality or salience of what is available from the point of view of the people involved. A growing number of observers, influenced by thinkers like Amartya Sen and John Rawls, argue that the fairness or *equity* of access and use, rather than the more or less equal distribution of information goods, may be a more useful foundation for studying inequities and formulating appropriate social policies. From the horizontal viewpoint, policy should consider values and content issues (Lievrouw, 2000; Schement, 1995) and how well people are able to make use of the resources they have in a particular context (Garnham, 1999; Besser, 1995).

Although this perspective may seem intuitively obvious (for example, no two engineers, day care workers, or historians will seek and use information in precisely the same way), it has generally been neglected in research and policy discussions on the grounds that such differences are a matter of personal choice or idiosyncrasy, and thus not suitable (or easy) objects for study or policy intervention. Still, they can have important social consequences, particularly as ICTs increasingly allow some people to tailor or customize available information to their interests and situations.

We conclude our discussion by proposing that information equity can be achieved only by integrating both perspectives in the formulation of information policy. We suggest five primary elements (access, skills, content, values, context) that should be incorporated into any analysis of equitable information access and use.

Equity vs. Equality

The concepts of equity and equality have long histories in social theory and research, yet they are seldom consistently defined. To complicate matters, notions of equity are often confounded with definitions of equality, as when Sen says that "The concepts of *equity* and justice have changed remarkably over history, and as the intolerance of stratification and differentiation has grown, the very concept of *inequality* has gone through radical transformation" (Sen, 1973, pp. 1–2; emphasis added).

For example, constitutional scholar Laurence Tribe (1988, citing Dworkin) uses the term *equality* to denote two distinct legal principles. On one hand is *equality of treatment*, the ideal embodied in the U.S. Constitution as "equal justice under the law." It is reserved for limited situations, such as voting, in which every person must be granted identical privileges or rights. On the other hand, he describes the *right to treatment as an equal*, a principle of American legal tradition that is not tied to any particular Constitutional language. It says that the state must treat each individual with equal *regard* as a person, no matter what his or her particular interests may be, and acknowledges that the conditions or outcomes of treatment may vary from case to case.

In discussions of information access and use, it may in fact be crucial to distinguish between equity and equality. The *Oxford English Dictionary* defines *equality* as "the quality or condition of being equal" and *equal* as "identical in magnitude, number, value, intensity, etc.; possessing a like degree of a (specified or implied) quality or attribute; on the same level in rank, dignity, power, ability, achievement, or excellence; having the same rights or privileges." This definition has the advantage of specifying the criteria by which equality might be measured or evaluated. For example, sociologist Charles Tilly (1998, p. 25) defines "human inequality" as the "uneven distribution of attributes among a set of social units such as individuals, categories, groups, or regions."

The *OED* definition of *equity*, on the other hand, is more nuanced: "the quality of being equal or fair; fairness, impartiality." Its etymology derives from the Greek *epiky*, meaning "principles of reasonableness and moderation in the exercise of one's rights." Unlike equality, it is more difficult to specify universal criteria for "reasonableness and moderation" that would make it possible to assess absolutely whether a social situation is equitable or not, or to make comparisons across situations with regard to their relative degrees of equity.

However, as Michael Gorman (2000) notes, when it comes to discussions of information access and use, the concept of equity does have one important edge over equality: equity, or fairness, of access to information across individuals or groups is attainable, whereas strict equality of access is not. In our view, this characteristic of attainability or possibility is precisely what makes equity a more useful term for both scholarly research and pragmatic policy making. It has the advantage of other "terms of art" in legal and policy discussions, such as the "public interest" or "reasonable doubt," which can be adapted flexibly as times and circumstances require.

We also agree with our *ARIST* predecessor, Ron Doctor (1992, p. 52), that equity is the more appropriate term because "equity embodies the idea of justice according to natural law or right as opposed to equality which means identical in value." Clearly, where information is concerned very few social situations exist in which information resources can be characterized as identical in value.

By the term "information equity," then, we mean the fair or reasonable distribution of information among individuals, groups, regions, categories, or other social units, such that those people have the opportunity to achieve whatever is important or meaningful to them in their lives. To the extent that information is unfairly distributed, people are denied such opportunities and information inequity exists. In such circumstances, policies should be formulated to promote more equitable information access and use.

Why Equity?

Why do we care about information and social equity? The main answer is that equitable access to information is, in principle, a fundamental and necessary (though not sufficient) condition for effective personal achievement and social participation, in whatever contexts and to whatever degree people consider important. As economist and philosopher Amartya Sen points out, "every plausibly defendable ethical theory of social arrangements tends to demand equality in *some* 'space,' requiring equal treatment of individuals in some significant aspect—in terms of some variable that is important in that particular theory" (Sen, 1992, p. 130; emphasis in the original). In information studies and a few other fields, information access is that important variable, that significant "space." Indeed, it is difficult even to conceive of other "spaces" for equality that would not require access to information as a prerequisite, including economic opportunity, creativity, self-sufficiency, freedom, security, or psychological well being.

So information equity, in our view, has value in and of itself. But another key reason why we are concerned with equity is that inequities of access and use have important social consequences. As Deborah Young (2001, p. 8) points out, "it is the causes and consequences of some pattern of inequality, rather than the pattern itself, that raises issues of justice." And chief among these "causes and consequences" of information inequity is the role that information plays in political participation and power, as Doctor (1992) argued so forcefully in the previous *ARIST* chapter on information and social equity. Indeed, this has historically been the primary justification of equity studies in library and information science research and library policies intended to promote equity (De la Peña McCook, 2001; Shera, 1974).

Democratic political systems, in particular, make claims to legitimacy partly on the basis of their citizens' ability to seek and obtain reliable, credible information about issues that affect them, information that allows them to interact with other citizens and with their governing institutions. The relationship between information and democracy has been set out in theories of the public sphere (Habermas, 1989), deliberative democracy (Dervin, 1994; Sunstein, 2001), and discourse democracy (Hagen, 1992; Lievrouw, 1994).

Indeed, the relationship between access to information and democratic political participation is so ingrained in the U.S. tradition that Americans have come to have "democratic expectations" about their sources of information (Gurevitch & Blumler, 1990). This premise is embodied in the "marketplace of ideas" concept and in key public institutions that have been established to ensure broad-based access to information (e.g., compulsory public education, land-grant universities, the U.S. Government Printing Office, public libraries, the speech and press freedoms of the First Amendment to the Constitution, and the U.S. Postal Service).

Certainly many other reasons also explain why the link between information and social equity is a perennial issue for study and debate, including interest in cultivating knowledge, art, culture, science, and technology. Space is too limited here to discuss them all. But for present purposes, we can say that no social arrangements, indeed, no culture or society, can exist without information; and we believe that a primary requirement for a "good society" is equitable information access and use.

Two Perspectives on Information and Equity

The Vertical Perspective

Most information equity research has taken the social, economic, and demographic characteristics of different groups as a point of departure. Such studies suggest that these characteristics influence, or can even determine, the group's information needs, access, and use; that is, groups with more socially or economically advantageous characteristics enjoy better information access and use than less advantaged groups. We do not attempt an exhaustive review of this literature here. But in this first part of the discussion we highlight a series of landmark studies that we think best illustrate the key problems, and the typical research strategies, of what we call "vertical" studies of information equity.

Information Rich and Poor

Concerns about information access and use have become more visible with the recent spread of new information technologies and services. However, these concerns are just the latest manifestation of a much older debate about the nature and prevalence of "information haves and have-nots" (Arunachalam, 1998) or the "information rich and poor" in society (Haywood, 1995).[2] In information studies, this line of research extends back at least to Bernard Berelson's (1949) study of library use in the U.S., where he found that library use was positively related to income, education, and other socioeconomic status (SES) variables.

As the language of "rich" and "poor" suggests, most of these studies assume (sometimes implicitly) that people with more wealth or other social advantages are better able to obtain and use information, just as they can other private goods and services. The studies also assume (if tacitly) that information has the characteristics of a private good or commodity that can be exchanged for other social or economic advantages. Technology has made information "costly to produce, but very cheap to reproduce, especially in digital form" (Shapiro & Varian, 1997, p. 5). Therefore, the reasoning goes, virtually any type of information can be treated as having material properties, and thus can be exchanged in market-type relationships.

The commodity view is commonly (although not universally) held in information studies (Meadow & Yuan, 1997), perhaps because it equates information with its recorded forms (i.e., documents or other material artifacts that are produced, managed, circulated, stored, and maintained).[3] Advocates claim that information must be treated as a good or commodity to ensure effective information management and retrieval (Buckland, 1991), or to formulate effective economic and policy decisions (Branscomb, 1994), given current technological systems and institutional structures.

In the mid-1970s, Childers and Post (1975) wrote their classic assessment of the "information poor in America." They framed their study using a model of information delivery resembling the linear sender-receiver model of communication, which casts individuals as receivers with needs for particular types of information: "Need is a construct, an abstraction that has been developed from a number of indirect observations such as what a person says he needs, or how he acts" (Childers &

Post, 1975, p. 15). Similar to Berelson's earlier findings, their survey data indicated that information poverty was associated with economic and social disadvantages.

Their findings also paralleled studies in communication research that examined differences in the consumption of mass media content by different social groups (Dervin & Greenberg, 1972; Siefert, Gerbner, & Fisher, 1989). Most notably among these studies, Tichenor, Donohue, and Olien (1970) developed the "knowledge gap" hypothesis. This hypothesis states that flows of information into a community are likely to produce "an increase of the gap in information acquisition between members of lower and upper socioeconomic status (SES), thereby exacerbating the existing inequities" (Viswanath, Kosicki, Fredin, & Park, 2000, p. 28; see also Viswanath & Finnegan, 1996). According to the knowledge gap theory, the education level of different groups in the community is among the most important factors affecting their exposure to information. Subsequent knowledge gap studies have suggested that people's interest in, or motivations about, a particular topic, and the extent of their interpersonal ties within the community, are just as influential as education in determining which groups know about a topic.

By 1977 sufficient studies of the characteristics of library users had been published that Zweizig and Dervin (1977) could conduct the first meta-analysis of this research. They found that, although results varied somewhat according to the research design and how survey questions were asked, all of the studies had obtained data about library users' demographics (e.g., age, sex, race, marital status, SES, and education). Across the entire set of studies they analyzed, education level was the strongest predictor of library use. However, education was so closely correlated with SES variables such as income or occupation that it was difficult to distinguish the effects of SES from education.

Zweizig and Dervin also found that library use correlated positively with heavy reading habits, extensive social networks (i.e., community involvement), certain information use variables (the number of information needs and potential information sources named by the respondents), and selected personality measures (achievement motivation and open-mindedness). However, library use was only moderately correlated with the user's distance from the library and length of residence in the community. Zweizig and Dervin (1977) concluded that studies of library users' characteristics were unlikely to provide data that would help libraries reach new audiences or be more accountable to their communities.

Despite Zweizig and Dervin's skepticism about SES and other demographic factors, however, the association between material wealth or social status and access to information has remained a key assumption in subsequent studies of information access and equity. International policy organizations, including the Organisation for Economic Co-operation and Development (OECD), UNESCO (United Nations Educational, Scientific, and Cultural Organization), and others, routinely associate access to information resources and services (e.g., telephone service or education) with demographic variables or SES data. In a recent report on intra- and cross-national "gaps" in information access and use issued by the Social Responsibilities Discussion Group of the International Federation of Library Associations and Institutions (IFLA), Kagan (1999, p. 1) underlines the relationship between wealth and information access:

> To a greater or larger extent all countries have information gaps. The United States and South Africa are examples of two countries that have extremely skewed distribution of wealth, resulting in excellent information services for some and poor or non-existent services for others.

He then goes on to define the "information poor" as

> (1) The economically disadvantaged populations of the developing countries (The South); (2) Rural people who are often geographically isolated by lack of communication and transportation systems; (3) Those disadvantaged by cultural and social poverty, especially the illiterate, the elderly, women, and children; (4) Minorities who are discriminated against by race, creed and religion; and (5) The physically disabled.

The IFLA report is consistent with the historical concern among public librarians that poorer communities must be well served to help those groups participate in democratic processes. De la Peña McCook (2001) has called this the "democratizing function" of libraries. She traces the evolution of American public library policies and practices, and finds evidence to support four factors that Jesse Shera (1974, pp. 221–222) identified previously as links between the American universal schooling movement and the movement for tax-supported public libraries:

> (1) The growing awareness of the ordinary man and his importance to the group; (2) the conviction that universal literacy is essential to an enlightened people; (3) a belief in the practical value of technical studies; and (4) an enthusiasm for education for its own sake.

De la Peña McCook suggests that librarians must understand the socioeconomic context of poverty in order to design and deliver effective information and outreach services.

The American Library Association's (ALA) recent equity policies have also concentrated on the needs of social groups with economic, gender, race, physical, or geographic disadvantages (for examples, see the Web site for the ALA Office of Information and Technology Policy, http://www.ala.org/oitp/). In 1990 the ALA adopted a policy that specifically addressed library services for the poor, again with the aim of improving their political enfranchisement and participation: "It is crucial that libraries recognize their role in enabling poor people to participate fully in a democratic society, by utilizing a wide variety of available resources and strategies" (American Library Association, 1999, online).

In recent years, some equity researchers have moved away from broad-based social surveys and analyses to study communities and groups in depth using ethnographic techniques such as interviewing or participant observation. Like the larger-scale studies, however, these projects are generally motivated by the premise that social disadvantages produce informational disadvantages.

For example, following the lead of the earlier "knowledge gap" studies, Elfreda Chatman investigated what she called the "information worlds" of the working poor, older women, prisoners, and low-skilled workers (Chatman, 1985, 1987, 1992, 2000; Chatman & Pendleton, 1995). She found that these groups' social and cultural norms influence their behavior in ways that can adversely affect their access to information, and so contribute to "information poverty" (Chatman, 1996).

Similarly, Lipinski (1999b) found that people who need legal assistance but cannot afford computer-assisted legal research, including prisoners and other "lower order litigants," are less able to find and cite unpublished precedents online to prepare their cases than are "upper order litigants."

In recent case studies, gender has been proposed as a factor in both the provision of and access to information services (Harris, 1995/1996; Shade, 1998). Ethnic and language groups have been compared in terms of their information access and use (Liu, 1995). Chu (1999) argues that linguistic minorities' literacy practices differ from those of majorities, and therefore influence minorities' access to information. Other analysts have suggested that certain members of minority language or inner-city communities may act as information "gatekeepers" for other members, and have a profound influence on the availability and flow of information within a community (Agada, 1999; Metoyer-Duran, 1991, 1993a, 1993b).

The 1990s and the Digital Divide

In the last decade, studies of information access and use by different social groups have been overshadowed to some extent by the growing importance of new information technologies, particularly networked computing and multimedia available via the Internet and the World Wide Web. In the 1990s these systems and services diffused well beyond their original bases in research, higher education, and a few major industries into diverse workplaces, homes, and leisure activities, especially with the advent of wireless services.

Figures from the OECD illustrate the scope of the changes, both in the U.S. and abroad. In 1988, American information technology (IT) industries were already growing at more than double the rate of the overall U.S. economy. At that time they represented 8.2 percent of U.S. gross domestic product; but by the mid-1990s, on average, they accounted for over one-quarter of total real economic growth each year. In 2000, the Organisation for Economic Co-operation and Development (2000, p. 2) noted that the U.S. "is the lead country in terms of IT expenditures and IT share as a share of GDP. Owing to the size of the U.S. market, its IT market structure and growth are similar to those of the OECD as a whole."

Again, the primary concern, even in this context of spectacular technological growth, has been that poor and disadvantaged groups are relatively less able to access and use IT. As early as 1991, Doctor (1991, p. 216) warned:

> As a society we are giving inadequate attention to ensuring that as new computer and telecommunications technologies become more pervasive, their benefits are distributed in ways that don't exacerbate existing disparities between the rich and the poor.

Today, more than a decade later, it is difficult to inventory the variety of information resources supported by new technologies. Content and services that were once clearly demarcated (and regulated) according to the technological systems and institutions that produced and distributed them (e.g., print, broadcasting, still and motion film and video, audio recordings, artworks, telephony) have converged. Hybrid systems can now generate and deliver digital content in almost any form. The conventional boundaries of the institutions and industries associated with these technologies have also softened as the result of cross-ownership, innovative alliances among firms, and the development of new forms of organizing that take advantage of ICTs. All of these changes have affected the availability of information sources and technologies among different social groups.

The information "gaps" of an earlier era have been recast as the "digital divide." The U.S. National Telecommunications and Information Administration (NTIA) employed the term "digital divide" as early as 1995 in its original *Falling Through the Net* report, and in subsequent updates, to describe differences in access to telecommunications and Internet resources in different American households (U.S. Department of Commerce. National Telecommunications and Information Administration, 1995, 1998, 1999). The NTIA has taken an explicitly vertical approach to the problem, defining the digital divide as "the disparities in access to telephones, personal computers (PCs), and the Internet across certain demographic groups" (U.S. Department of Commerce. National Telecommunications and Information Administration, 1999, online). More simply, it is "the divide between those with access to new technologies and those without" (U.S. Department of Commerce, 1998, online).

Likewise, the Organisation for Economic Co-operation and Development (2001, p. 5) defines the digital divide as "the gap between individuals, households, businesses and geographic areas at different socioeconomic levels with regard both to their opportunities to access information and communication technologies (ICTs) and to their use of the Internet for a wide variety of activities." Critics charge that "society should not be separated into information haves and have-nots" along economic lines (U.S. Congress. Office of Management and Budget, 2001, online). More bluntly, the digital divide has been called "cyberapartheid" (Putnam, 2000, p. 175). Others believe that IT creates both digital divides and digital opportunities, but that bridging the divides is a necessary precondition for the blossoming of creativity worldwide: "To begin with, universal access must be defined, ideally, as a basic necessity, if not a right" (Ishaq, 2001, p. 2).

In the late 1990s, several major survey studies began to correlate Internet and telecommunications access with income, education level, race/ethnicity, age, employment, Internet experience, and computer ownership, among other variables (e.g., Cooper & Kimmelman, 1999; Hoffman, Kalsbeek, & Novak, 1996; Hoffman & Novak, 1998; Katz & Aspden, 1997a, 1997b, 1998; Kraut, Scherlis, Mukhopadhyay, Manning, & Kiesler, 1996; National Public Radio, 1999). Recently, foundations and research universities have undertaken national-scale survey research in the U.S. that tracks respondents' attitudes and beliefs about the Internet as well as their activities online (e.g., Howard, Rainie, & Jones, 2001; Nie & Erbring, 2000; University of California Los Angeles. Center for Communication Policy, 2002). Generally speaking, and in line with previous research, these studies have found that Internet access and use are positively related to favorable demographic traits or higher socioeconomic status (although some recent studies have shown that the large racial, gender, and income gaps observed in the mid-1990s are narrowing, e.g., Birdsell, Muzzio, Krane, & Cottreau, 1998; Hoffman & Novak, 1998).

Within information studies, it is argued that important roles exist for public libraries in any community-wide effort to bridge the digital divide (Bishop, Tidline, Shoemaker, & Salela, 2000). Gladieux and Watson (1999, p. 5) conclude that "the result of new technologies may be to deepen the divide between educational haves and have nots," and that the market will not solve the problem. They call for public policy that will narrow the digital divide between whites and minorities, and between the wealthy and the poor. Barraket and Scott (2001) argue that to ensure equity of information technology access in academic libraries, more resources must be directed toward infrastructure, training users in the appropriate use of ICTs, and effective support.

Limitations of the Vertical Perspective

We have reviewed just a sample of "vertical" equity studies, including studies of the digital divide, that have been conducted to date. But what seems clear, even from this selected survey, is that most of them either assume or present evidence to support the hypothesis that social and economic characteristics are related to, or influence, information access and use. More affluent, better-educated, or higher-status individuals and groups are found to have access to more information sources, a wider range of media and content consumption choices, and more online access than other groups. (They are even more frequent library visitors.) The publicity surrounding the digital divide has simply served to bring these perennial problems of informational inequity center stage.

The vertical approach has a great deal of intuitive and pragmatic appeal, especially if information is treated as an objective good, like other material goods. And of course there is a long tradition in social research of using demographics or other group characteristics as indicators or predictors of social participation, behavior, and attitudes. But disadvantages also occur in using terms like "gaps," "haves and have-nots," "rich and poor," or "divides" to discuss information resources and technologies.

As McCreadie and Rice (1999) point out, to varying degrees most current studies of information access assume or argue for a sort of reinforcing "Matthew effect" (Merton, 1968, 1988), or power law of cumulative advantage, in which greater social and economic advantages are assumed to entail more or better information access and use. ("More" and "better" are often operationalized simply as the frequency of library visits or hours spent engaged in media use, such as reading, watching television, or searching Web sites online.) In turn, so the argument goes, better access and use enhance users' social and economic resources, and thus reinforce their material advantages and circumstances.

Yet owning information or having access to particular sources or technologies may not confer any particular benefit per se. Information resources are valuable only insofar as they are meaningful or useful to the people who have access to them. The ability to derive a benefit from a resource depends to a great extent on people's skills, experience, and other contextual factors.

Moreover, the wealth/poverty, rich/poor metaphor may encourage the perception that information "wealth," like other types of wealth, is finite and cumulative. It suggests the possibility to measure with some precision just how much more or less information one person or group has or uses than another.[4] Carried to its logical conclusion, the wealth/poverty metaphor implies that information access and use among very low status or severely disadvantaged groups may approach zero, whereas elites may have far more information, which they may hoard or redistribute. At best, this seems to be a somewhat incomplete account of the complex role that information sources and technologies play in people's lives.

The Horizontal Perspective

If most studies of information equity to date have tied information access and use to social and economic status, a rival school of thought has also developed over the last decade. We call this alternative approach the horizontal perspective because its adherents see significant differences in information access and use among members of social groups as well as up and down the socioeconomic ladder, because of both the nature of information and the varying capacity of individuals to benefit from it.

From the horizontal perspective, information is not just a good or commodity like any other; it also has characteristics of a public good that anyone may use without depleting what is available for others. "Information can be both a private or public good, and many of the debates on access to it hinge on which of these factors should condition its use" (Haywood, 1995, p. 83). Therefore, information equity cannot be achieved by the redistribution of material resources—information services and systems—alone. Rather, equity is achieved only when people are able to participate effectively in whatever aspects of society, and to whatever extent, they desire. Consequently, the task for researchers is to assess the quality as well as the distribution of available resources, and whether and how well people use them. The goal of policy is to ensure that individuals are able to accomplish their particular ends and purposes, and participate effectively in society, given the information resources available to them.

In this part of the discussion we review the main philosophical and theoretical influences on the horizontal perspective, as well as recent research and scholarship that takes the horizontal approach.

Theoretical and Philosophical Influences

Within information studies, the origins of the horizontal perspective can be traced to what Dervin and Nilan (1986) describe as a paradigm shift in studies of information seeking and use that occurred in the 1970s. Dissatisfied with certain core assumptions of library and information science research, and with a growing sense of epistemological uncertainty about whether "information is discovered or constructed" (Dick, 1999, p. 309), some researchers began to move away from the traditional expert-driven, top-down design of information organization, storage and retrieval systems (Swanson, 1997). Instead of trying to adapt information seekers to existing systems, the new "user studies" seek a better understanding of the seekers themselves, how they subjectively understand the world and construct meaning, as well as the intricate variability of human social contexts and information-seeking behavior (Bates, 2001; Fidel, 2001). The new paradigm redefined "information [as] a subjective phenomenon, constructed at least to some extent by the user, and not an objective phenomenon" (Cole, 1994, p. 465).

Therefore, the shift also involved a rejection of the view of information as an objective good. Such a view, critics said, does not account for certain intangible forms of information in society that are socially constructed, context dependent, and contingent, and that help people solve problems in their everyday lives (e.g., institutional arrangements, social relationships, cultural norms, facts, ideas [Dervin, 1976]). Furthermore, they argued, information separated from its context is distorted at best and meaningless at worst (Agre, 1995; Dervin, 1980, 1983). Therefore, it is counterintuitive and even socially questionable to treat all types of information as goods to be owned and exchanged.

The horizontal perspective, thus, is grounded in a phenomenological and constructivist view of information. But it has also been influenced by the political economy of information, especially the critique of information as a commodity developed in social theories of information society and the economics of information (e.g., Antonelli, 1992; Arrow, 1984; Bell, 1973; Lamberton, 1971, 2002; Slack & Fejes, 1987). For example, critical communications scholar Herb Schiller (1983, p. 538) has insisted that "information is a social good, a vital resource that benefits the total community when made freely available for general public use." Similarly, Oscar Gandy (1988, p. 108) has proposed that

> To understand and be understood is the most basic human right, one which must be secured for all as we emerge into this postindustrial, information society. It is the right upon which all other human rights ultimately come to depend, and it may be shown to have always been central, at least in theory, to the functioning of democratic society.

A related concern in horizontal studies of equity is the justice or fairness of information access and use. In recent years the work of political philosopher John Rawls, and of the economic philosopher and Nobelist Amartya Sen, has been widely influential in this area. The two scholars have been engaged in a friendly dialogue for decades, as they have refined their respective positions regarding equality and justice (e.g., Rawls, 2001; Sen, 1992). Their thinking informs a growing body of work regarding information and equity, and so their main points are summarized here.

According to Sen (1973, p. 3), any definition of inequality entails both objective and normative aspects: "it becomes very difficult to speak of inequality in a purely objective way, and the measurement of the inequality level could be intractable without bringing in some ethical concepts." The central ethical concept in contemporary discussions of equality/equity is justice, and John Rawls's (1999, 2001) formulations of *distributive justice* and *justice as fairness* are cited by many observers.

Put simply, Rawls defines equality as "a particular principle of distributive justice—that which starts from the *prima facie* assumption that all people may legitimately make the same claims on social resources" (Hochschild, 1981, p. 46). He calls for the fair distribution of certain "primary goods," including "the basic rights and liberties ... freedom of movement and prerogatives of offices and positions of authority and responsibility[;] income and wealth ... [and] the social bases of self-respect" (Rawls, 2001, pp. 58–59).

Rawls's criterion of fairness is based on what he calls the "original position"; that is, terms of social cooperation are fair when they are the product of "an agreement reached by free and equal citizens engaged in cooperation, and made in view of what they regard as their reciprocal advantage, or good" (Rawls, 2001, p. 15). To ensure parity in such discussions, Rawls suggests a hypothetical test, the "veil of ignorance," in which participants do not know their own interests, ranks, or resources and so must take the point of view of others in the group or society in order to arrive at a fair agreement.

Sen (1999, p. 112) paraphrases this process: "Fairness for a group of people involves arriving at rules and guiding principles of social organization that pay similar attention to everyone's interests, concerns, and liberties." He accepts Rawls's concept of fairness as a point of departure, but disagrees that equality is best achieved by the fair distribution of primary goods. Famously, he asks: "Equality of what?" (Sen, 1973, 1992), and argues that such goods do not confer any advantages or state of being in and of themselves. Rather, they are a means to an end.

Sen points out that the ability of individuals to use primary goods to achieve their particular ends varies drastically from person to person, group to group, and situation to situation. There is a difference between an individual's state of well being and her or his *achievement* of well being, or agency (Garnham, 1999). Sen's principal concern is creating and maintaining individual agency; and he believes that it is more important to preserve and enhance each actor's choices than to distribute some ostensibly "essential" bundle of goods that actors may or may not consider meaningful or useful in a given situation.

Therefore, Sen says, the proper focus of any theory of social justice should be what he calls people's "functionings" and "capabilities." "Functionings are what a person does or is. Capabilities are the set of alternative functionings a person has (his or her real opportunities)" (Garnham, 1999, p. 117). Capabilities, and whether they can be exercised, are necessarily defined from the actor's point of view. Equity, then, would entail the fair distribution of opportunities to achieve whatever people may value doing or being, i.e., the fair distribution of *capabilities*, rather than of primary goods as Rawls suggests, because even the most scrupulously equal distribution of material resources will not result in equity of opportunities.

A growing number of policy researchers have adopted Sen's capabilities framework, or similar concepts, in their analyses. For example, the OECD views the cultivation of "human capital" as the key to enduring economic development (Healy, 1998), where human capital is defined as the cultivation of individual ability (Coleman, 1990). Many experts who study universal service in telecommunications and public service obligations in broadcasting now recognize that:

> Information is not like food or energy of which everybody needs a bare minimum (an information ration of sorts) in order to survive. Information only has value when a recipient has some need for it *and the capacity to process it*. Otherwise information is a resource that is of no use. (Sawhney, 2000, p. 162; emphasis added)

Nicholas Garnham advocates the capabilities approach as a new direction for social policy in communications that departs from its traditional focus on the allocation and distribution of resources like telephone dial tone or high-speed bandwidth. These resources, he argues, have already been left mainly to market forces. Communications policy, he says, must "get beyond the superficial indexes of access and usage that we so often use ... these are crude indicators and do not get to the heart of the matter" (Garnham, 1999, pp. 120–121). Although it is possible and desirable, within the capabilities approach, to specify some set of "subsistence" resources to which each member of a society in a given place and time must have access (including communication resources), "access is not enough" (Garnham, 1999, p. 121). More important, he says, is

> the ability of people actually to make use of these options, to achieve, the relevant functionings ... We need to think of newspapers and broadcasting as enablers of a range of

functionings rather than as providers of a stream of content to be consumed. (Garnham, 1999, p. 121)

A similar stance has been adopted in some library and information policy circles. A decade ago, Doctor (1991, p. 217) noted that access to technology by itself is not enough to ensure equity:

> Access will be of little benefit to large portions of the population, unless it is accompanied by equipment and training that allow effective use of that access. What we need then is a "right to access" in the broader sense of a "right to *benefit* from access (emphasis in the original)."

In a recent report to the National Library of Canada on access, equity, and the Internet, Vincent Mosco argues that Canadian social and information policy should pay as much attention to cultivating individuals' abilities and interests as to the provisions of telecommunications and Internet services:

> It is important to broaden our definition of access from the traditional idea that access means the availability of a particular set of hardware and software technologies. In a deeper sense, *access requires a set of capabilities*, intellectual, social, and cultural, from basic literacy to higher education, that are necessary to make effective use of the Information Highway. (Mosco, 2000, p. 1, emphasis added)

Social Capital and Public Goods

These combined influences—a phenomenological, subjective view of information; the critique of information commodification from political economy; a view of social justice as fairness rather than strict equality; and the capabilities approach—have led some information equity researchers to look beyond the simple distribution of resources as a solution for inequity problems. One focus is the role that people's social networks play in their information access and use, and the related concepts of social capital and public goods.

Broadly speaking, social capital is one type of capacity, in Sen's sense. It is the benefit people derive from having relationships with others in society. It "is not a single entity, but a variety of different entities ... [that] all consist of some aspect of social structure, and facilitate certain actions of individuals who are within the structure" (Coleman, 1990, p. 302). Political scientist Robert Putnam (2000, p. 21) suggests that "social capital—that is, social networks and the associated norms of reciprocity—comes in many different shapes and sizes with many different uses." And a crucial form of social capital is "the potential for information that inheres in social relations" (Coleman, 1990, p. 310), that is, what members of a social network know, and may express and share in their interactions with one another.

Several sociologically oriented writers have begun to make the case for the role of social networks in information equity (e.g., DiMaggio, Hargittai, Neuman, & Robinson, 2001; Putnam, 2000; Wellman, Salaff, Dimitrova, Garton, Gulia, & Haythornthwaite, 1996). Obviously, for most people the first and most credible information sources are family members, friends, neighbors, co-workers, fellow church or club members, and so on. Even when people do consult documentary sources, such as news media, Web sites, advertising, or library collections, they typically "check out" the information they find with other people they trust. Therefore, social networks are information sources, and they also perform an important "filtering" or contextualizing function for their members.

Social networks are also powerful information resources because they are greater than the sum of social relations and reciprocal exchanges within the group. They help shape the character or sensibility of the wider communities in which they exist (Coleman, 1990). The larger or more extensive the network, the greater its value to each individual member as a source of information and social capital. That is, social networks and the social capital they confer on their members have important *externalities*, which give them the quality of *public goods* (Putnam, 2000, p. 20). Indeed, a number of writers today argue that many types of information, technological systems, knowledge, and cultural heritage should properly be considered public, rather than private, goods (Anton, Fisk, & Holmstrom, 2000; Introna & Nissenbaum, 2000; Lessig, 1999a, 2001; Serageldin, 1999; Spar, 1999; Stiglitz, 1999; Sy, 1999; van den Hoven, 1998).

Private and public goods differ in two important respects. Characteristically, private goods are *rival in consumption*—that is, a good consumed by one person becomes unavailable for anyone else. They are also *excludable*, that is, some people can be prevented from consuming them. Food, clothing, and most other types of material goods and property are treated as private goods.

Public goods, in contrast, are *nonrival in consumption*: one person's use of the good does not deplete what is available for others. And public goods are *nonexcludable*, meaning that no one can practicably or reasonably be prevented from using them. In *The Wealth of Nations*, Adam Smith (1993) offers the classic example of a lighthouse as a public good. Its beams cannot be restricted to being seen by just some ships and not others; and one ship's use of the lighthouse as a guide does not keep any other ship from using it as well. More contemporary examples include traffic signs, broadcast television and radio signals, and the Internet, as Lawrence Lessig (1999b, online) observes: "It's out there for the taking; and what you take leaves as much for me as there was before."

Certainly, then, to the extent that information and its related technologies fulfill these criteria, they are public goods. To understand the significance of information as a public good, we can compare it with another familiar good, water. Sax (1970) argues that water belongs to a distinct and special category of property that serves as a community resource and can never fully be privatized. He cites three reasons for this special treatment.

First, water has unique physical characteristics. Unlike other important resources (e.g., petroleum), it has no physical substitute. And bodies of water act as a public commons that provides access to waterways for navigation, fishing, and recreation. Second, water has historically been given special legal treatment. The public trust doctrine, in particular, has helped to ensure universal access to water resources for navigation and sustenance. Third, water is a "heritage resource," that is, communities see water as part of their legacy. They feel strong attachments to water resources just as they do to antiquities or other cultural property.

Does information fulfill these three criteria for being uniquely "public"? Certainly, it can be said that there is no substitute for information in human affairs and life experience. As Braman (1989, p. 239) notes, it is a constitutive force in society: "Information is that which is not just embedded within a social structure, but creates the structure itself." Information also has the characteristics of a public commons, a feature that was recognized by the framers of the U.S. Constitution as a justification for both the First Amendment and Article I Section 8, which provides for copyright and the public domain to "promote science and the useful arts."

The legal and institutional history of information is also analogous to that for water. It has been treated as both a community resource to be used by everyone, and as private property and a commodity. In the U.S., important institutions (public education, public libraries, the postal service) and laws and regulations (the First Amendment to the Constitution, the public service and universal service obligations of broadcast and telecommunications carriers) safeguard the broad availability of all types of information. In 1813, Thomas Jefferson noted the "peculiar character" of information:

> No one possesses the less, because every other possesses the whole of it. He who receives an idea from me, receives instruction himself without lessening mine; as he who lights his taper at mine, receives light without darkening me. That ideas should freely spread from one to another over the globe, for the moral and mutual instruction of man, and improvement of his condition, seems to have been peculiarly and benevolently designed by nature ... Inventions then cannot, in nature, be a subject of property. Society may give an exclusive right to the profits arising from them, as an encouragement to men to pursue ideas which may produce utility, but this may or may not be done, according to the will and conventions of the society, without claim or complaint from anybody ... The exclusive right to invention [is] given not of natural right, but for the benefit of society (T. Jefferson, letter to Isaac Macpherson, 1813).

Similarly, in a dissent in *International News Service vs. Associated Press*, Justice Louis Brandeis commented that "the general rule of law is, that the noblest of human productions—knowledge, truths ascertained, conceptions, and ideas—become, after voluntary communication to others, free as the air to common use" (*International News*, 1918).

Finally, there is no question that information, like water, is a heritage resource. It is the basis and inspiration for artworks, science, culture, and politics. Indeed, it is virtually impossible to define the concepts of *cultural heritage* or *cultural property* without accounting for the role that information plays in their designation. For example, the Hague Convention Article I Section (a), the governing international regime for the disposition of cultural heritage properties, imputes intangible but expressible significance to such properties. It thus suggests that the protection and preservation of cultural heritage property in fact preserves an intangible, informational interest (Hague Convention, 1954).

The Horizontal Perspective:
The Digital Divide and Intellectual Property

Considering all the various streams of research that have informed the horizontal perspective, it is perhaps unsurprising that scholars in this camp take a different view of the extent and significance of the digital divide. As Haywood (1998, p. 25) has observed about global data networks: "The world has always been a place of haves and have-nots and [I] can see no way that internetworking is going to change this very much."

Lentz (2000) identifies two competing accounts of the digital divide. One emphasizes computer and Internet consumption and argues that the divide is disappearing. The other focuses more on continuing barriers to access and use: "Policy should focus at least as much on the context and content of technology use as it has thus far on the increased distribution of computing resources" (Lentz, 2000, p. 355). Alexander Kouzmin (2000, p. 167) agrees that the complex reality of the digital divide requires a new approach: "There is a need for a new intellectual paradigm and policy platforms of a dynamic and contingent nature which address emerging structures created by socioeconomic and technological changes in highly volatile environments."

Other observers note that despite the rapid dissemination of hardware and systems, the differences in access and use persist because training and human support are neglected. Poor and low-status groups still have less access to computer networks and online services, but "this problem might disappear before we can create a presidential commission to study it ... there is a divide in this country, but it's not digital. It's in basic academic skills and high-quality schools" (Finneran, 2000, p. 30).

In an analysis of two statewide surveys conducted in 1998, Erik Bucy found that Internet access was indeed lowest among single mothers, members of lower socioeconomic groups, and older respondents. Yet, he argued, "social access" to the Internet is just as important as physical access to systems: "Beyond the physical hardware needed to go online, social access to the Internet requires that citizens have the cognitive ability and technical skills necessary to profit from a complex media environment" (Bucy, 2000, p. 60).

The structure of information systems, and of the information available from online sources, is another concern for those who take the horizontal view. Van Alstyne and Brynjolfsson (1996) warn against the "cyberbalkanization" of social groups on the Internet; while Lievrouw (1998, p. 84) observes that networked computing and telecommunications allow people to

> resort to "our own devices" both in the sense of our personal agendas, strategies, interests, and interpretations, and of the ICT tools that help us realize them ... those of us with the right educational and technological resources [can] avoid exposure to disagreement, difference, or other information that does not serve our direct purposes or reflect our individual views of the world.

Robert Putnam (2000, p. 179) cautions that "the commercial incentives that currently govern Internet development seem destined to emphasize individualized entertainment and commerce rather than community engagement." Social capital cannot be cultivated if we confine our interactions to exchanges with "people who share precisely our interests—not just other BMW owners, but owners of BMW 2002s and perhaps even owners of turbocharged 1973 2002s, regardless of where they live and what other interests they have and we have" (Putnam, 2000, p. 177). University of Chicago law professor Cass Sunstein (2001, p. 201) agrees:

There are serious problems if information is seen as an ordinary consumer product. The simple reason is that in a system in which individuals make choices among innumerable options based only on their private interest, they will fail to learn about topics and views from which they may not much benefit, but from which others would gain a great deal.

Given these myriad factors, the National Society of Black Engineers has developed what is perhaps one of the more comprehensive approaches to equity policy. The group supports a four-part program of access, skills, values, and content to help communities employ digital technology (Institute of Industrial Engineers, 2000). Another advocacy group, Bridges.org, recently released a report that outlines key factors essential for "real access," including physical access, relevant content, sociocultural factors, trust, a supportive legal/regulatory framework, strong local and macroeconomic environments, and political will (Bridges.org, 2001).

As these studies indicate, content—and not just the forms or channels of information—is another critical element of access from the horizontal viewpoint (McCreadie & Rice, 1999). Some policy researchers have argued that information service providers (including libraries) cannot continue to be content-neutral and still provide adequate information access. This bias toward the "conduit metaphor" (Day, 2000) prevents libraries and other information services from serving the real needs of their communities; instead, to provide access, researchers and policy makers must find out what particular content is considered necessary for participation in various community contexts (Sawhney, 2000; Schement, 1995). According to Lievrouw (2000, pp. 155–156), "we should move beyond the current conduit-centered notion of access in universal service to a more participatory notion of discourse, which assumes that some content is essential for social participation."

Content is also implicated in recent debates about the extension of intellectual property rights to more diverse types of information, and over longer terms of ownership. Critics warn that information technology has allowed more and more types of information to be privatized and thus removed from public access: "Public information is fast being commoditised and privately held in the commercialization of cyberspace"

(Stevenson, 2000, p. 3). Indeed, by 1988, Herb and Anita Schiller (1988, p. 146) had already noted that:

> An economic struggle with major cultural implications, underway for 20 years, and now intensifying, goes relatively unnoticed in the national media. It pits the fundamental principle of American libraries—free access to information— against the interests of the private information suppliers and their advocates in government. The privateers seek profit from the sale of information to those who have the means to pay for it.

Only a few years later, Jessica Litman (1994, p. 429) decried what she saw as an "intellectual property epidemic"; and Pamela Samuelson (1991, p. 23) identified six features of digital media that were "likely to bring about significant changes in the [intellectual property] law," including the ease of replication, ease of transmission and multiple use, plasticity, equivalence, compactness, and nonlinearity of works in digital form.

In fact, over the last decade the scope and duration of copyright and patent protections have expanded steadily, due in large part to the development of technological systems to control access and duplication of digital materials—so-called "anti-circumvention technologies" that effectively privatize forms of information that were previously difficult or impractical to own. The *Sonny Bono Term Extension Act*, the *No Electronic Theft Act*, and the *Digital Millennium Copyright Act* in the U.S., and the European Union's database protection legislation (Lessig, 1999a; Lipinski, 1998; Litman, 1994, 2001; Samuelson, 1991, 1994) have led some to conclude that "attempts to extend legal protection to basic facts and other public domain information demonstrate that the public space is slowly [being] reduced" (Lipinski, 1999a, p. 63).

Today, the rapidly expanding horizon of intellectual property claims has been characterized as a zero-sum "information arms race with multiple sides battling for larger shares of the global knowledge pool. The records of scholarly communication, the foundation of an informed democratic society, are at risk" (Hess & Ostrom, 2001, p. 45). On the other hand, however, because facts and ideas exist as information whether they are rendered in material form or not, "members of the general public commonly find copyright rules implausible, and simply disbelieve them" (Litman, 2001, p. 29). There is still a popular sense that "most innovations and inventions are based on ideas that form the common property of humanity" (Quéau, 2000, p. 1).

Discussion and Implications

To summarize, then, in the previous sections we surveyed what we believe are two general schools of thought regarding studies of information equity. On one hand, the "vertical" approach tends to view information as a bundle of tangible, material goods that are exchanged privately as commodities (i.e., private goods); information technology has made it possible to privatize and control more types of information than ever before. A person's information access and use are, to a large extent, determined by her or his demographic traits, economic resources, and social status. Therefore, information equity can be best achieved by an even distribution of resources and technologies across different social groups.

The horizontal school of thought, on the other hand, is more likely to see information as subjective and context dependent, a community resource that is nonsubstitutable and necessary for human life, culture, and heritage (i.e., a public good). The use of technology to extend property rights to ever more types of information, therefore, threatens access to and uses of information that are essential for effective social and political participation. A person's access and use depend mainly on her or his capacity to understand and benefit from information and information technology in a particular situation. Information equity, then, is best achieved by assuring that all individuals have the background and skills to use information effectively for their particular ends and purposes, and that essential types of content remain freely available to everyone.

Obviously, there are, always have been, and likely always will be economic, social, and political inequities. But if equity is a desirable social goal, both the vertical and horizontal dimensions of access and use must be considered. The distribution of resources and systems (perhaps thought of as primary goods) should be complemented by efforts to foster social and human capital and capacities, and the provision of relevant content. At a minimum, we propose that five elements or factors should be considered in any evaluation of information equity.

The first element is clearly indicated by the decades of studies that show consistent and enduring disparities in information access and use between higher and lower socioeconomic groups. Without question, like other resources, information and information technologies are distributed unevenly; problems of information access and use are exacerbated by economic and social disadvantages. As long as information resources and technologies are distributed primarily on an ability-to-pay, market basis, these disparities will persist and are likely to grow. Therefore, continuing efforts must be made to ensure a more even distribution of information resources in society.

Second, it is equally clear that if people lack the skills and background to understand or use the information resources that are available, even the most strictly apportioned distribution of resources is meaningless. Research and policy must assess people's abilities to use the resources they have, and provide a wider range of learning opportunities for those who wish to take advantage of them.

A third factor is related to skills and background. People's capacities depend a great deal on the values they share, including support of open information resources, open inquiry, and the norms of social reciprocity and trust that make information sources credible. Education and training must incorporate the values that support information seeking, as well as convey technical skills.

Fourth, the available content must be contextually relevant and meaningful in people's lives. Some evidence suggests, for example, that a small but substantial proportion of Internet users have become "Internet dropouts" because they do not find the information online to be useful or interesting. A similar phenomenon has been observed with certain ethnic and language groups, including African-Americans (Spooner & Rainie, 2000). Research and policy should be directed to identifying what is considered essential information in various communities, and creating conditions that ensure the wide availability of such information.

Finally, much more needs to be known about the social and life contexts that shape people's information needs and interests. Certainly, a great deal of work has been done that investigates the information-seeking patterns of particular groups, primarily professionals, students, and academics. But these efforts should be expanded to include more complex everyday life contexts. These contexts are not stable, and people may inhabit or move among several contexts simultaneously, so it is critical to understand how people navigate among contexts, how contexts affect each other, and any common elements of this movement.

The framework advocated here has several implications for the evolving field of information studies. First, this approach to information equity would necessarily expand the domain of research and policy analysis beyond traditional concerns with the management and distribution of systems and services. Researchers would also need to investigate the interests, orientations, practices, and complex social relations among individuals and social groups to gain a deeper appreciation of how people obtain, understand, and use information.

Of course, this was the clear agenda behind the paradigm shift in library and information science in the 1970s described previously (Dervin & Nilan, 1986). And librarianship has a long tradition of research and service aimed at developing the skills of information seekers and library users; for example, various types of literacy or after-school programs and services. But we wish to suggest that research and policy should do more than teach people how to adapt or reframe their interests to fit existing systems and resources. More basic research is needed to learn about unconventional, socially based information resources (social networks, for example), and how to help individuals and groups design and use resources that better suit whatever people value doing or being. It requires a creative, flexible approach to hypothesizing about information needs, uses, and sources that moves beyond documents and systems to relationships, cultural practices, and how ideas diffuse in communities.

The second implication is organizational, and to some extent hinges on the first. Conventional or taken-for-granted organizational forms and processes should be rethought and redesigned. Experts in urban planning, organization studies, and economics have identified new organizational forms, such as informal alliances, information hubs, and network firms, which take advantage of information technology and infrastructure as well as the networks of social relations and expertise among individuals and groups. Such organizations change shape, dissolve, reconfigure, or reincorporate as circumstances and needs require, according to the abilities and relationships of the people within them. Increasingly, libraries, archives, and other types of cultural institutions may need this same kind of flexibility to engage effectively with the communities they serve.

To some extent, the digital library projects of the last decade were intended to lay the infrastructure for just such new ways of distributing and delivering information resources. Networked computing and telecommunications services promised to free information from geographic space and organizational "territories," and digital libraries were meant to take advantage of this dynamic (Borgman, 2000). However, as the "new economy" bubble has deflated in the 2000s, incumbent institutions have moved to shore up their traditional prerogatives and controls over content, markets, infrastructure, regulatory regimes, behavior, and so on, that they appeared to be losing to small, unconventional challengers in the 1990s (Putting IT in its place, 2001). Libraries and other cultural institutions are unlikely to be immune to the current wave of retrenchment and centralization, and so digital libraries are likely to remain tied as adjunct or ancillary services of established institutions (government agencies, educational/research institutions, private firms, nongovernmental organizations) for the foreseeable future. New avenues for organizational innovation will be needed.

The third implication of the dimensional view of equity has to do with the nature and training of information professionals. Information studies must educate information professionals who combine both traditional technical and organizational skills with an almost anthropological or sociological sensitivity to social relationships and change. The combination of vertical and horizontal equity concerns requires that information professionals develop an ability to interact with diverse individuals and groups so that they can facilitate, broker, or navigate those groups' various interests and practices—again, to achieve whatever people may value doing or being, in whatever contexts and to whatever degree people consider important. Information practice should include not only identifying and accessing existing resources, and teaching people to be "users" of those established resources; it will also require the ability to recognize and bring into play a heterogeneous range of social, cultural, and documentary information resources—interpersonal and family networks, informal links among experts, and sources of local and universal knowledge.

To conclude, then, the environmental and dimensional approach to information and social equity builds on a foundation of earlier work, but is also an attempt to open up new questions and issues for research, policy, and practice. We hope we have provided a starting point for a new and fruitful discussion.

Endnotes

1. Although we use the terms "horizontal" and "vertical" in our discussion of information equity, we do not want to suggest that these aspects are independent or orthogonal. Indeed, they are necessarily interrelated because one's vertical opportunities or circumstances may influence one's horizontal interests and activities, and vice versa. Although we use these terms, we will try to avoid the problems that led Tilly (1998) to criticize the concepts of horizontal and vertical social mobility proposed by his teacher, Pitirim Sorokin (1959). Tilly objects to the labels horizontal and vertical because they suggest that there are clear steps or ranks in each dimension (Sorokin's social strata); thus creating a matrix of slots or positions into which individuals can be classified. Certainly, a number of the "vertical" studies reviewed here do in fact regard relative social status, and therefore information access and use, in this ranked or stepwise fashion. But in our view, the two aspects are more continuous and fluid. We use the terms "horizontal" and "vertical" more as heuristic concepts than as absolute scales for measurement.

2. We encourage readers to review the previous *ARIST* chapter on equity (Doctor, 1992) for a comprehensive survey of information and equity research prior to the early 1990s, especially with regard to power and democracy.

3. Although, as Meadow and Yuan (1997) observe, to call information a commodity simply describes one of its attributes, and not its essential nature.

4. Perhaps the most remarkable attempt to measure information in this sense at the whole-society level (i.e., the production and consumption of characters, words, or documents) was made by Japanese researchers between the 1960s and 1990s, using measures such as the "johoka index" (Ito, 1981) and the "information activity index" (Kurisaki & Yanagimachi, 1992).

Bibliography

Agada, J. (1999). Inner-city gatekeepers: An exploratory survey of their information use environments. *Journal of the American Society for Information Science, 50*, 74–85.

Agre, P. E. (1995). Institutional circuitry: Thinking about the forms and uses of information. *Information Technology and Libraries, 14*, 225–230.

American Library Association. (1999). ALA policy manual. Policy 61: Library services to the poor. Retrieved February 1, 2002, from www.ala.org/alaorg/policymanual/poorservice.html.

Anton, A., Fisk, M., & Holmstrom, N. (2000). *Not for sale: In defense of public goods.* Boulder, CO: Westview Press.

Antonelli, C. (Ed.). (1992). *The economics of information networks.* Amsterdam: North-Holland.

Arrow, K. J. (1984). *Collected papers, vol. 4: The economics of information.* Oxford, UK: Blackwell.

Arunachalam, S. (1998). Information haves and have-nots. *EDUCOM Review, 33*(6), 40–45. Retrieved February 1, 2002, from http://www.educause.edu/ir/library/html/erm9863.html.

Barraket, J., & Scott, G. (2001). Virtual equality? Equity and the use of information technology in higher education. *Australian Academic & Research Libraries, 32,* 204–213.

Bates, M. J. (2001, November). Do we know it all? An examination of the state of user studies. Talk presented at the Annual Meeting of the American Society for Information Science and Technology, Washington, DC.

Bell, D. (1973). *The coming of post-industrial society: A venture in social forecasting.* New York: Basic Books.

Berelson, B. (1949). *The library's public.* New York: Columbia University Press.

Besser, H. (1995). The information superhighway: Social and cultural impact. In J. Brook & I. Boal (Eds.), *Resisting the virtual life: The culture and politics of information* (pp. 59–70). San Francisco: City Lights.

Birdsell, D., Muzzio, D., Krane, D., & Cottreau, A. (1998, April/May). Web users are looking more like America. *The Public Perspective,* 33–35.

Bishop, A. P., Tidline, T. K., Shoemaker, S., & Salela, P. (2000). Public libraries and networked information services in low-income communities. *Library & Information Science Research, 21,* 361–390.

Borgman, C. L. (2000). *From Gutenberg to the global information infrastructure: Access to information in the networked world.* Cambridge, MA: MIT Press.

Branscomb, A. (1994). *Who owns information? From privacy to public access.* New York: Basic Books.

Braman, S. (1989). Defining information: An approach for policymakers. *Telecommunications Policy, 13,* 233–242.

Bridges.org (2001). *Spanning the digital divide: Understanding and tackling the issues.* Retrieved January 2, 2002, from http://www.bridges.org/spanning.

Buckland, M. K. (1991). Information as thing. *Journal of the American Society for Information Science, 44,* 351–360.

Bucy, E. P. (2000). Social access to the Internet. *Press/Politics, 5,* 50–61.

Chatman, E. A. (1985). Information, mass media use and the working poor. *Library & Information Science Research, 7,* 97–113.

Chatman, E. A. (1987). The information world of low-skilled workers. *Library & Information Science Research, 9,* 265–283.

Chatman, E. A. (1992). *The information world of retired women.* Westport, CT: Greenwood Press.

Chatman, E. A. (1996). The impoverished life-world of outsiders. *Journal of the American Society for Information Science, 47,* 193–206.

Chatman, E. A. (2000). Framing social life in theory and research. *New Review of Information Behaviour Research*, *1*, 3–17.

Chatman, E. A., & Pendleton, V. E. M. (1995). Knowledge gaps, information-seeking and the poor. *Reference Librarian*, *49/50*, 135–145.

Childers, T., & Post, J. A. (1975). *The information poor in America*. Metuchen, NJ: Scarecrow Press.

Chu, C. M. (1999). Literacy practices of linguistic minorities: Sociolinguistic issues and implications for literacy services. *Library Quarterly*, *69*, 339–359.

Cole, C. (1994). Operationalizing the notion of information as a subjective construct. *Journal of the American Society for Information Science*, *45*, 465–476.

Coleman, J. S. (1990). Social capital. In *Foundations of social theory* (pp. 300–321). Cambridge, MA: Belknap Press.

Cooper, M., & Kimmelman, G. (1999). *The digital divide confronts the Telecommunications Act of 1996: Economic reality versus public policy*. Washington, D.C.: Consumers Union. Retrieved November 15, 2000, from http://www.consunion.org/other/telecom2-0299.htm.

Day, R. E. (2000). The "conduit metaphor" and the nature and politics of information studies. *Journal of the American Society for Information Science*, *51*, 805–811.

De la Peña McCook, K. (2001). Poverty, democracy and public libraries. In N. Kranich (Ed.), *Libraries: The cornerstone of democracy*. Chicago: American Library Association. Retrieved January 2, 2002, from http://www.cas.usf.edu/lis/faculty/PDandPL.html.

Dervin, B. (1976). The everyday information needs of the average citizen: A taxonomy for analysis. In M. Kochen & J. Donohue (Eds.), *Information for the community* (pp. 19–38). Chicago: American Library Association.

Dervin, B. (1980). Communication gaps and inequities: Moving toward a reconceptualization. *Progress in Communication Sciences*, *2*, 73–112.

Dervin, B. (1983). Information as a user construct: The relevance of perceived information needs to synthesis and interpretation. In S. A. Ward & L. J. Reed (Eds.), *Knowledge structure and use: Implications for synthesis and interpretation* (pp. 153–183). Philadelphia: Temple University Press.

Dervin, B. (1994). Information <—> democracy: An examination of underlying assumptions. *Journal of the American Society for Information Science*, *45*, 369–385.

Dervin, B., & Greenberg, B. S. (1972). The communication environment of the urban poor. In F. G. Kline & P. J. Techenor (Eds.), *Current perspectives in mass communications research* (pp. 195–233). Beverly Hills, CA: Sage.

Dervin, B., & Nilan, M. (1986). Information needs and uses. *Annual Review of Information Science and Technology*, *21*, 3–33.

Dick, A. L. (1999). Epistemological positions and library and information science. *Library Quarterly*, *69*, 305–323.

DiMaggio, P., Hargittai, E., Neuman, W. R., & Robinson, J. P. (2001). Social implications of the Internet. *Annual Review of Sociology*, *27*, 307–336.

Doctor, R. D. (1991). Information technologies and social equity: Confronting the revolution. *Journal of the American Society for Information Science, 42,* 216–228.

Doctor, R. D. (1992). Social equity and information technologies: Moving toward information democracy. *Annual Review of Information Science and Technology, 27,* 43–96.

Fidel, R. (2001, November). Do we know it all? An examination of the state of user studies. Talk presented at the Annual Meeting of the American Society for Information Science and Technology, Washington, DC.

Finneran, K. (2000). Let them eat pixels. *Issues in Science and Technology, 16,* 30.

Gandy, O. H. (1988). The political economy of communications competence. In V. Mosco & J. Wasko (Eds.), *The political economy of information* (pp. 108–124). Madison, WI: University of Wisconsin Press.

Garnham, N. (1999). Amartya Sen's 'capabilities' approach to the evaluation of welfare: Its application to communications. In A. Calabrese & J.-C. Burgelman (Eds.), *Communication, citizenship and social policy: Rethinking the limits of the welfare state* (pp. 113–124). Lanham, MD: Rowman & Littlefield.

Gladieux, L. E., & Watson, S. S. (1999). *The virtual university and educational opportunity: Issues of equity and access for the next generation.* Washington, DC.: The College Board.

Gorman, M. (2000). *Our enduring values: Librarianship in the 21st century.* Chicago: American Library Association.

Gurevitch, M., & Blumler, J. G. (1990). Political communication systems and democratic values. In J. Lichtenberg (Ed.), *Democracy and the mass media* (pp. 269–289). Cambridge, UK: Cambridge University Press.

Habermas, J. (1989). *The structural transformation of the public sphere.* (T. Burger, Trans.). Cambridge, MA: MIT Press.

Hagen, I. (1992). Democratic communication: Media and social participation. In J. Wasko & V. Moco (Eds.), *Democratic communications in the information age* (pp. 16–27). Norwood, NJ: Ablex.

Hague Convention for the Protection of Cultural Property in the Event of Armed Conflict (1954, May 14). 249 United Nations Treaty Series 240.

Harris, R. (1995/1996). Service undermined by technology: An examination of gender relations, economics and ideology. *Progressive Librarian, 10/11,* Retrieved August 21, 2001, from http://www.libr.org/PL/10-11_Harris.html.

Haywood, T. (1995). *Info-rich info-poor: Access and exchange in the global information society.* London: Bowker-Saur.

Haywood, T. (1998). Global networks and the myth of equality: Trickle down or trickle away? In B. Loader (Ed.), *Cyberspace divide: Equality, equity and policy in the information society* (pp. 19–34). London: Routledge.

Healy, T. (1998, June/July). Counting human capital. *OECD observer, 212.* Retrieved December 7, 1999, from http://www.oecd.org/publications/observer/212/Article8_eng.htm.

Hess, C., & Ostrom, E. (2001, November). *Artifacts, facilities, and content: Information as a common pool resource.* Paper presented at the Conference on the Public Domain, Duke University Law School, Durham, NC.

Hochschild, J. (1981). *What's fair? American beliefs about distributive justice.* Cambridge, MA: Harvard University Press.

Hoffman, D. L., Kalsbeek, W. D., & Novak, T. P. (1996). Internet and Web use in the U.S. *Communications of the ACM, 39*(12), 36–46.

Hoffman, D. L., & Novak, T. P. (1998, 17 April). Bridging the racial divide on the Internet. *Science, 280* (5362), 390–391.

Howard, P., Rainie, L., & Jones, S. (2001). Days and nights on the Internet: The impact of a diffusing technology. *American Behavioral Scientist, 45,* 383–404.

Institute of Industrial Engineers (2000, November). Addressing the "digital divide." *IIE Solutions, 32*(11), 15.

Introna, L. D., & Nissenbaum, H. (2000). Shaping the Web: Why the politics of search engines matters. *The Information Society, 16,* 169–185.

Ishaq, A. (2001). On the global digital divide. *Finance & Development, 38*(3), 1–6. Retrieved April 31, 2002, from http://www.imf.org/external/pubs/ft/fandd/2001/09/Ishaq.htm.

Ito, Y. (1981). The *Johoka shakai* approach to the study of communication in Japan. In G. C. Wilhoit & H. de Bock (Eds.), *Mass communication review yearbook, 2,* 671–698.

Kagan, A. (1999, August). *The growing gap between the information rich and the information poor, both within countries and between countries.* A composite policy paper of the Social Responsibilities Discussion Group, International Federation of Library Associations and Institutions. Retrieved November 21, 2000, from http://www.ifla.org/VII/dg/srdg/srdg7.htm.

Katz, J. E., & Aspden, P. (1997a). Motives, hurdles, and dropouts. *Communications of the ACM, 40*(4), 97–102.

Katz, J. E., & Aspden, P. (1997b). A nation of strangers? *Communications of the ACM, 40*(12), 81–86.

Katz, J. E., & Aspden, P. (1998). Internet dropouts in the USA: The invisible group. *Telecommunications Policy, 22,* 327–339.

Kouzmin, A. (2000). Information technology and development: Is the "Digital Divide" an inevitability? *Public Administration and Development, 20,* 167–169.

Kraut, R., Scherlis, W., Mukhopadhyay, T., Manning, J., & Kiesler, S. (1996). The HomeNet field trial of residential Internet services. *Communications of the ACM, 39*(12), 55–65.

Kurisaki, Y., & Yanagimachi, H. (1992). The impact of information on the economic development of sub-regional centres: A trial application of the 'information activity' index to the 43 cities in Japan. In I. Snyder (Ed.), *Page to screen: Taking literacy into the electronic era* (pp. 53–79). London: Routledge.

Lamberton, D. L. (1971). *The economics of information and knowledge.* Harmondsworth, UK: Penguin.

Lamberton, D. L. (2002). The economics of information and industrial change. In L. A. Lievrouw & S. Livingstone (Eds.), *The handbook of new media: Social shaping and consequences of ICTs* (pp. 334–349). London: Sage.

Lentz, R. G. (2000). The e-volution of the digital divide in the U.S.: A mayhem of competing metrics. *Journal of Policy, Regulation and Strategy for Telecommunications Information and Media, 2*, 355–377.

Lessig, L. (1999a). *Code and other laws of cyberspace.* New York: Basic Books.

Lessig, L. (1999b, February). Code and the commons. Keynote speech given at the conference *Media Convergence*, Fordham Law School, New York, NY. Retrieved July 15, 2001, from http://cyber.law.harvard.edu/works/lessig/fordham.pdf.

Lessig, L. (2001). *The future of ideas: The fate of the commons in a connected world.* New York: Random House.

Lievrouw, L. A. (1994). Information resources and democracy: Understanding the paradox. *Journal of the American Society for Information Science, 45*, 350–357.

Lievrouw, L. A. (1998). Our own devices: Heterotopic communication, discourse and culture in the information society. *The Information Society, 14*, 83–96.

Lievrouw, L. A. (2000). The information environment and universal service. *The Information Society, 16*, 155–160.

Lipinski, T. A. (1998). Information ownership and control. *Annual Review of Information Science and Technology, 33*, 3–38.

Lipinski, T. A. (1999a). The commodification of information and extension of proprietary rights into the public domain: Recent legal (case and other) developments in the United States. *Journal of Business Ethics, 22*, 63–80.

Lipinski, T. A. (1999b). The information rich, the information poor and the legal information underclass: Access to unpublished precedent and use of CALR (Computer Assisted Legal Research). *Proceedings of the ETHICOMP99 conference.* Retrieved November 21, 2000, from http://www.ccsr.cse.dmu.ac.uk/conferences/ccsrconf/abstracts99/lipinski.html.

Lipinski, T. A. (2000). The developing legal infrastructure and the globalization of information: Constructing a framework for critical choices in the new millennium Internet—Character, content and confusion. *Richmond Journal of Law and Techology, 19*, Winter. Retrieved August 21, 2001, from http://www.richmond.edu/jolt/v6i4/article2.html.

Litman, J. (1994). Mickey Mouse emeritus: Character protection and the public domain. *University of Miami Entertainment and Sports Law Review, 11*, 429–435.

Litman, J. (2001). *Digital copyright.* Amherst, NY: Prometheus Books.

Liu, M. (1995). Ethnicity and information seeking. *Reference Librarian, 49/50*, 123–134.

McCreadie, M., & Rice, R. E. (1999). Trends in analyzing access to information. Part I: Cross-disciplinary conceptualizations of access. *Information Processing & Management, 35*, 45–76.

Meadow, C. T. & Yuan, W. (1997). Measuring the impact of information: Defining the concepts. *Information Processing & Management, 33*, 697–714.

Merton, R. K. (1968, January 5). The Matthew effect in science. *Science, 159* (3810), 56–63.

Merton, R. K. (1988). The Matthew effect in science, II: Cumulative advantage and the symbolism of intellectual property. *Isis, 79,* 606–623.

Metoyer-Duran, C. (1991). Information-seeking behavior of gatekeepers in ethnolinguistic communities: Overview of a taxonomy. *Library & Information Science Research, 13,* 319–346.

Metoyer-Duran, C. (1993a). Information gatekeepers. *Annual Review of Information Science and Technology, 28,* 111–150.

Metoyer-Duran, C. (1993b). *Gatekeepers in ethnolinguistic communities.* Norwood, NJ: Ablex.

Mosco, V. (2000, February). *Public policy and the information highway: Access, equity and universality.* A report to the National Library of Canada, Contract no. 70071-9-5107. Retrieved August 16, 2001, from http://www.carleton.edu/~vmosco/pubpol.htm.

National Public Radio. (1999). Survey shows widespread enthusiasm for high technology. Results of the NPR/Kaiser/Kennedy School Technology Survey. Retrieved April 6, 2000, from http://www.npr.org/programs/special/poll/technology/index. html.

Nie, N. H., & Erbring, L. (2000, February 17). *Internet and society: A preliminary report.* Stanford, CA: Stanford University, Stanford Institute for the Quantitative Study of Society. Retrieved March 15, 2000, from http://www.stanford.edu/group/siqss.

Organisation for Economic Co-operation and Development. (2000). *OECD Information Technology Outlook 2000: Highlights.* Retrieved July 7, 2001, from http://www.oecd.org/dsti/sti/it.

Organisation for Economic Co-operation and Development. (2001). *Understanding the digital divide.* Paris: OECD. Retrieved April 21, 2001, from http://www.oecd.org.

Putnam, R. D. (2000). *Bowling alone: The collapse and revival of American community.* New York: Simon & Schuster.

Putting IT in its place. (2001, August 11). *The Economist, 360* (8234), 18–20.

Quéau, P. (2000, January). Who owns knowledge? Defining the world's public property. *Le Monde diplomatique.* Retrieved August 21, 2001, from http://www.monde-diplomatique.fr/en.

Rawls, J. (1999). *A theory of justice* (Rev. ed.). Cambridge, MA: Harvard University Press.

Rawls, J. (2001). *Justice as fairness.* Cambridge, MA: Belknap Press.

Samuelson, P. (1991). Digital media and the law. *Communications of the ACM, 34*(10), 23–28. Retrieved July 7, 2001, from http://www.eff.org/IP/Video/digital_media_and_law.paper.

Samuelson, P. (1994). The NII intellectual property report: National Information Infrastructure. *Communications of the ACM, 37*(12), 21–27.

Sawhney, H. (2000). Universal service: Separating the grain of truth from the proverbial chaff. *The Information Society, 16,* 161–164.

Sax, J. (1970). The public trust doctrine in natural resource law: Effective judicial intervention. *Michigan Law Review*, *68*, 471–565.

Schement, J. R. (1995). Beyond universal service: Characteristics of Americans without telephones, 1980–1993. *Telecommunications Policy*, *19*, 477–485.

Schiller, H. I. (1983). The privatization of information. *Mass Communication Yearbook*, *4*, 537–568.

Schiller, H. I., & Schiller, A. R. (1988). Libraries, public access to information and commerce. In V. Mosco & J. Wasko (Eds.), *The political economy of information* (pp. 146–166). Madison, WI: University of Wisconsin Press.

Sen, A. (1973). *On economic inequality*. Oxford, UK: Clarendon Press.

Sen, A. (1992). *Inequality reexamined*. Cambridge, MA: Harvard University Press, for the Russell Sage Foundation of New York.

Sen, A. (1999). Global justice: Beyond international equity. In I. Kaul, I. Grunberg, & M. A. Stern (Eds.), *Global public goods: International cooperation in the 21st century* (pp. 116–125). Oxford, UK: Oxford University Press.

Serageldin, I. (1999). Cultural heritage as public good: Economic analysis applied to historic cities. In I. Kaul, I. Grunberg, & M. A. Stern (Eds.), *Global public goods: International cooperation in the 21st century* (pp. 240–263). Oxford, UK: Oxford University Press.

Shade, L. R. (1998). A gendered perspective on access to the information infrastructure. *The Information Society*, *14*, 33–44.

Shapiro, C., & Varian, H. R. (1997). *U.S. government information policy*. Berkeley, CA: University of California. Retrieved July 7, 2001, from http://www.sims.berkeley.edu/~hal/Papers/policy/policy.html.

Shera, J. H. (1974). *Foundations of the public library: The origins of the public library movement in New England, 1629–1855*. Hamden, CT: Shoestring Press.

Siefert, M., Gerbner, G., & Fisher J. (Eds.). (1989). *The information gap: How computers and other new communication technologies affect the social distribution of power*. New York: Oxford University Press.

Slack, J. D., & Fejes, F. (Eds). (1987). *The ideology of the information age*. Norwood, NJ: Ablex.

Smith, A. (1993). *Inquiry into the nature and causes of the wealth of nations*. New York: Oxford University Press.

Sorokin, P. (1959). *Social and cultural mobility*. Glencoe, IL: Free Press.

Spar, D. L. (1999). The public face of cyberspace. In I. Kaul, I. Grunberg, & M. A. Stern (Eds.), *Global public goods: International cooperation in the 21st century* (pp. 344–363). Oxford, UK: Oxford University Press.

Spooner, T., & Rainie, L. (2000). *African-Americans and the Internet*. Retrieved March 11, 2002, from the Pew Internet and American Life Project Web site: http://www.pewinternet.org/reports/pdfs/PIP_African_Americans_Report.pdf.

Stevenson, T. (2000). *Whose digital future? Players and bystanders*. Retrieved January 2, 2002, from http://www.metafuture.org/articlesbycolleagues/TonyStevenson/Stevenson%20Whose%20digital%20future.htm.

Stiglitz, J. E. (1999). Knowledge as a global public good. In I. Kaul, I. Grunberg, & M. A. Stern (Eds.), *Global public goods: International cooperation in the 21st century* (pp. 308–325). Oxford, UK: Oxford University Press.

Sunstein, C. (2001). *republic.com*. Princeton, NJ: Princeton University Press.

Swanson, D. R. (1997). Historical note: Information retrieval and the future of an illusion. In K. Sparck Jones & P. Willett (Eds.), *Readings in information retrieval* (pp. 555–561). San Francisco: Morgan Kaufmann.

Sy, J. H. (1999). Global communication for a more equitable world. In I. Kaul, I. Grunberg, & M. A. Stern (Eds.), *Global public goods: International cooperation in the 21st century* (pp. 326–343). Oxford, UK: Oxford University Press.

Tichenor, P. J., Donohue, G. A., & Olien, C. N. (1970). Mass media flow and differential growth in knowledge. *Public Opinion Quarterly, 34,* 159–170.

Tilly, C. (1998). *Durable inequality*. Berkeley, CA: University of California Press.

Tribe, L. (1988). *American constitutional law* (2nd ed.). Mineola, NY: Foundation Press.

University of California Los Angeles. Center for Communication Policy. (2002). *The UCLA Internet report: "Surveying the digital future."* Los Angeles: Center for Communication Policy, University of California, Los Angeles. Retrieved February 17, 2002, from http://www.ccp.ucla.edu/.

U.S. Congress. Office of Management and Budget (2001). *OMB watch and information policy website*. Washington, DC: U.S. Congress, Office of Management and Budget. Retrieved July 7, 2001, from http://www.ombwatch.org/info/aboutinfo.html.

U.S. Department of Commerce. (1998). *The emerging digital economy*. Washington, DC: U.S. Department of Commerce. Retrieved July 7, 2001, from http://www.ecommerce.gov/emerging.htm.

U.S. Department of Commerce. National Telecommunications and Information Administration (1995). *Falling through the net: A survey of the "have nots" in rural and urban America*. Washington, DC: U.S. Department of Commerce, National Telecommunications and Information Administration. Retrieved June 9, 1999, from http://www.ntia.gov/ntiahome/fallingthru.html.

U.S. Department of Commerce. National Telecommunications and Information Administration (1998). *Falling through the net II: New data on the digital divide*. Washington, DC: U.S. Department of Commerce, National Telecommunications and Information Administration. Retrieved June 9, 1999, from http://www.ntia. doc.gov/ntiahome/net2/fallingthru.html.

U.S. Department of Commerce. National Telecommunications and Information Administration. (1999). *Falling through the net: Defining the digital divide*. Washington, DC: U.S. Department of Commerce. Retrieved November 15, 2000, from http://www.ntia.doc.gov/ntiahome/fttn99/contents.html.

Van Alstyne, M. & Brynjolfsson, E. (1996). Electronic communities: Global village or cyberbalkans? *Proceedings of the 17th International Conference on Information Systems*. Retrieved February 7, 2002, from http://web.mit.edu/marshall/www/papers/CyberBalkans.pdf.

van den Hoven, J. (1998). Distributive justice and equal access: Simple vs. complex equality. In L. D. Introna (Ed.), *Proceedings of the Computer Ethics: Philosophical Enquiry (CEPE '98) Conference*. London: London School of Economics and Political Science.

Viswanath, K., & Finnegan, J. R. Jr. (1996). The knowledge gap hypothesis: Twenty-five years later. *Communication Yearbook, 19*, 187–227.

Viswanath, K., Kosicki, G. M., Fredin, E. W., & Park, E. (2000). Local community ties, community-boundedness, and local public affairs knowledge gaps. *Communication Research, 27*(1), 27–50.

Wellman, B., Salaff, J., Dimitrova, D., Garton, L., Gulia, M., & Haythornthwaite, C. (1996). Computer networks as social networks: collaborative work, telework, and virtual community. *Annual Review of Sociology, 22*, 213–238.

Young, I. M. (2001). Equality of whom? Social groups and judgments of injustice. *Journal of Political Philosophy, 9*(1), 1–18.

Zweizig, D., & Dervin, B. (1977). Public library use, users, uses: Advances in knowledge of the characteristics and needs of the adult clientele of American public libraries. In M. J. Voigt & M. H. Harris (Eds.), *Advances in Librarianship, 7*, 231–255.

Index

3-D representations, *see* domain
    knowledge visualizations

A

Abdul-Rahman, A., 482, 485
Abell-Seddon, B., 263
academic career reviews and e-jour-
    nal publishing, 160–162
access to information, *see* hypertext;
    indexing; information equity
access to resources, *see* also
    indexing
    e-journals, 144–146, 150–151,
        153, *see* also licensing
        e-journals
    in museums, 270, 283
    limitations of early systems,
        263–264, 266
    music information retrieval
        facets, *see* also music infor-
        mation retrieval (MIR)
        editorial, textual, biblio-
        graphic, 323–325

        harmonic, 321–322
        pitch and temporal, 317–321
        timbral, 322–323
ACM (Association for Computing
        Machinery) Digital Library,
        151–152
ACS (American Chemical Society),
        144–145, 168
activity theory, 417
Adamic, L. A., 96
Adams, C., 279, 486
Adams, K. C., 63–64, 80
Affelder, L. O., 419
Agada, J., 510
Agosti, M., 92
Agre, P. E., 515
Ahonen, H., 62
Akahori, K., 74–75
ALA (American Library Association)
        Office of Information and
        Technology Policy, 509
Albert, R., 95, 240
Albrechtsen, H., 242, 400
Alferes, J.J., 74
Allamanche, E., 324–325

F

J

Q

R

Further Reading in Information Science & Technology

Proceedings of the 65th Annual Meeting of the American Society of Information Science & Technology (ASIST)

A new awareness of the importance of the free flow of necessary and time-sensitive information and the technologies that support it is upon us. Information organization, access, and transfer are recognized more than ever as essential elements in all aspects of business and daily interaction. The ability of our institutions to react depends on an information infrastructure that is stable, secure, and adaptable. The information technologies which we have begun to take for granted have, when challenged, been dynamically adapted to new situations. The 2002 ASIST conference proceedings provide information on these and other information phenomena and their contribution to the transformation of our society.

2002/608 pp/softbound/ISBN 1-57387-167-2
ASIST Members $47.60 • Non-Members $59.50

Historical Information Science
An Emerging Unidiscipline

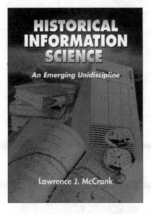

By Lawrence J. McCrank

Here is an extensive review and bibliographic essay, backed by almost 6,000 citations, about developments in information technology since the advent of personal computers and the convergence of several Social Science and Humanities disciplines in historical computing. Its focus is on the access, preservation, and analysis of historical information (primarily in electronic form) and the relationships between new methodology and instructional media, technique, and research trends in library special collections, digital libraries, electronic and data archives, and museums.

2002/1200 pp/hardbound/ISBN 1-57387-071-4 • $149.95

Evaluating Networked Information Services

Techniques, Policy, and Issues

"An excellent tool for assessing policies and programs."
–Library Bookwatch

Edited by Charles R. McClure and John Carlo Bertot

As information services and resources are made available in the global networked environment, there is a critical need to evaluate their usefulness, impact, cost, and effectiveness. This new book brings together an introduction and overview of evaluation techniques and methods, information policy issues and initiatives, and other critical issues related to the evaluation of networked information services.

2001/300 pp/hardbound/ISBN 1-57387-118-4
ASIST Members $35.60 • Non-Members $44.50

Statistical Methods for the Information Professional

By Liwen Vaughan

For most of us, "painless" is not the word that comes to mind when we think of statistics, but author and educator Liwen Vaughan wants to change that. In this unique and useful book, Vaughan clearly explains the statistical methods used in information science research, focusing on basic logic rather than mathematical intricacies. Her emphasis is on the meaning of statistics, when and how to apply them, and how to interpret the results of statistical analysis. Through the use of real-world examples, she shows how statistics can be used to improve services, make better decisions, and conduct more effective research.

Whether you are doing statistical analysis or simply need to better understand the statistics you encounter in professional literature and the media, this book will be a valuable addition to your personal toolkit. Includes more than 80 helpful figures and tables, 7 appendices, bibliography, and index.

2001/240 pp/hardbound/ISBN 1-57387-110-9
ASIST Members $31.60 • Non-Members $39.50

Editorial Peer Review

Its Strengths and Weaknesses

By Ann C. Weller

This important book is the first to provide an in-depth analysis of the peer review process in scholarly publishing. Author Weller (Associate Professor and Deputy Director at the Library of the Health Sciences, University of Illinois at Chicago) offers a carefully researched, systematic review of published studies of editorial peer review in the following broad categories: general studies of rejection rates, studies of editors, studies of authors, and studies of reviewers. The book concludes with an examination of new models of editorial peer review intended to enhance the scientific communication process as it moves from a print to an electronic environment. *Editorial Peer Review* is an essential monograph for editors, reviewers, publishers, professionals from learned societies, writers, scholars, and librarians who purchase and disseminate scholarly material.

2001/360 pp/hardbound/ISBN 1-57387-100-1
ASIST Members $35.60 • Non-Members $44.50

Introductory Concepts in Information Science

By Melanie J. Norton

Melanie J. Norton presents a unique introduction to the practical and theoretical concepts of information science while examining the impact of the Information Age on society. Drawing on recent research into the field, as well as from scholarly and trade publications, the monograph provides a brief history of information science and coverage of key topics, including communications and cognition, information retrieval, bibliometrics, modeling, economics, information policies, and the impact of information technology on modern management. This is an essential volume for graduate students, practitioners, and any professional who needs a solid grounding in the field of information science.

2000/127 pp/hardbound/ISBN 1-57387-087-0
ASIST Members $31.60 • Non-Members $39.50

The Web of Knowledge
A Festschrift in Honor of Eugene Garfield

Edited by Blaise Cronin and Helen Barsky Atkins

Dr. Eugene Garfield, the founder of the Institute for Scientific Information (ISI), has devoted his life to the creation and development of the multidisciplinary Science Citation Index. The index, a unique resource for scientists, scholars, and researchers in virtually every field of intellectual endeavor, has been the foundation for a multidisciplinary research community. This ASIS monograph is the first to comprehensively address the history, theory, and practical applications of the Science Citation Index and to examine its impact on scholarly and scientific research 40 years after its inception. In bringing together the analyses, insights, and reflections of more than 35 leading lights, editors Cronin and Atkins have produced both a comprehensive survey of citation indexing and analysis and a beautifully realized tribute to Eugene Garfield and his vision.

2000/544 pp/hardbound/ISBN 1-57387-099-4
ASIST Members $39.60 • Non-Members $49.50

Intelligent Technologies in Library and Information Service Applications

By F.W. Lancaster and Amy Warner

Librarians and library school faculty have been experimenting with artificial intelligence (AI) and expert systems for 30 years, but there has been no comprehensive survey of the results available until now. In this carefully researched monograph, authors Lancaster and Warner report on the applications of AI technologies in library and information services, assessing their effectiveness, reviewing the relevant literature, and offering a clear-eyed forecast of future use and impact. Includes almost 500 bibliographic references.

2001/214 pp/hardbound/ISBN 1-57387-103-6
ASIST Members $31.60 • Non-Members $39.50

Information Management for the Intelligent Organization, 3rd Edition

By *Chun Wei Choo*

The intelligent organization is one that is skilled at marshalling its information resources and capabilities, transforming information into knowledge, and using this knowledge to sustain and enhance its performance in a restless environment. The objective of this newly updated and expanded book is to develop an understanding of how an organization may manage its information processes more effectively in order to achieve these goals. The third edition features new sections on information culture, information overload, and organizational learning; a new chapter on Knowledge Management (KM) and the role of information professionals; and numerous extended case studies of environmental scanning by organizations in Asia, Europe, and North America. This book is a must-read for senior managers and administrators, information managers, information specialists and practitioners, information technologists, and anyone whose work in an organization involves acquiring, creating, organizing, or using knowledge.

2001/352 pp/hardbound/ISBN 1-57387-125-7
ASIST Members $31.60 • Non-Members $39.50

Historical Studies in Information Science

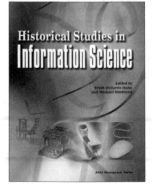

Edited by Trudi Bellardo Hahn and Michael Buckland

The field of information science has a broad history spanning nearly a century. *Historical Studies in Information Science* focuses on the progression of this dynamic and evolving industry by looking at some of its pioneers. This informative volume concentrates on the following areas: Historiography of Information Science; Paul Otlet and His Successors; Techniques, Tools, and Systems; People and Organizations; Theoretical Topics; and Literature.

1998/317 pp/softbound/ISBN 1-57387-062-5
ASIST Members $31.60 • Non-Members $39.50